Management

Management

Second
Edition

William F. Glueck
The University of Georgia

 The Dryden Press   Hinsdale, Illinois

Text and cover design by
James Buddenbaum Design
Index by Wanda Giles

Grateful Acknowledgment is made to the following people and organizations for the use of photographs: Photo of Frederick W. Taylor, page 16,
courtesy of Charles D. Wrege, Rutgers University. Photos of Frank Gilbreth
and Lillian Gilbreth, page 17, courtesy of Frank B. Gilbreth. Photo of Elton
Mayo, page 17, courtesy of Baker Library, Harvard University. Photo of
Jesse Hill, Jr., page 34, courtesy of Board of Regents. Photo of Jay
VanAndel, page 64, courtesy of Amway Corp. Photo of E. Hirst Mendenhall,
page 72, courtesy of Mr. Mendenhall. Photo of Mary Jane Mendenhall,
page 73, courtesy of Ms. Mendenhall. Photo of Edgar F. Kaiser, page 74,
courtesy of Kaiser Steel Corporation. Photo of Reginald H. Jones, page
100, courtesy of General Electric. Photo of A.P. Giannini, page 160, courtesy of Bank of America. Photo of Joseph Irwin Miller, page 224, courtesy of
Cummins Engine Co., Inc. Photo of Harry Blair Cunningham, page 257,
courtesy of K mart Corporation. Photo of Fremont A. Shull, page 374,
courtesy of Mr. Shull. Photo of Alfred P. Sloan, Jr., page 383, courtesy of
General Motors. Photo of Larry Greiner, page 421, courtesy of Mr. Greiner.
Photo of Sheldon A. Davis, page 432, courtesy of Mr. Davis. Photo of H.
Ross Perot, page 462, © Karsh, Ottawa; reprinted by permission. Photo of
Leonard R. Sayles, page 512, courtesy of McGraw Hill Book Company.
Photo of George Eastman, courtesy of Eastman Kodak Company. Photo of
J. C. Penney, page 670, courtesy of J. C. Penney Company. Photo of
William Cooper Procter, page 688, courtesy of Procter & Gamble.

To My Friends
In the Academy of Management
Who Have Been So Supportive in My Work

Preface

This is a book about management: the effective utilization of human and material resources to achieve the enterprise's objectives. There are many books on management. Let me explain briefly the approach and emphasis of this one to help you use it more effectively.

First, this book contrasts and compares the job of managers, entrepreneurs, and family business executives. Second, the book uses many examples and illustrations to help you understand effective management in the specific, not just in general. It includes the best theory and research on effective management, and it applies this knowledge to typical managerial situations to help you understand how to make use of it.

Third, this management book emphasizes some aspects of management more than many other books. These topics include:

- The manager's role in relating to the environment as negotiator and spokesperson.
- Understanding yourself and others at work with regard to personality, motivation, perception, and learning.
- Effective management of your time.
- Effective use of management by objectives.
- Designing challenging jobs and job enrichment.
- Leadership techniques for influencing employees and interpersonal influence techniques for relating effectively to colleagues and superiors.
- Effective communication approaches, including effective oral and written communication, effective listening and effective reading skills.
- Managing human resources.
- Managing your career and preparing for careers in the nonbusiness sector.

Last, each chapter begins with a list of learning objectives and a chapter outline. The objectives indicate what you should know after reading the chapter. The outline provides an overview of what you will read. The summary at the end of each chapter reinforces this overview.

Each chapter also provides thoughtful questions on the text and relevant problems—in the form of either fictitious cases or specific exercises to help you assess your understanding of the material presented. Your instructor may supplement this text with one or two companion volumes published by The Dryden Press: *Study Guide to Accompany Management*, Second Edition, which Sally Coltrin and I have authored, and *The Managerial Experience: Cases, Exercises, and Readings*, Second Edition, which Lawrence Jauch, Sally Coltrin, and I wrote.

Additional materials are available to instructors from The Dryden Press:

- *Instructor's Manual for Management*, Second Edition, which contains objectives, lecture outlines, Test Banks A and B, transparency masters, and answers to discussion questions, exercises, and cases.
- *Transparency Acetates*
- *Computer Test Bank*
- *Dialogues in Management*, which consists of interviews with such prominent people as Studs Turkel and Colonel Sanders
- *Instructor's Manual for The Managerial Experience: Cases, Exercises, and Readings*, Second Edition.

The Second Edition: How Is It Improved?

Many fine colleges and universities used the first edition of this book. For that, I am very grateful. Many users wrote me with suggestions for improvement. Some of these people are listed in the acknowledgments section. I have tried to incorporate all of these suggestions.

Let me briefly mention some of the changes in this new edition. The book has been thoroughly rewritten. The material and references have been updated in every chapter.

The use of the three models of management has disappeared from many chapters. In those where it remains, the titles of the models have been changed. In addition, tables and charts have been clarified, and fewer topics have been covered in each chapter. Those topics that remain are treated in more depth. To enhance the text's relevance, a number of applications have been added.

And finally, the following topics have been either added or given more substantial coverage:

- Mintzberg's research on the management process (Chapter 1).
- The history of management thought (Chapter 1).

- The impact of feelings on human behavior (Chapter 5).
- Planning and objectives (Chapter 7).
- Management by objectives (Chapter 7).
- Strategic planning (Chapter 8).
- Quantitative decision-making tools (appendix to Chapter 9).
- Decision making (including an appendix on Janis and Mann's conflict theory of decision making in Chapter 9).
- Matrix organizations (Chapter 11).
- Stages of development theories that relate to organizing the total enterprise (Chapter 12).
- Organizational change and development (Chapter 13).
- James McGregor Burns's extensive summary of leadership (Chapter 14).
- Fiedler's theory of leadership (Chapter 14).
- Delegation of authority (Chapter 14).
- Developing the political skills of a manager (Chapters 14 and 15).
- The management of committees (Chapter 16).
- Effective written communication (Chapter 17).
- Effective listening skills (Chapter 17).
- Control (Chapter 18).
- Budgetary control (Chapter 19).
- Staffing and management of human resources—employees (Chapter 20).
- The development of managerial resources and managers' careers—including dual career couples (Chapter 21).

Management is an exciting topic. I wrote this book in the hope of exciting you over the prospect of becoming a manager, entrepreneur, or family business executive. I hope you like the book and do choose a career in management.

Acknowledgments

A book is always the product of many people. I have been helped by many of my friends in the Academy, especially Lawrence Jauch, Southern Illinois University, Carbondale, and Sally Coltrin, University of North Florida. In addition, I had the benefit of several excellent reviewers, including Carl R. Anderson, University of North Carolina; Bernard M. Bass, State University of New York at Binghamton; Paul L. Harmon, The University of Utah; Jane W. Hass, University of Florida; J. Duane Hoover, Texas Tech University; Raymond G. Hunt, State University of New York at Buffalo; LeRoy Johnson, Washington State University; Marvin Karlins, University of South Florida; Donald A. Ryktarsyk, Schoolcraft College; Richard M. Steers, University of Oregon; and William B. Zachary, San Jose State University.

I wish to thank those responsible for creating such a stimulating work environment at the University of Georgia: my faculty colleagues, my students, Management Department Chairman Richard Huseman, and Dean William Flewellen, Jr.

A special word of thanks to my outstanding administrative assistant, Jean Hanebury. She is helpful in so many ways that my books are strongly influenced by her comments, critiques, and general support.

Finally, I wish to thank my children—Melissa, Bill, David, and Lisa—for the motivation and support they provide me for my work.

William F. Glueck
Athens, Georgia
January 1980

Contents

Part Two   **Understanding the Managerial World**

Part Six   **Controlling Organizational Resources**

Part Seven   **Managing Human Resources**

Part 1   Understanding the Managerial Task

1

Part 1 introduces you to the world and task of the manager, entrepreneur, and family business executive. A brief look is taken at management theories in historical perspective. The various types and levels of managers are examined and compared. And managerial functions—what it is society expects managers to do—are defined. The ways the manager, entrepreneur, or family business executive performs these functions are compared and contrasted.

Now

Part 1	**Understanding the Managerial Task**	**Managerial Job** **Job of Entrepreneur and** **Family Business Executive**
Part 2	Understanding the Managerial World	The External Environment of Management The Internal World of Management Understanding Human Behavior Understanding Motivation
Part 3	Planning the Organization Resources	Objectives Plans and Policy Making Decision Making
Part 4	Organizing the Enterprise's Resources	Organization and Coordination of Work Delegation of Authority Organizational Change
Part 5	Leading and Interpersonal Influences	Leadership of Employees Relationships with Peers and Superiors Relating to Groups Effective Communications
Part 6	Controlling Organizational Resources	Nonbudgeting Control Budgeting Control
Part 7	Managing Human Resources and Your Career	Managing Your Resources Managing Your Career

The Future

Chapter 1   An Invitation to Management

1

Learning Objectives

1. Define management and differentiate it from other phenomena.
2. Understand the functions all managers perform.
3. Place important management theories in historical perspective.
4. Develop a plan of your own to increase your managerial knowledge.

Chapter Outline

Some Questions about Management
What Is Management?
Management Functions and Roles
Mintzberg's Research
The Importance of Management
The Challenge to Management
Becoming a Manager
Avoiding Managerial Obsolescence
Management and You
Management Theories and Research
Historically Significant Management Theories
Modern Management Theories
How Relevant Are Management
Theory and Research?
Some Answers to the Questions about Management
Summary
Questions

This book is about managers, entrepreneurs (people who found their own businesses), and family business executives: who they are, what they do, and how they do their jobs. It is also an invitation to you to enter the field of management and learn how to make a success of the business enterprises in which you become involved.

Some Questions about Management

In a recent study by Barnett and Taguiri, 2,500 persons aged nine to seventeen were questioned about their concepts of management.[1] They were first asked to select a career that appealed to them and to state specifically whether they would like to be managers. Five of the other questions they were then asked are listed below. I would like you to write down your own answers to these questions. Later in the chapter you will have a chance to compare your answers with those of the respondents in Barnett and Taguiri's study.

1. What is a manager? What does a manager do at work?
2. Why would you choose a management career as compared to other careers? Specify which characteristics of a management career are most attractive.
3. What kind of person makes a good manager? A successful one?
4. How does someone become a manager? What career paths lead to management?
5. What kind of life-style does a manager have compared to other people in society?

Good management is important for all enterprises, including organizations in the not-for-profit and public sector of the economy. The president of United Airlines and the entrepreneur who owns and operates Stage 54 Disco must be good managers to make their businesses profitable. The administrator of Valley View Hospital (a not-for-profit institution) and the director of the U.S. Department of Labor's Bureau of Labor Statistics (a public office) must also be highly skilled in management to keep their organizations running smoothly. While the primary focus of this book is on effective management of businesses, the appendix to Chapter 21 does include a discussion of some of the similarities and differences between management of for-profit enterprises and management in the public and not-for-profit sectors.

What Is Management?

At one time in North America, Europe, and Japan the world of work was highly individualized. Farmers produced food for themselves and their families and, if they were lucky, had a surplus to sell to others. Craft workers produced their goods alone. Individuals who needed homes built them alone or with the help of their families. Even the government was individualized, consisting of a lord or knight. Sometimes cooperatives were formed to accomplish a specific purpose such as building a road or church or fighting off an enemy, but these lasted only a brief period of time.

In many of the developing nations, this work pattern still exists. In the developed countries, a few people continue in this individualized pattern—small farmers and independent carpenters, for example—but generally the work world is more complex.

Products such as Boeing 747 airplanes, television sets, and heating and air-conditioning systems are not produced efficiently by individual people. Similarly, services such as power for our homes and offices, cable TV systems, insurance against accidents, and complex investment of currencies and real estate can rarely be performed by lone individuals. The complexities of producing modern-day goods and services call for the joint effort of many people; seldom does one person have the required funds and abilities.

Management Functions and Roles

The individual who owns and operates a small business is responsible for it in all its aspects. When a business is large and involves many employees, it is often difficult to determine who will make certain decisions and assume certain responsibilities. Questions such as the following arise:

1. Who is responsible to the government, the community, and the stockholders for seeing that the firm and its employees act in a legal, ethical, and responsible way in all dealings?
2. Who is responsible for seeing that employees work together in harmony and receive adequate funds, materials, and supplies to get the job done? And who is charged with seeing that the employees are working hard and well and finding satisfaction and opportunities for growth and fulfillment in their work?
3. Who is responsible for deciding what the enterprise should be

accomplishing—which needs of society it should serve? Who decides how those who provide money, materials, and labor are to be satisfied?

4. Who gets the people to do the right tasks? Who relates these tasks to each other? Who is responsible for changing outmoded ways of doing things? Who is responsible for seeing that matters affecting employees and their work are conveyed to all concerned?

5. Who is responsible for resolving human, technical, marketing, financial, and other problems?

6. Who sees to it that the funds, materials, equipment, and other resources belonging to stockholders, suppliers, and others are not stolen, misused, or poorly used? And who is responsible for seeing that the objectives set are achieved on time?

7. Who sees to it that the people needed to do the work are at the workplace, are well trained, and are equitably rewarded for their work?

The answer to each of the above questions is one of the following: the manager, the entrepreneur, or the family business executive. These seven questions outline what it is society, employees, and other managers expect managers to do—in other words, basic management functions. In Table 1.1 these functions are named and numerically correlated with the questions. The chapters of the book in which they are discussed are also noted. Formal definitions of the management functions are given below.

Table 1.1
Management
Functions

Management Functions	Book Chapters
1. Relating to the environment	Chapter 4
2. Setting objectives and planning	Chapters 7, 8
3. Decision making and problem solving	Chapter 9
4. Organization	Chapters 10-13
5. Leadership, interpersonal influence, and communication	Chapters 14-17
6. Control	Chapters 18, 19
7. Human resource management and staffing	Chapters 20, 21

Relating to the environment includes all processes through which the manager represents the business enterprise to the various facets of the society in which it exists—government, local community, suppliers, unions, stockholders, customers, and pressure groups—and negotiates with them to acquire the resources, supplies, and support necessary for the enterprise's survival.

Decision making entails a choice between two or more alternatives. Decision making includes the processes of thought and deliberation that lead to decisions. Problem solving is a form of decision making.

Planning is the managerial activity which helps the firm prepare for the future. It includes (a) determining objectives for the firm; (b) examining the environment and forecasting changes; and (c) developing policies, procedures, and plans to help achieve the objectives in view of the changing environment.

Organization is the process by which people and the tasks they perform are related to each other. It consists of dividing up work among groups and individuals (division of labor) and linking the efforts of those groups and individuals (coordination).

Leadership and interpersonal relations Leadership is the set of interpersonal behaviors designed to influence subordinates to cooperate in the achievement of the enterprise's objectives. Interpersonal relations is that set of behaviors designed to influence peers, superiors, and nonsubordinates to cooperate in achieving the enterprise's objectives.

Control is the managerial process that ensures effective use of the enterprise's resources and achievement of its objectives. It includes three elements: (a) establishing standards for measurement, (b) developing measurement procedures to determine progress toward enterprise objectives, and (c) acting to reinforce success and correct shortcomings.

Staffing and human resource management are the processes of assuring that competent employees are selected, developed, and rewarded to achieve enterprise objectives. Effective human resource management includes providing a work climate in which employees can experience satisfaction and development.

All these tasks or functions are important and performed by all managers. But which of them take the most time from managers? In a study of more than four hundred managers at all levels in a dozen firms of all sizes, Thomas Mahoney and his associates collected the data arranged in Table 1.2.[2] Chapter 2 will make clear that the percentage of time spent on specific management functions may vary depending on the level of the manager within the firm (see Table 1.2).

Mintzberg's Research

Henry Mintzberg observed five top managers for one week. He analyzed their behavior and contends that they perform the functions shown in Table 1.3.[3]

How do Mintzberg's managerial roles relate to the managerial processes listed in Table 1.2? As can be seen in Table 1.4, which places the two different conceptions of management functions in perspective, some of

Table 1.2
Percentage of Time
Spent by Managers on
Management
Functions

Management Functions	Percent
Relating to the environment	1.8
Setting objectives and planning	19.5
Decision making and problem solving	6.0
Organization and coordination	15.0
Leadership and interpersonal influence	28.4
Communication[a]	12.6
Control[a]	12.7
Human resource management and staffing	4.1

[a] Mahoney did not use precisely these categories of management functions in the study.
Source: Adapted with permission from Thomas Mahoney et al., "The Job(s) of Management," *Industrial Relations 4* (February 1965): 97–110.

Mintzberg's roles are split up among several traditional functions. Others are very similar to the traditional functions.

But in Mintzberg's view, firms place far less emphasis on certain functions than other management theorists suggest. For example, he claims little planning goes on in firms. Since both the traditionally cited management functions and Mintzberg's management roles contribute to an understanding of what management is, they will be combined to form the basis of the following discussion. For purposes of organization, however, Mintzberg's roles will be considered in the context of the traditional functions.

Table 1.3
Mintzberg's
Managerial Roles

1. Interpersonal Roles
   A. Figurehead: Symbolic duties as head of the organization such as ceremonial duties Queen Elizabeth performs for the United Kingdom.
   B. Leader: Human resource management, motivational influences, and leadership duties.
   C. Liaison: Relating to the external environment to establish image, gather resources, etc.
2. Informational Roles
   A. Monitor: Collects information and organizes it for use in decision making.
   B. Disseminator: Distributes relevant information to those who need it.
   C. Spokesperson: Explains the unit's policies to external organizations.
3. Decisional Roles
   A. Entrepreneur: Strategic decision maker.
   B. Disturbance Handler: The decision maker of last resort for problems.
   C. Resource Allocator: Distributes resources as needed to achieve the ends of the business.
   D. Negotiator: Negotiates for resources outside the organization and to settle internal conflicts.

Source: Adapted from *The Nature of Managerial Work* by Henry Mintzberg. Copyright © 1973 by Henry Mintzberg. By permission of Harper & Row, Publishers, Inc.

Table 1.4
A Comparison of
Managerial Processes
and Mintzberg's
Managerial Roles

Traditional Managerial Processes	Mintzberg's Roles
Relating to the environment	Liaison; spokesperson; negotiator
Setting objectives and planning	Entrepreneur
Decision making and problem solving	Disturbance handler
Organization and coordination	Resource allocator
Leadership/interpersonal influences/ communication	Figurehead; leader; monitor; disseminator
Control	Resource allocator; negotiator
Human resource management and staffing	Leader

In sum, we can say that

management is the effective utilization of human and material resources to achieve the enterprise's objectives.[4]

And, as has already been indicated, management is accomplished by performance of the managerial processes or functions defined above.

How the manager, entrepreneur, or family business executive performs the managerial task is influenced by many factors, especially the following:

- The personal world and background of the manager.
- The organizational world in which the manager works—the kind of tasks done, the kind of people working there, the kind of resources available.
- The nature of the society in which the organization functions.

Chapters 2 and 3 will discuss these factors in more detail.

The Importance of Management

For enterprises to survive, they must achieve their objectives. All enterprises are responsible to certain groups, such as stockholders, for their performance. The manager is the link to these groups. The manager guides the enterprise, especially in times of trouble. Some writers feel that management is unnecessary—that employees themselves can do the work of management. But historians and social scientists have yet to find an enterprise that survived very long without developing a hierarchy of management.

On the other hand, many have argued that management—good management—is the key difference between the success and failure of enterprises. Some securities analysts attribute major differences in stock prices to stockholders' evaluation of managers. The great economist, Joseph Schumpeter, referred to management and entrepreneurs as "the engine of growth." And Peter Drucker, a well-known management consultant, calls management the life-giving organ of the enterprise's body.

Source: Drawing by Drucker; © 1974 The New Yorker Magazine, Inc.

"I'd like an album praising Management."

Firms can fail because of inadequate funds, improper marketing, incompetent product design, and for many other reasons. But they often fail because the basic managerial tasks are performed poorly or not at all. Indeed, Jacques Servan-Schreiber warned in *The American Challenge* that American multinational corporations would overwhelm European business because of the superior skills of American management.[5] So management itself can be a comparative advantage to a company or society.

The Challenge to Management

Some social scientists would like to wish management away and have society run by self-regulating teams. Others do not like the red tape and slow reaction time of large organizations. They blame these conditions on management and, accordingly, are critical of careers in management.

The 1930s gave rise to the issue of legitimacy of management. If the managers did not own the enterprise and if ownership was distributed among millions of stockholders, to whom was management responsible? Recent revelations of executives using corporate funds for illegal campaign contributions to politicians have led us to ask this question once again. Conflicts of interest also hurt the managerial image. We occasionally hear of corporate managers who have their purchasing agents place lucrative contracts with firms they secretly own.

But look at it this way: Does the incompetence of one physician make the entire medical profession worthless? And just because one lawyer exploits a widow by charging excessive fees for probating and processing a will, should you reject a law career? No.

There have always been those who questioned the legitimacy of management, or its value. But business needs competent, ethical managers who will make enterprises more productive. I hope you will be among them.

Becoming a Manager

I have just finished a brief description of why managers and management exist and what management is. Now let's discuss how you can become a manager. As with many jobs which do not require licensing by the state, management can be learned in several ways:

On-the-job training In this approach a person who appears to have potential is hired and then trained by an experienced manager. On-the-job training involves coaching and counseling, and frequently a gradual, step-by-step introduction to all the aspects of the job. The position of assistant manager is often a convenient vehicle for on-the-job managerial training.

Formal coursework In this approach, the potential manager studies in a college or in a firm's training program.

A combination of formal coursework and on-the-job training Most firms use this approach because there are some aspects of management which are more efficiently and effectively learned in class and others which are better learned on the job. Those most suitable to classroom teaching are the more scientific aspects of management, including decision-making tools, management by objectives, and human resource management. Effective interpersonal relations and communication practices are more arts than sciences and thus are better learned on the job. The distinction here is somewhat artificial, however, because all of management can be learned most effectively by first studying what is known in theory and then practicing the application of theory to on-the-job situations.

What part can this book play in your becoming a manager? It summarizes the theoretical aspects of management and provides cases to simulate on-the-job practice. Cases are included on the assumption that they will help you learn more quickly and allow you to make your mistakes here rather than on the job in working through the problems they present. The book is *not* a substitute for the art of management learned on the job.

Are books on management worthwhile? Consider the following:

- *Item:* Employers continue to pay premium salaries to people who have had courses in management. And they pay even higher salaries to those with graduate degrees in management. Employers do not pay premium salaries because they are generous. This is one of the ways they tell us that you can learn management in the classroom.
- *Item:* Employers give schools of business and management money to encourage the research and teaching of management. Would they do that if it made no sense to teach courses in management?
- *Item:* Employers spend billions of dollars each year in management development programs using books like this one to improve managerial skills.
- *Item:* Professors of management are often told: "I wish I had read your book (or taken your course) years ago. I was appointed a manager but didn't know the job. If only I knew then what I know now. . . ."

Management courses try to develop the skills and attitudes of effective, successful managers in their students. Could a person learn these skills and attitudes on the job? Sure. But this process would take longer and would not be as well organized as a management course. You are not born with management knowledge, and it is not just common sense. On the job the primary emphasis is on getting the job done, not on learning about the job.

I cannot tell you all you need to know about management in this book. But I can provide information that will give you a head start. You will have to put this knowledge to use to become a successful manager. I hope this book will help you understand what a manager is, how a manager works, and why certain managers are successful.

Avoiding Managerial Obsolescence

All fields change and develop, and effective managers need to continue to read and study to improve and update their management skills. It is also important to keep up with management theory and research by reading journals and going to conferences. The journals in the following list are among those to which you might subscribe in order to keep your management knowledge current:

- *Academy of Management Journal*
- *Academy of Management Review*
- *Business Horizons*
- *Business Week*
- *California Management Review*
- *Fortune*
- *Harvard Business Review*
- *Journal of Management Studies*

- *Management Review*
- *Organizational Dynamics*

Management and You

Each of us must choose a career. Our careers play an important role in the development of our self-image. As Chapter 21 points out, there are many possible career choices: blue-collar jobs (machinist), white-collar/clerical jobs (order processer), gray-collar service jobs (computer repair), technical jobs (medical technologist), and managerial or professional jobs.

One of the objectives of this book is to make you aware of the excitement of a managerial job so you will want to choose a career in management. Another is to help you learn how to be a successful manager. Our world desperately needs more effective managers, entrepreneurs, and family business executives. As you read the text, think about management—what it is like and whether you can see yourself as a manager. We have already defined management and outlined what it is about. What can management mean for you?

On the positive side, managers generally receive many rewards for their work: good pay and benefits and prestige from peers, subordinates, and society. Studies show that managers are among those most satisfied with their work in our society. Management positions provide more freedom and autonomy than most. They also provide the opportunity to work with people to help achieve important objectives. Finally, management jobs offer a variety of experiences and activities and are rarely dull.

Chapter 6 will discuss work motivation in more detail than is possible here. The following list briefly summarizes the needs many individuals have that can be satisfied in a managerial job:

- Physiological needs: The pay and benefits provide a good standard of living.
- Social and affiliation needs: Managers usually work with people and find the social aspects of their jobs enjoyable.
- Ego/status needs: Managers receive respect from others and society, which enhances their own self-respect. Getting important things done satisfies an individual's achievement needs. For some, it also satisfies a need for power.
- Self-fulfillment needs: Managers usually have a high degree of autonomy and freedom plus the chance to use all their skills. For these reasons a management career often results in a high level of personal fulfillment.

To be successful, however, most managers must work hard, keep their skills updated, and be willing to meet the challenges of change in personnel and in work. The last chapter in the book asks you to consider a managerial career. It also describes how to plan a successful career. It is my hope that as you read about management you will accept the management challenge.

Management Theories and Research

Now that you know something of the basic functions, challenges, and rewards of management, we will put management into a historical perspective. What we know about management comes from two sources: theories and research.

A theory is a scientifically acceptable schema useful in understanding phenomena and predicting future happenings.

In most subjects you have studied you have learned theories. Examples include Freud's theories about human beings, Darwin's theories of the origin of the species, and Toynbee's theories about human history. Sometimes theories are developed before research is done. Then research is performed to test them. They may be proved, modified, or rejected on the basis of the research.

Research is investigation or experimentation aimed at the discovery and interpretation of facts.

Sometimes the findings of research in several areas lead a scholar to develop a theory. Both approaches to developing a body of knowledge—theory and research—are useful. In this book, you will find examples of both theories and research that will help you understand management as well as predict problems and devise fruitful solutions in the future. Important management theories are presented below; results of research will be given in later chapters.

Historically Significant Management Theories

To begin with, let's briefly review several important theories that have significantly influenced management research and thinking. It is difficult, if not impossible, to grasp modern management theory and research without an understanding of its historical heritage. The focus here will be on the evolution of management theory since the late 1800s.

Prescientific Management

Managers and scholars have been giving advice on how to manage business enterprises throughout history. The Egyptians, the Chinese, the Persians, Greeks, Romans, Germans, and others offered insights into the management of large enterprises. Their ideas influenced the nineteenth- and twentieth-century theorists whose scientific management, principles of management, and human relations theories are discussed in this section. Notable among the nineteenth-century theorists were:

Robert Owen An early nineteenth-century British industrialist and management theorist, Robert Owen asserted that the best way to improve productivity was to improve the lives of employees—the vital machines, as he called them. This he tried to do by reducing the work day, improving workers' housing and purchasing power, and having employees rated openly on their contributions to each day's performance. The ratings were to serve two purposes: reward good performance with recognition and encourage managers to focus on problem areas.

Charles Babbage A nineteenth-century British mathematics professor, Charles Babbage was interested in the world of work. He studied factory work and advocated specialization, which, he maintained, would lead to increased employee skill development and so to greater productivity. Specialization is the approach to job design which breaks tasks into simplified parts. Babbage theorized that scientific study of work could lead to vast improvements in the world of work.

Scientific Management

At the turn of the century, a group of writers tried to make management more scientific by applying engineering approaches to job design. They were aided by early industrial psychologists, who were applying testing procedures to personnel selection. This group focused on effective design of the employee's task. A number of persons were involved in developing this new approach, but especially notable were:

Frederick W. Taylor Taylor followed in the footsteps of Babbage, although it is not clear whether he was aware of Babbage's work or not. He studied individual production tasks in order to streamline them and thus increase productivity and profits. At the same time he stressed the importance of reducing fatigue and increasing employee compensation.

To achieve these goals, Taylor and his associates conducted time and motion studies to design each task for maximum efficiency, outlining the right steps and refining tools. Then they used the developing science of industrial psychology/personnel management to match the requirements of each newly designed job with an employee who proved through testing to have the proper abilities. This made management responsible for making decisions on job design, selection, training, and work procedures and eliminated the vagaries of instinct and habit from such decisions. Employees had previously been left to perform these tasks as they saw fit. Taylor and his associates became theorists, practitioners, researchers, and propagandists for scientific management.

Frank and Lillian Gilbreth Close associates of Taylor, these two theorists and practitioners applied scientific management to all aspects of their life,

including the rearing of their twelve children. The scientific management of their family life has been memorialized in the book *Cheaper by the Dozen.* The Gilbreths specialized in motion analysis. Lillian Gilbreth applied their theories both in the consulting business and later in her career as a home economist—to designing kitchens and doing housework.

The scientific management movement focused the responsibility for work on management instead of on the worker or union. It emphasized efficient task performance and the responsibility of management to plan, organize, and control the employees' tasks.

Principles of Management

At about the time of World War I, certain people began to reflect on their experiences as managers and to describe and define managerial tasks. The major emphasis of this group was on the effective performance of managerial tasks. Prominent among these theorists was:

Henri Fayol A French executive who wrote about what managers do based on self-observation and the observation of other managers, Fayol divided the tasks a manager performs into two catagories, as shown in Figure 1.1: business functions and managerial functions.

Fayol theorized that all these functions are essential to the survival of the body corporate. He also pointed out that far less was known about the managerial functions than about business functions, even though the former are vital to the success of the enterprise. As he saw it, the business functions are more important at lower levels of management, and the managerial functions become progressively more important as the management level gets higher. Fayol and later writers in this school—James Mooney and Alan Reilly, Luther Gulick and Lyndal Urwick, and Chester Barnard—focused on the managerial functions as separate and important tasks.[6]

Human Relations

In the 1920s and during the Great Depression some social scientists, led by Elton Mayo, began to study how employees reacted to managerial incentive schemes, job design, and working conditions. This group of theorists emphasized the human side of management and tended to counterbalance the technical engineering emphasis of the scientific management movement. They believed management should focus on *people.*

Elton Mayo One of the most significant human relations studies done at this time took place at Western Electric's Hawthorne Works under the direction of Elton Mayo and associates such as Fritz Roethlisberger. Their

Figure 1.1
Fayol's Business
and Managerial
Functions

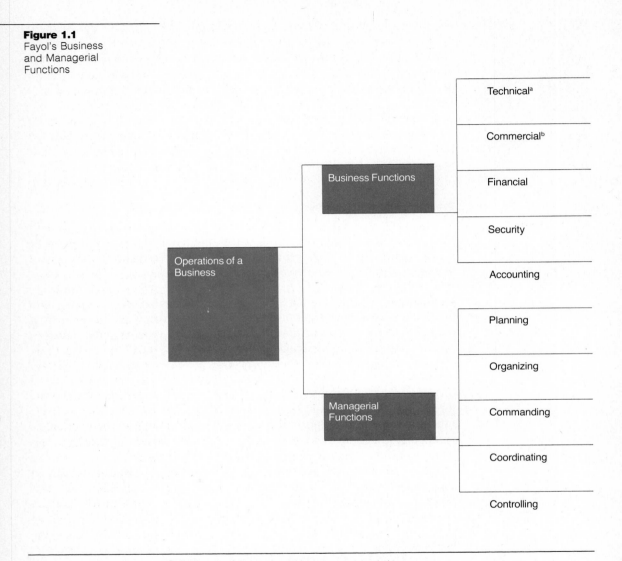

[a] Production operations management, in contemporary terminology.
[b] Marketing, in contemporary terminology.

approach followed along the lines of Robert Owen's—stressing the human factor in production—but with a different emphasis. Mayo's earlier anthropological work had centered around the importance of teamwork and group activity for survival. In the series of experiments he designed to determine how productivity might be improved, his earlier findings were reconfirmed.

Initially, he tried to improve the work lives of employees by a variation of Owen's and Taylor's approach—improvements in the physical environment (lighting, for example) and reduction of fatigue (rest breaks, for example). What he discovered, however, was that productivity was affected not by these factors but rather by communication and interaction within social groups at work. In fact, he found that work design, the approach of scientific management, had a negative impact as a result of the isolation it imposed on employees. Although the work of Mayo and this school focused on the task and not on management functions as such, Mayo emphasized that it is management's responsibility to humanize the work environment if productivity and satisfaction are to be achieved.

Modern Management Theories

The management theories and research of the past twenty-five years or so have tried to integrate the findings of scientific management, principles of management, and human relations movements.[8] As Harold Koontz has observed, a "management theory jungle" arose when each of these groups went off in its own direction and ignored the others. The modern followers of scientific management were emphasizing scientific decision making, the use of computers, and quantitative decision tools. The most recent crop of human relations theorists were concentrating on organizational development. And the principles people were succeeded by those who believe one needs to study many managers scientifically before "principles" can be advocated.

Two somewhat overlapping theories attempt to integrate what we know about management today. One is the *systems approach*. Drawing on work from many fields, including biology, this approach analyzes the functions of the total enterprise in terms of systems—inputs, processing, and outputs—with a view toward improving their operations.

Systems theorists point out that most units within an organization (a system) interact with each other and are therefore dependent on each other. For example, the solution to a problem in production will have an impact on other subsystems such as marketing. If production experiences an increase in costs per unit and tries to resolve this problem by producing goods in larger batches, marketing's orders may not be shipped on time. If, as a result, orders are lost, sales go down (affecting the marketing subsystem) and profits go down (affecting the financial system).

Another emphasis of the systems approach is that most organizations are open systems. That is, the organization (system) depends for its inputs (money, materials, employees) on other systems. It cannot solve a production problem without considering whether other systems will ship necessary materials on time or at the right price. In addition, the organization (system) sells its outputs (goods or services) to other systems (customers). If it wishes to survive, it must respond to both the systems that supply it and those it supplies.

Systems theory is a way of looking at and integrating the management functions (planning, organizing, etc.) and the management schools of thought (scientific management, human relations, principles of management) in order to analyze how a manager organizes her or his thoughts and actions.

The other major current theory is called the *contingency approach*. Contingency theorists have abandoned the principles of management approach of Henri Fayol. Fayol and his group were looking for effective techniques to manage any kind of business at any time; contingency theorists believe this is impossible. Their approach is to spell out the conditions of the task (scientific management), the people (human relations), and the managerial job (principles of management) as parts of the whole management situation (systems emphasis) and integrate them all into an effective management solution.

Thus contingency theorists believe that there are many effective ways to perform the various management functions. Consider planning, for instance. Which way should you plan? The contingency theorist argues that you choose Planning Method 1 because that is the best way to plan in your firm's environment, with your firm's people, with your firm's resources, with your firm's managerial values, and for a specific problem. Later chapters will discuss the contingency approach in more detail.

The contingency approach is generally favored today. Still, it is far from acceptable to everyone.[12]

How Relevant Are Management Theory and Research?

Knowledge about management theory and research comes from the field of management itself and from other fields of study as well. Those interested in advancing the practice of management have used the research of organizational psychologists, social psychologists, organizational sociologists, a few social anthropologists and political scientists, and some economists. Those interested in quantitative management tools have benefited from the work of engineers, statisticians, and mathematicians. Some managerial insights can be gained from the work of historians and novelists, too.

Many persons are not happy with the present status of management theory and research. Some management theorists—Leonard Sayles, for instance—feel that it is pedestrian and not well developed.[7] Others, like William Ryan, believe it fails to focus on matters central to the interests and uses of most managers.[8] In fact, there is much in management theory that is neither earthshaking nor practical. What I have tried to do here is summarize the best of what is available, especially that which is relevant to problems most managers face.

Some Answers to the Questions about Management

Here is how the 2,500 respondents (ages nine to seventeen) in the Barnett and Taguiri study answered some of the questions they were asked about management. Their answers were accurate in many ways. The percentage indicating they would choose management careers was greater among older age groups and among those whose parents were managers. About 40 percent of the males and 10 percent of the females wanted to be managers, preferring high-level management positions or running their own business. How do your answers compare to these young people's?

1. What is a manager? What does a manager do at work?

   Respondents to the study mentioned six major activities of managers in the following frequencies: top man (54 percent), supervises (39 percent), organizes (15 percent), divides work (10 percent), helps people (10 percent), and makes decisions (6 percent).

2. Why would you choose a management career as compared to other careers?

   Specify which characteristics of a management career are most attractive.

   The group's reasons for choosing a managerial career were opportunity for leadership (42 percent), high salary (25 percent boys, 12 percent girls), challenge (14 percent), responsibility (12 percent), and the opportunity to work with people (12 percent). Surprisingly, ownership, financing, and responsibility for the firm were infrequent responses.

3. What kind of a person makes a good manager? A successful one?

   The qualities ascribed to a good (successful) manager were competence, leadership, honesty, thoughtfulness, understanding, patience, energy, and self-assurance. Overall, the respondents' reactions on this question were realistic and objective.

4. How does someone become a manager? What career paths lead to management?

   The responses to this question on career pathways to management also showed realism: by serving an apprenticeship (28 percent), by working hard (23 percent), through special education (19 percent), by being appointed (18 percent), by showing technical competence (15 percent), and by exhibiting leadership qualities (12 percent).

5. What kind of life-style does a manager have compared to other people in society?

   Most respondents thought that managers work harder than other people, that their work is more useful than many other people's, and that they earn more. They saw managers as respected in their communities and materially affluent.

The high level of these young people's knowledge about management and their realistic responses were the most dramatic findings of the study. This chapter and others later in the book will provide more complete answers to the above questions, but those of the respondents are certainly reasonable, if abbreviated.

Summary

Chapter 1 introduced you to the world of the manager. *Management was defined as the effective utilization of human and material resources to achieve the enterprise's objectives.* Managers, entrepreneurs, and family business executives work in all kinds of enterprises. The primary focus of this book is on the effective business manager in the private sector. Because managers in the public and not-for-profit sectors perform similar functions, most of the book will apply to these managers as well. An appendix to the book will make the areas of divergence clear.

Managerial functions—what it is managers are expected to do—were defined and compared to various research results. These management functions include:

- Relating to the environment
- Setting objectives and planning
- Decision making and problem solving
- Organization
- Leadership, interpersonal influence, and communication
- Control
- Human resource management and staffing

All of these tasks or functions are important and performed by all managers, but some tasks take more time. Leadership and interpersonal influence claim the largest share. This book is organized according to the above list of functions.

The ways managers, entrepreneurs, and family business executives perform these functions is influenced by their personal world and background, the organizational world in which they work, and the kind of society their organization functions in. A manager can learn to perform these functions through on-the-job training, formal course work, or a combination of both.

Management has met some of the criteria that would permit it to qualify as a profession, but it does not license its practitioners or have a formal conduct board to deal with incompetent and/or unethical managers.

Managers do receive rewards for their work, though: good pay, benefits, and prestige. They must work hard, keep their skills updated, and be willing to meet the challenges of changes in personnel and their work in order to succeed.

The chapter closes with a brief look at management theories and research in historical perspective. Prescientific management, scientific management, principles of management, and the human relations approach are introduced through their most prominent contributors. Two somewhat overlapping theories—the systems approach and the contingency approach—represent current attempts to improve and synthesize earlier theories. The systems approach emphasizes the interactions and reciprocal effects of all the parts of a firm. The effects of a problem in marketing will be felt in production, personnel, and finance, for example. These ramifications will in turn be filtered back to have an effect on marketing.

The contingency approach spells out the conditions of the task (scientific management), the people (human relations), and the managerial job (principles of management) as parts of the whole management situation (systems emphasis), and integrates them all into an effective solution.

With this basis we can learn more about who managers are. Chapter 2 introduces us to managers, their characteristics and activities, and Chapter 3 compares and differentiates the role of the entrepreneur and family business executive.

Questions

1. Give your own definition of a manager's job. What are the decisions and responsibilities of the typical manager?
2. List the managerial functions and define each in your own words. Can you think of practical examples for each function?
3. How does Mintzberg's research on managers' functions equate with the managerial functions listed above? How does he feel about the planning function?
4. Assume you are the manager of a local business asked to speak to a class of freshman business majors. How would you convince them that management is important?
5. Describe the methods by which you can become a manager. Which method do you think is best? Why?
6. You are the same manager as in Question 4 speaking to the same class. Tell them what needs a managerial career could satisfy for them and how each of these needs would be satisfied.
7. What bases did Robert Owen and Charles Babbage lay for management as it is known today?
8. Compare and contrast these management theories: scientific management, principles of management, and human relations. Why do you think each is a useful approach to management?
9. Briefly define the systems approach and the contingency management approach. How does each try to integrate the historical management theories?
10. Which do you think is the most effective approach, given today's challenges to managers—the systems or the contingency approach?

Notes   [1]Rosalind Barnett and Renato Taguiri, "What Young People Think about Managers," *Harvard Business Review* 51 (May–June 1973): 106–118.

[2]Thomas Mahoney et al., "The Job(s) of Management," *Industrial Relations* 4 (February 1965): 97–110.

[3]Henry Mintzberg, *The Nature of Managerial Work* (New York: Harper & Row, 1973).

[4]There are, of course, many definitions of *management*. This is just one. Terminology is a problem in an applied social science field like management. To clarify terminology, see Arthur Bedeian, "An Historical Review of the Efforts in the Area of Management Semantics," *Academy of Management Journal* 17 (March 1974): 101–114.

[5]Jacques Servan-Schreiber, *The American Challenge* (New York: Atheneum, 1968).

[6]Chester I. Barnard, *The Functions of the Executive* (Cambridge, Mass.: Harvard University Press, 1938); Luther Gulick and Lyndal Urwick, eds., *Papers on the Science of Administration* (New York: Institute of Public Administration, 1937); and J. D. Mooney and Alan Reilly, *The Principles of Organization,* rev. ed. (New York: Harper & Bros., 1947).

[7]Leonard Sayles, "Whatever Happened to Management?" *Business Horizons* 13 (April 1970): 25–34.

[8]William Ryan, "Management Practice and Research: Poles Apart," *Business Horizons* 20 (June 1977): 23–29.

References   ### Some Questions about Management

Rosalind Barnett and Renato Taguiri, "What Young People Think about Managers," *Harvard Business Review* 51 (May–June 1973): 106–118.

Management Functions and Roles

Thomas Mahoney et al., "The Job(s) of Management," *Industrial Relations* 4 (February 1965): 97–110. Henry Mintzberg, *The Nature of Managerial Work* (New York: Harper & Row, 1973).

Becoming a Manager

"Company Courses Go Collegiate," *Business Week,* February 26, 1979. William Glueck, "Management Development," *Foundations of Personnel* (Dallas: Business Publications, 1979). Ronald Gribbins and Shelby Hunt, "Is Management a Science?" *Academy of Management Review* 3 (January 1978): 139–144. Craig Lundberg et al., "Contemporary Management Training in Large Corporations," *Training and Development Journal* 27 (September 1973): 34–38.

Management Theories and Research

Eugene Stone, *Research Methods in Organizational Behavior* (Santa Monica, Calif.: Goodyear, 1978).

Historically Significant Management Theories

Charles Babbage, *On the Economy of Machinery and Manufacturers* (London: Charles Knight, 1832). Chester I. Barnard, *The Functions of the Executive* (Cambridge, Mass.: Harvard University Press, 1938). Orlando Behling and Mabry Miller, "An Alternate Approach to the History of Management Thought," *Proceedings of the Academy of Management* (1978). Henri Fayol, *General and Industrial Administration* (New York: Pitman, 1949). Louis Fry, "The Maligned F. W. Taylor: A Reply to His Many Critics," *Academy of Management Review* 1 (July 1976): 124–129. Robert Fulmer and Daniel Wren, "Is There Anything 'New' in Management?" *Journal of Management* 2 (Fall 1976): 71–75.

Frank B. Gilbreth, Jr., and Ernestine Gilbreth Carey, *Cheaper by the Dozen* (New York: Thomas Y. Crowell, 1948). Luther Gulick and Lyndal Urwick, eds., *Papers on the Science of Administration* (New York: Institute of Public Administration, 1937). Dalton McFarland, "Whatever Happened to the Efficiency Movement," *The Conference Board Record* 13 (June 1976): 50–54. Elton Mayo, *The Social Problems of an Industrial Civilization* (Cambridge, Mass.: Division of Research, Graduate School of Business Administration, Harvard University, 1947). John Mee, *A History of Twentieth Century Management Thought* (Columbus: Ohio State University Press, 1959). J. D. Mooney and Alan Reilly, *The Principles of Organization,* rev. ed. (New York: Harper & Bros., 1947). Richard Sterba, "Clandestine Management in the Imperial Chinese Bureaucracy," *Academy of Management Review* 3 (January 1978): 69–77. Frederick W. Taylor, *Scientific Management: The Principles of Scientific Management* (New York: Harper & Bros., 1947). Philip Van Auken and Duane Ireland, "An Historical Review of Management Philosophy," *Proceedings of the Academy of Management* (1978). Charles Wrege and Anne Marie Stotka, "Cooke Creates a Classic: The Story behind F. W. Taylor's Principles of Scientific Management," *Academy of Management Review* 3 (October 1978): 736–749. Daniel Wren, *The Evolution of Management Theory* (New York: Ronald Press, 1972). Daniel Wren and Robert Hay, "Management Historians and Business Historians: Differing Perceptions of Pioneer Contributors," *Academy of Management Journal* 20 (September 1977): 470–475.

Modern Management Theories

Joseph Allen and Bennet Lientz, *Systems in Action* (Santa Monica: Goodyear, 1978). W. Jack Duncan, "Methodological Orientations and Management Theory," *Academy of Management Journal* 15 (September 1972): 337–348. William Greenwood, "Future Management Theory," *Academy of Management Journal* 17 (September 1974): 503–513. Harold Koontz, "The Management Theory Jungle," in *Toward a Unified Theory of Management* (New York: McGraw-Hill, 1964). Justin Longenecker and Charles Pringle, "The Illusion of Contingency Theory as a General Theory," *Academy of Management Review* 3 (July 1978): 679–683. Fred Luthans and Todd Stewart, "A General Contingency Theory of Management," *Academy of Management Review* 3 (July 1978): 683–687. Lee Preston and James Post, "The Third Managerial Revolution," *Academy of Management Journal* 17 (September 1974): 476–486. Jon Shepard and James Houghland, Jr., "Contingency Theory: 'Complex Man' or 'Complex Organization'?" *Academy of Management Review* 3 (July 1978): 413–427. Leland Wooten, "The Mixed Blessings of Contingency Management," *Academy of Management Review* 2 (July 1977): 431–441.

How Relevant Are Management Theory and Research?

Samuel Culbert, "The Real World and the Management Classroom," *California Management Review* 19 (Summer 1977): 65–78. Stephen Robbins, "Reconciling Management Theory with Management Practice," *Business Horizons* 20 (February 1977): 38–47. William Ryan, "Management Practice and Research: Poles Apart," *Business Horizons* 20 (June 1977): 23–29. Leonard Sayles, "Whatever Happened to Management?" *Business Horizons* 13 (April 1970): 25–34.

Chapter 2   The Manager's Job

Learning Objectives

1. Decide which level manager you would like to be—supervisor, middle manager, or top manager—and know what each choice would entail in terms of skills and challenges.
2. Differentiate the manager's job according to task assignment.
3. Relate how personal differences influence each manager's approach to the job.
4. Examine the environment to see how environmental differences shape the managerial job.

Chapter Outline

Differences in Managerial Jobs
Levels of Management
The Supervisor
The Middle Manager
The Top Manager
Differences by Task Assignment
Managerial Jobs and Personal Differences
Managerial Jobs and Organizational Differences
Managerial Jobs and Environmental Differences
Successful Managers
Summary
Questions
Appendix: Jobs Classified by Task and Kinds of Work Pressure
Case: Making It: The Easy Way

Differences in Managerial Jobs

I want you to fantasize. I want you to imagine that you are in a job interview with a recruiter from a company you want to work for very much. The recruiter has asked you for the expected information: your background, grade point average, experience, extracurricular activities in college. Then the recruiter asks: "What kind of position would you like with our company?" You respond: "I'd like to be a manager with your company." The recruiter questions you again: "What kind of a managerial position do you feel you are ready for now? What kind do you aspire to five years from now?"

You pause. These are tough questions to answer and standard ones for recruiters to ask. In order to respond to the recruiter, you need to understand how specific types of managerial positions differ. This chapter is designed to help you achieve that understanding. It will also help you in relating the information presented in the book to specific managerial positions.

Chapter 1 introduced you briefly to the job of a manager. Chapter 2 describes the various positions of managers in more depth; Chapter 3 will differentiate the tasks of entrepreneurs and family business executives from those of managers.

Though the managerial functions such as planning, organizing, and controlling have a role in all managers' positions, there are important differences among managerial jobs. You need to realize these differences in order to be able to choose the managerial job that is right for you. You can also increase your effectiveness in each management job you hold if you understand how it differs from others.

Table 2.1 outlines the different levels of management in the typical organization structure. Managers usually enter the organization as supervisors and are promoted upwards toward top management. Table 2.1 also suggests the differences in various management tasks. Sample job titles are given for each managerial level and task in Table 2.1.

Table 2.1
Differences in
Managerial Jobs by
Level and Task Type

Task Type

Level	General	P/OM[a]	Finance	Marketing	Personnel	Accounting	Logistics
Top	President	Vice-President	Vice-President	Vice-President	Vice-President	Controller	Vice-President
Middle	Division Head	Production Planning Manager	Cash Management Manager	Market Research Manager	Labor Relations Manager	Taxation Manager	Physical Distribution Manager
Supervisory	—	Foreman	District Supervisor of Finance	District Sales Manager	Benefits Supervisor	Accounting Supervisor (Plant Level)	Warehouse Supervisor

[a]Production/operations management.

The Supervisor

The greatest number of managers are supervisors. They have various titles: foreman, ward nurse, department chairperson, section chief, and so on. Robert Douglas, pictured on page 29, is a supervisor in a hospital. Supervisors are in charge of the employees who actually perform most of the work in the organization; in this respect all supervisory positions are similar. Supervisors are managers of employees and resources. The supervisor's job is the one most people who enter management start with. In many ways it is an exciting job. It is where the action is—the firing line. When the supervisor attends to problems and makes decisions, there is immediate feedback, and this can be rewarding.

In addition, the personality and experience of a manager, the organization, and the environment are all factors that create differences in management positions. We may sum up the ways in which management jobs differ as follows:

- *Differences in level* There are three levels in a firm: top managers, who are responsible for a firm's total performance; middle managers, who supervise groups of units; and supervisors, who manage a work unit.
- *Differences in tasks* There are many different management tasks: money management (finance), people management (personnel), and others. Managers' jobs vary according to the different tasks they perform.
- *Personal differences* Personality, experience, and education of managers differ.

Robert Douglas

Robert Douglas, supervisor of the admissions office at County Hospital, is a graduate of West Chester State College, where he majored in business administration. He worked part-time in a local hospital to finance his college education. He joined County as an assistant in the admissions department upon graduation. He has been admissions supervisor for the past five years.

   As admissions supervisor at County Hospital, Douglas is responsible for total coordination of the in-patient admission operations, including pre-admission forms, admissions interviews, room assignment, and insurance information processing. He supervises a staff of five admissions clerks and two secretaries. He assigns work schedules, hires and trains new personnel, and evaluates overall performance.

- *Organizational differences* Types of objectives and missions of organizations differ.
- *Environmental differences* The environments of organizations differ.

This chapter will discuss all these differences in the above order. It will also discuss the successful manager and how to become a successful manager.

Levels of Management

The president of General Motors is called a manager. He or she supervises hundreds of thousands of employees. The supervisor of ten clerks in an insurance office is also called a manager. But their jobs are not the same. Managerial jobs differ according to how high the manager is in the organization. Although some experts like to look at four levels of management, we will concentrate on three: the supervisor, the middle manager, and the top manager. Our purpose is to look at the *differences* between the three levels.

   Studies indicate that supervisors are busy, experience frequent interruptions, and often have to shift back and forth between tasks. They spend most of their time with subordinates, some with peers, and little with superiors or outsiders. For example, consider Table 2.2, which outlines 11½ minutes of a typical supervisor's day. Pat is one of fifty-six supervisors in an auto plant who were observed by Robert Guest and Frank Jasinski.[1]

   Note that Pat had personal contacts with thirteen persons and tried to solve eight problems in thirteen different places all in 11½ minutes. It tends to be that way throughout Pat's day.

   When the researchers figured up the amount of time Pat and his fellow supervisors spent talking about different topics, they found that most time was spent on technical *task details* such as quality of work and work

Table 2.2
A Few Minutes in a
Typical Supervisor's
Day

Time	Description
2:15 p.m.	Pat checks with Scheduler S. Looks at hourly report of number of cars coming through body shop.
2:16	Walks over to R (repair man) on pickup line and checks to see if earlier repair trouble was corrected.
2:17	Calls over inspection foreman to show him a hole missing in a piece. Inspection foreman acknowledges he will notify the trim department.
2:19	Pat tells repair man to locate the hole by eye until it comes through all right.
2:19½	Pat has a drink.
2:20	Pat walks over to Station 5 and asks his utility man how many men he still has to relieve.
2:20½	Moves along the line—Stations 5, 6, 7—checking visually on the quality of work.
2:21	Checks a loose nut on a fixture at Station 7. Speaks with operator.
2:22	Man at Station 3 calls for materials.
2:22¼	Pat tells man at Subassembly Bench E to make up more material.
2:23	Walks over to MH (stock man). Tells stock man the line is getting low on hinges. They discuss the number short and agree there are enough for tomorrow.
2:25	Pat walks from MH to Station 1 and makes visual inspection of the car body to check on the hole discussed earlier at the pickup line.
2:26	Pat sees foreman from preceding section and tells him about the missing hole.
2:26½	A hand signal from Welder W.

Sources: After Robert H. Guest, "Of Time and the Foreman," *Personnel* 32 (1955–1956): 478–486. Adapted by permission of the publisher from *Personnel* 32 (1955–1956), © 1955–1956 by American Management Association, Inc.

progress and supervisory/human resource duties of the employees such as personnel and employee job performance. The supervisors spent 58 percent of their time with people: 30 percent with subordinates, 23 percent with peers and others, and 5 percent with superiors.

The physical activities of the supervisors were also analyzed carefully. The results obtained are shown in Table 2.3. As you can see, the primary physical activities are talking, looking, and manipulating machines.

In one study, Thomas Mahoney and associates asked supervisors what managerial functions they performed.[2] Their responses, translated into the terms used in this text, are summarized in Table 2.4.

In sum, supervisors lead an active, hectic, often interrupted worklife, spending most of their time communicating and caring for the problems of the moment. There have been no studies of supervisors of staff activities. (For definition of staff, see task assignment section later in the chapter.) Their jobs are no doubt different in character. It seems reasonable to believe such jobs are less hectic, less active, and less splintered than the line supervisor's job.

Activity	**Percent of Time**
Talking	46.6%
Looking	20.9
Manipulating	9.6
Walking	6.9
Handing, Carrying	5.6
Reading	2.9
Telephoning	2.4
Writing	2.1
Standing	1.0
Signaling	0.8
Listening	0.6
Showing	0.4
Sitting	0.2
Total	100.0%

Table 2.3
How Supervisors
Spent Their Time
Physically

The Middle Manager

Middle managers are those managers above the supervisors and below the top manager and those who report directly to the top manager. The job of middle management is to manage managers—to act as a buffer between the top managers and supervisors. Linda Richardson, pictured on page 32, is a middle manager.

The jobs of most middle managers seem to be almost opposite to those of top managers or supervisors. The differences are apparent not only from their job behavior but also from their own perceptions of their jobs. Lyman Porter and Edwin Ghiselli describe the self-perceptions of middle and top managers as follows:

Careful planning, thoughtful actions and well-controlled behavior characterize the self perceptions of middle management. . . . Middle management people see themselves as individuals who seldom take rash actions that are not well thought out beforehand. They consider proposed actions from all angles and aspects before they move ahead. They can be counted on not to make hasty or unfounded decisions. They seem to place more reliance on operating within the rules and conditions of the system

Functions	**Percent of Time**
Leadership/interpersonal relationships	57%
Planning	15
Controlling	10
Organizing	5
Other managerial functions	13

Table 2.4
Managerial Functions
Performed by
Supervisors

Linda Richardson

Linda Richardson, compensation manager at Modern Industries, graduated from Michigan State University with a degree in personnel administration in 1964. After graduation she joined the United States Air Force, where she spent three years as a personnel assistant. After leaving the Air Force, she went to work for Modern Industries as a compensation supervisor. She was promoted to compensation manager after seven years. Among her present duties are responsibilities for developing and administering the total compensation package for salaried personnel in the firm.

rather than plunging ahead on their own ideas when these have not been previously tested. . . . In summary, they seem to describe themselves as stable and dependable individuals who try to avoid making mistakes on the job or elsewhere. . . . [3]

J. H. Horne and Tom Lupton analyzed the work lives of sixty-six middle managers.[4] Their findings provide some insights into the job of the middle manager. Their data indicate that the middle manager spends the most time on controlling, organizing, and coordinating and the least time on planning and objective setting. The primary activities of middle managers are defining, creating, collecting, assembling, integrating, and regulating the necessary resources. Table 2.5 provides a breakdown on how they spend their time:

Table 2.5 How Middle Managers Spend Their Time	**Activity**	**Percent of Time**
	Talking with one person	25%
	Discussion with more than one person	19
	Formal meetings	10
	Telephone discussions	9
	Completing paperwork	14
	Reading materials	10
	Thinking/reflecting	2
	Inspections	2
	Other	9

Source: Adapted from J. H. Home and Tom Lupton, "The Work Activities of 'Middle' Managers: An Exploratory Study," *Journal of Management Studies,* February 1965, p. 26. Reprinted by permission.

Table 2.6 Purpose of Middle Managers' Activity	**Purpose**	**Percent of Time**
	Information (giving, seeking, etc.)	42%
	Advice (giving, seeking, etc.)	6
	Decisions (giving, confirming, reviewing, etc.)	8
	Instructions (giving, receiving, confirming, etc.)	9
	Plans (coordinating, reviewing, etc.)	11
	Explanations (seeking, preparing, etc.)	15
	Other	9

Source: J. H. Horne and Tom Lupton, "The Work Activities of 'Middle' Managers: An Exploratory Study," *Journal of Management Studies*, February 1965, p. 26. Reprinted by permission.

The middle managers studied indicated their activities had a number of purposes. These purposes and their relative significance are noted in Table 2.6.

Horne and Lupton found that middle managers spend most of their time talking face to face informally to exchange information to help them organize and control resources (see Table 2.6). They also found that the closer the middle managers are to top management, the higher the percentage of time they spend away from their firm. For example, upper middle managers spent 10 percent of their time away from the company.

Middle managers have much less physical activity and more paperwork and meetings than supervisors. The job of the middle manager is less hectic, more reflective, and less active. In view of these differences, you can see that being a successful supervisor does not necessarily mean that you will be successful at middle management.

The Top Manager

An individual who is successful first as a supervisor and then as a middle manager may eventually reach the top. Top managers have job titles like chairman of the board, president, executive vice-president, hospital administrator, or secretary of state. The top managers are the chief policy-making officers of an enterprise. Jesse Hill, pictured on page 34, is a top manager.

Jesse Hill, Jr.

Jesse Hill, Jr., has been a member of the University of Georgia Board of Regents from the State-at-Large since 1973, when he was appointed to serve the unexpired portion of a board member who resigned. Hill was born in St. Louis, Missouri, on May 30, 1926. He received the B.S. degree in mathematics from Lincoln University and the M.B.A. degree in actuarial science and business administration from the University of Michigan. He was awarded the honorary LL.D. degree from both Morris Brown College and Clark College.

He is, and has been since 1973, president and chief executive officer and chairman of the Executive Committee of Atlanta Life Insurance Company, Atlanta. He joined Atlanta Life in 1949, and, after serving as actuarial assistant, acting actuary, and actuary, became vice-president-actuary and a member of the Board of Directors in 1970.

He is president of the Atlanta Inquirer, Inc., and president of Enterprise Investments. He is also president of the Atlanta Chamber of Commerce and a member of the Boards of Directors of Delta Air Lines, National Service Industries, Rich's and H. J. Russell Enterprises.

He is a member of the Boards of Directors of the National Urban Coalition, Opportunity Funding Corporation, National Urban League, Southern Christian Leadership Conference, and Martin Luther King Center for Social Change.

He is a member of the Board of Trustees of Big Bethel A.M.E. Church, Atlanta, and is the superintendent of the Sunday School of that church.

He is a member and past president of the National Insurance Association and is a member of the American Academy of Actuaries, the Southeastern Actuarial Club, and the Atlanta Actuarial Club.

He is a past chairman of the National Alliance of Businessmen for metropolitan Atlanta and north Georgia, a past member of the Board of Directors of the Metropolitan Atlanta Rapid Transit Authority (MARTA), past chairman of MARTA's Acquisition Committee, and past chairman of the Atlanta Crime Commission.

He received in 1972 the Temple Award, established by an endowment from the Hebrew Benevolent Congregation, for his contribution to improvement of human relations in Atlanta. He has also received numerous other awards from civic and civil rights organizations.

He is an Army veteran of the Korean War.

Source: Adapted from *The System Summary*, a publication of the University System of Georgia 14 (May 1978): 11–12.

In a recent study conducted by *Fortune*, it was found that top managers are highly educated: 67 percent had academic work beyond a bachelor's degree; almost 50 percent had a master's and/or doctoral degree.[5] Typically the degrees were in business. Some had degrees in law or engineering. The top managers normally came from the middle class. Frequently, their fathers had been in business or a profession. The study found that the typical top manager of a major business was from fifty to sixty-five years of age and had spent most of his/her life with the current company. The successful top manager worked long hours each week. The median was fifty-five to sixty-five hours per week. Table 2.7 details the specific findings.

In their study, Porter and Ghiselli examined the self-perceptions of top managers. They concluded:

Table 2.7
Background Information on Successful Top Managers

Educational Factors

Degrees Received	**College Majors**[a]
28% college degree	49% undergraduate: business
19% postgraduate study	33% graduate: business
24% master's degree	28% law
24% doctorate	27% engineering
5% attended college	26% economics

Background Factors

Father's Occupation	**Socioeconomic Background**
39% business executive	43% lower middle class
25% professional	41% upper middle class
12% skilled laborer	9% poor
7% farmer	5% wealthy
7% clerical	2% other
8% head of same corporation	
2% unskilled laborer	

Individual Factors

Hours Worked per Week	**Primary Functional Emphasis**
41% 45–54	28% marketing
38% 55–64	25% finance
14% over 65	19% P/OM
7% under 45	14% legal
	14% other

Age	**Crucial Factors in Success**[b]
34% 55–59	80% experience with present company
26% 60–64	34% experience with another company
22% over 65	14% organizing this company
15% 35–50	10% inheritance/family influence
3% below 35	6% ownership influence in company

[a] May have more than one degree.
[b] May have a multiple background.
Source: After Charles Burck, "A Group Profile of the Fortune 500 Chief Executives," *Fortune*, May 1976, pp. 172, 174, 176. Used by permission.

Members of top management perceive themselves as active, self-reliant, and generally willing to take action on the basis of their own faith in themselves and in their abilities, rather than simply on the basis of the weight of the objective evidence. They are willing to take risks when they think they have good, original ideas, and they possess the confidence that their decisions will lead to success. They are not easily discouraged and are able to capitalize on opportunities. In their social relations they are candid and straightforward and show confidence here as well as in the performance of their duties on the job. They picture themselves as behaving in a cultured and refined manner toward others without having to appear to ingratiate themselves.[6]

A recent article in the *Wall Street Journal* describing J. Peter Grace, president and chief executive officer of W. R. Grace and Company (1978 current assets $1,358,842 millions), offers some additional insights into the character and life-style of a top manager. At the time of this article (1975), Grace was sixty-two years old and had worked for the family firm for thirty years. He was regularly working eighty hours per week, putting in 112 hours per week during the two annual budget months.

No one says it's easy to work for Peter Grace. Except for infrequent breaks for his beloved horseplay, Mr. Grace hates to waste a single minute that could be used for work. Colleagues say he carries a special key that makes the elevator to his 48th floor office move faster by skipping stops; that saves a minute for work. Mr. Grace spends the 35-minute limousine ride between his Long Island estate and his Manhattan office dictating memos to a secretary (he has eight) who rides with the chauffeur. On frequent business trips via corporate jet, Mr. Grace becomes so absorbed in his work that he sometimes forgets to eat—so underlings don't eat either. (In many ways a softhearted man, Mr. Grace has been known to apologize for such carelessness.)

Underlings are expected to have instant answers to Mr. Grace's numerous questions. . . . What's more, Grace executives routinely compile massive statistical reports that Mr. Grace scrutinizes from cover to cover (it is said that he rejected one such report because a single punctuation mark was misplaced). . . .

His colleagues say Peter Grace has changed remarkably little over three decades and that he appears to enjoy every minute of his job. Says Mr. Griswold: "Peter gets a hell of a kick out of being a big businessman; he likes the recognition that he isn't just a rich playboy." Mr. Grace himself says that as long as he holds his job he'll continue to work as hard as he does now. There's no point, he says, in working less hard than one is able.[7]

There have been a number of studies of the top manager's job; these are summarized in Table 2.8. Generally, they have shown that most top managers' jobs are similar to supervisors' jobs in their activity level and hectic quality.

Table 2.8
Major Findings of Studies of Top Managers' Jobs

Author of Study	Carlson	Mintzberg	Copeman et al.	Case	Stieglitz	Connors and Hutts	Business Management
Major Finding	hectic job: 44% time away from the firm, 65% away from office; long hours, much of it in consultation, most of time with frequent interruptions	hectic job with frequent interruptions; often out of office	hectic job: in a typical hour the top manager has 3 visitors, 4 phone calls	time spent as follows: 56% in conference (usually with employees) 12% lunch (usually working lunches) 8% reading & dictating reports 7% reading & dictating mail 5% making decisions & thinking	top management work takes long hours	spent time as follows: 36.0% out of office 25.8% planning; when in office, most of the time was in conference; 3.2% alone in office	hectic job: typical executive— worked 63-hour week (10 away from office); attended 2–5 meetings weekly; received interrupting phone calls (typically 2 hours daily); spent less than 2 hours a day alone

Sources: After Sune Carlson, *Executive Behavior* (Stockholm: Strömbergs, 1951); Henry Mintzberg, "The Manager's Job; Folklore and Fact," *Harvard Business Review*, July–August 1975, pp. 49–61; G. Copeman, H. Luijk, and F. Haneka, *How the Executive Spends His Time* (London: Business Publications, 1963); Fred Case, "An Executive Day," *California Management Review*, Fall 1962, pp. 67–70; Harold Stieglitz, *The Chief Executive and His Job* (New York: National Industrial Conference Board, 1969); Edward Connors and Joseph Hutts, "How Administrators Spend Their Day," *Hospitals* 41 (February 16, 1967): 45–50, 141; and "How 179 Chief Executives Waste Their Time," *Business Management*, March 1968, pp. 12–14.

Some have speculated that one reason top executives often "jump channels" and deal with supervisors rather than middle managers is that the two jobs are similar in activity level and the individuals in them may thus have similar personalities. Top managers spend most of their time with peers, outsiders, and to a lesser extent, subordinates. This is in contrast to supervisors, who spend most of their time with subordinates and peers, and middle managers, who spend most time with subordinates and peers.

What percentage of time do top managers spend in the management functions? Mahoney and his colleagues found that top managers portioned their time among the various management functions as indicated in Table 2.9.[8] As you can see, Mahoney and associates found the top managers spending the most time in planning and leadership functions and the least time in organizing/coordinating functions.

As we have seen, managerial positions vary with respect to their emphasis on certain functions depending on their level in the firm. Most of the supervisor's time is spent on task details such as quality and quantity of work. Therefore, the supervisor is most closely involved with employee job performance and relating to subordinates. The middle manager is a buffer between the other two levels. Most of his/her time is spent controlling, organizing, coordinating, integrating and regulating necessary resources.

Top managers are most involved with the planning and leadership functions. They spend most of their time with peers and outsiders. The jobs are physically and psychologically different too, supervisors and top managers having more hectic and fragmented jobs, while middle managers, though sometimes subject to higher levels of frustration, can work at a somewhat slower pace.

Differences by Task Assignment

The second dimension of managerial jobs we will examine in this chapter is task type. First, let's distinguish between line and staff executives.

A line executive is one who is part of the direct chain of command.

Table 2.9
How Top Managers Divide Their Time Among Management Functions

Function	Percent of Time
Planning	28%
Leadership/interpersonal relationships	22
Organization and coordination	12
Control	14
Other	24

Source: Thomas Mahoney et al., "The Jobs of Management," *Industrial Relations* 4 (February 1965): 97–110. Reprinted by permission.

Typically, line managers supervise those aspects of the firm's activities directly related to the production of the goods or services which the enterprise offers society. Production/operations management, marketing, financial management, and general management are generally considered line functions. Basically, line executives have the most power in the enterprise.

A staff executive is one whose role is to provide counsel, advice, and expertise to help line executives and their units achieve organizational objectives.

A large number of staff positions can exist: for example, personnel/labor relations, accounting, logistics, administrative services, management information services, public relations, research and development, legal counsel, and engineering. Staff units and their executives exert influence by persuasion. Occasionally staff units are given authority to enforce laws and company policies in certain decision areas.

Space does not permit exploration of all the possible differences among managers of different task types. A few pieces of research may illustrate some of these differences. In studies mentioned earlier, Horne and Lupton took a look at how middle managers' jobs differ by task type.[9] Table 2.10 is a reformulation in our terms of what they found.

There are significant differences between line and staff positions in the time spent performing the management functions. Line departments spend much more time controlling (they have the power to do so) and much less in planning and organizing. The reverse is true in personnel, the staff function. Chapter 14 discusses the relationship between line and staff in more depth.

With regard to time away from the office, there are again clear-cut differences. But they are not line and staff differences. Personnel and engineering managers are home based. Marketing and purchasing managers are often away from the office.

Table 2.10
Average Percentage of Managerial Functions by Task Type

Task Type	Managerial Function (Percent)			
	Planning	Organizing	Controlling	Other
Production/operations management (line)	17%	19%	46%	18%
Marketing (line)	14	17	53	16
Finance (line)	15	12	60	13
Personnel (staff)	33	26	20	21

Source: Based on J. H. Horne and Tom Lupton, "The Work Activities of 'Middle' Managers: An Exploratory Study," *Journal of Management Studies*, February 1965, p. 23. Reprinted by permission.

Rosemary Stewart has studied differences in managerial jobs by task type for many years.[10] She finds that we can see differences in jobs along the following dimensions:

1. The extent and nature of contacts with other people on the job.
2. The work pattern.
   a. Self-generating work versus responding to others' work.
   b. Degree of fragmentation.
3. Uncertainty.
   a. Number of crises.
   b. Amount of control over problems.
   c. Amount of valid information to do the job.
   d. How far ahead the manager can plan.
4. Responsibility.
   a. Direct responsibility for resources.
   b. Shared or individual responsibility.
5. Demands on private life—to be away from home, transferred often, etc.

Using these task dimensions, she has defined the seven basic task job types listed below.

Job Type I: Manager of a Separate Unit

Type I.1 (internal unit): Most of the time of this type of manager (a typical example is a plant manager) is spent contacting subordinates. Type I.2 (external unit, such as branch bank manager): This manager has internal contacts but also must find and deal with customers.

Both these types of managers have little contact with peers and organizational politics. There is little role conflict. (Role conflict is a condition in which the person receives conflicting expectations about what his or her job is and how it should be performed.) In these types of jobs, responsibility for performance is clearly defined. Thus when these managers make mistakes, it is very clear that they are at fault.

Job Type II: Field Supervision

This manager is responsible for several units in an area. Type II is normally a higher-level job. Important aspects of the Type II job are people management, dealing with known contacts, and large demands on personal time because of travel. There are few peers to relate to. Some of these jobs are highly structured; others are more unstructured.

Job Type III: People Management

The contacts of personnel managers are primarily downward and upward.

There are a few peer contacts and a few external contacts. A large percentage of time is spent with known contacts.

Job Type IV: Work Flow Jobs

A large number of these jobs exist in factories and home offices. Contacts are with peers and subordinates. There is heavy peer dependence. Role conflict is a serious problem. There are six job categories in Job Type IV. These are described in the appendix to the chapter (Exhibit 2.1).

Job Type V: Solo Jobs

A few managers, usually specialists, work alone on their projects.

Job Type VI: Consulting and Advisory Jobs

These managers work primarily with top managers. Many contacts are required. (Some advisory jobs exist in IV.) Advisors can exist in structured, regular relationships or unstructured relationships.

Job Type VII: External Jobs

In these jobs, the major factor is external contact. These jobs have conflict and uncertainty. There are three categories of this type of job: VII.1: People management is important; external contacts are crucial. Time away from the company is great. VII.2: These jobs—purchasing, government relations, and advertising—involve many external contacts. VII.3: A few managers, usually public relations and general managers, spend most or all of their time away from the firm in making and maintaining contacts. These seven jobs are described in more detail (relationships, characteristics, types and examples) in the appendix to the chapter (Exhibit 2.1).

All managerial jobs have some stresses. To be successful as a manager you need to choose a position that has the kinds of problems you can live with; this is not as difficult as it might sound. Exhibit 2.2 in the appendix describes the kinds of pressures experienced in each of Stewart's seven job types.

Managerial Jobs and Personal Differences

After the organization has defined a managerial position in level and task, an individual occupies it. Consider two supervisors of a production unit. Tom, sixty-four years old and a graduate of the "school of hard knocks," has been with the company forty-four years. He is outgoing, bowls with members of his work unit, lives in their neighborhood, is optimistic, and sees his career as successful and himself as a professional supervisor. Joe is twenty-one years old, a graduate of the University of Missouri-Rolla in mechanical engineering. He is quiet, uses words sparingly, and is younger by ten years than the youngest of his new work group. He does not believe in fraternizing with employees.

Would you expect Joe and Tom to deal with disciplinary problems, planning, and control similarly? They probably will not. Each manager brings to the job education, experience, abilities, motivations, and personalities that are different. This will influence how each manages. The impact of these differences will be explored in more depth in other chapters, particularly Chapters 5 and 6.

Managerial Jobs and Organizational Differences

The objective of this section is to make you aware that differences in the work organization's objectives, task, and work climate influence the managerial task and make it different in some ways. This is important. You may believe you can move from one enterprise to another and use the same managerial style in the new job that you used in the old one. But, generally speaking, more effective managers adjust their managerial style (interpersonal and managerial skills) according to the enterprise's objectives, task, and climate.

Years ago, Peter Drucker made this point well when he asked—rhetorically, of course—if there would be any adjustments necessary if we made these managerial transfers:

- Harry Truman: from White House to Kremlin
- Joseph Stalin: from Kremlin to Vatican
- Pius XII: from Vatican to White House

As a human being you have many characteristics like other people's. These similarities are important. Differences are equally important. Are work organizations all the same? In some ways, yes. They all strive to achieve objectives, perform tasks, have a work climate. But these specific aspects of organizations are not all the same.

Consider a manager who moves from Exxon to the Orthodox Church of North and South America (see Table 2.11). The manager would notice many similarities after the job change. He or she would be paid a salary. The job descriptions might be similar; similar equipment might be used. The manager would probably supervise a work group in both places. But there would be differences—some slight, some significant. The boss's title would be different. The boss's clothing would be different. The traditions of the organization would be different in view of differences in objectives and history. The number of employees would also differ.

Table 2.11
Comparison of the
Orthodox Church of
North and South
America and Exxon

Organizational Element	Orthodox Church	Exxon
A. Objectives	1. solvency 2. satisfied employees and members 3. growth in number of souls saved and depth of spiritual experience 4. survival 5. influence in the world 6. preservation of liturgies and traditions of Christ and the Orthodox Church	1. profitability 2. satisfied employees and clients 3. growth in profits and sales 4. survival 5. influence in the community 6. innovations in marketing and products
B. Time duration	since the time of Christ; established in Orthodox form in 3rd century and in America in 18th century	since mid-19th century
C. Stable pattern of interactions	yes	yes
D. Hierarchies of managers	council of patriarchs, patriarch of Constantinople, patriarchs of metropolitans, priests, members	board, chairman of the board, president, vice-president, middle managers, supervisors, employees
E. Tasks	1. teach Christ's doctrines 2. administer the sacraments 3. conduct liturgies, etc.	1. explore for petroleum 2. refine petroleum products 3. distribute petroleum products, etc.

In her studies of managerial jobs, Stewart has found significant differences in managerial job demands in various organizations.[11] In Table 2.12, for example, contrast the relatively great demands subordinates place on the police inspector, hospital inspector, and chain store manager with the light demand on the bank manager. As Table 2.12 shows, the number of contacts, pressure exerted by bosses, and other factors in managerial positions also vary with the nature of the organization.

It is fairly easy to see differences between organizations in two different sectors. But there are significant differences between organizations within the same sector. Consider AT&T and Laidlaw Products (a small manufacturer of fly swatters), the largest employer in the United States and one of the smaller ones. There are major differences between them in number of levels of hierarchy, amount of specialization, amount of paper work, formality of communications, and many other factors.

As is pointed out later in the book, organizations are like people in that they go through a life cycle: a lean and energetic youth, a prosperous and vigorous middle age, a fragile and tenuous old age. This makes for further differences.

Table 2.12
Pressures on
Managers
in Different
Sectors

Job Title	Police Inspector	Hospital Administrator	Bank Manager	Store (Chain) Manager
Behavioral demands made:				
By subordinates	⊗	⊗	○	⊗
By peers and other seniors	⊗	●	○	○
By boss(es) dependence	○	●	○	○
By external contacts	●	⊗	●	○
By short-term contacts	●	⊗	●	○
By conflicting demands	●	●		
On private life	●	○	⊗	○
By exposure	●	⊗	●	⊗
Totals	13	10	9	3

Key	● High	⊗ Medium	○ Low

Scoring: 2 for high, 1 for medium. Exceptions: exposure—4 for high and 2 for medium; conflicting demands—1 for high (more conflicts than usual) and 0 for medium.

Differences in work climate also lead to differences in the managerial jobs. The term *climate* is hard to explain, so let me give you a parallel example you are probably familiar with.

If you looked around to select the college you were going to attend, you probably noticed differences in atmosphere, spirit, or what management people call work climate or character. There are differences of this kind between work organizations too—or, if they are large enough, between parts of organizations. Each organization develops a "culture" of its own, with its own language, ceremonies, and ways of doing things. So when you start to work for an organization, you are entering a different world.

I believe work climates develop because of the following factors:

- *The history and evolution of each enterprise is different.* A coal-mining firm develops in a different way from a cookie factory.

- *The crises in one enterprise differ from those of another.* Fashion design firms face more crises than nut and bolt factories.

- *The age of the enterprise differs.* The older the enterprise, the more tradition-bound it is. For instance, the U.S. Navy has a longer history than the Peace Corps.

- *The leadership in each enterprise is different.* Leaders tend to attract other managers much like themselves, who then institutionalize their way of doing things. Consider the Federal Bureau of Investigation and

Table 2.13
Definition of a "Good Manager" in Two Businesses

Factor	Corporation 1	Corporation 2
1. Managerial work values	You and the company are one. You and work are synonomous. Therefore good managers take work home, come in on Saturdays and Sundays, skip vacations.	Good managers are well organized. Therefore they get their work done at the office. If they take work home or skip vacations, they must be inefficient.
2. Money values	Money is something you invest. A good manager uses the budget to achieve the firm's objectives and can make a good case for more funds each quarter because he or she has been so successful.	Money is a scarce resource. It needs to be used carefully. The good manager is one who uses it so wisely that a budget surplus can be returned to the home office at the end of the quarter.
3. Equipment values	Equipment used symbolizes the corporation and its success. Since we are successful, we must always have the latest equipment, whether it is typewriters, computers, or company cars.	Equipment is a means to an end. Use it until it is used up. Good maintenance will make it last longer.
4. Manager's personal behavior off the job	You represent your company at all times. You must appear to be reliable and dependable. Therefore you will not get divorced, you will be active in community charities, you will dress formally, you will never drink to excess, you will be active in your church, you will not get into debt, etc.	Your personal life is your own. As long as you stay within the law and do your job during work hours you will be rewarded.

Source: Based on a 1965 series of lectures by Eugene Emerson Jennings.

J. Edgar Hoover, IBM and Thomas Watson Sr., the University of Chicago and Robert M. Hutchins.

The values and behavior patterns that make up a work climate affect how work gets done in organizations. Consider Table 2.13. Table 2.13 is included to illustrate the significant differences in values which can exist between two businesses. These value differences normally arise from the value differences between different founders. Founders typically hire employees who hold the same values. Thus the existing values are reinforced by the employees. The people working at a firm reinforce each other in these values until such time as the society changes.

To sum up, when you go looking for a managerial job, remember that the world of work is a cafeteria of organizations offering a variety of choices. The key is to match yourself to the right organizations, and this takes knowledge of yourself, knowledge of organizations, and some luck.

Managerial Jobs and Environmental Differences

Managerial jobs differ too because the environments of their organizations differ. Consider these dimensions of the environment:

Dependence on others The more dependent an organization is on resource suppliers, regulators, clients/customers, and competitors, the more pressure the managers receive from the environment.

Technology Managerial jobs vary too because of differences in technology. Technology varies from routine to nonroutine. A typical example of routine technology is the assembly line. In this type of technology, the manager's job focuses on maintenance of the assembly line and training and staffing with relatively unskilled employees. A typical nonroutine technology is the job shop. In this case, each order comes in with specifications from the customer—for example, for a specialized replacement part. In the job shop, the employees are highly skilled and managers have more planning and scheduling to do than with the routine assembly line.

Volatility Environments vary in volatility. Some industries such as pop records and fashions are subject to frequent and extreme changes while others such as manufacturers of washboards change only slightly, if at all. The skills necessary to operate in a volatile industry are quite different from those needed in a slow and steady business.

As you will see in later chapters, all the managerial functions are affected by environment.

Thus managers have many things in common, especially the managerial functions they perform. But significant variation occurs because of differences in level, task, and personal, organizational, and environmental factors.

Successful Managers

The preceding section made you aware of how difficult it is to define and predict success in management, given all the differences in managerial situations. Nevertheless it makes sense to ask what a successful manager is. Let me describe three managers:

- *Manager 1* Age fifty-eight. Born in a slum. Father died when he was six. Started selling papers at age seven. Paid his own way through college. Graduated in 1929. Held a series of jobs. Joined a major grocery chain. Rose through the ranks to a middle management job. Liked it and refused further promotions. His unit is rated above average in performance and employee satisfaction.

- *Manager 2* Age thirty-five. Middle-class background. Head of branch office of H&R Block Tax Service. Branch was losing money when she came two years ago. Since then she has cut the loss in half. Branch rated in bottom 10 percent in terms of performance. Had been in bottom 5 percent when she arrived. Employee satisfaction rating below average for the company.

- *Manager 3* Age forty-one. Lower-class background. Graduated with B.S. in nursing two years ago, R.N. two years before that. Took over a hospital ward where performance was rated much below average but employee satisfaction was high. Now the ward is rated number 1 in performance. Employee satisfaction is rated below average for the hospital.

Which of these three managers is the most successful? Why? After thinking about these questions, consider the following points:

- *Success is defined by the person.* If you ask five children in a slum what it would take to be successful in a job, you will get one set of answers. Ask five students at private high schools in Winnetka, Illinois; Darien, Connecticut; or upper-class suburbs elsewhere and you will get a different answer. Personal success is one measure of managerial success.

- *Success is defined by the organization and by society.* Organizations usually describe successful managers as those whose units have achieved or exceeded the organization's objectives. These vary, but can be defined in terms of efficiency (for example, low costs) and effectiveness (for example, satisfied clients, customers, employees).

- *A manager can be successful by his or her own definition, but less successful by the organization's or society's definition.*

- *A manager can be successful in reaching some objectives and less successful in reaching others.*
  The criterion problem is a serious one: Is success meeting objectives or making progress toward meeting them? Which objectives are the most important: client satisfaction, low cost, employee satisfaction, or profitability?

- *Many organizations, especially smaller and medium-sized ones, never really define what managerial success is and may not tell the manager when he or she is successful.* To them, success is so vague that they do not want to try to define it.

It is easier to define managerial success for a supervisor than for a middle manager. For example, some organizations equate success for the supervisor's unit with success for the supervisor. In general, the higher an individual manager is in an organization, the harder it is to define success for the manager.

So your first problem in trying to become a successful manager is to define success for yourself. Then you need to match yourself with an enterprise whose definition of success fits yours.

Now, the next question is: What does it take to be a successful manager? Figure 2.1 illustrates the factors that I believe contribute to managerial success.

To be successful, managers need certain abilities, both those that are innate and those developed by education, experience, and training. A successful manager needs technical, interpersonal, and conceptual abilities. The specific abilities necessary for managerial success are discussed in Chapter 5.

Successful managers have certain attitudes and motivations. (See Chapters 5 and 6.) Naturally, organizational rewards—pay, promotion, etc.—and organizational climate affect the manager's motivation and attitudes.

Note that the model in Figure 2.1 does not list *hard work*. This is assumed under motivation and abilities. Most successful managers work hard. But it does not follow that the harder you work, the more successful you are. Success depends on other factors as well. For instance, will the Oakland Athletics hire the player who bats .350 and practices 2 hours a week or the one who practices 20 hours a week and bats .500? Will the salesperson who sells his or her quota by working four days a week be kept on rather than the one who works six days a week and does not make his or her quota? What do you think? The notion that hard work equals success is clearly a myth.

Success is also a function of the right match between the individual's abilities and the job he or she takes. People are different. A person is successful when his or her strengths are matched by the needs of the job. Some people are more creative than others and are bored by detail. Such individuals will be more successful in jobs that require more creativity than working as, say, a quality control supervisor in a nut and bolt factory. Most psychologists make this point, and Chapter 10 discusses it in more detail.

Figure 2.1
Factors in
Managerial Success

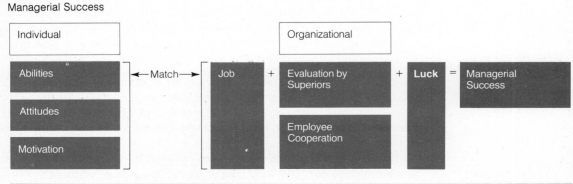

Interpersonal influence is another factor in success. Other things being equal, if your employees like you and work with you, this will help you succeed. Chapter 13 discusses how to achieve employee cooperation. Similarly, if your superiors like you, this too will help you succeed. You just learned that managerial success is hard to define. If the superiors of two managers being considered for promotion like one (and that one is a member of the same clubs, goes to the same church, belongs to the same social group, etc.), he or she has an edge. Depending on how you interpret this, it will make you a cynic, a realist, or an angry young manager.

Still, just as ability, hard work, and motivation alone do not equal success, so the boss's smile is not everything either. Look at it this way: With many professors, whether you get a B or a C when you are on the borderline might be affected by whether they like you. But a professor cannot give you an A if you are a D student because he or she likes you. It is the same with managerial success. You have to get close to the success category in terms of results, ability, and so on to have an edge. This is discussed further in Chapter 14.

The last factor, luck, is almost never mentioned in reference to managerial success. Why? Because it is hard to study, and managers would rather believe their own ability propelled them into successful careers. Nonetheless, luck is a significant factor. The boss's unexpected heart attack putting you in the home office five years early has little to do with your ability. Your joining a company whose R&D department stumbles onto

Source: King Features Syndicate, Inc. 1974.

the formula for cheap gasification of coal when you are just ready for promotion is not entirely a matter of ability either. The fact is, some success results from happening to be in the right place at the right time.

I discuss the role of luck in success because it is a factor and because unless you are aware of it you will not be able to fairly assess your prospects for success. If you do not consider the role luck plays, you may begin to blame lack of promotion entirely on lack of ability and think, "I don't have it." This can become a self-fulfilling prophecy. Obviously luck can be over-estimated too. We all know people who blame an F in algebra on bad luck when they did not study for the exam.

Abilities, attitudes, motivation, evaluation by superiors, cooperation of employees, and luck—how should each of these factors be weighted? Which is the most important? The answer is that you need them all. I will not try to assign weights to all those factors that contribute to managerial success.

Summary

All managers' positions involve the performance of the managerial functions such as planning, organizing, and controlling. But there are differences among managerial jobs, and this chapter describes these differences in depth. The chapter is also designed to be used as a guideline in planning your managerial career and helping you become a success.

First, differences exist in the different *levels* of managerial positions in the typical organization. There are three basic levels: supervisory, middle management, top management. The greatest number of managers are supervisors. Most people who enter management start as supervisors. Supervisors are busy, experience frequent interruptions, often shift back and forth between tasks, and spend most of their time with subordinates and peers. They lead active, hectic, often interrupted worklives, spending most of their time communicating and caring for the problems of the moment.

Middle managers are those managers above supervisors and below top managers. The job of the middle manager is to manage managers—to act as a buffer between the top manager and the supervisors. Compared to supervisors, middle managers are far less physically active and far more involved in paper work and meetings. Their job is less hectic, more reflective, and more frustrating.

The top managers are the chief policy-making officers of the enterprise. Top managers spend most of their time with peers, outsiders, and to a lesser extent, subordinates. The top manager's schedule is hectic, like that of the supervisor.

Second, managerial jobs differ by *task type*. A line executive is one who is part of the direct chain of command. A staff executive is one whose role is to provide counsel, advice, and expertise to help line executives and their units to achieve organizational objectives. Basically, line executives have the most power in the enterprise. Staff units and their executives exert influence by persuasion.

Third, after an organization has defined a managerial position in level and task, *personal differences* enter the picture. Each manager brings to the job different education, experience, abilities, and motivations, and a unique personality.

Differences in *the organization's objectives, task, and work climate* influence the managerial task and make it different in some ways. In some ways organizations are all the same; they all have objectives, perform tasks, and have a work climate. But there are differences too—in the history and evolution of the firm, the crises it has faced, its age, and its leaders.

Finally, the degree of an enterprise's *dependence* on others, its *technology,* and its *volatility* are environmental factors which serve to differentiate managerial jobs.

A number of factors affect managerial success. To be successful a manager must have certain attitudes, motivations, and abilities; work hard; find the right organization; know the right people; and be lucky.

You can now use the knowledge you have gained in this chapter about the different dimensions of managers' jobs to answer the questions put by the recruiter at the beginning of this chapter: "What kind of managerial position do you feel you are ready for now? Which kind do you aspire to five years from now?" You should also be able to formulate your own definition of managerial success and determine what you need to work on to enhance your chances. In the next chapter we will look at the special situations that differentiate entrepreneurs and family business executives from other managers. Perhaps you are better suited to one of these careers.

Questions

1. You are a supervisor in a large manufacturing plant. Describe what a typical day would be like in terms of managerial functions. How would you spend most of your time? With whom?
2. What is a middle manager? How do middle managers spend most of their time? What activities are most important at this level according to Horne and Lupton?
3. Use your knowledge of the *Fortune* study of 500 chief executive officers to describe the typical top manager (background, education, age, etc.).
4. What management functions do top managers view as most important according to Mahoney? Given your new knowledge about the top manager's job, do you think the emphasis on planning is justified?
5. What is a staff executive? A line executive? Give examples of each. How does this difference in task assignment affect the role a manager plays—for example, who is more powerful?

6. What dimensions did Stewart use to differentiate managerial jobs by task type? What are the seven basic types of jobs she has described along these dimensions?
7. Do you think you will handle your management responsibilities the same way another manager with a different background but the same type job would? How would personal differences affect the way each of you would perform the same type job?
8. Think about a firm or company whose organization you are familiar with. In what dimensions is it the same as other organizations? What organizational factors would be unique to this particular firm?
9. Managerial jobs are influenced by differences in the environment of the organization. What are these environmental dimensions? Illustrate each one.
10. Given the different factors that influence managerial success, explain how you would try to plan your own successful management career.

Notes

[1]Robert Guest, "Of Time and the Foreman," *Personnel* 32 (May 1956): 478–486; and Frank Jasinski, "Foreman Relationships outside the Work Group," *Personnel* 33 (1956–1957): 130–136.

[2]Thomas Mahoney et al., "The Jobs of Management," *Industrial Relations* 4 (February 1965): 97–110.

[3]Lyman Porter and Edwin Ghiselli, "The Self Perceptions of Top and Middle Management Personnel," *Personnel Psychology* 10 (1957): 397–406. Reprinted by permission.

[4]J. H. Horne and Tom Lupton, "The Work Activities of 'Middle' Managers: An Exploratory Study," *Journal of Management Studies* 2 (1965): 14–33.

[5]Charles Burck, "A Group Profile of the Fortune 500 Chief Executives," *Fortune*, May 1976, pp. 172–177, 308–312.

[6]Porter and Ghiselli, "The Self Perceptions," p. 401. Reprinted by permission.

[7]"J. Peter Grace," *Wall Street Journal,* April 2, 1975, p. 7. Reprinted with permission of *The Wall Street Journal,* © 1975 Dow Jones & Co., Inc. All rights reserved.

[8]Mahoney, "The Jobs of Management."

[9]Horne and Lupton, "The Work Activities."

[10]Rosemary Stewart, "The Manager's Job: Discretion vs. Demand," *Organizational Dynamics* 2 (Winter 1974): 67–80; and "Management Education and Our Knowledge of Managers' Jobs," *International Studies of Management and Organization*, Summer 1975, pp. 73–89.

[11]Stewart, "The Manager's Job" and "Management Education."

References

The Supervisor

James Driscoll et al., "The First Level Supervisor: Still the Man in the Middle," *Sloan Management Review,* Winter 1978, pp. 25–37. Robert Guest, "Of Time and the Foreman," *Personnel* 32 (May 1956): 478–486. Frank Jasinski, "Foreman Relationships outside the Work Group," *Personnel* 33 (1956–1957): 130–136. Brian Kay, "Key Factors in Effective Foreman Behavior," *Personnel* 36 (1959): 25–31. Emmanuel Kay and Herbert Meyer, "The Development of a Job Activity Questionnaire for Production Foremen,"

Personnel Psychology 15 (1962): 411–418. Thomas Mahoney et al., "The Jobs of Management," *Industrial Relations* 4 (February 1965): 97–110. D. L. Marples, "Studies of Managers: A Fresh Start?" *Journal of Management Studies* 4 (1967): 282–299. Harry O'Neil and Albert Kubany, "Observation Methodology and Supervisory Behavior," *Personnel Psychology* 12 (1959): 85–95. Quenton Ponder, "The Effective Manufacturing Foreman," *Proceedings of the Industrial Relations Research Association* (1957), pp. 41–54. Karl Price, "Characteristics of Corporate Executives: A Research Note," *Academy of Management Journal* 15 (September 1972): 318–381. Darrell Roach, "Factor Analysis of Rated Supervisory Behavior," *Personnel Psychology* 9 (1956): 487–498. C. E. Sequeira, "Functions of a Supervisor," *Indian Journal of Applied Psychology* 1 (1964): 46–54. Weld Turner, "Dimensions of Foreman Performance: A Factor Analysis of Criterion Measures," *Journal of Applied Psychology* 44 (1960): 216–223. W. L. Wallace and J. V. Gallagher, *Activities and Behaviors of Production Supervisors* (New York: Psychological Corporation, 1952).

The Middle Manager

Tom Alexander, "The Impresario of Peachtree Street," *Fortune*, February 13, 1978, pp. 112–115. G. Copeman, H. Luijk, and F. Haneka, *How the Executive Spends His Time* (London: Business Publications, 1963). Melville Dalton, *Men Who Manage* (New York, Wiley, 1961). Randall Dunhan, "Reactions to Job Characteristics," *Academy of Management Journal* 20 (1977): 42–65. Edward Faltermeyer, "The Man Who Keeps Those Maytag Repairmen Lonely," *Fortune*, November 1977, pp. 192–195, 197 ff. J. H. Horne and Tom Lupton, "The Work Activities of 'Middle' Managers: An Exploratory Study," *Journal of Management Studies* 2 (1965): 14–33. Raymond Katzell et al., "Organizational Correlates of Executive Roles," *Journal of Applied Psychology* 53 (1968): 22–28. Joe Kelly, "The Study of Executive Behavior by Activity Sampling," *Human Relations* 17 (1964): 277–287. Thomas Mahoney et al., "The Jobs of Management," *Industrial Relations* 4 (February 1965): 97–110. D. L. Marples, "Studies of Managers: A Fresh Start?" *Journal of Management Studies* 4 (1967): 282–299. Richard Martin, "The Managers," *Wall Street Journal*, April 18, 1977. David Moment and Dalmar Fisher, *Autonomy in Organizational Life* (Cambridge: Schenkman, 1975). Stanley Nealey and Fred Fiedler, "Leadership Functions of Middle Managers," *Psychological Bulletin* 70 (1968): 313–329. Diana Pheysey, "Activities of Middle Managers: A Training Guide," *Journal of Management Studies* 9 (1972): 158–171. Lyman Porter and Edwin Ghiselli, "The Self Perceptions of Top and Middle Management Personnel," *Personnel Psychology* 10 (1957): 397–406. Leonard Sayles, *Managerial Behavior* (New York: McGraw-Hill, 1964). Hugo Uyterhoeven, "General Managers in the Middle," *Harvard Business Review*, March–April 1972, pp. 75–85.

Top Managers

R. Beishon and A. Palmer, "Studying Managerial Behavior," *International Studies of Management and Organization* 2 (Spring 1972): 38–64. Joseph Bower, *Managing the Resource Allocation Process* (Homewood, Ill.: Irwin, 1972). Gary Brumback and John Vincent, "Factor Analysis of Work Performed Data for a Sample of Administrative, Professional, and Scientific Positions," *Personnel Psychology* 23 (1970): 101–107. Charles Burck, "A Group Profile of the Fortune 500 Chief Executives," *Fortune*, May 1976, pp. 172–177, 308–312. John Campbell et al., *Managerial Behavior* (New York: McGraw-Hill, 1970). Sune Carlson, *Executive Behavior* (Stockholm: Strömbergs, 1951). Fred Case, "An Executive Day," *California Management Review*, Fall 1962, pp. 67–70. Wallace Clement, *The Canadian Corporate Elite* (Toronto: McClelland and Stewart, "The Carleton Library," 1975). Edward Connors and Joseph Hutts, "How Administrators Spend Their Day," *Hospitals* 41 (February 16, 1967): 45–50, 141. G. Copeman, H. Luijk, and F. Haneka, *How the Executive Spends His Time* (London: Business Publications, 1963). "David Packard of Hewlett Packard," *Nation's Business*, January 1974, pp. 37–42. "How 179 Chief Executives Waste Their Time," *Business Management*, March 1968, pp. 12–14. "J. Peter Grace," *Wall Street Journal*, April 2, 1975. Thomas Mahoney et al., "The Jobs of Management," *Industrial Relations* 4 (February 1965): 97–110. Henry Mintzberg, "The

Manager's Job: Folklore and Fact," *Harvard Business Review*, July–August 1975, pp. 49–61. Robert Rock, *The Chief Executive Officer* (Lexington, Mass.: Lexington Books, 1977). Harold Stieglitz, *The Chief Executive and His Job* (New York: National Industrial Conference Board, 1969). Sandra Van Der Merwe, "A Portrait of the Canadian Woman Manager," *Business Quarterly* 43 (Autumn 1978): 45–52. Ray Wilkie and James Young, "Managerial Behavior in the Furniture and Timber Industries," *International Studies of Management and Organization* 2 (Spring 1972): 65–84.

Differences by Task Assignment

J. H. Horne and Tom Lupton, "The Work Activities of 'Middle' Managers: An Exploratory Study," *Journal of Management Studies* 2 (1965): 14–33. Diana Pheysey, "Activities of Middle Managers: A Training Guide," *Journal of Management Studies* 9 (May 1972): 158–171. Rosemary Stewart, "The Manager's Job: Discretion vs. Demand," *Organizational Dynamics* 2 (Winter 1974): 67–80; and "Management Education and Our Knowledge of Managers' Jobs," *International Studies of Management and Organization* , Summer 1975, pp. 73–89. Donald Thain, "The Ideal General Manager," *Business Quarterly* 43 (1978): 75–81; and "The Functions of the General Managers," *Business Quarterly* 43 (1978): 53–61.

Managerial Jobs and Organizational Differences

Leonard Nadler, "The Organization as a Micro Culture," *Personnel Journal*, December 1969, pp. 949–956. Edwin Samuel, *See How They Run: The Administration of Venerable Institutions* (London: Woburn Press, 1976). Rosemary Stewart, "To Understand the Manager's Job: Consider Demands, Constraints, Choices," *Organizational Dynamics* 4 (Spring 1976): 22–32. Harrison Trice et al., "The Role of Ceremonials in Organizational Behavior," *Industrial and Labor Relations Review* 23 (October 1969): 40–51. Robert Wright, "The Application of a Conceptual Scheme to Understand Organization Character," *Academy of Management Journal,* December 1968, pp. 389–399.

Successful Managers

William Anthony, "Living with Managerial Incompetence," *Business Horizons,* June 1978, pp. 57–64. L. L. Cummings and Donald Schwab, *Performance in Organizations* (Glenview, Ill.; Scott, Foresman: 1973). Edwin Ghiselli, *Explorations in Managerial Talent* (Pacific Palisades, Calif.: Goodyear, 1971). Barbara Karmel and Douglas Egan, "Managerial Performance: A New Look at Underlying Dimensionality," *Organizational Behavior and Human Performance* 15 (April 1976): 322–334. Pradip Khandwalla, "Style of Management and Environment: Some Findings," mimeographed (Montreal: McGill University, 1974). Harry Levinson, *The Exceptional Executive* (Cambridge, Mass.: Harvard University Press, 1968). Felix Lopez, "The Anatomy of a Manager," *Personnel*, March–April 1976, pp. 47–53. John McCarthy, *Why Managers Fail and What to Do about It* (New York: McGraw-Hill, 1978). Robert McMurray, *The Maverick Executive* (New York: AMACOM, 1974). Michael Maccoby, "The Corporate Climber Has to Find His Heart," *Fortune,* December 1976, pp. 98, 101, 104 ff. John Morse and Francis Wagner, "Measuring the Process of Managerial Effectiveness," *Academy of Management Journal* 21 (1978): 23–35. Lawrence Sank, "Perceived Trait Co-Occurrences According to Managerial Role: A Structural Representation," *Journal of Vocational Behavior* 7 (1975): 189–200; and "Effective and Ineffective Managerial Traits as Obtained as Naturalistic Descriptions from Executive Members of a Super Corporation," *Personnel Psychology* 27 (1974): 423–434. V. Srinivasan et al., "Measurement of a Composite Criterion of Managerial Success," *Organizational Behavior and Human Performance* 9 (1973): 147–167. Thomas Wheelen et al., "Skills of an Executive," mimeographed (Charlottesville, University of Virginia, McIntire School, 1978). William Williams and Dale Seiler, "Relationships between Measures of Effort and Job Performance," *Journal of Applied Psychology* 57 (1973): 49–54.

Appendix 2.1

Jobs Classified by Task and Kinds of Work Pressure

Here are two exhibits which you can use along with the text material on Stewart's managerial job classifications. Exhibit 2.1 describes her seven job classifications in more detail, giving relationships, characteristics, types, and examples. Exhibit 2.2 details the types of pressures experienced in various job types. For example, in Job Type A the plant manager experiences no high pressure and is subject to mild pressure because of fragmented work pattern, high contact time, and the fact that his or her mistakes are clearly identified. Compare this job with Job Type F, the regional training manager. She has high stress from work pattern (requiring self-starting), from high contact time, short-term relationships, role conflict, and high demands on private life. If fragmentation of work pattern is a problem you cannot live with, avoid a job like E, production manager. If high demands on private life are a problem, avoid a job like D.

Exhibit 2.1

Managerial Jobs Classified by Task (Excludes top management job where the occupant can largely adapt the role as he wishes.)

Job Types[a]	Relationship, Direction of[b]	Main Characteristics	Subdivisions	Main Characteristic(s) of Subdivisions	Examples of Jobs
A B	*Responsibility for separate unit* [downward] (outward) (up)	Few or no peer relations. Little or no role conflict. Evaluation possible.	1. Primarily internal contacts	People management high. Hard information. Responding to known contacts.	Retail store manager. Some works manager.
			2. Entrepreneurial.	External contacts, particularly customers. Can balance self-starting and responding.	Branch bank managers. Some general managers.
C D	*Field supervision* (area responsibility for separate units) [downward and up]	No interlocking subs. Few or no peer relations. People management high. Known contacts. Demands on private life.	1. Structured.	Responding. Similar tasks. Hard information.	Superintendent, retail chain stores. Various area management jobs.
			2. Relatively unstructured.	High uncertainty. Self-generating.	Regional director of overseas operations.
E	*People management* (relatively self-contained dept. or section) [down] (up)	People management key relationship. High contact time. Fragmented. Responding.	(Could be subdivided by leadership situation.)		Some administrative jobs. Some production management.
F G	*Work-flow jobs* [downward and sideways] (up)	Peer dependence. Obtaining cooperation without authority. Role conflict. Meetings. Known contacts.	1. Line management.	People management high.	Chief engineer, chief accountant, production manager.
			2. Service Staff Int. a. Non-selling customers come to you.	Time deadlines. Responding.	Some computer management. Transport manager.
			b. Selling.	Self-generating. Role conflict very high.	Training manager. Some personnel. Some computer management.
			c. Ext.	External contacts, time deadline.	Service manager.
			3. Coordinator (nonsubs).	Peer dependence very high.	Product manager.
			4. Control (over nonsubs),	Risk unpopularity. Role conflict very high.	Quality control manager. Some accounting.
	Solo jobs [alone]	Sustained attention. High alone time. Plan work.			Some planning jobs. Various specialist jobs.
H I	*Consulting and advisory* [upward] (sideways and downward)	Sustained attention. Time with senior management. Wide contacts.	1. Structured, continuing.	Known contacts, hard information. Low uncertainty.	Some accounting jobs.
			2. Unstructured, often one-shot jobs.	Risk incurring unpopularity. No, or low, people management. Self-generating.	Internal consultancy and special assignments.
	External jobs [outward]	Conflict objectives. External contacts high. Uncertainty high.	1. People management important.	People management high. Demands on private life.	Some sales management.
			2. Dealing with specialist contacts.	Conflict job objectives very high. Known contacts.	Purchasing manager. Advertising manager.
			3. Public relations, varied contacts.	Short-term relations. Demands on private life.	Public relations. Some general managers.

[a]See Exhibit 2.2 for explanation of Job Types A–1. Excludes top management job where occupant can largely adapt the role as he or she wishes.
[b]Main direction in [ ], other in ( ).

Source: Adapted by permission of the publisher from Rosemary Stewart, "The Manager's Job: Discretion vs. Demand," *Organizational Dynamics*, Winter 1974, p. 70. © 1974 by AMACOM, a division of American Management Associations.

Exhibit 2.2
Amounts and Kinds of
Work Pressure in
Various Jobs

Job Type	Examples
A	Plant manager, small subsidiary, 50 subordinates, process plant.
B	Branch bank manager.
C	Area manager, retail chain stores.
D	Regional director, overseas operations, four medium-size subsidiary companies, two newly acquired.
E	Production manager, 6 subordinates, light engineering.
F	Regional training manager, large company, 8 subordinates.
G	Management accountant, with an advisory and policing function, reporting to higher management, 3 subordinates.
H	Internal consultant on special assignment, 3 subordinates.
I	Group accountant, 2 subordinate accountants, 40 people reporting to them, works mainly with general manager.

Ratings of Jobs

The chart rates each job type (A–I) on 12 dimensions across three levels of pressure: High, Mild, and Low. Each dimension is shown between a "High Pressure" descriptor (left) and a "Low Pressure" descriptor (right), with columns A B C D E F G H I repeated under each of the High, Mild, and Low zones.

	High Pressure			High (A–I)									Mild (A–I)									Low (A–I)									Low Pressure

Work Pattern

1. Self-starting — High zone: D, F, H; Mild zone: B, H, I; Low zone: C, E, G — **Responding**
2. Fragmented — High zone: C, E; Mild zone: B, C, E; Low zone: G, H, I — **Not fragmented**
3. Time deadlines — High zone: D; Mild zone: B, C; Low zone: F, G, H, I — **No time deadlines**

Amount of Uncertainty

4. High — High zone: C, E; Mild zone: B, C, E, F; Low zone: D, H, I — **Low**

Exposed

5. No one to consult — High zone: C; Mild zone: H, I; Low zone: A, B, C, D — **People to consult**
6. Mistakes identified — High zone: A, B; Mild zone: C, E, F; Low zone: G, H, I — **Mistakes not identifiable**

Relationships

7. High contact time — High zone: A, B, C; Mild zone: D, E, F; Low zone: G, H, I — **Low contact time**
8. Short-term relations — High zone: C; Mild zone: D, E; Low zone: F, G, H, I — **Long-term contacts**
9. Conflict objectives (external contacts) — Mild zone: D, E; Low zone: G, H, I — **No conflict objectives**
10. Role conflict — High zone: D, E, F; Mild zone: B, C; Low zone: G, H, I — **No role conflict**
11. Unpopularity incurred — High zone: E, F; Mild zone: C, D; Low zone: G, H, I — **No need to risk unpopularity**

Demands on Private Life

12. High — High zone: D, F; Mild zone: C, E; Low zone: G, H, I — **Low**

Case

**Making It:
The Easy Way**

Mr. Smith eased into his chair hoping to find a respite from the tension that had become his steady companion. To his disappointment, home offered no sanctuary from unpleasant reality. His bank was in trouble. What a few years ago had been one of the fastest-growing banks in the nation now stood on the precipice. He mused on the previous month's events: the anger of the stockholders at their last meeting, the rumors that the directors were looking for a "sacrificial lamb," and the slights received from his colleagues. Even his personal secretary seemed to behave as if his future was a foregone conclusion. He wondered why he had been singled out. Although a supporter of the policy currently under attack, he had not made the final decision. Was he to be made the scapegoat for the bad judgment of others? Was it his fault that the economy had taken an unexpected downturn? As his indignation mounted, he erupted. "They seem to think I manufactured this recession," he shouted. As his composure slowly returned to him, he continued to brood over his now uncertain future.

**Mr. Smith's
Career**

Mr. Smith started his career in banking as a clerk in an obscure branch of a large regional bank in New England. Although he possessed only a high school education, he was considered very bright and ambitious by his superiors. This was made evident by his rapid promotion to assistant manager of a larger branch.

One of Mr. Smith's traits was the premium he placed on knowing the right people. While assistant manager he had many opportunities to speak with the bank's regional manager. Mr. Smith never failed to take advantage of all such meetings. It was at these times that he was at his charming best with compliments flowing freely. On occasion, the branch's manager would be taken aback by the lack of subtlety of this flattery. However, he said nothing to Mr. Smith about it.

It became obvious that Mr. Smith's strategy was successful when, on one visit, the regional manager asked him to be his partner in a golf match with two other officers of the bank. This was the first of many such social meetings with superiors. Mr. Smith made every attempt at these gatherings to be introduced to as many executives of the bank as possible. Almost all grew to like Mr. Smith because of his energy and spontaneous wit. More than one executive referred to him as a "comer" or a "boy with a future." Mr. Smith fully appreciated the value of these contacts, and many later served him in good stead by way of recommendations for promotion.

While assistant manager, Mr. Smith was involved in an incident that might have damaged his otherwise promising career. A new teller, Mrs. Jones, had come to him asking for the key to the vault. A regular patron, Mrs. Peters, had come to cash a five-thousand dollar check made out to cash. Mrs. Peters was the secretary of a local restaurant owner, Mr. Unger, and frequently drew money from the owner's large account for business purposes. Mrs. Jones matched the signature on the check to the file signature of Mr. Unger. Although they were alike, Mrs. Jones could not cash the check because she was a new teller and therefore had a limited amount of cash in her till. It was then that she approached Mr. Smith in order to get additional cash from the vault. After checking to see if it truly was the said patron, whom he was familiar with, Mr. Smith gave her the key and resumed his duties.

It was not many days later that the investigation began. The restaurant owner had claimed that the check had been stolen and the signature forged. Since his secretary had disappeared, it was suspected that she had indeed stolen and forged the check and thereafter left town. Insurance investigators soon arrived to question all parties involved. Mrs. Jones explained what had transpired and was confident that her story would be corroborated. Mr. Smith, however, explained that he did not recall Mrs. Jones ever coming to him about the matter. Furthermore, he stated that he was not familiar with the secretary in question and had previously chided the teller for lack of concern for bank policy. He confided to the investigator that, "She's been a problem ever since she got here. I don't know how we've put up with her this long." The investigator interviewed other employees and Mr. Smith's superior, but none could shed light on what had actually occurred. Although the testimony was contradictory, Mr. Smith's superiors believed his explanation. In light of this incident and the unfavorable evaluation it produced, Mrs. Jones's relationship with the bank was terminated at the end of her probationary period.

As he advanced in the organization, Mr. Smith often reflected back on this incident. Although he felt a certain amount of guilt for his actions, he believed it was the type of decision one had to make to get ahead in a tough, competitive world.

Mr. Smith held the position of assistant manager for a relatively brief period before he was again promoted. This time he would be the manager of his own branch. He continued to gain popularity among bank officers throughout this time. Much time was spent mingling with executives who would normally consider it an affront to their sense of protocol to socialize with a low-level manager.

Mr. Smith's rise in the organization was becoming meteoric. After a transfer to another branch, he was given responsibility for a district that included several branches. Within five years he held the post of assistant vice-president, and this promotion was followed four years later by a vice-president's chair. Throughout his climb up the organizational ladder, Mr. Smith had counted on and received the aid and support of his influential friends. Finally, he was nearing the top. It had taken the former clerk a mere fourteen years to achieve what he had strived for.

After having held a vice-presidency for two years, Mr. Smith was sought after for his views on a proposal being considered by the bank's top management. In recent years, competitors had been expanding more rapidly than Mr. Smith's bank. The change of policy being considered would involve seeking a higher volume of loans even though it might mean accepting a higher degree of risk. The bank's policy had always been to accept only the most credit-worthy applicants. Mr. Smith sincerely believed this proposal was the type of measure needed if the bank was to meet the growth rates of competitors. He endorsed the proposal and could be counted on to advocate it when asked at meetings. Through the efforts of Mr. Smith, though limited, and its other backers a final decision was reached accepting the new strategy.

A few years later, a recession struck the United States. It became apparent that the growth policy had been too risky when many of the bank's customers defaulted on their loans. The easy-credit strategy had led to a large volume of shaky loans to poor credit risks. As the recession deepened, the bank's financial position began to deteriorate and there was speculation from many sources that insolvency was a possibility that could not be ruled out if firm corrective action was not undertaken soon. The price of the bank's stock began a fall that appalled stockholders. On the eve of the annual stockholders' meeting, the Board of Directors met to discuss the details of the program of corrective action to be outlined to the distraught stockholders. One of the items was the elimination of one or all of the officers most directly responsible for the current crisis. They agreed that executives whose past performance was excellent should not be terminated if this had been their only serious error in judgment. On the other hand, officers without solid records of achievement in their present positions would be given a different sort of consideration. It was felt that this action would appease the stockholders and help to rebuild confidence in the bank.

Source: Francis A. Yeandel, St. Mary's College, Notre Dame, Indiana.

Problems
1. Is Smith successful?
2. Do you believe that Smith's behavior is typical executive behavior?
3. "If I had to do what Smith did to get ahead, I'd rather not get ahead." Comment.
4. Do the Smiths of the world make their firms more effective or less effective?

Chapter 3   Entrepreneurs and Family Business Executives

3

Chapter 2 discussed one kind of manager—the individual who has no family ties to the firm or enterprise and did not help create it. This chapter considers the management job of the individual who either creates a firm or an enterprise (an entrepreneur) or is related to its entrepreneurial founder (family business executive). The purpose here is threefold: (1) to introduce you to one part of the managerial world, (2) to help you understand more thoroughly the managerial functions, and (3) to introduce you to success factors in these jobs. The discussion will focus first on entrepreneurs and then on family business executives.

Who Is an Entrepreneur?

An entrepreneur is an individual who creates a new firm and continues to manage it until it is successful. Karl Vesper[1] has described nine types of entrepreneurs:

1. *Solo self-employed entrepreneurs.* The independent theatrical agent, plumber, or physician illustrates this category.
2. *Workforce builders.* Those who start and build up independent machine shops, commuter airlines, engineering service firms are entrepreneurs of this type.
3. *Product innovators.* Tektronix, Hewlett-Packard and many similar (and dissimilar) companies were founded by entrepreneurs with new products.
4. *Unutilized resource exploiters.* Mining prospectors, war surplus dealers, and real estate developers would all fit within such a category and, at the same time, illustrate its potential diversity.
5. *Economy of scale exploiters.* Discount store builders of the "50s" and mail order operators illustrate this type.
6. *Pattern multipliers.* Formulas of the MacDonald Brothers and of Colonel Sanders were exploited by franchise entrepreneurs. In an earlier age, chain builders multiplied patterns in other ways.
7. *Takeover artists.* If the company continues beyond its founder, it is because it has either been absorbed by a larger company or has been

Jay VanAndel

Jay VanAndel, chairman of the board of Amway Corp., Ada, Michigan, founded the corporation in 1959 with his longtime friend, Richard DeVos. Amway is the manufacturer of more than 150 household cleaning and personal care products distributed in the United States, Canada, and a number of other countries through a direct selling organization of some 250,000 independent distributors.

VanAndel is a graduate of Morningside College, Sioux City, Iowa; Pratt Business School, Pratt, Kansas; and Yale University, New Haven, Connecticut (Aviation Cadet School). In developing the business, he was especially active in the areas of finance, research, manufacturing, distribution, and law. He wrote almost all the original sales manuals, training bulletins, advertising brochures, and labels for Amway. In his thirty-year business history, VanAndel has conducted or participated in thousands of sales training meetings and still maintains a worldwide speaking schedule. He makes many recordings of speeches for use in sales training.

taken over by another entrepreneur of another type.

8. *Capital aggregators.* Specialists in marshaling front money can start businesses like banks and insurance companies that require large resource aggregations.

9. *Speculators.* Although they often do not start or build businesses, those who trade in ownership paper of various types sometimes do build fortunes and thereby become known as a type of entrepreneur.

Note that Types 6, 7 and 9 are not the founders of the business. They make successful firms out of relatively unsuccessful ones and are in this sense the creators of the new firm.

Entrepreneurial firms are more important today than ever before. They (and small businesses generally) represent 94 percent of firms employing 60 percent of the labor force and create a majority of new ideas, products, and services. One hundred fifty-eight entrepreneurships are created each hour (and they go out of business at about that rate, too). Jay VanAndel, pictured here, is an example of a successful entrepreneur.

Are You an Entrepreneurial Manager?

To find out if you have the traits of an entrepreneurial manager, answer these eight questions:

1. Do you have a tendency to have difficulty relaxing on holidays?

Figure 3.1
Factors In
Entrepreneurial
Success

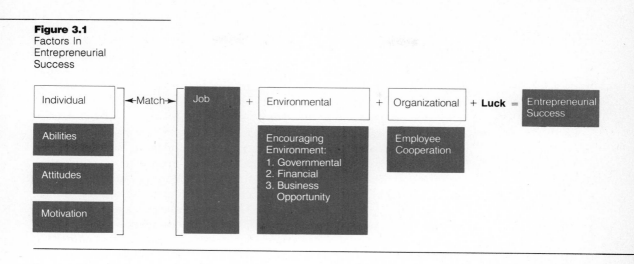

2. Do you have a tendency to become annoyed when people are late for appointments?
3. Do you get upset when you see anything wasted?
4. Do you dislike getting drunk?
5. Do you have a tendency to think about work matters outside working hours?
6. Do you have a preference for competent but difficult work partners over congenial but incompetent ones?
7. Do you have a tendency to become angry over inefficiency?
8. Do you have a life pattern of working hard to be at the top in your area of endeavor?

George Hines, who developed these questions for his research into the traits of entrepreneurs, found that successful entrepreneurs said yes to six or more.[2] Unsuccessful entrepreneurs said yes to three or less.

Figure 3.1 lists factors that contribute to entrepreneurial success. It restates Figure 2.1, where the formula for managerial success was given. Let's examine each of these factors.

**Abilities,
Attitudes, and
Motivation**

Entrepreneurs must have certain managerial *abilities,* including human resource skills, communication skills, and conceptual skills. Indeed, the latter are particularly important; they make it possible for the entrepreneur to visualize a new business. Dun & Bradstreet attributes more than 90 percent of entrepreneurial failures to lack of abilities to perform the managerial functions. Entrepreneurs also need high levels of energy, and if they are in technical businesses, they need technical skills.

Entrepreneurs gain some of these skills while working for other organizations—what some experts call the incubator organizations. These organizations provide experience. Often technical entrepreneurs are pushed out of the incubator organizations, influencing their attitudes and motivations. Technical entrepreneurs are individuals who get into a business of their own because they create a new product or service. If their incubator organization does not support their pet project—their creation—a conflict develops, causing them to leave.

Certain *attitudes* and *motivations* make entrepreneurs successful. As suggested above, these attitudes and motives arise out of their past experiences. Entrepreneurial models are a contributing factor—fathers, uncles, or family friends who have created their own businesses. Some ethnic groups (Greeks, Italians, Jews) have a high percentage of entrepreneurial role models because prejudice and discrimination have closed traditional managerial roles to them. Several studies indicate that entrepreneurs have a hard time working effectively for others because they did not relate well to fathers, teachers, and authority figures in general. The typical male entrepreneur is married. The typical female entrepreneur is not. Women are most often motivated to become entrepreneurs by entrepreneurial role models or by the need to support themselves. A major barrier to entry for women entrepreneurs is credit discrimination.

Psychologist David McClelland has studied the entrepreneurial personality and concludes the most dominant psychological drive motivating the entrepreneur is a high need for achievement.[3] This need to achieve will be discussed in more detail in Chapter 6, but the following traits summarize the entrepreneurial personality, according to McClelland:

- *Desire for responsibility* Entrepreneurs prefer to use their own resources in their own way to accomplish personal goals. They assume accountability for results and will perform well in a group only if they can personally influence the results in some specific way.

- *Preference for moderate risks* Entrepreneurs set goals which require high performance but which they feel sure they can reach.

- *Perception of probability of success* Entrepreneurs possess great confidence in their ability to achieve success. To insure success, they study the facts and form judgments about them. When facts are not available, they rely on their self-confidence.

- *Stimulation by feedback* Entrepreneurs are stimulated to higher levels of performance by feedback (good or bad) on how they are doing. They want to know how effective their efforts are as the task progresses.

- *Energetic activity* Entrepreneurs have a higher than average level of energy. They engage in novel ways of getting the task done, are active and mobile, and tend to be acutely aware of the passage of time.

- *Future orientation* Entrepreneurs search for and anticipate future possibilities by optimistically planning and thinking ahead.
- *Skill in organizing* Skill in organizing work and people for achieving goals is characteristic of entrepreneurs. They are highly objective about choosing the right individual to perform each task. An expert will be chosen over a friend to insure that the job is done efficiently.
- *Attitude toward money* For entrepreneurs, financial reward is second to the sense of achievement. They value money as a concrete symbol of a challenging objective accomplished and a testimony to their competence.

Environment

Entrepreneurs have abilities, attitudes, and motivations they match up with the right jobs. Like managers, they need employee cooperation and luck; but more than managers, they are especially dependent on a supportive *environment*.

There are three crucial environmental factors. The first is a government that enacts tax and other policies that allow entrepreneurs to develop and in some cases provides financial and other forms of encouragement. The helpful government also tries to encourage a successful economic society through the use of modern macroeconomic fiscal and monetary employment and manpower policies. The second factor is capital. No business can succeed without the money to buy materials, hire workers, rent or buy a workplace, pay marketing expenses, and so on. Entrepreneurs are especially vulnerable financially. They must save the money they need or borrow it from friends, family, bankers, or venture capitalists. The final success factor is the entrepreneurial idea. Successful entrepreneurs know their markets. Business opportunities exist either in genuinely new enterprises or in competing with ineffective firms. In addition to these three vital factors, a supportive environment in terms of spouse, family, and friends is also conducive to entrepreneurial success.

Can Entrepreneurship Be Learned?

In Chapter 1, I raised the question of whether you can learn how to be a manager from books and in the classroom. The answer I gave was that many managerial attitudes and techniques can be learned in this way. But managerial success also requires the ability to use managerial techniques well and at the right time—the art of management.

Learning to be a successful entrepreneur is similar to learning to be a manager. There is evidence that many aspects of entrepreneurship can be learned. McClelland and David Winter have shown that you can even teach entrepreneurial motivation in the classroom.[4] Of course some aspects of entrepreneurship are learned best in practice. For example, it is very difficult to teach someone how to create the idea or product that leads to the establishment of a business. But a lot can be taught about how to get going financially and legally, how to organize the business, and the like. In sum, much, but not all, that will help you to be a successful entrepreneur can be taught.

The Entrepreneurial Job

In Chapter 2, I described managerial jobs. Now we will look at an entrepreneur's day. In *Working*, Studs Terkel described Ken Brown, who at age twenty-six was president of four corporations: American Motorcycle Mechanics School, Evel Knievel's Electrocycle Service Centers, Triple A Motorcycle Leasing, and AMS Productions. Some of these are rather large franchises. Ken quit school at sixteen, worked for a big company for one year, and opened up his own repair shop at seventeen. He got into the motorcycle business because he felt that it had potential. At twenty-six he had all that wealth could buy—two chauffeured Cadillacs, a Corvette, a condominium in Skokie, a house in Evanston, a ranch in Arizona. Ken's own description of his work habits appears in Terkel's book as follows:

I usually get out of here at one o'clock in the morning. I go home and eat dinner at two. I do my best thinking at night. I can't fall asleep until seven in the morning. I turn the TV on. I don't even pay attention to it. They got the all-night movies. You actually feel like an idiot. I just sit there in the living room, making notes, trying to put down things for the next day to remember. I plan ahead for a month. Maybe I'll lie down in bed about four in the morning. If something comes in my head, I'll get up and start writing it. If I get three, four hours' sleep, I'm okay.

That's when I come up with my ideas. That's when I put this Electrocycle idea together. I sold Sun Electric on the idea of building them for me. Then I sold Evel Knievel on the idea of putting his name on it. . . .

I'm down at the office Saturdays too. Sundays, about half the time. The other half of the time maybe my wife and I will go horseback riding or visit a friend's house. Even when you're visiting with them, you can't get away from your work. They ask about it. It's kind of a good feeling. There's not too many Sundays like that. I've been traveling more than ever with these franchises. . . .

It wasn't easy. When other people were going out and just having fun and riding motorcycles and getting drunk and partying, I was working. I gave up a lot. I gave up my whole youth, really. That's something you never get back.

People say to me, "Gee! You work so damn hard, how can you ever enjoy it?" I'm enjoying it every day. I don't have to get away for a weekend to enjoy it. Eventually I'll move out to Arizona and make that my headquarters. I'm young enough. I'll only be thirty-one in five years. I can still do these things—horseback riding, looking after animals. I like animals. But I'll never retire. I'll take it a little bit easier. I'll have to. I had an ulcer since I was eighteen.

[Indicates bottle of tablets on the table. It reads, "Mylanta. A palliative combination of aluminum, magnesium, hydroxide to relieve gastric hyperacidity and heartburn."] I chew up a lot of Mylantas. It's for your stomach, to coat it. Like Maalox. I probably go through twenty tablets a day.

I guess people get different thrills out of business in different ways. There's a lot of satisfaction in showing up people who thought you'd never amount to anything. If I died tomorrow, I'd really feel I enjoyed myself. How would I like to be remembered? I don't know if I really care about being remembered. I just want to be known while I'm here. That's enough. I didn't like history, anyway.[5]

Note some of the characteristics of the entrepreneur's work pattern. Ken worked very hard, but he fit his hours to his preferences. He was his own boss.

Entrepreneurs have more time alone than managers. Typically, they spend 36 percent of their time alone, 15 percent doing things like observing or traveling. They spend time talking and listening, too: 9 percent with customers, 4 percent with suppliers, 9 percent with other managers, and 27 percent with other employees. But when asked what they do when alone, they say they spend this time thinking, reading, calculating, or writing.

Entrepreneurs have much less interruption than managers, and much more time to plan, to make decisions alone. They write their own job descriptions. And they seem to have more fun. As one entrepreneur, Anthony Ross, says, "I can't wait to get in in the morning."[6]

Challenges Entrepreneurs Face

Entrepreneurial firms face problems similar to those experienced by managerial firms: They hire and fire people, market goods and services, pay taxes, and so on. Certain challenges they face, however, are unique. Frederick Webster's analysis of the entrepreneurial venture, diagrammed in Figure 3.2, is useful in describing these challenges.[7]

Webster's venture has six stages. Stage 1 brings the first crisis, one that few managers face: the start-up crisis. Managers seldom face the level of trauma that entrepreneurs experience when they start a business. Entrepreneurs must have a product or service they believe they can sell in competition with established giants or other entrenched competitors. Coming up with the idea for a viable enterprise is not easy. And this is the crucial entrepreneurial act: the creation of a new product or service; the creation of new uses for existing products or services; the creation of a new delivery system for existing products or services; the creation of new locations for existing products or services; the creation of a new environ-

Figure 3.2
Stages in an
Entrepreneurial
Venture

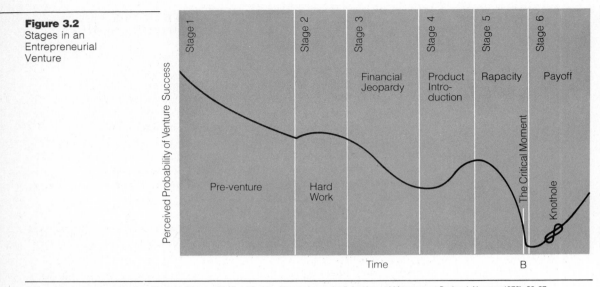

Source: Adapted by permission from Frederick Webster, "A Model for New Venture Interaction," *Academy of Management Review* 1 (January 1976): 26–37.

ment for an existing product or service; or some combination of these possibilities. After entrepreneurs hit upon some ideas, they evaluate them and, if necessary, negotiate with the environment (for example, an inventor) to set the business up.

In Stage 2 the entrepreneur spends his or her time getting the enterprise organized, a process that takes hard work and enthusiasm.

Stage 3 leads to the next crisis: the financial crisis. Getting someone to lend you the funds to take over a franchise or start a new firm is a problem. In effect, the entrepreneur is seeking venture capital, and venture capital firms have been less risk-oriented in recent years than they used to be. Webster calls this the stage of financial jeopardy.

Stage 4 consists of introducing the product, which often includes overdue payables, initial market success, and a lot of hope.

Stage 5 is the next crisis. In Webster's opinion this is *the* time for success or failure. More money problems arise, and the entrepreneur wants to get the financial backers out of the enterprise. This is the stage where the entrepreneur performs the rapacious act. Rapacity covers the actual seizing of the firm by disenfranchising, forcing to resign, or firing such people as the inventor and other directors or financial backers. This shortstops any claim they may have on future financial gains once the product or service is successful. If it gets through this "knothole," the enterprise can enter the payoff period.

Stage 6, though beyond the knothole, presents entrepreneurs with another problem managers do not face. The problem arises when the business grows so large that the entrepreneur can no longer effectively make all the key decisions. This has been called the delegation/leadership crisis: once the firm is off the ground, it is hard to let go of what you have built. Your money and ego are involved. Your name is on the door. Your checking account is paying the bills. It is hard to delegate certain decisions to others—they might ruin the company. Yet if the business grows, the entrepreneur must turn over some authority to others. There are only so many hours in a day, and if the entrepreneur does not delegate the least important decisions, or those he knows the least about, the firm will not prosper or grow. Some entrepreneurs "solve" this crisis by stopping growth at the point where they can still control everything. Others go through the crisis and slowly, painfully begin to delegate decisions.

So, although running your own business may sound very attractive, you need to be aware of the crises and challenges only entrepreneurs face. You also must be realistic about the long hours and high risks involved. For those with the right abilities, motivations and attitudes, and environment and luck, it is really worth it!

The World of the Family Business Executive

Let's begin our discussion of family business executives with three definitions:

- The **family business executive** is *someone who enters a firm founded by a relative while that relative is still running the firm or someone who enters a firm whose ownership is controlled by his or her family.*

- A **family-run firm** is *one whose major ownership influence is a family; most or all of its key executives are family members.*

- The **family-influenced firm** is *one whose major ownership influence is a family; some of the key executives are family members.*

You probably are under the impression that family businesses are small. In fact, they come in all sizes. With regard to large family-run or -influenced firms, one recent study of the *Fortune* 500—the largest firms in the United States—found that over 42 percent of publicly held firms are controlled by one person or family.[8] Another 17 percent are possibly controlled by a family. Larger percentages of medium or smaller firms are family-controlled. By the way, these percentages do *not* include companies with fewer than 500 shareholders who need not disclose their financial figures. Large family-controlled firms with relatively few shareholders, such as Hallmark Cards, Hughes Aircraft, Bechtel, Hearst, and Cargill, for example, add to the ranks of family businesses, making their actual number even more significant than those percentages indicate.

E. Hirst Mendenhall

E. Hirst Mendenhall, realtor, has been active in real estate for over thirty years. He has engaged in the listings and sales of residential, commercial, and income properties, in making numerous formal real estate appraisals, in handling completely the land development of three city residential homesite subdivisions and a lake cottage subdivision development, and in personally handling property management for owners of several hundred rental properties in the small university city of Columbia, Missouri.

Mendenhall has been conferred the national designation C.R.B.M. (Certified Real Estate Brokerage Manager) by the Realtors National Marketing Institute. He also possesses the G.R.I. (Graduate, Realtors Institute) designation. He was recognized by the Columbia, Missouri, Board of Realtors with its Realtor of the Year honor. He served five years as a national officer of the National Institute of Real Estate Brokers, both on the national board of governors and as a regional vice-president.

Mendenhall is a member of Phi Delta Theta fraternity and Sigma Delta Chi journalism fraternity. He was graduated from the University of Missouri in 1941; was a combat flyer in World War II (he flew sixty-five combat missions and was awarded the Distinguished Flying Cross among other medals); is a recent past president of the Columbia, Missouri, Kiwanis Club; and is an active member of the United Missouri Methodist Church.

Family-run and family-influenced firms are likely to continue to have their management tied to the family or family-approved executives. The family is likely to influence company objectives and policies, promotions, and similar issues. America provides many examples of businesses built by individuals for themselves and for their families. A few of these are included in the following list:

Family-Run Firms

- Mars, Inc., with sales of almost $2 billion, was founded by Forest Mars. It produces candy, including five of the six top-selling candy bars.
- After Six, which controls about 60 percent of the rental tuxedo business, is run by the Rudofker family.
- J. E. Rhoades and Sons, a firm run for 277 years by the Rhoades family, makes belting for industrial uses. Sales are about $3,000,000 yearly.
- Levi Strauss and Co. is run by the Haas family. Sales of its famous Levis bring in about $1,682,019 yearly.

Mary Jane Mendenhall

Mary Jane Mendenhall, a fourth generation realtor, earned a
B.S. in Business Administration at the University of Missouri.
Following graduation she became personnel director of U.S.
Engineers, Panama Canal Zone, for one year and later owned
her own accounting business. She entered the real estate
business in 1955 and has participated in subdividing, building,
and management. She is primarily interested in residential sales,
and her gross volume of sales in 1978 exceeded $20 million.
She is also a real estate speculator in the buying and
remodeling of homes.

   She has held all offices in the Columbia Board of Realtors
and several elective positions in the National Association of
Realtors, women's council division. She is active in civic affairs
and was the first woman to hold the Realtor of the Year award.
She also received the Columbia Citizen of the Year award,
outstanding businesswoman in Missouri award, and many other
awards.

- Field Enterprises, which is run by the Field family, includes such
  businesses as Marshall Field retailers, newspapers, television stations,
  coal mines, paper, and real estate. The two Field brothers running Field
  Enterprises receive $1.6 million in dividends each per year.

Hirst and Mary Jane Mendenhall, pictured here, are family executives in a
family-run firm.

Family-Influenced Firms

- IBM, influenced by the founding Watson family.
- RCA, until recently headed by the son of General Sarnoff, the founder.
- Armco Steel, Inc., whose chief executive officer is from the founding
  Verity family.
- Beech Aircraft, headed by the cofounder, Olive Beech, from 1950
  onward.

Edgar F. Kaiser, pictured on page 74, is an example of a family member
currently running a family-influenced firm.

**Advantages of a
Family Business**

Family businesses survive and prosper because they have many advantages. From the company's and community's point of view, some of these
advantages include:

- Financial flexibility and freedom from disclosure.

Edgar F. Kaiser

Edgar F. Kaiser is chairman of the boards of Kaiser Steel Corporation, Kaiser Foundation Health Plan, Inc., and Kaiser Foundation Hospitals; chairman of the board of liquidating trustees of Kaiser Industries Corporation; chairman emeritus and honorary director for life of Kaiser Aluminum & Chemical Corporation, Kaiser Cement Corporation and Kaiser Resources Ltd.; and vice-chairman and trustee of the Henry J. Kaiser Family Foundation.

He joined the Kaiser companies in 1930 as superintendent of a pipeline project in Kansas, advanced through various managerial assignments, and subsequently played an important role in the construction of Hoover, Bonneville, and Grand Coulee Dams, in Kaiser shipbuilding operations during World War II, and in auto manufacturing.

Kaiser served as a director of BankAmerica Corporation, San Francisco, from 1969 to 1979. He is a director emeritus and past chairman of SRI International. He is also an honorary member of the Business Council, an honorary director and past vice-president of the Oakland–Alameda County Coliseum, chairman emeritus and past chairman of the Oakland Symphony Orchestra Association, a member of the advisory board of the Oakland Museum Association, a director of the San Francisco Opera Association, a trustee and former chairman of the Bay Area Council, and a member of the New Oakland Committee.

Kaiser has received numerous awards and honors for his leadership in promoting economic and social well-being, both at home and abroad. For his efforts to expand the availability of low and moderate income housing, President Johnson awarded Kaiser the Presidential Medal of Freedom in 1969.

Kaiser was born on July 29, 1908, in Spokane, Washington. He attended the University of California, Berkeley, majoring in economics. In 1969, the University of California conferred on Kaiser the honorary degree of Doctor of Humane Letters and named him Alumnus of the Year. Kaiser also holds honorary degrees from the University of Portland, Pepperdine College, Mills College, Golden Gate University, and the University of the Pacific.

Other awards he has received include one of the Ten Outstanding Young Men of the Year in the U.S.–1943 (Junior Chamber of Commerce); Industrialist of the Year–1966 (California Museum of Science and Industry); Construction's Man of the Year–1968 (Engineering New-Record); The Hoover Medal–1969; Grand Officer of the Republic of Ivory Coast–1972; Manufacturer of the Year–1976 (California Manufacturers Association).

- Easier/simplified accounting procedures.
- Speedy response time to changes in the environment if power is clear and the family agrees.
- Ability to keep trade secrets protected.
- Ability to create long-term bonds between family executives and key customers.
- Ability to create long-term bonds between family executives and key suppliers.
- Ability to create long-term bonds between family executives and the community.
- Stability and persistence of values and the institutions.
- Ability to create a positive corporate image.

Advantages to the family members who choose to join the family business may include:

- Security of position.
- Status in the community.
- Good compensation and dividends.
- Identification with corporate objectives.

Problems in Family Enterprises

The advantages for firm, family members, and community described above exist in the *best of circumstances*. But problems can exist too. Those considering a career with a family enterprise would do well to determine if the advantages outweigh the problems before deciding to enter the firm or to stay in it after the advantages/problems ratio shifts. The following paragraphs describe some of the more significant problems that may arise.

Dominance of Younger Family Executives by Older Executives

A common source of difficulty in the family business is the relationship between generations, as the following Lichty cartoon suggests. Obviously many parents do get along with their children in their business relationships. So this may not be a problem for you, if you become involved in a family business. But think about this. You are an employee. Your boss is mean to you one day. You probably curse him and try to forget it. You may learn to hate him. Still, you live with it and hope you will be transferred. But what if the boss is your father and you are not going to be transferred? Your level of frustration may get very high, and if you begin to hate your father you may face severe guilt feelings.

"My son, who just graduated, is joining the firm, Finchley! He has all
the answers, but the staff will continue to ask ME the questions!"

Now look at it from the boss's point of view. You remember your
employee when you changed her diapers, spanked her, corrected her
algebra, paid her speeding ticket. You know all her weaknesses. Can you
trust her with your creation, the extension of your ego, your business?

If it is true that many entrepreneurs had difficult relationships with their
fathers, it may also be that they have a strong need to show their children
that they are competent. They may need to be "the boss" at all times and
to continually remind their children who gave them their jobs. This is
hardly a prescription for healthy interpersonal relations.

Paternalism

Some family businesses create a paternalistic environment in which
long-time employees are protected if they have been loyal, perhaps in spite
of current incompetence. The paternalistic attitude of entrepreneurial and

"The toughest part of this job is keeping dad convinced that nepotism is OK."

family firms toward their employees is a mixed blessing. Most such firms go out of their way to reward the loyal nonfamily employee who has been with the company a long time. For the employee, this may mean greater security, benefits, and compensation than are available elsewhere. On the part of the employers, it often indicates real human concern for employees' problems and willingness to help out in times of need, a condition rare in managerial firms, especially large ones.

A negative aspect of paternalism is the difficulty it causes in easing out or firing employees who are no longer competent. The entrepreneur or the family members never forget the employee who risked working for them when they started out or in their difficult times. Some employees exploit this feeling and coast for the rest of their lives with little fear of retribution.

Nepotism and Overcompensation of the Family

Some entrepreneurial and family firms become "the employer of last resort" for the whole family. Whether competent or not, hardworking or not, Cousin Charles and Niece Mary must be put on the payroll, preferably in high-status, high-paying jobs. This can increase the firm's overhead costs, but even more important, it can disillusion competent employees and cause high turnover. Indeed, serious problems develop in family firms where authority of office is based only on ownership and not on competence.

Equally problematical is the situation in which family members are paid larger salaries than their productivity can justify. This may serve to reduce the productivity and satisfaction of employees producing as much but paid less in salary and benefits.

Management Succession and Sibling Rivalry Problems

Trouble may result when two family members close in age enter the business and only one good position exists. Rivalry may develop between them, and the entrepreneur, without realizing it, may feed this rivalry. Such rivalries can become intense when the boss has to decide who will take over when he or she dies or retires. The inability to resolve the problem of succession (along with estate taxes) is one of the reasons many entrepreneurial firms sell out.

Intrafamily Rivalry

A major obstacle for both family and nonfamily executives to overcome is intrafamily friction. At times the family may split on key issues, with some family executives and board members taking one side, others taking the other side. Managers can be caught in the middle. Harry Levinson describes this situation as follows:

Perhaps more critical for the health of the business are the factional divisions that spring up in the organization as associates and subordinates choose the family members with whom they want to be identified. (Often, however, those who take sides discover that in a crisis the family unites against "outsiders," including their partisans, who are then viewed as trying to divide the family.)

If the nonfamily employees or board members decide not to become involved in a family fight and withdraw from relations with its members until the conflict is resolved, the work of the organization may be paralyzed. Worse yet, the dispute may eventually embroil the entire organization, resulting in conflicts at the lowest levels, as employees try to cope with the quarrels thrust on them.

Now the business has become a battleground that produces casualties but no peace. Such internecine warfare constitutes a tremendous barrier to communication and frustrates adequate planning and rational decision making.

A business in which numerous members of the family of varying ages and relationships are involved often becomes painfully disrupted around issues of empires and succession. Its units tend to become family-member territories and therefore poorly integrated organizationally, if at all.[9]

Difficulties may also arise when family members who see the business mainly as a source of dividends resist innovations for fear of reducing those dividends. Thus the objectives of the enterprise become opposed to the personal objectives of family members.

The Nonfamily Executive

Often the nonfamily executive in a family enterprise is confronted with a lack of promotion opportunities. Certain key positions will never be open to the nonfamily executive, regardless of his or her merit. These positions are reserved for family members, who frequently are younger and less experienced than the nonfamily executive. This is less of a problem for a nonfamily executive working for an entrepreneur—after all, the entrepreneur built the business, and the executive respects that. But the entrepreneur's son or daughter may not be so easy to respect and in fact may not deserve respect. Thus the nonfamily executive must not have a strong need for promotional forms of recognition, particularly if the family always practices nepotism.

Managing Successfully in a Family Business

What does it take to be a successful family business executive like Edgar Kaiser? As Figure 3.3 illustrates, the family business executive is in a position somewhere between the entrepreneur and the manager. The family business executive needs all the ingredients of managerial success. The main modification is that the entrepreneurial personality of its leaders begins to blend into a managerial personality over time. This occurs when the entrepreneur dies, leaving the business to his or her heirs, who of

Figure 3.3
Factors in Family
Business Success

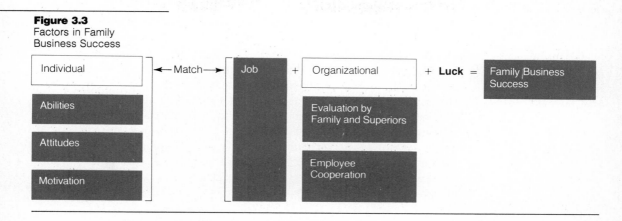

course have different personalities. A second major change is in organizational factors. The family business executive must be well evaluated by superiors and/or the family members directly involved in management or ownership of the enterprise.

All the same success factors that affect managers, and more, affect family business executives. R. David Yost, himself a boss's son, offers the family business executive some good advice on how to achieve success:[10]

- Work harder and longer than anyone else, especially during your first six months.
- Make it a point to work for someone other than a relative in your first job.
- Do not become a spy for the family.
- Refer to your relatives by the same names that everyone else uses.
- Do not bypass the chain of command to get to your relatives.
- Do not make family references on or off the job.
- Do not speak with more authority than you have in your present job.
- Avoid mixing family and business relationships.
- Expect most people to credit your success to being related to the right person.

Of course many of the problems inherent in a family business can be avoided. The Lanes of *Sunset* magazine apparently managed to resolve them successfully. Some parents get along well with their children even under the stressful conditions of a family business. And there is a big advantage in ownership relations *if* the interpersonal relationships can be worked out.

I worked for a family business and left it because the dominance problem was too difficult. If you are considering entering the family business and past relationships indicate that this will be a problem, do not join the business directly after school. Work for another firm for a few years and build your own track record. Then negotiate your way into the business if you are still interested.

Think your decision over carefully before joining the family firm. Consider this: How many sons or daughters succeed at the same jobs as their parents? Think of presidents, pianists, football players, and so on. Generally the comparison that results when children enter the same field as a parent is too hard on them. Though they are just starting out, they are compared to a successful, established person. And then if they succeed at the job, there is little recognition. People say, "Of course John made it. His dad set it up for him." Thus a crucial variable of success in a family business is family relationships and respect for the newly entering family member.

The family business executive can enhance the success of the firm by following this advice:

- Professionalize management practices. Amateurs cannot successfully compete in the marketplace. This book discusses effective planning, organizing, leadership, and control principles essential to professionalism.

- Use a professional leadership approach to mitigate the problems of dominance over younger family executives and paternalism.

- Employ professional planning and objectives setting to help reduce the problems of rivalry within the family regarding outcomes.

- Develop professional human resources policies on compensation or hiring of family members and of nonfamily executives.

- Create a management succession plan based on the competence of the people involved. Current leaders should do so while still in power rather than leaving a vacuum.

Family business firms which are managed to achieve business objectives and not just to satisfy family objectives can overcome most of the problems of family business and use to advantage its unique aspects.

Summary

Chapter 3 has compared and contrasted the worlds of the entrepreneur and the family business executive with each other and with that of the business manager. Now you can evaluate these three different types of managerial roles to decide which might be the best career goal for you.

An *entrepreneur* is an individual who creates a new firm and continues to manage it until it is successful. The entrepreneurial firm is more important today than ever before.

Entrepreneurs must possess certain abilities, motivations, and attitudes in order to succeed. They must have the skills of the business manager as well as self-confidence and the ability to control their own fate. The entrepreneurial venture is especially dependent on a favorable environment, particularly helpful government policies and an adequate supply of capital. The final success factor is the entrepreneurial idea; successful entrepreneurs know their market.

Stages in the entrepreneurial venture include: pre-venture, hard work, financial jeopardy, product introduction, rapacity, and payoff. Remember that entrepreneurs must put in long hours and assume high risks to make their ventures pay off.

The *family business executive* is one who enters a firm founded by a relative while that relative is still running the firm or the ownership of the firm is controlled by his or her family. The family business executive may work in a *family-run* or *family-influenced* firm. In the former case, *most or all* of the firm's key executives are family members. In the latter instance *some* of the key executives are family members.

There are distinct advantages to the firm, the community, and to the family members in the family business situation: stability and persistence of values and institutions, security of position, status in the community, for example. There are also problems unique to the family enterprise. These include:

- dominance of younger firm executives by older executives
- paternalism
- nepotism and overcompensation of the family
- management succession and sibling rivalry
- problems for nonfamily executives such as inability to advance

The crucial variables for success in a family business are family relationships and respect for family members who enter the firm. The use of professional management practices and leadership approaches is suggested to help these firms achieve business objectives and to overcome their unique problems.

In order to be successful, all managers, whether business managers, entrepreneurs, or family business executives, must meet many challenges from the environment. Chapter 4 presents these environmental challenges and the various roles managers must play in facing them.

Questions

1. What is an entrepreneur? Give some examples of different types of entrepreneurs based on Karl Vesper's research.
2. Describe the entrepreneurial personality in terms of David McClelland's findings.
3. Why is the entrepreneur especially dependent on a supportive environment?
4. If you chose to be an entrepreneur, how would you spend your time? How would your activities differ from those of the managers described in Chapter 2?
5. State Frederick Webster's stages of an entrepreneurial venture, and explain what happens during each stage.
6. Knowing now what it is to be an entrepreneur, tell why you will or will not become one. What success factors do you have and lack for being an entrepreneur?
7. You are a family business executive. How does your position differ from that of other managers?
8. What is a family-run firm? A family-influenced firm? Give examples of each.
9. What advantages does a family business have from the company's point of view? From the community's point of view? From a family member's point of view?

10. There are many unique problems which arise for the family member who joins the family business. List these and explain why each is a problem. What kind of problems exist for the nonfamily executive in these firms?

11. R. David Yost gave some advice for a family member about to enter the family business. What advice did he give? Do you believe it is sound?

12. Now that you know what a family business executive is, tell why you will or will not become one. What success factors do you have and lack for being a family business executive?

Notes

[1] Karl Vesper, "Strategic Management: New Ventures and Small Business Commentary," in *Strategic Management: A New View of Business Policy and Planning,* ed. Charles Hofer and Dan Schendel (Boston: Little, Brown, 1979).

[2] George Hines, "Achievement Motivation, Occupations, and Labor Turnover in New Zealand," *Journal of Applied Psychology* 58 (December 1973): 313–317.

[3] David C. McClelland, *The Achieving Society* (New York: Free Press, 1967).

[4] David McClelland and David Winter, *Motivating Economic Performance* (New York: Free Press, 1969).

[5] Studs Terkel, *Working* (New York: Pantheon, 1974), pp. 463–464. Reprinted by permission.

[6] George de Mare and Joanne Summerfield, "I Love Every Minute of It! I Can't Wait to Get In in the Morning," *Across the Board* 14 (February 1977): 44–52.

[7] Frederick Webster, "A Model for New Venture Interaction," *Academy of Management Review* 1 (January 1976): 26–37.

[8] Robert Sheehan, "Proprietors in the World of Business," *Fortune,* June 14, 1967, pp. 178–183, 242 ff.

[9] Harry Levinson, "Conflicts That Plague Family Businesses," *Harvard Business Review,* March–April 1971, p. 95. Copyright © 1971 by the President and Fellows of Harvard College; all rights reserved.

[10] R. David Yost, "Family Affair," *MBA,* November 1975, pp. 11–14.

References

Who Is an Entrepreneur?

Gurney Breckenfeld, "The New Entrepreneur: Romantic Hero of American Business," *Saturday Review,* July 22, 1978. Arnold Cooper, "Strategic Management: New Ventures and Small Business," in *Strategic Management: A New View of Business Policy and Planning,* ed. Charles Hofer and Dan Schendel (Boston: Little, Brown, 1979). David Kaskoff, "Legends from the Gilded Age," *Saturday Review,* July 22, 1978. Frederick Klein, "Still Getting Started," *Wall Street Journal,* December 5, 1975. John O'Connell, "Still a Tiny Piece of the Action," *MBA,* January 1976. Ross Robertson, "The Small Business Ethic in America," in *The Vital Majority,* ed. Deanne Carson (Washington, D.C.: Government Printing Office, 1973). Alexander Ross, *The Risk Takers: The Dreamers Who Build a Business from an Idea* (Toronto: *Financial Post*/Macmillan, 1975). Studs Terkel, *Working* (New York: Pantheon, 1974). Karl Vesper, "Strategic Management: New Ventures and Small Business Commentary," in Hofer and Schendel, eds., *Strategic Management: A New View of Business Policy and Planning.* Roy Wilkie and James Young, "Managerial Behavior in the Furniture and Timber Industries," *International Studies of Management and Organization* 2 (Spring 1972): 65–84.

Are You an Entrepreneurial Manager?

Traits characteristic of entrepreneurial managers are discussed in the following publications: G. Jay Anyon, *Entrepreneurial Dimensions of Management* (Wynnewood, Pa.: Livingston, 1973). Robert Brockhaus, "The Effect of Job Dissatisfaction on the Decision to Start a Business," *Proceedings of the Academy of Management* (1978). Orvis Collins and David Moore, *The Organization Makers* (New York: Appleton-Century-Crofts, 1970). Arnold Cooper, "Strategic Management: New Ventures and Small Business," in Hofer and Schendel, eds., *Strategic Management: A New View of Business Policy and Planning.* John Deeks, "Educational and Occupational Histories of Owner-Managers and Managers," *Journal of Management Studies* 9 (May 1972): 127–149. Manfred DeVries, "The Entrepreneurial Personality: A Person at the Crossroads," *Journal of Management Studies* 14 (February 1977): 34–57. Roger Dunbar, "One Man, Two Organizations: The Fool on the Hill" (International Institute of Management, Preprint Series, April 1976). George Hines, "Achievement Motivation, Occupations, and Labor Turnover in New Zealand," *Journal of Applied Psychology* 58 (December 1973): 313–317. John Hornaday and John Aboud, "Characteristics of Successful Entrepreneurs," *Personnel Psychology* 24 (Spring 1971): 141–153. John Hornaday and Charles Bunker, "The Nature of the Entrepreneur," *Personnel Psychology* 23 (Spring 1970): 47–54. P. S. Hundal, "A Study of Entrepreneurial Motivation," *Journal of Applied Psychology* 55 (August 1971): 317–323. Rudolf Knoepfel, "American and European Entrepreneurs and Managers," *Managerial Planning,* November/December 1974, pp. 1–14. David C. McClelland, *The Achieving Society* (New York: Free Press, 1967). David McClelland and David Winter, *Motivating Economic Performance* (New York: Free Press, 1969). J. R. Mancuso, "What It Takes to Be an Entrepreneur," *Journal of Small Business Management* 2 (October 1974): 16–22. Edward Nicholson, Jr., et al., "Social and Attitudinal Differences between Entrepreneur and Business Hierarchs," *Proceedings of the Southern Management Association* (1973), pp. 182–193. James Schreier, *The Female Entrepreneur* (Milwaukee: Center for Venture Management, 1975). Eleanor Brantley Schwartz, "Entrepreneurship: A New Female Frontier," *Journal of Contemporary Business* 5 (Winter 1976): 47–76. Norman Smith, *The Entrepreneur and His Firm* (East Lansing: Michigan State University Press, 1967). Abraham Zaleznick and Manfred DeVries, "What Makes Entrepreneurs Entrepreneurial?" *Business and Society Review* 17 (Spring 1976): 18–23.

Can Entrepreneurship Be Learned?

G. Jay Anyon, *Entrepreneurial Dimensions of Management* (Wynnewood, Pa.: Livingston, 1973). Clifford Baumback et al., *How to Organize and Operate a Small Business* (Englewood Cliffs, N.J.: Prentice-Hall, 1973). Merrill Douglas, "Relating Education to Entrepreneurial Success," *Business Horizons* 19 (December 1976): 40–44. Douglas Durand, "Training and Development of Entrepreneurs," *Journal of Small Business Management* 12 (October 1974): 23–26. Herbert Kierulff, "Can Entrepreneurs Be Developed?" *MSU Business Topics,* Winter 1974, pp. 39–44. David McClelland and David Winter, *Motivating Economic Performance* (New York: Free Press, 1969). Joseph Mancuso, *Fun and Guts* (Boston: Addison-Wesley, 1973). Roger Ricklefs, "Entrepreneurial Coaching," *Wall Street Journal,* July 31, 1978. James P. Roscow, "Can Entrepreneurship Be Taught?" *MBA,* June–July 1973, pp. 12, 16, 50, 51. Karl Vesper, "A Multidisciplinary Experiment in Management Education," *Proceedings of the Academy of Management* (1973), pp. 284–290. Richard White, *The Entrepreneur's Manual* (Radnor, Pa.: Chilton, 1977).

The Entrepreneurial Job

Studs Terkel, *Working* (New York: Pantheon, 1974). George de Mare and Joanne Summerfield, "I Love Every Minute of It! I Can't Wait to Get In in the Morning," *Across the Board* 14 (February 1977): 44–52.

Challenges Entrepreneurs Face

Hans Camenzind, "The Agony and Ecstacy of a Startup," *MBA,* October 1974. Arnold Cooper, "Strategic Management: New Ventures and Small Business," in Hofer and Schendel, eds., *Strategic Management: A New View of Business Policy and Planning.* Alan Filley and Robert House, *Managerial Process and Organizational Behavior* (Chicago: Scott, Foresman, 1976), chapter 22. Richard Henderson, "The Best of Two Worlds: The Entrepreneurial Manager," *Journal of Small Business Management* 12 (October 1974): 4–7. Frederick Klein, "Getting Started," *Wall Street Journal,* November 6, 1974. Small Business Administration, *The First Two Years: Problems of Small Firm Growth and Survival,* prepared by Kurt Mayer and Sidney Goldstein (Washington, D.C.: Government Printing Office, 1961). A. E. B. Perrigo, "Developing Corporate Strategy for Small Businesses," *Journal of Business Policy* 3 (Summer 1973): 57–63. Frederick Webster, "A Model for New Venture Interaction," *Academy of Management Review* 1 (January 1976): 26–37.

The World of the Family Business

Benjamin Becker and Fred Tillman, *The Family Owned Business* (New York: Commerce Clearing House, 1975). Phillip Burch, *The Managerial Revolution Reassessed* (Lexington: D. C. Heath, 1972). "C. William Verity of Armco Steel," *Nation's Business,* August 1973, pp. 51–58. Edward Grether, "Four Men and a Company: Levi Strauss since World War I," *California Management Review* 20 (Fall 1977): 14–20. Walter Guzzardi, Jr., "Ford: The Road Ahead," *Fortune,* September 11, 1978, pp. 36–48. Frederick Klein and Harlan Byrne, "Dynastic Duo: Brothers Share Control of Field Enterprises through Unusual Pact," *Wall Street Journal,* August 17, 1978. Urban Lehner, "Stepping Out: Tuxedo Firm . . ." *Wall Street Journal,* October 24, 1975. Rush Loving, Jr., "Here Comes Another Kaiser," *Fortune,* February 1977, pp. 156–160, 162 ff. "Mars," *Business Week,* August 14, 1978. John Reeder, "Corporate Ownership and Control: A Synthesis of Recent Findings," *Industrial Organization Review* 3 (1975): 18–27. "Running a Family Business for 274 Years," *Nation's Business,* July 1976, pp. 31–34. Robert Sheehan, "Proprietors in the World of Business," *Fortune,* June 15, 1967, pp. 178–183, 242 ff. "Where Management Style Sets the Strategy," *Business Week,* October 23, 1978. Maurice Zeitlin, "Corporate Ownership and Control: The Large Corporation and the Capitalist Class," *American Journal of Sociology* 79 (March 1974): 1073–1119.

Advantages of the Family Business

Theodore Cohn and Roy A. Lindberg, *Survival and Growth* (New York: Amacom, 1974). Robert C. Dailey, Thomas E. Reushling, and Robert F. DeMong, "Uncertainty and the Family Corporation," *Journal of General Management* 4 (Winter 1976–1977): 60–67. Robert Donnelley, "The Family Business," *Harvard Business Review,* July–August 1964, pp. 93–105.

Problems in Family Enterprises

Monroe Bird, "Major Problem Areas as Perceived by Presidents of Small Manufacturing Firms," *Academy of Management Journal* 16 (September 1973): 510–515. O. G. Dalaba, "Lengthening Your Shadow," *Journal of Small Business Management* 11 (July 1973), pp. 17–21. Everett Groseclose, "You Have Problems? Consider the Plight of Nation's S.O.B.s," *Wall Street Journal,* March 20, 1975. Howard Klein, *Stop! You're Killing the Business* (New York: Mason and Lipscomb, 1974). Harry Levinson, "Conflicts That Plague Family Businesses," *Harvard Business Review,* March–April 1971, pp. 90–98. Robert E. Levinson, "What to Do about Relatives on Your Payroll," *Nation's Business,* October 1976, pp. 55–60. Chris McGivern, "The Dynamics of Management Succession: A Model of Chief Executive Succession in the Small Family Firm," *Management Decision* 16 (1978), pp. 32–42. "When a Family Company Outgrows the Family," *Business Week,* August 1, 1977, pp. 68–69.

Managing Successfully in a Family Business

Louis B. Barnes and Simon A. Hershon, "Transferring Power in the Family Business," *Harvard Business Review,* July–August 1976, pp. 105–114. Bernard Barry, "The Development of Organization Structure in the Family Firm," *Journal of General Management* 3 (Autumn 1975): 42–60. Robert E. Levinson, "How to Make Your Family Business More Profitable," *Journal of Small Business Management* 12 (October 1974): 35–41. Justin G. Longenecker and John E. Schoen, "Management Succession in the Family Business, *Journal of Small Business Management* 16 (July 1978): 1–6. Seymour Tilles, "Survival Strategies for Family Firms," *European Business,* April 1970, pp. 9–17. R. David Yost, "Family Affair," *MBA,* November 1975, pp. 11–14.

Case for Chapter 3

Hartley Foods

Jane Hartley joined the family firm three years ago after graduating from the University of Southern California. She spent two years in the army between high school and college (to get away from home). She majored in business at USC and graduated in the top 10 percent of her class.

James Hartley, Sr., Jane's grandfather, is president of the firm. Uncle George is treasurer. Uncle Errol is sales manager. Jane's father was killed in an accident several years ago. The firm, a food wholesaler, employs 100 people.

Jane has done all kinds of jobs. While she was in school she worked on the loading docks, filled orders, drove a truck, and took telephone orders. Since joining the firm she has done bookkeeping, pricing, purchasing, and advertising. She has tried very hard to do a good job, but her grandfather and uncles have not given her much feedback on her performance.

Jane knows that Uncle George has two sons in college, and both have told Jane that they plan to enter the firm. Uncle Errol has a daughter who plans to go to work for Hartley when she finishes her M.S. in accounting at the University of Oregon.

Jane is single. Her salary is below what her college classmates are making. Recently she overheard several nonfamily department heads talking. One said he feared that he was going to be fired to make room for Jane. As he put it, "Jane's OK, I guess, but we all know that she's only getting ahead at Hartley because of her name." The others agreed. Jane wonders if she really has a future at Hartley and why she is staying on there.

Problem

You are a friend of Jane's from USC days. She has asked you for your advice on what she should do. Give Jane your advice and an explanation or justification for it.

Case for Part One

**McDougall
Knitting Mills**

Howard McDougall, now eighty-five years old, had founded McDougall Knitting Mills in London, Ontario, when he was twenty-six years old. The firm was engaged in the manufacture of quality woolen sweaters, scarves, mittens, wrist and ankle protectors, and men's and boys' hose. It maintained a small factory and sold its own products, as well as competitive lines from other manufacturers, through its own retail store located in the downtown shopping district.

The firm also sold by mail order, circulating an annual catalog among rural customers in Canada and the United States. The bulk of sales had, from an early date, resulted from this mail order activity, although there were a few scattered retail outlets as well. These latter outlets were usually country stores which sold goods on consignment, but the firm had, however, always preferred to deal directly with the ultimate consumer. The founder was convinced, after some fifty-nine years of successful operation, that this preferential policy had strengthened the position of his firm.

McDougall was a native of Ireland. He had been the sole proprietor, manager, and controller of the firm since its inception. The business had been his dominant interest in life and, indeed, to many observers it seemed to be a reflection of his alter ego. Throughout the years all of the employees of the firm had answered only to him. His decisions had always been final and irrevocable.

Recently, McDougall had suffered two serious heart attacks. Even though his doctors had advised him after his first attack that he should take life easier and turn active management of the firm over to someone else, McDougall insisted on going to his factory every day, and he continued to supervise all work down to the smallest detail. He had at that time a staff of nineteen full-time employees, many of whom had been with him for more than thirty years. They were skilled knitters and set-up workers, and all were imbued with a deep respect for and sincere personal loyalty to McDougall.

The main retail outlet, located in an expensive downtown section of the city, had been under the management of Gregory Holmes for fifty-two years. Holmes, whose title was general sales manager, was theoretically responsible for all sales activities in the firm. For many years he had refused to make decisions on any problems unless an exact precedent existed. If there was no precedent, he referred the decision to McDougall.

However, Holmes was considered to be thoroughly proficient in looking after the mail order activities. He possessed an intimate knowledge of McDougall's rural customers, including their requirements and the ability of the firm to fill their orders. But while the store was ideally located, it was poorly arranged to facilitate effective displays of merchandise. Old-fashioned in every respect, Holmes did not evidence any interest in modern retailing methods for attracting customers, improving sales, or reducing selling expenses. It was conceded by everyone, however, that he was honest, loyal, and faithful and that he knew the products from A to Z.

During his more active days, McDougall had been an outstanding citizen of the community. He had served several terms on the city council, and he had been prominent in the work of his church and many service clubs. As he had grown in years, his activities outside his business had first decreased and then finally stopped completely. Later, even his business had begun to reflect his age. Since he had been a strong leader for many years, none of his employees had been called upon to exercise any imagination or anticipatory foresight in any of the firm's activities, and so the relative position of the firm had begun to show a gradual decline. A point had been reached, some years ago, when bank credit no longer was being extended because it had become apparent to the bankers that the McDougall Knitting Mills Ltd. no longer had the benefit of effective management direction. Nevertheless, the firm continued to produce much as before. Many orders arrived each day from the firm's rural customers and it was apparent that a considerable residue of good will was associated with the firm's name. Thus, while no new catalog had been issued for the past two years nor any effective advertising for the past five years, the business had continued on its own momentum and reputation of former years, providing a good income for McDougall and his employees.

Within the past eighteen months, a new competitor, Evergreen Knit Goods Ltd., had built a new factory in London, leased a modern well-equipped store in a good location, and placed four traveling salesmen on the road. It was apparent that Evergreen Knit Goods Ltd. was in a good position to capture the market formerly held by McDougall Knitting Mills Ltd.

The position of the McDougall Knitting Mills Ltd. was further complicated by the fact that McDougall had transferred the ownership of the firm to his wife thirty-five years ago. When she died, twelve years after the transfer, the shares of ownership were distributed equally to their three children. The children, however, had never taken any interest in the operation of the firm, having felt that the ownership had been left to them in trust for the use of their father.

After his second heart attack, McDougall himself began to realize that some changes were required. He approached his son-in-law, Andrew Jones, and asked him to join the firm and assume direction of the management. At that time Jones was anxious to enter a business of his own and since his wife already owned one-third of the firm, had readily agreed. Jones signed an agreement with one of the other shareholders whereby Jones would be able to buy out this shareholder (at a stipulated price) after one year of operation under the direction of Jones. He also had obtained agreement from both the other shareholders that during the first year under his management he would have a free hand to make any necessary changes required to rehabilitate the firm.

McDougall then agreed that Jones would enter the firm as executive assistant to McDougall until such time as he had obtained a full grasp of the business. During this period he would supervise all manufacturing activities, promote the sale of the firm's products in an aggressive manner, and generally restore public and customer confidence in the firm and its products.

Furthermore, it was agreed that McDougall would personally announce the managerial changes to the employees of the firm and that a written notice afterward would be circulated for everyone to read and initial. Jones agreed to submit a draft of this notice the very next day, since McDougall now was anxious to act at once.

That evening, when discussing the situation with his wife, Jones said, "You know, this job is not going to be an easy one . . . sure, I have a lot of administrative experience, but I have had none in the knitting business or the woolen business. How can I learn the tricks of these trades quickly? . . . On top of that, every one of the employees there is old enough to be my father—and for that matter, even my grandfather. How can I best get them to cooperate with me, individually as well as a group? . . . Then there is the whole competitive situation and especially the Evergreen Knit Goods Ltd. Those fellows are sharp characters and I'm sure they're out to capture our customers. What measures can I take to stop these fellows quickly and decisively? . . . And, you know your father . . . do you really believe he'll go along with the many changes which will be needed if the firm is to be rescued? Should I wait for a year before doing anything about present policies, or should I tackle your father at once on policy changes? . . . If I don't get busy right away, how can I stop the Evergreen fellow? . . . And that reminds me of another problem: Gregory Holmes! How should I go about getting his cooperation in the "face-lifting" operations that are needed in our sales and promotion activities? . . . How should I write the announcement so that I will have freedom to act quickly and decisively and yet not upset any of the employees or your father? . . . And I have to do this tonight before your father gets another idea and changes his mind about me. . . ."

Source: William Pershing, © 1979 W. A. Pershing, University of Alberta, Edmonton, Alberta, Canada.

Problems

1. Will Jones be able to be an effective manager of McDougall? Under what conditions? How likely are these conditions to exist?
2. Will banks begin lending to McDougall now?
3. If you were Jones, would you have made the decision he did?
4. You are Jones. The instructor will assign someone to be McDougall. Time: three months after you began working there. You have a number of suggestions for modernizing (and you think saving the firm from ever-increasing Evergreen competitions). You propose them and try to convince McDougall of their usefulness.

Part 2

Understanding the Managerial World

2

Part 2 is aimed at helping you understand the manager's world. This world is both external and internal. The external environment—society, customers, government, suppliers, competitors, and the local community—impacts on how the managerial task is organized. The internal world of the manager also influences his or her performance. Thus, the various aspects of human behavior, the uniqueness of each person, and motivation are introduced.

Chapter 4   Relating to the Environment

Introduction

Perhaps in simpler times the entrepreneur or manager could ignore much of what went on outside the company. But a glance at any newspaper will give you an idea of how the *environment influences firms* today:

- The Sierra Club lobbies to prevent the harvesting of redwoods in California. This pressure group has affected the operations of the lumber firms and the jobs of their employees.

- A group of consumers is lobbying to get a law passed prohibiting the sale of the Battlestar Gallactica line of toys and other toys which shoot projectiles. This could affect Mattel Toy Company (producer of the Battlestar Gallactica line of toys) and other toy companies in what they offer the public.

- The Environmental Protection Agency has banned the use of the pesticide 2-4-T at least temporarily. This will affect how Weyerhauser manages its forests. It is likely to increase the cost of wood and all of the products made from it, such as furniture, newspapers, greeting cards, books, and houses.

- The United Mine Workers Union struck the coal firms. This shut many mines, increased coal prices and the cost of heating homes, even shut factories, and forced people to leave their (freezing) homes. But mostly, it prevented firms such as Peabody Coal from producing and selling coal and railroads such as Chessie from hauling it.

- Stockholders of Gulf Oil revolted and got the board to fire its top manager. This affected the career of this executive and may affect the future behavior of Gulf executives regarding payments to political campaigns.

- There was a revolution in Iran. This has reduced the shipment of crude oil to petrochemical firms and increased the price of this raw material to all industries using it, such as plastics. The oil has also become available only irregularly with severe impact on production scheduling, inventory costs, and sales.

- A community votes not to change its zoning laws and thus prohibits a new plant from being built there.
- Eastern Airways, as it opened its Atlanta to San Francisco flight on its new Airbus, offered its customers a $49 fare one way. This led Delta to lower its price too—for a limited number of customers.

Other news items indicate how the *enterprise influences the environment*.

- More and more top executives of firms have gone to state capitals and Washington to speak with and influence legislators. They are engaging in *interpersonal influence*.
- Often, the fund drives for charities are led by business executives. They are engaging in *community work*.
- Mobil Oil sponsors TV programs to get its message across to customers. Mobil is engaging in *advertising* and *image building*.
- The Kellogg Foundation gives funds to community organizations and hospitals. The image of Kellogg cereals may benefit from this *philanthropy*.
- *Lobbyists* for real estate interests influence members of Congress not to change depreciation rates on rental property. This is paid for by real estate brokers.
- The manager is active in trade associations and tries to influence other firms including competitors to police unethical behavior.

To fully understand management and the organizations which managers run, you need to understand the organization's environment. To be a successful manager today, you need to know how the environment influences the organization and how to influence that environment.

The enterprise must seek its supplies (money, people, raw materials, equipment) from other enterprises or from other sources outside the enterprise. The enterprise must be legitimized by a government. It is located in a community. It has competitors to fight with and clients to satisfy. These usually exist *outside* the boundaries of the enterprise. They can and do influence the managerial job. And managers try to influence them in order to make their enterprise more successful and their life easier.

A few enterprises are so powerful and so self-contained that they do not spend much time dealing with the environment; but in this interdependent world of ours they are few and declining in number. Many managers spend much of their time trying to predict the future environment and influence it. The more dependent a firm is, the more time it needs to analyze, relate to, and try to influence the environment.

This is not the last time I will touch on this topic. In Chapters 2 and 3 it was pointed out that managerial attitudes and behavior are influenced by the enterprise's environment. In Chapters 5 and 6 I will discuss how people differ in motivation and attitudes as a result of differences in culture and history. In Chapter 8 you will see how managers perform strategic planning, a conscious attempt to plan how the enterprise will deal with environmental opportunities and threats. Finally, in Chapters 10 through 13 I will indicate how environmental factors influence organizational structure and lead to organizational change.

Environmental influences, like most other influences in our life, are perceived. They are not absolute. Karl Weick calls this enacting the environment.[1] What he means is this: Managers receive many cues from inside and outside the organization. The top manager chooses the factors he or she wishes to focus on, and this becomes the environment. If the manager makes a mistake in choosing what to observe, react to, and influence in the environment, significant problems can arise. Who within the Tennessee Valley Authority would have thought that the snail darter would delay the generation of more electricity? How many managers seriously worried about the ecology movement as part of the environment in 1965? How many are aware of it in 1980?

The major elements in the external environment which most businesses must be aware of include:

- Societal values and pressure groups
- Government bodies
- Customers/clients
- Suppliers (stockholders, bankers, raw material and subassembly providers, unions, etc.)
- Local community
- Competitors

Certain internal factors can influence which of these external factors are most critical to the success of the enterprise:

- *The volatility of the environment of the firm* In a fast-changing business such as fashion merchandising, the customer component may be the most significant external factor to follow. In a slow-changing business such as aluminum smelting, the key factors might be the government or suppliers.
- *The technology of the business* High-technology businesses such as electronics may need to focus on suppliers more closely than low-technology businesses like wood products.
- *The size of the firm* The pressure society and the government exert on a firm may depend on its size. Large firms like General Electric are more visible than smaller firms like a 100-employee job shop in Peoria.
- *The complexity or diversity in offering of products/services* The number and types of products or services offered influences how many sets of factors (customer groups, suppliers) the firm must monitor and relate to.

- *Corporate objectives* To a significant degree, a firm's objectives influence how it relates to the environment. I will discuss this in more detail in Chapter 7. For example, if one of a firm's objectives is social responsibility, it will spend more funds on beautifying its site and in philanthrophy than will a firm which does not include social responsibility among its objectives.

The Manager's Roles in Relating to the Environment

The manager plays several roles in relating to the environment. In Henry Mintzberg's terms the manager is a liaison, spokesperson, and negotiator.[2] As a liaison person the manager gets known in the environment and thus helps establish and personify the firm in the environment. The manager receives praise on behalf of the whole organization when it is doing well and receives blame when it is failing. If a firm or football team does poorly, it is probably due to the failures of many. Yet it is the coach or the president of the firm who is fired. For example, the chief executive officer of Lockheed was asked to resign during the period of exposure and near bankruptcy, and he did.

As a spokesperson, the manager steps forward when the organization is called upon to respond to an accusation or accept thanks for an action. In this symbolic role, the manager satisfies the need people have to see someone "in charge" who can "do something" relative to environmental challenges.

As a negotiator, the top manager is reactive and proactive. The reactive manager scans the environment and makes decisions on how to respond to the demands of factors in the environment such as the government and competitors. The proactive manager scans the environment, determines what pressures are coming, and takes active steps to deflect forces which will be harmful and reinforce those which will be helpful. Both of these aspects of the negotiator's role involve a two-step process: (1) scanning the environment to determine what is happening that is influencing or may influence the firm and (2) diagnosing the significance of these forces so as to set priorities on how to respond to or anticipate these.

The manager's need to influence various institutions, groups, and individuals outside the enterprise will be described in Chapter 8. Managers must plan their time and programs of influence carefully, or they may find themselves spending their time trying to influence relatively unimportant groups. The most significant groups are those on which the firm is most dependent.

Like any other aspect of the managerial job, external relations will benefit from planning. The first step is conscious setting of priorities: asking various management groups to determine where the firm should place its energies and spend its time first—that is, which areas are most significant.

The second step is determining which mechanisms of influence will be used and which managers will be involved. This is planning implementation. For example, the vice-president for marketing may be assigned to relate to consumer groups, the vice-president–general counsel to relate to the state legislature, the vice-president for personnel and organization planning to relate to the unions, and the vice-president for finance to relate to stockholders.

Although there is little direct proof that planning this aspect of management will lead to greater effectiveness, research has shown that planning has been beneficial in other aspects of management. It seems reasonable to conclude that it would help in managing external relations.

An effective negotiator may take advantage of any of the various approaches listed below:

- *Direct interpersonal influence* In this approach, the manager gets to know key people in the external organization. The manager uses his or her powers of persuasion to influence these people and their organizations. American Telephone and Telegraph (AT&T) is a firm which utilizes this approach well.[3]

- *Community work* Managers are expected to be active in community groups—United Fund, PTA, League of Women Voters, church and synagogue, and similar organizations to become known and to be able to defend their organization's point of view.

- *Advertising and image building* By sponsoring television and radio programs, Junior Achievement, and ads in newspapers, the firm's interests can be expressed. Good corporate images can help in dealing with external factors.

- *Philanthropy* Some organizations dispense scholarships, give to cultural organizations, establish parks, etc., to improve the firm's influence in the community and society.

- *Direct action* Some businesspersons have run for office to make sure that antibusiness laws are not passed. They may also sponsor lobbyists to persuade various organizations of the firm's point of view.

The above is a general description of these approaches. I will give you some concrete examples as we now discuss influencing specific external organizations. One executive who has done an excellent job in the spokesperson and negotiator role is Reginald Jones, pictured on page 100.

Relating to Society

Whether a businessperson can negotiate with the environment or try to influence it as a spokesperson is partially a result of the position of the manager or entrepreneur in society at the time. This conditions the attitudes and behavior of the manager or entrepreneur in negotiations with the environment.

Reginald H. Jones

Reginald H. Jones is chairman of the board and chief executive officer of the General Electric Company. A graduate of the Wharton School of the University of Pennsylvania, he joined General Electric's business training course in 1939 and served as a traveling auditor. He was elected a vice-president of the company in December 1961 after a career in general management positions with the company.

Following a series of assignments in the apparatus area, he was named general manager of the air conditioning division in 1956. Two years later, he was appointed general manager of the General Electric supply company division. When the construction industries division was formed January 1, 1964, he was made its general manager. He continued to head both divisions until he was named to head the components and construction materials group in 1967. He was named vice-president—finance for the company on May 1, 1968.

Jones was elected a senior vice-president on June 1, 1970, and made a member of the board of directors on August 1, 1971, and vice-chairman of the board and member of the corporate executive office on March 1, 1972. He was elected president of the company on June 23, 1972, and chairman and chief executive officer on December 15, 1972.

Jones was born in the United Kingdom on July 11, 1917, and came to the United States as a child. He is chairman of the Business Council and co-chairman of the Business Roundtable. In May 1979, President Carter named Jones chairman of the President's Export Council. He is a member of the Advisory Committee for International Monetary Reform, a trustee of the University of Pennsylvania, chairman of the board of Overseers of the Wharton School, and an active layman in the Congregational Church.

The prevailing evaluation of business has ranged from "The business of this country is business"—in which businesspeople were very influential—to "Business is dull, dirty, and beneath the dignity of important people." In a society where business is revered, businesspeople can (if they choose to) negotiate with and influence the environment effectively. In an antibusiness society the businessperson is on the defensive and usually reacts to the environment rather than trying to influence it positively.

There are examples of societies at both extremes, some in-between, and some (including our own) where attitudes toward business are cyclical. Examples of antibusiness societies include classical Greece, imperial Rome, medieval Catholic Europe, and Ottoman Turkey. Middle-of-the-road attitudes prevailed in Byzantium, Russia under the Czars, and England from 1600 to 1800. Probusiness societies include Protestant Europe in the nineteenth century (especially Scotland, Holland, Switzerland, Scandinavia, and Germany) and the United States from 1865 to 1929.

With regard to the United States and Canada, business was most influential in good times and was given credit for the general prosperity. The periods when businesspeople had the greatest influence were 1860–1900, 1900–1929 (the high point), and 1953–1961. Men like John Jacob Astor, J. P. Morgan, Henry Ford, Thomas Watson, and George Humphrey were highly influential in society and could affect government policy.

The prevailing attitude toward business in a society is a result of business behavior, of course. Public opinion of business is influenced by certain groups in society, particularly authors—novelists and journalists. There is much evidence that in the U.S., at present, these influentials portray businesspersons in a negative light. This is true of a significant percentage of humanities and social sciences faculties in many universities. Louis Banks points out that business must do a better job presenting its case in the media if the societal values are not to become even more negative.[4]

Besides relating to customers, government, suppliers, competitors, and the local community, managers must relate to some institutions and groups which for the sake of simplicity we shall call pressure groups. These groups can have an indirect effect on the success of a business. They include agricultural groups, intellectual groups, environmental groups, the poor, the aged, and voluntary pressure groups like churches and the YMCA. The Gray Panthers and the National Association of Retired Persons, for example, might try to influence insurance companies about the cost of health and auto insurance as well as lobby the government about social security increases.

Some businesses are directly involved with agricultural groups such as the Farm Bureau, the National Farmers Organization, and the Grange. Farm implement manufacturers, fertilizer companies, and seed companies clearly have an interest in relating to these groups of potential customers.

Businesses sometimes lobby for, sometimes against the programs advocated by agricultural groups in state capitals or in Washington. There have been few direct clashes between business and agriculture in recent years, however.

This is not so with other groups in society. The organized pressure groups favoring environmental protection and improvement and similar objectives have lobbied, advertised, and organized against specific business actions. Their greatest impact has been on auto makers (emissions), chemicals (pollution), utilities (nuclear power), airframe corporations (SST, Concorde), petroleum (Alaska pipeline, offshore oil drilling), coal (strip mining), and defense manufacturing. In general, these groups favor improvement of the quality of life and the reduction of pollution in all its forms—chemical, noise, visual (billboards), and so forth.

These issues have divided the business community. Many if not most businesspeople favor cleaner air, more beautiful land, and a quieter environment. The affected industries usually argue that they favor these objectives too but differ on the attainable goals for economic reasons.

The businesses involved use all the influence mechanisms available to them to plead their case: interpersonal relations, image building, lobbying, and others. In some cases they have also used threats: "If you require a particular level of air purity, we will close the plant. It will no longer be cost effective."

Business needs to do a better job of stating its case and trying to influence environmental groups. Of course in some instances (for example, the steel works in Gary, Indiana), the case is difficult to make and the firm should comply with the regulations or close the plant.

Another "pressure group" that has arisen in the past ten years is the urban poor. This group has publicized the urban crisis and urged or demanded that business improve urban living conditions by helping with urban renewal, job training, minority entrepreneurship programs, and more jobs. The response from business is directly related to the "social responsibility consciousness" of managers. This issue is described further in Chapter 7.

The final group with which business can interact is made up of the intellectuals and media influence leaders. Important television, radio, newspaper, and magazine opinion leaders can have a significant impact on the future of business. If, for example, they all coalesced behind a demand that the oil companies be nationalized, this would greatly influence voters (who are consumers) and legislators. To a lesser extent, some intellectuals such as scientists and professors can have an effect on business, usually by influencing key people in the media.

Business managers should try to influence these groups. The most effective method is to have intelligent, persuasive spokespeople develop interpersonal relationships with them. Other methods are less fruitful.

Often the demands of different pressure groups conflict. In such cases

"One pressure group wants us to withdraw sponsorship of our TV show, another pressure group wants us to continue sponsorship of our TV show, and still another pressure group wants us to add more noodles."

business must choose a side and get ready for attacks from those who do not agree with their choice.

Relating to Customers

As you well know, the customer has a highly significant impact on the firm's method of operating. Means used to influence customers vary according to how many customers the firm has. Firms can become very dependent on one or a few customers. The major defense manufacturers sell their products to the government (or perhaps a few governments). The success of major airplane manufacturers depends on their ability to sell planes to perhaps ten airlines. Contrast these firms with General Foods, which sells Maxwell House coffee to millions of consumers and thousands of wholesalers.

When a firm has only a few clients, the main method it uses to influence them is interpersonal influence. Community work, advertising, and image building may also be employed. When a firm has millions of customers, the individual consumer is much less influential. If General Foods loses a few customers, many more can be acquired through TV advertising.

Irresponsible or inefficient service and poorly designed or unsafe products have led to the reappearance of the consumer movement. In this movement, blocks of consumers join together to exert pressure on an enterprise or industry. The consumer movement has had its ups and downs. Between 1879 and 1905 the movement was strong: 100 bills to regulate the food and drug industry at the state level and the Pure Food and Drug Act at the federal level were passed. Then the movement declined. It reappeared in the Depression, retrenched in the 1940s and 1950s, and reappeared again in the late 1960s and 1970s. Major consumer groups in the late 1970s include the Consumer Federation of America, the National Consumers League, and the Consumer Union of the United States. These groups expose irregularities, sue the enterprises involved, and lobby for their causes. Ralph Nader has been very active in this area through his Center for Responsive Law.

There is also a movement to set up a cabinet-level Department of Consumer Affairs to "protect the consumers of America." Advocates of this new agency argue that this unit would better enforce truth-in-advertising laws and product liability legislation and warranties, as well as pure food and similar legislation.

In the past, businesses have responded to the consumer movement by trying to make sure the enterprise was not guilty of deception or illegal acts. Some enterprises supported voluntary organizations such as Better Business Bureaus (BBBs) to alert the consumer to fraud and exert pressure on offending businesses. Although BBBs are fairly successful, they tend to operate "behind the scenes." Thus they are not generally perceived as a powerful force in protecting consumers.

Recently, however, BBBs became more influential when ninety-two of the 134 in existence set up arbitration boards in 1972. Typically these boards are composed of lawyers, educators, and a sample of businesspersons and housewives. The FTC recently required Joseph's Furniture Company (New York) to submit a consumer dispute to one of these boards. Whirlpool, B. F. Goodrich, and 13,000 other businesses are now using them. The courts have supported their rulings too.

How does business relate to the consumer? Business has taken several approaches to consumer relations. Some companies have created consumer ombudsmen or -women who see to it that the consumer gets a "fair shake." Others have widely advertised a toll-free "consumer hotline." For example, Whirlpool urges its customers to call about service or product complaints and promises to take action.

Strict enforcement of the laws by government would also help. Why do some people believe that creation of a Consumer Department will ensure greater compliance with the laws? Both consumers and honest business-people should lobby for better enforcement of the present laws before creating new laws or new bureaucracies.

Business needs to try to relate to the consumer movement. Instead of hiring private detectives to try to trap Ralph Nader in some compromising act, General Motors would have been more effective in combatting

Nader's charges if it had investigated them and made its case known to the public and Congress. Businesses should develop interpersonal relationships with major consumer groups so that they have a "pipeline" to these influential groups. They should offer to cooperate in sponsoring independent studies of the charges made by such groups as Consumers Union. Their present stance casts them in the role of selfish interests vigorously trying to protect themselves while producing unsafe or useless goods and services. This is a losing position.

Government Influences on Business

Government at all three levels (federal, state—in Canada, provincial—and local) influences business. In the United States, federal, and in Canada, provincial legislation has had the greatest impact on business success. Governmental units can influence managers in many ways. I will discuss four here: regulation, subsidization, competition, and management of the economy.

All three levels of government can regulate businesses. Cities can impose licensing requirements, and local government zoning restrictions can prevent a firm from expanding. States or provinces can also regulate an industry or company, and of course the federal level can and often does regulate business. It takes a government charter to open a business, and various government agencies regulate almost every aspect of almost any business.

Among the recent popular movements that have changed or increased government regulation of business are the environmental movement (Environmental Protection Agency), the antitrust movement, the civil rights movement (Equal Employment Opportunity Commission), and the women's rights movement (also covered by the EEOC). Between 1960 and 1975 eighty-eight *significant* laws were passed regulating business activity. (A sampling is given in Table 4.1 on page 106.) These laws supplemented many others already in existence, and all are enforced by government agencies—some new, some old.

These laws and regulations have had various effects on businesses. For some, they have meant heavy costs: red tape and the forms that must be filled out take time and money. And, for example, when a business spends money to meet the Environmental Protection Agency's standards, it reduces the funds it can invest in increasing productivity. Murray Weidenbaum has shown that most of the objectives of legislation could be more efficiently achieved by other means.[5]

Regulation also directs how and how much some businesses compete. The deregulation of airlines appears to be increasing competition and lowering prices. Recently the U.S. federal government required that

Table 4.1
Some Significant
Legislation Regulating
Business, 1960–1975

Civil Rights Act of 1960
Federal Hazardous Substances Labeling
  Act of 1960
Fair Labor Standards Amendments of
  1961, 1966, and 1974
Federal Water Pollution Control Act
  Amendments of 1961
Oil Pollution Act of 1961 and Amendments
  of 1973
Food and Agriculture Act of 1962
Air Pollution Control Act of 1962
Antitrust Civil Process Act of 1962
Drug Amendments of 1962
Clean Air Act of 1963 and Amendments of
  1966 and 1970
Equal Pay Act of 1963
Civil Rights Act of 1963
Food Stamp Act of 1964
Automotive Products Trade Act of 1965
Federal Cigarette Labeling and Advertis-
  ing Act of 1965
Water Quality Act of 1965
Clean Water Restoration Act of 1966
Fair Packaging and Labeling Act of 1966
Federal Coal Mine Safety Act Amend-
  ments of 1966
Financial Institutions Supervisory Act of
  1966
Oil Pollution of the Sea Act of 1966
Age Discrimination in Employment Act of
  1967
Air Quality Act of 1967
Agricultural Fair Practices Act of 1968
Consumer Credit Protection Act of 1968
Natural Gas Pipeline Safety Act of 1968
Radiation Control for Health and Safety
  Act of 1968
Cigarette Smoking Act of 1969

Child Protection and Toy Safety Act of
  1969
Federal Coal Mine Health and Safety Act
  of 1969
Natural Environmental Policy Act of 1969
Tax Reform Act of 1969
Bank Holding Act Amendments of 1970
Bank Records and Foreign Transactions
  Act of 1970
Economic Stabilization Act of 1970 and
  Amendments of 1971 and 1973
Environmental Quality Improvement Act of
  1970
Fair Credit Reporting Act of 1970
Investment Company Amendments of
  1969
Noise Pollution and Abatement Act of
  1970
Occupational Safety and Health Act of
  1970
Securities Investor Protection Act of 1970
Water and Environmental Quality Im-
  provement Act of 1970
Export Administration Finance Act of
  1971
Consumer Product Safety Act of 1972
Equal Employment Opportunity Act of
  1972
Federal Environmental Pesticide Control
  Act of 1972
Noise Control Act of 1972
Agriculture and Consumers Protection
  Act of 1973
Emergency Petroleum Allocation Act of
  1973
Highway Safety Act of 1973
Water Resources Development Act of
  1974

Source: From Albert Seelye, "Societal Change and Business-Government Relationships," pp. 5–13, *MSU Business Topics*, Autumn 1975. Reprinted by permission of the publisher, Division of Research, Graduate School of Business Administration, Michigan State University.

physicians write prescriptions in generic (chemical/pharmaceutical) names rather than brand names. Most ethical drug manufacturers like Eli Lilly had based their strategy on branded drugs. This could change substantially how these companies do business. And if the Federal Communications Commission widens the AM radio band, it will mean more stations.

**Government
Subsidy, Support,
and Taxation**

Governments can directly affect the profitability of an enterprise through their tax policies. Increases in taxes reduce the amount of money available to purchase goods and services. Selective tax policies (subsidies) can keep enterprises afloat or even make them profitable. The U.S. government subsidizes, directly or indirectly, airlines, railroads, and many other businesses. It can accomplish this by purchasing the output of an enterprise or by giving loans to firms such as Lockheed and Penn Central.

The Government as Competitor

The government can nationalize an enterprise and put it out of existence, as Britain did to British Leyland (its largest auto firm) and as several Latin American governments have done. Or the government can compete directly with private firms. Consider these instances:

Government Enterprise	Private Enterprise
U.S. Postal Service	United Parcel Service
TVA	Peabody Coal, Union Electric
U.S. Employment Service	Chusid Employment Agency
Public Broadcasting Service	National Broadcasting Company
Government arms factories	Remington Arms Company
Yellowstone National Park	Disney World
National Park Service	KOA
Military and Transport Service	Flying Tiger
U.S. Military Commissary	Safeway Stores
British Leyland Motors	Ford Motors (U.K.)
Veterans Administration hospitals	Doctors' hospitals

The list can easily become quite long. As governments move toward ownership of business, they can squeeze out the private sector.

The Government as Manager of the Economy

Various economists advocate different government economic policies. The monetarists, for instance, urge the government to make stabilizing the money supply a major economic policy. On the other hand, Keynesian economists—whose theories stem from John Maynard Keynes, an English economist—advocate the use of fiscal and monetary methods to increase aggregate demand in slack times and dampen it in peak times. In recent decades, governments have been influenced by Keynesian economics, but they have used only the first half of the Keynes approach. In managing the economy through government fiscal and monetary policies, they have used deficits and easy money in an attempt to increase employment. Inflation and wage and price controls have been the results. These policies clearly affect business's ability to make a profit and survive—as do all government economic policies.

Relating to the Government

Now we will take a look at the six ways managers relate to government. In relatively large firms top managers and government relations specialists do the relating. In other firms top managers are responsible for this function directly and through their trade associations. The objective of these relationships is to protect the interests of the business and to influence government policy.

Business has recently become more active in trying to influence the federal government because the federal government has begun to have a greater impact on business than it did twenty years ago. And as John Alpin and W. Harvey Hegarty have shown, business is having more impact on Congress for the following reasons:[6]

- Congressional deliberations are more open than they used to be. Therefore, members of Congress are being held responsible.
- There is greater turnover in Congress than in the past. As a result members of Congress are more responsive to constituents than they used to be.
- Committee chairpersons are less powerful than they used to be.
- Members of Congress are being assigned to committees based on their expertise.
- Congress is more powerful relative to the president than it used to be.

Interpersonal Influence

The first approach managers use in relating to government is interpersonal influence. They get to know government officials, politicans, and leaders of groups that can influence legislation. They try to use the mechanisms of interpersonal influence to get government officials to like them and trust them. They socialize with these officials and provide them with information in an attempt to enlist their support. The manager may play golf with government officials, invite them to lunch or for a few drinks at the country club, and in general develop a program of relatively frequent social interaction with these individuals.

It is not easy to develop a dialog between business and government leaders, even through interpersonal relationships. They tend to talk past each other rather than to each other. Differences in terminology are a problem. So are differences in educational background and objectives. Nonetheless, it is vital to the survival of the private sector that managers make their case known to government officials.

Advertising and Image Building

A second approach—which has an indirect influence on the political process—is to advertise and try to build a good image for the company with the general public (i.e., the voters). News programs are sponsored on TV, ads are placed in magazines and on the radio to get the enterprise's point of view across. As with all ads, some are good, others poor. Many times it is hard to evaluate the costs and benefits of campaigns of this type.

Lobbying

A manager can influence proposed new legislation (or amend past legislation) by writing, calling, or visiting legislators and trying to influence the actual writing of the law. More frequently, the manager supports his or her trade association's efforts in this regard. The association hires a lobbyist who knows the lawmakers and the legal process. The lobbyist is there when the law is being drafted and argues for a particular version of the bill.

All elements of our society employ lobbyists: farmers, unions, teachers, environmentalists, and others. Ralph Nader is, in effect, a lobbyist. Businesspeople must see that their side is heard too. An example of how lobbyists can influence legislation may be seen in the strip mining industry's ability to affect legislation regulating its industry.

The key question is how lobbyists are used. Ethical businesspeople take steps to see that efficient, respected, honest lobbyists are hired to plead their case.

Direct Political Action

Another form of influence is political activity. Businesspeople can be active in politics and even run for office. Many well-known politicians were prominent businesspeople when they ran for office. Examples include Senators Charles Percy (R-Illinois, formerly at Bell and Howell), and Lloyd Bentson (D-Texas, formerly an insurance entrepreneur). Many state legislators are entrepreneurs and family business executives. Business executives who do not hold public office can exercise political power by influencing how shareholders relate to government and mobilizing them to take action. Shareholders are voters too. Some executives have found it very effective to encourage extensive mail and postcard campaigns to members of Congress. The businessperson may also accept political appointments—examples include Michael Blumenthal, Roy Ash, William Simon, and many others. There are dangers in direct political activity by business executives, however. The enterprise can lose the time and talents of executives in this way, and customers of other political persuasions may be antagonized.

Becoming a Government Business

In earlier periods entrepreneurs would seek to become the government's exclusive agent. The East India Company (British and Dutch) helped develop America, and Aristotle Onassis ran Greece's Olympic Airways in this way.

Illegal Action

The final method some managers use to influence the government is to bribe, frighten, or blackmail politicians or government officials into going along with their enterprise's preferences. Frequently, these techniques are used to get laws administered (or ignored) in such a way as to favor the enterprise over others. This activity is discussed further in Chapter 7. Suffice it to say here that successful businesses can operate without resorting to these illegal methods.

Relating to Suppliers

The firm is dependent to a greater or lesser extent on the suppliers of its needs: money, materials and equipment, and people. Thus a business is dependent on stockholders and bankers, materials and equipment suppliers and unions, and its managers must be able to relate to these people.

Relating to Stockholders and Bankers

In entrepreneurial and family businesses the managers are the stockholders. In some family businesses the managers are the major stockholders, but other family members hold important blocks of stock. Again, these family members are often on the board of directors. The various objectives of these stockholders often strongly influence decisions on issues such as dividend policy, growth policy, and philanthropy. As discussed in Chapter 3, the relationships can become difficult if personal differences among family members are translated into differences among managers or board members. Sometimes the only way such differences can be settled is to buy out minority stockholders with a bank loan or some similar mechanism. Since these stockholders can combine and get voting control of the enterprise, interpersonal relationships with these individuals are often carefully cultivated. Sometimes positions in the company are created for relatives in order to influence their attitudes. Again the method of interpersonal influence is used.

As indicated in Chapters 2 and 3, in many middle-sized and larger firms certain individuals own major blocks of stock. If one stockholder owns 25 percent and the other 75 percent is owned by several thousand people, the major stockholder *potentially* can have a great impact on the management. Normally, interpersonal methods are used to influence major stockholders. Board positions are often offered too.

Stockholders usually regard ownership of stock as an investment, not a means of controlling the enterprise. Most of the nation's 30-odd million stockholders have neither the knowledge nor the inclination to try to affect management policy. A few large shareholders do.

Enterprises try to influence most stockholders through advertising, image building, and good annual reports. Some larger enterprises have executives in charge of stockholder relations. These individuals often pay special attention to major shareholders and watch the trading in the stock carefully to see if problems are developing.

When a few large stockholders can influence a corporation (as the Mellons can influence Gulf Oil), the top managers must spend some of their time communicating with these individuals and influencing them interpersonally.

A newer group that could *potentially* influence managers is the top executives of financial institutions: mutual funds, pension funds, endowment and philanthropic funds, and insurance and investment companies. These institutions own almost 50 percent of all stocks and are responsible for two-thirds of the trading on the stock exchanges. The managers of these institutions, a relatively small group, could make or break a firm. If they decided to "dump" 50 percent of the company's stock within a brief period, the firm's cost of capital would skyrocket. Financial managers and top managers try to influence these individuals directly and indirectly through interaction with stockbrokers and financial analysts. It is not beyond the realm of possibility that these people might demand changes in management and threaten to dump stock if the changes are not made. To the extent that an enterprise's stock is "closely held" by such individuals, it is well for the manager to try to influence them.

Finally, most enterprises need additional funds from banks from time to time. These firms need to cultivate relationships with bankers who can provide loans when necessary. Generally this takes the form of interpersonal relations. Bankers may also be asked to serve on the enterprise's board, an honor that can lead to a favorable attitude toward lending needed funds to the enterprise.

Thus stockholders and bankers, the sources of funds, need to be influenced by enterprises, large, medium, and small, through interpersonal relations, advertising and image building, and exchange relationships.

Relating to Suppliers of Materials and Equipment

Many managers view their suppliers of materials and equipment as dependent on them—the purchasers. In many cases they are. If there are hundreds of companies trying to sell you lumber, you may see yourself as "in the driver's seat" and expect the suppliers to cultivate you.

In fact, however, in many cases there are only a limited number of suppliers who can provide you with the equipment and materials you need at the price you can pay for the quality you need and in the time you need it. Often there are really only one or two suppliers. It is very important to develop good relations with these suppliers so that when you need a favor (such as an emergency shipment) the supplier will try to help.

Managers should also examine the relationships between suppliers and the enterprise's purchasing agents. Purchasing is an area in which unethical people can develop bribery relationships to the detriment of both the enterprise and supplier relations. Nonpurchasing managers should visit with supplier executives at conventions and other times to see if the supplier relationship is sound.

Whether an enterprise is dependent on a few suppliers or many, effective exchange relationships can lead to better shipping arrangements, early warning of major changes in prices, and speedy information about technological or marketing developments. Thus managers make an investment toward enterprise effectiveness if they develop friendly, professional relationships with their equipment and materials suppliers.

In sum, the usual and appropriate methods of influencing these suppliers are interpersonal relationships, effective purchasing arrangements, and perhaps advertising and image building.

Relating to Unions

If the enterprise is unionized, it makes sense to relate frequently and effectively with union leaders. Otherwise the only contacts might be negative adversarial relationships at contract time and confrontations over serious grievances. If the differences between managers and union leaders in socioeconomic characteristics (social class, education, age, values, income) are not bridged, conflict between the two groups can be accentuated.

Business managers attempt to influence union members through image building, advertising, and interpersonal influence. They can try to influence union leaders through interpersonal influence. Managers should get to know union leaders socially. They should sound them out regularly on their feelings and those of their members. The steel industry's labor problems were reduced when the steel union presidents golfed with the steel company presidents. Again, what is suggested here is not the unethical or illegal exercise of influence but simply getting to know and understand the other person so that working relationships will improve. This is the job of personnel managers (the local union president, business representatives, and officers), supervisors (the respective shop stewards), and company presidents and regional and/or international union presidents.

If the enterprise is not unionized, it is useful to develop alternative mechanisms to determine employee complaints and concerns. An ombudsman or -woman is one such mechanism. Other mechanisms include elected employee committees and suggestion systems. The best approach is to develop good personnel management practices. Chapters 20 and 21 discuss some of these.

Relating to Competitors

Enterprises compete for customers or clients with other enterprises. A major variable in a firm's success or failure (and existence) is the degree to which it competes effectively.

How should managers relate to competitors? First of all, relationships with competitors are influenced by the law and by the values of top management. In most of the world and throughout history (and in most nonbusiness sectors of society), cooperation with competitors has been the norm. Competition has been viewed as undesirable. Thus guild societies such as those established in medieval Europe and by the Moravians in this country gave monopolies to craftsmen to ensure quality work and "fair return." Many European societies have seen trusts and monopolies as desirable and efficient, although the Common Market now has an antimonopoly commission. It is only the teaching of Adam Smith, as enacted in the United States antitrust laws, that sees monopoly as bad. If two hospitals got together and agreed to divide the market, with one specializing in heart work and another in kidney work, this plan would be applauded. If two businesses agreed to do this, their executives could go to jail.

In spite of the antitrust laws, "combinations in restraint of trade" take place in secret hotel rooms and prices and territories are sometimes agreed upon by competitors. The *Wall Street Journal* reported recently on the "gypsum trust."[7] And you may have heard about the "electrical conspiracy," in which some General Electric and Westinghouse executives were punished for price and territory fixing. The Federal Trade Commission has accused a series of industries of monopolistic practices. A recent case in point is the paper craft industry.

There has been concern for some time about the concentrations of power that exist in some industries. The theory—and often the practice—is that fewer enterprises can (if they choose to) keep prices high and service or product variety low. This is often accomplished through mergers. There is much evidence that many lose in a merger—not only the customers but also the stockholders of the acquiring company. The main beneficiaries of mergers are the stockholders of the acquired company (in the short run) and the top executives of the acquiring company.

Obviously, managers in the United States must obey the antitrust laws scrupulously, even while seeking to change them—if they are so inclined.

How, then, can managers relate legally to their competitors? They can do so through their industry trade associations. There are many issues that can be legitimately resolved through the trade association. For example, if the industry has an inefficiently large number of product types the association may seek to standardize them. The association may fund research for safer working conditions, more efficient machinery, more efficient hiring of salespeople, and similar projects. It may also lobby and attempt to influence legislation.

Managers should get to know their competitors. From time to time they can help each other. For example, a firm with a surplus can sell to a competitor whose plant has burned down. Both firms will benefit. In general, some cooperation is desirable for all concerned, as long as it is legal and ethical.

Relating to the Local Community

The enterprise and the local community are highly interdependent. The local community influences zoning and similar matters. More importantly, the local community is the major source of the enterprise's labor force.

Table 4.2
Conditions Leading to
Community
Involvement

	More Involvement	**Less Involvement**
Type of Business	Family Local markets Extractive or distributive	Absentee-owned Regional or national markets Manufacturing
Interbusiness Relations	Centralization of influence Cohesion of interests	Fragmentation Factionalism

City Characteristics	Small- or medium-sized
	Limited industrialization
	Economically undiversified
	Minimal heterogeneity of population
	Limited unionization of blue-collar
	  workers
	One-party predominance
	Non-partisan politics
	Limited differentiation of polity from
	  family and economic interests
	Limited organization of interests
	  countervailing those of business
	South, Southwest, or Midwest
		Large
		Highly industrialized
		Diversified
		High degree of heterogeneity
		
		Extensive unionization
		Two or more vigorous parties
		Partisan politics
		High degree of differentiation
		
		High degree of countervailing organi-
		  zation
		East or Northeast

Source: From "Business and the Local Community" by Rogers and Zimet in *The Business of America*, edited by Ivar Berg, copyright © 1968 by Harcourt Brace Jovanovich, Inc., and reproduced with their permission.

Enterprises that are perceived as good places to work probably attract better employees. The local community is also the firm's physical environment. The more desirable a place it is, the more likely that people will be willing to work there. In turn, the enterprise can help make the community a better place to work. Finally, the local community provides clients and customers for goods and services.

Businesspeople place different priorities on relating to the local community. Some say, "It's our responsibility to be involved," while others maintain, "Business's business is to do its job." The degree of involvement also varies widely. Involvement in a company town is much higher than in New York City, for example.

The research on business involvement in the local community is summarized in Table 4.2. Note the variety of ways businesses can be involved, depending on the type of business, the interrelationships, and the kind of local community in question.

The variety of ways in which businesspeople can get involved is almost unlimited. Some of the most significant possibilities include:

- Direct political action
- Philanthropy

- Advisory services (to the city, voluntary associations, etc.)
- Support of bond issues and civic improvement
- Support of charity drives
- Providing executives for city or voluntary agencies

The number and variety of possible community support situations are so large that the enterprise should set priorities and concentrate its support in the most fruitful areas.

In general, the mechanisms available for community relations are similar to the mechanisms useful in government relations. Direct political action and lobbying are infrequently employed, but interpersonal influence and advertising and image building are common techniques.

The one addition to the methods discussed earlier is encouraging managers to join civic groups and volunteer to help the community. The enterprise can provide funds for advertising in support of community actions and send letters of support to its employees.

Sometimes business takes the lead in civic improvement. For example, the Pittsburgh rejuvenation project was led by the business community. The pharmaceutical firm of Smith, Kline and French supported an urban renewal program around its Philadelphia headquarters. And Hallmark bought some slums near its headquarters in Kansas City, tore them down, and redeveloped the area for shopping and better housing units.

Some large enterprises have set up their own community relations programs. AT&T, for example, trains its executives in community relations and then encourages them to become active in voluntary groups such as charity organizations, blood banks, the Rotary Club, the YMCA, PTAs, the Jaycees, and the United Fund. It encourages them to run for part-time offices such as positions on zoning boards and school committees. AT&T also provides the schools with free texts and training programs. It is not known how much all this costs. AT&T's New York headquarters budgeted $10 million for this work in 1975 alone, but this figure does not include the cost in time of executives released from work.

The community usually benefits from these kinds of activities, and the enterprise benefits to the extent that the community views it as a responsible employer and source of goods and services.

Summary

Reading the newspaper or watching TV, you have been bombarded with all kinds of items about pressure groups, lobbyists, and environmental threats. Chapter 4 has summarized these environmental challenges the manager must face every day and introduced the roles and tools the effective manager must use to meet them.

The major elements in the external environment which most businesses must be aware of include:

- Societal values and pressure groups
- Government bodies
- Customers/clients
- Suppliers (stockholders, bankers, raw material and subassembly providers, unions, etc.)
- Local community
- Competitors

Internal factors, too, such as the volatility of the firm's business, the technology, the firm's size, the complexity or diversity of products and services, and corporate objectives can influence which of these external factors are most critical to the enterprise's success.

In relating to the environment, the manager is a spokesperson and negotiator. In the former role, the manager receives the praise when the organization is doing well and the blame when it is not. In the latter, the top manager can be *reactive,* scanning the environment for threats and opportunities and responding to them, or *proactive,* trying to deflect forces which will be harmful and reinforce favorable ones. To do both, the executive must scan and diagnose the elements in the environment.

Once the environmental situation has been diagnosed, how can an effective negotiator influence the significant groups mentioned above? The approaches include: direct interpersonal influence, community work, advertising and image building, philanthropy, and direct action.

Each of the major elements in the firm's environment presents certain challenges, and certain methods are most effective in responding to each of these challenges. A few enterprises are so powerful and so self-contained that they do not spend much time dealing with the environment. These are very few and declining in number, however. Most managers spend much of their time trying to predict and influence the future environment.

An appendix to the chapter introduces you to the environment of the international manager.

Questions

1. Why is it necessary for today's managers to understand how the environment influences the organization and how to influence the environment? Cite specific situations to support your answer.
2. "Environmental influences, like most other influences in our life, are perceived." What does this statement mean to you as a manager trying to deal with the environment?
3. What major elements in the external environment should the effective manager be aware of?
4. Explain how internal factors of the specific firm can influence which of the external factors are most critical to its success.
5. Define and differentiate the spokesperson and the negotiator roles.

What do scanning and diagnosing the significance of the forces in the environment have to do with the negotiator role?

6. List and explain the series of approaches available to the effective negotiator for managing external relations.

7. How would society's prevailing attitude toward business at any given point in time affect you as a manager?

8. What approaches are most effective in relating to customers?

9. You hear complaints every day about the impact of government on business. How would you handle governmental influences on your firm?

10. What are the appropriate means of relating to stockholders? Bankers? Materials and equipment suppliers? Unions?

11. How can managers relate legally to their competitors?

12. As a representative of your company's image, how would you plan to relate to your local community?

Notes

[1] Karl Weick, *The Social Psychology of Organizing* (Reading, Mass.: Addison-Wesley, 1969).

[2] Henry Mintzberg, *The Nature of Managerial Work* (New York: Harper & Row, 1972).

[3] Sanford L. Jacobs, "Best Foot Forward: On the Job or Off, AT&T People Polish the Company Image," *Wall Street Journal,* April 16, 1975; and Sandra L. Holmes, "Executives Should Be Seen and Heard," *Business Horizons* 20 (April 1977): 5–8.

[4] Louis Banks, "Taking on the Hostile Media," *Harvard Business Review,* March–April 1978, pp. 123–130.

[5] Murray Weidenbaum, "The High Cost of Government Regulation," *Business Horizons,* August 1975, pp. 43–51.

[6] John C. Alpin and W. Harvey Hegarty, "Planning Effective Strategies to Influence Federal Legislation," paper based on research project, Indiana Executive Program (Bloomington: Graduate School of Business, Indiana University, 1979).

[7] David McClintick, "Busting a Trust," *Wall Street Journal,* October 3, 1975.

References

Business and the Changing Environment

Joseph R. Monsen, *Business and the Changing Environment* (New York: McGraw-Hill, 1973). Jeffrey Pfeffer and Gerald Salancik, *The External Control of Organizations* (New York: Harper & Row, 1978). Karl Weick, *The Social Psychology of Organizing* (Reading, Mass.: Addison-Wesley, 1969).

The Manager's Roles in Relating to the Environment

Sanford L. Jacobs, "Best Foot Forward: On the Job or Off, AT&T People Polish the Company Image," *Wall Street Journal,* April 16, 1975. Sandra L. Holmes, "Executives Should Be Seen and Heard," *Business Horizons* 20 (April 1977): 5–8. Richard A. Mittenthal and Brooke W. Mahoney, "Getting Management Help to the Nonprofit Sector," *Harvard Business Review,* September–October 1977, pp. 95–103. Henry Mintzberg, *The Nature of Managerial Work* (New York: Harper & Row, 1972).

Relating to Society

Hermann Krooss, *Executive Opinion: What Business Leaders Said and Thought, 1920–1960* (New York: Doubleday, 1970). David Macmillan, *Canadian Business History* (Toronto: McClelland and Steward, 1972). Louis Banks, "Taking on the Hostile Media," *Harvard Business Review,* March–April 1978, pp. 123–130. Bruce Cook, "Big Business and the Bad Guys on Television," *Wall Street Journal,* February 23, 1979. Wilson C. McWilliams and Henry A. Plotkin, "The Historic Reputation of American Business," *Journal of Contemporary Business* 5 (Autumn 1976): 1–46. Gerald R. Rosen, "The Growing Clout of 'Do Good' Lobbies," *Dun's Review,* April 1977, pp. 44–50, 113. H. R. Smith, "Novelists and Businessmen: Schizophrenia in the Complex Society," *Journal of Contemporary Business,* Autumn 1976. "What Black Leaders Want from Business," *Business Week,* October 10, 1977, pp. 85–88, 92. Richard B. Wirthlin, "Public Perceptions of the American Business System: 1966–1975," *Journal of Contemporary Business,* Summer 1975, pp. 1–14.

Relating to Customers

Max Brunk, "Consumerism and Marketing," in *Issues in Business and Society,* ed. George Steiner (New York: Random House, 1972). Richard T. Hise, Peter L. Gillett, and J. Patrick Kelly, "The Corporate Consumer Affairs Effort," *Consumer Affairs* (Summer 1978), pp. 17–26. Scott Maynes, "The Power of Consumers," *Business Horizons,* June 1972, pp. 77–86. R. Joseph Monsen, *Business and the Changing Environment* (New York: McGraw-Hill, 1973), chapter 3. Robert L. Simison, "The Final Word: Arbitration for Consumers Is Spreading as Better Business Bureaus Offer Service," *Wall Street Journal,* April 21, 1975, p. 24.

Government Influences on Business

John C. Alpin and W. Harvey Hegarty, "Planning Effective Strategies to Influence Federal Legislation," article based on research project, Indiana Executive Program (Bloomington: Graduate School of Business, Indiana University, 1979). Roy L. Ash, "A Business Guide to Political Action," *Management Review,* May 1977, pp. 20–23. John Connally, "The Case for the L-1011 Lockheed Transport Loan Guarantee," in *Hearings before the Senate Banking, Housing and Urban Affairs Committee on S1891,* 92d Congress, 2d session, June 1971. Richard Eels and Clarence Walton, *Conceptual Foundations of Business* (Homewood, Ill.: Irwin, 1974), chapter 14. John R. Emshwiller, "New Allies: Shareholders Unite to Help Utility Firms Battle Regulators and Consumer Groups," *Wall Street Journal,* April 13, 1978, p. 46. Neil Jacoby, *Corporate Power and Social Responsibility* (New York: Macmillan, 1973). Robert A. Leone, "The Real Costs of Regulation," *Harvard Business Review,* November–December 1977, pp. 57–66. Robert E. MacAvoy, "Business Strategy and Inflation: Finding the Real Bottom Line," *Management Review,* January 1978, pp. 17–24. Thomas McCraw, "Regulation in America: A Review Article," *Business History Review* 49 (Summer 1975): 159–183. John C. Perham, "A Unique Job Swap for Executives," *Dun's Review,* May 1977, pp. 89–91. Reed Powell and K. Tim Hostwick, "The Business Executive's Role in Politics," *Business Horizons,* August 1972, pp. 49–56. William Proxmire, "The Lockheed Bail Out: A Threat to Free Enterprise," speech before the National Federation of Independent Business, Washington, D.C., May 18, 1971. Alfred Seelye, "Societal Change and Business-Government Relationships," *MSU Business Topics,* Autumn 1975, pp. 5–11. George Steiner, "New Patterns in Government Regulation of Business," *MSU Business Topics,* Autumn 1978, pp. 53–61. Jerrold G. Van Cise, "For Whom the Antitrust Bell Tolls," *Harvard Business Review,* January–February 1978, pp. 125–130. Murray Weidenbaum, "The High Cost of Government Regulation," *Business Horizons,* August 1975, pp. 43–51.

Relating to Suppliers

William F. Glueck, *Personnel: A Diagnostic Approach* (Dallas: Business Publications, 1978), chapter 19. Thomas Kochen, "Determinants of Power of Boundary Units in an Interorganizational Bargaining Relationship," *Administrative Science Quarterly* 20 (September 1975): 434–452. William E. Lucado, "The Energy Situation: Implications for Strategic Planning," *Business Horizons,* April 1975, pp. 26–30.

Relating to Competitors

Peter W. Bernstein, "Competition Comes to Accounting," *Fortune,* July 17, 1978, pp. 88–96. Peter Caudle, "U.K. Chemicals: Strategic Planning or Industrial Strategy," *Long Range Planning* 10 (December 1977): 31–39. Kenneth J. Hatten, Dan E. Schendel, and Arnold C. Cooper, "A Strategic Model of the U.S. Brewing Industry: 1952–1971," *Academy of Management Journal* 21 (1978): 592–610. Neil Jacoby, *Corporate Power and Social Responsibility* (New York: Macmillan, 1973). David McClintick, "Busting a Trust," *Wall Street Journal,* October 3, 1975. Desmond Martin and William Kearney, "External Policy and Control in Large Scale National Trade Associations," *Journal of Business Administration* 1 (Summer 1969): 29–37; and "Who Makes the Decisions in Trade Associations?" *Atlanta Economic Review* 19 (September 1969): 10–13.

Relating to the Local Community

James S. Bowman, "Business and the Environment: Corporate Attitudes, Actions in Energy-Rich States," *MSU Business Topics,* Winter 1977, pp. 37–49. Keith Davis and Robert Blomstrom, *Business and Society* (New York: McGraw-Hill, 1975), chapter 17. Eugene Litwak and Henry Meyer, "A Balance Theory of Coordination between Bureaucratic Organizations and Community Primary Groups," *Administrative Science Quarterly* 16 (June 1966): 31–58. Neil Maxwell, "Conservation vs. Fertilizer: Fierce Opposition to New Mining Stymies Phosphate Industry Expansion in Florida," *Wall Street Journal*, July 14, 1976, p. 32. David Rogers and Melvin Zimet, "The Corporation and the Community," in *The Business of America,* ed. Ivar Berg (New York: Harcourt, Brace and World, 1968), pp. 37–80. Vermont Royster, "Thinking Things Over: Mirror, Mirror on the Wall," *Wall Street Journal,* December 3, 1975.

The Manager in an International Environment

Jose De LaTorre and Brian Toyne, "Cross-National Managerial Interaction: A Conceptual Model," *Academy of Management Review,* July 1978, pp. 462–474. George England et al., *The Manager and the Man* (Kent, Ohio: Kent State University Press, 1974). Richard Farmer, "International Management," in *Contemporary Management,* ed. Joseph McGuire (Englewood Cliffs, N.J.: Prentice-Hall, 1974). Mason Haire et al., *Managerial Thinking* (New York: Wiley, 1966). Frederick Harbeson and Charles Myers, *Management in the Industrial World: On International Analysis* (New York: McGraw-Hill, 1959). W. Warren Haynes et al., *Management,* 3d ed. (Englewood Cliffs, N.J.: Prentice-Hall, 1975), chapter 27. Allen I. Kraut, "Some Recent Advances in Cross-National Management Research," *Academy of Management Journal* 18 (September 1975): 538–549. Peter Kuin, "The Merger of Multinational Management," *Harvard Business Review*, November–December 1972, pp. 89–97. Joseph La Palombara and Stephen Blank, *Multinational Corporations in Comparative Perspective: A Research Report* (New York: The Conference Board, 1977). Don Lebel et al., "Small Scale Industries and Developing Countries," *California Management Review* 17 (Fall 1974): 32–40. I. A. Litvak and C. J. Maule, "Branch Plant Entrepreneurship," *Business Quarterly,* Spring 1972, pp. 44–53. R. Hal Mason, "Conflicts between Host Countries and the Multinational Enterprise," *California Management*

Review 17 (Fall 1974): 5–14. Joseph Massie and Jan Luytjes, *Management in an International Context* (New York: Harper & Row, 1972). Howard Perlmutter and David Heenan, "How Multinational Should Your Top Managers Be?" *Harvard Business Review,* November–December 1974, pp. 121–134. David Rutenberg, "Organizational Archetypes of a Multinational Company," *Management Science* 16 (February 1970): B337–B349. Hans Schollhammer, "Organization Structures of Multinational Corporations," *Academy of Management Journal* 14 (September 1971): 345–365. Prokash Sethi and Richard Holton, "Country Typologies for the Multinational Corporation," *California Management Review* 15 (Spring 1973): 105–117. Samir Youssef, "Contextual Factors Influencing Control Strategy of Multinational Corporations," *Academy of Management Journal* 18 (March 1975): 136–143.

Appendix 4.1

The Manager in an International Environment

Some people contend that management is the same through all ages and in all countries. In many ways this is true, but the differences are more important than the similarities. The differences are especially important when managers are working at sites away from their home country. Management practices abroad are constrained by four sets of differences:

- *Educational factors* Examples include the number of skilled employees available, attitudes toward education, and literacy level. Educational deficiencies in some countries can lead to a scarcity of qualified employees and/or a lack of educational facilities to upgrade potential employees.

- *Behavioral factors* Societies differ in factors such as attitudes toward wealth, the desirability of profits, managerial role, and authority.

- *Legal-political factors* Laws and political structures differ and can encourage or discourage private enterprise. Nations also differ in degree of political stability. Some countries are very nationalistic (and xenophobic). Such countries can require local ownership or, if they are so inclined, expropriate foreign enterprises.

- *Economic factors* Economies differ in basic structure, inflation rate, ownership constraints, and the like.

Before entering into a foreign venture managers should examine these constraints as they affect each aspect of management and prepare a matrix like that in Exhibit 4.1. It is obvious that not all factors are going to be different in each country. There will be some overlap in attitudes and practices. The degree of difference seems to decrease in more economically developed countries.

We can divide the nations of the world into three economic categories: fully developed, developing, and less developed. The fully developed nations include the United States and Canada, Australia, New Zealand, Israel, Japan, South Africa, and most European countries (the United Kingdom, Austria, West Germany, France, the U.S.S.R., Belgium, Luxembourg, the Netherlands, Switzerland, Italy, Sweden, Denmark,

Exhibit 4.1
The Firm/Environment
Matrix

Local Environment Constraints

FIRM AND MANAGERIAL FUNCTIONS	Educational	Behavioral	Legal-Political	Economic
Planning	a_1	a_2		
Control				
Organization				
Staffing				
Direction				
Marketing				
Production and Procurement				
Research and Development				
Finance				
Public and External Relations				a_{40}

Each block a_1, a_2, . . ., a_{40} is a potential interface problem between the firm and its environment.

Source: From Richard N. Farmer, "International Management" in *Contemporary Management: Issues and Viewpoints*, by McGuire, © 1974, p. 300. Reprinted by permission of Prentice-Hall, Inc., Englewood Cliffs, New Jersey.

Norway, Finland). In these countries the American or Canadian manager will find fewer differences in educational, behavioral, economic, and legal-political factors than he or she is likely to encounter in developing or less developed countries.

The developing nations are those that are well along in economic development but not yet fully developed. Examples include Brazil, Mexico, Argentina, Venezuela, Chile, Spain, Portugal, Nigeria, Saudi Arabia, Iran, Libya, India, Singapore, Taiwan, the countries in Eastern Europe (Yugoslavia, Romania, Poland, East Germany, Czechoslovakia), Korea, and possibly China. These countries provide more constraints in all four categories than developed countries.

Third World nations—the less developed countries—are the most difficult to work in because of significant constraints in all four categories. The remaining ninety or so countries in the world are in this group. A sample list would include Egypt, Pakistan, Bolivia, Paraguay, Bangladesh, Upper Volta, and Sudan.

To be successful abroad, the manager must learn about the country where he or she will be working. There are many sources of this kind of information.

So knowledge of differences among nations in the four constraints listed earlier is essential for success abroad. Equally important (and more difficult to obtain) are proper attitudes toward other countries and their cultures. The United States is the most powerful and one of the most affluent countries in the world. Canada is equally affluent. Managers working abroad may develop a mind set like the following:

U.S./Canada	Characteristic	Host Nation
Strong	Strength	Weak
Wealthy	Wealth	Poor
Advanced	Managerial Practice	Primitive
Important	Culture	Insignificant

A manager with this set of attitudes may try to transfer North American ways of doing things directly to the host country without considering the four constraints. The more significant the differences between the manager's home country and the host country in the four constraints, the more likely they are to cause problems for the unperceptive manager.

Effective international managers adapt their managerial practices to conditions in the host country. Just as the tools of management science do not work on very unstable problems, so leadership styles that are effective where employees are educated and achievement oriented may not work where employees are uneducated and nonachieving. The willingness to adapt managerial practices to the needs of the environment or culture joined with knowledge of the legal-political and economic factors is likely to lead to success overseas.

The Multinational Corporation

A small number of firms are *multinational;* that is, much of their business and/or profits may come from overseas. These firms have regional headquarters for whole areas of the world (for example, ABC Europe, ABC Asia, etc.). They develop worldwide strategies in order to survive and grow. It is estimated that 15 percent of gross world product is produced by multinational corporations.

Most multinationals are owned and controlled primarily by individuals in one country. A few are transnational (for example, Shell and Unilever); their ownership is split among individuals in several major countries. Successful multinationals grow because they develop good managers who respect other nations and their cultures as they establish their management structures and build their marketing, financial, and operating strategies. They have learned to strike a proper balance between executives who are citizens of the host country and executives from the home office.

Multinationals have been critized, however, for not developing a global management group. The members of such a group would be on the same pay scale, evaluated on the same criteria, kept on the same management inventory, and given experience around the world. Instead, the present pattern is to have the home office staffed primarily by executives of the home country, the local branch staffed primarily by host country nationals, and very few "third world" nationals in management positions anywhere. It is argued that to be successful, multinational corporations need a core group of globally oriented executives and professionals who can work anywhere. This may be true, but knowledge of the four constraints (economic, political-legal, behavioral, and educational) is necessary for success in most overseas assignments, and this is very difficult to develop if you spend two years in Mexico followed by two years in Japan, two in South Africa, and then two in Belgium.

The multinational corporations are still evolving the most effective mechanisms of international policy and personnel development. More research is needed before we can say much more about effective multinational management.

Case for Chapter 4

Amax and Crested Butte, Colorado

Crested Butte is a former mining town of 1,000 persons who have restored its Victorian buildings. Many of Crested Butte's leaders and townspeople are transplanted—educated former New Yorkers, Californians, and ex-Atlantans. Crested Butte is nestled beneath Mt. Emmons in an unspoiled valley almost entirely surrounded by National Forest land.

Amax, a firm with assets of $3 billion, wishes to develop a $1 billion mine to process molybdenum from the mountain. The world market for molybdenum (moly for short) is $7 billion and rising at 7 percent a year. Amax produces half the world's supply of moly, and Mt. Emmons is

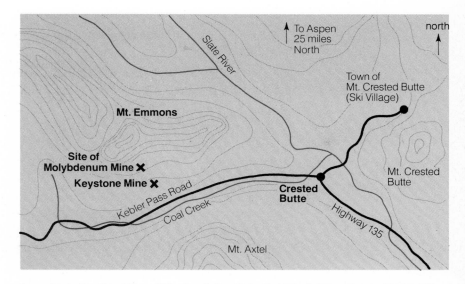

Source: Adapted from Roger Williams, "A Tiny Town Battles a Mining Giant," *New York Times Magazine*, March 4, 1979, p. 17.© 1979 by the New York Times Company. Reprinted by permission.

believed to contain the world's largest deposit of moly. Moly is used to give durability to steel. It also reduces corrosion, helps it resist severe temperatures, and makes it lighter. In World War II, it was considered the country's most strategic metal, and troops surrounded the moly mines to prevent possible Nazi sabotage. If the mine is built, 2,000 workers will be employed in the construction process, and 1,300 people will be needed to run it once built.

Presently, the Crested Butte area is supported by recreation; 1,500,000 campers, hikers, fishermen, backpackers, and others visit the area every year. Some of the locals believe the mine and its associated waste products—perhaps 200–300 million tons—will ruin the area for recreation. It also will destroy the wilderness, they think. At present, there is little unemployment. Many locals believe that the doubling of their town's and county's population will bring all the problems of growth they came to "the Butte" to avoid: unemployment, housing cost increases, and drugs.

The company has faced many challenges from those who oppose the mine, including:

- Bumper stickers against Amax.
- Proposals to build a much smaller mine—one which Amax says is uneconomical.
- Shots taken at executives' homes.
- The opposition of a paraplegic mayor who received national publicity.
- The opposition of the city council.
- Attempts of state and county planning boards to prevent or control the mine.

The company has been involved in the following legal activities to try to develop the mine:

- The expenditure of $800,000 to unpollute a creek which the previous mine owners polluted.
- The construction of a $2,000,000 water treatment plant to clear up water pollution further.
- Full-page advertising in local papers and the production of *Moly News*, its monthly newsletter.
- The use of unarmed security guards.
- Participation in Colorado Review Process, a government planning organization promoting balanced growth of jobs, housing, transportation, sewerage, etc.
- Contribution of $100,000 to the County Planning Commission toward a computerized planning system.
- Employment of spokespersons to explain Amax's position.

- Tours for thirty-six town and county officials to see how other mining towns adapted.

Still the locals are fighting the mine.

Source: Adapted from Roger Williams, *New York Times Magazine*, March 4, 1979, p. 17.
© 1979 by the New York Times Company.

Problem

You are Stan Dempsey, spokesperson for Amax. You were in charge of environmental controls during the construction of the most environmentally sound mine in the world. Design a program for improved negotiator and spokesperson roles for Amax.

Chapter 5   Understanding Human Behavior

Learning Objectives

1. Learn to evaluate yourself and your employees in terms of the model of human nature and the personality.
2. Remember environmental conditions such as rearing and wider cultural influences affect each individual.
3. Understand how biology affects your functioning as a manager.
4. Develop some insight into personality to aid you in evaluating your own and employees' behavior.
5. Gain and use in your career as a manager a basic knowledge of certain mental constructs such as abilities, aptitudes, perception, attitudes and of the interaction of reason and emotion in determining behavior.
6. Understand that learning and teaching are basic to the manager's role and to the accomplishment of any new task.

Chapter Outline

Introduction   Chapter 4 discussed how the world outside the firm influences it and how the manager's role includes relating to the environment. This chapter is the first part of a two-chapter sequence designed to help you understand the world inside the firm—the human world of managers and employees.

Chapters 5 and 6 are basic to understanding all of management, for most of management focuses on getting things done through people, the human resource. People manage the firm's other resources too. In order to be an effective manager, entrepreneur, or family business executive it is absolutely vital to understand how and why people behave as they do.

Research from many fields contributes to an understanding of human behavior: organizational behavior,[1] psychology, biology, philosophy, to mention a few. By using this body of knowledge, you will be able to identify and anticipate human problems and thus prevent management problems. You will often be able to look at and understand why an employee is ineffective on the basis of a simple checklist like the following:

1. Does he or she lack abilities?
2. Does he or she not understand the situation because of differences in perception, attitudes, or personality?
3. Does he or she lack motivation?

Once you have determined the cause of the problem, you will know whether you need to transfer, retrain, or counsel the employee.

One conclusion you may draw from this chapter is that dealing with individual differences is a problem. It is also a challenge. The information in this chapter should help you meet that challenge by observing the following points:

1. *You can welcome individual differences.* They give you the ability to fit a variety of talents to a variety of jobs.
2. *You can listen with understanding to employees and thus clarify and reduce conflicts.*

3. *You can recognize and accept different views of the causes and solutions of problems.*

4. *You can indicate the procedures and ground rules you will use to resolve differences.*

One major individual difference needs to be discussed in a chapter of its own, namely, motivating employees. This is the subject of Chapter 6.

A Model of Human Nature

In Chapters 2 and 3, we presented a model of managerial success. The first part of the model was a simplified version of the human factors affecting managerial success. This part of the model will be the focus of Chapters 5 and 6. It is expanded in Figure 5.1 to indicate the complexities of human nature. Figure 5.1 will serve as the model of human nature to be used in these chapters.

Note, the individual variable in the success formula is called the personality. Each of the variables in Figure 5.1—environmental influences,

Figure 5.1
A Model of Human
Nature and Personality

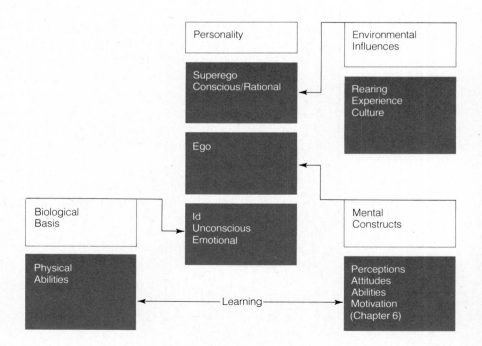

biological basis, personality, and mental constructs—will be discussed in depth in the following sections. Their influences on the person and their application to management will be explored in detail.

Environmental Influences on Human Behavior

Social scientists differ in the emphasis they place on the environment's impact on human actions. According to some, the human being is a piece of clay molded by the environment. Ivan Petrovich Pavlov, John B. Watson, and B. F. Skinner number among those who have emphasized the environmental conditioning of behavior. Other psychologists assert that the environment is not a significant influence on behavior. Some theorists even see human beings as animals who respond to situations instinctively. Others view them as having free will to respond or not respond to stimuli.

Although the environment is an important influence on human behavior, some have overemphasized it, calling it the *primary* influence. It is actually only one of a number of factors that shape behavior. A person acts in response to his or her own internal inclinations, choices, *and* environmental influences. Kurt Lewin stated this principle as Behavior = $f(P, E)$: behavior is a function of the person and the environment.[1] Sometimes the person's needs and choices predominate and lead him or her to act. At other times environmental forces strongly influence behavior, But all behavior is caused by a *combination* of the personal consent of the actor plus environmental influences.

How people are reared at home and what they are taught at school and in their church or synagogue also affects their personality and behavior. The wider culture influences individual behavior and attitudes, too. For example, Southeast Asian cultures are more fatalistic than Western cultures. Personal experiences also affect the way people act, especially in relation to others.

We are almost all social animals. There are a few people who manage to develop in isolation—most major religions have mystics who worship, work, and write alone in the desert or on a mountaintop. But most of us develop our abilities, motives, perceptions, and personalities as a consequence of interacting with others. When dealing with an individual, the manager must recognize that feedback from the individual's work group will determine his or her responses, at least in part.

Biological Basis of Human Behavior

Human behavior is influenced by the physiology and biology of the body. We inherit certain physical characteristics that influence our ability to play basketball, do heavy physical labor, and perform other tasks. We also may inherit many of our mental abilities. Carl Jung believed we inherit attitudes and ideas, too, but most experts disagree.[2]

Let's review briefly the biological basis of human behavior with a simplified model of the nervous system as shown in Figure 5.2. Nervous tissue consists of two types of cells: glial cells and neurons. These cells are organized into the various components of the nervous system: the brain, the spinal cord, and the peripheral nervous systems. The agents of change in the system are electrochemical. A sensory signal entering the brain speeds along a neuron as a tiny electrical current. When the signal reaches the end of one neuron it must be transmitted across a minute gap called a synapse to another neuron. The electrical current activates transmitter chemicals at the nerve endings, and those chemical substances cross the synapse, passing a replica of the original impulse to the neighboring neuron. Suppose you accidentally shut your finger in your desk drawer. A neuron in your finger sends a message to the next and so forth until the message reaches your pain receptors. At that point you grimace in pain and use an appropriate expletive. You have probably already pulled back your hand. All of this takes place in microseconds.

The brain is a complex entity whose functioning is understood only imperfectly at present. One site of the brain—the frontal lobe—is concerned with expressive behavior, the activity which the living organism exhibits as a result of the impact of external and internal environmental stimuli. This is the part of the brain which enables the person to engage in characteristic motor behavior. The parietal cortex is concerned with body image and the integration of sensory systems throughout the body. The

Figure 5.2
Diagram of the Brain

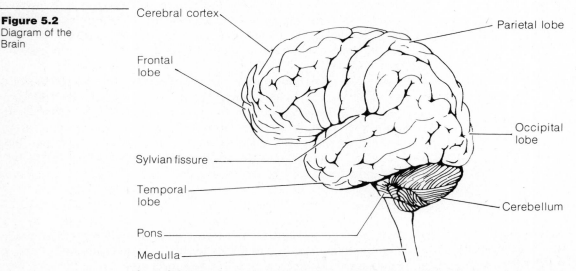

Source: C. P. Noback and R. J. Demarest, *The Human Nervous System*. Copyright © The McGraw-Hill Book Company, 1967, p. 52.

area which controls vision is the occipital cortex. The temporal lobe has to do with hearing, language, and music appreciation, and it controls the capacity to understand and manipulate numbers.

Perhaps the most exciting aspect of the brain is revealed in the research neurosurgeons have done on human memory. Through electrical stimulation of the temporal lobe they have brought back patients' memories of specific points in their lives. In these experiments, the patients have recalled past experiences in full detail, leading scientists to conclude that experiences are never forgotten, just repressed by more recent overlapping memories.

Finally, the integration of various impulses from throughout the body is controlled by the limbic lobe. The limbic lobe also plays a role in regulating emotional response. Much more work is necessary in this area, however, for emotional behavior is also governed by a more primitive site in the brain that cannot be easily investigated.

Thus, from the biological point of view, human behavior is a complex set of patterns of motor activity in response to sensory stimulation. To some extent the biological aspects of human behavior can be controlled or modified when necessary as a result of breakthroughs in the fields of science and medicine.

Personality and Human Identity

You will understand yourself and your employees better and thus be a better manager if you understand personality. Think of personality as a person's *unifying mechanism* that provides identity and affects behavior.

Personality is the pattern of stable states and characteristics that influences an individual's behavior toward goal achievement. Each person has unique ways of protecting these states.

There is much debate about the development of personality. Various experts have argued that personality is influenced genetically (through heredity); by internal mental development; by interaction with others in the family, in the peer group, and at work; and by the general environment and culture. All of these influences are shown in Figure 5.3. Note that personality is viewed as more or less *stable* and *consistent* over time. Obviously personality changes and develops, but it tends to evolve gradually.

There are many well-known theories of personality—Carl Jung's, George Kelly's and the humanists, such as Carl Rogers, Gordon Allport, Rollo May, and Abraham Maslow.[3] All are important, but the best known theory is that of Sigmund Freud.[4] Figure 5.3 reproduces a simplified version of Figure 5.1. The terms used in both figures are Freud's.

According to Freud, the mind is composed of the following:

Figure 5.3
Personality and Human
Behavior

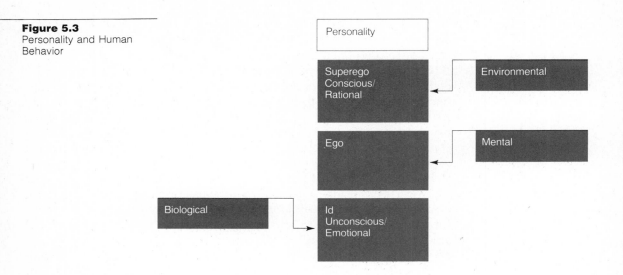

1. *The preconscious:* items in the mind that can be recognized only through Freud's association method.
2. *The conscious:* thoughts, feelings, and desires that we can learn about ourselves through introspection.
3. *The unconscious:* ideas and wishes that cannot be learned through introspection but can be determined from dreams, hypnotism, and Freudian therapeutic techniques.

Freud taught that we act in response to conscious and unconscious motives. The conscious is guided by a reasoned reality principle. The unconscious is guided by a hedonistic pleasure principle. Freud and most of the psychoanalytic school teach that the personality of the human being develops out of conflict. At first Freud taught that conflicts take place between the sex instinct and ego instincts (such as hunger and pain). Later he argued that the conflict that influences personality development is between the life instinct (a combination of sex and ego instincts) and the death or destruction instinct.

Various theorists have argued that the personality has levels. In the eighteenth century the Anglican bishop and philosopher Joseph Butler argued that the human being is guided by three levels in the self:

1. Instincts.
2. Regulating/controlling principles: benevolence, cool self-love.
3. Conscience: the ultimate controlling principle.

That is, the self at its "basest" level relies on instincts; as it develops, it begins to regulate the instincts, and conscience then regulates the "regulators."

Freud's analysis of personality is similar. At the base is the *id*—primitive, instinctual, governed by the pleasure principles, and greedy. Since the id is not rational, it is childish, never satisfied, demanding, destructive of others and self, often greedy and brutal. Adults generally act in response to the id only infrequently. When they do, they tend to place the id in the third person or explain the act away: "I was not myself" or "It made me angry." Note that in Figures 5.1 and 5.3 the id is linked to the biological.

As a person learns to separate unreality from reality in childhood, the *ego* develops. According to Freud, this is the self-oriented "executive of the mind"—rational and logical, but providing for the id's needs, given the circumstances. In essence, the ego is a mediator between the realities of the world and the id's demands. It also regulates mental and motor functioning, integrates inner motives and conflicting needs, protects the person with defense mechanisms, and masters the person's goals. The ego develops by creating an effective perceptual system that enables the person to adjust to the *reality principle:* awareness of things, tolerance of tension, expectation of punishment, and the associated inhibition of action. Although the ego contains no energy, Freud contended that it could control behavior by means of the approach-avoidance conflict, turning the energy of the id against itself. Note the connection between mental activity and the ego in the two figures.

As a child develops and absorbs parental and cultural attitudes and values, he or she develops a *superego*. Freud described this as consisting of the conscience and the ego ideal. The superego tells the individual what behavior is acceptable. It may be quite strict; it may even be committed to the destruction or close control of the id. It operates in terms of what it has been taught is right or correct, not just out of fear of punishment. People who violate their superego's prohibitions may punish themselves (feel guilty).

Freud said that the ego's role is to mediate between the id and the superego. A personality becomes sick when either the id or the superego becomes dominant, a condition that results in a personality disorder. When too much energy is expended by the ego in mediating between the id and the superego, a person's work or personal development will suffer.

The id, ego, and superego are in more or less constant conflict in Freud's view. When the ego feels pressure it adjusts by means of a series of defense mechanisms, thus protecting the conscious from the unconscious. Four common defense mechanisms are

1. *Repression* One of the less useful defense mechanisms, repression forces the concern from the conscious mind or forces deliberate forgetfulness. Since problems cannot be solved this way, repression simply postpones them and does not aid personality development. Sometimes a person employs perceptual defenses in the same way.

2. *Rationalization* Instead of facing up to the problem in question, the ego may redefine the situation and thus prevent it from reaching the conscious mind. Essentially the ego finds excuses or explains away the problem. Thus this mechanism is not conducive to problem solution or personality development either.

3. *Reaction formation* If a person recognizes that the existence of a certain problem is uncomfortable, the ego may repress it and substitute its opposite. For example, if a person dislikes Germans but is upset by this feeling, he or she may claim to like Germans.

4. *Projection and introjection* The ego is using projection when a person denies that he or she has a particular emotion or acts in a particular way and "blames" it on something (or someone) else. This normally takes place when admitting the feeling or action would cause the person serious anxiety. Projection is a safety valve, but it does not help the person adjust to personality development. In the opposite function, introjection, the person "takes in" something from the outside, makes it his or her own (*my* country, *my* teacher), and sees it as part of himself or herself. Sociologists call this process *internalization* (especially of values), and it is an important part of the socialization process—growing up.

Freud contended that the person can be understood by understanding how energy affects personality and behavior. Energy is contained in the *libido* (drive), the life-maintaining, pleasure-seeking energy that becomes attached to or withdrawn from various goals or objects. According to Freud, the human personality could be understood by examining the amount of libido attached to or withdrawn from specific objects and activities (likes and dislikes). Tension occurs when the libido is not immediately satisfied. It can arise from the environment or be innate (an impetus). The person seeks the objects necessary to remove tension and restore himself or herself to equilibrium. In a hungry infant, the tension resulting from the need for food requires immediate attention if equilibrium is to be restored. As the personality develops, the reality principle comes into play: the person learns that postponement of immediate gratification may lead to greater gratification later on.

A manager can use knowledge of personality to understand and influence employees' behavior. Understanding personality is particularly helpful in the leadership phase of the managerial process. Chapter 14 will present this practical application in more detail.

Mental Constructs of Human Behavior

Some theorists see the human being as very rational, a sort of walking electronic calculator. Others view the human being as primarily emotional and intuitive. Although we have included reason and emotion under the mental constructs, this interpretation is simplified. Both interact with the biological basis of behavior. The ability to reason can be affected by such biological problems as brain trauma or mental retardation, and emotional behavior is clearly related to hormonal activity as well as mental perceptions.

The Human: A Rational and Emotional Mix

In this book we assume that people are both rational and emotional. Centuries before Christ, Aristotle described the human being in that way. More recently Hegel, a very conservative philosopher, and Marx, a radical thinker, elaborated on and supported the view that we are a balance of reason and emotion. As we have seen, Freud described human behavior as deriving from conscious motives (rational) and unconscious motives (emotional).

Feelings are the subjective awareness of our own emotional state.

They are signals which direct us toward goodness, safety, pleasure, and group survival. Feelings are guides in our decision making. They influence our perception of the world in which we live. In a recent book, Willard Gaylin has shown how feelings influence human behavior.[5] Table 5.1 is a table I created to present a synopsis of Gaylin's discussion of twelve crucial feelings. It lists the sources of the feelings and their uses to the individual and describes how people deal with these feelings. It also describes how I think feelings affect the managerial process.

As Table 5.1 indicates, motivation at work is influenced by feeling anxious, feeling guilty, feeling ashamed, and feeling proud. Group behavior is affected by feeling anxious, feeling touched and hurt, or feeling moved. Motivation for planning may come from feeling upset. In human resource management it is important to know if employees are feeling tired, bored, or used.

In sum, our response to the world is affected by our feelings. We are less rational than most of us dare to recognize, and we can use our feelings best by assuming a middle position between total suppression (holding everything in) and total expression ("letting it all hang out"). It is not enough to be aware of the objective factors shaping ourselves and our employees. As effective managers, we must also consider the significant impact of human emotions.

Aptitudes and Abilities

Individuals do not all possess exactly the same abilities and aptitudes.

Abilities are skills people possess.

Aptitudes are potential skills which have not been developed yet.

Aptitudes and abilities appear on both the biological side and the mental side of our model (see Figures 5.1 and 5.3).

Table 5.1
Feelings and Their Relevance to Management

I. Feelings That Direct Us to Survival and Obligations of Group Living

Feeling	Sources of the Feeling	How People Manage the Feeling	Value of the Feeling	Relevance to Management
Anxious (Anticipation of future unpleasant events.)	1. Change in sense of self. 2. Separation anxiety (constant reassurance of approval needed). 3. Awareness of inevitable vulnerability (death).	1. Rationalization; control. 2. Displacement; blaming others; phobias. 3. Delusions. 4. Somatization (conversion to physical symptoms). 5. Spending money. 6. Sexual activity. 7. Oral gratification (eating).	Alerts; buoys; motivates; gives direction to action.	Motivation; creation of climate for planning.
Guilty (Behavior a failure in judgment of ego.)	1. Genetic regulation of fear (to avoid punishment). 2. Learned precepts of right and wrong. 3. Self-disappointment.	1. Avoiding undesirable acts of commission and omission. 2. Experiencing guilt after failure or evil acts.	Shapes personal goodness and generosity (guardian of goodness).	Motivation of employees; control/ discipline experiences.
Ashamed (Consequence of or anticipation of public chastisement for evil acts.)	1. Fear of public exposure for wrongdoing. 2. Exposure violating innate and learned need for privacy.	1. Powerful feeling of identity with the community.	Facilitates socially acceptable acts.	Motivation, especially for group action; regulation; and control/ discipline problems.
Proud (Sense of self-respect, self-esteem, and self-confidence; pleasurable sense of mastery.)	1. Self-acceptance and self-value. 2. Activities and achievements. 3. Public acknowledgment of value. 4. Innate sense of worth, accentuated by parental encouragement.		Encourages maturity—the willingness to give up comfortable dependence and seek rewards.	Intrinsic motivation.

II. Feelings That Are Caution Signals

Feeling	Sources of the Feeling	How People Manage the Feeling	Value of the Feeling	Relevance to Management
Upset (An awareness of change in the psychological threshold; psychological equivalent of physiological irritability—overreaction to physical stimulus.)	1. Fear; apprehension. 2. Unexpected guilt. 3. Anger. 4. Hurt feelings.		Warns self of unpreparedness; warns others to tread lightly.	Creation of climate for planning; regulation of group behavior.
Tired (Emotional exhaustion, total weariness and depletion.)	1. Depression; hopelessness; helplessness; absence of feeling. 2. Loss of confidence in the future.	1. Caring for self. 2. Seeking caring from others. 3. Indulging self. 4. Modifying conditions.	Warns that life-style is not healthy—psychic resources are being spent faster than they are being earned.	Indication of need for change in job and life-style; understanding of implications necessary for human resource management.

Continued from previous page (Sources of the Feeling):

3. Bankruptcy of self-esteem and self-confidence in control of future.
4. Loss of respect for self as supplier of pleasure in life.

Feeling	Sources of the Feeling	How People Manage the Feeling	Value of Feeling	Relevance to Management
Bored (Response to perception of life as meaningless, empty.)	1. Lack of confidence in self as source of pleasure. 2. Anxiety.	1. Liberation from self. 2. Oral gratification (eating). 3. Fantasy. 4. Changing alternatives. 5. Increasing pleasure.	Warns of and so creates awareness of need.	Human resource management; indication of need to change job design or job.

Envious (Bitter resentment toward a person who is superior in some characteristic.)	1. Oedipal complex.
	2. Sibling rivalry.
	3. Following pattern of reactions:
	  a. Feeling of deprivation.
	  b. Desired characteristic in another person.
	  c. Impotence in face of this disparity.
	  d. Competition/paranoia relative to the other person.
		1. Becoming aware of personal strengths.
		2. Identification with person who is object of envy.
		3. Loving person who is object of envy.
				Dysfunctional effect on group activities and cooperative efforts; factor in Machiavellian competition; indication of the problems inherent in certain leadership styles.

Used (Sense of being viewed as less than a person—significant only in services and products offered.)	1. Treatment as a means, not an end. 2. Being "put down."		Warns that personal worth is threatened.	Indication of overuse of behavior modification and overly mechanistic reward system.

III. Feelings as Signals of Success

Feeling	Sources of the Feeling	How People Manage the Feeling	Value of Feeling	Relevance to Management
Touched and hurt (Positive impact of human contact; feeling of closeness.)	1. Survival needs of childhood.		Guides toward affection and joyous aspect of involvement; helps enrich life.	Motivation for group and interpersonal interactions.
Moved (Deep, intense emotion arising from significant experience with people, the arts, nature, etc.)	1. Excitement of discovery (derivative of childhood).		Evokes existential joy.	Motivation for group and interpersonal interactions.
Good (Lightness, buoyancy, aliveness, enthusiasm, optimism, peace, hope, involvement, mastery, self-confidence.)	1. Sensate pleasure. 2. Discovery. 3. Expansion, mastery, growth. 4. Creativity. 5. Immersion. 6. Fusion with people in group. 7. Transcendental experience.		Encourages life behavior.	Motivation to enjoy work and life.

Source: Adapted from Willard Gaylin, *Feelings* (New York: Harper & Row, 1979). Copyright © by Willard Gaylin. By permission of Harper & Row, Publishers, Inc.

You have probably noticed that some tasks are easier for you than for others. Perhaps math comes easily to you and languages come more easily to a friend. Some people seem to grasp mechanical concepts readily. Others never quite understand them. Psychologists refer to this diversity in abilities and aptitudes as individual differences. Just as we differ in appearance, we also differ in relative amounts of abilities and aptitudes.

Psychologists have spent many years studying similarities and differences in such abilities as

- *Mechanical ability*—perception and manipulation of spatial relations; ability to visualize how parts fit together into a whole; comprehension of mechanical relationships.
- *Motor coordination ability*—the ability to move the body effectively to perform physical acts.
- *Mental abilities*—general intelligence; logic or reasoning; verbal ability; numerical ability.
- *Creative abilities*—musical and artistic abilities; psychophysical abilities; esthetic judgment.

Are abilities and aptitudes innate or learned? Where do they come from? On one side are some ethologists, biologists, and psychologists who argue that aptitudes are transmitted through the genes—that we inherit our abilities from our ancestors. How better to explain the Bach family's musical abilities? At the other extreme are many sociologists, psychologists, and anthropologists who argue that abilities are learned. Recently these views have tended to converge. According to psychologist Lyman Porter and his associates,

Traditionally psychologists have classified behaviors [abilities] into those that are innate and those that can be altered and learned. This way of thinking seems to be outmoded. . . . Thus it now seems reasonable to think of human response capacities in terms of a continuum. At one end of the continuum are those responses that are relatively uninfluenceable as a result of training and experience (for example, response time and finger dexterity). And at the other end are those that are relatively open to change and not significantly constrained by genetic or physical equal factors (such as interpersonal skills).[6]

Do some groups of people have more or fewer of certain abilities? Various studies allege to have found such differences. But as Norman Maier has observed,

Whether or not the distributions of ability between sexes and races differ and whether or not differences reported are due to biological, cultural or educational factors are questions that cannot be answered at this time. For practical purposes, the answers would prove of little value. . . . Race and sex offer no meaningful clues for selection since individual differences are the important variables.[7]

Dealing Effectively with Differences in Ability

As managers, we seek high performance from our employees and enterprises. The following formula states the ingredients in high performance:

$$\text{Human performance} = \text{Ability} \times \text{Motivation} \times \text{Role clarity.}$$

Most management experts have found that managers overemphasize the ability side of the equation. That is, they too easily attribute failure to lack of ability. But failure is often a result of lack of motivation. A person who is strongly motivated but deficient in ability will often make up for this deficiency by working very hard (see Chapter 6).

Selection and *training* are the two ways managers can best utilize human aptitudes and abilities in matching employees with jobs. In most cases an aptitude can be developed into an ability through training and experience. In some cases it makes more sense to select people who already have the necessary abilities. Not all people have all the abilities required for a particular job. Nor does a manager always have the time or money to train a person without the needed ability.

Perception

Figures 5.1 and 5.3 show perception as a mental process.

Perception is the chief mechanism by which human beings come to know the world outside themselves.

Perception "translates" the stimuli received by the senses into impressions of the world. The model for this process appears in Figure 5.4.
The manager's world is full of tasks which require interaction and communication with others. To survive, the manager must do these tasks well. Yet people see the same things and the same people differently, and they behave according to what they believe they see, not the "objective reality," as the cartoon on page 142 illustrates. To be efficient, a manager must understand how people perceive events, objects, and other people.

Briefly, let us summarize some relevant facts about perception.

Figure 5.4
Perception Model

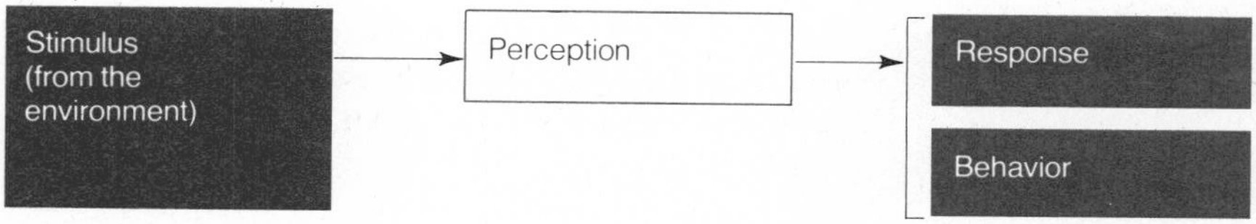

We organize our perceptions. Perceptions result from "filling in" of stimuli to give us closure. We do not initially perceive a "car". We see its color, shape, and size, and these "add up" to the perception "car" through closure. Some perceptual differences result from different closures by different people.

We try to give stability and constancy to our perceptions by finding patterns. It is easier for a person to operate if his or her perceptions do not change too often. This need leads us to see the world with stable perceptions even if doing so results in some distortion. When it is clear to the person that the world has changed, the perception is adjusted.

We respond to perceptual stimuli selectively. It is impossible to respond to all the cues we receive from the environment. We focus on selective stimuli and respond to those that are familiar to us, appeal to our internal feelings and attitudes, and fit the situation of the moment. The way we respond selectively is influenced by:

- *Grouping and context* The perceiver will group objects by similarity or closeness. Contrasting light and dark shades (figure and ground) establish a context that influences what is perceived. Perceptual differences arise from attention to different parts of objects or from different ways of grouping them.

- *The source of the information* The perceiver will weigh perceptual evidence coming from respected (or favored) sources more heavily than that coming from other sources.

- *Emotional factors* In making abstract or intellectual judgments, the perceiver may be influenced by emotional factors, perceiving what he or she likes as correct. The perceiver may not even realize all the factors influencing him or her at the time.

- *Irrelevant cues* When required to form difficult perceptual judgments, the perceiver may respond to irrelevant cues to arrive at a judgment. For example, it has been shown that the trait of smiling or not smiling is often used as a cue to judge a person's honesty.

We respond differently to people than we do to objects. People affect the observer's perceptions, while objects do not. A car does not change as it is being observed and perceived; a person can and often does. Our perceptions of other people are influenced in a number of ways: (1) We tend to perceive others as similar to us, projecting our own characteristics onto them. (2) We almost always base our perceptions of other people on first impressions, usually without adequate information. (3) Our perceptions of people tend to be consistent—we try to evaluate them as good or bad, warm or cold, and so on, and then stick to our initial evaluation. (4) These perceptions (warm-cold, good-bad, etc.) are based on past experiences with the type of person perceived. (5) The most recent perception is the strongest impression of a person (other than the first impression). (6) Our perceptions may be influenced by peer group attitudes. (7) The roles we play influence how we perceive others. (8) The influence of the culture we belong to may cause us to base our perceptions on prejudices against whole groups of people of different race, religion, age, or sex.

Differences in Perception: A Challenge to Management

Understanding perceptual differences can enhance your effectiveness as a manager. Indeed, there is hardly a single managerial function which is not influenced by perception. Consider these few examples:

With regard to dealing with the environment, the manager sees a union as restricting the freedom to shift employees and thus increasing costs and cutting job creation. The employee may see the union as a source of job security and better working conditions. The manager who wishes to prevent a union from forming must change the perception of the employee or provide for the employee's security and monetary needs without a union.

In planning, two managers must respond to a report delivered about future problems. One manager knows and trusts the individual who gives the report. The other has never met her and forms a poor impression. Which manager is likely to let his or her plans be influenced by the report?

In leadership, a manager must try to get an employee to change to a new way of doing business: using a computer. The employee perceives the computer as a threat to his job. The manager must change this employee's perception of the computer in order to change the employee's unproductive behavior (criticizing the computer, saying it cannot do the job, for instance).

In controlling, the firm puts in a new control and budgeting system to project costs and budget accordingly. Some employees may perceive the system as a check to see if they are cheating.

In human resources management, the manager may see female and minority employees as capable of doing skilled mental work. The white male employees may stereotype them as incapable. Before the manager can implement equal employment opportunity programs effectively, this stereotype must be changed.

Attitudes

Another mental construct is shown in Figures 5.1 and 5.3

Attitudes are learned predispositions to objects. They are beliefs about the object and an evaluation of the usefulness of the object.

Attitudes exist because they serve these purposes:

- *Economy* Attitudes give order to people's mental processes and thus help them make sense of the many stimuli that are constantly bombarding them.
- *Self-realization* Attitudes help people deal with their psychological problems and inner conflicts.
- *Ego defense* Attitudes contribute to a person's identity.

Attitudes do influence perceptions and they can influence behavior. There has been much research on this. Some feel the results are contradictory. But in a recent thoughtful analysis of 109 studies of the relationship between attitudes and behavior, Icek Ajzen and Martin Fishbein found that where properly measured, strongly held attitudes can be used to predict behavior.[8]

Let's examine two attitudes and assess how they might affect behavior: work attitudes and managerial attitudes toward employees.

Work Attitudes

Historically, two opposing attitudes toward work have been held by employees:

1. *Work is a means to an end.* It is usually unpleasant, but we must work to reach the ends we desire and to pay our living costs.
2. *Work is an end in itself and is very satisfying.* A person gains self-fulfillment through work.

The first view has been the predominant one throughout history. In early societies work was regarded as degrading, fit only for the masses, whose lot it was. Workers were slaves or low-caste, ignorant, irresponsible, or unprincipled people. The Judeo-Christian view that work was a consequence and a means of expiating ancient sins is typical of these early attitudes. Later Christianity argued that work was a means of earning one's way in life, but it also was desirable to work to gain wealth in order to serve less fortunate individuals through charity.

Attitudes toward work and a job are developed from the total culture, from an individual's experiences, and from attitudes he or she sees in friends and family. Generally, the findings of social science indicate that Americans regard work as one of the most important parts of life. No major groups of able-bodied males (or, increasingly, females) between the ages of twenty-five and sixty-five are without work. Moreover, unemployment for any length of time is regarded as disastrous, even by the unskilled manual workers whose work is least desirable.

Today's employees have varying work attitudes. Some employees identify with work; their attitude is that work is an end in itself. Others see work as a means to another end. Although work attitudes probably differ by age, sex, race, education, and experience, the attitude that work is a means to an end is probably more widespread among blue-collar workers than among white-collar workers. The attitude that work is an end in itself is found among many professional, technical, and managerial people and other white-collar workers. If you can determine the attitudes which are related to specific behaviors and if you find that they are strongly held, you can better predict employee behavior and make decisions. Knowledge of employee attitudes toward work is very useful to the manager. For example, enlarging jobs and delegating responsibility to employees is more likely to be successful if employees feel that work is satisfying in and of itself than if they believe work is merely a means to other ends. The latter attitude calls for closer supervision and control systems.

Attitudes toward Employees

A second set of attitudes which are important for managers to understand are attitudes toward employees. There are a number of ways to express these attitudes. Douglas McGregor's concept of "Theory X" and "Theory Y" attitudes is a well-known example.[9]

According to McGregor, Theory X people hold this set of attitudes toward employees:

- People are by nature indolent.
- They lack ambition, dislike responsibility, prefer to be led.
- They are self-centered, indifferent to organizational needs.
- They are by nature resistant to change.
- They are not very bright and lack creative potential.

According to Theory Y, on the other hand,

- People are ambitious.
- They seek responsibility.
- They recognize and accept organizational goals.
- They are dynamic and flexible.
- They are intelligent and possess creative potential.

Management attitudes toward employees can affect managerial behavior. The manager who holds Theory X attitudes is likely to adhere to the following principles:

- Management is responsible for organizing the elements of productive enterprise—money, materials, equipment, people—in the interest of the organization's economic ends.
- With respect to people, this is a process of directing their efforts, motivating them, controlling their actions, and modifying their behavior to fit the needs of the organization.
- Without this active intervention by management, employees would be passive—even resistant—to organizational needs.

Planning, organization, and control would be done in traditional ways as described later in the book by a Theory X manager.

If, on the other hand, the manager holds Theory Y attitudes, the manager's behavior could be quite different. Some examples of Theory Y attitudes and how they might affect managerial behavior include:

- Management is responsible for organizing the elements of productive enterprise—money, materials, equipment, people—in the interest of the organization's economic ends. But management need not do all the planning and other managerial functions.
- Employees are not by nature passive or resistant to organizational needs. They have become so as a result of experience in organizations.

- Motivation, potential for development, the capacity for assuming responsibility, and readiness to direct behavior toward organizational goals are all present in people. Management does not cause these traits to form.

Theory Y managers will perform planning and other managerial functions quite differently from Theory X managers.

Learning

What is learning and how does it affect the manager's job?

Learning is the process by which the individual acquires skills, knowledge, and abilities; it results in a relatively permanent change in behavior.

Learning was shown connecting the mental and physical spheres in Figure 5.1 because both mental and physical abilities can be improved by learning.

The human being begins to learn at birth (and perhaps before) and can continue to learn until death. Where and how we learn influences the kind of people we become. We learn first at home. Family and friends, the neighborhood in which we grow up, and local child-rearing practices lead us to have certain expectations about working conditions. They also affect our preferences regarding leadership style, organization practices, and other aspects of management. Later we learn at school, in church or synagogue, and through work or quasi-work experiences.

North American society is learning oriented. Its values are strongly tied to the learning ability of its citizens. You have probably been exposed to economics and the "economic person." This model portrays a creature forever thirsting for more goods and services—a thirst that is never satiated. Human potential theorists have a parallel model: "the learning person"—an individual ever thirsting for more learning and thus greater self-development. Many psychologists believe human beings use only 5 to 10 percent of their capacity. As Herbert Otto puts it, "the ultimate creative capacity of the human brain may be, for all practical purposes, infinite."[10]

The section on aptitudes and abilities should have made you aware that certain skills and abilities are harder for some of us to acquire than others. In general, individuals have different learning capacities, learn at different rates, and learn in different ways at various stages in life. So although the learning potential of almost everyone may be very great, every kind of learning is not equally easy or desirable for each of us.

We are not equally motivated to learn all things at all times. A manager trying to develop abilities of a particular type in a group of employees will discover that some will learn more quickly than others because of differences in aptitudes and motivation.

What conditions are conducive to adult learning? The answer to this question depends partially on what and how much "learning theory" you accept. Pavlov introduced the concept of *classical conditioning*. In his experiments on the salivation of dogs, he discovered that a neutral stimulus (one that does not produce a response) when consistently paired with a nonneutral stimulus that does produce a response, eventually produces the response evoked by the nonneutral stimulus. More sophisticated theories have stressed the significance of operant conditioning. In operant conditioning aspects of an individual's behavior that are directed toward a stated goal are rewarded, while other aspects are ignored. Through repeating this pattern of rewards again and again, the individual is guided to the goal.

Leslie This and Gordon Lippitt have used relevant material from learning theorists and other training specialists in compiling the following list of ways to improve learning at work:

- The fact that all human beings can learn must be accepted. Most normal human beings can choose whether they will learn at any time in their lives; people can and do learn.

- The individual must be motivated to learn. This motivation involves two factors: awareness of the need to learn based on the individual's own inadequacy in this regard and a clear understanding of what needs to be learned.

- Learning is an active process. The individual learns better when more of the senses are utilized in the effort and involvement in the learning process increases.

- Normally, the learner must have guidance. Learning is more efficient if it is not by trial and error. Guidance can speed the learning process and provide feedback as well as reinforce appropriate learning and prevent inadequate behavior patterns from developing.

- Appropriate materials for sequential learning (cases, problems, discussion outlines, reading lists) must be provided. The trainer is an aid in an efficient learning process.

- Time must be provided to practice learning. Learning requires time to assimilate what has been learned, to accept it, to internalize it, and to build confidence in what has been learned.

- Learning methods should be as varied as possible. It is boredom that destroys learning, not fatigue. Any method—whether old-fashioned lecture or programmed learning or the jazziest computer business game—will begin to bore some learners.

    The learner must secure satisfaction from the learning and must see that the material is useful in terms of personal needs.

- The learner must get reinforcement of correct behavior. As behavioral psychologists have shown, learners learn best with fairly immediate reinforcement of appropriate behavior. The learner must be rewarded for new behavior in various ways—pay, recognition, promotion.

- Standards of performance should be set for the learner. Benchmarks for learning will provide goals and give a feeling of accomplishment when reached.

- Different levels of learning are appropriate at different times and require different methods.[11]

How Learning Relates to Management

Managers, especially at the supervisory and middle managerial levels, teach. As a manager you must select people who may require training for new jobs. You must choose people for promotion to jobs that may require a significant amount of learning. And you will have an influence in determining rewards such as pay and promotion, which can serve to reinforce learning. In addition, you will have to decide whether to accept or reject job opportunities that require you to engage in additional learning. Willingness to learn is greater in certain life phases, and so is the ability to serve as a mentor.

A manager must understand, too, that there are individual differences in ability to learn and that when and where something is learned and how it is rewarded affect whether and what a person learns. Indeed, managers have many opportunities to apply learning principles in the course of their work.

The Uniqueness of Each Person

Each individual is unique. The way a human being thinks and acts is determined by his or her unique personality, abilities, attitudes, and motives—all of which can change and develop. Because individuals are unique, understanding human behavior is not easy. Many people are quite complex. Yet successful managers must try to understand each person they work with, looking at that person as an individual with unique abilities, perceptions, learning potential, and personality. Successful managers try to plan, communicate, and control in the light of these characteristics. They learn to manage differently in response to differences in employees, superiors, and peers. This is part of what is termed the contingency approach to management.

Summary

Human nature is influenced by the environment, biology, personality, and mental processes. Each of these areas is examined, and the managerial implications of its effects are given.

Environmental conditions which affect each individual include rearing, wider cultural influences, and personal experiences. Managers need to be aware of these influences and the fact that humans are social beings, constantly interacting with each other.

Human behavior is influenced by our bodies and biology. Differences in physical make-up and the way the nervous system functions have an impact on a person's abilities to perform a task.

Another dimension of the human is personality. *Personality* is a pattern of stable states and characteristics of a person that influence his or her behavior toward goal achievement. Each person has unique ways of protecting these states. Sigmund Freud taught that we act in response to conscious and unconscious motives. In Freud's terms the mind is composed of the id, the ego, and the superego. The *id* is the primitive instinctual base of the personality. It is childish, never satisfied, demanding, greedy, and destructive of others. The *ego* is the self-oriented, rational, and logical "executive of the mind" that provides for the id's needs. The *superego*, which develops as the child absorbs parental and cultural attitudes and values, tells a person what behavior is acceptable. These three are in more or less constant conflict and various defense mechanisms help the ego adjust and protect the conscious against the unconscious. Knowledge about personality constructs can be used to help understand and influence employees' behavior.

The human being is a mixture of the emotional and the rational. Both interact with the biological bases of behavior. The ability to reason can be affected by such things as brain trauma; hormonal activity influences emotional behavior.

Abilities and aptitudes also differ for each individual. *Abilities* are skills people possess. Aptitudes are potential skills which have not been developed yet. Examples include mechanical ability, motor coordination ability, mental abilities, and creative abilities. Abilities appear on both the biological side and the mental side of the model. So they are to some extent inherited (innate). But most can be developed or learned. Effective managers use *selection* (choosing people with the abilities needed and matching them to the job) and *training* (developing aptitudes into abilities needed for the job) to match individual differences in ability with the needs of a job.

Perception is the chief mechanism by which human beings come to know the world outside themselves. It translates the stimuli received by the senses with impressions of the world. We behave according to what we believe we see, not the "objective reality." We organize our perceptions; we try to give stability and constancy to our perceptions by finding patterns; and we respond differently to people than to objects. There is hardly a single managerial function which is not influenced by perception.

Understanding differences in how people perceive events, objects, and other people will enhance your effectiveness as a manager.

Attitudes influence our perceptions and can influence our behaviors. They are learned predispositions to objects. Attitudes are beliefs about the object and an evaluation of the usefulness of the object. Attitudes give order to a person's constructs and help make sense of the many stimuli that are constantly bombarding the individual. They help a person deal with his or her psychological problems and inner conflicts. Attitudes contribute to a person's identity. If strongly held attitudes closely correspond to behavior and have been properly measured or assessed, attitudes can predict behavior.

Work attitudes and managerial attitudes toward employees are both important in management. The two opposing work attitudes held by individuals are: (1) work is a means to an end, and (2) work is an end in itself and is very satisfying.

Two opposing managerial attitudes toward employees illustrated are Douglas McGregor's Theory X and Theory Y. Theory X managers see people as lazy, lacking in ambition, unwilling to assume responsiblity, and resistant to change. Theory Y managers have a more positive view; they believe people are industrious, ambitious, ready to assume responsibility, and willing to accept change. Understanding attitudes is important in management. If you can learn the attitude which is related to a behavior and determine that it is strongly held, you can better predict behavior and make decisions.

Learning is the process by which the individual acquires skills, knowledge, and ability; it results in a relatively permanent change in behavior. Learning links the mental and physical spheres of our model. Individuals have different learning capacities, learn at different rates, and learn in different ways at various stages in life. Knowledge about learning is particularly important to managers because they must select people for new jobs that may require training. Managers, especially at the middle and supervisory levels, teach. And you as a manager must accept or reject job opportunities that require additional learning.

Chapter 5 has introduced you to the environmental, biological, mental, and personality influences that individuate each person. Chapter 6 will deal with motivation, the other part of the managerial success formula.

Questions

1. Explain the various past and present environmental influences which help make you the unique person you are.
2. Describe how the nervous system operates. Specify which areas of the brain direct which functions. For example, memory.
3. Define personality. How did Freud structure personality?

4. Describe the defense mechanisms used to protect the conscious from the unconscious.
5. Is being emotional necessarily counterproductive to a career as a manager?
6. What are the important managerial applications of your knowledge of ability and aptitude?
7. What is perception? How are perceptions organized? Give some personal examples of how your own perceptions would affect you as a middle manager.
8. What are the two basic attitudes regarding work? How would you handle an employee who seemed to work just to get a paycheck?
9. Differentiate between Theory X and Theory Y managerial attitudes toward employees. What kind of manager will you be?
10. How does learning relate to your career as a manager? To your own advancement on the job?

Notes

[1]Kurt Lewin, *A Dynamic Theory of Personality: Selected Papers by Kurt Lewin* (New York: McGraw-Hill, 1935).

[2]Carl Jung, *Psychological Types* (New York: Harcourt, Brace and World, 1923); and *Man and His Symbols* (New York: Doubleday, 1964).

[3]Carl Rogers, *On Becoming a Person* (Boston: Houghton Mifflin, 1961); Gordon Allport, *Personality and Social Encounter* (Boston: Beacon Press, 1964); Rollo May, *Psychology and the Human Dilemma* (Princeton, N.J.: Van Nostrand, 1967); and Abraham Maslow, *Motivation and Personality* (New York: Harper & Bros., 1954).

[4]Sigmund Freud, *The Standard Edition of the Complete Psychological Works of Sigmund Freud,* ed. James Strachey, 24 vols. (London: Hogarth Press, 1953).

[5]Willard Gaylin, *Feelings* (New York: Harper & Row, 1979).

[6]Lyman Porter et al., *Behavior in Organizations* (New York: McGraw-Hill, 1975), p. 61.

[7]Norman Maier, *Psychology in Industrial Organizations* (Boston: Houghton Mifflin, 1973), pp. 159–160.

[8]Icek Ajzen and Martin Fishbein, "Attitude-Behavior Relations: A Theoretical Analysis and Review of Empirical Research," *Psychological Bulletin* 84 (1977): 888–918.

[9]Douglas McGregor, *The Human Side of Enterprise* (New York: McGraw-Hill, 1960).

[10]Herbert Otto, "New Light on Human Potential," *Saturday Review,* December 20, 1969, pp. 14–17.

[11]Leslie This and Gordon Lippitt, "Learning Theories and Training," *Training and Development Journal* 20 (April 1966): 2–11; (May 1966): 1–10. Reproduced by special permission from the April and May 1966 *Training and Development Journal.* Copyright 1966 by The American Society for Training and Development, Inc.

References

Environmental Influences on Human Behavior

L. L. Cummings, "Toward Organizational Behavior," *Academy of Management Review*, January 1978, pp. 90–98. Kurt Kourosh Motamedi, "Toward Explicating Philosophical Orientations in Organizational Behavior (OB)," *Academy of Management Review,* April 1978, pp. 354–360.

Biological Basis of Human Behavior

This section was researched and coauthored by Jean Marie Hanebury. Harold Saxton Burr, *The Neural Basis of Human Behavior* (Springfield,Ill.: Charles C Thomas, 1960). Gene Bylinsky, "A Preview of the 'Choose Your Mood' Society," *Fortune,* March 1977, 220–224, 226 ff. Alan Cornwell, *Biology, Man, and Society* (London: McGraw-Hill, 1974). Basil E. Eleftherious and Richard L. Sprott, eds., *Hormonal Correlates of Behavior* (New York: Plenum Press, 1975). C. R. Evans and A. D. J. Robertson, eds., *Brain Physiology and Psychology* (Berkeley: University of California Press, 1966). "A Genetic Defense of the Free Market," *Business Week,* April 10, 1978, pp. 100–104. Philip M. Groves and George V. Rebec, "Biochemistry and Behavior: Some Central Actions of Amphetamine and Antipsychotic Drugs," *Annual Review of Psychology* 27 (1976): 91–127. Julian Jaynes, *The Origin of Consciousness in the Breakdown of the Bicameral Mind* (Boston: Houghton Mifflin, 1976). Asterios G. Kefalas and Waino W. Soujanen, "Organizational Behavior and the New Biology," *Academy of Management Journal* 17 (September 1974): 514–527. Vincent Mallardi, *Biorhythms and Your Behavior* (Philadelphia: Media America, 1975). Allan Mazur and Leon S. Robertson, *Biology and Social Behavior* (New York: Free Press, 1972). "Memory Hormone?" *Time,* February 27, 1978, p. 57. Armand M. Nicholi, Jr., ed., *The Harvard Guide to Modern Psychiatry* (Cambridge, Mass.: Harvard University Press, Belknap Press, 1978). "The Pain Killers," *Time,* December 4, 1978, p. 96. Richard A. Schaffer, "Mastering the Mind," *Wall Street Journal,* August 12, 1977, p. 1. Brian Sullivan, "Remarkable Brain Experiments Reveal Much," *Athens Banner-Herald/Daily News,* September 24, 1978, p. 1C. "Why You Do What You Do—Sociobiology: A New Theory of Behavior," *Time,* August 1, 1977, pp. 54–58, 63. Edward Wilson, *On Human Nature* (Boston: Harvard University Press, 1978); and *Sociobiology: The New Synthesis* (Boston: Harvard University Press, 1975).

Personality and Human Identity

Gordon Allport, *Personality and Social Encounter* (Boston: Beacon Press, 1964). Raymond Cattell, "Personality Pinned Down," *Psychology Today,* July 1973, pp. 40–46. John Dollard and Neal E. Miller, *Personality and Psychotherapy: An Analysis in Terms of Learning, Thinking, and Culture* (New York: McGraw-Hill, 1950). Eric Erikson, *Childhood and Society,* rev. ed. (New York: W. W. Norton, 1963). Sigmund Freud, *The Standard Edition of the Complete Psychological Works of Sigmund Freud,* ed. James Strachey, 24 vols. (London: Hogarth Press, 1953). Martin L. Hoffman, "Personality and Social Development," *Annual Review of Psychology* 28 (1977): 295–321. Carl Jung, *Psychological Types* (New York: Harcourt, Brace and World, 1923); and *Man and His Symbols* (New York: Doubleday, 1964). George Kelly, *The Psychology of Personal Constructs,* 2 vols. (New York: W. W. Norton, 1955). Alastair MacIntyre, "Carl Jung," in *The Encyclopedia of Philosophy,* ed. Paul Edwards (New York: Macmillan, 1967). E. Jerry Phares and James T. Lamiell, "Personality," *Annual Review of Psychology* 28 (1977): 113–140. Otto Rank, *The Trauma of Birth* (London: Routledge & Kegan Paul, 1929). Carl Rogers, *On Becoming a Person* (Boston: Houghton Mifflin, 1961). Ross Stagner, *Psychology of Personality,* 4th ed. (New York: McGraw-Hill, 1974). Joseph Stein, *Effective Personality: A Humanistic Approach* (Belmont, Calif.: Brooks/Cole, 1972). Abraham Zaleznik and Manfred DeVries, *Power and the Corporate Mind* (Boston: Houghton Mifflin, 1975), chapter 10.

The Human: A Rational and Emotional Mix

Willard Gaylin, *Feelings* (New York: Harper & Row, 1979). W. Walter Menninger, "The Power of Emotions; the Role of Feelings," in *Man and Work in Society,* ed. E. L. Cass and F. G. Zimmer (New York: Van Nostrand Reinhold, 1975), chapter 6, pp. 194–204.

Aptitudes and Abilities

Anne Anastasi, *Differential Psychology* (New York: Macmillan, 1970); and *Common Fallacies about Heredity, Environment, and Human Behavior* (Iowa City: American College Testing Service, 1973). J. P. Das et al., "Simultaneous and Successive Synthesis," *Psychological Bulletin* 82 (1975): 83–103. Steven Goldberg, *The Inevitability of Patriarchy* (New York: Morrow, 1973). Alison Jolly, *The Evolution of Primate Behavior* (New York: Macmillan, 1972). Asterios Kefalas and Waino Suojanen, "Organizational Behavior and the New Biology," *Academy of Management Journal* 17 (September 1974): 514–527. James McConnell, *Understanding Human Behavior* (Hinsdale, Ill.: Dryden Press, 1977). Norman Maier, *Psychology in Industrial Organizations* (Boston: Houghton Mifflin, 1973). Ashley Montague, ed., *Man and Aggression*, 2d ed. (New York: Oxford University Press, 1973). Robert Ornstein, *The Psychology of Consciousness* (New York: Viking Press, 1973). Lyman Porter et al., *Behavior in Organizations* (New York: McGraw-Hill, 1975). Steven Rose, *The Conscious Brain* (New York: Knopf, 1973).

Perception

Albert H. Hastorf et al., *Person Perception,* ed. Charles Kiesler (Reading, Mass.: Addison-Wesley, 1970). Harold Leavitt, *Managerial Psychology,* 3d ed. (Chicago: University of Chicago Press, 1972). James McConnell, *Understanding Human Behavior* (Hinsdale, Ill.: Dryden Press, 1977), chapters 10 and 11. Paul F. Secord and Carl W. Backman, *Social Psychology,* 2d ed. (New York: McGraw-Hill, 1974). H. Tajfel, "Social and Cultural Factors in Perception," in *The Handbook of Social Psychology,* ed. Gardner Lindzey and Elliot Aronson, 2d ed., 5 vols. (Reading, Mass.: Addison-Wesley, 1969), 3: 315–394.

Attitudes

Icek Ajzen and Martin Fishbein, "Attitude-Behavior Relations: A Theoretical Analysis and Review of Empirical Research," *Psychological Bulletin* 84 (1977): 888–918. Elliot Aronson, "The Theory of Cognitive Dissonance: A Current Perspective," in *Advances in Experimental Social Psychology,* ed. Leonard Berkowitz, 4 vols. (New York: Academic Press, 1969), 4: 1–34. Roger Bennett, "Orientation to Work and Organizational Analysis: A Conceptual Analysis, Integration and Suggested Application," *Journal of Management Studies,* May 1978, pp. 187–210. Leon Festinger, *A Theory of Cognitive Dissonance* (Stanford, Calif.: Stanford University Press, 1957). Charles A. Kiesler, *The Psychology of Commitment* (New York: Academic Press, 1971). Douglas McGregor, *The Human Side of Enterprise* (New York: McGraw-Hill, 1960). William McGuire, "The Nature of Attitudes and Attitude Change," in *The Handbook of Social Psychology,* ed. Gardner Lindzey and Elliot Aronson, 2d ed., 5 vols. (Reading, Mass.: Addison-Wesley, 1969), 3: 136–314. Gerald R. Salancik and Jeffrey Pfeffer, "A Social Information Processing Approach to Job Attitudes and Task Design," *Administrative Science Quarterly* 23 (June 1978): 224–253. William Scott, "Attitude Measurement," in *The Handbook of Social Psychology,* ed. Gardner Lindzey and Elliot Aronson, 2d ed., 5 vols. (Reading, Mass.: Addison-Wesley, 1969), 3: 136–314. Richard E. Nisbett and Stuart Valins, *Perceiving the Causes of One's Behavior* (New York: General Learning Press, 1971).

Learning

Edward Fiske, "Study Ties Child Learning to the History of Science," *New York Times,* June 15, 1975. Asterios Kefalas and Waino Suojanen, "Organizational Behavior and the

New Biology," *Academy of Management Journal* 17 (September 1974): 514–527. Herbert Otto, "New Light on Human Potential," *Saturday Review,* December 20, 1969, pp. 14–17. J. L. Phillips, *The Origins of Intellect: Piaget's Theory* (San Francisco: Freeman, 1969). Lloyd R. Peterson, "Verbal Learning and Memory," *Annual Review of Psychology* 28 (1977): 393–415. Leslie This and Gordon Lippitt, "Learning Theories and Training," *Training and Development Journal* 20 (April 1966): 2–11; (May 1966): 1–10.

Case for Chapter 5

Eastern Canadian Oil Company, Ltd.

Eastern Canadian Oil Company is a medium-size independent oil dealer with headquarters in Toronto, Ontario. An interesting incident took place in the Quebec province. The best dealer/salesman in this region is Jacques Flambeau. His sales increase each month has been phenomenal, especially in view of the tough competition recently. But a memo (Exhibit 1) from Toronto was received by Armand Leclercq, Jacques's sales manager. Before passing this report on to Jacques, Armand penciled in (in French): "Jacques, please don't let me down. Comply."

Two weeks later Leclercq got a phone call from Vaughn, Assistant to the Vice President of Marketing. Jacques had sent in the first week's report on time but had missed the second week. Leclercq called Flambeau and asked him to come to his office at 9 the next morning.

Armand recalled that Jacques has told him many times that if he had to waste time on reports, he lost sales, and a good salesperson gets results—that reports were just bureaucratic red tape. Jacques is 45 years old and has worked in sales for ECOC for 20 years, and his customers are extremely loyal to him. Leclercq is 40, with 15 years experience with ECOC.

Exhibit 1

TO: Armand Leclercq
FROM: Owen Vaughn
SUBJECT: Jacques Flambeau's Reports

As you know, all salesmen are to mail to our office weekly their sales reports, call reports, and expense reports. You get copies of these.

As you no doubt noticed, Flambeau gets his expense accounts in on time, but his other reports are a month late. At least once each week, I've been sending him letters which he ignores!

You recognize that these reports are vital to our analysis, budgeting, sales projection, and purchasing—in fact, to our whole management information and control system. Please see that he complies at once or I will be forced to notify your superior, the regional manager.

Sincerely,

Owen Emerson Vaughn
Assistant to Vice President of Marketing

Problems

1. How do you explain the behavior of Leclercq and Vaughn?
2. Plan the meeting strategy for Leclercq for the next day. What would you do to affect the behavior?

Chapter 6   Motivation and the Manager

Learning Objectives

1. Understand how individual needs, the job, and the environment determine what motivates people to work.
2. Learn how to apply Maslow's hierarchy of needs, Alderfer's E-R-G theory, and consistency theory in managing employees' individual needs.
3. Relate Herzberg's motivators to job design as an incentive.
4. Know how to develop a behavior modification reinforcement schedule to reward an employee's work behavior.
5. Be able to explain how the interactive theories—manifest needs theory, equity theory, and expectancy theory—explain motivation as the result of a combination of factors, specifically, individual needs and the environment.

Introduction

Motivation explains why some people work hard and well and others perform poorly. Three critical factors affect motivation: individual needs, the nature of the job, and the work environment.

Individual needs are important motivators. In fact, for many top managers, they are the most significant motivating factors. Remember the description of J. Peter Grace in Chapter 2? He found great personal satisfaction in the hectic, long hours he put into his career. Amadeo Peter Giannini, whose profile appears on page 160, is another example of a top manager whose success resulted from his efforts to meet his individual needs. Contrast the life-style and work habits and attitudes of these two top managers with those of a person who feels no such job-related needs, an employee who does just enough to satisfy the supervisor and no more.

Job design and the work environment are also important in motivation. If job design is such that the employee sees no significance or value in his or her work and the work environment is unpleasant, the employee's motivation to perform well is adversely affected. The impact of the work group, rewards, and supervisory style are all important aspects of the work environment. In *Working,* Studs Terkel has quoted a steelworker's description of his job—a poorly designed job in a poor work environment:

You're on your feet all day, on concrete . . . oh you get tired. Your feet get tired. Your eyes get tired. . . . They work us twelve days in a row 7–3. . . . You're just a number out there. Just like a prison. . . . A lot of people don't know your name . . . you're just badge 44–065. Of course, there are accidents . . . you eat dust and dirt and take all the things that go with it. . . . The workplace is not inside a building. It's just under a roof. There's no protection against the wind or snow. The roof is so leaky they should provide you with umbrellas. . . . They're forcing you to work harder by making cutbacks. . . . Everyone looks forward to retirement. That's all they talk about is retirement. . . . What have I done in my forty years of work? . . . Here I am almost sixty years old and I don't have anything to show for it. . . . I think I've been a good worker. But they don't appreciate it. They don't care.[1]

Amadeo Peter Giannini

Why do businessmen work so hard? Their standard answer, that they are responsible for producing profits, is true—and also a crashing oversimplification. Two other motives: they like the game for its own sake, and they like helping people. Nobody's life personifies these two motives better than that of Amadeo Peter Giannini, the boy fruit peddler who built the biggest nongovernment bank in the world. He was both friendly and combative, a combination that revels in business activity.

As a young man, Giannini bought produce in rural California so shrewdly that he could retire at thirty-one, with a fortune of $300,000 and a comfortable $20,000 house in San Mateo. He quarreled with his fellow directors of a tiny North Beach bank serving the Italian community, and started a rival, the Bank of Italy, to serve the small customer. Its assets multiplied sixty times in ten years. Giannini pioneered in branch banking and consumer loans. In 1930 the Bank of Italy became the Bank of America. Giannini retired again, and was ill in Europe when he learned that the group he had put in control was dismembering his holding company, Transamerica Corp. He regained control after one of the most tumultuous proxy fights in U.S. corporate history. Toward the end of his life he noticed that he had almost a million dollars and quickly gave half of it away. "Hell, why should a man pile up a lot of goddamned money for somebody else to spend after he's gone?"

Source: "A Hall of Fame for Business Leadership," *Fortune*, January 1975, p. 68. Reprinted by permission.

This chapter will discuss the theories and research on how each of the motivating factors—individual needs, the nature of the job, and the work environment—affect a person's motivation and how a manager can sometimes influence the way an employee performs through these factors. All three are important, and all three interact.

What Is Motivation?

Motivation has meant many things over the years. In general, it refers to the process or factors (motives) that influence people to act. Psychologists view motivation as the process of (1) arousing behavior, (2) sustaining behavior in progress, and (3) channeling behavior into a specific course. Motives induce the self (or will) to act and so result in behavior.

Motivation is the inner state that energizes, channels, and sustains human behavior.

Though this definition sounds simple enough, it is anything but simple, as the following facts about motivation reveal:

The person changes over time, and the environment also changes, influencing his or her motives. Thus a person's motivation is not fixed over time. Consider how important one need (money) might be to a person at various points during a twenty-five year period.

- Age 21 Bachelor, good salary, low expenses, happy-go-lucky, "have-a-good-time" orientation.
- Age 23 Gets married, decides to buy home and furnish it.
- Age 26 Furnishes home, makes house payments; no money problems.
- Age 29 Wife has twins, both severely retarded, which must be cared for in an institution.
- Age 31 Wife has normal child.
- Age 32 Wife has normal child.
- Age 50 Normal children begin college while retarded children are still institutionalized.

During this period there were times when money was very short, others when it was plentiful. This person's reaction to money as an incentive varied with his need for it at the time, of course. And his other needs and desires could also change over time.

Motivation is rarely traceable to a single motive. Often motives involved are in conflict. This can lead to several outcomes. Different motives may bring about the same behavior or similar behaviors. In different cases the same need can result in different behaviors. For example, in the first instance, did you work to get a 4.0 average this term because you have a high need to achieve or because you were promised a new car by your parents? Or did both of these factors enhance your motivation? In the second case, a need for social interaction could result in any one of a number of responses—going to church, a party, home for the weekend, etc.

The person performing the act may not be fully conscious of the motives leading to the act. Thus motivation can be explained in terms of either conscious rational processes or unconscious, emotional or instinctual methods. The most useful approach is to assume that both the conscious and the unconscious are involved and that each helps explain certain aspects of behavior.

Needs and motives lead to behavior which in some cases reduces the motivation for that behavior and in other cases increases the motivation. For example, a person who has a need for food eats. In most cases, there is no desire after eating to eat again right away. But if a person has a need for social interaction and experiences rewarding social interaction, motivation to seek social interaction may increase. Managers try to reward good performance on the job so that employee motivation to work well and hard will be constantly renewed.

Why Managers Should Motivate

Managers want to know about motivation for several reasons. First, they must understand individuals' motives in order to know how to get them to join the organization. Second, they must know how to motivate employees to stay with the organization. They must see that jobs and working conditions allow employees to meet their individual needs. One way they do this is to make employee satisfaction and development an organizational objective (see Chapter 7). Third, together with ability, training, and correct job placement, motivation often leads to effective employee performance. Two extreme positions can be taken in considering motivation—that motivation is the key to management or that it should be ignored. The truth lies in between.

A Model of Motivation Factors and Theories

Figure 6.1 portrays the factors affecting work motivation and the theories which attempt to explain it. As you will note, some theories (and supporting research) concentrate on one factor. Others are concerned with more than one of the factors. We will look first at the three theories which concentrate on how individuals' needs affect motivation; then we will look at a theory which focuses on how job design and working conditions affect motivation. Next we will consider an approach which tries to tie environmental factors to motivation. Last we will examine three theories which try to integrate and show how the three factors effect motivation in an interactive way.

Individual Needs and Motivation

As indicated in Figure 6.1, there are three major theories whose approach is this: If you want to understand what motivates a person, you should understand their needs or wants. The first of these is Abraham Maslow's theory.

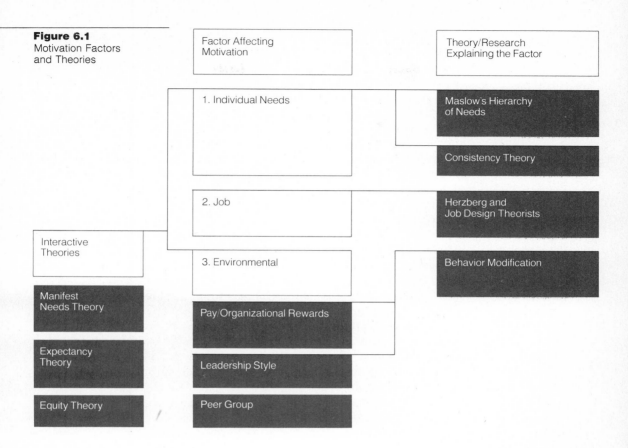

Figure 6.1
Motivation Factors
and Theories

Maslow's Hierarchy of Needs

Although Maslow originally developed his theory in clinical work, it is the most widely known theory to be applied in management situations. Maslow's theory is a "need" theory of motivation.[2] That is, it argues that we behave in order to satisfy certain needs.

Maslow was interested in delineating the source of these needs. He concluded that some needs are *innate*.

Innate needs are inherited or unlearned needs such as the need for food and water.

Other needs are *acquired* or learned.

Acquired needs are needs we learn as we experience life, the need for social recognition, for example.

According to Maslow, there are five types of needs: (1) *Physiological needs* are innate. Basic to all human beings is the need for food, water, rest, exercise, shelter (protection from the elements), and sex. If these needs are not satisfied, most people are not motivated by "higher" needs. When you are cold and hungry you cannot afford the luxury of concern about needs such as self-actualization and self-confidence. (2)*Safety and security needs* are partly innate and partly inherited. They include freedom from bodily harm and freedom from arbitrary loss of employment. The remaining three types of needs are learned. (3) *Social needs* come into play after physiological and safety needs are reasonably well satisfied. These learned needs include the needs for friendship, affection, and interaction and acceptance by peers. Most people need to be with others at least part of the time they are at work. (4) *Ego/esteem* needs, which become significant once social needs are met, include the need for self-respect, self-confidence, and a stable and positive self-evaluation. The respect and appreciation of others are also ego/esteem needs, for they provide an individual with status and reputation. (5) *Self-actualization* is the individual's highest need—the need to realize one's potential, to become what one wants to become, to know one is using all one's talents well, and to be creative. Like ego/esteem and social needs, the need for self-actualization is learned. It is usually the last to be fulfilled.

In Maslow's view, humans strive to satisfy their needs in a specific order, or *hierarchy*. That is, one set of needs must be satisfied first before the others function to motivate behavior. Figure 6.2 illustrates Maslow's hierarchy; the needs are listed according to their priority for satisfaction from bottom to top. Thus physiological needs usually must be satisfied before safety needs can influence behavior, and so on. If a need is not satisfied, it produces tension. Psychologists call the state in which needs are unfulfilled *deprivation*. An effort to reduce the tension that occurs when a need is unfulfilled and so restore equilibrium results in behavior that responds to the unmet need.

Maslow theorized that once a need is satisfied, it no longer motivates behavior. Psychologists apply the term **relative gratification** to *the state of satisfaction in which a need no longer motivates behavior*. Maslow also recognized that there are individual differences in the strength of each need. For example, workers who have experienced a layoff may have greater security needs than those who have not had such an experience. Deprivation over a long period of time can lead to overemphasis or fixation on the need which is not satisfied.

People's needs can change with changes in their life circumstances, according to Maslow. Whatever the situation, he felt, the most important need—the need for self-actualization—is unlikely to be satisfied. He conceded, however, that some few people may be motivated by this need even when their lower needs are not satisfied. In such cases the lower needs are suppressed.

Is Maslow's theory valid? Most managers say it makes sense to them. But it is a very hard theory to prove. Maslow himself said (in 1965):

Figure 6.2
Maslow's
Hierarchy of Needs

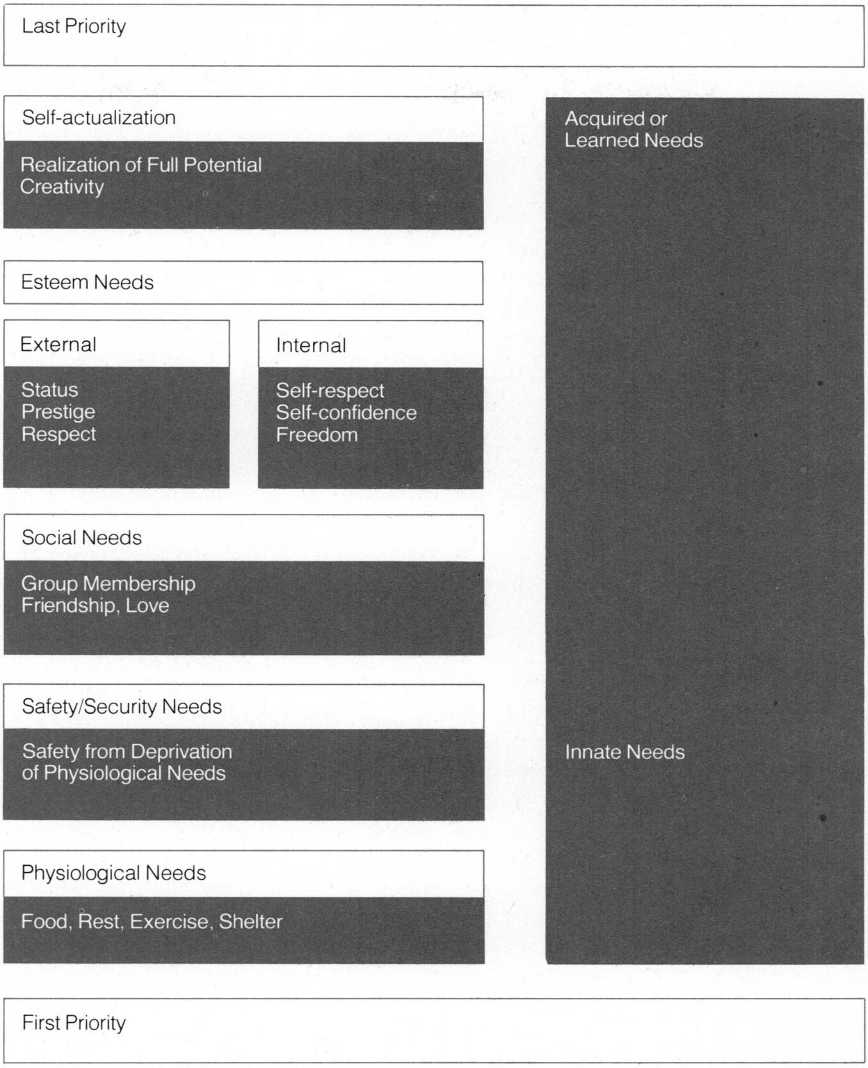

Last Priority

Self-actualization

Realization of Full Potential
Creativity

Acquired or
Learned Needs

Esteem Needs

External

Status
Prestige
Respect

Internal

Self-respect
Self-confidence
Freedom

Social Needs

Group Membership
Friendship, Love

Safety/Security Needs

Safety from Deprivation
of Physiological Needs

Innate Needs

Physiological Needs

Food, Rest, Exercise, Shelter

First Priority

I of all people should know just how shaky this foundation for the theory is as a final foundation. My work on motivation came from the clinic, from a study of neurotic people. The carry-over of this theory to the industrial situation has some support from industrial studies, but certainly I would like to see a lot more studies of this kind before feeling finally convinced that this carry-over from the study of neurosis to the study of labor in factories is legitimate. The same thing is true of my studies of self-actualizing people—there is only this one study of mine available. There were many things wrong with the sampling, so many in fact that it must be considered to be, in the classical sense anyway, a bad or poor or inadequate experiment. I am quite willing to concede this—as a matter of fact, I am eager to concede it—because I'm a little worried about this stuff which I consider to be tentative being swallowed whole by all sorts of enthusiastic people, who really should be a little more tentative in the way that I am.[3]

Maslow's critics take issue with his theory that once a lower need is satisfied, the next higher need becomes the crucial motivator, maintaining there is little evidence to support such a conclusion. They also question the order of his hierarchy of learned needs. Summarizing his own and others' research, Clayton Alderfer has revised Maslow's hierarchy as shown in Table 6.1.[4]

Note that Alderfer's Levels 1 and 2 are substantially the same as Maslow's. Level 3 combines Maslow's higher needs. Alderfer calls his formulation the E-R-G theory (for existence, relatedness, and growth needs). Maslow's theory, especially as modified by Alderfer's E-R-G formulation, has received moderately good research support. Since it focuses only on the individual needs and not on the job and environmental factors influencing motivation, the level of research support is not surprising.

Consistency Theory

A modernized version of what was called equilibrium, or balance, theory, consistency theory asserts that people are motivated to act to keep themselves in balance. Its modern spokesperson, Abraham Korman, has described the basic principles of consistency theory thus:

1. Motivational processes are a function of the drive to be consistent with an individual's belief systems about the nature of the self, others, and the world.
2. Belief systems leading to differing levels of achievement, creativity, and aggression are a function of and develop in the same types of environments.
3. Changing environments in certain directions specified by the theoretical model will result in changes in achievement, creativity, and aggression.[5]

Note that in the first principle stated above the basic motive for all acts is to keep oneself in balance or consistent with one's self-image (developed by the self and others). Put simply, the individual tries to maintain his or her

Table 6.1 Alderfer's Hierarchy	**Alderfer**	**Maslow**
	Level 3: Growth needs	Self-actualization and self-esteem
	Level 2: Relatedness needs	Social and status needs
	Level 1: Existence needs	Physiological and some safety/security needs

self-image. Korman has elaborated on the other two principles with the following observations:

- People of high self-perceived competence and positive self-image should be more likely to achieve on task performance than those who have low self-perceived competence, low success expectancy and low self-image concerning the task or job at hand, since such differential task achievement would be consistent with their self-cognitions. This assumes that task performance is seen as valued.

- People who have beliefs that there is one set of rules to guide behavior in this world and that there is one way of looking at the world are more likely to be opposed to creative change, change in general, and to those people or things that are different or constitute a change from themselves, since such change would be inconsistent with their belief systems.

- People who have beliefs that people, in general, are not desirable, cannot be trusted, and must be controlled by threats and punishments are more likely to develop aggressiveness toward others and are more likely to engage in generally hostile interpersonal behavior, since such types of behavior would be consistent with their belief systems about people.[6]

Figure 6.3 provides a schematic diagram of consistency theory. Korman has presented a good deal of research that tends to support his theory. Though promising, however, consistency theory still requires further refinement.

Applications of Need Theories to Management

There are a number of ways in which managers can apply Maslow's or Alderfer's needs hierarchies. The first step, of course, is to find out what needs employees have through interviews and other methods.

When employees' *physiological needs* are not being met, management may choose to provide employees with counseling on how to improve their money management so they can better provide for the basics—food and shelter for themselves and their families. It may also consider offering

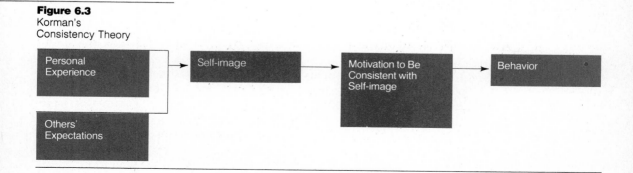

Figure 6.3
Korman's
Consistency Theory

Personal Experience

Others' Expectations

Self-image

Motivation to Be Consistent with Self-image

Behavior

higher pay and greater benefits. When employees' *safety needs* are not being met, firms can improve physical working conditions, especially health and safety programs. Employee health and safety may be adversely affected by negative attitudes toward work and management. Policies and leadership styles to which employees react favorably enhance employee health and safety.

If *social needs* of employees are not being met, managers may want to lay out the work stations or offices so employees can interact on the job. They may also encourage socializing during coffee breaks or strengthen orientation and training programs so that employees get to know their coworkers. If *esteem needs* are not being met, management may wish to give employees the opportunity to improve their skills and advance. This they can do by offering more training and development programs. Status symbols such as titles, privileges, and clothing can harm self-esteem if they are inadequate. They should be assessed on this basis and improved where necessary. The *self-actualization* needs of most employees will not be fulfilled. The key to encouraging self-actualization is placing persons in positions which match their self-concepts.

If you accept consistency theory, you will consider a couple of aspects of the work environment carefully. Korman argues that people prefer to work with others whom they feel are most like themselves. This implies that management should permit some employee impact on how work groups are formed. Of course carried too far or improperly handled, such a policy could lead to discrimination and equal employment opportunity problems. Consistency theory also leads to the conclusion that managers should seek to reinforce employees' self-concepts through appropriate placement. For example, the positions with the greatest challenges should be matched with those individuals who view themselves with confidence and expect to achieve well.

Job Factors and Motivation

As shown in Figure 6.1, the second factor which some researchers believe influences motivation is the job itself. The best-known theorist associated with this view is Frederick Herzberg, who did a study in which he asked 200 engineers and accountants what factors at work satisfied them the most.[7] The factors indicated in the responses were classified either as motivators or as hygiene factors.

Hygiene factors—supervisory style, interpersonal relations, salary, personnel policies, physical working conditions, and job security—must be present and "satisfied" before employees can be motivated. But these factors do not motivate greater productivity. People are motivated to work only when job satisfiers (motivators) are present in the work situation. These motivators are (1) the nature of the work itself, (2) the achievement of an important task, (3) responsibility at work, (4) recognition of work, and (5) opportunity for advancement. Thus Herzberg and others contend that designing jobs which are more varied, have more freedom and responsibility and receive feedback lead to better-motivated employees.

The movement to design jobs in this way is called job enrichment and job enlargement. How this is done—and the conditions under which it is successful—will be discussed in greater detail in Chapter 10. The evidence that job design alone motivates is mixed. That is because individual and environmental factors contribute to motivation too.

Environmental Factors and Motivation

The environment is the third major influence on employee motivation shown in Figure 6.1. There are a large number of conditions in the environment which could possibly affect the motivations of employees. The three most likely are:

- Pay/reward policies
- Leadership style
- Peer group interactions

The behavior modification theory of motivation addresses the first two, although this is not the only theory applicable to these areas.

Behavior Modification Approaches to Motivation

Today's behavior modification is an outgrowth of behaviorism in psychology. Its current and major theorist is B. F. Skinner.[8] The basic theory can be diagrammed in this way:

It teaches that people respond to their environment, and their behavior can be influenced by the consequences of their responses. Thus management can motivate desired employee behavior by structuring specific consequences for specific types of behavior. Four types of consequences may be used to accomplish this:

Positive reinforcement The manager gives positive reinforcers such as money, recognition, praise, and promotions to those who perform well. The reinforcers must result from performance, and the greater the performance, the greater the reinforcement. This is also called the carrot approach.

Avoidance learning The manager responds to undesirable employee behavior in a manner unpleasant for the employee. An employee who

Source: © 1979 King Features Syndicate.

notices that certain behavior results in such undesirable outcomes as criticism by supervisors or disciplinary layoffs will stop this behavior. Behavior modification theory contends that the employee is motivated to perform the desired behavior to *avoid* the consequences of the undesired behavior. This method of strengthening positive behavioral outcomes is often called the stick approach. Some people get the carrot and stick mixed up at times.

Punishment The manager withholds rewards or arranges a negative consequence because performance did not take place or was inadequate. Punishment differs from positive reinforcement or avoidance learning in that it relies on the withdrawal of a positive reinforcer or the presentation of a negative reinforcer.

Extinction The manager withholds reinforcement from behavior that was previously but is no longer desired. Skinner prefers this method for reducing undesirable behavior to punishment.

W. Clay Hamner recommends six rules for making behavior modification effective:[9]

1. *Do not reinforce or reward all people in the same way.* Since people desire different rewards, the rewards they desire must be paired with the desired behavior.
2. *Do not fail to use reinforcement.* Failure to reinforce has reinforcing consequences; nonreinforcement can have the effect of extinction or punishment.
3. *Be sure to tell a person what he or she can do to receive reinforcement.* Behavior modification will not work well if the desired behavior is not known by the employee.
4. *Be sure to tell a person what he or she is doing wrong.* When the supervisor does this, the employee knows what must be done to obtain reinforcement.
5. *Do not punish in front of others.* To do so doubles the punishment; the employee is disciplined and also loses face in the eyes of others.
6. *Make the consequences equal to behavior.* To be effective, reinforce-

ment must be equitable—neither too great nor too small relative to the significance of the behavior.

The most effective approach in behavior modification is to use a *partial reinforcement schedule* in which reinforcement occurs after some but not after every behavior performed. This can be done in two ways. In a *fixed ratio schedule* rewards are given only when a specific desired number of behaviors have occurred (for example, piecework pay schemes). In a *variable ratio schedule,* reinforcement occurs after a reasonable number of behaviors are performed. The number varies around an average. For example, if you choose to reinforce on an average of once every 12 times, you could reinforce after 8 times, 16 times, then 12 times.

Many companies are trying to use the behavior modification approach now, and some contend they have great success. These include Emery Air Freight, 3M, Frito Lay, A-M, and B. F. Goodrich. There has been some research which bears out this approach. It has also been criticized by Edwin Locke because it ignores the human's ability to think and thus interferes with the simple model proposed by the behavior modification approach.[10]

The major management applications of behavior modification are in two areas: leadership style and pay/rewards. If you accept behavior modification, your primary emphasis as a manager will be on positive reinforcement. This is discussed in much more detail in Chapter 14. It has significant implications for pay policies. Chapter 20 will discuss the advantages and disadvantages of incentive pay schemes which behavior modification people would advocate.

The final influence in the environment recognized by behavior modification theorists is the peer group. A work group can have norms that motivate individual performance. The group's internal workings are such that they can reinforce more productivity or less productivity. This is discussed in full detail in Chapter 16.

Interactive Motivation Theories

Three theories attempt to relate the effect on motivation of more than one of the factors shown in Figure 6.1. Manifest needs theory, equity theory, and expectancy theory are all concerned with the interaction of individual needs and factors in the environment.

Manifest Needs Theory

Manifest needs theory was originally developed by Henry Murray and later refined by J. W. Atkinson.[11] Its current advocate and researcher is David McClelland.[12] Two basic premises are the foundation on which manifest needs theory is built:

- Most mentally healthy adults have a large reservoir of potential energy.
- Most mentally healthy adults have basic motives or needs that channel and regulate the flow of potential energy. These needs or motives are relatively stable and are learned, not innate.

There are three basic needs which an individual might have. *The need for power* results in a strong desire to influence people. (While effective managers usually have a strong need for power, they generally avoid using power for personal gain. Instead, they use it to stimulate their employees to be more productive.) *The need for achievement* results in a desire to do something better or more efficiently than others. Effective achievers are characterized by:

- Desire for personal responsibility for decisions and results
- Desire to take moderate risks
- Desire for feedback on results (good or bad)
- High energy, willingness to work hard
- Tendency to initiate decisions

The need for affiliation leads to a desire for friendly and close interpersonal relationships.

Manifest needs theory contends that while people within a culture may have the same needs, there are major differences in the relative strength of those needs. Each need is in effect a motive for a pattern of action or behavior that results in a specific kind of satisfaction. The feeling resulting from achievement is a sense of accomplishment. The feeling resulting from affiliation is the warmth of being well received by others. Power brings the feeling of being in control, of being influential.

According to the manifest needs theory, the likelihood that a person will perform a task successfully depends on a combination of

- The strength of the motive (need).
- The subjective probability of success at the task. (How likely does the employee feel that he/she will be able to achieve success at the job?)
- The strength of the incentive value of success. (How strongly does the employee perceive the cue that aroused the motive [need]?)

Also important is the environment (climate) of the work situation. The trigger that activates a particular motive is the situation with which the person is dealing. Aspects of the environment—support, conflict, rewards—arouse different motives. For example, George Litwin and Robert Stringer found that the effects of certain characteristics in the environment on arousal of motives in managers are as shown in Table 6.2.[13]

Table 6.2
The Effect of the
Environment on
Arousal of Motives

Aspects of the Environment	Motives		
	Need for Power	**Need for Achievement**	**Need for Affiliation**
Warmth	No effect	No effect	Aroused
Support	No effect	Aroused	Aroused
Conflict	Aroused	Aroused	Reduced
Reward	No effect	Aroused	Aroused
Responsibility	Aroused	Aroused	No effect

Source: Adapted by permission from George Litwin and Robert Stringer, *Motivation and Organization Climate* (Cambridge, Mass.: Harvard University Press, 1968), chapter 8. Copyright © 1968 by the President and Fellows of Harvard College; all rights reserved.

Manifest needs theorists assert that the most successful managers have the highest need for power, moderate to low need for achievement, and low need for affiliation. Successful salespersons and entrepreneurs have high need for achievement and moderate need for power. They have low need for affiliation. David McClelland claims that high need for affiliation leads to selective interpretation of policies and rules and ineffective management. Research strongly supports McClelland's theory. There is also strong evidence that his training programs based on this theory are successful in motivating managers to achieve more. Further research is needed, but the theory shows promise.

Management Applications of Manifest Needs Theory

The managers who wish to apply manifest needs theory will take two basic steps. First, they will create a climate in their organizations which will lead to the motivation they desire in their employees. Second, they will match employees with a high need for power with managerial positions and employees with high needs for achievement with positions requiring responsibility while working alone (or in nonsupervisory positions), for example, in sales, systems analysis, and R&D.

Equity Theory

Like manifest needs theory, equity theory focuses on the individual needs factor and the environmental factors, particularly rewards. What we call equity theory has had several other names in the past: social comparison theory, exchange theory, distributive justice theory. Its central theme is that rewards such as pay are important motivators of behavior.

According to equity theory, the major cause (motive) leading to job performance and satisfaction is the degree of equity or inequity the employee perceives in the workplace. An employee perceives equity by calculating the *ratio of his or her inputs to the outcomes as compared to the ratio (inputs/outcomes) of his or her reference person or reference group*. Note the emphasis on the perceived ratio rather than the actual ratio.

Examples of inputs include effort, experience and training, seniority, skill, education, and social status. Examples of outcomes are pay, seniority, rights, benefits, job status, status symbols and perquisites, and satisfying supervision. Negative outcomes such as monotony and poor working conditions are subtracted from the positive outcomes. The person seeks to maximize positive outcomes and minimize effort.

A person perceives an inequity when he or she is underrewarded or overrewarded. The perceived inequity is greater when the person is underrewarded than when he or she is overrewarded. Inequity is a source of tension. The greater the perceived inequity, the greater the motivation to reduce the tension. Inequity is rarely reduced by changing the reference person or group. The person who perceives inequity can best reduce tension by changing his or her calculations of the ratio. Sometimes a close examination of the situation will result in the discovery of factors affecting the ratio that were not considered, thus making this possible.

What happens if inequity is perceived and the individual does not reduce it by changing reference persons or changing the ratios? There are several possibilities:

- A person who is overpaid in an hourly pay system will perceive inequity and will produce more than the equitably paid person.
- A person who is overpaid in a piece rate system will produce higher-quality products than the equitably paid person.
- A person who is underpaid in an hourly system will decrease his or her inputs.
- A person who is underpaid in a piece rate system will produce a large number of lower-quality products.
- If the magnitude of the inequity is large and there are no other means of reducing it, the person will leave the field.
- If the inequity is fairly large and there are no other means of reducing it, the person will reduce the inequity through increased absenteeism.

Equity theory has received relatively good support in research.

Management Applications of Equity Theory

Equity theory has been applied primarily in determining pay rates. It can also be applied to the distribution of other rewards, such as praise and promotion. Managers have some control over reward systems. To the extent that they try to equitably reward employees for their efforts, this should contribute to employee motivation.

Sometimes, though, individual supervisors cannot adequately influence the reward structure. For example, benefits and pay structures are often fixed in spite of various inputs such as education and skill level. Equity theory helps explain how employees are likely to respond in such cases (increased absenteeism, lower quality of work). Supervisors can try to increase equity by improving on the outcomes that they can control—praise, perquisites, status symbols, tedium, and monotony—in order to offset those they cannot. Thus equity theory provides a manager with significant insights into the relationship between rewards and employee effort. It is, however, somewhat narrow in its emphasis on visible rewards and probably overemphasizes conscious responses.

Expectancy Theory

The expectancy theory of motivation also emphasizes the interaction of individual needs and environmental factors. The description of it given here relies on the work of David Nadler and Edward Lawler.[14]

According to expectancy theory, employees are motivated to perform by three beliefs.

- Employees believe that their behavior will lead to external or internal outcomes. This belief is called *performance-outcome expectancy*. Examples of external outcomes are changes in pay, promotion, praise by supervisor, or change in peer support. Internal outcomes can include the feelings of achievement or accomplishment.
- Employees believe that they can perform at the expected level of performance. This belief is called the *effort-performance expectancy*.
- Employees believe that these outcomes have values to them. This belief is called a valence.

This relationship can be expressed as a formula:

$$\text{Motivation} = f(\text{Expectancy} \times \text{Valence})$$

That is, motivation is a function (f) of the two expectancies and the valence. Somewhat complicating this rather simple formula is differences in abilities among employees. People with more ability need not be as motivated (or expend as much effort) as those with lesser ability.

Management Applications of Expectancy Theory

Expectancy theory has received much research support and theoretically could influence pay programs, job design, group relationships, leadership styles, and other management functions. Managers who wish to apply this theory must take these steps:

- Figure out what outcomes each employee values.
- Determine what kinds or changes in level of behavior are desired.
- Make sure that the desired level of performance is reasonably attainable.
- Link the desired outcomes to desired performance.

- Analyze the total situation for conflicts in expectancy; that is, determine whether the employee's expected outcome conflicts with your own.
- Make sure that changes in outcome are large enough.
- Check the system for its equity.

Though strongly supported by research, expectancy theory is not without problems. It may be that it goes too far in assuming employees are very rational in their decision making. And the assumption that employees have enough information to make these decisions well may also be somewhat extravagant. Additionally, expectancy theory is complex to research, much less to implement in practice.

Summary

Motivation explains why people work hard and well or poorly. By definition, *motivation* is the inner state that energizes, channels, and sustains human behavior. Three critical factors affecting motivation are:

- individual needs
- the job
- the environment

This chapter discussed the theories and research which will help you understand how each of these factors affects a person's motivation and how a manager can use these factors to influence employees' motivation. All three factors are important and interactive. Although the above definition of motivation seems quite simple, you should remember these facts:

1. A person and the environment change over time thus influencing the person's motives.
2. Motivation is rarely traceable to a single need or motive.
3. Needs and motives lead to behavior which in some cases reduces motivation to behave and in other cases increases the likelihood of more behavior.

Maslow's hierarchy of needs and Alderfer's revision of this hierarchy (E-R-G theory) focus on individual needs. Maslow postulated two kinds of needs, innate or unlearned needs and acquired needs. Physiological needs, which are innate, must be met before safety and security needs, which are partly learned and partly innate, can be satisfied. Social needs, ego/esteem needs and self-actualization or self-fulfillment needs are acquired, and according to Maslow they become a concern only after the others are met. There is little support for Maslow's contention that once a lower need is satisfied the next higher need becomes a motivator or for the accuracy of his hierarchy's order. Alderfer's revision grouped Maslow's needs into three categories: existence, relatedness, and growth needs. But there is moderately good support for the existence of these individual needs.

Korman's consistency theory applies to the individual needs, too. This theory is a modernized version of equilibrium or balance theory and proposes that people act to keep themselves in balance.

Some of the managerial applications of these theories which relate to the individual and motivation include:

- Improving physical working conditions to satisfy employees' safety needs.
- Increasing the level of training and development to meet employees' esteem needs.
- Reinforcing employees' self-concept by appropriate placement.

The best-known motivation theorist concerned with the job itself is Frederick Herzberg. His theory evaluated the job in terms of hygiene factors (supervisory style, salary, physical working conditions) and motivators (job satisfiers) such as the nature of the work itself, and opportunity for responsibility, recognition, advancement. Thus Herzberg and others contend that designing jobs which are more varied and provide some freedom, responsibility, and feedback leads to better-motivated employees.

Behavior modification theorists teach that people are influenced by their environment and that management can structure consequences of behavior on the job to influence (motivate) employee performance positively. This can be done through pay/reward policies and leadership style. Another important environmental influence as far as behavior modification theory is concerned is the peer group. Peer pressure based on the group's norms often influences what motivates greater or lesser performance.

Manifest needs theory, equity theory, and expectancy theory are attempts to describe the interaction of the environment and individual needs in motivation. McClelland's manifest needs theory considers how environmental factors and individual needs combine to form basic human motives: the need for power, for achievement, and for affiliation. In applying this theory, the manager rates positions according to the degree to which they fulfill each of these needs and then seeks individuals with the corresponding needs to fill them.

Equity theory states that the major cause (motive) leading to job performance is the degree of equity or inequity the employee perceives in the workplace. The employee calculates inputs and compares these to outcomes, seeking to maximize positive outcomes and minimize effort. This theory is applied primarily in determining pay scales.

Finally, expectancy theory assumes three factors influence employee behavior: performance-outcome expectancy, valence, and effort-performance expectancy. The employee believes his or her efforts lead to outcomes which have value to him or her. The theory may be relevant to pay programs, job design, leadership styles, and other management functions.

All of these motivation theories have managerial applications, as we have noted. But you must remember that well-motivated employees are only part of our success formula. In addition, none of the theories involves all factors. Even the interactive theories did not take the job into account. With these cautions in mind, you may nonetheless want to apply motivation theories to increase your effectiveness as a manager.

Turn now to Part 3 for a discussion of planning and decision making.

Questions

1. Define motivation. What are the three critical factors affecting motivation? Is motivation usually traceable to a single need?
2. What are some of the reasons you as a manager would want to know more about motivation? How would you use your knowledge to get the job done?
3. Maslow's hierarchy of needs deals with individual needs and motivation. List his hierarchy of needs and describe in your own terms how it is supposed to operate.
4. What kinds of criticism has Maslow's hierarchy of needs received based on research? Explain how Alderfer's E-R-G theory modified Maslow's hierarchy.
5. What are the basic contentions of consistency theory? Do you think your motivation to work stems from a feeling of being in balance?
6. How does job design affect an employee's motivation according to Herzberg?
7. How could you use behavior modification to influence an employee to produce more? Which of the factors influencing motivation is involved—individual needs, the job, or the environment?
8. List some of the rules you would follow to make sure your behavior modification scheme is effective. How often would you reinforce the desired behavior?
9. Explain how manifest needs theory combines the individual needs factor and environmental factor in motivation. How could you use it to hire a new salesperson for your firm?
10. Use your knowledge of equity theory to explain what you would do if you felt you were overcompensated on the job.
11. How would you go about using expectancy theory to help motivate your employees?

Notes

[1] Studs Terkel, *Working* (New York: Pantheon, 1974), p. 118.

[2] Abraham H. Maslow, "A Theory of Human Motivation," *Psychological Review* 50 (July 1943): 370–396; *Motivation and Personality* (New York: Harper & Bros., 1954).

[3] Abraham H. Maslow, *Eupsychian Management* (Homewood, Ill.: Irwin, Dorsey Press, 1965), p. 95.

[4]Clayton P. Alderfer, "A Critique of Salancik and Pfeffer's Examination of Need-Satisfaction Theories," *Administrative Science Quarterly* 22 (December 1977): 658–672.

[5]Abraham Korman, *The Psychology of Motivation* (Englewood Cliffs, N.J.: Prentice-Hall, 1974), p. 226.

[6]Ibid., pp. 227–228.

[7]Frederick Herzberg, *The Motivation to Work* (New York: Wiley, 1959).

[8]B. F. Skinner, *Science and Behavior* (New York: Macmillan, 1952); and *Beyond Freedom and Dignity* (New York: Knopf, 1971).

[9]W. Clay Hamner, "Reinforcement Theory and Contingency Management in Organizational Settings," in *Organizational Behavior and Management,* ed. Henry Tosi and W. Clay Hamner (Chicago: St. Clair Press, 1974); and "Worker Motivation Programs," in *Contemporary Problems in Personnel,* ed. W. Clay Hamner and Frank Schmidt (Chicago: St. Clair Press, 1974).

[10]Edwin A. Locke, "Myths in 'The Myths of the Myths about Behavior Mod in Organizations,'" *Academy of Management Review* 4 (January 1979): 131–136; and "The Myths of Behavior Mod in Organizations," *Academy of Management Review* 2 (October 1977): 543–553.

[11]Henry Murray, *Explorations in Personality* (New York: Oxford University Press, 1938); and J. W. Atkinson, *An Introduction to Motivation* (New York: American Book, 1964).

[12]David McClelland, *The Personality* (New York: Dryden Press, 1951).

[13]George Litwin and Robert Stringer, *Motivation and Organization Climate* (Cambridge, Mass.: Harvard Business School, 1968).

[14]David Nadler and Edward Lawler, "Motivation: A Diagnostic Approach," in *Perspectives on Behavior in Organizations,* ed. J. Richard Hackman et al. (New York: McGraw-Hill, 1977).

References

What Is Motivation?

Abraham K. Korman, Jeffrey H. Greenhaus, and Irwin J. Badin, "Personnel Attitudes and Motivation," *Annual Review of Psychology* 28 (1977): 175–196. Richard Steers and Lyman Porter, eds., *Motivation and Work Behavior* (New York: McGraw-Hill, 1979).

Individual Needs and Motivation

Clayton P. Alderfer, "A Critique of Salancik and Pfeffer's Examination of Need-Satisfaction Theories," *Administrative Science Quarterly* 22 (December 1977): 658–672. Clayton P. Alderfer, Robert E. Kaplan, and Ken K. Smith, "The Effect of Variations in Relatedness Need Satisfaction on Relatedness Desires," *Administrative Science Quarterly* 19 (March 1974): 507–532. Douglas Hall and K. E. Nougaim, "An Examination of Maslow's Need Hierarchy in an Organization Setting," *Organizational Behavior and Human Performance* 3 (February 1968): 12–35. Gerald H. Huizinga, *Maslow's Need Hierarchy in the Work Situation* (The Netherlands: Wolters-Noordhoff nv Groningen, 1970). E. E. Lawler and J. L. Suttle, "A Causal Correlational Test of the Need Hierarchy Concept," *Organizational Behavior and Human Performance* 7 (June 1972): 265–287. A. H. Maslow, *Eupsychian Management* (Homewood, Ill.: Irwin, Dorsey Press, 1965); *Motivation and Personality* (New York: Harper & Bros., 1954); and "A Theory of Human Motivation," *Psychological Review* 50 (July 1943): 370–396. Vance F. Mitchell and Pravin Moudgill, "Measurement of Maslow's Need Hierarchy," *Organizational Behavior and Human Performance* 16 (August 1976): 334–349. Roy Payne, "Factor Analysis of Maslow Type Need Satisfaction Questionnaire," *Personnel Psychology* 23 (Summer 1970): 251–268. Gerald R. Salancik and Jeffrey Pfeffer, "An Examination of Need-Satisfaction Models of Job Attitudes," *Administrative Science Quarterly* 22

(September 1977): 427–456. Benjamin Schneider and Clayton Alderfer, "Three Studies of Measures of Need Satisfaction in Organizations," *Administrative Science Quarterly* 18 (December 1973): 489–505. L. W. Slivinski, "Attitudes of Managers in the Canadian Public Service," *Studies in Personnel Psychology* 1 (Spring 1969): 71–92. J. T. Trexler and A. J. Schuh, "Longitudinal Verification of Maslow's Motivation Hierarchy in a Military Environment," Experimental Publication System (Washington, D.C.: American Psychological Association, 1969), ms. no. 020A. Mahmoud Wahba and Lawrence Bridwell, "Maslow Reconsidered: A Review of Research on the Need Hierarchy," *Organizational Behavior and Human Performance* 15 (April 1976): 212–240. John P. Wanous and Abram Zwany, "A Cross-Sectional Test of Need Hierarchy Theory," *Organizational Behavior and Human Performance* 18 (February 1977): 78–97. J. C. Wofford, "The Motivational Basis of Job Satisfaction and Job Performance," *Personnel Psychology* 24 (Autumn 1971): 501–518. Yoel Yinon, Aharon Bizman, and Martha Goldberg, "Effect of Relative Magnitude of Reward and Type of Need on Satisfaction," *Journal of Applied Psychology* 61 (June 1976): 325–328.

Consistency Theory

L. A. Festinger, *Theory of Cognitive Dissonance* (Evanston, Ill.: Row, Peterson, 1957). Fritz Heider, *The Psychology of Interpersonal Relations* (New York: Wiley, 1958). Abraham Korman, *The Psychology of Motivation* (Englewood Cliffs, N.J.: Prentice-Hall, 1974): and "Hypothesis of Work Behavior Revisited and an Extension," *Academy of Management Review* 1 (January 1976): 50–63. Abraham K. Korman, Jeffrey H. Greenhaus, and Irwin J. Badin, "Personnel Attitudes and Motivation," *Annual Review of Psychology* 28 (1977): 175–196. C. E. Osgood and P. H. Tannenbaum, "The Principle of Congruity in the Prediction of Attitude Change," *Psychological Review* 62 (January 1955): 42–55.

Job Factors and Motivation

John P. Campbell et al., *Managerial Behavior* (New York: McGraw-Hill, 1970). Marvin Dunnette et al., "Factors Contributing to Job Satisfaction and Dissatisfaction in Six Occupational Groups," *Organizational Behavior and Human Performance* 2 (May 1967): 143–174. Mitchell Fein, "Job Enrichment: A Reevaluation," *Sloan Management Review*, Winter 1974, pp. 69–88. George Graen, "Instrumentality Theory of Work Motivation," *Journal of Applied Psychology Monograph* 53, part 2 (April 1969): 1–25. Benedict Grigalumas and Frederick Herzberg, "Relevancy in the Test of the Motivator Hygiene Theory," *Journal of Applied Psychology* 55 (February 1971): 73–79. Pehr Gyllenhammer, "How Value Adapts Work to People," *Harvard Business Review*, July–August 1977, pp. 102–113. J. Richard Hackman, "The Design of Work in the 1980's," in *Motivation and Work Behavior*, ed. Richard Steers and Lyman Porter (New York: McGraw-Hill, 1979): and "Work Design," ibid. Frederick Herzberg, *The Motivation to Work* (New York: Wiley, 1959); and "One More Time: How Do You Motivate Employees?" *Harvard Business Review*, January–February 1968, pp. 53–62. Robert House and L. A. Wigdor, "Herzberg's Dual-Factor Theory of Job Satisfaction and Motivation," *Personnel Psychology* 20 (Winter 1967): 369–390. Rabindra N. Kanungo, Gerald J. Gorn, and Henry J. Dauderis, "Motivational Orientation of Canadian Anglophone and Francophone Managers," in *Behavioral Issues in Management*, ed. H. C. Jain and R. N. Kanungo (Toronto: McGraw-Hill Ryerson, 1977). J. M. Pennings, "Work Value Systems of White-Collar Workers," *Administrative Science Quarterly* 15 (December 1970): 397–405. Donald Schwab and H. G. Heneman III, "Aggregate and Individual Predictability of the Two Factor Theory of Job Satisfaction," *Personnel Psychology* 23 (Spring 1970): 55–65. H. M. Soleman, "Motivation-Hygiene Theory of Job Attitudes," *Journal of Applied Psychology* 54 (October 1970): 452–461.

Environmental Factors and Motivation

Richard Beatty and Craig Schneier, "A Case for Positive Reinforcement," *Business Horizons* 18 (April 1975): 57–66. Orlando Behling, "Operant Conditioning Approaches to Employee Behavior: Some Issues of Research Methodology," *Organization and Administrative Sciences* 6 (Winter 1975–1976): 43–46. Leonard Berkowitz, "Social Motivation," in *Handbook of Social Psychology,* ed. Gardner Linzey and Elliot Aronson, 2d ed., 5 vols. (Reading, Mass.: Addison-Wesley, 1969), 3: 50–135. W. Clay Hamner, "Reinforcement Theory and Contingency Management in Organizational Settings," in *Organizational Behavior and Management,* ed. Henry Tosi and W. Clay Hamner (Chicago: St. Clair Press, 1974); and "Worker Motivation Programs," in *Contemporary Problems in Personnel,* ed. W. Clay Hamner and Frank Schmidt (Chicago: St. Clair Press, 1974). W. Clay Hamner and Ellen P. Hamner, "Behavior Modification on the Bottom Line," *Organizational Dynamics* 4 (Spring 1976): 3–21. Judi Komaki, William M. Waddell, and M. George Pearce, "The Applied Behavior Analysis Approach and Individual Employees: Improving Performance in Two Small Businesses," *Organizational Behavior and Human Performance* 19 (August 1977): 337–352. Barry Ledwidge, "Cognitive Behavior Modification: A Step in the Wrong Direction?" *Psychological Bulletin* 85 (March 1978): 353–375. Edwin A. Locke, "Myths in 'The Myths of the Myths about Behavior Mod in Organizations,'" *Academy of Management Review* 4 (January 1979): 131–136; and "The Myths of Behavior Mod in Organizations," *Academy of Management Review* 2 (October 1977): 543–553. Fred Luthans, "An Organizational Behavior Modification Approach to Organizational Development," *Organization and Administrative Sciences* 6 (Winter 1975/1976): 47–53. Fred Luthans and Robert Kreitner, *Organizational Behavior Modification* (Chicago: Scott, Foresman, 1975). Terence R. Mitchell, "Cognitions and Skinner: Some Questions about Behavioral Determinism," *Organization and Administrative Sciences* 6 (Winter 1975–1976): 63–72. Walter Nord, "Beyond the Teaching Machine: Operant Conditioning in Management," *Organizational Behavior and Human Performance* 4 (November 1969): 375–401; and "Some Issues in the Application of Operant Conditioning to the Management of Organizations," *Organization and Administrative Sciences* 6 (Winter 1975–1976): 55-62. Craig Schneier, "Behavior Modification in Management: A Review and Critique," *Academy of Management Journal* 17 (September 1974): 528–548. B. F. Skinner, *Science and Behavior* (New York: Macmillan, 1952); and *Beyond Freedom and Dignity* (New York: Knopf, 1971).

Manifest Needs Theory

J. W. Atkinson, *An Introduction to Motivation* (New York: American Book, 1964). J. W. Atkinson and Norman Feather, eds., *A Theory of Achievement Motivation* (New York: Wiley, 1966). J. W. Atkinson and J. O. Raynor, *Motivation and Achievement* (New York: Holt, Rinehart and Winston, 1974). George Litwin and Robert Stringer, *Motivation and Organization Climate* (Cambridge, Mass.: Harvard Business School, 1968). David McClelland, *The Personality* (New York: Dryden Press, 1951). David McClelland and David H. Burnham, "Power Is the Great Motivator," *Harvard Business Review* 55 (March–April 1976): 100–110. David McClelland and David Winter, *Motivating Economic Achievement* (Glencoe, Ill.: Free Press, 1971). Henry Murray, *Explorations in Personality* (New York: Oxford University Press, 1938). Paul Wish and J. E. Hasazi, "Motivational Determinants of Curricular Choice Behavior in College Males," *Proceedings of the Eastern Psychological Association* (1972).

Equity Theory

J. Stacy Adams, "Inequity in Social Exchange," in *Advances in Experimental Social Psychology,* ed. Leonard Berkowitz, vol. 2 (New York: Academic Press, 1965); "Toward an Understanding of Inequity," *Journal of Abnormal and Social Psychology* 67 (October 1963): 422–436; and "Effects of Overpayment: Two Comments on Lawler's Paper,"

Journal of Personality and Social Psychology 10 (September 1968): 315–316. Michael R. Carrell, "A Longitudinal Field Assessment of Employee Perceptions of Equitable Treatment," *Organizational Behavior and Human Performance* 21 (February 1978): 108–118. Michael R. Carrell and John E. Dittrich, "Equity Theory: The Recent Literature, Methodological Consideration, and New Directions," *Academy of Management Review* 3 (April 1978): 202–210. Martin Evans and Larry Molinari, "Equity Piece Rate Overpayment and Job Security: Some Effects on Performance," *Journal of Applied Psychology* 54 (April 1970): 105–114. Paul Goodman and Abraham Freedman, "An Examination of Adams' Theory of Inequity," *Administrative Science Quarterly* 16 (September 1971): 271–288. Sam Gould, "An Equity-Exchange Model of Organizational Involvement," *Academy of Management Review* 4 (January 1979): 53–62. George Homans, *Social Behavior* (New York: Harcourt, Brace and World, 1961). Elliot Jacques, *Equitable Payment* (New York: Wiley, 1961); and *Measurement of Personality* (London: Tavistock Institute, 1956). R. Dennis Middlemist and Richard B. Peterson, "Test of Equity Theory by Controlling for Comparison Co-Workers' Efforts," *Organizational Behavior and Human Performance* 15 (April 1976): 335–354. Richard Mowday, "Equity Theory Predictions of Behavior in Organizations," in *Motivation and Work Behavior*, ed. Richard Steers and Lyman Porter (New York: McGraw-Hill, 1979). Robert Pritchard, "Equity Theory: A Review and Critique," *Organizational Behavior and Human Performance* 4 (May 1969): 176–211. Karl E. Weick, Michel G. Bougon, and Geoffrey Maruyama, "The Equity Context," *Organizational Behavior and Human Performance* 15 (February 1976): 32–65.

Expectancy Theory

Paul J. Andrisani and Gilbert Nestel, "Internal-External Control as Contributor to and Outcome of Work Experience," *Journal of Applied Psychology* 61 (April 1976): 156–165. Orlando Behling, Chester Schriesheim, and James Tolliver, "Alternatives to Expectancy Theories of Work Motivation," *Decision Sciences* 6 (July 1975): 449–461. John Campbell and Robert Pritchard, "Motivation Theory in Industrial and Organizational Psychology," in *Handbook of Industrial and Organizational Psychology,* ed. Martin Dunnette (Chicago: Rand McNally, 1976). Terry Connolly, "Some Conceptual and Methodological Issues in Expectancy Models of Work Performance Motivation," *Academy of Management Review* (October 1976): 37–47. Jack M. Feldman, H. Joseph Reitz, and Robert J. Hilterman, "Alternatives to Optimization in Expectancy Theory," *Journal of Applied Psychology* 61 (December 1976): 712–720. Gerald R. Ferris, Terry A. Beehr, and David C. Gilmore, "Social Facilitation: A Review and Alternative Conceptual Model," *Academy of Management Review* 3 (April 1978): 338–347. Christopher R. Forrest, L. L. Cummings, and Alton C. Johnson, "Organizational Participation: A Critique and Model," *Academy of Managment Review* 2 (October 1977): 586–601. W. Clay Hamner and Lawrence W. Foster, "Are Intrinsic and Extrinsic Rewards Addictive? A Test of Deci's Cognitive Evaluation Theory of Task Motivation," *Organizational Behavior and Human Performance* 14 (December 1975): 398–415. Herbert Heneman III and Donald Schwab, "Evaluation of Research on Expectancy Theory Predictions of Employee Performance," *Psychological Bulletin* 78 (July 1972): 1–9. Richard E. Kopelman, "Across-Individual, Within-Individual, and Return on Effort Versions of Expectancy Theory," *Decision Sciences* 8 (October 1977): 651–662. Edward Lawler, *Motivation in Work Organizations* (Monterey, Calif.: Brooks/Cole, 1973). Bronston T. Mayes, "Incorporating Time-Lag Effects into the Expectancy Model of Motivation: A Reformulation of the Model," *Academy of Management Review* 3 (April 1978): 374–380. Terrence Mitchell, "Expectancy Models of Job Satisfaction, Occupational Preference and Effort," *Psychological Bulletin* 81 (1974): 1053–1077. Paul M. Muchinski, "The Consistency of Intrasubject Valence and Instrumentality Measures: A Methodological Consideration," *Academy of Management Journal* 20 (June 1977): 321–327. David Nadler and Edward Lawler, "Motivation: A Diagnostic Approach," in *Perspectives on Behavior in Organizations*, ed. J. Richard Hackman et al. (New York: McGraw-Hill, 1977). Lawrence H. Peters, "Cognitive Models of Motivation, Expectancy Theory and Effort: An Analysis and Empirical Test," *Organizational Behavior and Human Performance* 20 (October 1977): 129–148. Robert D.

Pritchard, Philip J. DeLeo, and Clarence W. Von Bergen, Jr., "A Field Experimental Test of Expectancy-Valence Incentive Motivation Techniques," *Organizational Behavior and Human Performance* 15 (April 1976): 355–406. Leon Reinharth and Mahmoud A. Wahba, "A Test of Alternative Models of Expectancy Theory," *Human Relations* 29 (March 1976): 257–272. Frederick A. Starke and Orlando Behling, "A Test of Two Postulates Underlying Expectancy Theory," *Academy of Management Journal* 18 (December 1975): 703–714. Victor Vroom, *Work and Motivation* (New York: Wiley, 1964). M. A. Wahba and Robert House, "Expectancy Theory in Work and Motivation," *Human Relations* 27 (February 1974): 121–147.

Cases for Chapter 6

**A Tale of
Fred and Wil**

The following two cases illustrate two types of employees with different motivations. They both cause problems for management in their own ways.

**Fred Mengel,
Tennessee
Revenue Officer**

An office of the Tennessee State Department of Revenue is located in Memphis, Tennessee. This unit is responsible for the collection of Tennessee taxes for the region and for enforcement of the tax laws.

One of the employees of this office is Fred Mengel. Fred, a civil service employee, is 51 years old. He has worked for the State of Tennessee for twenty years. He could not afford to go to college, but he has taken all the training the department offers and has occasionally attended night courses at Memphis State University, especially when the state paid for the course and if it raised his pay grade.

Fred was divorced some years ago. Between his job and his inheritance he has more than enough money to live and retire on. He has no children and his parents are dead. His wife moved to California after the divorce. Fred likes television. Every Thursday night he plays cards with friends. On Saturdays he usually has a date to go dancing or to a movie. Fred feels that life is quite pleasant, especially when nobody pushes him.

The preceding is a preliminary description of a problem employee to the casewriter by his superior, Bernie Lovell. Bernie is 38 years old, a graduate of Memphis State with a master's degree. Bernie has been Fred's boss for a year. He has discussed "the Fred problem" with his two previous supervisors, Walter Rogers and Forrest Quigley. Their analysis is the same as his.

As Bernie sees it, Fred is a classic case of the ineffectual employee that you cannot do anything about. But he pulls morale and performance down. Bernie says,

Fred is the twenty-year civil service veteran. You really can't do anything about him. He slides through his job, never straining himself for anyone or anything. He drifts in about on time. He fiddles around his desk for half an hour or so. He starts the 9:30 coffee break early and stretches it late. He does the same at lunch and at the afternoon coffee break. He starts getting ready to leave 45 minutes early with the going to the rest room and straightening up his desk routine. He has never, *never* left late. He has a good time with a circle of friends at breaks and lunches. He calls them during the day too, though I've never caught him at it.

Fred knows how to work the system. He does just enough so you can't do anything about him. Have you ever tried to discipline a civil servant, much less a twenty-year veteran?

I've tried to talk to him. His attitude, never spoken, is: I've seen bosses come and go and I'm still here. I'll listen, appear hurt, may even agree to try harder, but there's nothing you can do and we both know it. We're playing a game.

Fred's job involves routine checking of tax payments. He has never received either a bad performance evaluation or a good one. It is always average, slightly above, or slightly below.

But Bernie is perturbed because the other employees tend to emulate Fred after a while. Even if they are enthusiastic and hardworking at first, pretty soon they begin to follow his behavior patterns.

Wil Michaels of Foreign Autos, Inc.*

Ralph Johnson, Sr., owner of Foreign Autos, Inc., was sitting alone in his office late one Friday night pondering what he should do about Wil Michaels, who had been with Foreign since its inception thirty years ago.

History

Foreign Autos, Inc., a medium-size sales and service dealership for several makes of prestigious foreign automobiles, was founded in Virginia soon after World War II. From the sale of his very first automobile, Ralph Johnson, Sr., realized a potential market existed among consumers who found themselves ready to purchase durables, especially automobiles, after the hardships of the war ended. Ralph knew that in order to develop a successful auto business, he must not only sell autos but also must be prepared to offer service commensurate with the prestigiousness of these autos. To do this Ralph very carefully hired auto mechanics who were familiar with his products. This was not an easy task for Ralph, a salesman with a degree in Business Administration from a midwestern university. But with the help of a former army buddy, he was able to locate two mechanics who were familiar with foreign autos. Hendrick, a former mechanic from Munich, Germany, was a middle-aged widower who lost his wife just prior to the war and was able to emigrate to the United States. Hendrick was happy

*This case was prepared by Professor Mary Ann Lederhaus of the University of Northern Florida, Jacksonville.

to have the opportunity to work on engines with which he was so familiar. Although his ability to communicate was restricted by his heavy German accent, he welcomed the opportunity to teach his trade to a young mechanic from Wisconsin, Wilson Michaels.

Hendrick and Wil carried the service end of Foreign Autos for almost five years. One day, however, in a conference with Mr. Johnson, both men requested an oil change and grease mechanic to relieve them of these more mundane duties. Foreign Autos had grown to the point where Hendrick and Wil were working ten to twelve hours a day and barely meeting customer time demands. A grease mechanic, they felt, would allow them to handle the mechanical work in a more efficient manner. Ralph, who was somewhat surprised at the request, said he certainly would look into the matter and apologized to Hendrick and Wil for not spending more time with his service responsibilities.

Ralph, Sr., realized then that he could not be a salesman and a service manager at the same time. Therefore, he was willing to relinquish his sales duties to his son and his service duties to a newly-hired service manager. So by 1966 the family business had burgeoned into a corporation with six salesmen headed by Ralph, Jr., as sales manager and five mechanics headed by Don Evans as service manager. Although Hendrick retired just prior to Don's coming, Wil, now a twenty-year veteran, remained as a valuable product of Hendrick's careful teaching.

Although attrition had been minimal prior to 1966, Foreign Autos, Inc., experienced considerable turnover in its service department during the following ten years. It lost three service managers during that time, and none of the mechanics other than Wil had more than three years with Foreign.

Ned Thomas, Foreign's current service manager, was a young mechanic with a two-year associate degree in auto repair. In addition, Ned minored in business management at college. Although Ralph felt Ned was well qualified to handle the service manager's job, problems continued in the service department.

The Issue

Ned stormed into Ralph's office late last week and told Ralph that he had to get rid of Wil. While Wil was an outstanding mechanic, the other mechanics would not work with Wil. "Wil is trying to show us up," said one young mechanic. "I've been here only two months, but I can see it already. He comes in at 7:00 A.M. and works 'til 6:00 at night, or later. That stuff can be done the next day."

"He won't even eat lunch with the rest of us guys," said the air-conditioning mechanic. "He eats while he works. Granted, a lot of people ask for Wil because he's been here so long, but if he would not tinker on a job, he would get through. The other day he was fixing a door lock and he said it just didn't sound right when he got it back together, so he took the whole thing apart again. Hell, it worked and that's what matters."

"This is creating a problem, Ralph," said Ned. "Let me cite a few other instances."

"One day about two weeks ago a lady came in to get new wiper blades. She walked into the service area and was greeted by a big hello from Wil. You've got to admit, Wil's mighty friendly. To make a long story short, Wil left his job and put the wiper blades on for her. We've got people to do those small tasks. It was okay for him to retorque her engine after the head replacement, but why this nonsense? We've got a minimum charge for labor and he put those blades on for just the cost of the parts. We'll go bankrupt this way."

"You'll probably remember last Friday night when we all were going to leave exactly on time to go to the ball game—well, Wil was still working on this car he promised to have done. He had all the major work done by 4:45. Instead of quitting, he started tinkering with the seat belt adjustment. The customer told Wil that he would be very happy to bring the car in some other more convenient time—but, no, Wil had to fool around with that, too. You know, I don't leave until all the mechanics are gone, but I just couldn't stay and I decided to leave about ten after five. I don't know how long he kept the cashier there, on top of which he had me blocked in the parking lot with his car. Boy, I burned rubber when I got out of there!"

"What concerns me most right now, Ralph, is that I overheard some of the guys planning to place one of Wil's wrenches in the cowl behind the fan. You know what that will do."

"I guess this problem is just getting too big for me to handle. I'd fire him immediately, but I learned in business school not to overstep my authority, so I'm coming to you to ask you to do it."

Ralph's train of thought suddenly was interrupted by the pile of mail on his desk. He had been so involved in his thoughts about his service department he failed to look through the day's mail. Only bills, he thought, until he came to a post card—a glossy color print of Vancouver—addressed to—Wil! Curiosity forced him to read the card—"We're having a lovely trip—no car trouble thanks to your wonderful service, time and effort on our car. We'll always be your loyal customers."

Ralph turned back to his thoughts. He really didn't know what to do. Should he say something to Wil tomorrow during their fishing trip?

Problems

1. What motivates Fred?
2. What motivates Wil?
3. As a manager, how would you attempt to modify the behavior of Wil (or would you)? What theoretical framework would guide you in the effort?

Case for Part Two

Chris Logan, City Engineer

For ten months Christopher Logan had been the acting city engineer–public works director of Culligan City, Florida. He had had the title of assistant city engineer–public works director during the first five years with the city, but no one had the title now. Before coming to the City, he had been for twelve years an engineer with the Florida State Department of Transportation. He had substituted "years of experience in a responsible position" for an engineering degree to become eligible to take the state exam, and six years ago he became a registered engineer.

Chris had memberships in both the American Society of Civil Engineers (ASCE) and the Florida Engineering Society (FES). As his wife was president of the FES Auxiliary, he attended most of the monthly meetings and occasionally went to some of the ASCE meetings as well.

The City Engineering–Public Works Department office was located in the city hall. Among the 39 subordinates who reported to Chris there were two or three secretaries and four graduate engineers. These engineers had all passed the first part of the state professional registration examination but still needed to accumulate four years of experience before taking the second half.

Some engineering turnover occurred. Last year one man went to Saudi Arabia. Chris Logan had helped write civil service examination questions when the position was filled again. The Personnel Department advertised the opening in professional journals and the local newspapers. The new staff engineer had been selected by the department from among those who had made the five highest scores on the examination.

Now Chris Logan was being interviewed by a college professor looking for classroom material. He responded to the question, "What do you do?" by saying,

I am an engineer for Culligan City—because it is my profession. I am an engineer even though I use my engineering background and training in the administration of an engineering department.

Departmental Activities

In response to the question, "What kinds of activities occur in your department," Logan replied,

This department is responsible for the design and construction of public work type projects which include roads, storm drainage systems, sewers, water systems, and recently added is the gas system. We also design and construct recreation projects such as tennis courts and related parking areas. We perform large maintenance projects on city buildings such as roofs. We have a plumbing system replacement over in the city jail going on at the present time. We also control, at least I have to check and make sure that our consulting engineers who are doing the major sanitary treatment sewage plants, are performing as required. So they are technically under my control.

This was a different group of people from Logan's 39 subordinates. These consulting engineers were hired by the city to do specific things—in this particular case to design roughly $20 million worth of sewage treatment plants.

Discussing the department generally, Logan continued.

We actually perform the surveying required for our projects, then do the design and drafting work to draw up the plans; and our engineers prepare the specifications for the projects. We advertise and let the bid on the construction projects—$3½ million last year—and then we inspect and lay out the construction projects—a survey layout sort of thing. We inspect and also, to some extent, test the materials used in the projects, and, of course, supervise payments to the contractor.

At the same time, another of our responsibilities is to respond to citizen complaints. This department is very heavily involved in annexations of additional property to the city. As city engineer, I act in the capacity of an advisor to the city manager and the city commission on any engineering related matter. I am required to attend all commission meetings and, of course, all related functions that go with that. I also act as advisor in an engineering context for all other city departments that require engineering, which is a very broad term. The Parks and Recreation Department, for example, requires plans and estimates on its park properties which are extensive. They occasionally require vertical elevations, horizontal alignment, and so on for their various projects such as ball parks. We also assist them in making estimates for budgeting.

The Traffic Engineering Department looks to us to construct sidewalks, to revise intersections, to perform surveying work perhaps related to alignment of streets. Although the Traffic Engineering Department is responsible for intersections, we design and build the intersections in this department. They design the traffic aspects of the intersection.

For example, they might say, "We need an intersection with 12-foot lanes, with 25- or 50-foot radius. We need to have a storage area at least 500 feet long. Now you build it." We take their needs and design the drainage, the payment type and thickness, and so on. And we actually make it fit the property that we have to build on. They are looking at the project as if they were up in an airplane and looking down on it, and saying how the traffic is going to move and what widths and lanes are required, and so on. And we take that and translate it into something on the ground. It's a cooperative effort you might say. It absolutely is. We work very closely together.

"Do you get along well with the Traffic Department?"

"Yes, as a matter of fact, we get along good with all the departments."

"Do you deal more with Traffic than you do with any other department?"

There are several others which I did not mention. The Utilities Department is responsible for the water and sewage systems billing, minor maintenance of the water system, and control of the sewage treatment plants. They actually run them, in other words. Now, they look at us to build related facilities. For example, I am doing some gas repair work at the present time. They also control the gas system. They would look to us for performing the construction work related to new systems and additions to the present system. In major maintenance work such as replacement of an entire system and related work, we would serve as their engineer. They would say, "O.K., we would like to move a line from here to here. Here's what we would like to do. You do it." We would supervise the construction. I must say that that's in a period of transition right now, because we have just "inherited," so to speak, the gas construction and actually have not performed any of this type of work.

Although Logan was describing the relationship with other departments, the crew that actually did the construction work was that of an outside contractor. Any project over $5,000 had to be advertised and usually resulted in hiring outside contractors to do the work. The city crews were not designed for construction. They were primarily responsible for maintenance of existing systems. Major new construction and major maintenance was done by outside contractors.

   Asked if the city was ever criticized for being in competition with private industry, Logan responded,

We have been on occasion. But it is our system and it is our construction and we can build it if we want to. In competition with private industry means that we would be competing with them for money, which we are not. We are not going out, for example, and bidding against them on other jobs. That would be competition. We have work that has to be done. It can either be done by the city forces or we can hire someone else to do it. But it is our system, and we can build it if we want to. And I don't really feel that it is in competition with private industry.

That's like saying in your home, you want a door put on your cabinet. You have two options: you can put the door on your cabinet or you can go out and hire a carpenter to put it on. You certainly are within your rights to put your cabinet door on, and you are not in competition with private industry. You are simply doing something that needs to be done in your own facility. You might decide that it would take you forty hours, and it might take someone else two hours who had the proper equipment. If you consider your time valuable, it would cost less to hire someone outside to do it. And we use that philosophy a lot. There are many times when it would take our crews and tie them up from maintenance and keep them from doing the things that they need to do, so we simply contract for it.

Intergroup Relations

Logan discussed his view of departmental conflict:

One thing that can cause conflict between departments is having different goals. What might be very important to me might be nothing for someone else. For example, we had a preconstruction conference this morning for plumbing fixtures for the jail. Now that was probably one of the most important things to the jail system and police system that you can imagine—not having a commode in one of the jail cells. Very important to them. It is insignificant to us in our $3½ million construction program. You are talking about $10,000 worth of fixtures. It is totally insignificant to us, and I'm sure that on occasion they have been upset with us because we haven't given this the attention that they think it deserves. So, we are serving the Police Department in that we are providing engineering for their facilities, and we are doing it at our convenience not theirs. There is a possibility for conflict if your goals and objectives are different and/or if something is more important to you than it is to another department. *"How does one go about resolving those issues? I'm sure it must happen occasionally."*
That's one thing I think the administration does or tries to do. For example, if a department director is unhappy with the status of one of his projects, he can always go to the assistant city manager whom he is assigned to and say, "This guy is just not doing me right. I need all of us to sit down and talk about it, because what is important to me is not important to him. And it's not getting done the way I think it should be." I've done that before. We have said, "O.K., we realize that this is most important to your department, but we have five departments that we are working for—in addition to our own systems that we are trying to improve and maintain."

Construction projects in drainage, for example, were strictly the responsibility of Logan's department. In this particular case he was talking about major streams from five or six major basins in the city. Each of these basins ultimately connected into a stream which flowed into the bay or gulf. The maintenance of those streams and development of the pipes and bridges crossing them was his responsibility. So in addition to working for the other departments and the administration, he also had areas of his own responsibility. He said he would like to think that those responsibilities were at least equal with the other departments' if not ahead of them.

We have sat down with directors before and said, "Look, we have 87 projects to accomplish this year, and you have one that you have just come up with that you want done right now. We have your other projects scheduled at various times during the year along with all the other projects. If you want to bump one of your projects—either completely out or change the schedule on your projects—then we'll try to work this one in. But we are not going to continue to do all of your projects and take someone else's project and throw it aside in order to shove in a different one for you." We have had to tell them this in no uncertain terms, because in any organization you have aggressive people and nonaggressive people. The nonaggressive ones will say,"Here's my list and do the best you can," and the aggressive ones will say, "Here's my list, I'll be back next week and give you an additional list. I'll be back after that with another list, and I want you to do my stuff and let everyone else's go," which of course we cannot do. It's human nature. The squeaking wheel strategy sometimes works. At the beginning of this year we set a program trying to allocate space as best we could to each department.

"When you set it up, did you go to each and ask for their priorities?"
Yes, then we made our own priority list based on what their priorities were. The unfortunate thing is that priorities change. Even during the year.

"What is your connection and relationship with the Building Department?"
There's no actual connection except that sometimes we advise them. Yet we have similar activities. For example, when the sanitary sewer line is on private property, it is inspected by the Building Department. We pick it up at the point it leaves private property and comes onto public property. It is our responsibility to oversee, inspect, and so on the construction that occurs within the public right-of-way.

"And so you would do the same kind of building inspection for sewage and whatever on public property that Building does on private property?"
Yes.

"It is fairly clear, but isn't there a chance of disagreement as to where one department's authority stops and the other one's picks up?"
We work very closely and get along very well with all of the public directors. We assist them and they assist us. For example, Building is going to inspect our plumbing project at the jail on which we opened bids and had a preconstruction conference about this, this morning. As an assistance to us they are going to actually inspect that for us because we are not plumbing fixture inspectors. It can go both ways. If they feel, after looking at something that has been designed by an engineer or an architect, that they need engineering assistance to determine if it is structurally adequate, such help is provided by us. Not long ago a swimming pool was to be built in the Ocean Park Estates subdivision very near the sea wall. The asked us to review the plans and approve it for construction because it might cause structural failure in the sea wall. As it turned out, there were problems. We made the suggestions for corrections. The corrections were made and approved by us. We inspected it and they proceeded with the pool construction. So it's a related and interconnected operation.

While we do not have a direct connection with the Building Department, we do have an association with them. The Building Department controls the Certificates of Occupancy of buildings. If we are having problems with the public works system related to any structure, we can request Building to hold Certificate of Occupancy, and they will do so. Again, this is just a cooperative effort. We are trying to accomplish an excellent public works system for the city, and all the other departments work with us to try to do this.

"Are you saying that one way they do this on an unofficial basis is when you ask them to hold up on the occupancy of the building? They have a little more muscle than you do so they can help you get done what you need done?"

That's right. It isn't written anywhere, so it is not necessarily an official procedure. It's just a thing we use in order to accomplish the things that we have to do.

"The Building Department, because of such opportunities as this, is more of an enforcement agency than you are?"

Yes. The occupancy itself is really the important goal of the developer. Without that he really has nothing. If he cannot occupy his building, he does not have anything, because to have an empty building is nothing but a liability.

"My guess is that once they are in that building, the chance of getting them to do something after that is nearly impossible."

Yes. Experience has shown that once they occupy the building, then they no longer are responsive to anything unless they just happen to feel like they want to do it. And we have not been able to force them out. Taking it to court is just a time-consuming waste of effort.

"You probably have something to do with the legal department, too."

We work closely with the legal department because of several things. (1) The property acquisitions are handled through this department. We have a registered real estate broker who acts as our right-of-way agent and is a part of this department. He acquires right-of-ways and property, and he also acquires all of the park property, for example. If a fire station needs property to build an addition, he acquires the land. We then assist the fire department by drawing up the basic area needs. They use that information to go to an architect and say "O.K., this is what we are thinking about, now can you give us a price for the design work based on what we have done?" But you see, we have already done a great deal of design work before they ever get to the architect.

"And then once the architect is through, you put it out on bids. The contractor then constructs the building which meets the Building Department's inspection regulations."

Right, and they are inspected just like private facilities.

"And when they are through, to whom does the building belong?"

The building then belongs to the Fire Department. The Building and Maintenance Department of the city, which is a part of Central Services, will do the maintenance. They take care of it after we have done our job.

"How do you spend your time?"

That's very difficult to say. It varies, of course, depending upon the workload we have. I would say that probably 95 percent of my own time is spent in administration and five percent in engineering. There are times when special projects come along that require more attention than that, but primarily I am an administrative officer. Some days, for example, I spend all of my time with customers. I spend a lot of time with budgeting functions—who has money to do what? This morning I have been on the phone twice regarding budgeting. In the preconstruction conference, for example, it came up (and I conduct all the preconstruction conferences myself) that some additional work may be needed to be done. The building and maintenance supervisor was there, and he said he had been having problems. "In addition to installing the gold plated johnnies there (they are stainless steel and are located in the security cells), I have been having trouble with valves and I would like to get them replaced at the same time." This was not a part of the contract, and I did not know if we had money available. I called someone in Budgeting to see how much money we actually had. As it turned out we did have money, so we ordered the valves.

How do I spend my time? A large portion of time I spend going through my paperwork, handling mail, and trying to perform jobs requested by other departments. It is not uncommon for me to write five to ten letters a day, sometimes more and sometimes less, but an average of ten; I receive approximately 20 to 50 telephone calls a day. Of course I receive mail each morning that has to be reviewed and information either dispersed to other persons for work or I have to sit and assign the duties myself. At the present time I do not have an assistant, so consequently most of the work that I would delegate to an assistant I must do part of it myself. I normally work from 8:30 until 6:00 at night, and occasionally I take work home. But that's a workaholic problem that I have to deal with.

Right now I am preparing for two court appearances next week representing the city in a condemnation suit, and we are now finishing the acquisition of some property. It is very important that I prepare the maps, which are being done under my direction, and I must make sure that we have all the information. It could make a difference of some $200,000. It is very important that I be prepared for that even if I must let some of the other paperwork go.

The second court case that I have to attend to next week is related to some drainage problems. The drainage structure was constructed by the developer, and it has caused damage to a downstream property owner. The downstream property owner is suing the developer, who is at the same time bringing the city in as a party to the suit. I must go in defense of the city's position. Those are some of the things I am doing right now. I have also just finished the budgeting process trying to outline capital improvements for next year's projects. Some $2½ million worth of just plain drainage and construction projects. We also required each department director to come up with the various projects they need done around the city.

"Do you put some sort of priority on these cases?"

Not at this point. It is a question of "here are the things that need to be done, and here is how much they cost." Later on in the budget hearings they will be prioritized. We will decide which ones are the most important. There is rarely enough money to do everything that we would like to. At this time raising taxes is strictly not very popular.

"How much time do you figure you spend with your own department people as opposed to outside?"

I don't spend nearly as much as I would like to with the internal organization. Day-to-day, face-to-face contact probably takes up ten percent of my time.

"Now take the other ninety percent and divide it—if you can—with the state, county people, other department heads, the public, etc."

O.K., another ten to fifteen percent for outside contact. Much of that is spent with persons in the administration. I've been working very closely with the assistant city managers, for example, working on a sewer agreement for one small neighboring town. I've done two or three things related to that this morning. So, much of my outside contact is really with other persons in the city. Very little of it is with property owners, etc. A small percentage is spent with the outside. The other 75 percent I'm here at my desk working, trying to respond to letters, make sure that my projects are going correctly, doing administrative sort of work related to my budget, responding to complaints, handling directions from administration, planning the work that has to be done, and actually seeing that it is done.

"Out of the departments in the city, which ones do you spend the most time with?"

Probably Parks and Recreation and Traffic Engineering.

"And as a final question to this interview, what is your biggest problem?"

If it were two years ago I would have a different answer than I do now. Functioning in an acting position for ten months as I have, one of my biggest problems is making sure that the work all gets done—because we do have an extremely large number of assignments for an Engineering Department. We are expected to do many many things related to all of the activities in the city and must see that they all get done. This is one of the biggest problems. Two years ago I would have said that our biggest problem was trying to get our programs approved and get funding for everything that we wanted to do. That is not as big a problem now. The budgeting process has changed for one thing, and we do seem to get our projects funded. We do have a good direction also in the sense that our master drainage plan is finished. So on the whole, I'm fairly optimistic that this department is now and can continue accomplishing its mission and goals.

With a pleasant expression, Logan stood up, shook hands with the professor, and left the office for a late lunch.

Source: This case was written by Dorothy Harlow and Ellen Kimmel, University of South Florida, Tampa.

Problems

1. What kind of personality does Chris have? Does it help or hinder his job performance?
2. Suppose the job remains essentially the same. What kind of a person would you suggest be hired as his assistant?
3. Is Chris a professional's professional? Is this an asset or liability?
4. Does operating in the public sector bother Chris? How do you account for his ability to operate?
5. Do you think Chris is a good manager? Why or why not?

Part 3   Planning the Organization Resources

3

As the model indicates, you have arrived at the point where we can discuss the planning of the organization's resources. The practice of managerial skills—planning objectives, strategies, policies, and procedures and decision making—is part of what managers do each day. They use their interpersonal skills and knowledge of people in this activity.

Planning takes time and effort. But effective planning and good decision making are the cornerstones of the successful manager and firm.

Chapter 7 Planning Objectives

Learning Objectives

1. Know what the planning process involves.
2. Avoid problems that will prevent you from setting realistic, measurable, attainable objectives.
3. Understand the basic principles of management by objectives (MBO).
4. Decide what kind of manager you will be in terms of ethics—profit oriented or socially conscious.

Chapter Outline

A Model of the Planning Process
Participation in Planning
Why Planning?
Planning Leads to Organizational Success
Planning Benefits Employees
Planning Helps a Manager Cope with Change
Planning Is Necessary for Effective Performance of Management Functions
Why Managers Do Not Plan
Is Planning Everything?
Determining Objectives
What Are the Objectives of Businesses?
Objectives Are Multiple
How Are Objectives Determined?
Management by Objectives
What Is MBO?
Starting an MBO Program

Establishing Measurable Objectives
Negotiating Objectives
Reinforcement of MBO
Evaluation and Reward
Why Does MBO Work and What Benefits Does It Provide?
Problems with MBO
Ethical Behavior of Executives
Recent Examples of Unethical Business Behavior
Are All Managers Unethical?
What Can Be Done to Improve Ethical Behavior?
Social Responsibility as a Business Objective
The Profit Ethic
The Social Responsibility Ethic
Planning and Evolution of Social Responsibility Programs
Summary
Questions
Case: MBO: A Failure?

A Model of the Planning Process

With this chapter we begin a three chapter sequence on planning and decision making. Chapter 7 introduces the topic and discusses the first phase of planning: setting objectives. Chapter 8 discusses the other phases of planning. Chapter 9 covers the processes involved in decision making. We discuss planning as the first management function because although the management functions are all interrelated, planning acts as a stimulus on the others.

Planning is a set of managerial activities designed to prepare the enterprise for the future and ensure that decisions regarding the use of people and resources (the means) help achieve enterprise objectives (the ends).

The set of managerial activities that comprise planning can be modeled as shown in Figure 7.1. All these phases in the planning process are interrelated. The first three are discussed separately in this text so that they can be explained more clearly. Feedback comes from the control system described in Chapter 18 or from communication and management information systems described in Chapter 17.

Figure 7.1
A Model of the Planning Process

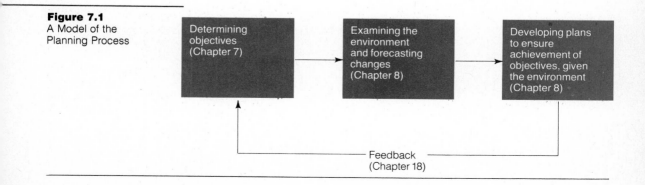

In an entrepreneurial firm and most small and medium-sized firms (whether corporate or family businesses), the top manager is responsible for planning. In all enterprises, objectives are the responsibility of top management. So, too, is examining the environment, although corporate staff and middle managers may assist in this task. The development of detailed plans—specific policies, procedures, and rules, for example—is done by corporate staff and middle and supervisory managers. Management responsibilities for the various planning phases are outlined in Figure 7.2 as a form of summary.

Participation in Planning

Whatever the level at which they are involved in planning, managers differ in the amount of participation they seek from immediate subordinates. The *traditional* manager believes that the manager is not only responsible for the management functions but also uniquely qualified by training and experience to do the best planning. So this manager does the planning alone and then communicates the plans to employees. Like the traditional manager, the *consultative* manager believes that the manager is responsible for the management functions. Yet the consultative manager also believes

Figure 7.2
Planning Responsibilities by Level of Manager

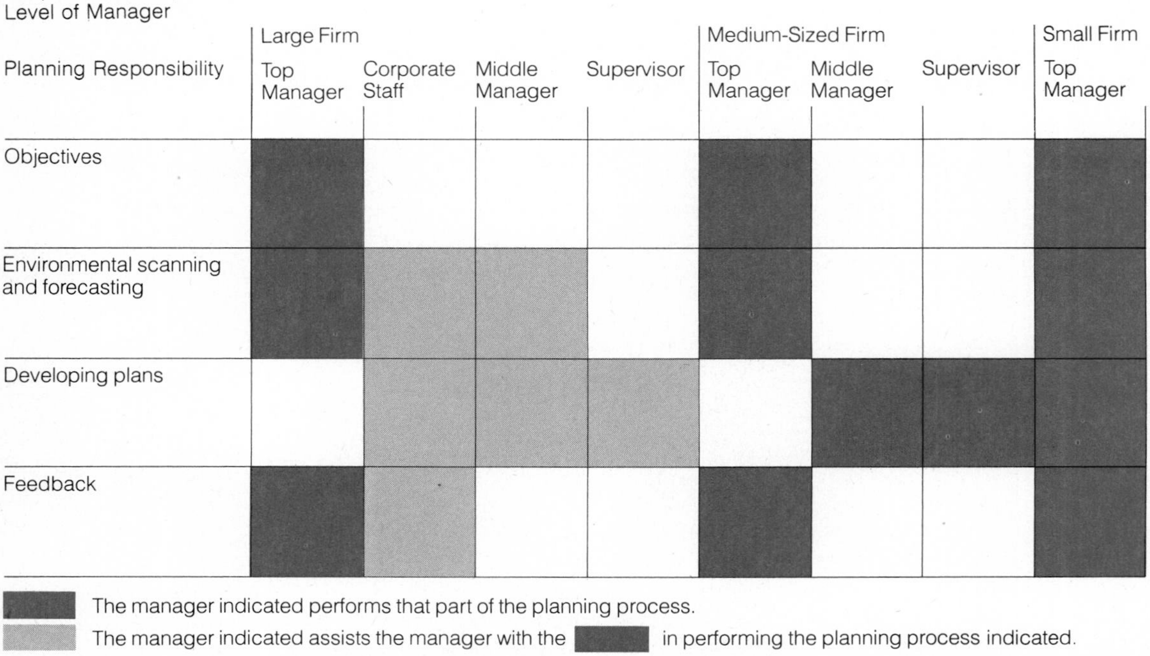

Planning Responsibility	Large Firm				Medium-Sized Firm			Small Firm
	Top Manager	Corporate Staff	Middle Manager	Supervisor	Top Manager	Middle Manager	Supervisor	Top Manager
Objectives	Performs				Performs			Performs
Environmental scanning and forecasting	Performs	Assists	Assists		Performs			Performs
Developing plans		Assists	Assists	Assists		Performs	Performs	Performs
Feedback	Performs	Assists			Performs			Performs

■ (Performs) The manager indicated performs that part of the planning process.
▨ (Assists) The manager indicated assists the manager with the ■ in performing the planning process indicated.

that although he or she is well qualified by training and experience, the employees have something to contribute. So this manager discusses planning needs and asks for employee suggestions before developing the plans. The *participative* manager believes that the work group is responsible for performance of the managerial functions. Therefore planning and the other managerial tasks are performed by the work group. The manager's role is that of coordinator.

Which planning approach is appropriate for a manager depends on several factors, including the manager's attitude toward subordinates, the qualifications of the manager and the employees, and time constraints. *Managerial attitudes* toward people (as discussed in Chapter 5) are important. Managers with Theory X attitudes tend to be traditional regarding participation, for example. It is also essential to consider the *qualifications of the employees and the manager.* If the employees are highly trained and experienced, as much or more so than the manager, the participative model makes more sense. And finally, *time pressures* can inhibit participative or consultative approaches.

The approaches to participative management are used in setting objectives, planning and policy making, and decision making. Later in the chapter, the best-known approach used by consultative managers, management by objectives, will be discussed in significant detail.

Why Planning?

Managers plan for four reasons:

- Planning leads to organizational success.
- Planning leads to feelings of success and satisfaction by employees.
- Planning helps a manager cope with change.
- Planning is necessary for effective performance of the other management functions.

Planning Leads to Organizational Success

Planning does not guarantee success. But studies have shown that companies that plan consistently outperform nonplanners. Before citing these studies, however, let me make a commonsense argument for planning with two sample situations.

- If two football teams of equal ability are going to meet two weeks hence, which do you think will have the best chance of winning: Team 1, which has scouted the other team, trains its players on Team 2's strengths and weaknesses, and prepares plans to exploit its weaknesses and isolate its strengths; or Team 2, which ignores its opponents?

Source: Reprinted by permission of Newspaper Enterprise Association.

- Two salespeople are competing for an order. One studies the client's organization and determines its needs and how the purchasing agent operates. The other comes to the enterprise with a standard pitch. Assuming that their products are about equal in value, who gets the order?

I am making this argument at length because managers tend to put off planning or never do it at all. Yet the results of not planning can be as unsatisfactory for managers and their organizations as for the Eskimos shown building their igloo in the Thaves cartoon. The two studies cited in Table 7.1 underline the importance of planning in organizational success. These and other studies indicate that, other things being equal, planning pays off in terms of greater success. But not only is the company's success greater; the manager's ability to *predict* is better. This helps the manager deal effectively and so find favor with bankers and security analysts. And this, in turn, helps the enterprise get the resources it needs.

Planning Benefits Employees

Not only employers gain from planning; so do employees. Comprehensive planning systems lead to definition of objectives. Knowing the objectives of the enterprise helps employees relate what they are doing to meaningful outcomes (ends). The planning process requires managers to define the enterprise's objectives. If employees are involved in this process, they can more effectively tie what they are doing (the means) to the firm's objectives (the ends). Employees who know what is expected of them feel successful and find their work meaningful when they achieve well-defined objectives. Success of this sort usually increases job satisfaction and the employee's interest in the success of the organization. In fact there is good evidence that the greater the extent to which employees identify with work (as described in Chapter 5) and are involved in planning, the greater their feelings of success and satisfaction when objectives are achieved.

Table 7.1
Two Studies Which
Found That Strategic
Management Leads to
Organizational
Effectiveness

Karger and Malik Study

Delmar Karger and Zafar Malik studied 273 firms in the chemical and drugs, electronics, and machinery industries. All were $50 to $500 million corporations. Those practicing planning were contrasted with those who were not. (That is to say, the firms which emphasized planning were contrasted with those which did not.) In the machinery and electronics industries, those firms which planned had much higher profits and sales than those which did not. Results for the drug and chemical group were also more positive for the planners.

Thune and House Study

Stanley Thune and Robert House studied eighteen matched pairs of medium-size to large companies in the petroleum, food, drug, steel, chemical, and machinery industries. The firms in each pair were about the same in size and growth rate. Initially, none of the firms used planning. One firm in each pair introduced it during the study. The researchers observed the pairs before the introduction of planning and for seven years thereafter. They found that the firms which introduced and used planning significantly outperformed their own past results and those of the others on most measures of success such as return on equity, earnings-per-share growth, and return on investments. On no measure of success did the planners underperform the nonplanners.

Sources: Delmar Karger and Zafar Malik, "Long Range Planning and Organizational Performance," *Long Range Planning* 8 (December 1975): 60–64; Zafar Malik and Delmar Karger, "Does Long Range Planning Improve Company Performance?" *Management Review* 8 (September 1975): 27–31; and Stanley Thune and Robert House, "Where Long Range Planning Pays Off," *Business Horizons* 13 (August 1970): 81–87.

**Planning Helps
a Manager Cope
with Change**

No doubt you have run across lots of articles about how fast the world is changing and how the speed of the changes is accelerating. There is change in all sectors. Consider technological change. We hear about chemical, physical, and material changes occurring every day. The economy changes too: A full business cycle ran its course between 1972 and 1976. Governments fall and government policies change. As firms get larger, the amount of money it takes to enter a business increases. Longer lead times are necessary to make decisions. Social norms and attitudes also change. Consider how the attitudes toward large and small cars and toward cigarettes have changed over the past ten years. Finally, competitive structures change. Each year about 15 percent of all businesses fail. The number and types of competitors change. An example is computer manufacturing: In 1972 this industry included firms like General Electric, RCA, and Xerox. By 1976 these companies had left the industry. Only two of the computer firms presently in existence may be left by 1983.

Enterprises, like civilizations, rise, stabilize, decline, and disappear. So managers have to cope with a changing environment. This is done best through planning. The manager who is able through planning to anticipate and prepare for some of the numerous possible changes in the business world has more control than the manager who does not look and plan ahead.

Planning Is Necessary for Effective Performance of Management Functions

Without planning, organization and control—two other vital management functions—cannot be effective. Chapters 10 and 11 will show that organization depends for effectiveness on a number of factors, including the strategy the firm chooses to follow. Strategy (a type of plan) determines organizational structure.

Control involves holding employees accountable for resources and evaluating whether they have used them well or poorly so that rewards can be distributed accordingly. How can we evaluate employees' effectiveness if we do not tell them what they are expected to accomplish with the resources they control? Designing standards for evaluation is in fact setting objectives (part of the planning process). Without well-defined objectives, evaualation will be too subjective. (A superior can always find some reason to criticize a subordinate.) Effective planning enables managers to design good control and evaluation systems for their enterprises.

Why Managers Do Not Plan

Human beings are the only creatures we know that can understand that there is a future and anticipate it. Yet many managers with the skills and foresight needed for planning resist such activity. There are a number of reasons for this ironic situation.

- Managers have a lot to do. Planning is only one of several activities competing for the manager's attention.
- Managers prefer to act on immediate problems because they generate immediate feedback. If a customer makes a rush order and the manager helps out, the customer's thanks are given *now*. Planning deals with future events, and the rewards (if any) are deferred into the future. Most of us prefer to take our rewards now rather than later.
- Planning, good planning, is hard work.
- Plans can be used to measure results (control). Sometimes managers do not want anyone else to know that their plans were poorly thought out or could not be accomplished.
- Planning often involves thinking, paperwork, and time alone—activities most managers do not like or have precious little of. Managers tend to prefer to be doers, not thinkers.

Planning takes time and effort. It is best done as a separate activity when few interruptions are likely to occur. This is another reason managers do not like to perform planning activities. Effective managers find hideaways and private moments in which to do their planning. Otherwise they become fire fighters, spending all their time putting out fires instead of preventing them.

Planning and nonplanning are actually two different managerial philosophies. Nonplanners blame the things that are always happening to them on bad luck. They are a bit like the student who does not make out a course schedule and then finds out that the accounting course meets at the same time as the computer programming course.

I once worked for a food business that did not do much planning. When the salespeople wanted to spend time planning, they were berated for wasting time in the office instead of calling on customers. But which customers? Which products should get the most attention? Which new accounts should be accepted? No one knew, and the sales staff went through a series of crises because the wrong orders were taken, customers did not get the right amount of the right product at the right time, and so forth. After planning was initiated, the salespeople's work life settled down and goals were met.

Is Planning Everything?

Planning does not automatically lead to success. As I hope is clear by now, lots of factors contribute to success. One is having enough resources; another is luck. Planning *contributes* to the success of an enterprise. But planning alone is not sufficient to ensure success.

Moreover, planning is more important to some enterprises than others. Three principles can be applied in determining where planning is most essential:

1. The larger the enterprise, the more significantly planning contributes to its effectiveness.
2. The more volatile the enterprise's environment, the more significantly planning contributes to its effectiveness.
3. The more complex the enterprise's product or service line, the more significantly planning contributes to its effectiveness.

In sum, where problems are greatest, planning pays off the most. It is conceivable that an energetic entrepreneur running a small, single-product-line business in a slowly changing industry can be effective with a minimum of planning. Thus the Ace Washboard Company, employing fifty people and making a product that has hardly changed in forty years, can be successful without much planning. General Electric has to plan.

Sometimes, however, no planning is better than bad planning. Bad planning can consist of preparing too many policies and standardizing the planning process; this leads to inflexibility and wastes time and money. But since most managers do not spend much time planning, few enterprises involve themselves in this kind of planning.

In sum, planning usually contributes to managerial success, though it is not a guarantee of success.

Determining Objectives

Objectives are those ends which the organization seeks to achieve by its existence and operations.

They are also constraints on actions by the firm. For example, if a firm's objectives include minimum market share of 20 percent for each product group and if the firm wishes to grow by acquisition, it is limited to acquiring other firms whose market share is more than 20 percent. Effective objectives are:

- *Measurable* Rather than vague statements, they are operational and specific.
- *Attainable* They are high enough to be challenging but not so high that employees give up.
- *Consistent with the firm's resources* They are reasonable, given the wherewithal of the enterprise. (American Motors in 1980 does not set objectives which would require General Motors' resources.)

Objectives are the beginning point of planning. We set objectives for the same reasons we plan. And we set objectives so that planning can take place effectively. Planning will take place whether objectives are well formulated or not. But it will be much less valuable without well-thought-out objectives.

What Are the Objectives of Businesses?

Many of the most common objectives of business have been discussed. Table 7.2 shows how business executives surveyed in two studies ranked twenty-three potential objectives in importance.

Let's briefly summarize the findings of James Dent and George England shown in Table 7.2. As you will note, the executives surveyed did not rank many potential objectives at all. Profit is the leading objective, but *not the only one*. Service in the form of good products or services and employee welfare was also emphasized.

Dent found that large businesses stressed public service more than small businesses. The executives of unionized firms stressed employee welfare more than those in nonunionized firms. Also, if the firms had more white-collar than blue-collar workers, their executives were less profit oriented than those in firms with more blue-collar than white-collar workers. Finally, Dent's study revealed that more successful firms focused *outward* to stress meeting the competition and producing good products. Less successful firms focused on *internal* efficiency.

England did not find the differences in ranking of objectives based on organizational differences that Dent found. His differences were explained as individual managerial differences.

In comparing these studies we see only a few major differences, and

Table 7.2
Business Objectives

Potential Objectives	Dent Study	England Study
I. Profitability Objectives		
Maximize net profit over a short period	A	A
Maximize net profit over a long period	A	A
Maximize the dividends for the shareholders	C	—
Maximize the company's net assets and reserves	—	—
II. Marketing and Sales Objectives		
Maximize the company's rate of sales growth	B	B
Provide the best-quality products or services possible	A	—
Be a market leader, for example, first in market with new products or services	B	B
Have the most satisfied customers	—	—
Maximize the market share	—	—
III. Efficiency and Innovation Objectives		
Be the most efficient firm in the industry	C	A
Run a stable organization	B	B
Be the leading innovator in the industry	—	B
IV. Employee-Related Objectives		
Provide high rewards and benefits to the employees	A	C
Create a friendly and pleasant workplace	A	C
Have satisfied employees	A	C
Prevent unionization or further unionization	—	—
V. Social Responsibility Objectives		
Be a socially responsible company	C	C
Be of service to the community	C	C
VI. Other Objectives		
Maximize the company's prestige	—	—
Be influential in local community decisions	—	—
Provide income or jobs for owning family members	—	—
Keep government out of this business	—	—
Keep tax payments to a minimum	—	—

A = Most important third of objectives ranked.
B = Middle third of objectives ranked in importance.
C = Least important third of objectives ranked.
Sources: Based on James Dent, "Organizational Correlates of the Goals of Business Managers," *Personnel Psychology* 12 (Autumn 1959): 365–393; and George England, "Organizational Goals and Expected Behavior of American Managers," *Academy of Management Journal* 11 (June 1967): 107–111.

some of these are due to the fact that the two researchers did not provide the executives with the same list of objectives. The major differences are these: Dent's executives ranked employee welfare objectives considerably higher than the executives in the later England study. And England's executives put much more emphasis on efficiency than Dent's executives did. There appears to be remarkable consistency in the ranking of objectives, however, considering differences in time, sample, and specific objectives listed.

Objectives Are Multiple

As was just discussed and shown in Table 7.2, most firms pursue multiple objectives. There is no doubt that profitability is always a significant objective. But almost all the evidence indicates that *no sizable firm exists for more than a very short time if its only objective is profit maximization.*

Since firms have multiple objectives, management must establish a hierarchy of objectives. That means it must calculate the trade-offs at any one point in time between any two objectives—for example, profitability and employee satisfaction—and establish which is more important. The hierarchy obtained thus ranks the objectives to be achieved in the short and long runs to guide management decisions. The result, an overall balancing of objectives to achieve corporate success, is often called organizational effectiveness.

What then is organizational effectiveness or success? That is hard to define. Most writers on the subject do not give complete measures of organizational success. There is no Nobel prize (yet) for the best-managed company. So when is a company successful? *An organization is successful if it survives and if it meets its objectives.* The gut measure of success is survival. If you fold, no one will call you successful. No one rushed to declare Shah Reza Pahlavi a success in 1979; similarly, few would call Studebaker Motors a success, and the same applies to many other long-forgotten enterprises. Survival is easy to determine. It is more difficult to discover whether a firm has been successful in meeting its objectives, however. There may be many organizational objectives. The relevant variables may be numerous as well. And the criteria used in such an evaluation may be subject to individual preference or interpretation.

Source: Drawing by Ross; © 1976 The New Yorker Magazine, Inc.

"The choice is yours, ladies and gentlemen. Will you take the regular dividend or will you take whatever is behind that curtain?"

The success of an enterprise in meeting its objectives can be evaluated either objectively or subjectively. An objective evaluation is based on the measurement of specific criteria. For example, we can evaluate a business as successful to the degree that criteria such as return on investment or market share improve relative to past performance and/or relative to performance by similar firms. An example of this approach is the *Forbes* rating system. Each year, in its January 1 issue, *Forbes* magazine "measures management" by combining financial and marketing indexes and rating every major company both within its own industry and in comparison with industry as a whole. In the forest products industry, for example, it ranked Fort Howard Paper first and Union Camp second in 1978. It rated Southwest Forest Industries twenty-second (out of twenty-two). *Business Week* makes similar ratings each quarter, and *Fortune* rates the "Fortune 1,000" firms.

Another approach is to ask "experts" which firms are the most successful. This is a subjective approach; it is based on the opinion of these people. *Dun's Review*'s list of the five or ten best-run American companies is an example of this method.

Both objective and subjective approaches to assessing success become more difficult when more than one aspect of the business is considered. For example, taking two measures of success, efficiency and production effectiveness, we could rate four firms as shown in Figure 7.3.

However, a number of problems are involved in the measurement of success (organizational effectivess).

- *Stability of criteria* A criterion emphasized at one point in time may not be valid later on.

- *Time* Which is to be used—a short-run or long-run measurement?

- *Precision and variety of measurement* Not all measures are easy to compute, and there are different ways of computing them.

It is a lot easier to measure success when a company shows consistent results on most of the variables assessed in most years. In fact the research indicates that there is a high intercorrelation among organizational

Figure 7.3
Efficiency and
Production
Effectiveness

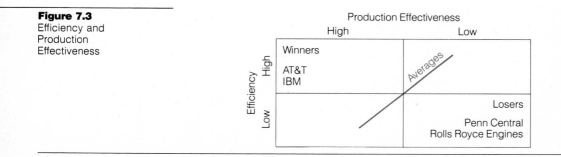

variables. If you are a "winner" on three measures, chances are you are a winner on all measures.

I would add that to me the most critical problem is the trade-off among measures. Suppose, for example, that you are measuring success on the basis of the criteria shown in Table 7.3. Admittedly, success is hard to determine, especially when you have eight measures of success and at the end of 1979 you see three up, three down, and two even. In such a case the firm is declared successful if the three measures that are up are the most important. It is easy to recognize success when most indicators are + or −, but very hard when you get results like these. In general, organizations feel that they are successful if the most important indicators are positive.

How Are Objectives Determined?

Two simple theories have been advanced to explain how objectives are determined. Traditional economists have suggested that the firm's objectives are simply the objectives of the entrepreneur or top manager. Chester Barnard believed that objectives were formed when a consensus about what the objectives were arose from the employees.[1] This is a sort of "trickle up theory."

The theory we shall discuss here is that of the traditional economists— that objectives are formulated by the top managers of the firm. These executives do not choose the objectives in a vacuum. Their choices are affected by four factors.

1. The external environment
2. The enterprise's resources
3. Internal power relationships
4. The attitudes (value systems) of the top executives

Table 7.3
Measuring Success: Percentage of Objectives Achieved

Criterion	Percentage of Objectives Achieved	
	1978	1979
Production effectiveness		
Production output	110%	105%
Market share	12	13
Efficiency		
Return on capital	6	7
Efficiency in utilization of equipment	95	90
Adaptiveness		
Rate of production innovation	50	65
Satisfaction		
Clients	80	
Employees	75	75
Development		
Training investments	90	90

Let's discuss each of these influences and then summarize how objectives are formulated.

The first factor is the external environment. Managers who wish to maximize profits may have to modify this objective because of forces in the environment such as pollution control, excess profits, antitrust, consumer labeling, and other regulations. Trade unions, another element in the environment, may require higher than market wage rates, featherbedding, fringe benefits, more holidays, and the like. Competitors may sell other products or services at unrealistically low prices and spend excessive amounts on advertising. Suppliers may become monopolized and charge outrageous prices. So the environment places limitations on the objectives firms set.

The enterprise's resources, the second factor, also affect the formulation of objectives. Larger and more profitable firms have more resources with which to respond to forces in the environment than do smaller or poorer firms.

In addition, internal power (political) relationships—the third factor—affect the firm's objectives. The direction management takes revolves around many questions of power and influence. First, how much support does management have relative to others in the organization? Does the management have the full support of the stockholders? Has management developed the support of employees and key employee groups? If so, management can set higher objectives that employees will help achieve. With support from owners who are willing to establish drastic sanctions to assure success, management can act to force employees to meet its objectives when employee support is lacking.

Objectives are also influenced by the power relationships between the strategists acting either as individuals or representatives of units within the organization. Thus, if there are differences of opinion on which objectives to seek or what trade-offs to make, the power relationships may help settle these differences. Richard Cyert and James March have theorized how this takes place.[2] They describe the firm as a coalition of interests and individuals with different needs and ways of looking at the world. They bargain with each other over objectives (among other things) using money, position, status, and power. Past experience, commitments, and policies are the base from which objectives are set.

The attitudes and preferences of the managers, the fourth factor influencing the choice of objectives, develop out of the education and experience of the managers, as described in Chapters 5 and 6. The Stevenson cartoon illustrates how a managerial attitude can influence corporate identity and advertising.

Some enterprises are strongly identified with certain attitude systems or ideologies. Such systems are essentially sets of attitudes about what is good or bad, desirable or undesirable. Firms with pronounced ideological

"I'm sick of the whole approach. Just tell the public we're cold and
aloof and we make a goddam good carburetor."

identities attract and retain managers who think along the same lines. The
corporate identity that arises thus affects the objectives set by executives.
One special aspect of executive attitudes—the application of ethical
behavior to management—will be discussed later in the chapter.

Objectives are not the result of managerial power alone. Nor do they
percolate up from the employees. Objectives result from the attempts of
managers to satisfy the needs of all groups involved with the enterprise.
These coalitions of interests (stockholders, employees, suppliers, customers, and others) have sometimes conflicting objectives. As the strongest
group in the coalition, managers try to reconcile these conflicts. Naturally
they cannot settle them once and for all. They can only "bargain" with the
various groups and try to produce a set of objectives which will satisfy all or
most of them at a given time.

Organizational objectives change as a result of:

- Increased demands from coalition groups that make up the enterprise.

- Changes in the aspiration levels of managers. On the basis of past
  achievements, managers may begin to believe the enterprise can do
  more. Or they may look at and decide to match or exceed the
  achievements of relevant competitors or other enterprises.

- A crisis in the firm or its environment. Objectives can change drastical-
  ly, for example, when a firm's market disappears or its reason for being
  ceases. When the polio vaccine was invented, the objectives of the
  National Foundation for Infantile Paralysis had to change dramatically.

Of course, objectives are not set from scratch each year. The most recent set of objectives is the reference point managers use. They consider incremental changes in light of the current environment, current demands of conflicting groups, and their own aspirations for the firm. No set of objectives can satisfy everyone. Nonetheless, with some effort managers can usually develop objectives that offer all or almost all concerned a satisfactory compromise.

Management by Objectives (MBO)

Earlier in the chapter I said that we would discuss in more detail the system the consultative manager uses to establish objectives: management by objectives (MBO). As indicated, MBO is a structured alternative to the traditional approach of having the top executive or boss set objectives.

Studies indicate that MBO is used by many firms, although not all of them use it as completely as is described here. Figure 7.4 presents a model of the MBO process. Let us examine each step of the process now.

What Is MBO?

Management by objectives (MBO), an approach which is popular today, really began to be used in the 1930s. Today it is applied to many aspects of management including control and employee evaluation. One of the most frequent applications of MBO is in setting objectives. When MBO is used, the manager must formulate *very specific, measurable* objectives for the

Figure 7.4
A Model of MBO

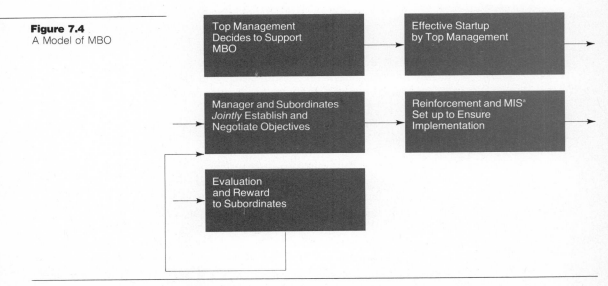

aMIS = Management Information System.

firm or work unit. In the MBO approach, which is modeled in Figure 7.4, the objectives are developed jointly by the manager and his or her superior. And it requires that information be provided about results achieved versus the original objectives.

Starting an MBO Program

Top managers must take the initiative in starting the MBO program, making it clear why they believe in it and indicating over and over that they are very interested in it.

An adequate training program in MBO is necessary for all employees. All parts of the organization must participate. This means that MBO cannot be implemented overnight.

In setting up an MBO system the following steps should be taken:

- Specify the objectives of the program.
- Name the departments and units that will participate.
- Clarify relationships between departments that are affected by MBO.
- Assign responsibility for MBO activities at each level; make sure job descriptions are clear.
- Establish time deadlines for each stage of MBO and check back to see that these are met.

Establishing Measurable Objectives

A crucial next step is to insist that *realistic, important, measurable* objectives be set at all levels of the enterprise. These objectives must meet five criteria:

1. They must be clear, concise, and unambiguous.
2. They must be achievable by the person concerned.
3. They must be interesting, motivating, and challenging.
4. They must be consistent with organizational policies, procedures, and plans.
5. They must be accurate in terms of what is actually desired by the enterprise.

The objectives should also be *team oriented;* they should not stimulate competition between employees in the same unit.

To meet these criteria a "cascade" approach is necessary. That is, before lower-level objectives can be set, clear, concise top-management objectives must be set, cascading down to long-range objectives, short-range objectives, and then unit objectives throughout the organization. Thus top management must set down a statement of organizational purpose including precise definitions of the firm's business, the strategies chosen, the organizational structure, the markets to be served, and measurable objectives (e.g., return on investment, market share, etc.). The following should also be defined:

- Profitability (specific measures)
- Markets (share of market, dollar volume, etc.)
- Productivity (outputs per employee)
- Facilities (square feet, etc.)

This process continues down to the departmental level, where objectives are specified for each unit. Specific objectives include the following:

- Sales volume (for instance, $3,000,000 total dollar revenues for 1979–1980)
- Share of market (15 percent of total dollar volume of industry sales in 5 countries)
- Market penetration (5 percent increase in the number of sales outlets carrying our product by January 1, 1981)
- Reduction in sales costs (3 percent less newspaper advertising by January 1, 1981)

The final step, then, is to set the objectives of each job in a conference between the employee and the supervisor. These objectives should be set in the following areas:

- Routine activities in key areas—for example, to limit waste to 3 percent of raw materials; to reduce the grievance rate by 5 percent.
- Creative activities—for example, to introduce a new computerized billing system by January 1, 1981, and thus reduce accounts receivable to ten days of sales on average.
- Personal development activities—for example, to learn FORTRAN by June 15, 1980; to use transcendental meditation daily in order to reduce stress by July 30, 1980.

At each level within the firm the objectives should be assigned priorities in case all cannot be accomplished. One possible weighting system is the following:

1. Critical objectives: must do
2. Necessary objectives: should do
3. Desirable objectives: need to do

Objectives that are most useful in MBO systems are measurable, relevant and important, challenging, and attainable. Thus they must be above the average level of achievement of pre-MBO days (assuming no serious changes in the environment), but not overly demanding. If the company has improved its market penetration 1 percent, 1½ percent, 2 percent, 2½ percent, and 3 percent in the past five years, 3½ percent is not challenging and 6 percent is probably unattainable. Four and one-half percent may be just right.

Negotiating Objectives

It is important for the superior to take MBO seriously. This means he or she must do the following:

- Come prepared to the meeting at which objectives are to be set and have objectives in mind.
- Put the employee at ease.
- Facilitate discussion by listening, summarizing progress at various points, minimizing criticism, and rewarding insight and self-criticism.
- List disagreements and work them out.
- Summarize in writing the objectives that have been agreed upon.

A good checklist for the objective-setting interview is presented in Table 7.4.

Table 7.4
Checklist for Objective-Setting Interview (Slusher and Sims)

Checklist 1—Before the Interview

What the Subordinate Should Do
- Develop preliminary objectives that have a clear performance standard and completion deadline.
- Provide the superior with a copy of the preliminary objectives prior to the interview.
- Prepare supporting data for each objective.
- Decide what resources and coordination will be necessary.
- List questions and problems for discussion with the superior.

What the Superior Should Do
- Decide whether each preliminary objective represents a priority need.
- Check for technical completeness of objectives. Is there a clear performance standard, completion deadline, and method of checking results?
- Judge whether performance standards are realistic (not too easy, not too difficult).
- Decide if the subordinate has sufficient authority in the objective area.
- Specify any required personnel coordination needed to achieve an objective.
- Determine if needed resources can be provided.
- Note whether foreseeable contingencies should be recognized.
- Consider the extent of personal support that the subordinate will require for improved performance.
- Examine the subordinate's other job responsibilities to see if any are being neglected.
- Determine whether additional objectives are appropriate.
- Insure that there are neither too few nor too many objectives in total.

Table 7.4
Checklist for
Objective-Setting
Interview (Slusher and
Sims)
(continued)

Checklist 2—During the Interview

What the Superior Should Do

- Select a convenient interview location and stress the meeting's importance. Be prompt and allocate sufficient time for an uninterrupted discussion.
- Begin with small talk to set the subordinate at ease; tailor the approach to the individual.
- Request that the subordinate explain each objective. Provide ample opportunity for developing insight into the objectives. Listen with interest and understanding.
- Ask questions based on prior preparation and new information. Encourage subordinate to respond and ask his [or her] own questions.
- Ask how superior can help subordinate do an even better job. Take notes on agreed support.
- Avoid placing the subordinate in a defensive position. Keep advice to a minimum. Avoid clashes over personality differences, weaknesses, and past mistakes; avoid arguments.
- Provide positive comments whenever possible. Be open about ideas. Seek self-awareness and mutual understanding. Help him [or her] gain insight into his [or her] behavior and its consequences. Concentrate on anticipated performance. Future improvement should be the focus.
- See that final objectives meet technical requirements (clear performance standard, completion deadline, and method of checking).
- Remember that setting objectives is a joint process. Compromise when possible. Be willing to change viewpoints.
- Be willing to resolve serious controversies (in the final analysis, there must be a boss).

What the Subordinate Should Do

- Present objectives vigorously.
- Be thorough and confident in discussing each objective.
- Accentuate the positive by emphasizing what should be done.
- Listen carefully to the superior's responses, both positive and negative. They are important indications of his [or her] priorities and perception of career development.
- Insist on final agreement. Do not leave questions hanging in the air. Use the opportunity to bring differences out into the open and resolve them.

Checklist 3—After the Interview

What the Subordinate Should Do

- Set up a method for regularly reviewing progress toward objectives.
- Renegotiate objectives when major changes occur.
- Let the superior know when progress is lagging.
- Let the superior know when a lack of coordination or resources requires action.

What the Superior Should Do

- Maintain a historical and current file on each subordinate's objectives.
- Develop checks and reminders for using with each subordinate to insure continuous progress.
- In a timely and informal way, let subordinates know that he [or she] is interested in week-to-week progress (however, avoid nagging).

Source: Allen Slusher and Henry Sims, "Commitment through MBO Interviews," *Business Horizons* 18 (August 1975): 5–12. Copyright, 1975, by the Foundation for the School of Business at Indiana University. Reprinted by permission.

It has been pointed out that MBO is not MBO if the supervisor sets the objectives: They must be *jointly* set. Research indicates that a large majority of employees will set higher objectives than their supervisors if given the chance.

Reinforcement of MBO

Research in MBO and behavioral science in general shows that any program works better if it is reinforced regularly. Feedback received once a year is less effective than quarterly or monthly feedback, as can be easily seen by considering the advantages of weekly grades over a single grade per term.

Reinforcement can take several forms:

- Letters from top executives thanking supervisors for carrying out the MBO program.
- Group meetings during which managers express renewed support for MBO.
- A letter from the president telling employees about MBO's great future.
- Memos from the personnel department offering refresher courses in MBO.
- Periodic performance reviews.
- Counseling sessions when objectives are behind schedule.

The Management Information System (MIS) is also used to ensure that the MBO program is adequately reinforced. This approach will be discussed in Chapter 18 as a control device.

Evaluation and Reward

The final step necessary to make MBO work is the review session in which objectives are matched against performance. Guidance on future achievements is given, and the employee is rewarded verbally and in other ways (pay, promotion, etc.) for achieving particular objectives. This is essential to employee motivation.

Why Does MBO Work and What Benefits Does It Provide?

According to Stephen Carroll and Henry Tosi, MBO works because, when it is properly implemented, the employee participates in the process and therefore accepts the company's objectives and becomes committed to achieving them.[3] Participation motivates many (but not all) employees to work for the objectives they help choose. Even instrumental employees are motivated by the process because it makes clear what is expected of them. They know what they need to do to be rewarded.

MBO also works because the communication system ensures that employees know how they are doing and what remains to be accomplished.

This can improve their performance. In addition, clearly set goals direct employees' attention to the results of their work. They also lead to higher levels of achievement by preventing arbitrary judgments of performance and improving the ability of all concerned to predict results. Many studies indicate that MBO goal-setting sessions, properly done, result in achievable goals and that motivation is positively affected when these goals are achieved: in other words, success breeds success. The employee sets the goal, reaches it, everyone knows it, and he or she is rewarded for it; this keeps the success momentum going.

What benefits does MBO provide? Table 7.5 lists the benefits along with the strength of research support for each claimed benefit.

Problems with MBO

Of course not everyone agrees that MBO is wonderful. Several studies have indicated that MBO does not always perform miracles. Some of the more typical problems that can undermine an MBO program include:

- Inadequate top management support
- Inadequate explanation of the program
- Poorly defined objectives
- Conflicting personalities

Table 7.5
Strength of Research
Support for Benefits
Claimed by MBO

MBO Benefit Claimed	Research Support for Benefit
Benefits for the Enterprise	
1. Focuses managers' efforts on right objectives.	Strongly positive
2. Improves the potential for achieving objectives such as profits.	Strongly positive
3. Provides the data to reward managers "objectively."	Strongly positive
4. Helps pinpoint human development needs.	Depends on how MBO is developed
5. Helps identify promotable managers.	Strongly positive
6. Facilitates the enterprise's ability to change.	Not tested enough
7. Helps coordinate the enterprise's efforts.	Not tested enough
Benefits for Superiors	
1. Helps the superior coach the subordinate.	Not tested enough
2. Helps eliminate vague performance appraisal tools.	Strongly positive
3. Motivates subordinates to perform better.	Strongly positive
Benefits for Employees (and Lower-Level Managers)	
1. Increases employee job satisfaction.	Mixed results
2. Clarifies what is expected of the employee.	Strongly positive
3. Provides measurable objectives that the employee is expected to achieve.	Strongly positive

- Insincere commitment by managers
- Inadequate reinforcement
- Overemphasis on paperwork

Inadequate Top Management Support

Time and again top managers see MBO as a panacea for all their problems. But although they decide to go ahead with it they delegate its operation to someone else. MBO will not work well without the participation and strong support of top management at the beginning and *regularly* during the year.

Inadequate Explanation of MBO

Some enterprises get off on the wrong foot by assuming that the employees know and understand MBO. They provide only a short, cursory explanation of it. If employees and supervisors do not understand the system and why it was introduced, it should be no surprise to learn that it does not work.

Poorly Defined Objectives

MBO works when *important, measurable* objectives are jointly agreed upon. It works less well if the objectives are too narrow or when, in an attempt to quantify every aspect of the job, the objectives chosen are short-term, unimportant, and hard to measure. Objectives may be hard to develop in very volatile environments. They are also hard to develop if the position's job description and responsibilities are vague.

Personality Conflicts

It is difficult to set up an MBO system when supervisors and subordinates have personality conflicts. MBO requires *joint* development of objectives. This is hard to do when the participants do not get along.

Insincere Commitment by Managers

For MBO to work, the superior must be committed to it. It will not work if a leader goes through the motions and, at the "joint" meeting, simply tells the subordinate his or her objectives. This turns MBO into a sham. The employee will resent it and view MBO as "playing games."

Inadequate Reinforcement of MBO

MBO works better when progress meetings are held frequently to provide feedback. Refresher training in the principles and techniques of MBO is also needed, and rewards must be tied to the achievement of objectives. What you learned about motivation in Chapter 6 and will learn about communication in Chapter 17 makes this obvious.

Overemphasis on Paperwork

A good way to kill MBO is to convert it into costly, technique-oriented paperwork. The essence of MBO is not paperwork but rather getting managers and employees together to agree on objectives. Some enterprises design lots of paperwork to provide evidence that MBO is being used—forms to be filled in (in several copies) at the beginning, after objective-setting and reinforcement meetings, at end-of-year reviews, and so forth. This increases the time necessary to operate MBO. Employees and managers will resist this "paper mill" and thus MBO itself. Paperwork must be kept to a minimum.

In sum, although implementation problems can develop, they can be avoided. Most of the findings of research on MBO are very positive. Managers would do well to use MBO to help develop objectives in particular and planning in general.

Ethical Behavior of Executives

Earlier in the chapter, I mentioned that we would discuss ethical behavior of business executives as an application of managerial philosophy and attitudes.

Ethical behavior is that set of acts which society considers right.

Fundamentally, ethics are based on the individual conscience and moral code that a person develops in the course of his or her upbringing. Societal prohibitions have some influence on an individual's code of ethics. Is ethical behavior the same as legal behavior? No. Actions can be legal but unethical; they can also be ethical but illegal. For example, campaign contributions by corporations are legal in Canada, though some Canadians may consider them unethical. Consumption of alcoholic beverages in the United States was illegal in 1923, but most citizens considered it ethical. Discrimination against Jews was legal in Germany in 1943, but unethical. So laws can be passed that violate the ethical codes of citizens, and unethical acts may not be covered by existing laws.

Most normative ethicians would argue that to be ethical a business person must obey the law. The executive who feels that a law is unethical must work to have it modified. The ethicians would also argue that an executive must avoid acts that are unethical (but not covered by any law) and must perform acts that are not required by law (but necessary from an ethical standpoint).

Sometimes it is hard to define ethical behavior. Perhaps some illustrations of unethical business practices will help.

The following cases recently reported in the news have been upsetting to those who believe that the future of our free enterprise system depends on ethical behavior:

Bribes and Kickbacks

Schlitz Brewing Company agreed to pay $750,000 in civil penalties and $110,000 in misdemeanors for violation of laws and ethics by illegal payoffs and kickbacks. Originally charged with three felonies and 743 misdemeanors, the company opted to make this settlement. The U.S. government claimed it had evidence that Schlitz paid off retail leaders such as Carson Pirie Scott & Co.'s Bar at O'Hare Airport (Chicago) to the tune of $3 million between 1967 and 1976.

Damon Corporation, the largest operator of medical laboratories, and other similar businesses were accused of paying kickbacks to physicians for use of their labs. Authorities in the state of Michigan estimate that about half of the labs in that state do likewise.

Theft and Allied Acts

Several ex-executives of the now bankrupt REA Express were indicted for conspiring through the use of false invoices, fictitious bills of lading, and dummy corporations to steal at least $1 million as the firm was going under. Instead of trying to save the corporation, they were helping destroy it.

The Interstate Commerce Commission has claimed that it can document the charge that a large number of interstate movers, with the cooperation of state employees, falsified the weights of shipments to cheat customers.

Frito Lay's chief purchasing agent was accused of making millions by ordering corn from a firm in which he was an owner (secretly).

The founder of Mattel pleaded no contest to the accusation that she falsified ten company reports from 1969 to 1974. She faces fines of up to $57,000. The purpose of the deception was apparently to create the impression of corporate growth and thus increase the price of the stock.

Falsification of Public Statements

Jim Montgomery recently reported on the trials and tribulations of being in public relations.[4] These persons are expected by some executives to lie, "stonewall," and cover up bad news from the public.

Political Bribes and Payoffs

Watergate is barely behind us. We all remember the extensive number of companies who used stockholders' funds to make donations directly to politicians or to their campaign committees.

Are All Managers Unethical?

The "robber barons" of the nineteenth century are evidence that unethical business practices are not a new issue. But are all business people unethical? The answer is no, not all business people are unethical. While some corporations have made illegal gifts to political campaigns, others have refused to do so.

Even in the same industries where some have violated the law and/or behaved unethically, others subject to the same pressures and the same governmental "recriminations" have refused to lower their standards of ethical conduct. Recent reports have shown how Ingersoll Rand carefully avoids any bribes or semblance of bribes overseas, how IBM turns down business in Latin America if it has to bribe to get it, and how Caterpillar's business is booming although it is known to be scrupulous in dealing with potential bribery situations. So although the newspaper reports are gloomy at times, remember that the emphasis on unethical business practices may only be a result of the fact that editors consider bad behavior more newsworthy than good behavior.

One example of an ethical executive is Joseph Irwin Miller, whose profile appears on page 224.

Recent studies by S. N. Brenner and E. A. Molander seem to indicate there is no decline and there may even be an increase in concern among executives that businesses act ethically.[5]

What Can Be Done to Improve Ethical Behavior?

Several approaches to improving business behavior have been suggested. There is some evidence of a general resurgence of religion as an important force in personal life, and some would encourage increased efforts by the churches to produce "religious managers." Ethics courses in business schools and executive programs would serve to reinforce this effort. This approach might help, but it might also be a long while before it showed results.

A second possible method of promoting ethical business behavior is rigorous enforcement of the laws by the SEC, the IRS, and other government agencies. Ralph Nader and Mark Green suggested that the Justice Department set up a Division of Corporate Crime to combat internal offenses and to take more vigorous antitrust action on bribery both here and abroad.[6] In addition, they insist, bigger fines and jail sentences for offending executives are necessary to prevent illegal and unethical acts.

Indeed, the government and corporate boards of directors must make

Joseph Irwin Miller

To come back from Yale and Oxford with a choice of jobs in several family businesses—that seems like an easy way to start. It wasn't easy for J. Irwin Miller, because the company he joined was broke and because nothing would ever be easy for him. Associates describe Miller as "highly competitive." What he competes against are his own standards, set by an inquiring imagination and a restless conscience. Miller wants everything—from a corporate-earnings statement to the ethics of business—to be better than it is.

Cummins Engine Co., at least, got better between 1934, when he became general manager, and 1977, when he retired as chairman. Now it's a billion-dollar business with 46 percent of the U.S. market in diesel engines for trucks and $380 million in overseas sales. Cummins has been profitable since 1937, and its return on stockholders' equity has been 12 percent or better in all but seven of the last thirty years.

Business and religion are intertwined in him and in his family history. His great-grandfather, a banker in Columbus, Indiana, founded the family fortune more than a hundred years ago. Both of Miller's grandfathers were Campbellite ministers. Miller's great-uncle, Will G. Irwin, multiplied the fortune with investments in an interurban railway and the Purity chain of food stores in California.

Irwin Miller was a shy boy with a stammer that persisted through the Taft School and Yale, where he "never got into the swing" of social life, concentrating on Latin and Greek. He went to Oxford for two years, gaining self-confidence and losing his stammer when he made the Balliol College crew.

He could have gone into preaching or teaching or the bank or the prospering Purity stores. He went into the unpromising engine company, in part because Clessie L. Cummins needed his help. As Will Irwin's chauffeur, Cummins had persuaded his boss to back him in making diesel engines. He was an inspired mechanic, but no businessman. Year after year Will Irwin had to put in more money.

In retrospect, Miller thinks his contribution was to connect Cummins's production with its potential markets. Many of the biggest truck manufacturers made their own engines. Miller said: "We're in the business of selling engines to engine-makers, which is surely not the easiest way to make a living." He did it by persuading trucking companies that they would reduce operating costs by specifying Cummins engines when they ordered trucks.

Much of Miller's thinking on ethical problems turns up in the concept of self-interest, which he sharply distinguishes from selfish interest. Self-interest respects the self-interest of others, and is, he points out, the premise of the Golden Rule. Cummins was one of the first manufacturing companies in its area to open non-janitorial jobs to black workers, and Miller personally helped to desegregate Columbus. His quiet influence in the town has been immense. For years the company has paid the design costs of many public buildings in Columbus, which has become a kind of living museum of the best contemporary architecture. Miller found time to play his Stradivarius violin and to delve with scholarly competence into theology and early church history. He was the first layman to head the National Council of Churches. He belongs to the wing of the Republican party that is too aware of the need and opportunity for change to call itself "conservative."

Not all the "hungry men" in U.S. business were born poor, and not all the hunger is for material gain.

Source: "Joseph Irwin Miller," *Fortune,* January 30, 1977, p. 97. Reprinted by permission.

the penalties for illegal acts clear: You will be fired, you will pay *large* fines, and you will go to jail if you violate laws and ethical precepts. Too often we read of a thief who stole $50 being sent to jail while executives who stole millions go on living in luxury and status. The punishment must fit the crime or law and ethics become a joke.

A third approach is for top management to set a good example itself. A set of policies—a code of conduct—should be established, followed, and enforced by top management and the board of directors. United Brands is trying this. Bank of America is doing it, too, and so is Bendix. Some feel that a code of conduct will work. But if executives violate laws with penalties, will they hesitate to violate codes of conduct? The fourth approach would be the rigorous enforcement of both laws and codes of conduct with the penalties for wrongdoing swift and severe. In some cases, when unethical and illegal behavior is discovered the culprits are fired and required to pay the money back. In others such actions are not taken.

The fourth approach requires all persons and groups involved with business in any way—employers, employees, and consumers—to actively fight criminal and unethical practices. Internal and external auditors must become more aggressive in order to learn about bribes and other illegal behavior. Ralph Naders of the world must be encouraged to find the thieves. Employees must be rewarded for turning in white-collar criminals who, as described earlier, often steal far more than the average stick-up thief. And stockholders must sue the offending corporate officers when their unethical behavior becomes known (as is happening more often now). All these pressures must be brought to bear if our business society is to survive. Unions will not allow a person with a criminal record to hold office. *Businesses should do the same.*

With all of these approaches, we can encourage and compel ethical business behavior on the part of executives. This will have positive results for executives, firms, and society.

Social Responsibility as a Business Objective

As mentioned earlier, social responsibility is considered by some managers to be an important objective of business. Those who take this view are motivated by what we call the social ethic. Those who do not, adhere to what is called the profit ethic.

The Profit Ethic

The profit ethic holds that the primary objective of a business is to maximize profits and serve the interests of its owners. The business of a business is to make money. If the enterprise pays out some of its profits to benefit society, this is a tax on profits, and only the government should tax. Of course managers should be socially responsible *as individuals,* but with their own money, not someone else's. Like Adam Smith, those who accept the profit ethic argue that when each business maximizes profits, this lowers the cost of everything and improves the economic well-being of all. Six reasons are given for this position:

1. The enterprise's profit is not the executive's own money. It is the stockholders' money. Managers are only the agents of the stockholders and have no legal right to spend money on social responsibility projects, notwithstanding the desirable ends of these projects. The money spent on such projects lowers the dividend and/or price of the stock. This denies the stockholder the use of this money, which is a rightful return on invested capital.
2. If one enterprise spends money on social responsibility projects and its competitors do not, this increases the costs of the socially responsible firm. It will have to raise its prices and thus will lose business. If the socially responsible firm is economically marginal, it will put itself out of business. If its prices are higher than those of the firm's overseas competitors, balance-of-payments problems may also arise.
3. Spending on social responsibility projects increases prices to all customers. In effect this is a tax, since customers lose the opportunity to spend this money on other goods.
4. Unlike government officials, politicians, and voluntary organization specialists, managers are neither trained in nor competent at judging which of the many socially desirable projects they should fund. Thus many of the projects they underwrite do not give maximum benefits to society.

5. Making businesses responsible for the welfare of society puts too much power in the hands of business executives. In effect it gives political-social power to those with economic power. A fundamental idea of a democratic society is *pluralism,* that is, a condition in which power is widely distributed among individuals and institutions.

6. Social responsibility is a movement toward socialism. People have progressed economically and socially under free enterprise regimes and have lost economical and often political power under socialist regimes.

It is important to note that most of these arguments do *not* hold for entrepreneurs and many family business executives. These executives can spend the enterprise's money as they please, if they spend it out of profits and do not pass it on as a cost to the consumer. Argument 4 may still hold, however.

The Social Responsibility Ethic

The social responsibility ethic holds that a business is responsible to many groups besides owners—including employees and customers. Therefore profit maximization is not the only objective of a business. Some profits should be diverted to social projects in the short run. Improvements in society will make it easier for the firm to survive and enjoy satisfactory long-run profits. People who hold the social ethic advance five reasons why executives and entrepreneurs should make social responsibility an objective of business and a part of the decision-making process:

1. Times have changed. People *expect* institutions (including business enterprises) to be socially responsible. Those that refuse will not survive the wrath of their clients or customers.

2. If business is not socially responsible, the public will press for more government regulation. So it makes sense to be socially responsible in order to prevent further government regulation of business.

3. In the long run a business's profits will be higher if it is socially responsible. For example, if a business in a ghetto does not hire members of the local minority group, it will lose business and suffer pilferage; it may even be burned down. Therefore it makes more sense to be socially responsible, even if it costs more in the short run.

4. Business should become involved in socially responsible projects because it has the financial resources to do so. Besides, business executives are efficient. After some initial training, business can do a better job of improving social conditions than other institutions.

5. Short-run profit maximization must be tempered by social responsibility. A firm will not have long-run viability unless the profit ethic is tempered with social responsibility.

Both sides make good points. Maybe this is why many executives wind up being pragmatists on social responsibility—acting in accordance with the social ethic when profits are exceptionally good or social conditions very bad, and in accordance with the profit ethic when the enterprise is up against the wall or when social conditions do not warrant a great deal of concern.

Those who favor the social ethic have found a number of areas where they can fulfill their responsibility to society. Some include:

- *Minorities and the poor* Training the unskilled, locating plants near the poor, purchasing supplies from minority-owned firms.
- *Philanthropy* Giving funds and other support to education, the arts, and similar causes.
- *Environmental improvement* Giving beyond the legal requirements to improve the aesthetic, social, and physical environments.

Planning and Evolution of Social Responsibility Programs

If an enterprise takes a pragmatic or pro–social responsibility position, it needs to determine its priorities. Since a goodly amount has been written on this issue, only a few words need be added here.

How do firms respond to social responsibility? Robert Ackerman has observed that enterprises go through three phases (see Figure 7.5).[7] The first phase begins when the top manager gets involved, makes speeches, maybe even gives money from corporate headquarters (with no impact on the operating divisions). The next occurs when the president appoints a staff executive responsible to the president to coordinate the firm's efforts in this area. The result may be almost no response or a token response. In the final phase the president builds social objectives into the firm's reporting and reward system. This produces results. Ackerman has also noted that a test case or confrontation will speed the movement from Phase 1 to Phase 3.

In sum, enterprises vary in their degree of acceptance of the social ethic, the profit ethic, or a profit ethic modified by a social ethic when economically possible. If the social ethic is accepted, it must be planned for and managed effectively.

Summary

Planning is a set of managerial activities designed to prepare the enterprise for the future and ensure that decisions regarding the use of people and resources (the means) help achieve enterprise objectives (the ends). The planning process involves determining objectives, examining the environment and forecasting changes, developing plans accordingly, and adjusting strategy as feedback on effectiveness indicates.

Planning is initially the responsibility of top management, but middle managers and supervisors plan too. There are three managerial styles regarding the participation of subordinates in planning. A *traditional*

Figure 7.5
Conversion of
Social
Responsiveness
from Policy to
Action

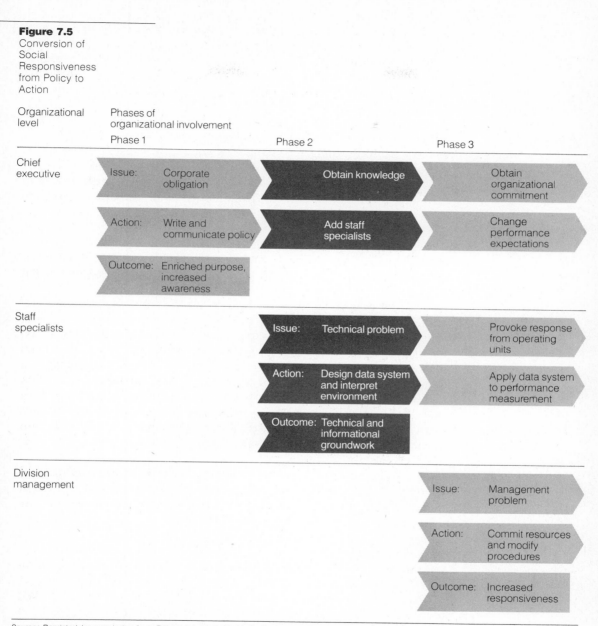

Organizational level	Phases of organizational involvement		
	Phase 1	Phase 2	Phase 3
Chief executive	Issue: Corporate obligation	Obtain knowledge	Obtain organizational commitment
	Action: Write and communicate policy	Add staff specialists	Change performance expectations
	Outcome: Enriched purpose, increased awareness		
Staff specialists		Issue: Technical problem	Provoke response from operating units
		Action: Design data system and interpret environment	Apply data system to performance measurement
		Outcome: Technical and informational groundwork	
Division management			Issue: Management problem
			Action: Commit resources and modify procedures
			Outcome: Increased responsiveness

manager accepts total responsibility for planning. The *consultative* manager also accepts the ultimate responsibility, but he or she involves the employees in the planning process to a limited extent. The *participative* manager requires the work group to take an active part in the planning process. The manager's attitudes toward people will determine the managerial style chosen.

Managers plan for four reasons: (1) Planning leads to organizational success. (2) Planning leads to feelings of success and satisfaction by employees. (3) Planning helps a manager cope with change. (4) Planning is necessary for effective performance of the other management functions.

Planning does not automatically guarantee success, but it *contributes* to the success of an enterprise. Planning is more important to some enterprises than to others. Where problems are the greatest, planning pays off the most.

The initial step in the planning process is setting objectives. *Objectives* are those ends which the organization seeks to achieve by its existence and operations. Effective objectives are measurable, attainable, and consistent with the firm's resources.

Some objectives of business include profitability, sales growth and marketing, efficiency and quality of products/services, employee relationships like job satisfaction, and social responsibility. No sizable firm exists for more than a short time if profitability is its only objective. Most firms pursue multiple objectives, which are placed in a hierarchy on the basis of their priority. Management must calculate trade-offs at any point in time.

The hierarchy ranks the objectives to be achieved in the short and long run. This balancing of objectives to achieve overall corporate success is often called organizational effectiveness. Organizational success is hard to define. But it can be said that an organization is successful if it survives and if it meets its objectives.

How are objectives determined? The top manager or entrepreneur sets the objectives. Their choices are affected by four factors: (1) the realities of the external environment, (2) the realities of the enterprise's resources, (3) internal power relationships, and (4) the attitudes (value systems) of top managers. Management does not begin with a completely new set of objectives every year. Rather, the existing set is evaluated, and incremental changes are made as the current environment and current demands of conflicting groups dictate.

The consultative manager uses the management by objectives (MBO) technique to set objectives for the firm. MBO is a structured alternative to the *traditional* approach. It is an involved process in which the manager and the employees set the objectives, clarify relationships, assign responsibility, and establish time deadlines for each aspect of the business. Setting realistic, important, measurable objectives is crucial. Most research on the effectiveness of MBO is very positive, but problems can arise due to inadequate top management support, inadequate explanation of MBO, poorly defined objectives, personality conflicts, insincere commitment by managers, inadequate reinforcement, and overemphasis on paperwork.

Ethics and the importance of ethical behavior are one aspect of managerial philosphy. *Ethical behavior* is that set of acts which society considers right. Based on an individual's conscience and moral code, ethics are influenced by societal prohibitions. Actions can be legal but unethical; they can also be ethical but illegal.

Some business executives consider social responsibility one of their objectives today. They adhere to the social ethic, which holds that a business is responsible to many groups besides owners: employees, customers, and the general public. The profit ethic, on the other hand, states that the business of business is to make money, not to improve society. Those who favor the social ethic have implemented their objectives a number of ways: through locating plants near the poor, philanthropy, and environmental improvement. Enterprises vary in their acceptance of the social ethic, the profit ethic, or a profit ethic modified by a social ethic. If the social ethic is accepted, it too must be effectively planned for and implemented.

Questions

1. What is planning? Who is involved in setting objectives? Examining the environment?
2. There are three managerial styles of participation with the immediate subordinates in planning. What are these? Which style do you think would be your choice?
3. You are the top manager of your own firm and have just been asked why you believe in planning. What reasons would you give and why?
4. You are the same top manager but you never seem to get around to the planning function. What are some of the reasons you give yourself to justify the lack of planning?
5. Define objectives. What characterizes *effective* objectives?
6. List as many business objectives as you can, ranking them in order of importance as you see them.
7. How would you evaluate the success of an enterprise objectively? Subjectively?
8. You are ready to sit down and choose the objectives for your own small firm. What four factors should you keep in mind as you make your choice? Why?
9. What is management by objectives? Do you think this would be a useful approach?
10. Compare and contrast the benefits and problems of MBO.
11. Is ethical behavior the same as legal behavior? What would you do to help improve ethical business behavior?
12. Contrast the profit ethic with the social ethic. Which do you feel you would favor as a manager?

Notes

[1]Chester Barnard, *Functions of the Executive* (Cambridge, Mass.: Harvard University Press, 1939).

[2]Richard Cyert and James March, *Behavioral Theory of the Firm* (Englewood Cliffs, N.J.: Prentice-Hall, 1963).

[3]Stephen J. Carroll and Henry L. Tosi, *Management by Objectives: Applications and Research* (New York: Macmillan, 1973).

[4]Jim Montgomery, "The Image Makers: In Public Relations, Ethical Conflicts Pose Continuing Problems," *Wall Street Journal*, August 1, 1978, pp. 1, 14.

[5]S. N. Brenner and E. A. Molander, "Is the Ethics of Business Changing?" *Harvard Business Review* 55 (January–February 1977): 57–71.

[6]Ralph Nader and Mark Green, "What to Do about Corporate Corruption?" *Wall Street Journal*, March 12, 1976.

[7]Robert Ackerman, "How Companies Respond to Social Demands," *Harvard Business Review* 51 (July–August 1973): 88–98.

References

Planning Leads to Organizational Success

This section is based on William Glueck, *Business Policy and Strategic Management* (New York: McGraw-Hill, 1980), chapters 1 and 3.

Planning Benefits Employees

Gary Latham and Gary Yuki, "A Review of Research on the Application of Goal Setting in Organizations," *Academy of Management Journal* 18 (December 1975): 824–845. Richard Steers and Lyman Porter, eds., *Motivation and Work Behavior* (New York: McGraw-Hill, 1979); and "The Role of Task Goal Attributes in Employee Performance," *Psychological Bulletin* 81 (May 1974): 434–452.

Determining Objectives

James Dent, "Organizational Correlates of the Goals of Business Managers," *Personnel Psychology* 12 (Autumn 1959): 365–393. "Doing Things Right the First Time Around," *Business Week*, March 12, 1979, p. 10. George England, "Organizational Goals and Expected Behavior of American Managers," *Academy of Management Journal* 11 (June 1967): 107–111. Robert Hoppock, "Reminiscences and Comments on Job Satisfaction," *Journal of Employment Counseling* 13 (June 1976): 50–57. Arne L. Kalleberg, "Work Values and Job Rewards: A Theory of Job Satisfaction," *American Sociological Review* 42 (February 1977): 124–143. Raymond Katzell et al., *Work, Productivity and Job Satisfaction* (New York: The Psychological Corporation, 1975). Thomas A. Kochan, L. L. Cummings, and George P. Huber, "Operationalizing the Concepts of Goals and Goal Incompatibilities in Organizational Behavior Research," *Human Relations* 29 (June 1976): 527–544. Dennis W. Organ, "A Reappraisal and Reinterpretation of the Satisfaction-Causes-Performance Hypothesis," *Academy of Management Review* 2 (January 1977): 46–53.

Objectives Are Multiple

Isidore Barmash, *Great Business Disasters* (New York: Ballantine Books, 1973). John Child, "Managerial and Organizational Factors Associated with Company Performance,"

Journal of Management Studies 11 (October 1974): 175–189; "Managerial and Organizational Factors Associated with Company Performance, Part II: A Contingency Analysis," *Journal of Management Studies* 12 (February 1975): 12–27; and "What Determines Organizational Performance?" *Organizational Dynamics* 3 (Spring 1975): 2–18. Merrill Douglass, "How Do You Measure the Effectiveness of a Business?" *Organizational Dynamics* 3 (Winter 1975): 47–50. Martin Gannon, "The Measurement of Performance in Multi-Unit Service Organizations." *Proceedings of the Midwest Academy of Management* (1970), pp. 263–272. Jai Ghorpade, *Assessment of Organizational Effectiveness* (Pacific Palisades, Calif.: Goodyear, 1971). Robert Heller, *The Great Executive Dream* (New York: Dell, 1972). Paul Hersick, "Organizational Effectiveness and the Institutional Environment," *Administrative Science Quarterly* 20 (September 1975): 327–344. M. C. Knowles, "Interdependence among Organizational Variables," *Human Relations* 28 (July 1975): 431–450. Paul Mott, *The Characteristics of Effective Organizations* (New York: Harper & Row, 1972). James Price, *Organizational Effectiveness* (Homewood, Ill.: Irwin Dorsey Press, 1968). Joel Ross and Michael Kami, *Corporate Management in Crisis: Why the Mighty Fall* (Englewood Cliffs, N.J.: Prentice-Hall, 1973). Bernard Reimann, "Organizational Effectiveness and Management's Public Values: A Canonical Analysis," *Academy of Management Journal* 18 (June 1975): 224–241. William Rushing, "Differences in Profit and Nonprofit Organizations: A Study of Effectiveness and Efficiency in General Short-Stay Hospitals," *Administrative Science Quarterly* 19 (December 1974): 474–484. Richard Steers, "Problems in the Measurement of Organizational Effectiveness," *Administrative Science Quarterly* 20 (December 1975): 546–558; and "When Is an Organization Effective? A Process Approach to Understanding Effectiveness," *Organizational Dynamics* 5 (Autumn 1976): 50–63. Ronald G. Storey, "The Effects of Firm Performance, Role, and the Firm X Individual Performance Interaction on Satisfaction in a Stable Environment," *Journal of Business Administration* 7 (Spring 1976): 61–81. Mahmoud Wahba and Harus Shapiro, "Managerial Assessment of Organizational Components," *Academy of Management Journal* 16 (June 1973): 277–284. R. J. Webb, "Organizational Effectiveness and the Voluntary Organization," *Academy of Management Journal* 17 (December 1974): 663–667.

How Are Objectives Determined?

Richard Cyert and James March, *Behavioral Theory of the Firm* (Englewood Cliffs, N.J.: Prentice-Hall, 1963). J. Craig Jenkins, "Radical Transformation of Organizational Goals," *Administrative Science Quarterly* 22 (December 1977): 568–586. Hans G. Krijnen, "Formulating Corporate Objectives and Strategies," *Long Range Planning* 10 (August 1977): 78–87. George Cabot Lodge, "Business and the Changing Society," *Harvard Business Review* 52 (March–April 1974): 59–72. Walter P. Margulies, "Make the Most of Your Corporate Identity," *Harvard Business Review* 55 (July–August 1977): 66–74. James Brian Quinn, "Strategic Goals: Process and Politics," *Sloan Management Review* 19 (Fall 1977): 21–37. H. Redwood, "Setting Corporate Objectives," *Long Range Planning* 10 (December 1977): 2–10. Herbert Simon, "On the Concept of Organizational Goals," *Administrative Science Quarterly* 9 (June 1964): 1–22. Richard M. Steers, "Factors Affecting Job Attitudes in a Goal-Setting Environment," *Academy of Management Journal* 19 (March 1976): 6–16. James Thompson, *Organizations in Action* (New York: McGraw-Hill, 1967).

Management by Objectives

Stephen J. Carroll and Henry L. Tosi, *Management by Objectives: Applications and Research* (New York: Macmillan, 1973). Rodney Chesser, *MBO as a Behavioral System* (D.B.A. diss., Michigan State University, 1971). Peter F. Drucker, *Management: Tasks, Responsibilities, Practices* (New York: Harper & Row, 1973), chapter 34. Herbert Hand and Thomas Hollingsworth, "Tailoring MBO to Hospitals," *Business Horizons* 18

(February 1975): 45–52. J. M. Ivancevich, "Longitudinal Assessment of Management by Objectives," *Administrative Science Quarterly* 17 (March 1972): 126–138; and "Changes in Performance in an MBO Program," *Administrative Science Quarterly* 19 (December 1974): 563–574. John M. Ivancevich et al., "Goal Setting: The Tenneco Approach to Personnel Development and Management Effectiveness," *Organizational Dynamics* 6 (Winter 1978): 58–80. Bruce A. Kirchoff, "MBO: Understanding What the Experts Are Saying," *MSU Business Topics* 22 (Summer 1974): 17–21. Edwin A. Locke, "The Ubiquity of the Technique of Goal Setting in Theories of and Approaches to Employee Motivation," *Academy of Management Review* 3 (July 1978): 594–601. Paul Mali, *Managing by Objectives: An Operating Guide to Faster and More Profitable Results* (New York: Wiley, 1972). Dale D. McConkey, "MBO—Twenty Years Later, Where Do We Stand?" *Business Horizons* 16 (August 1973): 25–36. Mark L. McConkie, "A Clarification of the Goal Setting and Appraisal Processes in MBO," *Academy of Management Review* 4 (January 1979): 29–40. R. Henry Migliore, *A Study of Management by Objectives in the Banking and Selected Manufacturing Industries* (Ph.D. diss., University of Arkansas, 1975). Jon Muczyk, "A Controlled Field Experiment Measuring the Impact of MBO on Performance Data," *Proceedings of the Academy of Management* (1975). Fred E. Schuster and Alva F. Kindall, "Management by Objectives: Where We Stand: A Survey of the Fortune 500," *Human Resource Management* (Spring 1974): 8–11. Douglas S. Sherwin, "Management of Objectives," *Harvard Business Review* 54 (May–June 1976): 149–160. Y. Krishna Shetty and Howard Carlisle, "Organizational Correlates of MBO Program," *Academy of Management Journal* 17 (March 1974): 155–160. Herbert Simon, "A Study of MBO in a Professional Organization," *Journal of Management Studies* 12 (February 1975): 1–11. Allen Slusher and Henry Sims, "Commitment through MBO Interviews," *Business Horizons* 18 (August 1975): 5–12. Richard M. Steers and Daniel G. Spencer, "Achievement Needs and MBO Goal-Setting," *Personnel Journal* 57 (January 1978): 26–28. Henry Tosi et al., "How Real Are Changes Induced by Management by Objectives," *Administrative Science Quarterly* 21 (June 1976): 276–306. Donald D. White, "Factors Affecting Employee Attitudes toward the Installation of a New Management System," *Academy of Management Journal* 16 (December 1973): 636–646. Ethan Winning, "MBO: What's in It for the Individual?" *Personnel* 51 (March–April 1974): 51–56.

Ethical Behavior of Executives

John E. Adair, *Management and Morality: The Problems and Opportunities of Social Capitalism.* (London: David and Charles, 1974). Andrew Alexander, "Firms Pay Millions to Check Integrity: In-House Probes Drain Ills and Funds," *Atlanta Journal,* Sunday, May 7, 1978, p. 14A. Peter Asch and Joseph J. Seneca, "Characteristics of Collusive Firms," *Journal of Industrial Economics* 23 (March 1975): 223–237. Raymond Baumhart, *Ethics in Business* (New York: Holt, Rinehart and Winston, 1960); and "How Ethical Are Businessmen?" *Harvard Business Review* 39 (July–August 1961). George C. S. Benson, "Business Ethics in American Society," *Journal of Contemporary Business* 4 (Summer 1975): 59–74. "The Big Rip-Off in Purchasing," *Dun's Review* 111 (March 1977): 76–77, 102–103. David K. Berlo, "Morality or Ethics? Two Approaches to Organizational Control." *Personnel Administrator* 20 (April 1975): 16–19. S. N. Brenner and E. A. Molander, "Is the Ethics Business Changing?" *Harvard Business Review* 55 (January–February 1977): 57–71. Albert Carr, "Can An Executive Have a Conscience?" *Harvard Business Review* 48 (July–August 1970): 58–64. Archie B. Carroll, "Linking Business Ethics to Behavior in Organizations," *Advanced Management Journal* 43 (Summer 1978): 4–11; "Managerial Ethics," *Encyclopedia of Professional Management* (New York: McGraw-Hill, 1979); and "Managerial Ethics: A Post Watergate View," *Business Horizons* 18 (April 1975): 75–80. Lindley Clark, Jr., "Innocents Abroad?" *Wall Street Journal,* April 14, 1976. Eberhart Faber, "How I Lost Our Great Debate about Corporate Ethics," *Fortune* 94 (November 1976): 180–189. William F. Glueck, "Ethics in Business: Have They Gone Out of Style?" *Survey of Business* 11 (January–February

1976): 8–12. Thomas Griffith, "Payoff Is Not 'Accepted Practice,'" *Fortune* 92 (August 1975): 122–125, 200–206 ff. Tony McAdams and Robert Miljus, "Growing Criminal Liability of Executives," *Harvard Business Review* 55 (March–April 1977): 36–40, 164, 166. Mary Susan Miller and A. Edward Miller, "It's Too Late for Ethics Courses in Business Schools," *Business and Society Review* 17 (Spring 1976): 39–42. Jim Montgomery, "The Image Makers: In Public Relations, Ethical Conflicts Pose Continuing Problems," *Wall Street Journal,* August 1, 1978, pp. 1, 14. Ralph Nader, "A Code of Professional Integrity," *New York Times,* January 15, 1971. Ralph Nader and Mark Green, "What to Do about Corporate Corruption?" *Wall Street Journal,* March 12, 1976. Robert H. Nelson, "The Economics of Honest Trade Practices," *Journal of Industrial Economics* 24 (June 1976): 281–293. John Newstrom and William Ruch, "The Ethics of Management and the Management of Ethics," *MSU Business Topics* 23 (Winter 1975): 29–37. Theodore V. Purcell, S. J., "Do Courses in Business Ethics Pay Off?" *California Management Review* 19 (Spring 1977): 50–58; and "A Practical Guide to Ethics in Business," *Business and Society Review* 13 (Spring 1975): 43–50. Hans Schoolhammer, "Ethics in an International Business Context," *MSU Business Topics* 25 (Spring 1977): 54–63. John Senger, "The Religious Manager," *Academy of Management Journal* 13 (June 1970): 179–186. Samuel Southard, *Ethics for Executives* (New York: Thomas Nelson, 1975). Christopher Stone, *Where the Law Ends* (New York: Harper & Row, 1975). George Strother, "The Moral Codes of Executives: A Watergate-Inspired Look at Barnard's Theory of Executive Responsibility," *Academy of Management Review* 1 (April 1976): 13–22. Jerry Wall, "What the Competition Is Doing: Your Need to Know," *Harvard Business Review* 52 (November–December 1974): 22–38, 162–166. Kenneth D. Walters, "Your Employees' Right to Blow the Whistle," *Harvard Business Review* 53 (July–August 1975): 26–34 and 161, 162. Clarence Walton, *Ethics and Executive* (Englewood Cliffs, N.J.: Prentice-Hall, 1969). James A. Waters, "Catch 20.5: Corporate Morality as an Organizational Phenomenon," *Organizational Dynamics* 6 (Spring 1978): 2–19. James A. Wilson, "Morality and the Contemporary Business System," *Journal of Contemporary Business* 4 (Summer 1975): 31–58.

Social Responsibility as a Business Objective

Kamal M. Abouzeid and Charles N. Weaver, "Social Responsibility in the Corporate Goal Hierarchy," *Business Horizons* 21 (June 1978): 29–35. Robert Ackerman, "How Companies Respond to Social Demands," *Harvard Business Review* 51 (July–August 1973: 88–98. Gordon J. Alexander and Rogene A. Buchholz, "Research Notes: Corporate Social Responsibility and Stock Market Performance," *Academy of Management Journal* 21 (September 1978): 479–486. Archie B. Carroll, "Setting Operational Goals for Corporate Social Responsibility," *Long Range Planning* 11 (April 1978): 35–38. Keith Davis, "Five Propositions for Social Responsibility," *Business Horizons* 18 (June 1975): 19–24; and "Social Responsibility Is Inevitable," *California Management Review* 19 (Fall 1976): 14–20. William E. Halal, "A Return-on-Resources Model of Corporate Performance," *California Management Review* 19 (Summer 1977): 23–34. Gerald D. Keim, "Managerial Behavior and the Social Responsibility Debate: Goals versus Constraints," *Academy of Management Journal* 21 (March 1978): 57–68. Edwin A. Murray, Jr., "The Social Response Process in Commercial Banks: An Empirical Investigation," *Academy of Management Review* 1 (July 1976): 5–15. Leonard H. Orr, ed., "Is Corporate Social Responsibility a Dead Issue?" *Business and Society Review* 25 (Spring 1978): 4–20. S. Prakash Sethi, "A Conceptual Framework for Environmental Analysis of Social Issues and Evaluation of Business Response Patterns," *Academy of Management Review* 4 (January 1979): 63–74. Frederick D. Sturdivant and James L. Ginter, "Corporate Social Responsiveness: Management Attitudes and Economic Performance," *California Management Review* 19 (Spring 1977): 30–39. Kenneth D. Walters, "Corporate Social Responsibility and Political Ideology," *California Management Review* 19 (Spring 1977): 40–51.

Case for Chapter 7

**MBO:
A Failure?**

Recently Francine Siemers, president of a medium-size machine tool manufacturing company, attended an industry convention. One of the major topics was management by objectives. Francine had heard about MBO but did not know much about it. The session consisted of a main speaker who described briefly what MBO was and how it was implemented and a panel of industry executives who each spoke about five minutes, praising MBO's results in their companies.

On the flight home Francine reflected on that session. It seemed relevant to her company's problems: declining achievement of objectives, people whose responsibilities overlapped, less than fully motivated employees, and the like. The speakers all seemed satisfied with how MBO worked at their companies. Francine decided to try MBO.

Francine called the usual Monday executive coordinating meeting to order. She spent ten minutes summarizing some of the news she had picked up on new products, personnel changes, and so forth. Then she launched into a fifteen minute description of how MBO could help the company. She made it clear that MBO would be their next major project.

As the other executives spoke up, it became apparent that serious problems had arisen while she was gone. Some important operating decisions had to be made about the new plant in Australia; there was the issue of the reorganization of the regional sales offices; and a decision had to be made on whether to offer to buy back the million shares of company stock as recommended by the treasurer.

So Francine took aside the vice-president of personnel, Nat James, and told him she was making him the MBO officer and that she wanted MBO operating in the company within three months.

Nat rushed out, bought some books on MBO, chose a set of forms to use, and sent out a letter stating that MBO would be the new policy and directing that each department adopt it within sixty days.

Francine has heard rumbling from the ranks about "this MBO joke." She does not understand what happened and has called Nat in for a meeting.

Problem

What advice would you give to Francine and Nat about what probably went wrong and how it might be corrected?

Chapter 8   Planning Strategies and Policies

Learning Objectives

1. Relate the level of the planner to the various time horizons—long-range, intermediate, short-range—and different types of plans.

2. Know how to use the environmental factors that have an impact on top managerial planning to identify threats to and opportunities for your chosen career.

3. Learn how to evaluate a local firm using the strategic advantage analysis process to look for advantages and weaknesses.

4. Understand how to analyze a firm in terms of what grand strategy and substrategy its managers are following and why.

5. Be able to plan implementation of such a strategy.

6. Learn what plans are made and implemented at the middle managerial and supervisory levels.

7. Recognize the importance of avoiding the pitfalls of inadequate feedback and inadequate attention to planning.

Introduction

Chapter 7 began our analysis of the planning process. It discussed how objectives are determined: the first step in planning. Figure 8.1 reproduces Figure 7.1 to show how Chapter 8 fits into the process.

We will now continue in our consideration of this process by looking at the next two steps: examining the present and probable future environment and then developing plans. The major plans we will look at are the strategies and policies which are set by top management. We will also look at the kinds of plans middle managers and supervisors make. Before we discuss these different kinds of plans, let's look at a key issue—whether managers actually do plan.

Do Managers Really Plan?

You would think that since I am asking you to read three chapters on planning and decision making, the answer would be yes. But a well-known management thinker, Henry Mintzberg (whom I have mentioned before) has argued that his studies show little evidence of planning.[1] Planning, he says, is only a vague objective of managerial work. Is he right?

Let me take you along while a colleague of mine, Neil Snyder of the

Figure 8.1
A Model of the
Planning Process

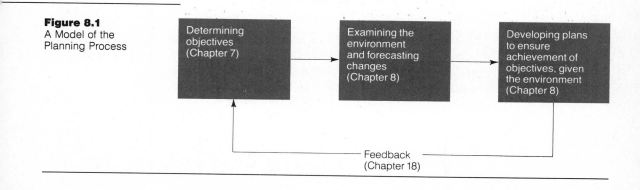

University of Virginia, and I observe the planning activities of two managers using Mintzberg's research approach.[2] I think this will help you understand planning better and also give you a feel for management research.

Neil and I chose to observe the chief executives of a hospital and a school system because these were two of the five roles Mintzberg observed in his research. Also, they were chosen because it is common knowledge that nonbusiness enterprises are less likely to follow business management principles than businesses. Thus, if the nonbusiness chief executives planned as part of their managerial activities, it would be a more significant argument against Mintzberg's position than if the same result was obtained from a business sample.

The school superintendent is a fifty-four year old man who has been in his current position for eight years. He entered this position after having served in the same capacity in another city for nine years. Prior to becoming a superintendent, he worked as an elementary school teacher, a counselor, and a principal. He holds a Doctor of Education (Ed.D.) degree. The school system that he manages serves an area with a population of 70,000, and it has a student enrollment of 10,000. The system employs approximately 1,300 individuals (600 professional and 700 non-professional), and the annual budget for the system is approximately $13 million.

The hospital administrator is a forty-seven year old man who has been in his current position for five years. He entered this position after having served for sixteen years as administrator of smaller hospitals. Prior to serving as an administrator, he received a B.A. degree and pursued graduate work in hospital administration. He manages a 140 bed hospital with approximately 650 employees, and he has an annual budget of approximately $11.5 million. The hospital was expanding and expansion was expected to be completed within three years.

We observed these chief executives for four days each. Each separate and distinct activity in which they engaged, the duration of each activity, and the purpose for each activity were recorded following Mintzberg's classification scheme and using his *chronological record*. Five separate and distinct activities were recorded: desk work, scheduled meetings, unscheduled meetings, telephone calls, and tours.

A *mail record* was used to describe the type and purpose of mail the manager sent out and received. Additionally, the sender of the mail and the attention it received from the manager were recorded there. The specifics with regard to telephone calls, scheduled meetings, unscheduled meetings, and tours were recorded in the *contact record*. For a detailed analysis of these activities, we recorded the purpose of each contact, the participants, the initiating party, the duration of the activity, and the place where the contact occurred.

In total, the managers engaged in 355 separate and distinct activities. There were 138 desk work sessions, 94 telephone calls, 24 scheduled meetings, 87 unscheduled meetings, and 12 tours. Additionally, they processed 220 pieces of mail (150 pieces of incoming mail and 70 pieces of outgoing mail).

For observational research to be fruitful, the observation period must be representative of the "normal" work period. The executives and their secretaries were asked to contrast the observed week with a normal work week for the executives. All four persons believed that the observed period was normal.

While Mintzberg claimed that the key to his study was the categorization of the purpose behind each activity, he did not focus on the purpose of *groups* of related activities. Neil and I feel that by viewing the managerial activities as discrete events and not attempting to relate them one to another, Mintzberg did not grasp the importance of or the purpose for the activities he observed.

The key to understanding managerial work is understanding managerial activities. To gain an accurate picture of managerial work, it is absolutely essential to view these activities in their totality. Focusing on the individual activities alone will inevitably lead to a different view of reality. Thus the researcher must trace through the maze of individual managerial activities to find a common thread linking activities. This is especially true in identifying activities associated with a planning program. After all, managers do not telephone in the abstract. They telephone to accomplish some goal.

To trace this common thread of purpose, Neil and I asked these chief executives to explain *what* they were doing and *why* each time they engaged in an activity. Care was taken not to project specific purposes by suggesting them to the subjects. Indeed, the chief executives became so accustomed to providing this information that they rarely had to be asked for the what and why after the first day of the observation periods.

Our Findings

A planning program is defined as those activities which are concerned specifically with determining in advance what actions and/or human and physical resources are required to reach a goal.

It includes identifying alternatives, analyzing each one, and selecting the best one. Let's examine the planning activities of both executives.

Planning and the School Superintendent

Prior to the observation period, the school superintendent had experienced difficulties with a black city councilman. The superintendent believed that the councilman was attempting to disrupt the publicly held school board meetings and to discredit him as superintendent. The councilman claimed that there was a concerted effort by the administration to make it difficult for blacks to become a part of the school system. In the past, the community had experienced some racial difficulties, and the superintendent wanted to avoid them in the future. Additionally, he has a strong personal conviction that the school environment should allow people of all races to learn to live and work together in harmony. The superintendent had written a letter to the councilman to arrange an informal meeting at which they could discuss privately the councilman's grievances.

On our first day of observation, the superintendent received a reply to his letter. The councilman stated that he would meet with the superintendent if certain conditions were met. The conditions were that a formal agenda be prepared and presented to him two days prior to the meeting, that they meet at a neutral site, and that he be allowed to bring with him other individuals. What was originally intended to be an informal meeting where two parties could reconcile their differences was developing into something different.

Given his desire to find an equitable solution to the problem, the superintendent contacted community leaders and knowledgeable insiders to inform them about the problem and to solicit their ideas and opinions for its resolution. Also, the superintendent obtained relevant personal information about the councilman. This enabled him to develop a more complete understanding of the councilman's motives and attitudes. Obtaining the ideas and opinions of others plus relevant personal information about the councilman was, according to the superintendent, of paramount importance in developing a strategy to handle the problem equitably.

During the observation period, 12.3 percent of the superintendent's phone calls (21.9 percent of the time he spent on the telephone) were devoted to obtaining the aforementioned information. The purpose of 16.3 percent of the unscheduled meetings (21.11 percent of the time spent in unscheduled meetings) was to gather information needed to plan an equitable strategy to deal with the councilman. At a regularly scheduled, weekly meeting, 44.8 percent of the time was spent analyzing alternatives for resolving the problem (3.43 percent of the time spent in all scheduled meetings was consumed in like fashion). In total, the school superintendent devoted 6.96 percent of the observation period to gathering and analyzing information necessary to develop an equitable strategy to handle the councilman. Thus, almost 7 percent of his time was spent in planning to deal with *one* future event. Additional time was spent planning for other events.

Planning and the Hospital Administrator

The hospital administrator was in the process of undertaking a building expansion program that would take three years to complete. The expansion would result in a 25 percent increase in the size of the hospital. A great deal of the administrator's time was spent with physicians, members of his staff, architects, and the Hospital Authority (his board of directors) planning how to construct the addition in a way that would allow room for future growth and facilitate efficient operation. He focused on both the current and future needs of the hospital, giving more emphasis to future needs.

During the observation period, 13.8 percent of the hospital administrator's telephone conversations (3.6 percent of the time he spent on the phone) related specifically to planning the most effective and efficient ways to meet the needs of the hospital. However, scheduled and unscheduled meetings were more frequently used for planning the expansion program. The reason was that the parties involved in the planning process needed to see blueprints in order to intelligently discuss alternatives. This necessitated sitting down and studying each alternative and its impact on the entire hospital.

Of the hospital administrator's unscheduled meetings, 23.7 percent were devoted to examining alternative ways of meeting the hospital's needs (44.1 percent of the time spent in unscheduled meetings). The purpose of 40 percent of the scheduled meetings (52.7 percent of the time spent in scheduled meetings) was to study the feasibility of different alternatives. During the observation period, the hospital administrator devoted 37.2 percent of his time to identifying alternatives and determining their feasibility. Again, additional time was spent on planning for additional future events.

Clearly, managers do plan. The findings of this and other research confirms that managers plan and that planning is part of the managerial activities, especially if top management creates a climate that encourages it. Planning has always been an important part of management. George Washington, pictured on page 244, is a classic example of an individual who planned and profited by planning.

Planning Horizons

All managers plan, but the future events they plan for differ in length of time. Firms can have plans for three time horizons: long range (more than

---

George Washington

A surfeit of other "firsts" has obscured the fact that George Washington was an excellent business man. His shrewd bets were mostly placed on the asset that he, a surveyor and farmer, knew best and deemed of "permanent value," namely land. After buying and selling land for years, he owned at his death some 64,000 acres, scattered from Mount Vernon to the upper reaches of the Ohio and even the Mohawk Valley. When he acquired a 1,200-acre tract near Pittsburgh, he noted that under it were coal deposits of "the very best kind." His account books tell more about him than many a romanticized portrait. In managing Mount Vernon, he made careful observations of yields per acre. He got out of tobacco, which he knew depleted the soil, and was one of the first in his area to plant alfalfa. He told his neighbors that, for farm work, mules were more efficient than horses. He worked out an elaborate system for the division of labor during a wheat harvest. His flour achieved brand recognition in the West Indies market; one grade he advertised as "Superfine." As a commander his success was largely attributable to the transfer of methodical habits he had learned as a civilian. On his arduous horseback rides into the Appalachians he not only sensed the westward destiny of the country but also concluded that trade among Americans was the best means of binding East and West together. Indeed, it was his attempt to develop water routes to the interior that prompted efforts toward a stronger national government, efforts that led to the Constitutional Convention of 1787, and to his own businesslike presidency.

George Washington, Gilbert Stuart, National Gallery of Art, Washington, Andrew W. Mellon Collection.

Source: *Fortune*, January 1975, p. 68. Reprinted by permission.

---

five years), medium range (one to five years), and short range (less than one year). In general top managers plan for the long run, middle managers for the intermediate term, and supervisors for the short term. George Steiner shows us (in Figure 8.2) the ideal time horizons for planning that managers of different levels should use.[3]

Note that Steiner developed these time horizons for the average medium-size company. The emphasis may not be great enough for the period beyond five years, especially for a very large firm. One study of planning in larger companies found that the actual time horizons for planning ahead depend on the following factors:[4]

- Lead time for the item or industry.
- Length of time required to recover capital funds invested in plant, equipment, and personnel training.

Figure 8.2
"Ideal" Allocations of Time for Planning in the "Average" Company

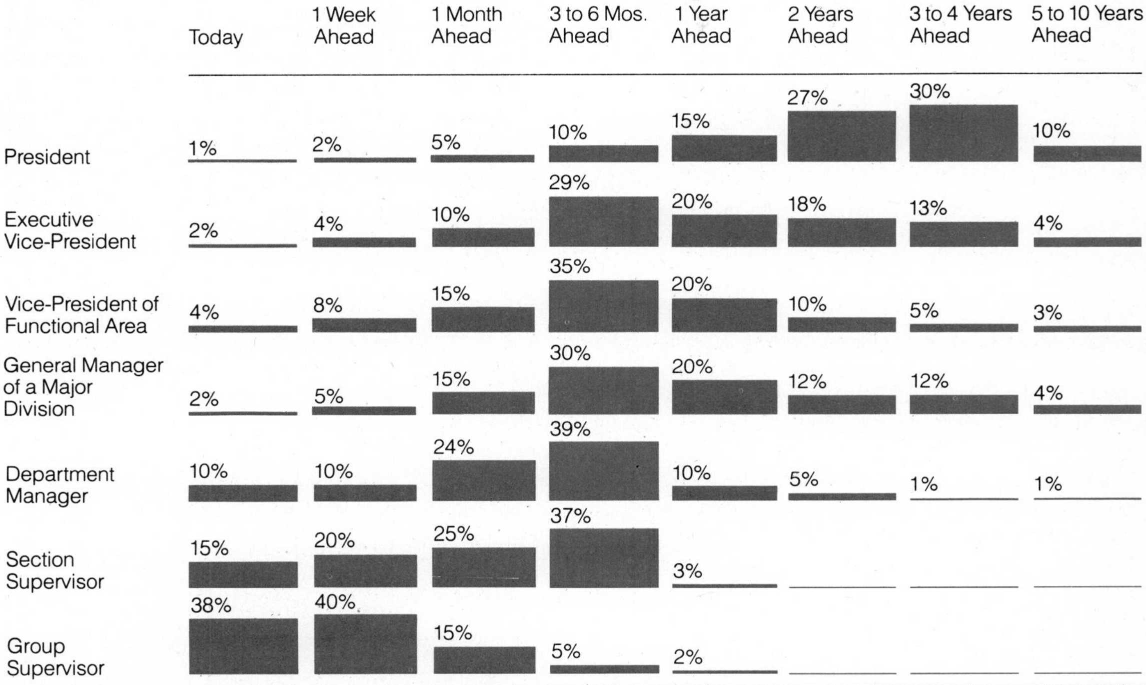

	Today	1 Week Ahead	1 Month Ahead	3 to 6 Mos. Ahead	1 Year Ahead	2 Years Ahead	3 to 4 Years Ahead	5 to 10 Years Ahead
President	1%	2%	5%	10%	15%	27%	30%	10%
Executive Vice-President	2%	4%	10%	29%	20%	18%	13%	4%
Vice-President of Functional Area	4%	8%	15%	35%	20%	10%	5%	3%
General Manager of a Major Division	2%	5%	15%	30%	20%	12%	12%	4%
Department Manager	10%	10%	24%	39%	10%	5%	1%	1%
Section Supervisor	15%	20%	25%	37%	3%			
Group Supervisor	38%	40%	15%	5%	2%			

Source: George A. Steiner, *Top Management Planning* (New York: Macmillan, 1969), p. 26. Reprinted by permission.

- Expected future availability of customers.
- Expected future availability of raw materials and components.

With regard to the first factor, the lead time—the amount of time required to ready a product for sale—for a new series of computers may be three to five years. The lead time for a new line of women's dresses may be six months to a year. Capital recovery in petrochemicals takes much longer than in most service industries. The lead time for customers of machinery and equipment firms like Cincinnati Milacron is much longer than in most consumer goods industries. And it takes ninety-nine years to replace some trees but much less time to replace other product components.

So the short-range plans of some firms are shorter than those of others. Utilities may have to plan new generators ten to twenty-five years in advance. *All but the very smallest enterprises prepare short-range plans. Some medium-sized and most large enterprises prepare long-range plans.* Large companies can and often do prepare short-, medium-, and long-range plans.

Types of Plans

Firms prepare plans which have different time horizons. They also prepare plans which have different purposes. These are different types of plans. Table 8.1 lists these different types of plans and shows you which level of managers prepare each type. As can be seen, some of the plans are developed entirely at one managerial level (for example, strategies); others are developed at several levels (for example, budgets). Later in the chapter I will describe in more detail what each of these types of plans are, how they are developed and used, and why. First, though, I'd like to describe the second step in the planning process: examining the environment and forecasting change, since this affects all types of plans. (See Figure 8.4, a model of the strategic planning process, later in the chapter.)

Examining the Environment

The environment includes organizations and forces outside the manager's work unit. The manager must examine it to see if objectives are realistic and to see how the environment will affect the plans he or she will make in Step 3.

Managers need to search the environment in order to determine (1) what threats to achieving the unit's objectives are developing and (2) how changes in the environment present opportunities for greater achievement of those objectives. Managers who do not keep up with change become self-satisfied and get left behind. Self-satisfaction is a good way to start an enterprise on a decline. Look what happened to the film companies when TV came in, to the steam locomotive companies when diesels came onto

Table 8.1
Types of Plans and Management Level of Preparation

Type of Plan	Level of Preparation		
	Top Management	Middle Management	Supervisor
Strategies	●		
Policies	●	●	
Procedures		●	
Rules		●	●
Projects	●	●	●
Programs	●	●	●
Budgets	●	●	●
Schedules			●

David Sarnoff

At 12:18 A.M. on April 15, 1912, a smart young radio operator working for the Marconi company in New York picked up a CQD signal (predecessor of the SOS) sent out by the *S.S. Titanic*. David Sarnoff alerted the world to the most shocking maritime disaster in history. Four years later Sarnoff picked up another kind of signal. He wrote a memo to his superiors saying he had a "plan of development which would make radio a 'household utility' in the same sense as the piano or phonograph." After the Radio Corp. of America bought out Marconi, Sarnoff became its general manager. His "radio music boxes," put on the market in 1922, grossed $83.5 million in the first three years. He formed the National Broadcasting Co. to help feed the box with news and entertainment. As early as 1923 his interest turned to television; he was to spend $50 million of RCA's money toward its development before a dollar came back. This gamble was to be overshadowed by another. RCA spent $130 million on a color television system that for years looked like a loser. The Federal Communications Commission had approved a different system sponsored by RCA's rival, CBS. Doggedly, Sarnoff fought on and finally won a reversal from the FCC. This intense, opinionated, driving man, who loved to be called "General" (he had served on Eisenhower's staff), had been born near Minsk, Russia. Like a million other Jewish immigrants, he knew poverty on New York's Lower East Side. At his funeral in 1971, John D.'s grandson, Governor Nelson Rockefeller, delivered Sarnoff's eulogy in Temple Emanu-El: "In David Sarnoff, the word 'visionary' meant a capacity to see into tomorrow and make it work."

Photo by Steve Shapiro, Time-Life Picture Agency, © Time Inc.

Source: *Fortune*, January 1975, p. 71. Reprinted by permission.

the scene, to A. B. Dick when Xerox grew. One manager who effectively examined the environment and persuaded his enterprise to anticipate the future was David Sarnoff (see accompanying picture and profile).

The environment to be examined varies with the level of the manager. The primary environments top managers must be concerned with are those outside the firm and the overall internal strengths and weaknesses of the firm. The environment which the middle manager examines is the superior's world (to make sure that resources and support will be given to the unit), units which feed into his or her unit at the peer level, subordinates' units, and firms and factors outside the firm which feed directly into the unit. For example, the middle manager who is a plant manager will examine the following units and forces, among others:

- The home office.
- Plants which supply the manager's plant with subassemblies.
- Warehouses and other plants where products are shipped.
- Subordinates.
- Trucking firms and other firms outside the company with which it is necessary to deal.

At the supervisory level, the environment examined parallels that of the middle manager, except supervisors examine units outside the firm only rarely. The primary environment includes:

- Superiors' units.
- Peer units.

The External Environment of the Top Manager

Among the aspects of the external environment which a top manager examines are economic factors, government and legal factors, market and competitive factors, and social factors.

Economic Factors

The state of the economy at present and in the future affects the fortunes of the firm. The major events which the manager must consider include:

- *The stage of the business cycle* The economy can be classified as being in a depression, recession, recovery, or prosperity.
- *The inflationary or deflationary trend in prices of goods and services* If inflation is very severe, wage and price controls can be imposed.
- *Monetary policies, interest rates, and devaluation or revaluation of the currency relative to other currencies.*
- *Fiscal policies* Tax rates for firms and individuals have a significant impact on a firm's objectives.
- *Balance of payments surpluses or deficits* The balance of payments is a crucial factor in foreign trade.

Each of these facets of the economy can help or hinder the achievement of a firm's objectives and the success or failure of the firm.

Government and Legal Factors

Federal, state or provincial, and local governments have a growing impact on business. They legislate on such matters as wage and price controls, equal employment opportunity, safety and health at work, how consumer credit is administered, where plants can locate, what plants can emit in the air, how much noise a product can make, whether and what kinds of advertising businesses can run, and other matters. These laws and regulations change how businesses operate on a day-to-day basis.

Actions by governments also affect the future choices of businesses. They can increase opportunities for or threats to a firm's success, sometimes both. Some examples of how government laws and regulations provide opportunities for business are listed below:

- Governments are large purchasers of goods and services.
- Governments subsidize firms and industries and thus help them survive and prosper.
- The government protects domestic producers against "unfair" foreign competition.

Market and Competitive Factors

Top managers first examine primary demand factors—those which affect the basic demand for a product or service. Among such factors are:

- Changes in population.
- Age shifts in population.
- Income distribution in the population.

They then look at what is happening in the competitive sphere, for example:

- Entry and exit of major competitors from competion with the firm.
- New substitutes for the product or service being introduced by the firm.

Supplier and Technological Factors

Some of the major issues involved in the supply of necessary resources and technology include:

- Changes in the availability and cost of raw materials.
- Changes in the availability and cost of money.
- Changes in the availability and cost of labor.
- Changes in the availability and cost of subassemblies.
- The amount and quality of technological change affecting the firm's products/services and/or how they are produced or created.

Social and Other Factors

Finally, the top manager also examines changes in values and attitudes of people (customers and employees) which can affect the firm.

- At one time, it was thought the normal thing for a family unit to do was have two to four children. This view is no longer as widely held as it was, and certain firms are significantly affected by this change: P&G (Pampers), Gerber (baby food), builders (houses vs. condominiums), Mattel (toys), and others.

- At one time, retired people, single people, widows, and widowers lived with relatives. Now there is a trend to live alone. This has a strong impact on builders, G.M., appliance manufacturers such as Hoover, food packers such as Campbell Soup, and others.

- At one time, most married women stayed home. Now, most work for pay. This has caused problems for firms that sold door to door—for example, Avon and Fuller Brush—and has increased business for a variety of firms: those that offer nursery school service, prepared foods, restaurants (two-employee families eat out more frequently), and home security systems, to name a few.

- Newer attitudes on the part of employees about how many hours they wish to work, the quality of life they expect at work, and the kind of supervisory style they expect can affect how strategies are developed and implemented.

How Do Managers Examine the Environment?

Management uses three methods to search the environment: information gathering, spying, and forecasting/modeling. Information gathering involves reading written material from company, industry, and government sources to determine potential changes. But managers prefer to gather information verbally, from the media (radio and TV), employees, clients, competitors, industry channel executives (e.g., wholesalers), consultants, bankers, and stockbrokers.

A second source of getting information is by using spies. These individuals can be the enterprise's employees, an employee of a competitor, a supplier, a customer, or a "professional" spy. The third method of information gathering focuses on formal forecasts and models of the future. The forecaster can be an enterprise employee, a forecasting service, or a consultant. We shall return to the subject of forecasting shortly.

These are the three sources. But which is used when, and how are they used? There have been a few studies of managers' information-gathering activities. Francis Aguilar studied how the executives in forty-one chemical companies in the United States and Europe gathered information to be used in forecasting the future.[5] He found that the primary way of gathering information is through verbal communication, usually from subordinates and friends in the industry. What written data are used come mostly from newspapers. Usually any information gathered by executives from subordinates is solicited. Information from outside often comes unsolicited, and it has greater impact. Other studies confirm these findings.

We know little about spying that is not mere sensationalism. But Jerry Wall, who studied 1,200 companies, argues that spying has not increased much since the late 1950s and that most of what took place then was not of the professional variety.[6] It usually consisted of questioning clients and competitors' salespeople.

Forecasting the Future

One of the tools which managers use to help predict and then plan for the future is forecasting.

Forecasting is the formal process of predicting future events that will significantly affect the functioning of the enterprise.

All the factors discussed regarding the environment are subject to forecasting techniques.

Forecasting Techniques

In a formal forecasting procedure the forecaster decides what to forecast, does the necessary research using various techniques, prepares a forecast, and then compares the forecast to later actuality and modifies his or her premises or techniques accordingly. Note that the output of the process is a forecast of future events that is used to plan the enterprise's operations.

In sophisticated forecasting systems several forecasts are prepared. This is called *contingency forecasting*. The several forecasts are based on different assumptions about major future events. For example, Forecast 1 may assume that OPEC will not shut off the supply of oil and that it will raise prices 7 percent per year. Forecast 2 may assume a 12 percent annual rise in oil prices.

In the following paragraphs we will consider different types of forecasting techniques. Forecasting techniques can be categorized as qualitative, historical/predictive, technological, or causal.

Qualitative Techniques

The qualitative approach uses an informed expert to predict some future occurrence. Sometimes the opinions of many "experts" are summed or weighted to arrive at a single forecast. But whatever quantitative techniques are used, the qualitative approach is always used by the decision maker. He or she must decide to accept, modify, or reject a prediction. In effect, a decision maker who rejects or modifies a qualitative forecast substitutes his or her judgment for the expert's findings.

Many enterprises have found that certain well-informed and savvy salespeople can make better predictions of future demand than experts using sophisticated computer models. The salespeople know the customers and their recent product decisions, and these can be adjusted more quickly than an econometric model can be rebuilt.

A more formal qualitative forecast can be prepared by using the Delphi technique. Delphi was originally developed by the Rand Corporation to forecast possible military events. The unit seeking a forecast identifies the experts whose opinions it wants to know. Each expert does not know who the others are. A coordinator mails a description of the subject of the forecast to each expert. The experts make their forecasts and the coordinator summarizes their responses, indicating the average (median) response and the range of the middle 50 percent of the answers. The experts are then asked to reconsider their predictions; if a prediction was not in the middle 50 percent, the expert is asked to give reasons for making that particular forecast. Even without this kind of feedback, studies indicate that these second responses tend to be closer together than the first group of predictions. This process continues (probably through three or four sets of predictions), and then the forecast is made on the basis of the median responses. Sometimes the "extreme" prediction on Round 1 becomes the final forecast if the reasons are good. Otherwise (and most frequently) the predictions get closer with each round. The Delphi technique is used to reduce the "crowd effect" or "group think" in which everyone agrees with "the expert" when all are in the same room

The key to the success of a qualitative forecast is the choice of experts. It is important to choose people who know the field and who have a history of making good forecasts.

Another type of qualitative forecast is the market survey. The enterprise can poll (in person or by questionnaire) customers or clients about expected future behavior. The University of Michigan asks people about their probable future purchases of cars, for example; political polls ask people about their probable future usage of government services, among other things. Forecasts based on such surveys are effective if the right people are sampled in enough numbers, if those sampled know what they want to do, and if the sample is taken close enough to the time at which the purchase would be made (or the service used, etc.). This method amounts to asking a set of "experts"—consumers or potential consumers—what they will do. If they are indeed "experts," the forecast will be a good one.

Quantitative Techniques

Trend Projection

A second approach to forecasting is quantitative projection of historical patterns into the future. The simplest way of using this approach is to project past data into the future. This can be done in a table or a graph. For example, if you want to predict future usage of the Xerox machine, examine past usage. If the machine has been used 60 times per day with an average load of 600 pages per day for the past week, you can confidently predict 60 uses and 600 pages per day for tomorrow.

Xerox usage is rarely exactly the same from day to day, however. You can make the forecast more sophisticated by examining the variations around the average. A closer look may indicate a pattern (see Table 8.2). Suppose one forecast was based on Week IV alone. A quick look,

Table 8.2
Xerox Usage

	Week I	Week II	Week III	Week IV
Monday	54/540	55/560	57/578	64/640
Tuesday	52/510	54/546	53/525	58/560
Wednesday	53/535	53/537	55/560	59/590
Thursday	50/490	51/500	54/540	57/570
Friday	55/570	56/565	58/580	62/635

however, reveals that usage is increasing. So computing *moving* averages is better than taking a simple average. This can be made more sophisticated by using weighted moving averages or exponential smoothing. As the data accumulate, they become easier to visualize if they are incorporated into a graph (See Figure 8.3). The extension of the trend line (which I have drawn in arbitrarily) is the forecast of future usage.

Look again at Table 8.2. It is clear that Monday and Friday are the busiest days, Wednesday somewhat less busy; Tuesday and Thursday are slower. In predicting things like sales, patterns of this type develop too. They are called *seasonal variations*. In sales of cranberry sauce these variations are dramatic; in soap sales less so. In forecasting the future the period for which the forecast is made can be adjusted to take seasonal variations into account. In really sophisticated trend projections long-run changes such as business cycle changes can be considered as well. Such projections are called *time series analyses*.

There is a big assumption behind trend analysis: that future conditions

Figure 8.3
Xerox Usage

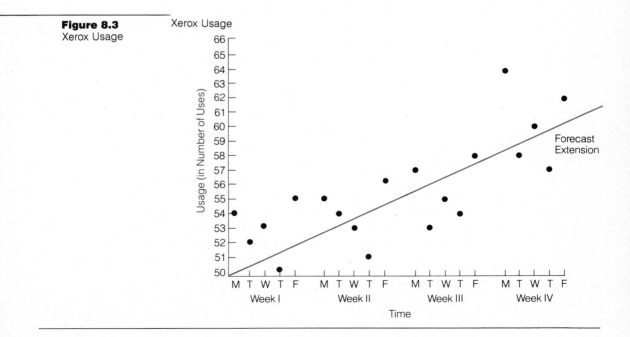

will be similar to past conditions. This is truer in some businesses (e.g., demand for telephones) than in others (e.g., demand for high-fashion merchandise). The method is less useful in cases in which this assumption is less justified.

Technological Forecasting

Some enterprises try to predict changes in technology—for example, what are the possible future uses of the minicomputer? This is called *technological forecasting*. The enterprise can use techniques like Delphi or simply extrapolate present technological trends. For example, if you examine the data on lumens per watt from the first lightbulb in 1880 to the fluorescent bulb in 1940, the trend is almost a straight line upward.

Technological forecasting has been somewhat successful where data have been available. Many experts can predict that a change is coming, but predicting *when* it will come is more crucial, and technological forecasting has done a poor job in this area. It may improve in the future, however.

Causal Modeling

The most technically sophisticated forecasts use statistical techniques and econometric modeling to forecast the future. This method involves studying the statistical relationship between the factor under consideration (for example, demand for baby food) and another factor (for example, birthrate). In statistical terms this relationship is called a *correlation*. The closer the correlation comes to "perfect" (1,000), the more accurate the forecast. If the correlation is good (say, 0.95) and the other factor is known, a forecast is possible. More sophisticated techniques that involve more than two factors can be used (multiple correlation or multiple regression). Again, the better the predictors and the closer the correlation, the better the forecast.

The most technically sophisticated forecasting technique is *mathematical/econometric modeling*. Specialists develop a series of equations that relate the essential functions of the enterprise. Once this is done, they can forecast the future by putting the model through a series of "what if" changes. This works *if* the model is accurate and *if* the rest of the environment does not change. But it is very expensive. Thus there are a number of possible forecasting techniques. How do you choose the right one, considering cost, accuracy, and other factors? Table 8.3 briefly summarizes some of the methods and offers some criteria for making the choice.

Developing Plans

After searching the environment for opportunities and threats the firm (or units within the firm) faces, the last step is to develop plans to achieve the

Table 8.3
Basic Forecasting
Techniques

	A. Qualitative Methods		B. Trend Projection	C. Causal Methods (Quantitative)	
	1. Delphi Method	**2. Market Research**	**1. Trend Projections**	**1. Regression Model**	**2. Econometric Model**
Description	A panel of experts is interrogated by a sequence of questionnaires in which the responses to one questionnaire are used to produce the next questionnaire. Any set of information available to some experts and not others is thus passed on to the others, enabling all the experts to have access to all the information for forecasting. This technique eliminates the bandwagon effect of majority opinion.	The systematic, formal, and conscious procedure for evolving and testing hypotheses about real markets.	This technique fits a trend line to a mathematical equation and then projects it into the future by means of this equation. There are several variations: the slope-characteristic method, polynomials, logarithms, and so on.	This functionally relates sales to other economic, competitive, or internal variables and estimates an equation using the least-squares technique. Relationships are primarily analyzed statistically, although any relationship should be selected for testing on a rational ground.	An econometric model is a system of interdependent regression equations that describes some sector of economic sales or profit activity. The parameters of the regression equations are usually estimated simultaneously. As a rule, these models are relatively expensive to develop and can easily cost between $5,000 and $10,000, depending on detail. However, due to the system of equations inherent in such models, they will better express the causalities involved than an ordinary regression equation and hence will predict turning points more accurately.
Accuracy Short term 0-3 months	Fair to very good	Excellent	Very good	Good to very good	Good to very good
Medium term 3 months- 2 years	Fair to very good	Good	Good	Good to very good	Very good to excellent
Long term 2 years and up	Fair to very good	Fair to good	Good	Poor	Good
Turning point identification	Fair to good	Fair to very good	Poor	Very good	Excellent
Applications	Forecasts of long-range and new-product sales, forecasts of margins.	Forecasts of long-range and new-product sales, forecasts of margins.	New-product forecasts (particularly intermediate- and long-term).	Forecasts of sales by product classes, forecasts of margins.	Forecasts of sales by product classes, forecasts of margins.
Data required	A coordinator issues the sequence of questionnaires, editing and consolidating the responses.	As a minimum, two sets of reports over time. One needs a considerable collection of market data from questionnaires, surveys, and time series analyses of market variables.	Varies with the technique used. However, a good rule of thumb is to use a minimum of five years' annual data to start. Thereafter, the complete history.	Several years' quarterly history to obtain good, meaningful relationships. Mathematically necessary to have two more observations than independent variables.	The same as for regression.
Cost	$2,000+	$5,000+	Varies with application	$100	$5,000+
Computer calculation required?	No	No	No	No	No
Time required to develop forecast	2 months+	3 months+	1 day-	Depends on ability to identify relationships.	2 months+

Source: John Chambers et al., "How to Choose the Right Forecasting Technique," *Harvard Business Review* 49 (July–August 1971): 55–60. Copyright © 1971 by the President and Fellows of Harvard College; all rights reserved.

objectives of the enterprise. In our consideration of this process we shall look at the plans of three management levels: top, middle, and supervisory.

At the top management level, the plans are strategies and policies. Figure 8.4 is a model of strategic planning, one of the most important jobs top managers perform. As you may note, Chapter 7 discussed Step 1, and we have just completed discussing Step 2A. We shall now examine the other steps in strategic planning. The output of the total process is a set of plans to achieve corporate objectives, a strategy.

A strategy is a unified, comprehensive, and integrated plan relating the strategic advantages of the firm to the challenges of the environment. It is designed to ensure that the basic objectives of an enterprise are achieved.

Policies are guides to decision making and action which spell out precisely how the strategy will come to be and set up a follow-up mechanism to make sure all of its aspects are put into effect.

Part of the policy-making process is resource deployment through the use of budgets. Decisions on which divisions, departments, or units are to receive how much money, which facilities, and which executives are all

Figure 8.4
A Model of the
Strategic Planning
Process

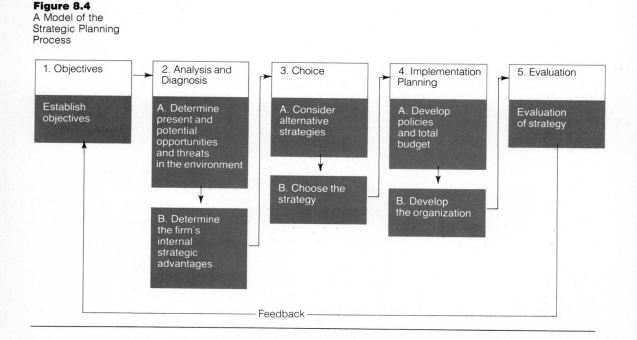

Harry Blair Cunningham

Technological advance has played such a large part in the rise of twentieth-century business that there's a tendency to assume the presence of an invention behind every important business innovation. Harry Cunningham's achievement in the ancient field of retailing is a reminder that business is still a matter of knowing what employees can do and how customers will react. The man who, by an innovation called K mart, revitalized the stagnant S.S. Kresge Co., did it without test tubes or patents.

Cunningham had not set out to be a retailer. He studied journalism during two years at Miami University, Ohio, then got a job on a newspaper in Harrisburg, not far from his birthplace, Home Camp, Pennsylvania. He met a Kresge executive and saw more chance of advancement there. Starting at the bottom as a stock boy in a Lynchburg, Virginia, store, he worked seventy, eighty, ninety hours a week. Promotions came fast. In 1957 he was given the title of "general vice president" with no specified duties and no staff. He seemed to be in line for the top job, but its incumbent, who didn't want a crown prince around the Detroit headquarters, suggested that he travel. Cunningham had noticed that many corporate executives competed so intently for the chief executive office that they didn't know what to do with it when they got it. He set out to find what the company needed; after two years of travel he had visited all except fourteen of Kresge's 725 stores.

Sebastian S. Kresge's successors had preserved the sound management he built before his retirement in 1925. (Kresge died in 1956 at ninety-nine.) But the chain's customers had been moving to the suburbs, stranding central-city stores. Though sales inched up year by year, profits inched down. Cunningham, searching for new directions, studied the discount stores that were booming, especially in New England. Here was, he soon concluded, an idea that Kresge, with its strong national organization, could carry further than the discounters. He did not trumpet this conclusion in a company that looked down on discounters. "If I had announced before being elected president my intention to take Kresge into discounting, I'm quite sure I would not have been elected president."

He wanted a broad management consensus to understand why and how Kresge should make a major shift. An executive group carried out an elaborate study of discounting and, before the first K mart opened in 1962, management's confidence in the idea was such that it had made an $80-million commitment for thirty-three K marts. The new stores carried fast-moving lines of nationally advertised goods, relying [on] a high turnover to keep prices down.

Kresge's sales volume had been $483 million in 1962, less

than half that of the Woolworth chain. In a few years Kresge overtook Woolworth, which moved slowly into discounting with Woolco stores. In 1977 Kresge, its name changed to K mart Corporation, had sales of $9 billion. Profits rose from $9 million in 1962 to around $300 million in 1977. There are now 1,367 K marts, including 161 opened in 1977. No large retailer in the last fifteen years has had a comparable record of growth.

Cunningham says that the key was his appreciation of Kresge's organizational strengths. For decades the company had given store managers more scope than they had in most rival chains, a policy that facilitated development of executive talent. Kresge's real-estate department had always been strong, and Cunningham relied on it to pick freestanding K mart sites outside of high-rent shopping centers.

Cunningham, who retired as c.e.o. in 1972, is now a director of several big companies, including K mart. In his two years of roving exile from headquarters, he did more than generate a bright marketing idea; he discovered that his organization had capabilities for change that nobody else had seen.

Source: *Fortune*, January 30, 1978, p. 95. Reprinted by permission.

aspects of resource deployment. One executive who developed a strategy and policies that had a positive effect on his company is Harry Blair Cunningham, pictured on page 257.

Our definition of strategy and policies implies one strategic decision and a set of policies. In general, this is the case. In a few large and complex firms with major subdivisions facing multiple environments, several strategies and sets of policies can be chosen. This process is called *contingency planning*. Here is how it works.

If one contingency (typically a set of economic and political conditions) comes to be, Strategy A and its associated policies are the plan. Strategy A's conditions may require stable government monetary and fiscal policies, prosperity, and a GNP growth rate of 3 percent. If instead there is a recession and a negative growth rate, Strategy B will be put into effect.

I said earlier that strategic planning is a top management job. By top management I mean the chairman of the board, corporate president, and chief operating vice-presidents. Some firms are so large and complex that they organize their divisions independently and the top officials of these divisions are thus top managers. General Electric calls these major units Strategic Business Units (SBUs). Many firms also have and use corporate planning staffs to help make strategy and policy decisions. Usually these staffs do studies of the environment, of internal strategic advantages, and of strategic alternatives. They may also recommend policies to be adopted.

Now let us discuss, however briefly, Steps 2B, 3, 4 and 5 of the strategic planning process shown in Figure 8.4.

Strategic Advantage Analysis and Diagnosis

Strategic advantage analysis and diagnosis is the process by which the strategists examine the firm's financial accounting, marketing/ distribution, production/operations, personnel/labor relations, and corporate resources to determine where the firm has significant strengths (and weaknesses) in order to most effectively exploit the opportunities and meet the threats the environment is presenting the firm.

No firm is equally strong in all its functions and divisions. Procter & Gamble is known for its superb marketing. Maytag is known for its outstanding productions and product design. American Telephone & Telegraph is known for its outstanding service and personnel policies.

Within a company, each of the divisions has varying strengths and weaknesses. General Electric was strong in jet engines and weak in computers a few years ago. General Motors is stronger in market control in automobiles than in appliances. Ford does better in automobiles than with its Philco electronics division.

Executives must look for what Chester Barnard called "the strategic factors."[7] Unless they are fully aware of their strategic advantages, they may not choose whichever of the many opportunities available at a given time is likely to lead to the greatest success. Unless they regularly analyze their weaknesses, they will be unable to face the environmental threats effectively.

Every firm has strategic advantages and disadvantages. Large firms, for instance, have financial strengths but tend to be much slower to move and less able to serve small market segments effectively than smaller firms. Advantages are analyzed and diagnosed at the corporate level in a single SBU firm. They will be analyzed at the SBU level by SBU executives and then reevaluated at the corporate level and compared across SBUs.

Management performs strategic advantage analysis and diagnosis to identify clearly the current strengths and weaknesses of the firm. Management also examines its most probable *future* strengths and weaknesses. This helps determine how relevant current policies and future policies are to:

- Corporate objectives.
- Competitors in similar businesses.
- Future environment.
- Product/service life cycle.

Most strategists are concerned with how they are placed strategically relative to competitors with similar businesses. It is vital that the proper comparisons be made. As research has shown, companies with a high degree of investment intensity are often less profitable than those with lower investment/sales ratios. Similarly, other differences exist if the firm used for comparison is substantially different.

It is also important to compare firms in businesses in the same or similar phases of the product service life cycle. It would be inappropriate to compare a firm whose main products or services are in the mature portion of the life cycle with a firm whose main products are in the growth phase of the cycle.

Data for analysis and diagnosis of the factors come from several sources. Data gathered in the environmental analysis and diagnosis stage of strategic planning constitute one source. Internal data generated in doing business and available from the management information system and the functional departments (such as marketing, personnel) are another good source.

Each function of the business is analyzed. For example, Table 8.4 presents the finance and accounting factors and Table 8.5 the marketing strategic factors to be analyzed and evaluated. Once managers analyze the results, they can begin to make decisions about the present status of divisions or product or service lines. One example of this kind of analysis is the "Business Portfolio or Growth Share Matrix" (Figure 8.5) done by the Boston Consulting Group (BCU).[8] BCG's research indicates that the larger the market share, the greater the profitability of a product/service line.

In the lower left corner of Figure 8.5 are the most profitable current products which generate more cash than it *costs* to operate (cash cows). In the upper left corner are the stars—the products of the future. Firms use cash from the cash cows to invest in the stars. Products in the lower right corner are the worst and should be liquidated by selling them off or stopping production (dogs). The hardest to decide on are the question

---

Table 8.4
Strategic Advantage Factors: Finance and Accounting

1. Total financial resources and strength.
2. Low cost of capital relative to industry and competitors because of stock price and dividend policy.
3. Effective capital structure, allowing flexibility in raising additional capital as needed; financial leverage.
4. Amicable relations with owners and stockholders.
5. Advantageous tax conditions.
6. Efficient and effective financial planning, working capital, and capital budgeting procedures.
7. Efficient and effective accounting systems for cost, budget and profit planning, and auditing procedures.
8. Inventory valuation policies.

Table 8.5
Strategic Advantage
Factors: Marketing and
Distribution

1. Competitive structure and market share: To what extent has the firm established a strong market share in the total market or its key submarkets?
2. Efficient and effective market research system.
3. The product mix: quality of products and services.
4. Product-services line: completeness, new product leadership, and product mix; phase of life cycle the main products are in.
5. Strong new product/service leadership.
6. Patent protection (or equivalent legal protection for services).
7. Positive feelings about the firm and its products/services on the part of the ultimate consumer.
8. Efficient and effective packaging of products (or equivalent in services).
9. Pricing strategy for products and services.
10. Efficient and effective sales force: close ties with key customers. How vulnerable are we in terms of concentration of sales to a few customers?
11. Effective advertising: Has it established the company's product-brand image to develop loyal customers?
12. Efficient and effective marketing promotion.
13. Efficient and effective service after purchase.
14. Efficient and effective channels of distribution and geographic coverage, including international efforts.

marks—some should be divested (sold off); others turned into stars. The goal in BCG analysis is to develop a balanced portfolio of products or divisions. It is desirable to have largest sales in cash cows and stars. Only a few question marks and a very few dogs can be tolerated.

Strategic Choice

When strategic analysis is complete then top managers are ready to enter Step 3, choice of the strategy. The first step in making the strategic choice

Figure 8.5
The Business
Portfolio or Growth
Share Matrix

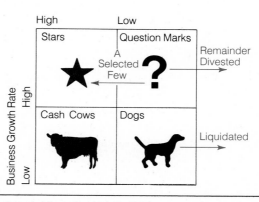

Source: Allan Gerald, "A Note on the Boston Consulting Group Concept of Competitive Analysis and Corporate Strategy," Intercollegiate Case Clearing House, ICCH 9-175-175, June 1976, p. 5. Reprinted by permission.

is to generate a reasonable number of strategies to consider given the environmental opportunities and threats and the strategic advantages and weaknesses of the firm. These will help fill the gaps or take advantage of the opportunities with which the firm is faced.

The central concern is the business the firm is in. The business definition will vary in complexity from the simple (a one-product or -service firm) to the very complex (a large firm involved in multiple businesses). Once the business the firm is in has been defined, the strategist must pose various questions: "Should we get out of this business entirely?" "Should we try to grow?" Answering such questions will help the strategist focus on the type of strategic alternatives the firm should pursue. Depending on the strategist, an active or passive strategy will be put into effect.

Where do strategic alternatives come from? They begin with alternatives (1) the strategist knows about, (2) the strategist thinks will work, and (3) are not major breaks with the past (unless the firm's situation is dire). The grand strategic alternatives and their substrategies are listed below in outline form:

I. *Stable growth strategies* A stable growth strategy is one that a firm pursues when it continues to pursue the same or similar objectives, increasing the level of achievement by about the same percentage each year as it has achieved in the past, continuing to serve the public in the same or similar sectors. The firm's main strategic decisions focus on incremental improvement of functional performance. Substrategies for stable growth are:

   A. *Incremental growth* The firm sets as its objectives the achievement level that was accomplished in the past, adjusted for inflation. These objectives usually approximate the industry average or somewhat less.

   B. *Profit (-harvesting) strategies* When the main objective of the SBU or firm is to generate cash for the corporation or stockholders, profit strategies are followed. If necessary, market share is sacrificed to generate cash.

   C. *Stable growth as a pause strategy* When the firm reduces the objectives to be achieved from the growth level to the incremental growth level in order to focus attention on improving efficiency and similar operations, this is known as a pause strategy.

   D. *Sustainable growth strategy* This is an incremental growth strategy chosen because the firm's executives believe that external conditions such as the availability of resources have turned unfavorable for growth strategy.

Whichever substrategy of the stable growth grand strategy is chosen, the firm will plan growth at about the past stable growth rate and no more.

II. *Growth strategies* A growth strategy is one that a firm pursues when it increases the level of its objectives to a level higher than an extrapolation of the past level into the future; when it serves the public in the same sector or can add additional product/service sectors; and when it focuses its strategic decisions on major functional performance increases. Substrategies of the growth strategy include:

A. *Internal growth strategies* An internal growth strategy is one in which the firm raises its level of objectives achievement higher than an extrapolation of its past level by increasing sales and profits of its present product/service line.

    1. *Diversification strategy* A diversification strategy is one in which the firm's objectives are at the growth level and are achieved by adding products or services internally to the prior product/service line. This can be accomplished by improving technology or marketing channels or increasing production or the number of customers.

B. *External growth strategies* When the firm raises its objectives to a level of achievement higher than that which an extrapolation of its past level suggests and does so by increasing sales and profits through merger, joint venture, vertical integration, or grow-to-sell-out strategy, this is known as an external growth strategy.

    1. *Merger* A merger occurs when two or more businesses combine. There are two types of mergers. One company may acquire the assets and liabilities of the other in exchange for stock or cash. Or both companies may be dissolved so that assets and liabilities can be combined and new stock can be issued.

    2. *Joint venture* A joint venture involves an equity arrangement between two or more independent enterprises which results in the creation of a new organizational entity.

    3. *Vertical integration* Vertical integration is a growth strategy characterized by the extension of the firm's business definition in two possible directions: A *backward* integration strategy has the firm entering the business of supplying some of the firm's present inputs. A *forward* integration strategy moves the firm into the business of distributing its output by entering the channels closer to the ultimate consumer.

    4. *Grow-to-sell-out strategy* Many entrepreneurs plan to develop their business into a growth company; when it reaches the fast growth rate apex, they sell out to a larger firm.

III. *Retrenchment and turnaround strategies* A retrenchment or turnaround strategy is pursued by a firm whose level of achievement is below its past level. Management will seek to increase the level of achievement if possible. If it wants to continue to serve the public in the same sector or product/service line, it may have to reduce its product or service line. Strategic decisions in a retrenchment or turnaround strategy focus on functional improvement and reduction of units with negative cash flows. The substrategies include the following:

A. *Turnaround strategies* Focus on improving the firm's efficiency.

B. *Divestment* The selling off or liquidation of an SBU or a major subpart of an SBU.

C. *Liquidation* The selling off or shutting down of the firm. When should a firm liquidate?

D. *Captive company* A firm becomes a captive company when it reduces its major functional activities and sells 75 percent or more of its products or services to a single customer.

IV. *Combination Strategy* A combination strategy is a strategy that a firm pursues when its main strategic decisions focus on the conscious use of several grand strategies (stable growth, growth, retrenchment) at the same time in several of its SBUs. Another type of combination strategy involves the use of several grand strategies at different future times. The firm's objectives and the business sector it serves may be the same or change depending on how it applies the grand strategies of growth and retrenchment.

Once a reasonable number of strategic alternatives are considered, the top managers choose a strategy. Strategic choice decisions are made in light of four selection factors: (1) managerial perceptions of external dependence, (2) managerial attitudes toward risk, (3) managerial awareness of past enterprise strategies, and (4) managerial power relationships and organization structure.

The extent to which the firm is dependent for its survival on owners, competitors, customers, the government, and the community is an important factor in the success of a management strategy. Thus management's view of external dependence—the first factor noted above—plays a major role in this selection process. Managers' attitudes toward risk, the second factor, vary greatly. Some feel risk is necessary for success. Others believe risk is a fact of life and some risk is desirable. Still others feel that high risk destroys enterprises and needs to be minimized. Which of these attitudes the firm's managers assume determines how innovative or risky their strategic choice will be. It will eliminate some strategic alternatives and highlight others.

Past strategies are the beginning point in strategy selection. Managerial awareness and evaluation of past strategies—the third factor—may eliminate some strategic choices. Power relationships and organization structure, the final dimension in the strategy decision process, are a key factor. Personalities get involved, and whom the boss likes and respects has an impact on which strategic choice is made. Sometimes, too, the powerful can shift blame to lower-level executives. Lower-level managers in the organization have some impact on strategic choice, and the amount of time the decision maker has to make the strategic decision also influences the final choice.

Implementation Planning

Enterprises which prepare functional policies and plans for implementing strategic choices will be more effective than those which do not. As noted in Figure 8.4, once a strategy has been chosen, the next step is implementation planning. Let's discuss briefly the development of policies, the first phase (4A in Figure 8.4) of implementation planning. Developing the organization, the second phase (4B), is the organizing function, which is examined in Chapters 10 through 13.

Functional policy implementation involves two processes: resource deployment and development of policies which actually put the strategy into effect. Strategists have the power and must determine how to distribute money, facilities, and executives among divisions, departments, or SBUs (resource deployment). There are two steps in the development of policies. First, management must spell out precisely how the strategic choice will come to be. Then a follow-up mechanism must be set up to make sure strategic choice and policy decisions will take place.

The policies the firm creates are decisional guides to action; they make the chosen strategy work. The critical element in functional policy making is management's ability to factor the grand strategy into policies that are compatible, workable, and not just "theoretically sound." Follow-through on functional policy implementation requires an effective information system, an appropriate control system, and a reward system which leads to accurate, complete feedback in time to act upon the data.

An enterprise could develop hundreds of policies to cover the important areas of the business. Note that a policy does not tell the manager how to handle a specific promotion or add a specific product. It is a general guide to action. It limits the choices of managers in most cases. But it does not limit them entirely. It serves as a guide to middle and supervisory managers in making certain choices.

Policies are developed to ensure that (1) the strategic decision is implemented; (2) there is a basis for control; (3) there is relative consistency and coordination of work; (4) the amount of time executives spend making decisions is reduced. In small and many medium-size enterprises, policies are generally understood and verbal. In large and some medium-size firms, they are often in written form and are distributed to managers. Without policy development, managers would make the same decisions over and over again. In addition, different managers might choose different directions, which could create problems. On the other hand, policies should never be so inflexible as to prevent exceptions for good reasons.

Minimally adequate policies consist of key functional decisions in at least six areas:

1. Finance and accounting
2. Marketing
3. Production/operations management
4. Research and development

5. Personnel
6. Logistics

By way of illustration, crucial accounting and finance policy questions for implementing a growth strategy are listed in Table 8.6. Policies which correspond to these questions are given in Table 8.7. The number of the policy question in Table 8.6 corresponds to the number of the appropriate response in Table 8.7.

Evaluation of Strategy

The last phase of the strategic planning process is evaluation.

Evaluation of strategy is that phase of the strategic planning process in which the top managers determine whether their strategic choice in its implemented form is meeting the objectives of the enterprise.

Evaluation takes place at both corporate and SBU levels. The evaluation process requires:

- Motivation to evaluate.
- A feedback system to provide the data for evaluation.
- Criteria for evaluation.
- Decisions about the outcome of the strategic evaluation.

Before evaluation will take place, the top managers must want to evaluate the performance. This motivation develops if they realize the strategy can fail and if they are rewarded for their performance relative to objectives.

Information in a usable form is necessary to evaluate the strategy. This requires an effective management information system and honest and complete reporting of the results of the strategy.

The criteria to use in the evaluation process according to Seymour Tilles are:[9]

1. Internal consistency.
2. Consistency with the environment.
3. Appropriateness, given the enterprise's resources.
4. Acceptability of degree of risk.

Table 8.6
Finance/Accounting Policy Questions Crucial to the Implementation of a Growth Strategy

1. Where will we get added funds to grow: internally or externally?
2. If externally, how? Where?
3. What will growth do to our cash flow?
4. What accounting systems and policies do we use?
5. What capital structure policy do we pursue? No debt or heavily levered structure?

Table 8.7
Examples of Finance
and Accounting
Policies

1. Additional funding needed for growth will be generated externally.
2. An equity issue of $100,000,000 will be offered in 1980.
3. If growth causes cash flow problems which the $100,000,000 does not satisfy, we will seek additional long-term debt. Our debt/equity ratio will be quite satisfactory after the $100,000,000 equity issue.
4. We will continue to use LIFO (last-in/first-out accounting) in view of the current inflationary economy.
5. The capital structure we follow will continue as in the past. We will seek to approximate the debt/equity ratio of the average firm in the industry. This will balance leverage with risk.

5. Appropriateness of time horizon.
6. Workability.

In attempting to make a quantitative evaluation of the effectiveness of corporate strategy with reference to the firm's own history or to a competitor's performance, the firm's performance on the following factors is relevant: net profit, stock price, dividend rates, earnings per share, return on capital, return on equity, market share, growth in sales, days lost per employee as a result of strikes, production costs and efficiency, distribution costs and efficiency, and employee turnover, absenteeism, and satisfaction indexes.

The evaluation can be based on objective or subjective criteria. Four sources of measuring achievement objectively when comparing the firm's results with those of similar firms include: Compustat, *Dun's Review, Fortune Magazine,* and *Forbes*'s "Annual Report on American Industry." A subjective approach would be to ask "experts" which firms are the most successful. But both objective and subjective methods become more difficult when more than one criterion is used to rate success.

Finally, note the feedback loop from evaluation to objectives in Figure 8.4. This indicates that through the control system, management information system, and strategic planning evaluation, managers can take action to correct flaws in the system where necessary: Thus, if objectives are too easily achieved, the manager should raise them. If they are impossible to meet, the manager should lower them. If they are attainable yet challenging, they are ideal.

**Middle
Management
Planning**

Top managers are directly responsible for strategic planning. They supervise middle management planning too. Middle managers do the planning which implements the major policies further down in the organization. They break down the big decisions into meaningful parts for divisions, departments, and units. The plans they produce include derivative policies, procedures, rules, programs, projects, and intermediate level budgets.

Derivative Policies

Middle managers implement the general policies made by top managers at their level. Assume, for example, the strategy chosen is growth and the top management policy is to grow in the toy division. Middle managers would develop the policies which affect the product groups within the toy division. For example, those products which could be marketed in the toy division under consideration are:

- sports equipment (for baseball and basketball)
- board games (Monopoly, for instance)
- electronic toys (items such as TV games)
- playground equipment (swings, slides, etc.)
- stuffed animals
- dolls
- adult toys

The middle managers would set policies that would determine which of these lines to emphasize and market and how they would be marketed. Related marketing policy decisions include direct sales policies, advertising policies, sales promotion policies, pricing policies, and channel policies. Of course middle managers must be sure they couple their operating plans and policies to the strategy.

Procedures and Rules

After the broadest policies are developed, some enterprises push the planning process further and develop procedures or rules. These are more specific plans that limit the choices of middle and supervisory managers still further. Procedures and rules are developed for the same reasons as policies in areas where problems have been severe in the past or in potential problem areas that management considers important enough to warrant this kind of attention.

A procedure or rule is a specific guide to action. It tells a manager how to do a particular activity. In larger organizations procedures are collected and put into manuals, usually called Standard Operating Procedures (SOPs).

Procedures or rules or methods (all mean approximately the same thing) exist to make sure policy decisions are carried out. Suppose, for instance, that a policy to implement top management's growth strategy was written thus: "In selecting potential supervisory managers the firm will normally hire college graduates." If managment feels that this is an important area in the company's growth strategy, it will develop procedures based on enterprise experience to get the best managers. Here are some examples:

- *Procedure 1* Only graduates of business and engineering schools should be hired.
- *Procedure 2* All potential managers should have a full-day site visit and be interviewed by at least five supervisory and middle managers.
- *Procedure 3* Preference should be given to veterans.
- *Procedure 4* Preference should be given to individuals who worked their way through school.
- *Procedure 5* Preference should be given to individuals in the top 5 percent of a graduating class.

If you stop and think about procedures for a moment, you can readily see how the overconscientious manager could soon develop procedures for every conceivable thing and then barely be able to find them, much less remember or effectively use them. If you have had a government job, been in the military, or worked for a very large organization, you know how procedures can slow you down. A balance must be struck between initiative and consistency. In my opinion formal procedural plans should be drawn up only in really serious decision areas.

I do not mean to imply that procedures and rules serve only to restrict managers' actions. In many cases they also free managers from having to make decisions in areas in which they have less competence or on matters they do not want to become involved with. In this way rules and procedures enable managers to concentrate on more important issues and on decisions for which they have greater competence.

Budgets

Budgets are plans which allocate money to specific activities. As indicated in Figure 8.2, budgets exist at all levels in the enterprise. Top managers set overall budget policies and approve the corporate budget. Middle managers are most involved in developing budgets for the enterprise. One of their budgetary responsibilities is to supervise the budgets of supervisory level managers. Since Chapter 19 considers budgets in substantial detail, not a great deal will be said about them here.

Chapter 19 emphasizes their importance as control devices. Yet while that is probably their primary purpose, budgets are also planning, resource deployment, and communication tools. For example, if top management says it supports a division's plans but then does not allocate the budget needed to accomplish those plans, it is sending the division a message. As indicated earlier, a major part of the policy process which assures the success of strategy in meeting the firm's objectives is resource deployment.

Projects and Programs

Middle managers also contribute to the planning and strategy implementation process by developing and/or implementing projects and programs.

A program is a detailed set of plans developed to accomplish a major objective.

This objective has a relatively short time horizon. Programs tend to be set up to meet the requirements of one-time (rather than recurring) issues.

A project is a program with less significant objectives, generally a shorter period of time, and usually less detail.

Both these terms are loosely used and may not be differentiated clearly in many firms.

One example of a project was described by Mark Dodosh.[10] In 1979, because of a number of changes in the oil market—including the Iranian revolution, nationalization of foreign oil firms by Arab countries, and the reduction of production by oil producers to drive prices up, the supply of oil was diminishing. Many firms created projects to acquire additional oil from additional sources. Failing this, they reduced production or service.

Now for an example to show you the difference between a project and a program: Many firms since the 1973 oil embargo have had "Project Conservation" programs, systematic programs for a moderately lengthy period that are intended to reduce the firms' use of and dependence on oil because of its cost increases. Steps taken have varied from finding substitutes to making better use of oil to using better insulation to using more efficient machines. These programs have been successful. For example, U.S. industry has reduced its petroleum use since 1973 to *below* its increase in production and in line with the GNP. In contrast, U.S. households use much *more* oil than their increase in income or GNP.

Supervisory Level Planning

Obviously, not all enterprises have middle-management planning. They may have no middle management. But in almost all enterprises supervisors must plan in order to get the work done. Where upper-level planning is done, the supervisor's planning takes top management's plans one step further, keeping the enterprise's objectives in view. Supervisors, even if there are middle managers, do some planning similar to that which middle managers do at their level. For example, they create unit budgets, usually of short duration—for a day, a week, or a month. They also create rules for their units. They may have projects to plan, too.

The kind of planning a supervisor is most often involved in, however, is scheduling the work of the unit. The supervisor divides up the total output he or she needs to produce by time period, then divides that up by the people available. To determine daily or weekly output, scheduling

Figure 8.6
Sales Department
Schedule

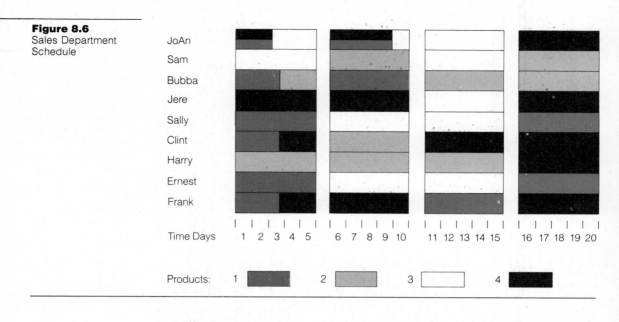

methods vary from simple to more or less complex. Among the tools used in scheduling are variations of the chart shown in Figure 8.6.

As you can see in Figure 8.6, the sales supervisor has scheduled the sales staff to cover all four products each week. The salespeople tend to specialize, however. Sam concentrates on Products 2 and 3. All products receive some emphasis each week, but during some weeks, because of sales patterns and contests, some products receive greater emphasis (for example, Product 3 during Week 3). Plans of this nature help the supervisor reach his or her sales objectives, guide the salespeople's efforts, and allow the salespeople to plan their calls and prepare their presentations and materials more efficiently.

Although it is an important tool, this kind of scheduling is not very complicated. Another tool, used in more complicated scheduling, is *network analysis*. The best-known network methods are PERT (program evaluation and review technique) and CPM (critical path method). Both use similar approaches, except that CPM relies on one estimate of the time required to get an activity done, while PERT uses more than one estimate. These scheduling aids were developed to help plan complicated projects in which coordination is necessary to get the project completed on time. They are used primarily for complicated planning of nonrepetitive projects. PERT is used particularly to handle significant scheduling problems. A procedure for the preparation of a PERT plan follows:

I. Prepare a list of all activities necessary to complete the project.
II. Design the PERT network (see Figure 8.7). Relate all the activities to

Figure 8.7
PERT Scheduling
Plan

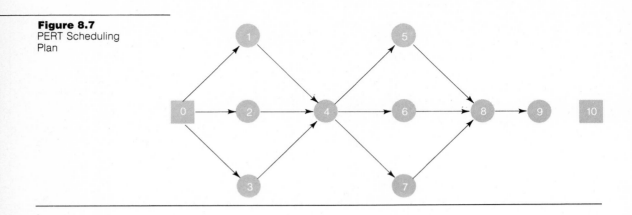

each other in the proper sequence. Perform as many activities concurrently as is practicable.

III. Estimate the time between "events" (how long will it take to get Activity 1 completed before it can link up with Activity 4?).

    A. Three people most familiar with the activity make three estimates:

        1. Optimistic time (the shortest time it could take if everything ran perfectly).

        2. Pessimistic time (the longest time it could take if everything went wrong, as Murphy's law predicts).

        3. The most probable time.

    B. Compute a weighted average of these times and insert it into the PERT network. The 10 in the box in Figure 8.7 indicates that the project is expected to take 10 weeks.

IV. Carefully monitor the times for each activity, paying special attention to crucial events, such as 4 and 8, that can prevent later activities from being completed.

Feedback and Planning

Throughout this chapter I have argued that planning leads to effectiveness. But no matter how good the plan and the planners, there are times when the environment changes, unanticipated events occur, or the plan simply does not work.

    Managers need feedback in order to know when to redirect their plans. One way to fill this need is through the use of feedback and control systems (described in Chapter 18). Another is to prepare several plans or sets of plans based on the most likely future events (not one future possibility but several contingencies). An example of this kind of contingency planning is the Apollo moonflight backup plans. In effect, contingency plans are prepared as follows:

- If A happens, follow Plan A.
- If B happens, follow Plan B.
- If C happens, follow Plan C.

This kind of system requires good feedback to let management know whether A, B, or C or perhaps a combination of two (AB) is happening. (In the latter case a hybrid Plan AB may be prepared.)

The crucial point is that planning in most enterprises is a dynamic event. Managers cannot plan at Point 1 in time and then simply follow the plan to the letter at Points 2, 3, and 4.

Pitfalls in Planning

Not every approach to planning is successful. George Steiner in a study of 215 companies and Paul Stonich in another study have found over fifty pitfalls in planning which if not avoided can lead to disasters.[11] Some of the major pitfalls are given in Table 8.8. Basically, what they all amount to is inadequate attention to planning by line managers. When line executives dump planning responsibilities on corporate staff the plans get buried. Any action can be overdone, underdone, or done with the wrong emphasis. Planning is no exception.

Table 8.8
Major Pitfalls in Planning

1. Top management's assumption that its planning responsibilities can be delegated.[a]
2. Neglect of strategic planning due to the overinvolvement of top management in current problems.
3. Inadequately defined corporate objectives.
4. Inadequate participation in planning by middle and supervisory line executives.
5. Inadequate use of plans for control purposes.
6. Failure to create a planning climate.
7. Too much paperwork and inflexibility in planning.

[a] One is the most important pitfall, two the next most important, etc.

Summary

Chapter 8 discusses examining the environment, forecasting changes, developing plans to ensure the achievement of objectives.

A *planning program* is defined as those activities which are concerned specifically with determining in advance what actions and resources are required to reach a goal. It includes identifying alternatives, analyzing each one, and selecting the best one.

All managers plan, but the plans differ in length of time. Some plans are short-range; others intermediate; others long-range. Some plans are developed entirely at one managerial level. Others are developed at several levels. Some plans have more flexible time dimensions; others have precise time constraints.

Before the strategic plan can be chosen, the environment must be searched for opportunities and threats. The environment to be viewed varies according to the level of the manager. The top manager's environment is primarily outside the firm—economic factors, government and legal factors, market and competitive factors, supplier and technological factors, and social and other factors. The middle manager's environment is the unit and the areas that infringe on or affect it. The supervisor's is a more circumscribed version of the middle manager's.

Managers use three methods to search the environment: information gathering, spying, and forecasting/modeling. *Forecasting* is one tool that managers use to help predict and plan for the future. It is the formal process of predicting future events that will significantly affect the functioning of the enterprise. Forecasting techniques can be categorized as qualitative, historical/predictive, technological, or causal.

After evaluating the environment, the actual plan is developed. These plans consist of a strategy and policies for its implementation. A *strategy* is a unified, comprehensive, and integrated plan relating the strategic advantages of the firm to the challenges of the environment. It is designed to ensure that the basic objectives of an enterprise are achieved. *Policies* are guides to decision making and action which spell out precisely how the strategy will be accomplished and set up a follow-up mechanism to make sure the strategy and policies will come into being. In large firms, several strategies or sets of policies can be developed to be used as appropriate for environmental conditions. This is known as contingency planning.

The next step in the planning process is strategic advantage analysis. *Strategic advantage analysis and diagnosis* is the process by which the strategists examine the firm's financial accounting, marketing/distribution, production/operations, personnel/labor relations, and corporate resources to determine where the firm has significant strengths (and weaknesses). With this knowledge, management can effectively exploit the opportunities and meet the threats that confront the firm.

Management performs strategic advantage analysis and diagnosis to identify clearly the current strengths and weaknesses of the firm relative to corporate objectives, competitors in similar businesses, future environment, and product/service life cycle. Once managers begin to analyze each function of the business from these perspectives, they can then begin to make decisions about the present status of divisions or product/service lines. (One approach outlined is that of the Boston Consulting Group's "Business Portfolio or Growth Share Matrix.")

Next a reasonable number of strategic choices must be generated for consideration. Of central importance is the business the firm is in and its complexity—whether it has a single product/service line or is engaged in a number of businesses.

Where do strategic alternatives come from? They begin with alternatives which (1) managers know about, (2) managers think will work, and

(3) are not major breaks with the past (unless the situation is dire). The grand strategies and their substrategies are each defined in the text. A list in outline form follows:

   I. Stable growth strategies
      A. Incremental growth strategy
      B. Profit (-harvesting) strategies
      C. Stable growth as a pause strategy
      D. Sustainable growth strategy
  II. Growth strategies
      A. Internal growth strategies (for example, diversification)
      B. External growth strategies
         1. Merger
         2. Joint venture
         3. Vertical integration
         4. Grow-to-sell-out strategy
 III. Turnaround strategies
 IV. Retrenchment strategies
      A. Divestment
      B. Liquidation
      C. Captive company
  V. Combination strategy

Strategic choice decisions are made in light of four selection factors: (1) managerial perceptions of external dependence, (2) managerial attitudes toward risk, (3) managerial awareness of past enterprise strategies, (4) managerial power relationships and organization structure. The amount of time the decision maker has in which to make the strategic decision influences the final choice too.

Once the choice is made, it must be implemented. Functional policy implementation involves two processes: resource deployment and development of policies to operationalize the strategy. In developing policies, the manager must spell out precisely how the strategic choice will come to be and set up a follow-up mechanism to make sure the strategic choice and policy decisions will take place.

The minimal policies which must be developed consist of key functional decisions in (1) finance and accounting, (2) marketing, (3) production/operations management, (4) research and development, (5) personnel, and (6) logistics. These policies are developed as a general guide to action and to ensure that the strategic decision is implemented, that there is a basis for control, that there is relative consistency and coordination of work, and finally, that the amount of time executives spend making decisions is reduced.

The last stage of the strategic planning process is evaluation. *Evaluation of strategy* is that phase of the strategic planning process in which the top managers determine whether their strategic choice in its implemented form is meeting the objectives of the enterprise. This process requires the motivation to evaluate, a feedback system to provide the data, criteria for evaluation, and decisions about the outcome of strategic evaluation. If evaluation and feedback indicate that the objectives are too easily achieved, they should be raised. If the objectives are unattainable, they should be lowered. Attainable yet challenging objectives are ideal.

Middle managers do the planning which implements the major policies further down in the organization. The plans they produce include derivative policies, procedures, rules, programs, projects, and intermediate-level budgets.

Supervisors do some planning even if there are middle managers. They create unit budgets (for a day, a week, a month). They create rules for their units and plan projects. The kind of planning a supervisor does most frequently is creating schedules for the work unit, essentially dividing up the total output needed by the total people available to determine the daily or weekly output.

Since the environment is constantly changing, planning must be dynamic, and managers need feedback in order to know when to redirect their plans. The major pitfalls in planning which can lead to disaster all amount to inadequate attention to planning on the part of line managers.

Questions

1. Summarize the author's replication of the Mintzberg study on planning. Do you believe planning is really necessary?
2. What are the time dimensions of planning? At which level is each type of plan likely to be found?
3. Why does a planner need to examine the external environment?
4. Each level of manager examines a somewhat different aspect of the environment. Explain.
5. You are a top manager. Which specific factors in the external environment would interest you?
6. What are the three methods management uses to search the environment? Which method do you think is most effective?
7. Outline the steps in formal forecasting and explain the quantitative techniques available for your use.
8. What is a strategy? A policy? At what stage in the planning process are you ready to choose a strategy?
9. Suppose you were the top executive of a large and complex firm. Why would you be likely to use the contingency approach to planning?
10. Why do managers need to perform strategic advantage analysis and diagnosis?
11. Which factors must you consider when comparing your firm to that of a competitor?

12. One example of an analysis of the present status of divisions or product/service lines is BCG's "Business Portfolio or Growth Share Matrix." How does this operate?
13. Where do strategic alternatives come from?
14. Briefly outline one of the grand strategies.
15. What are the four selection factors you must keep in mind as you make your strategic choice decision?
16. What is involved in functional policy implementation? What is the critical element in functional policy making?
17. Why does a manager need to develop policies?
18. Explain the evaluation phase of the strategic planning process. Why is this stage so important?
19. You are a middle manager at a large toy company. What types of plans would you be responsible for? Define each type.
20. Feedback is essential to effective planning. Do you agree? Why or why not?

Notes

[1]Henry Mintzberg, *The Nature of Managerial Work* (New York: Harper & Row, 1973).

[2]William Glueck and Neil Snyder, "Mintzberg and the Planning Literature: An Analysis and Reconciliation," Second International Research Seminar in Strategy, Saint Maximin Abbey, Aix en Provence, France (June 1, 1979).

[3]George Steiner, *Top Management Planning* (New York: Macmillan, 1969), p. 26.

[4]Robert H. Schaffer, "Putting Action into Planning," *Harvard Business Review* 45 (November–December 1967): 158–166.

[5]Francis Aguilar, *Scanning the Business Environment* (New York: Macmillan, 1967).

[6]Jerry Wall, "What the Competion Is Doing: Your Need to Know," *Harvard Business Review* 52 (November–December 1974): 22–38, 162–166.

[7]Chester Barnard, *Functions of the Executive* (Cambridge, Mass.: Harvard University Press, 1939).

[8]Allan Gerald, "A Note on the Boston Consulting Group Concept of Competitive Analysis and Corporate Strategy," Intercollegiate Case Clearing House, ICCH 9–175–175 (June 1976).

[9]Seymour Tilles, "How to Evaluate Corporate Strategy," *Harvard Business Review* 41 (July–August, 1963): 111–121.

[10]Mark Dodosh, "Crisis Planning," *Wall Street Journal,* March 2, 1979.

[11]George Steiner, *Pitfalls in Comprehensive Long Range Planning* (Oxford, Ohio: Planning Executives Institute, 1972). Paul J. Stonick, "Formal Planning Pitfalls and How to Avoid Them, Part I," *Management Review* 64 (June 1975): 4–11; and "Part II" 64 (July 1975): 29–35.

References

Do Managers Really Plan?

William Glueck and Neil Snyder, "Mintzberg and the Planning Literature: An Analysis and Reconciliation," Second International Research Seminar in Strategy, Saint Maximin Abbey, Aix en Provence, France (June 1, 1979).

Planning Horizons

Raimo Nurmi, "Developing a Climate for Planning," *Long Range Planning* 11 (June 1978): 48–53. Robert H. Schaffer, "Putting Action into Planning," *Harvard Business Review* 45 (November–December 1967): 158–166. George Steiner, *Top Management Planning* (New York: Macmillan, 1969), p. 26.

Examining the Environment

Francis Aguilar, *Scanning the Business Environment* (New York: Macmillan, 1967). Robert Collings, "Scanning the Business Environment for Strategic Information" (D.B.A. diss., Harvard Business School, 1968). Warren Keegan, "Scanning the International Business Environment" (D.B.A. diss., Harvard Business School, 1967). Jeffrey Pfeffer and Gerald Salancik, *The External Control of Organizations* (New York: Harper & Row, 1979), esp. pp. 71–89. Jerry Wall, "What the Competition Is Doing: Your Need to Know," *Harvard Business Review* 52 (November–December 1974): 22–38, 162–166.

How Do Managers Examine the Environment?

Jerry L. Wall and Bong-gon P. Shin, "Seeking Competitive Information," in William F. Glueck, *Business Policy and Strategic Management,* 3rd ed. (New York: McGraw-Hill, 1980).

Forecasting the Future

John Chambers et al., "How to Choose the Right Forecasting Technique," *Harvard Business Review* 49 (July–August 1971): 45–74. R. G. Coyle, "Systems Dynamics: An Approach to Policy Formulation," *Journal of Business Policy* 3 (Spring 1973): 40–48. Peter Drucker, *Management* (New York: Harper & Row, 1974), chapter 40. Erich Jantsch, "Forecasting and Systems Approach: A Frame of Reference," *Management Science* 19 (August 1973): 1355–1367. C. Jackson Grayson, "Management Science and Business Practice," *Harvard Business Review* 51 (July–August 1973): 41–48. F. L. Harrison, "How Corporate Planning Responds to Uncertainty," *Long Range Planning* 9 (April 1976): 88–93. Don Lebell and O. J. Krasner, "Selecting Environmental Forecasting Techniques from Business Planning Requirements," *Academy of Management Review* 2 (July 1977): 373–383. Richard D. Rippe, "The Integration of Corporate Forecasting and Planning," *Columbia Journal of World Business* 11 (Winter 1976): 54–61. Barbara Weaver and Wiley Bishop, *The Corporate Memory* (New York: Wiley, 1974). Steven C. Wheelwright and Darral G. Clarke, "Corporate Forecasting: Promise and Reality," *Harvard Business Review* 54 (November–December 1976): 40–43 ff.

Developing Plans

Guy Bernard, "A Method for Planning Long Term Strategy in Basic Industries," *Long Range Planning* 10 (April 1977): 46–55. David L. Currill, "Introducing Corporate Planning: A Case History," *Long Range Planning* 10 (August 1977): 70–77. Milton Leontiades, "What Kind of Corporate Planner Do You Need?" *Long Range Planning* 10 (April 1977): 56–64. Robert J. Litschert, "Role of Corporate Planner in Strategic Management," in William F. Glueck, *Business Policy and Strategic Management,* 3rd ed. (New York: McGraw-Hill, 1980). Jacob Naor, "How to Motivate Corporate Executives to Implement Long-Range Plans," *MSU Business Topics* 25 (Summer 1977): 41–49. W. Owen Nutt, "A Future for the Corporate Planner," *Long Range Planning* 10

(April 1977): 90–93. Stephen Rosen, "The Future from the Top: Presidential Perspectives on Planning, Part Three," *Long Range Planning* 7 (August 1974): 73–79.

Strategic Advantage Analysis

William F. Glueck, *Business Policy and Strategic Management,* 3rd ed. (New York: McGraw-Hill, 1980).

Strategic Choice

William F. Glueck, *Business Policy and Strategic Management,* 3rd ed. (New York: McGraw-Hill, 1980).

Implementation Planning

William F. Glueck, *Business Policy and Strategic Management,* 3rd ed. (New York: McGraw-Hill, 1980).

Middle Management Planning

John M. Hobbs and Donald F. Heany, "Coupling Strategy to Operating Plans," *Harvard Business Review* 55 (May–June 1977): 119–126.

Projects and Programs

Mark Dodosh, "Crisis Planning," *Wall Street Journal,* March 2, 1979.

Pitfalls in Planning

George Steiner, *Pitfalls in Comprehensive Long Range Planning* (Oxford, Ohio: Planning Executives Institute, 1972). Paul J. Storich, "Formal Planning Pitfalls and How to Avoid Them, Part I," *Management Review* 64 (June 1975): 4–11; and "Part II" (July 1975): 29–35.

Case for Chapter 8

The Restaurant Question

You are Justin Orman. You have just inherited $25,000 (after taxes) from your grandfather. You graduated from a good business school and have thought of entering the restaurant business because you like it. You would like to move to a warm climate, so you are considering several smaller Texas cities.

Your present first choice has a population of about 100,000. The city is not contiguous with others. You have heard that the population is about one-fourth upper class (incomes over $20,000), one-third lower class (incomes below $12,000).

At present there are twelve restaurants of the quality you would like to run in this city. Their characteristics are presented in Exhibit 1. Four of these restaurants have changed management in the past year. Three others (Numbers 2, 7, and 9) previously went bankrupt. You have heard that several of the restaurants are barely managing to continue operation.

You would like to run a very nice, rather expensive restaurant and cocktail bar with Greek decor. You are wondering if you should go ahead.

Exhibit 1
The Restaurant Question

Type of Restaurant	Seating Capacity	Liquor License	Years in Business
1. Chinese	100	yes	4
2. Chinese	75	yes	1
3. Steak	160	yes	8
4. Italian	60	yes	2
5. Steak/seafood	150	no	1
6. Vegetarian	50	no	new
7. German	100	yes	1
8. General	150	yes	3
9. General	100	no	1
10. General	125	yes	2
11. Barbecue	100	yes	3
12. Mexican	75	yes	2

Problems

1. What kind of planning should you do before you decide to go ahead on this project in this city?
2. What additional environmental search should you carry out?
3. What objectives should you set up? Can MBO be used here?
4. Can you ever make a decision like this on the basis of premises and studies alone?

American Hardware Supply

American Hardware Supply (AHS) is one of the largest wholesale hardware firms in the United States, with headquarters in a large eastern U.S. city. About two years ago, to help cover an area not previously represented in its chain, AHS bought a smaller wholesale hardware company in the Northwest.

The results reported by this division have been less than great, so top management sent a team of executives from headquarters to gain better insight into the operations of the division.

The setting of this case is the conference room. Top management is listening to what the investigative team has found out. The purpose of the meeting is to design plans for improvement of the division's operations. The team leader is delivering the report.

As you know, we purchased Northwest Supply two years ago. The top management of the firm stayed on per our request and consists of Ike Farmer, 63 years old. He blames most of Northwest's current problems on us. He contends that if we Easterners would just leave him and his team alone, they'd be doing fine. He sees us tying his hands with our admittedly rather complete policy manual, forms, and reports, none of which he'd ever had before two years ago. The rest of his team consists of guys who have worked for Ike for an average of fifteen years, mostly high school educated, up-from-the-ranks boys who learned "the hard way."

Here are some of the specific problems we found at the division:

Sales: The sales curve of the division has started to flatten. Sales grew 27 per cent in the 5-year period prior to our purchase and only 14 per cent in the last two years. This partly reflects heightened competition in the area.

Profits: Profits have been declining and are now in the lowest 20 percent of the industry. Last year the operation approached the breakeven point.

Warehouse: The warehouse is the oldest in the company, and it is inefficient. It is a multistory job, which requires a lot of elevator trips to fill orders. It is also 20 percent below the recommended size for the volume of business it handles. It would take $2 million to replace it.

Dealer Relations: The division has long-standing, close relations with dealers in the area. But it is not adding new dealers. Competitors are getting to them sooner. The division seems satisfied with its share of the market.

Finance/Accounting: The accounting department is only now adjusting to our accounting policies. The division is solvent, but with declining profitability. Without an addition of funds soon, its ratios will not look good.

Relations with Home Office: The division resists most incentives from the East, whether they have to do with advertising, accounting, or training. This causes a problem in view of our decentralization philosophy.

Overall Effectiveness: In general, the division is not meeting the objectives of the company, although it seems to be one of the leading wholesalers in the Northwest; that is, its results are as good as those of competitors in the area. Its turnover and absenteeism rates are better than average.

Problems

You are the president of AHS.
1. Which of these problems is the most important?
2. What additional information do you need to set your objectives and make your decisions?
3. What would you do about the Northwest Division?
4. Design an MBO system for AHS that will help deal with the division's problems.

Chapter 9   Decision Making

Learning Objectives

1. Learn to reorganize when a gap exists between a desired objective and the existing state.
2. Understand the necessity of formulating alternative solutions to a problem and how to choose the best alternative.
3. Learn how to make effective decisions.
4. Be able to implement your choice effectively and set up a feedback mechanism for evaluating the decision and the results.
5. Be able to evaluate your decisions in terms of all the factors which may affect an individual's decision-making process.
6. Become familiar with the group decision-making process and methods for effective group decision making.

Chapter Outline

Most aspects of management have decision making at their core. Indeed, some management experts equate management with decision making. What is decision making? What, in fact, is a decision?

A decision is a choice between two or more alternatives. Decision making is the process of thought and deliberation that leads to a decision.

Each day of your life you make decisions, both personal and professional. For example:

- You decide to go to work rather than sleep in.
- You decide to hire Sam and not John.
- You decide to purchase Item X instead of manufacturing it in your factory.
- You decide to introduce Product A into the line instead of Product B.

All of these are decisions: choices among alternatives. Let's briefly review why we are looking at decision making. Then we will examine the who, what, where, and how of decision making.

There are many reasons for learning about effective decision making. I will discuss four: (1) Managers spend a great deal of time making decisions. Thus if you want to improve your managerial skills you need to learn how to make effective decisions. (2) Like it or not, a manager is evaluated and rewarded on the basis of the number and importance of his or her decisions. (3) Because of the stresses and conflicts involved, many managers are reluctant to make significant decisions. They are beset by doubts and worry. They avoid decision making by rationalizing, procrastinating, or denying that they are responsible for the decisions. (4) Decisions are often poorly made for a number of reasons that have been summarized by Irving Janis and Leo Mann:[1]

- Decision makers are often distracted by irrelevant aspects of the choices.
- Managers are too easily swayed by how the information about risk is presented.

- Too often managers rely on stereotyping or faulty categories.
- Managers have an illusion of control. They are overoptimistic in their estimates of outcomes, often ignoring chance and luck.
- Stress from complexity of problems and fear of loss of self-esteem can affect decision-making quality.
- Managers tend not to discount irrelevant, useless information.

The object of learning about decision making is to make better decisions. A decision can be judged as good by either of two standards: (1) it fits the general criteria of a good decision at the time it is made; or (2) it turns out to be right later on.

Many managers believe they should be rewarded on the basis of the first standard only (a good decision at the time). But sometimes luck intervenes and decisions that were "right at the time" turn out to be wrong later. And sometimes managers make "wrong" decisions that through luck turn out to be right later. Thus inevitably managers are evaluated on the rightness of their decisions by both standards. In view of the many sources of error in decision making, it is worthwhile to learn how to make good decisions.

Making Good Decisions

How can you make good decisions? I will spend the whole chapter explaining this topic in detail. It is useful, however, to begin the chapter with Janis and Mann's seven steps to good decision making, which appear in Table 9.1 and to which I will refer as I proceed to outline the decision-making process.[2] The more of these steps that are violated in the decision-making process, the more likely it is that the decision will be poor.

Table 9.1
Seven Steps to Good Decision Making

The decision maker, to the best of his or her ability and within information-processing capabilities:

1. Thoroughly canvasses a wide range of alternative courses of action.
2. Surveys the full range of objectives to be fulfilled and the values implied in the choice.
3. Carefully weighs whatever is known about the costs and risks of negative consequences as well as the positive consequences that could flow from each alternative.
4. Intensively searches for new information relevant to further evaluation of the alternatives.
5. Correctly assimilates and takes account of any new information or expert judgment to which he or she is exposed, even when the information or judgment does not support the course of action initially preferred.
6. Reexamines the positive and negative consequences of all known alternatives, including those originally regarded as unacceptable, before making a final choice.
7. Makes detailed provisions for implementing or executing the chosen course of action, with special attention to contingency plans that might be required if various known risks were to materialize.

Source: Irving Janis and Leo Mann, *Decision Making* (New York: Free Press, 1977), p. 11. Reprinted by permission.

The Decision-Making Process

Because of the difficulties in making a decision, certain conditions must exist before a decision takes place. Kenneth MacCrimmon has listed four such conditions:[3]

1. A gap must exist between desired state and existing state.
2. The gap must be large enough to be noticeable and thus perceived as deserving attention.
3. The decision maker must be motivated to reduce this gap.
4. The decision maker must believe that she or he can do something about the gap.

If these conditions are met, then the decision-making process can function. The standard model of problem solving given in Figure 9.1 serves as the basis of our discussion.

Stage 1: Recognition of the Problem

The first phase of decision making is recognition that a problem exists. Very little research has been done on this phase.

One piece of research dealing with it is the study of fifty managers conducted by William Pounds.[4] Problem finding, as Pounds calls it, is a matter of identifying variances from objectives and defining their causes. The first stage in decision making is to recognize that a problem exists and to define it in terms of probable causes. The decision maker looks first for single then for multiple causes. Problems may be identified and then defined in either of two ways:

- *Working forward (versus working backward)* The most common approach is to work forward and project the results that are likely if the problem is not solved; this projection becomes the basis for the decision.
- *Means-ends factoring* The manager breaks the problem down into subproblems and solves each one individually. This method is useful only when there are not too many interrelationships among the parts.

Pounds found that three sources of information led to problem recognition:

Figure 9.1
The Decision-
Making Process

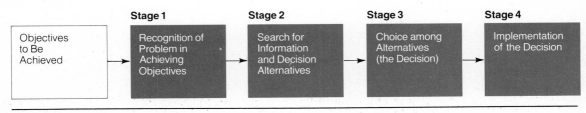

| Objectives to Be Achieved | **Stage 1** Recognition of Problem in Achieving Objectives | **Stage 2** Search for Information and Decision Alternatives | **Stage 3** Choice among Alternatives (the Decision) | **Stage 4** Implementation of the Decision |

- *Historical data* When the firm's or unit's performance declined relative to past performance, a decision was likely.

- *Planning data* When the results did not meet the planned objectives, a decision was likely.

- *Criticism* When outsiders pointed out problems or when the results were compared unfavorably to those of other similar enterprises, a decision was likely.

Problems that can affect this first stage in decision making have been studied by Charles E. Watson:[5]

- The decision maker ignores information and thus is blind to the problem.

- The wrong problem and/or causes are identified from the information.

- The decision maker skips over the problem recognition stage, attempting to solve the problem before it is clearly defined and recognized.

Note that even in Janis and Mann's seven rules of effective decision making in Table 9.1 there are no rules directly relevant to adequate problem definition. Decision making can fail if Stage 1 is ignored or inadequately completed.

Stage 2: Search for Information and Alternatives

This next stage begins to address the issue of what can be done about the problem. Of course managers begin to think this way *as* they are defining the problem. But the thought and the actions are different. For example, suppose the problem has been identified as failure to meet profit objectives. Beginning with problem definition, we note that the spread between costs and selling price is beginning to narrow. This can be caused by higher costs or price pressure in the marketplace or both.

At this point we begin to gather more information to determine the cause or causes of the problem and consider alternatives. If after some information is gathered it appears that costs are the culprit, *some possible alternatives* might be the following:

- Reduce raw material costs through better purchasing methods.

- Reduce raw material costs by producing our own raw materials.

- Reduce production costs by using more efficient machinery.

- Reduce production costs by hiring cheaper labor.

Decision trees (described in Appendix 2 to this chapter) can be helpful at this stage.

As indicated in Chapter 8, the information search is likely to be verbal, centering on subordinates and friends and acquaintances in the industry. The amount of search necessary depends on whether the problem is recurrent, routine, or new. If it is an old problem, the manager is likely to reinstitute successful past programs and focus on past patterns. If it is a new problem, he or she will search more widely and generate enough alternatives to fit his or her *decision mode* (to be described shortly). Specifically, given the decision maker's ability- and information-processing capacities, Janis and Mann's Rules 1, 4, and 5 (Table 9.1) for effective decision making apply.

Let's reflect on Rule 5 first: The decision maker must *correctly assimilate and take account of any new information or expert judgment to which he or she is exposed, even when the information or judgment does not support the course of action initially preferred.* The effective executive seeks out advice from experts inside the organization (including staff experts) and outside it. A pragmatic approach is to formulate a decision-making strategy which has built-in opposition to make sure that all sides of the issue are examined. Various persons and institutions have implemented this approach to seeing that the most reasonable alternatives are thoroughly investigated.

- Murray Lincoln, the dynamic developer of the Ohio Farm Bureau Federation, who guided its expansion into such organizations as Nationwide Insurance, suggested that every organization needs a "Vice-President of Revolutions," whose role is to question the way things are going and to propose and stimulate innovative decision making.

- President Franklin Roosevelt approached decision making by consciously asking two or so bright cabinet officers on different sides of a key issue to recommend positions he should take. In this way he received the best arguments on all sides of the issue.

- The Roman Catholic Church has a "devil's advocate" present to investigate and attempt to prevent the canonization of a person to sainthood.

This is one approach to seeing that the most reasonable alternatives are thoroughly investigated.

Rules 1 and 4 encourage thorough information seeking and problem solving: The decision maker must *thoroughly canvass a wide range of alternative courses of action* (Rule 1) and *intensively search for new information relevant to further evaluation of the alternatives* (Rule 4). I wish to point out that the effective executive uses all of her or his capacities in this pursuit; not only the rational, analytic, step-by-step thinking that is a basic part of management training but also intuition.

Subconscious, nonrational intuition is the basis for most of our actions. The step-by-step analytical approach is a special kind of thinking and decision making. Research studies by Joan Peters and associates have shown that overall, intuitive thinking is no more error prone than analytic.[6] Some of the most important breakthroughs in the history of science resulted from intuitive insights. Of course truly creative results come from

"I thought I was developing a real gift for gut level reactions to
management problems, but it was an ulcer."

intuition primarily when the decision maker is a creative person. There
are, however, some techniques for stimulating creative problem solving
and the effective use of intuition.

Several such techniques as noted by Irvin Summers and David White,
involve *free association.*[7] One method, *brainstorming,* calls for a heterogeneous group of six to eight people to discuss the problem. Judgment is
withheld and no evaluation or criticism of ideas is allowed when ideas are
first proposed. The objective is to generate numerous ideas. In *synectics,*
another method, a team of problem solvers carefully selected according to
the type of problem involved attempts to get at the heart of the problem
and uncover potential solutions by constructing personal, direct, symbolic,
and fantasy analogies and metaphors. There are many other lesser-known
free association techniques.

There are also a number of creative techniques that do not rely on free
association alone. One such approach to improving the creativity of
decision making is the *nominal grouping process*—so named because
initially the group involved does not interact vocally. In nominal grouping,
the larger group is divided into smaller groups (typically seven to ten

members). They do not speak as they sit at the conference table. Instead, they write their ideas about the problem or issue on paper. Individuals' written lists may be divided into lists centering around feelings (fear, anxiety, for instance) and lists focusing on organizational dimensions (structure, costs, resources).

As a next step, the chairperson calls on each member in turn to give one of her or his ideas. A recorder lists them on a flip chart in plain view of all. This continues until all ideas are listed. At this point the ideas (usually about twenty) are discussed. They are clarified, and the participants elaborate on or support various ones. In this clarification phase, some overlapping ideas are combined.

Finally, each person ranks the ideas. Each idea receives points for the rank assigned it by each individual (for example, 1st rank = 5 points, 5th rank = 1 point). The idea with the greatest number of points is designated as the solution. The fact that the procedure is relatively simple and easy to understand is a distinct advantage of the nominal grouping process technique. According to Andrew Van de Ven and André Delbecq, it has six distinct advantages:[8]

1. Noninteracting groups do not inhibit the performance of members, as may interacting (for example, brainstorming) groups.
2. Noninteracting groups do not tend to focus on a single train of thought, as may interacting groups.
3. Tension created because others in the group are industriously writing causes one to become fully involved in the task.
4. The process avoids early evaluation and the distraction of elaborate comments.
5. Round-robin procedure allows risk takers to state risky problems and self-disclosure dimensions early, thus making it easier for the less secure to engage in similar disclosure.
6. Use of personal and organizational categories encourages the stating of social-emotional dimensions.

As the above discussion has suggested, there are many ways of searching for information and alternatives in problem solving. Effective managers use all of their human capacities—analytic and creative, conscious and subconscious—and seek both individual and group involvement in this stage of the decision-making process.

Stage 3: Choice

Once a number of alternatives have been developed, the decision maker must choose one. The choice process may follow any of the decision-making modes described later in this chapter. Janis and Mann's Rules 2, 3, and 6 (Table 9.1) apply here.

I noted in Chapter 7 that meeting objectives is the purpose of decision making. Objectives are multiple, so the choice is made in light of multiple

THEY OFFERED ME A JOB AS A TOP LEVEL DECISION-MAKER, BUT I CAN'T MAKE UP MY MIND WHETHER OR NOT TO TAKE IT.

Source: Reprinted by permission of Newspaper Enterprise Association.

and often conflicting objectives. According to Rules 2 and 3, *the decision maker must survey the full range of objectives to be fulfilled and the values implied in each choice and carefully weigh whatever is known about the costs, risks, and benefits that could flow from each alternative.* Both analytical and intuitive thinking are appropriate. Indeed, the importance of carefully weighing all alternatives cannot be overemphasized. It explains Rule 6, according to which *the decision maker must reexamine the positive and negative consequences of all known alternatives, including those originally regarded as unacceptable, before making a final choice.* This is necessary in order to break away from past patterns. There is a strong tendency among decision makers to become increasingly committed to past decisions, as Barry Staw has pointed out.[9]

Stage 4: Implementation

Once a decision is made, the effective manager makes sure that he or she has communicated the decision, organized support for it, and assigned resources to implement it. The manager also designs a feedback system to ensure that he or she will be alerted if the decision is not being implemented (a control system) and/or can respond if the desired results do not flow from the chosen alternative. Janis and Mann's Rule 7 applies to this final stage in the decision-making process: *The decision maker must make detailed provisions for implementing or executing the chosen course of action, with special attention to contingency plans that might be required if various known risks were to materialize.*

One other process that takes place after choice is completed and encourages implementation is cognitive dissonance. After the decision is made, the mind consciously and unconsciously discounts the alternatives not chosen and reevaluates the chosen alternative as even more desirable. This helps the decision maker deal with past choice concerns and fears which could lead to a change in decision or worse—indecision.

What has been presented here, in Figure 9.1 and the text, is the most commonly used model for decision making. There are more detailed models to choose from, two of which are described in Appendix 9.1.

Factors Affecting the Decision-Making Process

The preceding four-step description of problem solving and decision making provides a background for more specific information on how to understand decision making. Obviously, decision making varies; that is, managers make decisions differently depending on several factors:

- Significance of the decision
- Time pressure
- Factors in the decision environment
- Factors affecting the decision maker(s)
  Decision mode
  Politics
  Individual or group process

Let's discuss each of these now. First, consider two aspects of the decision situation that affect how managers make decisions: the relative significance of the decision and time pressure.

Significance of the Decision

Thus far we have been discussing decisions as if they were all similar. But this is *not* the case. All managers make a series of decisions, some very significant, others insignificant, some in between. Consider, for example, two decisions of General Motors' Thomas Murphy and other top managers: one to support the Detroit United Appeal and the other to make General Motors the first line of cars to be "down-sized." Both could be called decisions, but, as you suspect, the decision-making process was not exactly the same in each case. The four steps in the process were probably covered in both cases, but the time and methods used certainly varied.

The relative significance of a decision is measured in three ways:

1. *Number of people affected* For an enterprise with 250 employees a very significant decision might affect 150 or more people; a significant decision could involve 50 to 149; and a minor one would affect 1 to 49.
2. *Relative impact of dollar amounts involved* A decision is significant if it affects the survival or profitability of an enterprise. A $99,000 decision may be minor to a big corporation, but to most family restaurants it would mean the difference between survival and failure.
3. *Time needed* Significance can also be measured by how long it takes to be educated to make good decisions (in school or on the job). It might take a week to learn how to make insignificant decisions, ten years to learn how to make significant ones.

It seems reasonable to conclude that effective managers will give more time, care, and attention to significant decisions than to insignificant ones. For example, they may not consider more than one or two quickly generated alternatives in making an insignificant decision. But they will consider more alternatives, take more time, and make more detailed calculations in making significant decisions.

Degree of Time Pressure

A second factor affecting the decision process and the quality of the decision made is how much time the decision maker has in which to make the decision. The deadlines are often set not by the manager but by others. Consider the following decision situations:

- A series of firms (including Eastern Airlines, Pan American Airlines, Texas International Airlines) are trying to merge with National Airlines. National's top management must accept or reject each merger offer within a relatively short time period.
- Bank E offers you a business loan with a less than ideal set of conditions but has a taker waiting if you do not accept now. Bank F has not decided whether it will give you a loan or what conditions it will require.

The manager in both examples must make decisions in time frames *set by others*. In other cases he or she may have more time to seek alternatives and choose among them.

When time pressures are significant, managers or entrepreneurs may be unable to gather enough information or to consider an adequate number of alternatives. Time pressures also affect the decision-making process itself. Three studies illustrate this. Peter Wright found that managers under time pressure put more weight on negative evidence than on positive evidence and considered fewer factors in making decisions.[10]

Of course these results could differ, depending on the alternatives being considered. Indeed, Richard Pollay and others who have researched this subject found that (1) in making difficult decisions managers take longer to select from two good alternatives and two poor ones than when all four alternatives are good, but (2) in making easy decisions managers take longer to select from four good alternatives than from two good ones and two poor ones.[11] Perhaps in the first case the job looks difficult when there are four good alternatives and they impulsively pick one, whereas with two bad alternatives they feel competent rejecting two and take their time choosing one of the remaining two. In the second case it may be that they feel more capable of making the decision and so take longer to compare four alternatives than two.

Finally, Lars Engwall found that executives in smaller firms made faster business decisions (in this case bidding for printing jobs) than executives in larger firms. This was attributed at least in part to the fact that the business was more important to the small firms than to the large firms.[12] All three studies illustrate that time pressures may lead to less analytic decision making. This may mean that some of the four steps in decision making are eliminated or just given bare coverage.

Factors in the Decision Environment

The environment in which the decision maker operates affects how he or she makes a decision. Various terms have been used to describe the environments. Here I will briefly define these terms and then apply them to show how decision making can vary depending on environmental conditions.

One way to categorize the environment for decision making is to scale it from *certain* to *uncertain* (see Figure 9.2). The degree of perceived uncertainty (and stress) in decision making increases as we move from left to right in Figure 9.2. Remember that what is certainty to one executive may be risk to another; differences are sometimes more perceived than real.

Certainty zone In a certain environment the decision maker knows all the alternatives and the outcomes of each. The decision is easy to make. It consists of choosing the alternative that maximizes the outcome desired by the decision maker. The decision maker simply applies the sophisticated tools described in Appendix 9.2 and looks at the results. Linear programming, inventory models, and breakeven analysis can be used effectively. The trouble is, few significant problems fit these characteristics. These decisions are routine decisions.

Risk zone In an environment of risk it is possible to detect the outcomes of various alternatives, but the probability of each outcome is not known. Thus it is necessary to appraise the likelihood of each outcome and make the decision on this basis, taking into account the kind of outcome desired. The number of such decisions managers make varies according to the kind of enterprise they work for and how they perceive the environment. Managers who make decisions of this type rely on past experience, trying to draw conclusions from problems that appear similar by using the best decision tools available. In risk situations PERT (see Appendix 9.2) and other tools such as statistical quality control and game theory can help in decision making.

Figure 9.2
The Certainty-Uncertainty Continuum

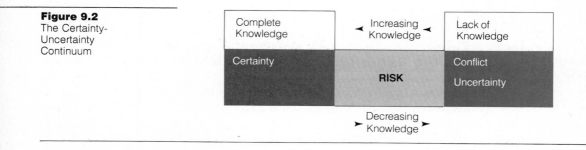

Conflict In conflict some of the outcomes are under the control of competitors or other groups. Many managerial decisions must be made in this category, though again, the number varies according to the type of enterprise. Fashion merchandising and electronics managers make many decisions of this type; in social security check processing few such decisions are made. Some normative decision theorists believe that game theory might help here, but game theory has not often been used successfully by practicing managers. In fact, sophisticated decision-making tools are almost worthless in a conflict-competition environment, although having more than one decision maker may help improve decision quality.

Uncertainty zone In an uncertain environment the probabilities of the various outcomes of alternatives are not known. Intuitive decision making, based on experience and creative ability, is required. Some managers contend that most of their decisions fall into this category since they lack information, time, or the ability to rationally "decide so often." Again, more than one decision maker may be necessary in cases such as these. Decisions that must be made in an uncertain environment are called nonroutine decisions.

With regard to the last three categories, decision makers use several strategies to deal with uncertainty:

- *Avoid uncertainty:* Ignore the sources of uncertainty and hope for the best—an uncommon strategy.

- *Reduce uncertainty to certainty:* Pretend that the future will be like the past and decide as in the past. This is a frequent strategy.

- *Reduce the uncertainty in the environment:* Negotiate with the source of uncertainty. Thus if supplies are uncertain the manager may sign a long-term contract (to reduce the uncertainty of future prices).

By now it should be clear how the degree of uncertainty in the environment affects decision-making style and accuracy. We turn next to factors which affect the person making the decision.

**Factors
Affecting the
Decision Maker**

The third set of factors affecting the decision are those which affect the decision maker directly. These include the attitudes, feelings, abilities and motives, and personality of the decision maker. They are particularly important in influencing the decision mode a person chooses to use. They also affect how the decision maker perceives and responds to the pressures and interpersonal influences received from others in the decision situation. Finally, they also have an impact on whether the decision maker chooses to make the decision as an individual or as part of a group.

The Decision Mode

The decision mode is the way an executive goes about making decisions. It is influenced by the extent to which the executive expects to achieve the *best* decision. Several modes will be described.

Maximizing

The theory behind this mode has been put forth by some economists, mathematicians, and management scientists. It may be summed up in two statements: (1) The decision maker is a unique actor whose behavior is not only intelligent but rational. The decision is the choice this actor makes, in full awareness, among all feasible alternatives, in order to *maximize* his or her advantages. (2) The decision maker therefore considers *all* the alternatives as well as the consequences that would result from all the possible choices, orders these consequences in the light of a fixed scale of preferences, and chooses the alternative that procures the maximum gain.

Those who accept this model believe that individuals are thorough in making decisions and that these decisions are always directly related in a *conscious* way to achieving a particular objective. If you are familiar with the economist's "economic man" seeking to maximize profits, you know this model. The decision maker is said to be "rational" because he or she knows the objectives and makes decisions systematically in order to achieve them.

To make decisions "rationally" a decision maker must fulfill the following four conditions:

1. Know his or her objectives and rank them in order of importance.
2. Know all possible alternative solutions to the decision problem.
3. Know the relative pros and cons of each alternative.
4. Always choose the alternative that maximizes attainment of the objective.

This theory has been criticized on the following grounds:

- Often the decision maker is not a unique actor but rather part of a multiparty decision situation.
- Decision makers are not rational or informed enough to consider *all* the alternatives or to know *all* the consequences.
- Research evidence indicates that multiple objectives are involved in decision making. How do you maximize multiple objectives *simultaneously?*

The theory is philosophically inadequate too. If you accept it, you must believe that everything you do is done to maximize pleasure and minimize pain. Philosophical and psychological evidence contradicts this. And no one has ever been able to construct a set of decision rules on the basis of this theory.

The maximizing theory ignores the evidence that decision makers rarely fulfill *any* of the conditions of the theory, much less all four. Decision makers rarely are intelligent enough, have enough time, or take an exclusively rational approach to decision making. Certainty in the environment is also necessary in this theory. So this is an infrequent decision mode.

When decisions are made this way, the management science tools described in Appendix 9.2 are used. Ultimately, of course, if management decisions can be made fully rational they can be made by computers.

Elimination by Aspects

This mode developed by Amos Tversky attempts to be as rational as possible given human abilities and the time pressures on the decision maker.[13] It combines the rational approach with simple decision rules, proceeding in the following steps:

1. Set your objectives.
2. Rank order your objectives.
3. Create as many alternatives as possible.
4. Take your first (most important) objective as a decision rule and eliminate all alternatives which cannot achieve this objective.
5. Take your next most important objective as a decision rule and eliminate all alternatives which cannot achieve this objective.
6. Continue this process until one alternative is left and this is your decision.
7. If you run out of objectives and still have more than one alternative, add desirable objectives.
8. If you run out of alternatives before you are through selecting one, either create more alternatives and start over or eliminate the least necessary objectives and choose the alternative that meets the greatest number of significant objectives.

Elimination by aspects is more realistic and more appealing philosphically than maximizing.

Satisficing

Many theorists have pointed out the shortcomings of the maximizing theory. They propose that managers make decisions "administratively," or *satisfice*. This decision mode uses the following process:

▪ The manager has a general idea of his or her objectives but does not rank these objectives because they are multiple and the ranks are subject to change.

- The manager investigates alternatives only until he or she finds a *satisfactory* solution, that is, one that satisfies the objectives minimally.

- The manager knows some of the pros and cons of the various alternatives but lacks the knowledge, information, and time to learn them fully.

- The manager chooses the first alternative he or she discovers that meets the objectives set. This choice is limited by the decision maker's values, attitudes, abilities, and experience.

- If the manager finds no alternatives that satisfy his or her minimum objectives in a reasonable time, he or she reduces the level of objectives sought and accepts the first alternative that satisfies the new level of objectives.

- The manager adapts his or her decisions from the present decision situation, making small, incremental changes from the present.

Thus the administrative decision maker operates with a simplified model of the world because of *bounded rationality,* or limitations in terms of ability and time. In essence, this mode is a simplification of the elimination by aspects mode using one alternative and not necessarily with a high expectation level of fulfilling even that one.

A variation of satisficing is the consecutive addition—"muddling through"—approach. It assumes you satisfice but always beginning from past approach and moving just slightly away from this present decision.

Satisficing is more realistic than maximizing. It is quasirational and has received some research support.

Using Intuition

The opposite of those who adhere to the maximizing mode, the intuitive manager makes decisions based on hunches, gut feelings, ESP, and other creative mechanisms. The intuitive manager may make decisions this way because he or she feels that this is the best way or because the decision problem seems to call for this decision mode. This mode has been called "sudden reorganization"; it has also been referred to as "heuristic."

Essentially, in intuitive decision making there is no systematic approach to the decision process. The mind is allowed to focus *generally* on the topic or else is deliberately taken away from the topic by means of analogies and other mechanisms. It is just the opposite of the rational management science approach.

There is evidence that this mode of decision making is often used by creative individuals. Research indicates that the characteristics of these individuals tend to include strong need for independence, high aspirations, very strong ego, high intelligence, self-control, and wide-ranging interests.

The use of hunches (or intuitive decision making) is widespread among top managers. Roy Rowan found that many top executives feel that intuition is an essential part of decision making.[14] As Robert Jensen, Chairman of the General Cable Company, said of a recent decision involving $300 million, "On each decision, the mathematical analysis only got me to the point where my intuition had to take over. . . . It's not that the numbers weren't accurate, but were the underlying assumptions correct?"

Bennett Goodspeed sells disciplined intuition to firms. He says, "Lead time is the most valuable thing a corporation can have. Yet by the time the numbers are in on any trend, the change is obvious to everyone." So intuition must be used to get lead time.

Rowan cites a recent study which found that more than 80 percent of CEOs who had doubled their company's profits within five years proved to have above average intuitive decision-making skills.

This is not to imply that only intuitive decision makers are creative. They just make decisions differently than "rational" decision makers do. Judging from the nature of the theory, you would not expect much empirical support for it. This assumption is correct, though case studies of decision effectiveness provide some support.

The ultimate form of intuitive decision making is to let the decision be made by chance. The Coptic Orthodox Church chooses the Patriarch of Alexandria by preselecting several reasonable choices, placing their names in a cup, holding a liturgy, and having a blindfolded child (called the Hand of God) choose one.

The acceptable decision mode in Western business is the rational or administrative mode, that is, the four-step approach detailed previously. In reality, however, many more decisions than managers may care to admit are made using the intuitive mode. "Executive dart boards" have sections labeled "yes," "no," "study it," "merge," "sell out," and so forth. Managers joke about making decisions by throwing a dart at the board, flipping a coin, praying, and the like. So do not be surprised when you find managers making decisions on the basis of hunches—intuitive decisions—especially on very uncertain volatile questions.

When to Use Each Mode

Table 9.2 indicates when each mode is used. Effective decision making involves matching the decision mode to the characteristics of the decision problem. As you note, the greater the tendency toward certainty, the more effectively the rational, analytical modes can be used. The less the time pressure, the more likely it is that rational maximization/rational modes can be used. If the decision is significant, it is highly desirable to use rational modes as one input. This does not mean, however, that only rational modes should be used. Even after the rational modes are used, the

Table 9.2
Relating Decision Modes to Degree of Certainty, Decision Significance, and Time Pressure

Decision Mode	Maximizing	Elimination by Aspects	Satisficing	Intuitive
Significance				
High	■	■		
Medium			■	
Low				■
Degree of Time Pressure				
High			■	■
Medium		■		
Low	■			
Degree of Certainty				
Certainty	■			
Risk		■		
Conflict			■	
Uncertainty				■

crucial process in decision making is weighing the possible alternatives. This, I believe, is always done intuitively.

The Political Dimension of Decision Making

As noted earlier, managers' decisions are influenced by those around them. This is true first in the sense of *political* constraints or limits. Managers are part of a system of constraints, and they naturally consider political dimensions in making decisions. Thus the organization in which the decision maker works limits the choices available to him or her. And when several people are involved in the decision they, too, are subject to certain constraints. They must find a solution by mutual adjustment and negotiation—in short, by political maneuvering.

Enterprises have been described as coalitions of interest groups and individuals.

A coalition is a group of two or more people or social units seeking to maximize their portion of the payoff from a particular decision.

No single alternative will maximize the return to all participants; no one has sufficient power to control the outcome unilaterally; and no one must be included in every winning combination. This concept stresses the political aspects of decision making. Members of the enterprise do not participate equally in this process. Managers are the most powerful members of the coalition, but some managers are more powerful than others.

In a coalition government two or more political parties share power and the government stays in office as long as those parties get along. Enterprises are like that. The manager needs the cooperation of others to do the job. These others therefore influence his or her decisions. And the more power the others have, the more they influence those decisions. (The political environment of the manager is discussed more fully in Chapter 14.)

Sometimes it is not a good idea to give in to political influences. There are times when a certain action is politically undesirable. In such cases effective managers make their case, try to persuade others, and then make the best decision possible under the circumstances. When fundamental issues are not involved, these managers do the politically desirable thing in order to build support that can be drawn upon when conflicts arise.

Source: Drawing by Fradon; © 1977 The New Yorker Magazine, Inc.

"'*No!*' shouted Mr. Bixbey, slamming his fist down on the table. The floor shook, the walls trembled. Mr. Watson turned ashen. '*Y-y-you m-m-mean w-w-we . . .*' The words wouldn't come out. He seemed to choke on each syllable."

You do not avoid "politics" by working only for nongovernmental enterprises. Politics exists in all organizations, though some groups are more political than others. Managers should seek the enterprise with the amount of politics they can live with (some thrive on it and seek out the most politicized enterprises). In any case, political realities influence some managerial decisions, and the typical manager has to live with this fact.

In a second sense, managers influence each other. They can be persuasive. They can try to convince the decision maker to change his or her tentative decision independent of the political aspect of decision making. Chapter 15 will discuss how one manager can influence others.

Individual versus Group Decisions

Who should make the decision: an individual or a group? There are several possible patterns:

1. The manager can make the decision alone.
2. The decision can be made by the manager after consulting with others involved.
3. Those affected by the decision can make the decision as a group (with the manager as one of the group members).

There are mixed feelings on the subject of group decision making. We all have heard that "two heads are better than one." We have also all heard that "a camel is a horse designed by a committee." Let's review the pros and cons of individual and group decision making.

Advocates of group decision making contend that group decisions have the following advantages:

- *Increased acceptance by those affected* Decisions made by a group more often than not are accepted by the group's members, who help implement them.

- *Easier coordination* Decisions made by groups reduce the amount of coordination necessary to bring the decision into play.

- *Easier communication* Decisions made by groups reduce the amount of communication necessary to implement the decision.

- *Greater variety of alternatives and solutions considered* Since "several heads are better than one," more solutions are discussed in a group situation.

- *More information processed* Because many individuals are involved, more data and information can be brought to bear on the decision.

These advantages lead the advocates of group decision making to conclude that group decisions are better—usually defined as *more accurate*—decisions.

But group decisions have their negative side, too. The following characteristics are usually cited as disadvantages of group decisions:

- *Group decisions take longer* There seems to be little doubt that groups are slower to arrive at decisions. One study found that groups took 50 percent longer than individuals to make decisions. Others have found that most executives believe group decisions waste time.

- *Groups can be indecisive* Some research indicates that groups may drag on and on and never make decisions because they can always blame other members of the group for lack of progress.

- *Groups can compromise* Groups can make decisions by compromising. This can lead to decisions that satisfy the "lowest common denominator" or conformity to peer pressure.

- *Groups can be dominated* The highest-status individual, if he or she chooses, can influence the group so that it ratifies his or her choices. This negates the advantages of group decision making.

- *Groups can play games* Some individuals may use groups to increase their self-image by playing off factions and trying to win "points." This too can negate the advantages of group decision making.

Certain characteristics of group decision making appear to be present at some times and not others. They include *risk taking* and *conflict and disagreement.* Some laboratory research indicates that groups are more willing to make risky decisions than individuals. Most executives feel, however, that individuals make more "hard" or "risky" decisions than groups. It appears to me that risk is a function of the values of the decision maker(s) at the time. Some individuals are averse to risk, while others prefer it. Sometimes groups cannot make decisions because of internal conflict and disagreements—a problem that individual decision making does not encounter.

In sum then, group decision making can be functional for some problems, less so for others. Groups are best used when the following conditions are present:

- When accuracy is particularly important. Speed is more important in some situations, accuracy in others. The group is usually more accurate than the individual decision maker.

- When the group is cohesive and works well together with a reasonable amount of conflict.

- When the coordinator facilitates the achievement of group objectives and keeps meetings on schedule.

- When the decision requires a number of skills and experiences unlikely to be present in one person (when *in fact* several heads are better than one).

- When the group is rewarded for making good decisions.

Whether you like it or not, you will spend much of your time as a manager making group decisions. Thus it's helpful to know the following techniques for improving the group decision-making process:

- Make sure that the higher-status individuals in the group are secure enough so they will not dominate the group's decision processes.
- Encourage each group member to express what he or she *really* feels—praise, criticism, or doubts. The chairperson can encourage this by expressing each of these feelings and accepting criticism of his ideas in a fruitful way.
- Coach the group to avoid personalizing conflicts.
- Make the group uneven in number (preferably five or seven).
- Include specialists from relevant areas.
- Clearly explain the objectives of the decision.

Two other approaches can improve group decision making. One has already been discussed: nominal grouping techniques.

A second approach is Delphi. In this approach, the group does not meet. A mailed questionnaire is used to get ideas. The chairperson combines the responses and reports the results. Typically this process goes three rounds of questionnaires in order to bring the group closer to consensus on which ideas are best.

Summary

This chapter has dealt with decision making, a process at the core of most aspects of management. *Decision making* is the process of thought and deliberation that leads to a decision. A *decision* is a choice between two or more alternatives.

Four reasons for learning about effective decision making were discussed: (1) Managers spend a great deal of time making decisions. (2) A manager is evaluated and rewarded on the basis of the number and importance of his or her decisions. (3) Managers are often reluctant to make decisions because of the stresses and conflicts involved. (4) Decision making is often poorly done for a number of reasons including distraction, information about risk, and stereotyping.

How can you judge if a decision is good or bad? A decision can be judged as good if it fits the general criteria of a good decision at the time it is made and it turns out to be right later on. The decision maker can use Janis and Mann's seven steps to good decision making to help insure a more effective decision making process and a better decision:

1. Thoroughly canvass a wide range of alternative courses of action.
2. Survey the full range of objectives to be fulfilled and the values implied in the choice.

3. Carefully weigh whatever is known about the costs and risks of negative consequences as well as the positive consequences.
4. Intensively search for new information relevant to further evaluation of the alternatives.
5. Correctly assimilate and take account of any new information or expected judgment.
6. Reexamine the positive and negative consequences of all known alternatives.
7. Make detailed provisions for implementing or executing the chosen course of action.

MacCrimmon suggests certain conditions must exist before a decision takes place. A gap must exist between the desired state and the existing state. It must be large enough to be noticeable and thus perceived as deserving attention. The decision maker must be motivated to reduce this gap. And the decision maker must believe that something can be done about the gap.

A model of the decision-making process outlines the stages leading to the choice among alternatives—the actual decision. First, the manager must recognize a problem exists, and the probable causes of the problem must be defined. Managers use historical comparison, planning data, and criticism to help recognize the existence of a problem.

Next the manager must begin to decide what to do about the problem. At this stage more information is gathered about the cause, and appropriate alternatives for dealing with the problem are formed. The effective manager uses rational, analytic, and intuitive approaches in this pursuit. Each of these methods is outlined in the chapter.

Once the alternatives have been generated, the decision maker chooses the one felt to be the most appropriate. This choice is made in the light of multiple and conflicting objectives. The effective decision maker keeps in mind the costs and risks of negative consequences as well as positive consequences of each alternative.

Once the decision is made, the manager makes sure it has been communicated, that support for it has been organized, and that the necessary resources have been assigned to implement it. A feedback system also has to be designed to ensure that the right decision is being implemented and that the desired results are being achieved.

The chapter continues with a discussion of the specific information on how to understand decision making. Managers make decisions differently depending on:

- Significance of the decision.
- Time pressure.
- Factors in the decision environment.
- Factors affecting the decision maker including his or her attitudes, personality, abilities and motives.

- Decision mode: maximizing, elimination by aspects, satisficing, using intuition.
- Politics of decision making.
- Individual or group involvement.

Since much of your time as a manager will be spent in making group decisions, the chapter closes with a brief overview of guidelines for improving the group decision-making process.

Appendix 9.1 outlines two more complicated models of the decision-making process. Appendix 9.2 describes quantitative tools you can use in the process.

Questions

1. Define decision. Define decision making. Why is the decision-making process so important to the manager?
2. What criteria would you use to judge if a decision were good or bad?
3. List MacCrimmon's four conditions which must exist before a decision will be made. Give a personal example to illustrate these conditions.
4. How, as a decision maker, would you recognize that a problem existed?
5. How, as an effective manager, would you proceed to formulate alternatives once you perceived the existence of a problem?
6. Which method of generating alternatives do you think is most appropriate—the rational, analytic, or intuitive approach to problem solving? Why?
7. Describe how you would implement your chosen alternative. Is a feedback system necessary at this stage of the decision-making process? Why or why not?
8. What factors influence the significance of a decision? How does time pressure affect the decision-making process?
9. Describe the various decision modes available. Which one do you think would be best for you?
10. How can you facilitate group decision making to ensure that the best decision is made?

Notes

[1]Irving Janis and Leo Mann, *Decision Making* (New York: Free Press, 1977), p. 11.

[2]Ibid., chapter 1.

[3]Kenneth MacCrimmon, "Managerial Decision Making," in *Contemporary Management,* ed. Joseph McGuire (Englewood Cliffs, N.J.: Prentice-Hall, 1974).

[4]William Pounds, "The Process of Problem Finding," *Industrial Management Review* 11 (Fall 1969): 1–19.

[5]Charles E. Watson, "The Problems of Problem Solving," *Business Horizons* 19 (August 1976): 88–94.

[6]Joan T. Peters, Kenneth R. Hammond, and David A. Summers, "A Note on Intuitive vs. Analytic Thinking," *Organizational Behavior and Human Performance* 12 (August 1974): 125–131.

[7]The discussion in this section of free association methods and the nominal grouping process is based on Irvin Summers and David White, "Creativity Techniques: Toward Improvement of the Decision Process," *Academy of Management Review* 1 (April 1976): 99–107.

[8]Andrew Van de Ven and André Delbecq, "Nominal versus Interacting Group Processes for Committee Decision-Making Effectiveness," *Academy of Management Journal* 15 (June 1972): 203–212.

[9]Barry M. Staw, "Knee Deep in the Big Muddy: A Study of Escalating Commitment to a Chosen Course of Action," *Organizational Behavior and Human Performance* 16 (June 1976): 27–44.

[10]Peter Wright, "The Harassed Decision Maker," *Journal of Applied Psychology* 59 (October 1974): 555–561.

[11]Richard Pollay, "An Experiment into Factors Affecting Decision Difficulty as Measured by Decision Time," mimeographed (Lawrence, Kansas: TIMS College of Organization, October 1, 1969).

[12]Lars Engwall, "Response Time of Organizations," *Journal of Management Studies* 13 (February 1976): 1–15.

[13]Amos Tversky, "Elimination by Aspects: A Theory of Choice," *Psychological Review* 79 (July 1972): 281–299.

[14]Roy Rowan, "Those Business Hunches Are More than Blind Faith," *Fortune,* April 23, 1979, pp. 110–113.

[15]Henry Mintzberg et al., "The Structure of Unstructured Decisions," *Administrative Science Quarterly* 21 (June 1976): 246–275.

References

Introduction

William A. Delaney, "Form vs. Substance: Some Guidelines for Managers," *Management Review* 67 (November 1978): 46–48. Donald Gerwin and Francis D. Tuggle, "Modeling Organizational Decisions Using the Human Problem Solving Paradigm," *Academy of Management Review* 3 (October 1978): 762–773. Kjell Gronhaug, "Water to Spain: An Export Decision Analyzed in the Context of Organizational Learning," *Journal of Management Studies* 14 (February 1977): 26–33. Thomas Isaack, "Intuition: An Ignored Dimension of Management," *Academy of Management Review* 3 (October 1978): 917–922. Irving Janis and Leo Mann, *Decision Making* (New York: Free Press, 1977). Brian Loasby, *Choice Complexity and Ignorance* (Cambridge, England: Cambridge University Press, 1976). Marjorie A. Lyles and Ian I. Mitroff, "Organizational Problem Formulation: An Empirical Study," mimeographed (Pittsburgh: University of Pittsburgh, 1978). Kenneth MacCrimmon, "Managerial Decision Making," in *Contemporary Management,* ed. Joseph McGuire (Englewood Cliffs, N.J.: Prentice-Hall, 1974). Henry Mintzberg, "Beyond Implementation: An Analysis of the Resistance to Policy Analysis," paper presented at the IFORS Conference (Toronto, June 1978); and "Strategy Formulation as a Historical Process," *International Studies of Management and Organization* 7 (Summer 1977): 28–40. Henry Mintzberg et al., "The Structure of Unstructured Decisions," *Administrative Science Quarterly* 21 (June 1976): 246–275. Andrew Oldenquist, "Choosing, Deciding, and Doing," *Encyclopedia of Philosophy* (New York: Collier Macmillan, 1967). Phillip Rosson, "Dealer Adoption of a New Car Franchise: An Exploratory Study," *Journal of Management Studies* 14 (October 1977): 329–340. Fremont Shull, André Delbecq, and L. L. Cummings, *Organizational Decision Making* (New York: McGraw-Hill, 1970), chapter 1.

Stage 1: Recognition of the Problem

William G. Dyer, "When Is a Problem a Problem?" *Personnel Administrator* 23 (June 1978): 66–71. Yoram Friedman and Eli Segev, "The Decision to Decide," *Journal of*

Management Studies 14 (May 1977): 159–168. William Pounds, "The Process of Problem Finding," *Industrial Management Review* 11 (Fall 1969): 1–19. Charles E. Watson, "The Problems of Problem Solving," *Business Horizons* 19 (August 1976): 88–94.

Stage 2: Search for Information and Alternatives

Douglas Dean and John Mihalasky, "Testing for Executive ESP," *Psychic* (November–December 1974): 21–25. John W. Dickson, "The Relation of Individual Search Activity to Subjective Job Characteristics," *Human Relations* 29 (October 1976): 911–928. Horst Geschka, Goetz R. Schaude, and Helmut Schlicksupp, "Modern Techniques for Solving Problems," *International Studies of Management and Organization* 6 (Winter 1976–1977): 45–63. Theodore T. Herbert and Ralph W. Estes, "Improving Executive Decisions by Formalizing Dissent: The Corporate Devil's Advocate," *Academy of Management Review* 2 (October 1977): 662–667. Thomas S. Isaack, "Intuition: An Ignored Dimension of Management," *Academy of Management Review* 3 (October 1978): 917–922. I. C. Macmillan, "General Management Policy and Creativity," *Journal of General Management* 3 (Winter 1976–1977): 3–10. Joan T. Peters, Kenneth R. Hammond, and David A. Summers, "A Note on Intuitive vs. Analytic Thinking," *Organizational Behavior and Human Performance* 12 (August 1974): 125–131. T. Richards and B. L. Freedman, "Procedures for Managers in Idea-Deficient Situations: An Examination of Brainstorming Approaches," *Journal of Management Studies* 15 (February 1978): 43–55.

Stage 3: Choice

John W. Dickson, "The Adoption of Innovative Proposals as Risky Choice: A Model and Some Results," *Academy of Management Journal* 19 (June 1976): 291–303. Barry M. Staw, "Knee Deep in the Big Muddy: A Study of Escalating Commitment to a Chosen Course of Action," *Organizational Behavior and Human Performance* 16 (June 1976): 27–44.

Stage 4: Implementation

Leon Festinger, *A Theory of Cognitive Dissonance* (Evanston, Ill.: Row Peterson, 1957).

Degree of Time Pressure

Lars Engwall, "Response Time of Organizations," *Journal of Management Studies* 13 (February 1976): 1–15. Richard Pollay, "An Experiment into Factors Affecting Decision Difficulty as Measured by Decision Time," mimeographed (Lawrence, Kansas: TIMS College of Organization, October 1, 1969). Peter Wright, "The Harassed Decision Maker," *Journal of Applied Psychology* 59 (October 1974): 555–561.

Factors in the Decision Environment

Robert Duncan, "Characteristics of Organizational Environments and Perceived Environmental Uncertainty," *Administrative Science Quarterly* 17 (September 1972): 313–327. Ray Jurkovich, "A Core Typology of Organizational Environments," *Administrative Science Quarterly* 19 (September 1974): 380–394. Kenneth MacCrimmon, "Managerial Decision Making," in *Contemporary Management,* ed. Joseph McGuire (Englewood Cliffs, N.J.: Prentice-Hall, 1974). Richard Tersine, "Organization Decision Theory: A Synthesis," *Managerial Planning* 21 (July–August 1972): 18–24, 40 ff.

The Decision Mode

Robert P. Abelson, "Script Processing in Attitude Formation and Decision Making," in *Cognition and Social Behavior,* ed. John C. Carroll and John W. Payne (New York: Lawrence Erlbaum, 1976): 33–45. John Bailey and Robert O'Conner, "Operationalizing Incrementalism: Measuring the Middles," *Public Administration Review* 35 (January–February 1975): 60–66. Lee Roy Beach and Terence R. Mitchell, "A Contingency Model for the Selection of Decision Strategies," *Academy of Management Review* 3 (July 1978): 439–449. John P. Edwards, "Strategy Formulation as a Stylistic Process," *International Studies of Manager and Organization* 3 (Summer 1977): 13–27. Amitai Etzioni, *The Active Society* (New York: Free Press, 1968). Lewis R. Goldberg, "Man versus Model of Man: Just How Conflicting Is That Evidence?" *Organizational Behavior and Human Performance* 16 (June 1976): 13–22. Catherine Gremion, "Toward a New Theory of Decision Making," *International Studies of Management and Organization* 2 (Summer 1972): 125–141. Luther Wade Humphreys and William A. Shrode, "Decision-Making Profiles of Female and Male Managers," *MSU Business Topics* 26 (Autumn 1978): 45–51. Robert Libby, "Man versus Model of Man: The Need for a Nonlinear Model," *Organizational Behavior and Human Performance* 16 (June 1976): 23–26; and "Man versus Model of Man: Some Conflicting Evidence," *Organizational Behavior and Human Performance* 16 (June 1976): 1–12. James March and Herbert Simon, *Organizations* (New York: Wiley, 1958), especially chapter 6. Enid Mumford and Andrew Pettigrew, *Implementing Strategic Decisions* (London: Longman's, 1975). Allen Newell and Herbert Simon, *Human Problem Solving* (Englewood Cliffs, N.J.: Prentice-Hall, 1972), especially pp. 789–867. Paul C. Nutt, "Models for Decision Making in Organizations and Some Contextual Variables Which Stipulate Optimal Use," *Academy of Management Review* 1 (April 1976): 84–97. Richard Tanner Pascale, "Communication and Decision Making across Cultures: Japanese and American Comparisons," *Administrative Science Quarterly* 23 (March 1978): 91–110. K. J. Radford, *Complex Decision Problems* (Reston, Va.: Reston Publishing, 1977). Roy Rowan, "Those Business Hunches Are More than Blind Faith," *Fortune,* April 23, 1979, pp. 110–113. Herbert Simon, *Administrative Behavior* (New York: Macmillan, 1961), especially chapters 1, 4, and 5. Amos Tversky, "Elimination by Aspects: A Theory of Choice," *Psychological Review* 79 (July 1972): 281–299.

The Political Dimension of Decision Making

George Kelley, "Seducing the Elites: The Politics of Decision Making and Innovation in Organizational Networks," *Academy of Management Review* 1 (July 1976): 66–73. Andrew M. Pettigrew, "Strategy Formulation as a Political Process," *International Studies of Management and Organization* 3 (Summer 1977): 78–87.

Individual versus Group Decisions

Panayiota A. Collaros and Lynn R. Anderson, "The Effects of Perceived Expertness upon Creativity of Members of Brain-Storming Groups," *Journal of Applied Psychology* 53 (April 1969): 159–163. N. C. Dalkey, *The Delphi Method: An Experimental Study of Group Opinion* (Chicago: Rand Corporation, 1969). James Davis, *Group Performance* (Reading, Mass.: Addison-Wesley, 1969). André Delbecq et al., *Group Techniques for Program Planning* (Chicago: Scott, Foresman, 1975). D. H. Gustafson et al., "A Comparative Study of Differences in Subjective Likelihood Estimates Made by Individuals, Interacting Groups, Delphi Groups, and Nominal Groups," *Organizational Behavior and Human Performance* 9 (April 1973): 280–291. George Huber and André L. Delbecq, "Guidelines for Combining the Judgment of Individual Members in Decision Conferences," *Academy of Management Journal* 15 (June 1972): 161–174. Andrew Van de Ven and André Delbecq, "Nominal versus Interacting Group Processes for Committee Decision-Making Effectiveness," *Academy of Management Journal* 15 (June 1972):

203–212. Ross Webber, "The Relation of Group Performance to the Age of Members in Homogeneous Groups," *Academy of Management Journal* 17 (September 1974): 570–574.

Appendix 9.1: More Detailed Models of Decision Making

Irving Janis and Leo Mann, *Decision Making* (New York: Free Press, 1977). Henry Mintzberg et al., "The Structure of Unstructured Decisions," *Administrative Science Quarterly* 21 (June 1976): 246–275.

Appendix 9.1

More Detailed Models of Decision Making

Although we have discussed the typical decision-making model, many researchers believe that decision making requires a more detailed analysis. I shall describe two more detailed models here.

Henry Mintzberg and associates have closely examined *complex* decision making on significant issues. Their research indicates the decision process involves the following four stages:[15]

Stage 1 *The identification phase* (recognition of the problem in our earlier model) consists of two steps:

A. *Decision recognition* Opportunities, problems, and crises are recognized, and this leads to decision-making activity.
B. *Diagnosis* Management seeks to comprehend the evoking stimuli and determine cause/effect relationships.

Stage 2 *The development stage* (search for information and alternatives) consists of:

A. *Search* The management looks for ready-made solutions to problems recognized in Stage 1.
B. *Design* Management develops custom-made solutions to modify the ready-made ones in 2A.

Stage 3 *The selection phase* (choice) consists of:

A. *Screening* A large number of ready-made alternatives must be reduced to a few feasible ones.
B. *Evaluation/choice* The feasible choices are investigated and a course of action is selected.
C. *Authorization* Official approval from higher up in the organization hierarchy is given the chosen course of action.

Stage 4 *Supporting phases* (implementation) consist of:

A. Decision control, which guides the decision process.

B. Communication, which provides input and output information necessary to maintain decision making.

C. Political strategy, which helps the decision maker survive in his or her environment.

The research of Mintzberg and associates reinforces the general model and adds enriching detail as well.

The second research summary and model for decision making is that of Irving Janis and Leo Mann. Exhibit 9.1 presents their model. Note that these authors list not only the stages but also key questions to be asked at each level. Their stages parallel those of the general model, except their Stages 3 and 4 are the same as Stage 3 (choice) in the general model description.

The framework in which the two researchers use the seven rules presented in Table 9.1 and the questions in Exhibit 9.1 is the conflict model of decision making shown in Exhibit 9.2, which focuses on all stages of decision making. If these stages of decision making are not adequately completed, the failure may result from one of the problems listed below:

- *Unconflicted adherence* can cause problem recognition or information search to be faulty or inadequate and lead to incomplete search, appraisal, and contingency planning.

- *Unconflicted change* can make problem recognition or the information search malfunction. If communication does not generate an anticipation of significant loss, or if social or self-approval is high, no stress for a decision will be generated.

Exhibit 9.1
Janis and Mann's Model for Decision Making

Stage	Key Questions
1. Appraising the challenge	Are the risks serious if I don't change?
2. Surveying alternatives	Is this (salient) alternative an acceptable means for dealing with the challenge? Have I sufficiently surveyed the available alternatives?
3. Weighing alternatives	Which alternative is best? Could the best alternative meet the essential requirements?
4. Deliberating about commitment	Shall I implement the best alternative and allow others to know?
5. Adhering despite negative feedback	Are the risks serious if I don't change? Are the risks serious if I do change?

Source: Irving Janis and Leo Mann, *Decision Making* (New York: Free Press, 1977), p. 172. Reprinted by permission.

Exhibit 9.2
A Conflict-Theory
Model of Decision
Making Applicable to
All Consequential
Decisions

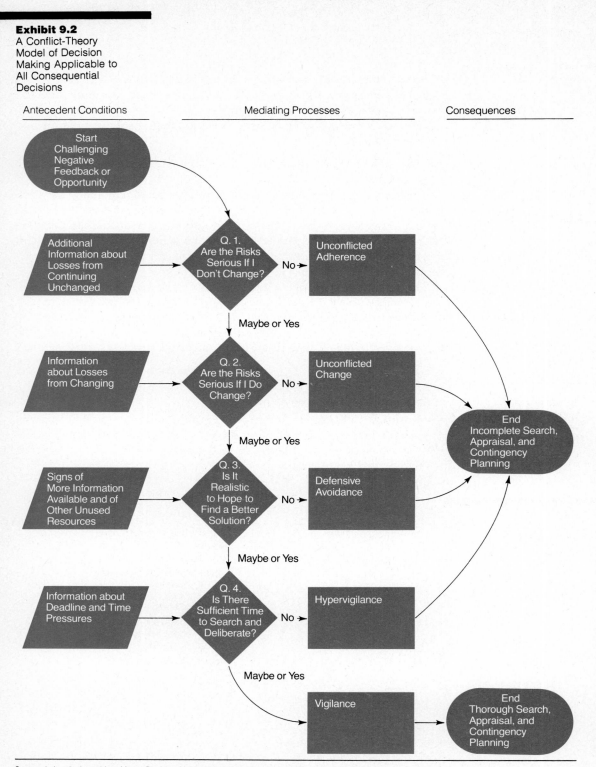

Antecedent Conditions   Mediating Processes   Consequences

Start
Challenging
Negative
Feedback or
Opportunity

Additional
Information about
Losses from
Continuing
Unchanged

Q. 1.
Are the Risks
Serious If I
Don't Change?

No →

Unconflicted
Adherence

Maybe or Yes

Information
about Losses
from Changing

Q. 2.
Are the Risks
Serious If I Do
Change?

No →

Unconflicted
Change

Maybe or Yes

Signs of
More Information
Available and of
Other Unused
Resources

Q. 3.
Is It
Realistic
to Hope to
Find a Better
Solution?

No →

Defensive
Avoidance

Maybe or Yes

Information about
Deadline and Time
Pressures

Q. 4.
Is There
Sufficient Time
to Search and
Deliberate?

No →

Hypervigilance

Maybe or Yes

Vigilance

End
Incomplete Search,
Appraisal, and
Contingency
Planning

End
Thorough Search,
Appraisal, and
Contingency
Planning

Source: Irving Janis and Leo Mann, *Decision Making* (New York: Free Press, 1977), p. 70. Reprinted by permission.

- *Defensive avoidance* can cause choice behavior to malfunction. In this case, the executive keeps himself or herself from receiving communication that could reveal the problem.
- *Hypervigilance* can make choice or implementation behavior malfunction. Hypervigilance is characterized as frantic preoccupation with the problem and time deadlines.

Appendix 9.2

Quantitative Approaches to Decision Making

Quantitative analysis provides managers with a means of assigning a cost or profit value to each of the alternatives of a decision. These assigned values assist managers as they attempt to weigh the alternatives in their decision deliberations. The alternative that is chosen will be the one that is believed to best contribute to the ultimate achievement of the organization's objectives.

Quantitative analysis is ordinarily used when the degree of time pressure is low, the decision is very significant, and the data required for the analysis are available. These data may be either known with *certainty,* or the probability of data outcomes can be estimated—a condition often referred to as *risk.*

In this appendix we shall examine four well-known and commonly used quantitative approaches to decision making. *Breakeven analysis* and *inventory models* are used under conditions of certainty, while *decision trees* and *payoff tables* are used under conditions of risk.

Breakeven Analysis

Breakeven analysis is a method of finding answers to questions such as how many products must we produce annually before total costs equal total revenue (before we break even)? Managers must often answer such questions when they are contemplating new activities such as planning for the introduction of new products.

Breakeven implies that neither a profit nor a loss occurs from a new activity: Total costs exactly equal total revenues. *Total costs* include certain fixed costs and variable costs. *Fixed costs* are annual costs that do not vary with levels of production output; for example, depreciation, insurance, executives' salaries, taxes, and maintenance. *Variable costs*—labor, materials, supplies, training, supervision, and fringes—are directly related to the level of production. As production output is increased, these costs increase; and as production output is decreased, they decrease. *Total revenues* are the income resulting from the new activity and are computed by multiplying the selling price per product times the number of products sold.

Exhibit 9.3 shows a breakeven analysis of a proposed new product. The analysis graphically plots the total revenue function (based upon a selling price of $6 per product) and the total cost function ($100,000 annual fixed costs and $4 per product variable costs). The *breakeven point*—quantity of products produced and sold where total costs equal total revenues—can be read off the graph at 25,000 products per year. If less than 25,000 products are sold per year, the firm operates at a loss (total costs are greater than total revenues). At production levels greater than the breakeven point the firm operates at a profit (total revenues are greater than total costs).

Perhaps the greatest strength of breakeven analysis is its simplicity. It is easily performed, easily explained, and quickly understood. In spite of its

Exhibit 9.3
A Breakeven Analysis
of a New Product

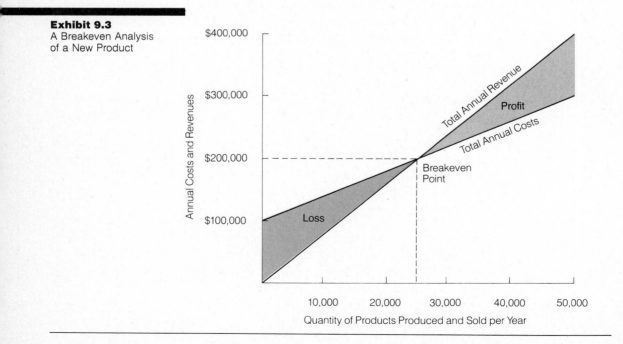

simplicity, breakeven analysis allows managers to answer such subtle questions as: What selling price will allow us to break even in our first year of production if we estimate that 25,000 units will be sold? How much must we reduce our annual operating costs to break even at our current level of annual sales?

Breakeven analysis does have some limitations. It may not be appropriate unless the selling price and variable cost per unit are constant (total revenue and total cost functions are linear) over a broad range of production levels. Additionally, it must be possible to estimate the elements of the revenue and cost functions with certainty. In spite of these linearity and certainty limitations, however, breakeven analysis remains one of management's most frequently used tools of analysis.

Inventory Models

Managers in all kinds of organizations must make decisions about their inventories. Banks, retailers, manufacturers, wholesalers, governments, and hospitals all have inventories, and the items kept in inventories include such diverse things as raw materials, supplies, final products, crude oil, merchandise, and money. An *inventory* is a reservoir of items held until needed to fill customers' orders or for use in the business.

Exhibit 9.4 shows how inventory levels for a particular item change over time. When an order of Q units of the item is received from a supplier, Q units are placed into inventory. As the item is used, the inventory level falls until another shipment is received from the supplier. This cycle of order receipt, item usage, falling inventories, and order receipt is repeated again and again.

Perhaps the most critical decision that managers must make about inventories is how many units of an item to order (Q) from a supplier. If Q is too large, average inventory level ($Q/2$) is too large and *carrying costs*

Exhibit 9.4
Changing Nature of
Inventory Levels

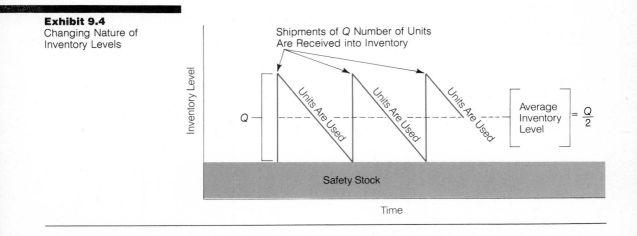

such as insurance, warehouse rent, finance charges, and taxes are excessive. If *Q* is too small, too many orders must be placed each year for the item, and *ordering costs* such as clerical, receiving, and expediting are excessive. Exhibit 9.5 shows how managers decide on an order quantity for a particular item.

As *Q* (the order quantity) increases for an item in Exhibit 9.5, annual carrying costs increase and annual ordering costs decrease. *Total annual stocking costs* (the total of carrying and ordering costs) are at a minimum when carrying costs and ordering costs are equal. The order quantity which results in a minimum total annual stocking cost is called the *economic order quantity* (EOQ). Managers therefore select EOQs for all of their items held in inventory in an attempt to minimize annual stocking costs.

Decision Trees

A decision tree is a graphic description of a management decision which is usually nonrecurring. The tree's branches show the decision alternatives that the managers must choose from and the possible outcomes of each alternative. The actual outcome of each alternative is not known with certainty, but probabilities may be assigned to each of the possible outcomes.

To illustrate, Exhibit 9.6 shows a decision tree of a management

Exhibit 9.5
Determining the
Economic Order
Quantity (EOQ)

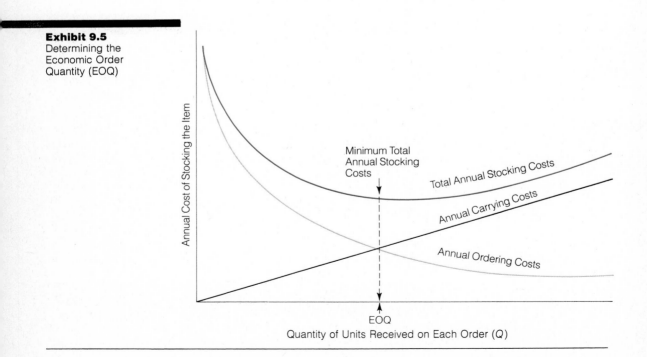

Exhibit 9.6
A Decision Tree of a
Facility Expansion
Decision

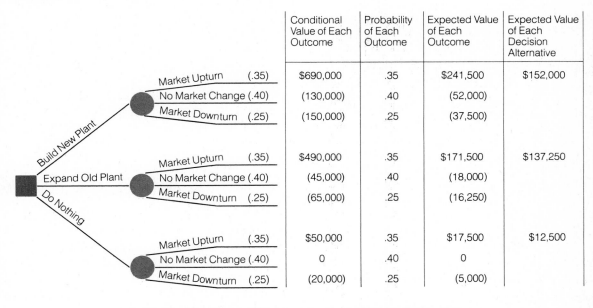

		Conditional Value of Each Outcome	Probability of Each Outcome	Expected Value of Each Outcome	Expected Value of Each Decision Alternative
Build New Plant	Market Upturn (.35)	$690,000	.35	$241,500	$152,000
	No Market Change (.40)	(130,000)	.40	(52,000)	
	Market Downturn (.25)	(150,000)	.25	(37,500)	
Expand Old Plant	Market Upturn (.35)	$490,000	.35	$171,500	$137,250
	No Market Change (.40)	(45,000)	.40	(18,000)	
	Market Downturn (.25)	(65,000)	.25	(16,250)	
Do Nothing	Market Upturn (.35)	$50,000	.35	$17,500	$12,500
	No Market Change (.40)	0	.40	0	
	Market Downturn (.25)	(20,000)	.25	(5,000)	

Build a New Plant Because This Alternative Has the Highest Expected Value

decision about a manufacturing facility expansion. The manager is considering three alternatives: build a new plant, expand the old plant, or do nothing. Each of these alternatives is affected by three possible market outcomes: market upturn, no market change, or market downturn. The probabilities of these outcomes are 0.35, 0.40, and 0.25 respectively. Expected values are computed for each decision alternative in the following steps:

1. Listing the conditional values of each outcome of the tree.
2. Computing an expected value for each outcome by multiplying its conditional value by its probability.
3. Summing up the expected values of the outcomes to each decision alternative.

As you can see, the decision tree analysis in Exhibit 9.6 indicates that a new plant should be built because this decision alternative has the highest expected value.

Decision trees are helpful to managers in two important ways. First, they help them see clearly which decision alternatives are available to them and the likely outcomes of each alternative. The expected value computed for each alternative helps managers weigh and decide among the alternatives. Structuring decisions in this way helps managers organize their thinking about them and thus be more systematic in their decision making.

However, a note of caution regarding the interpretation of decision trees is appropriate. The expected values of decision alternatives are only relative measures of value. For instance, the manager who selects the "build a new plant" alternative in the decision tree in Exhibit 9.6 will never actually experience a $152,000 return—the expected value of this alternative. The return will be either $690,000, ($130,000), or ($150,000), depending upon the actual market outcome. The expected value is, therefore, only a relative value of this alternative when compared to the other decision alternatives. Decision trees of decisions which are nonrecurring, "one-shot" decisions require careful interpretation of the meaning of expected values.

Payoff Tables

Unlike decision trees, which are usually used to analyze one-time decisions, payoff tables are often used to analyze recurring decisions. The decision maker usually is considering a few alternatives for meeting a few possible outcomes. Which outcome will actually happen is not known, but the probability of each outcome occurring can be estimated.

For instance, consider a retailer who is trying to decide how many units of an electronic calculator to stock next month. This stocking decision is repeated monthly. Historical sales for the item are:

Number of Units Demanded/Month (d)	Historical Data: Number of Times Each Quantity Was Demanded	Probability of Each Quantity Being Demanded P(d)
100	1	.1
200	1	.1
300	4	.4
400	3	.3
450	1	.1
Totals	10	1.0

The retailer estimates that whenever a customer's order for one or more calculators cannot be filled, a *shortage cost* of $5 per calculator in lost profits occurs. Whenever one or more calculators are stocked but not sold they must be carried over into the next month, and a *carryover cost* of $2 per calculator occurs.

Exhibit 9.7 demonstrates how payoff tables can help the retailer decide which stocking alternative (100, 200, 300, 400, 450) minimizes the total expected shortage and carryover costs for this calculator. The analysis

Exhibit 9.7
Payoff Table Analysis
of a Retailer's Stocking
Decision

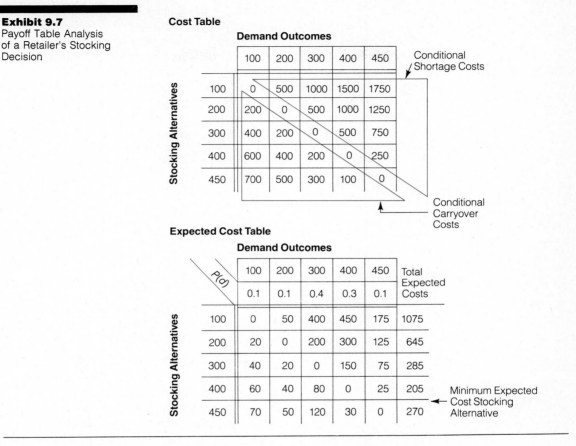

Cost Table

Demand Outcomes

Conditional Shortage Costs

Stocking Alternatives	100	200	300	400	450
100	0	500	1000	1500	1750
200	200	0	500	1000	1250
300	400	200	0	500	750
400	600	400	200	0	250
450	700	500	300	100	0

Conditional Carryover Costs

Expected Cost Table

Demand Outcomes

	P(d)	100	200	300	400	450	Total Expected Costs
		0.1	0.1	0.4	0.3	0.1	
100		0	50	400	450	175	1075
200		20	0	200	300	125	645
300		40	20	0	150	75	285
400		60	40	80	0	25	205
450		70	50	120	30	0	270

(Stocking Alternatives)

Minimum Expected Cost Stocking Alternative

involves two steps. First, a *cost table* is prepared, and second, an *expected cost table* is completed.

A cost table computes the shortage or carryover costs for each of the stocking alternatives (left hand margin) for each of the possible demand outcomes (top margin). Notice that when the stocking decision exactly meets the demand, neither shortage or carryover costs occur, and the total cost is zero. Therefore the NW-SE diagonal is all zeros. When demand exceeds the amount stocked, a $5 per unit shortage cost occurs. For example, a manager who had decided to stock 300 units when 400 units were actually demanded would be 100 units short. The shortage cost would be $5 per unit × 100 units, or $500. If, on the other hand, the manager had stocked more than was actually demanded, a carryover cost of $2 per unit would occur. For example, say that 300 units were stocked and 200 units were actually demanded. Supply would be 100 units long, and the carryover cost would be \$2 per unit $\times$ 100 units, or \$200. All of the other stocking-demand combinations are likewise computed in the cost table.

The expected cost table computes the *total expected costs,* both shortage and carryover costs, for each of the stocking alternatives. All of the boxes of the tables, except those of the expected cost column, are filled by multiplying the probabilities of each demand outcome column by the costs in the same column found in the cost table above. For example,

Cost from the 100-Unit Demand Column from the Cost Table	P(100)	Expected Costs for 100-Unit Demand Outcome
0	0.1	0
200	0.1	20
400	0.1	40
600	0.1	60
700	0.1	70

The other columns of the expected cost table are computed in the same way:

$$0.1(500,0,200,400,500) = 50,0,20,40,50$$
$$0.4(1000,500,0,200,300) = 400,200,0,80,120$$
$$0.3(1500,1000,500,0,100) = 450,300,150,0,30$$
$$0.1(1750,1250,750,250,0) = 175,125,75,25,0$$

The expected cost column is computed by summing across the stocking alternative rows. This expected cost column shows that a stocking alternative of 400 calculators exhibits the lowest expected cost.

Payoff tables are a powerful analysis tool for managers who must make recurring decisions under conditions of risk. They are particularly valuable when managers must decide among a few alternative stocking levels for such commodities as cash, consumer products, service levels, or standby machines; when stocking too many or too few units results in long and short costs; and when the actual number of units demanded is unknown but probabilities can be assigned to the possible demand levels.

Usefulness of Quantitative Approaches

The quantitative approaches discussed in this appendix can be useful tools of analysis in managerial decision making. It is important to recognize, however, that these and other quantitative approaches often oversimplify dirty and complex real problems into clean and simple ones for the purposes of analysis. When these models depart materially from reality, great care must be used in applying their solutions.

Quantitative approaches all have certain simplifying assumptions. These assumptions should be understood by those who use the solutions provided by quantitative analyses. It is not unreasonable for managers to expect an analyst to explicitly list all of the assumptions which underlie his or her analysis. In this way, they—the decision makers—can see for themselves how far the analysis departs from reality.

Quantitative analysis does not diminish the important role of managers in decision making. The solutions to quantitative analyses are not the decisions but rather an input to the decision making process. Managers must weigh and decide among the alternatives while considering a much broader view of the organization than may be possible in quantitative analysis. In the end, however, quantitative analysis imposes a structure on decision makers, and this structure often helps managers become more systematic in their decision making processes.

Source: Appendix 9.2 was written for this text by Norman Gaither, Associate Professor of Business Analysis and Research, Texas A & M University, College Station, Texas.

Case for Chapter 9

Scientific Decision Making

Bob Bates is the president of a company that makes subassemblies for large auto firms. Bates's firm is located in the upper midwestern United States. One thing that Bates has learned in business is that committee meetings are a big waste of time. So he always schedules them so that natural stopping times will keep them reasonably short. For example, he schedules them at 3:30 or 10:30 so that lunch and quitting time will cut the chatter. He has also found that Friday afternoon is a good time, since many people like to go away for the weekend.

At a recent Friday afternoon meeting it was 4:50 P.M. There was one more item on the agenda: a proposal by the production department for new machinery. The vice-president of production, Oscar Slusher, presented the proposal, which claimed that the new machinery would pay for itself in five years in labor cost savings. The machinery would cost $1 million. Sales vice-president Bert Smith was for the proposal.

The vice-president of finance, Sam Donaldson, was opposed to the plan. The following discussion ensued:

Donaldson: Wait a minute. Our rate of return is not good right now. We don't have much cash on hand. I'd have to borrow that money. The banks aren't happy with our balance sheets and income statements right now. I'm not sure they'd give us the money at all, and if they would, it would cost us 2 per cent above the prime interest rate. I don't believe we should borrow any more money until we get our ROI up. Besides, where are the figures to support this labor cost saving figure?

Slusher: This is a chicken-and-egg thing, Sam. How can we increase our ROI with the lousy machinery we've got? Our labor costs are killing us, and with competition the way it is, to get GM and Ford's business sales, we can't raise prices. We've got to get our costs down.

Donaldson: Yeah, but where are the figures to prove labor costs would go down $200,000 a year?

Smith: Figures, figures, figures! We've been here four hours now. I've got an important engagement shortly. I'm with Oscar. I heard the sales presentation from the machinery company and it sounded good to me.

Donaldson: "Important engagement," eh? Is she a blond or a brunette?

And did you give your wife that line about a conference in Houston again?

Smith: Sam, watch it!

Bates: It's getting late. Let's get back to the issue.

Donaldson: This is a lot of money. It *is* late. This can wait until next Friday's meeting, when I'd like to see the figures on where the cost savings will come from and I can check what the banks will . . .

Bates: All in favor say aye. . . . The proposal passes. Meeting adjourned.

Problem

Evaluate the approach used to make this decision. What suggestions do you have for improving future decisions at Bates's firm?

Case for Part Three

Send Razorback Divers and Swimmers to the NCAA Swim Meet?

The Southwest Conference annual swimming and diving competition was held in the Razorback pool in Fayetteville in March 1979. All the teams in the Southwest Conference entered except for Baylor. As expected, Southern Methodist swept practically all the events, winning the meet by an overwhelming margin. For some seventeen years SMU had dominated the conference, and 1979 was no exception.

The Razorbacks won fourth place, winning only one event—the fifty-yard free style. However, another swimmer did come in second, just behind a Longhorn swimmer who held a nationally ranked time in the 200-yard breast stroke event.

Three members of the Razorback diving team, who had met the national qualification standards while competing in the regular season, had finished sixth, eighth, and tenth in the Southwest Conference diving meet. SMU had placed the first five divers in the annual event.

Since the three Razorback divers had met the qualifying standards, despite their poor showing in the Southwest Conference meet, their coach, Ed Fedosky, had submitted a travel request of approximately $3,500 for the three divers, two swimmers, and two coaches to attend the NCAA Swimming and Diving Championship at Long Beach, California.

Lon Farrell, assistant athletic director, received the request from the swimming coach who reported to Lon for administrative matters in the Athletic Department. Lon immediately raised the question of whether the Department could afford to spend $3,500 to send seven athletes to the NCAA event in light of the poor showing of the three divers in the Southwest Conference swim meet.

Lon approached Frank Broyles, the athletic director, to register his objection to the request to send seven swimmers to the NCAA meet. Frank then had to decide what course of action to follow.

Two years ago the Razorback swimming coach had asked to take nine qualifiers, but he was allowed to take only four to the national event. Last year two of his divers who had qualified attended the national NCAA event. The swimming coach stated, "Fulfillment of national qualifying standards with permission from the coach of the respective sport (such as swimming, golf, track, and tennis) and first place conference finishers have both been previously used in assessing qualifiers for attending NCAA meets."

He continued, "We never really had an established policy, and it really never entered our minds that we would need one. This year I submitted a request to take five athletes—two swimmers and three divers—and two coaches, John Phillips, our diving coach, and me. I thought that the Athletic Department would have enough money to honor my request, although I know that our swimming budget of $34,000 did not include any provision to attend the NCAA meet."

Ed Fedosky continued, "Our swimming program is geared toward qualifying for the nationals. We try to do our best in the Southwest Conference meet, but SMU and Texas have so many guys already qualified for the nationals prior to the conference meet."

Lon Farrell, however, raised the question of whether sending the three divers and diving coach would accomplish anything for the Razorback swimming program. The budget that year was very tight and perhaps the money could be spent in a better fashion next year for improving the swimming program. "Why waste our limited financial resources on sending three divers and a coach to an NCAA meet when there isn't a chance that they will come anywhere close to winning?" He further knew that in 1978, when two divers were sent to the NCAA meet, they scored 56th and 64th on three dives out of 69 contestants. Another diver scored 57th out of 59. Two years ago, a Razorback swimmer scored 32nd out of 37 in the 100-yard breast stroke and 25th out of 31 in the 200-yard breast stroke. Another swimmer scored 44th out of 50 in the 100-yard butterfly, and 39th out of 40 in the 200-yard butterfly.

Frank Broyles, upon hearing the pleas of Lon Farrell and Ed Fedosky, instructed Farrell to call the University of Oklahoma to find out what their policy was in regard to sending individual athletes to NCAA events. Oklahoma reported that the Big Eight school followed the practice of sending only conference winners to national meets. Frank Broyles knew that the Southeast Conference schools generally but not always followed the same policy.

Further investigation revealed that SMU's budget for swimming was $26,000, not counting support from outside benefactors, while the Texas Longhorns spent more than the $34,000 budget of the Razorbacks. SMU followed the practice of sending only selected swimmers and divers to the national meet, regardless of whether they had qualifying scores (although everyone who went to the NCAA meet had qualified). Lon Farrell further rationalized that since SMU with its smaller budget did not send all of its qualifiers, why should the Razorbacks be different from SMU, the conference powerhouse in swimming?

Lon Farrell also knew that during the last year Frank Broyles had increased the swimming budget as well as the budgets for all nonrevenue sports. He also had approved a capital expenditure of $10,000 for a timing device for the swimming pool. Lon stated, "We are worried about the effect of the energy crisis on football gate receipts. Football receipts, as we all know, provide the revenue for all sports. Basketball, the Razorback's only other revenue sports program, lost $100,000 during the past year."

He added, "We are operating under financial handicaps that we've never had before. We estimate that next year's receipts will cover our expenses, but there are so many variables. A lot of things are changing, and we have to be prepared for them."

Frank Broyles stated, "I feel that we must establish a qualification standard that will be fair to the coaches, the athletes, and still be within the financial limits of the Athletic Department as to individual competition in national meets."

Frank also remarked, "I am interested in developing strong teams with sufficient numbers to win dual and triangular meets and the Southwest Conference championship. Perhaps any money saved can be wisely used to improve the overall swimming program."

He further wondered about what policy he would recommend to the Faculty Athletic Committee as he temporarily decided to send only conference champs to national meets and so notified the swimming coach.

Immediately the assistant diving coach was interviewed by a regional TV sports director. The coach, along with the three divers, commented, "It would have made a big difference to us if such a policy had been established before the season started. We divers stayed at the University during spring break to practice. Then we found out that we could not go to the nationals. We had trained all year for this meet."

About two weeks later the results of an informal survey which Lon Farrell made of other schools became known. He had written to several schools trying to determine what criteria athletic directors in the Big Ten, Big Eight, Southwest, and Southeast conferences used in determining what individuals they send to the NCAA championships in swimming, track, golf, and tennis. The results were as follows:

Schools Participating in Survey

1. University of Nebraska
2. University of Illinois
3. University of Tennessee
4. University of Houston
5. Southern Methodist University
6. University of Kentucky
7. University of Alabama
8. Kansas State University
9. University of Colorado
10. Michigan State University
11. Louisiana State University
12. University of Florida
13. University of Wisconsin
14. Iowa State University
15. Oklahoma State University
16. Purdue University
17. University of Michigan
18. Ohio State University
19. Indiana University
20. Rice University
21. University of Arkansas

Criteria Different Universities Use in Their Selection of Individuals to Participate in NCAA Championships in Swimming, Track and Field, Golf, and Tennis

Criteria[a] Used	Swimming	Track and Field	Golf	Tennis
Merely meet NCAA standards	(1)	(1)		
Meet NCAA standards and in estimation of coach and athletic director have chance to score points in nationals	(6)	(6)	(5)	(5)
Place 1st in conference meet or tournament	(5)	(7)	(7)	(7)
Place 1st or 2nd in conference meet or tournament and meet NCAA standards	(5)	(4)	(3)	(6)
Place 1st, 2nd, or 3rd in conference meet or tournament and meet NCAA standards	(4)	(5)	(4)	(4)
Send entire team if they win conference championship	(1)		(1)	(1)
Have a time or rating in the top ten in the nation	(1)	(1)	(1)	(1)
Selected by district committee			(3)	
Strictly up to coach but must come out of coach's budget.	(1)	(1)	(1)	(1)

[a] Some colleges reported more than one criterion.

Three weeks later the swimming coach, the assistant athletic director, and the athletic director met to discuss the situation. The swimming coach made the following statements:

1. This survey *does not* include the following teams that contribute to the quality of the meet:

South Carolina	Air Force
North Carolina State	Univ. of Pacific
Miami of Florida—	Long Beach State
NCAA Indiv. Champ.	Kent State
Miami of Ohio	Texas at Arlington
Southern Illinois	Florida State
Tulane	

2. Our program at Arkansas is geared to the NCAA qualifying times. This is what we strive for and is a main factor when trying to recruit the better athletes.

3. The NAIA's Championship was a "bust" this year because of the stringent restrictions placed on the teams for entering the meet. The number of heats for each event was held down to three or four, fewer participants were in attendance during the meet, enthusiasm was very low, and the final outcome was rather obvious from the beginning. Thus a very dull meet.

4. Tough conferences would eliminate most of the swimmers from the meet if only the 1st and 2nd place finishers attended. Seventy-five percent of the swimmers would know from the first day of practice that they would not be going to the NCAA meet and the greatest motivator would be lost. Such teams as SMU, Indiana, Tennessee, USC would be the only teams at the meet.

5. The reasons why there are a great many entries in the NCAA's who have not placed 1st or 2nd in their respective conferences are:

   a. Some swimmers are very versatile and qualify in several events during the season but are limited to only three events in their conference championships.

   b. Very few of our top teams ever "peak" *during* the season *or* for conference meets.

   c. The major tapering, peaking, psyching-up (including shaving) *must come only at one time* during the season. It is extremely difficult to peak twice during one season. (Oregon had a fantastic conference meet and did not score one point in the NCAA meet. Texas did not score one point in the NCAA meet—they missed their peak or hit it early against SMU. Only one swimmer from the Big 8 scored.) Some individuals consider the NAAU's as the big meet of the year and only shoot for that meet, which comes two weeks after the NCAA's.

Exhibit 1

Schedule of Revenues and Expenditures for Intercollegiate Athletics at the University of Arkansas, Year Ended June 30, 1981

Revenues:

Sports (a)

Football	$1,087,898.50
Basketball	35,702.27
Other Sports	1,482.04
Southwest Conference—Pool Division	180,000.00
Radio and Television	109,456.74
Programs and Concessions	77,305.40
Parking Lot	2,483.75
Gifts and Donations (b)	120,000.00
Other Revenue Items	133,215.65
Total Revenues	$1,747,544.35

Expenditures:

Administration and General	$ 309,697.44
Buildings and Grounds	65,195.77
Training Room and Publicity	25,474.33
Football	1,005,092.07
Baseball	52,920.73
Basketball	143,197.63
Track	75,794.98
Golf	21,604.14
Swimming	38,047.51
Tennis	23,841.51
Band	1,710.16
Radio and Television	36,753.14
Concessions	39,507.82
Scholarships (total expenditures of $403,233.70 included with sports)	
Total Expenditures	$1,838,837.23

Transfers—Additions (Deductions):

Student Fee Allocation	$ 166,500.00
Plant Additions and Improvements	(797.76)
Debt Service	(37,689.29)
Band Scholarships	(5,000.00)
Other Nonrecurring Transfers	(1,685.60)
Recovery of Indirect Costs	59,500.00
Total Transfers	$ 180,827.35
Change in Fund Balance	$ 89,534.47
Balance, July 1, 1980	5,905.11
Balance, June 30, 1981	$ 95,439.58

Notes: (a) Revenues are NET after guarantees and options.

(b) For educational scholarships.

d. Diving is something else. It is all subjective opinion by the judges. On any given day even the no. 1 diver in the country will miss only *one* dive and not get into the finals. This happened to a diver from Ohio State this year. In 1978 he won both 1-meter and 3-meter events. (There are 94 entries in diving this year. Each diver performs 3 dives and then the total is cut to 32 divers. Those divers do 5 more dives, and the list is cut to 12, who do 3 more dives in the finals.) An attempt is being made to allow those divers who meet the qualifying standards to perform all 11 dives before the "first cut." Time is a great factor in this situation.

6. I would like to make the following recommendations for future attendance:

a. Let $3,000 be added to the swimming budget for use only for the NCAA meet. (The farther the distance from Fayetteville, the fewer participants in attendance.)

b. Let swimmers and divers meet the NCAA qualifying standards to be eligible.

c. Let the decision determining those swimmers or divers who deserve the opportunity to represent the University of Arkansas at the NCAA championships be left to the coach.

Source: This case was written by Robert Hay, Lon Farrell, Ed Fedosky, and Frank Broyles, University of Arkansas, Fayetteville, Arkansas.

Problems

1. What should be the Athletic Department's policy on sending swimmers, golfers, track and field, and tennis athletes to NCAA meets?
2. What factors should be used to make these policy decisions?
3. Was Broyles's original decision well timed?
4. What are the swimming coach's objectives for swimmers? Frank Broyle's objectives?
5. Having decided the policy in Question 1 above, write a policy statement which includes objectives in the preamble. State the policy clearly and in the briefest effective manner.

Part 4   Organizing the Enterprise's Resources

4

After the manager has planned for the firm's resources, they must be organized. First we will deal with organizing and designing jobs. Then we will explore how these jobs are grouped into departments and units, how big work groups get, and how to get units to work together. The next logical step is organizing the total enterprise to function as effectively as possible given the strategic, internal, and external factors that affect it. Often organizational structure must be changed, so we also will address the causes, dimensions, and elements of change, as well as reactions to the change process.

Chapter 10 Organizing Jobs

10

Learning Objectives

1. Become familiar with the factors which affect job design.
2. Analyze a specialized job in terms of advantages and disadvantages.
3. Analyze an enriched job on the same basis.
4. Be able to prepare a job analysis, job description, and job specifications for a typical middle management position.

Chapter Outline

Organization and the Management Process
Factors Influencing Job Design
Employee Factors in Job Design
Economic Factors in Job Design
Technological Factors in Job Design
Union and Government Requirements
Managerial Objective, Strategy, and Philosophy
Job Design Strategies
Specialization Job Design Strategy
Job Enrichment Design Strategy
Rotation of Specialized Jobs
Sociotechnical Group Job Design
Which Design Strategy Should You Use?
Job Definition, Role Clarity, and Their Impact
Developing a Job Analysis
Developing a Job Description
Developing Job Specifications
Summary
Questions
Exercise: Job Design

**Organization
and the
Management
Process**

This is the beginning of a three chapter unit designed to enable you to become more effective at organizing. In Chapter 2 it was shown that organizing is a very important management function. Note that I did not say that managers spend a great deal of time organizing. Managers do spend some of their time organizing. If they do a good job at it, it does not take a great deal of their time. If they do a poor job, they spend much time dealing with the problems that result.

Organization is a cyclical kind of activity, not a regular daily occurrence. In general, what happens is that symptoms of organizational problems appear. The manager studies the symptoms, makes an organizational adjustment, then checks to see if the problem has been solved. Organization then recedes into the background until other symptoms arise or the manager decides to make strategy changes that will necessitate changes in organization.

The amount and types of organizational problems faced by managers vary with the kind of enterprise. This is related to the fact that as a small enterprise evolves into a large company, its organizational needs change.

Organizing is the management process by which the work is divided up among units and employees (division of labor) and then these units and jobs are linked together to form a unified system (coordination).

A number of organizational relationships that will be discussed are graphically described in Figure 10.1. The individual elements of each job must be organized (this is normally called job design); jobs must be organized into units or departments; departments must be organized into whole organizations; and organization design must be related to the effect of the environment. In our discussion here in Part 4 we shall begin with the simplest units requiring organization and proceed to the more complex. This chapter focuses on how a manager organizes tasks into jobs and how she or he goes about defining these jobs for employees and for purposes of organizing departments.[1]

Figure 10.1
Organizational
Relationships

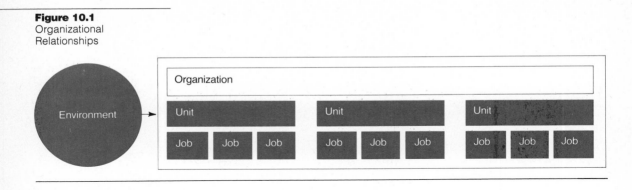

First let's define job design:

Job design consists of specifying the tasks of the job, the methods used on the job, and how the job relates to other jobs in the organization.

Jobs are designed by managers. Sometimes, especially in larger firms, the manager seeks the advice of specialized staff experts from the personnel department or from the engineering department. As shall shortly become clear, if the firm is unionized, unions help design and define the job. Finally, the more capable and experienced the employee holding the job, the more likely that he or she will have an impact on job design and job definition.

Factors Influencing Job Design

A large number of factors influence how we organize jobs. Figure 10.2 shows the major ones; each will be discussed in turn. Since most of the topics are covered in depth elsewhere in the book, the treatment is brief.

Employee Factors in Job Design

Two characteristics of employees affect job design: (1) ability and (2) attitudes and motivation (see Chapters 5 and 6). Jobs cannot be designed to require greater ability than the employees or potential employees can offer. For example, if the only people available for a job are unskilled, the job must be simplified to meet their skill levels or they must be trained to meet the minimum skill levels necessary. Of course an employee who wants to learn may be able to be trained. Thus if the present job design requires a skilled carpenter and none is available, the manager can train an unskilled person to do the whole job or break the job down into steps that a partially trained carpenter can perform. So employee abilities or willingness to be trained can limit the skill level to be designed into jobs.

Employees' work attitudes and motivations and needs are an equally

Figure 10.2
Factors Influencing
Job Design

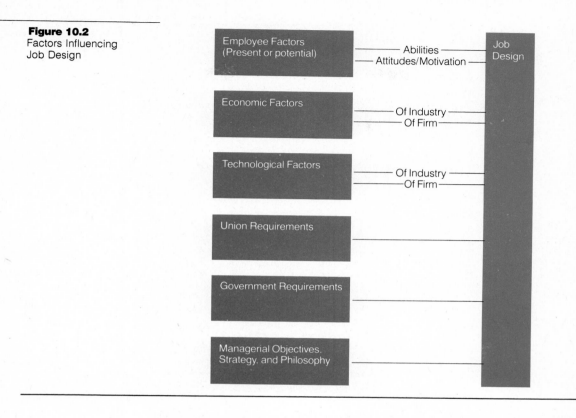

important consideration. Some jobs require employees who have a strong work ethic. Others may be adequately filled by employees who view work as purely instrumental. For example, routine jobs which require little initiative or responsibility but pay well may satisfy an employee whose primary needs as far as work is concerned are physiological and security needs. Work is the instrument that allows such an employee to meet those needs. But if employees identify their own success in terms of their success at work and expect to satisfy social and higher-level needs on the job, they will be dissatisfied with routine, less varied, less responsible jobs. Employee dissatisfaction can lead to higher turnover and absenteeism and perhaps lower levels of productivity.

Economic Factors in Job Design

The resources available to the enterprise and the economic environment also affect job design. Managers in some organizations have all the resources they need and the best equipment and working conditions available. Other managers must make do with very little. A manager of a research lab at IBM's research facility in New York has a different set of job design challenges than a supervisor in one of the old steel factories in

Source: Reprinted by permission of Sidney Harris, from Wall Street Journal.

"I find this work truly fulfilling in many ways—there's the exercise, the sense of accomplishment, and, most important, the opportunity to make lots of noise."

Gary, Indiana, or an almost-played-out coal mine in eastern Kentucky. Thus if new equipment is available to improve job design but the enterprise cannot afford it, job redesign will not take place. Maybe the enterprise cannot afford the services of a well-trained job design engineer. In theory we could improve the design of every job. But in practice the money may not be available.

Technological Factors in Job Design

Job design is affected by the technology of the enterprise and/or its industry. The technology consists of the equipment, work flow, tools, techniques, and procedures used to complete the work. In a government office the technology may include forms and typewriters. In an oil refinery it includes complicated automated machinery and computers as well as typewriters and forms.

Generally we can scale technology from craft work to machine tending to assembly lines to automation. The craftsperson pursues his or her work with simple tools. The machine tender services the machine. (This can develop into trouble shooting and emergency jobs.) The assembly line employee helps keep the line moving. The employee in an automated factory reads gauges, services the machine, and handles emergencies. To the extent that the job design is determined by technology, it is less flexible. It is easier to redesign craft work than assembly line work; it is easier to redesign order processing in a restaurant than at an automated factory.

Redesigning certain kinds of work becomes difficult when the firm has invested heavily in the current technology. Even if it does want to solve some problems of job design, it may be unable to replace costly machinery. This is especially true of automated, continuous process technology such as is found in petroleum and chemical firms and of assembly lines such as those found in the auto and similar industries. Even if funds are available for change, there may be no efficient technological alternatives—no new equipment or process available.

Union and Government Requirements

Up until now, the government has legislated only indirectly in the job design area. For example, certain requirements for safety can influence job design. Some advocates of job redesign want the government to mandate changes in it. But up until now, no requirements have been legislated.

Unions do influence job definition and indirectly job design. In many firms, unions define specific jobs—a machinist's job or an electrician's, for example. Interestingly enough, unions in Norway and Sweden have encouraged job redesign experiments (job enrichment). North American unions have been less active in this movement. Richard Peterson suggests that this is because the union staffs do not have expertise in job redesign.[2] Unions also feel they have little control over such experiments and fear that these attempts may win employees over to management's side, thus reducing the union's power. So up until now, unions have had little impact on job redesign.

Managerial Objective, Strategy, and Philosophy

The final factor which has a strong influence on job design is management. Some managers view employee satisfaction and development as a major corporate objective. The firm is likely to direct attention to the need for job design and redesign if this is one of its management's objectives and if its managerial philosophy is essentially humanistic. Management also will integrate its job design approach with its organizational philosophy in establishing organizational units as well as in establishing the total organization.

If management is primarily cost and efficiency oriented, it will not view job design and redesign as an important area of responsibility and consequently will not emphasize it. On a plant visit, for example, I observed several poorly designed jobs on the assembly lines. Some workers were working too hard because of poor placement of tools. When I pointed this out to the management, the response was, "It's always been that way. Besides, it's not an important job." Managers with attitudes like this put little time and effort into job design. When little is done in this area, jobs simply evolve, sometimes more or less efficiently, sometimes poorly.

Some firms do not redesign jobs to enlarge them because supervisory and middle management see this process as a threat to their authority. Fearing a loss of power, they may pressure top management not to get involved in job redesign. It is top management's responsibility to assess the total costs and benefits of job design. The considerations at issue are discussed below.

Job Design Strategies

Over the past several centuries, managements have used three basic job design strategies resulting in the categories of jobs noted in Figure 10.3. *Craft jobs,* which predominated until the Industrial Revolution, now constitute a very small percentage of jobs available. The Industrial Revolution brought about a shift away from craft to *specialized jobs.* Currently, specialized jobs dominate the market, although they may decline in number somewhat by 1999. Only a small percentage of the work force, especially in clerical and blue collar jobs, enjoy *enriched jobs,* which represent a movement back toward craft jobs. (See Figure 10.3 for a graphic portrayal of the historical trends for these job categories.)

To understand the job design strategies, it is essential to know the terms for specific factors involved in job content and organization. These are given in Table 10.1.

Figure 10.3
An Estimate of the Predominance of Basic Job Designs, 1650–2000

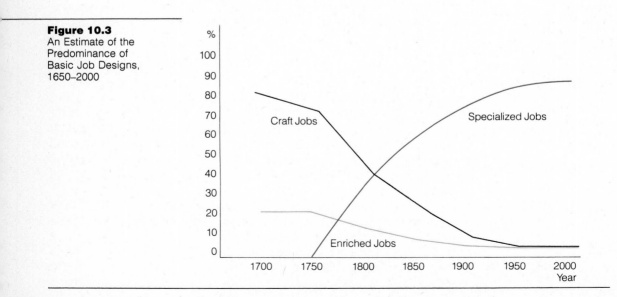

Table 10.1
Job Design Terms

Variety	Jobs differ in the degree of variety within the job. A job has variety if the number of motions performed is great and/or if the number of operations performed is great. A job is narrow and routine if just a few things are done over and over. Variety allows more creativity; requires more education, training, and experience; and provides more prestige.
	It is possible to design the job of processing welfare claims so that one person interviews the client, another checks the form, and another fills out vouchers: This provides little variety. A different way of designing the job is to have a single official handle the whole claim process: This offers more variety. Greater variety contributes to the fulfillment of Maslow's recognition and self-actualization needs (and McClelland's need for achievement). Recent technological changes often provide greater opportunity for job variety.
Cycle time	Cycle time is the time it takes to complete the job. Long cycle times tend to give more tasks identity.
Task identity/ wholeness	A job can provide a meaningful, whole experience or a very fragmented experience. Consider salad cooks. The job can be designed so that one cook washes the materials, another chops them up, a third mixes them, and a fourth puts them in bowls. Or all four cooks can wash, chop, mix, and bowl them. The latter is a "whole" job and is more meaningful. The cook can receive feedback: "We got a lot of compliments on your salads today." Whole jobs take more training and experience and provide more prestige.
	Erich Fromm hypothesized splintered jobs, in which people experience no variety and wholeness, lead to boredom. [a] Boredom (a state of insufficient inner productivity), according to Fromm, leads people to provide themselves with substitute satisfactions. Since for many people leisure is no substitute for work satisfaction, they turn to sadistic or destructive behavior. Fromm's analysis and others provide the rationale for job rotation, job enlargement, and job enrichment (to be described shortly). Wholeness helps fulfill Maslow's recognition and self-actualization needs and McClelland's need for achievement.
Knowledge/ skill required	Some jobs are designed so that they require a great deal of experience, skill, and knowledge. Others call for little. Recognition and self-actualization needs are not likely to be fulfilled in jobs where low levels of knowledge or skill are required.
Human interaction	Some jobs are designed so that people work closely together and can enjoy social interaction and develop friendships. Other jobs are designed so that people must work in teams. For example, you can design the painter's job to have one painter work on one side of a house and another on the opposite side. Or you can team them up and have them paint the same side at the same time. (The equipment available can affect this aspect of job design.) Thus jobs can be designed to help fulfill the need for affiliation (social need).
Freedom and control	Jobs vary in the amount of freedom the employee is given. Some jobs allow the employee to decide what to do, when to do it, and how to do it as long as the job gets done by the set time and within cost and quality limits. Thus the employee controls job pace, tools used, and other factors as long as he or she does not hold up another person's work and serves clients in a reasonable time. On the other hand, a job can be programmed. A salesperson, for example, can be told when to start work, which calls to make when and in what order, what sales pitch to use, and so on. Or you can say, "Sue, by Friday you need to call on your customers in Arkansas. Here's the sales budget. If you need help, call me." One design uses control; the other, freedom. Freedom on the job helps employees fulfill their needs for power and achievement and higher-level needs in general.
Responsibility/ autonomy	Closely related to freedom is responsibility. The employee who is given freedom must be made responsible for the results. This is often called *autonomy*. Freedom does not work unless Sue knows that if she does not call on the Arkansas customers by Friday there will be adverse consequences. This serves the same motivational needs as freedom.

[a] Erich Fromm, *The Anatomy of Human Destructiveness* (New York: Holt, Rinehart and Winston, 1973).

Specialization Job Design Strategy

Historically, jobs have been designed three ways, as shown in Table 10.2, which gives an example of one job (making a chair). As you will note, in craft work, each employee makes a whole product. This was the way all jobs were until the Industrial Revolution. Today, there are a few craft workers around. For example, some people buy handmade kitchen cabinets designed and made by a skilled carpenter. But few jobs are craft jobs today.

The miracle of the Industrial Revolution was the shift from craft jobs to work simplification jobs. The revolution substantially reduced the costs of goods so that many more people could afford to own them and employees who made them could earn much more money. Work simplification breaks craft jobs down into small parts, as in the example of the chair in Table 10.2. Other examples are the job of checking forms in a welfare office, the job of washing the lettuce in a restaurant kitchen, and the programming of a salesperson's job described in Table 10.1. All are simplified tasks.

Job design engineers believe this kind of design yields production efficiencies such as the following:

- Less skilled (and lower-paid) workers can perform these jobs.
- More workers are available to do these jobs.
- As a person does the same job over and over, he or she gets better at it and can produce more products of sufficient quality in the same time.
- The work gets done sooner. (Can you imagine one person producing a missile guidance system using the craft approach?)
- Productivity increases because the employee does not lose time shifting from one task (and pattern of action) to another.

Figure 10.4 relates the job design factors listed in Table 10.1 to specialized jobs. Human interaction is listed in the middle because specialized jobs vary significantly in the degree to which they involve this factor.

The job design engineer uses time and motion study, ergonomics, and other tools to find the best way to do these specialized jobs. (*Ergonomics* is the study of ways to make work less taxing physiologically.) The engineer designs the total workplace, including tool design and arrangement, conveyors, and the like. He or she designs jobs using appropriate

Table 10.2
Ways of Making a Chair

Craft Design	Job Enrichment		Work Simplification
	A	**B**	
Each chair is made entirely by one person.	Each major chair part (for example, the chair back) is made by one employee.	Each complete part (for example, chair legs) is made by one employee.	Each employee performs a few operations on one part of the chair (for example, runs the sanding machine on left chair legs).

Figure 10.4
Specialization Job
Design

Job Design Factors		Profile	
		High	Low
Variety	(Long)		(Short)
Cycle Time	(Whole)		(Splintered)
Task Identity			
Knowledge Required			
Human Interaction			
Freedom and Control			
Responsibility/Autonomy			

movements and the best employee-machine engineering to reduce fatigue and improve output. The engineer also fits the job to the employee, taking into consideration the employee's physical and mental characteristics.

Much of the increase in our standard of living is clearly due to the efficiencies created by specialized jobs. As people produce more using the same capital resources, prices fall. As people are more efficient, they can be paid more. So both society and employees benefit.

In addition, many jobs are so complex that specialization is essential. This is true of high technology fields, medicine, and many industries. Specialization has made it possible for people to operate with lasers, walk on the moon, perform brain surgery, and place telephone calls by satellite. At the same time, specialization has resulted in expanded job opportunities for persons with few skills and little education; they can support themselves better than ever before.

The machine driven assembly line such as that used by auto manufacturers is the most highly specialized production operation. Studies show that many of the employees on such assembly lines held craft or enriched jobs prior to taking these specialized jobs. These employees obviously prefer specialized jobs with higher pay to craft or enriched jobs with less pay.

**Rotation of
Specialized Jobs**

Job rotation is not a way to design a job but rather a system of arranging work, usually specialized jobs. In the job rotation system, each employee is periodically shifted from one job to another. This periodic reassignment has several advantages:

- *Flexible assignments* Employees learn other jobs so they can fill in for absent employees. This system requires more training than work simplification. It also requires more complex scheduling than work simplification.

- *Easier staffing* Jobs that involve heavy physical exertion or exposure to unpleasant working conditions may be difficult to staff if the job is held by the same person for eight hours a day. A person might be able to stand it for only four hours. Maybe two employees could rotate jobs every two hours.

- *Less boredom and monotony* Simplified jobs can become boring, and this sometimes reduces productivity and satisfaction. Rotation of jobs provides some variety and is less costly to implement than job enlargement.

An example of this approach to job design is provided by Alcan Aluminium of Canada, which enhances its white collar jobs by rotating people onto task forces, using several promotional ladders (one for managers, one for scientists, etc.) and experimenting with career planning that includes extensive job rotation as part of the plan.

Although most people recognize the advantages of specialized jobs, some design specialists point out that educational levels have been rising. These theorists believe that specialization creates jobs beneath the ability of an educated population. This, they argue, makes it impossible for many to satisfy their higher needs on specialized jobs. Of course, one must not confuse number of grades completed with higher-level abilities. There is much evidence that the educational process has not improved automatically as people stay in schools longer. Performance on the competency based tests shows that large numbers of individuals with four years of high school are unable to read and do mathematics at levels corresponding to grade school levels in the early 1900s. The feeling that specialized jobs do not offer an opportunity for full use of human abilities has led to the job enrichment approach to job design.

Job Enrichment Design Strategy

Depending on which source you consult, a small percentage (perhaps 5 percent) of employers are experimenting with job enrichment. Job enrichment is a movement back toward designing craft jobs. (See Table 10.2 for two examples.) Figure 10.5 profiles jobs designed under an enrichment strategy. Compare it with Figure 10.4, and you will see how different the job enrichment strategy is from specialization.

There are two approaches to job enrichment. One is to increase the *horizontal loading* of a job. This is sometimes called increasing the *job scope* or job enlargment. For example, in the diagram below, Job 1 has five

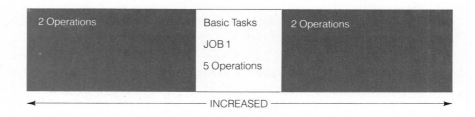

| 2 Operations | Basic Tasks
JOB 1
5 Operations | 2 Operations |

← —————————————————— INCREASED —————————————————— →

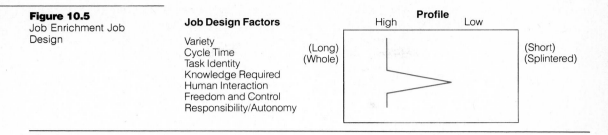

Figure 10.5
Job Enrichment Job Design

For instance, an employee might be expected not only to perform certain operations on the product but also to order the materials necessary for these operations and inspect them for quality control purposes. Essentially, this type of enrichment takes some of the authority from supervisors (or other departments) and adds it to the job. Thus it can increase an employee's freedom and control, responsibility and autonomy.

operations. To enlarge its scope, four operations could be added: two from the job which precedes it and two from the job which follows. Horizontal loading serves to increase variety, lengthen cycle time, provide the task with more wholeness and identity, and increase the knowledge necessary to perform it.

The second approach to enrichment is to increase the *vertical loading* of a job, as shown for Job 2 in the diagram below. Increased vertical loading gives the employees more responsibility for the tasks on which they work. This second approach is usually called job enrichment. But the literature uses both terms similarly. So I will call the approach which uses either or both strategies job enrichment.

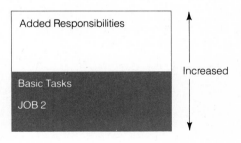

For instance, an employee might be expected not only to perform certain operations on the product but also to order the materials necessary for these operations and inspect them for quality control purposes. Essentially, this type of enrichment takes some of the authority from supervisors (or other departments) and adds it to the job. Thus it can increase an employee's freedom and control, responsibility and autonomy.

There are some well-known examples of this approach. At Air Canada, maintenance crews were given the responsibility for deciding when to replace aircraft windows. Management had previously been responsible for this. At AT&T, key punchers were randomly assigned portions of all key punch tasks sent to the department. Enrichment was achieved by assigning an entire key punch task—for example, payroll—to one key puncher. Thus each task was given more wholeness.

The advantages claimed for job enrichment are attributed to the fact that employees experience greater need satisfaction. Enrichment advocates claim the following benefits for their design strategy:

- More work is produced.
- Work of higher quality is produced.
- Employees are absent less frequently.
- Employees work for the company longer.
- Employees are more satisfied and developed.

Sociotechnical Group Job Design

One type of enrichment redesigns jobs not for individuals but for groups of employees. The objective is to create autonomously working groups who share responsibility for tasks. The technology is part, but not the final determinant of the job design. When the group's work is designed in this way, members plan the flow of work and set the production scheduling together. And they often share pay. This is a return to the way work was done before the specialization movement took hold. It reverses the trend of making management responsible for these tasks and contradicts all the scientific management movement stands for. Advocates of group job design (such as Tavistock Institute in London, and the Work Psychology Institute in Norway) claim that their approach leads to more productive and satisfied employees. Experiments have been tried abroad (Atlas Copco Mining in Sweden) and in the U.S. (Procter & Gamble in Albany, Georgia, and Lincoln Electric in Cleveland, Ohio). But, at present, group job design is not a widely used strategy.

Which Design Strategy Should You Use?

Research indicates that all job design strategies can be effective. Most jobs are designed with the specialization approach. Specialization is currently the norm for job design. What about job enrichment? Is it the wave of the future? Job enrichment does *not* always lead to favorable results, particularly in the instances listed below:

- *Some employees may not wish enriched jobs.* They may be instrumentally motivated. This is a crucial variable. It is not known what percentage of employees really desire job enrichment. Given an opportunity to have more variety, more responsibility, and more autonomy, workers respond differently. Cultural differences are one factor that determines whether they react negatively or positively. Some research indicates that employees from rural backgrounds or with a strongly ingrained work ethic respond favorably to enrichment. Still, no single factor has been found to account for all the differences in employee response.

- *Technological costs may not offset the benefits.* Technology limits job enrichment. Most successful experiments with enrichment have involved production where product components were small, few tools were required, and assembly times were fairly lengthy. Job enrichment is very difficult to accomplish in the manufacture of larger products such as cars, refrigerators, and engines. In such cases the most efficient method is a moving assembly line—the specialization approach.

- *Most jobs that are increasing in number are not easy to enrich.* These include secretarial, retail sales, restaurant, bookkeeping, and office-cleaning jobs. Generally speaking, applications of job enrichment are in declining sectors of the economy.

- *Lack of motivation and job satisfaction may not be the source of employee problems in meeting desired levels of productivity.* Indeed, poor production control or some other management deficiency may be the cause.

- *Unions may oppose enrichment, and thus the benefits of enrichment may not come to be.*

- *Supervisors may oppose enrichment, and thus enrichment's positive outcomes may be reduced.*

- *There is little evidence that specialization always leads to monotony or boredom and thus to dissatisfaction.* Studies have shown that some aspects of job enrichment increase employee satisfaction and some aspects *decrease* satisfaction.

- *Job enrichment can lead to problems of role conflict and ambiguity.*

These factors help explain why relatively few employers have embraced job enrichment.

When will job enrichment work? The crucial variables which determine whether job enrichment can work assuming technological and economic factors are not adverse include: (1) cooperation and encouragement of the union and management at all levels and (2) work ethic attitudes on the part of the employees. If these conditions exist, management's job design strategy may well be to move slowly and with the participation of all involved toward enrichment of some jobs. Table 10.3 provides some guidelines for choosing either the specialization or job enrichment strategies based on employee attitudes. Note that there are three cases of specialization described: one where employees are instrumentally oriented, another where they have a low to moderate commitment to the work ethic, and still another where attitudes are mixed. Most of the likely conditions regarding job enrichment strategies are given in the one cell. Remember that to be successful, job design must match the predominant employee attitude.

Table 10.3
Guidelines for
Selecting Job Design
Strategies

Present Job Design Strategy	Employee Attitudes	Likely Result	Managerial Action
Specialization 1	instrumental workers	good to satisfactory outcomes	none
Specialization 2	low to moderate work ethic values	moderate to low outcomes	A. job rotation B. hiring preference for instrumental workers
Specialization 3	A. some high-work-ethic employees B. some low-work-ethic employees	A. low outcomes B. good to satisfactory outcomes	A. job enrichment B. none
Job enrichment	A. some high-work-ethic employees B. some low-work-ethic employees	A. good to satisfactory outcomes B. moderate to low outcome	A. none B. specialization

Job Definition, Role Clarity, and Their Impact

At the beginning of the chapter we described how managers were involved with two processes of organizing jobs: job design and job definition. As just discussed, job design involves how we group tasks into jobs.

Job definition is the process by which we communicate the tasks and standards of performance of the tasks to employees.

The purpose of job definition is role clarity. By role clarity, we mean the mutual understanding between manager and employee of exactly what the employee's tasks and their minimum performance levels are. Studies have found that role clarity has a positive and significant impact on:

- Job satisfaction of employees.
- Absenteeism and turnover.
- Job stress for employees.
- Organizational effectiveness.

Believe it or not, in many organizations employees in many jobs have only a general idea of what the job is and what is expected of them. Effective job definition avoids this role ambiguity. By forcing managment to figure out how each employee fits into the organization, it contributes to overall organizational effectiveness.

Role ambiguity can result from a number of causes, some of which are listed below:

- Different people within the organization may define a job differently, thus putting different and sometimes conflicting demands on the employee. For example, expectations of the employee's superior, peers, and subordinates may all vary.

- The supervisor alone may expect different types of performance at different times, thus again placing conflicting demands on the employee.
- The supervisor and the organization never really define what is expected on the job. Some research indicates that this causes employees the most stress of all.
- There is a bad match between employee and job. The demands made are too great for the employee's abilities. In this case, a new placement is the solution.

With the exception of the last, all the above reasons for role ambiguity can be remedied by two managerial actions: (1) the development of a job description which is comprehensive and clear and (2) verbal communication between the supervisor and employee about the job description and job expectations. It may also be necessary to involve peers and other employees in the clarification process. A management by objectives approach is one way of enhancing communication in such cases (see Chapter 7). Let's discuss the development of an effective job description. The job definition process begins with job analysis.

Developing a Job Analysis

Job analysis is the process by which a job analyst gathers data about a job.

These data include activities; the tools and equipment used; job-related items such as materials used, products made, services rendered; work performance; working conditions; and requirements for the job such as knowledge, skills, experience, and personal attributes. One or more of the following seven methods may be used in analyzing a job:

1. Examination of previous job analyses or job descriptions of the position and/or other records.
2. Observation of the job and the job occupant.
3. Interviewing the job occupant and/or supervision by one or more analysts.
4. Structured or open-ended questionnaires to be completed by job occupants and/or supervisors.
5. A log or diary kept by the job occupant.
6. Recording job activities on film or with audio means.
7. Analyzing equipment design information from blueprints and design data.

Methods 1, 4, and 7 are the quickest but may develop less reliable data than others. Methods 2, 3, 5, and 6 are more accurate but more costly. As far as observation and other data gathering techniques are concerned, it has been found that proper work-sampling techniques add to the quality of the data's reliability and validity. Whatever the method(s) used, the data collected are recorded on a job analysis schedule such as that shown in Table 10.4.

The Department of Labor's *Handbook for Analyzing Jobs* has guidelines for analyzing jobs and 298 work fields as related to the *Dictionary of Occupational Titles*. This approach emphasizes systematic verbal description of the functions performed on the job.

Developing a Job Description

Job descriptions are prepared after job analyses are completed.

A job description is a written statement which details the duties and responsibilities of a job.

A good source of reference to use for writing job descriptions and job specifications is *The Dictionary of Occupational Titles,* which is published by the U.S. Department of Labor. In its latest form, it contains almost 40,000 titles and almost 25,000 actual job descriptions. More than half of these are in production and transportation, followed by professional, technical, managerial, and unclassified positions. Many enterprises use these as guides, sometimes even copying their own job descriptions from the *Dictionary*. Table 10.5 is an example of a job description.

As you can see, a general description of the job and its responsibilities is

Table 10.4
Excerpts from U.S. Training and Employment Service: Job Analysis Schedule for a Dough Mixer

Job Summary:
Operates mixing machine to mix ingredients for straight and sponge (yeast) doughs according to established formulas, directs other workers in fermentation of dough, and cuts dough into pieces with hand cutter.

Description of Tasks:
1. Dumps ingredients into mixing machine. Examines production schedule to determine type of bread to be produced, such as rye, whole wheat, or white. Refers to formula card for quantities and types of ingredients required, such as flour, water, milk, vitamin solutions, and shortening. Weighs out, measures, and dumps ingredients into mixing machine.
2. Operates mixing machine. Turns valves and other hand controls to set mixing time according to type of dough being mixed. Presses button to start agitator blades in machine. Observes gauges and dials on equipment continuously to verify temperature of dough and mixing time. Feels dough for desired consistency. Adds water or flour to mix measuring vessels and adjusts mixing time and controls to obtain desired elasticity in mix.
3. Directs other workers in fermentation of dough: Prepares fermentation schedule according to type of dough being raised. Sprays portable dough *trough* with lubricant to prevent adherence of mixed dough to trough. Directs *dough mixer helper* in positioning trough beneath door of mixer to catch dough when mixing cycle is complete. Pushes, or directs other workers to push, troughs of dough into fermentation room.
4. Cuts dough. Dumps fermentated dough onto worktable. Manually kneads dough to eliminate gases formed by yeast. Cuts dough into pieces with hand cutter. Places cut dough on proofing rack and covers with cloth.
5. Performs miscellaneous duties: Records on work sheet number of batches mixed during work shift. Informs *bake shop foreman* when repairs or major adjustments are required for machines and equipment.

Table 10.5
Job Description of a
Personnel Manager

Department: Personnel
Date: Jan. 1, 1979
General description of the job
Performs responsible administrative work managing personnel activities of a large state agency or institution. Work involves responsibility for the planning and administration of a personnel program which includes recruitment, examination, selection, evaluation, appointment, promotion, transfer, and recommended change of status of agency employees and a system of communication for disseminating necessary information to workers. Works under general supervision, exercising initiative and independent judgment in the performance of assigned tasks.

Duties of the job
- Participates in overall planning and policy making to provide effective and uniform personnel services.
- Communicates policy through organization levels by bulletin, meetings, and personal contact.
- Interviews applicants, evaluates qualifications, classifies applications.
- Recruits and screens applicants to fill vacancies and reviews applications of qualified persons.
- Confers with supervisors on personnel matters, including placement problems, retention or release of probationary employees, transfers, demotions, and dismissals of permanent employees.
- Supervises administration of tests.
- Initiates personnel training activities and coordinates these activities with work of officials and supervisors.
- Establishes effective service rating system, trains unit supervisors in making employee evaluations.
- Maintains employee personnel files.
- Supervises a group of employees directly and through subordinates.
- Performs related work as assigned.

presented in a short summary form, followed by a list of the specific duties a person in the position has. To be of any value, a job description must be kept up to date. It must also be complete. And finally, it must be based on specifically desired behaviors (job objectives).

**Developing Job
Specifications**

Job specifications are prepared from job descriptions.

**Job specifications are a written statement listing the qualifications a
person needs to perform a given job effectively.**

Table 10.6 is an example of job specifications for the job described in Table 10.4.

Job specifications clarify the skills and experience necessary to perform a job effectively, including the number of months or years of experience as well as the specific education or training required. If the position requires physical effort, this effort is specified—for example, the amount of weight to be lifted. Where appropriate, the responsibility section also includes the

Table 10.6
Job Specifications for
Personnel Manager

General Qualification Requirements
- *Experience and training*   Should have considerable experience in personnel administration. Four years is a minimum.
- *Education*   Graduation from a four-year college or university, with major work in personnel or business administration.
- *Knowledge, skills, and abilities*   Considerable knowledge of principles and practices of personnel administration; selection and assignment of personnel; job evaluation.

Responsibility
- Supervises a department of three personnel professionals and one clerical employee.

amount of assets and equipment for which the individual in the position is responsible. Finally, for many jobs, job conditions such as the degree of environmental unpleasantness (heat, dust, etc.) are given.

Care must be taken in writing job specifications to avoid any improper form of employment discrimination. Specifically, it is necessary to avoid the following:

- Violation of the equal employment opportunity laws.

- Sex stereotyping in job titles. (For example, flight attendants, not stewardesses, assist passengers on airplanes; and postal carriers, not mailmen, deliver the mail.)

- Listing more than absolute minimum requirements for effective performance. (Thus graduation from college should not be listed unless the enterprise's records show that the job has never been performed effectively by a person who did not graduate from college and, in addition, it is unthinkable that such a person could competently fill the position.)

- Listing lengthy experience requirements (for example, ten years) unless no one with less experience could possibly perform the job effectively.

- Basing job specifications on the *opinions* of personnel or operating officers rather than on the experience of the enterprise.

Properly prepared job analyses, job descriptions, and job specifications are a good first step toward achieving role clarity. Making sure that communication lines are open and communication is taking place between employees at all levels—both through the formal MBO process and through less formal channels—will assure the desirable level of role definition and prevent role ambiguity and its consequences.

Summary

Chapter 10 began a three chapter unit on effective organizing. *Organizing* is the management process by which the work is divided up among units and employees (division of labor) and then these units and jobs are linked together to form a unified system (coordination). This chapter dealt with how a manager organizes tasks into jobs and how these jobs are defined for employee understanding and organizing departments.

Job design consists of specifying the tasks of the job, the methods used on the job, and how the job relates to other jobs in the organization. It is performed by managers, sometimes with the advice of specialized staff experts from personnel or engineering departments. Factors which influence job design include: (1) employee factors such as abilities and attitude/motivation; (2) economic factors such as available resources; (3) technological factors—equipment, work flow, tools, techniques; (4) union requirements; (5) government requirements; and (6) managerial objectives, strategy, and philosophy.

In order to understand job design strategies, certain terms regarding job content and organization must be understood. Each of these terms— *variety, cycle time, task identity/wholeness, knowledge/skill required, human interaction, freedom and control, responsibility/autonomy*—was defined in Table 10.1.

There are three basic job design strategies; one relies on craft jobs, another on specialization, and the third on enrichment. Jobs get more specialized by a process called *work simplification*, in which complete jobs are broken down into "small," simplified parts. Specialization is believed to yield the following production efficiencies: (1) Less skilled workers can be used. (2) More qualified workers are available. (3) Repetition of the same job results in production of more products of sufficient quality in the same amount of time. (4) The work gets done sooner. (5) Productivity increases because employees do not lose time shifting from one task to another.

Job rotation is sometimes used with specialization to allow more flexible assignments and easier staffing as well as to alleviate monotony and boredom for employees.

In contrast to the specialization approach to job design, job enrichment is a strategy that moves backward toward craft job design. Enrichment is accomplished either by increasing the *horizontal* loading of a job or by increasing the *vertical* loading of a job. Advocates of job enrichment claim that because more of an employee's needs are satisfied by this approach, the employee will (1) produce more work, (2) produce work of higher quality, (3) be absent less frequently, and (4) be more satisfied and developed.

Which design strategy should you use? Research indicates that all job design strategies can be effective. Most jobs are designed with the specialization approach. The job enrichment approach is likely to work when there is cooperation and encouragement at all levels on the part of union and management, and when employees have a strong work ethic.

Once the job is designed, it must be defined. *Job definition* is the process by which we communicate the tasks and standards of performance to employees. The purpose of job definition is to provide role clarity, a mutual understanding between manager and employee of exactly what the tasks and minimum performance levels are. In order to avoid role ambiguity it is important to develop comprehensive and clear job descriptions and have supervisors and employees discuss the descriptions with each other relating them to their own expectations. In the case of a bad match between employee and job, a new placement is the solution.

The job definition process begins with job analysis. *Job analysis* is the process by which a job analyst gathers data about a job. Job descriptions are prepared after the job analysis is completed. A *job description* is a written statement which details the duties and responsibilities of a job. It is imperative that the job description be kept up to date, be complete, and be based on job objectives.

Job specifications are prepared from job descriptions. *Job specifications* are written statements which list the qualifications a person needs to perform a job effectively. They clarify the skills and experience necessary to perform the job effectively.

If job analysis, job description, and job specifications are properly completed and prepared, role clarity should be easy to achieve.

Once the job has been designed, analyzed, and described, and job specifications have been written, the next stage of the organizing process is to group jobs into work units. This is discussed in Chapter 11.

Questions

1. Define organizing. What are the three stages in the organizing process in which you as a manager are likely to be involved?
2. What is job design? What factors influence job design? Give examples of each.
3. On what specific dimensions or factors do jobs differ?
4. Explain the specialization approach to job design, its advantages and disadvantages. Would you like to hold this type of job?
5. Do you think the job rotation system is a good approach to arranging specialized jobs? Why or why not?
6. "Job enrichment is a movement back toward craft job design." Justify this statement using your knowledge about the job enrichment technique of job design.
7. Under what circumstances is the job enrichment approach likely to be effective? Under what conditions is it likely to lead to unfavorable results?
8. Do you agree that the purpose of job definition is role clarity? How can you avoid role ambiguity in defining a job?
9. What factors would you consider in analyzing a job?
10. What is a job description? List the criteria you would use to develop a *good* job description.
11. What do job specifications do? Can job specifications have a significant impact on employment discrimination?

Exercise for Chapter 10

Job Design

To analyze job design, it is necessary first to do a job analysis and write a job description. This exercise will lead you through the appropriate steps.

1. Visit a firm which employs at least fifty persons.
2. Choose three jobs which have at least three persons with the same job title.
3. Prepare a job analysis for each of these three jobs. First, observe the employees for at least one-half hour and interview them individually or as a group. Then review available records, prior job analyses, and so forth. Data to be analyzed include:
   a. Work activities (procedures used, physical motions, human interactions).
   b. Machines, tools, equipment used.
   c. Job-related materials used, products made, or services performed.
   d. Job context—working conditions, inventories, and so forth.
4. The job analysis for each of the three jobs should include at least the following items:
   a. Job title.
   b. Job summary: one paragraph describing the general duties of the job.
   c. Descriptions of tasks: detailed step-by-step descriptions of the physical duties performed by the employee using the descriptions of the tasks from Part c above.
5. For each of the three jobs prepare a job description that includes a description of job content: job content factors which can be used include:
   a. Information input needed on the job.
   b. Mental processes used on the job.
   c. Work output (physical activities required).
   d. Relationships on the job (contacts required, and so forth).
   e. Job context (safety; pleasantness/unpleasantness).
   f. Other characteristics.

Now use the data you have collected to complete your job design analysis:

1. Is this job primarily a job designed with work simplification or job enrichment in mind? Why?
2. Would the present employees prefer a change more toward simplification or enrichment? Why or why not?
3. If the answer to Question 2 is yes, redesign the job to meet the new approach.
4. Return to the workplace. Show the job descriptions, job analyses, and job redesign to:
   a. The supervisors of the employees studied.
   b. The employees studied.
   Record the reactions of each person involved to your analyses, descriptions, and redesign.
5. Prepare final job analyses, job descriptions, and job designs acceptable to the supervisors and employees involved.

Notes

[1]For a discussion of the purpose and possible future direction of job design, see Louis E. Davis, "Job Design: Overview and Future Direction," *Journal of Contemporary Business* 6 (Spring 1977): 85–102.

[2]Richard Peterson, "Practical and Methodological Problems in Job Design," *Journal of Contemporary Business* 6 (Spring 1977): 67–83.

References

Employee Factors in Job Design

Randall B. Dunham, "Reactions to Job Characteristics: Moderating Effects of the Organization," *Academy of Management Journal* 20 (March 1977): 42–65. William E. Gallagher, Jr., and Hillel J. Einhorn, "Motivation Theory and Job Design," *Journal of Business* 49 (July 1976): 358–373. J. Richard Hackman, "The Design of Work in the 1980s," in *Motivation and Work Behavior,* ed. Richard Steers and Lyman Porter (New York: McGraw-Hill, 1979). J. Richard Hackman and J. L. Suttle, eds., *Improving Life at Work* (Santa Monica, Calif.: Goodyear, 1976), pp. 96–162. Donald P. Schwab and L. L. Cummings, "A Theoretical Analysis of the Impact of Task Scope on Employee Performance," *Academy of Management Review* 1 (April 1976): 23–35. Special Task Force to the Secretary of HEW, *Work in America* (Cambridge, Mass.: MIT Press, 1977). Richard Steers and R. T. Mowday, "The Motivational Properties of Tasks," *Academy of Management Review* 2 (October 1977): 645–658. Richard Steers and D. G. Spencer, "The Role of Achievement Motivation in Job Design," *Journal of Applied Psychology* 62 (August 1977): 472–479. Arthur Turner and Paul Lawrence, *Industrial Jobs and the Worker* (Boston: Harvard Business School, 1965).

Technological Factors in Job Design

Richard Peterson, "Practical and Methodological Problems in Job Design," *Journal of Contemporary Business* 6 (Spring 1977): 67–83. Denise M. Rousseau, "Technological Differences in Job Characteristics, Employee Satisfaction, and Motivation: A Synthesis of Job Design Research and Sociotechnical Systems Theory," *Organizational Behavior and Human Performance* 19 (June 1977): 18–42.

Union and Government Requirements

John Child, *Organization* (London: Harper & Row, 1977), chapter 2. Richard Peterson, "Practical and Methodological Problems in Job Design," *Journal of Contemporary Business* 6 (Spring 1977): 67–83. Leonard A. Schlesinger and Richard E. Walton, "The Process of Work Restructuring and Its Impact on Collective Bargaining," *Monthly Labor Review* 100 (April 1977): 52–55. Bernard J. White, "Innovations in Job Design: The Union Perspective," *Journal of Contemporary Business* 6 (Spring 1977): 23–35.

Specialization Job Design Strategy

Jean Champagne, "Adapting Jobs to People: The Alcan Experiment," *Monthly Labor Review* 96 (April 1973): 49–52. Louis E. Davis and James C. Taylor, *Design of Jobs*, 2d ed. (Santa Monica: Goodyear Publishing Co., 1979). David Folker, "Does the Industrial Engineer Dehumanize Jobs?" *Personnel* 50 (July–August 1973): 62–67. Stephan Konz, "Fitting the Job to the Man," *Industrial Engineering* 3 (January 1971): 10–15. Norman Maier, *Psychology in Industrial Organizations*, 4th ed. (Boston: Houghton Mifflin, 1973), chapter 11. Robert F. Schaeffer, "Reevaluating 'Meaningless' Work," *Personnel Administrator* 22 (January 1977): 51–53. David A. Whitsett, "Where Are Your Unenriched Jobs?" *Harvard Business Review* 53 (January–February 1975): 74–80.

Job Enrichment Strategy

Lloyd S. Baird, "Relationship of Performance to Satisfaction in Stimulating and Nonstimulating Jobs," *Journal of Applied Psychology* 61 (December 1976): 721–727. Elliot Carlson, "Job Enrichment: Sometimes It Works," *Wall Street Journal*, December 13, 1971. Kae H. Chung and Monica F. Ross, "Differences in Motivational Properties between Job Enlargement and Job Enrichment," *Academy of Management Review* (January 1977): 113–122. Thomas Cummings and John Bigelow, "Satisfaction, Job Involvement, and Intrinsic Motivation: An Extension of Lawler and Hall's Factor Analysis," *Journal of Applied Psychology* 61 (August 1976): 523–525. Thomas Cummings and Suresh Srivastva, *Management of Work: A Socio-Technical Systems Approach* (Kent, Ohio: Kent State University Press, 1977). Claude Durand, "Employer Politics in Job Enrichment," *International Studies of Management and Organization* 5 (Fall 1975): 66–86. R. N. Ford, "Job Enrichment Lessons from AT&T," *Harvard Business Review* 51 (January–February 1973): 96–106. Linda Frank and J. Richard Hackman, "A Failure of Job Enrichment," *Journal of Applied Behavioral Science* 2 (October–November–December 1975): 413–436. J. R. Hackman, "Is Job Enrichment Just a Fad?" *Harvard Business Review* 53 (September–October 1975): 129–138. J. R. Hackman et al., "A New Strategy for Job Enrichment," *California Management Review* 17 (Summer 1975): 57–71. J. Richard Hackman and Greg R. Oldham, "Motivation through the Design of Work: Test of a Theory," *Organizational Behavior and Human Performance* 16 (August 1976): 250–261. J. Friso den Hertog and Philips Gloeilampenfabricken, "The Search for New Leads in Job Design: The Philips Case," *Journal of Contemporary Business* 6 (Spring 1977): 49–66. Frederick Herzberg, "One More Time: How Do You Motivate Employees?" *Harvard Business Review* 46 (January–February 1968): 53–62. David Jenkins, *Job Power: Blue and White Collar Democracy* (New York: Doubleday, 1973). "Job Redesign on the Assembly Line: Farewell to Blue Collar Blues," *Organizational Dynamics* 2 (1976): 51–56. E. E. Lawler III, J. R. Hackman, and S. Kaufman, "Effects of Job Redesign: A Field Experiment," *Journal of Applied Social Psychology* 3 (January–March 1973): 49–62. Edwin A. Locke, David Sirota, and Alan D. Wolfson, "An Experimental Case Study of the Successes and Failures of Job Enrichment in a Government Agency," *Journal of Applied Psychology* 61 (December 1976): 701–711. Bowen Northrup, "Battling Boredom: Auto Plant in Sweden Scores Some Success with Worker 'Teams,'" *Wall Street Journal*, March 1, 1977, pp. 1, 36. Greg R. Oldham, J. Richard Hackman, and Jone L. Pearce, "Conditions under Which Employees Respond Positively to Enriched Work," *Journal of

Applied Psychology 61 (August 1976): 395–403. D. A. Ondrack, "Energy Occupational Values," *Academy of Management Journal* 16 (September 1973): 423–432. William Paul et al., "Job Enrichment Pays Off," *Harvard Business Review* 47 (March–April 1969): 61–78. Samuel Rabinowitz, Douglas T. Hall, and James G. Goodale, "Job Scope and Individual Differences as Predictors of Job Involvement: Independent or Interactive?" *Academy of Management Journal* 20 (June 1977): 273–281. Howard Schwartz and Leopold Gruenfeld, "Psychological Assumptions and Utopian Aspirations: A Critique of *Work in America*," *Administrative Science Quarterly* 20 (March 1975): 126–130. James C. Taylor, "Job Design in an Insurance Firm," *Journal of Contemporary Business* 6 (Spring 1977): 37–48. Noel M. Tichy, "When Does Work Restructuring Work? Organizational Innovations at Volvo and GM," *Organizational Dynamics* 5 (Summer 1976): 63–80. Denis D. Umstot, Cecil H. Bell, Jr., and Terence R. Mitchell, "Effects of Job Enrichment and Task Goals on Satisfaction and Productivity: Implications for Job Design," *Journal of Applied Psychology* 61 (August 1976): 379–394.

Which Design Strategy Should You Use?

James Biggane and Paul Stewart, "Job Enlargement: A Case Study," in *Design of Jobs,* ed. Louis Davis and James Taylor (Baltimore: Penguin, 1972). Milton R. Blood and Charles L. Hulin, "Alienation, Environmental Characteristics, and Worker Responses," *Journal of Applied Psychology* 51 (June 1967): 284–290. Louis Davis, "Readying the Unready," *California Management Review* 13 (Summer 1971): 27–36. Lex Donaldson, "Job Enlargement: A Multi-Dimensional Process," *Human Relations* 28 (July 1975): 593–610. Mitchell Fein, "Job Enrichment: A Reevaluation," *Sloan Management Review* 15 (Winter 1974): 69–88. Robert Ford, "Job Enrichment Lessons from AT&T," *Harvard Business Review* 51 (January–February 1973): 96–106. *Motivation through the Work Itself* (New York: American Management Association, 1969). A. Geijer and V. Hauser, *Democratie Industrielle* (Stockholm: Lands Organizationen I Sverige, 1971). Judson Gooding, "Blue Collar Blues on the Assembly Line," *Fortune,* July 1970, pp. 69–71, 112–117. Michael Gordon and Richard Arvey, "The Relationship between Education and Satisfaction with Job Content," *Academy of Management Journal* 18 (December 1975): 888–892. Neil Herrick, "The Other Side of the Coin," paper presented at the Invitational Seminar of Profit Sharing Research Foundation (Evanston, Ill.: November 17, 1971). Charles Hulin, "Individual Differences and Job Enrichment: The Case against General Treatments," in *New Perspectives in Job Enrichment,* ed. John Mahler (New York: Van Nostrand/Reinhold, 1971). Carl Jacobs, "Job Enrichment at Xerox Corporation," paper presented at the International Conference on the Quality of Work Life (New York, September 24–29, 1972). Robert Janson, "Job Enrichment in the Modern Office," in *New Perspectives in Job Enrichment,* ed. John Mahler (New York: Van Nostrand/Reinhold, 1971). Sar Levitan and William Johnston, "Job Redesign, Reform, Enrichment: Exploring the Limitations," *Monthly Labor Review* 96 (July 1973): 35–41. John Mahler, *New Perspectives in Job Enrichment* (New York: Van Nostrand/Reinhold, 1971). F. G. Miller et al., "Job Rotation Raises Productivity," *Industrial Engineering* 5 (June 1973): 24–26. William Reif and Robert Monczka, "Job Redesign: A Contingency Approach to Implementation," *Personnel* 51 (May–June 1974): 18–28. H. L. Shepard and N. Q. Herrick, *Where Have All the Robots Gone?* (New York: Free Press, 1972). Rollin Simonds and John Orife, "Worker Behavior versus Enrichment Theory," *Administrative Science Quarterly* 20 (December 1975): 606–612. H. R. Smith, "From Moses to Herzberg: An Exploration of Job De-Enrichment," *Proceedings of the Academy of Management* (1973). Patricia Smith and C. Lemm, "Positive Aspects of Motivation in Repetitive Work," *Journal of Applied Psychology* 39 (October 1955): 330–333. Gerald Susman, "Job Enlargement: Effects of Culture on Worker Responses," *Industrial Relations* 12 (February 1973): 1–15. Arthur Turner and A. Miclette, "Sources of Satisfaction in Repetitive Work," *Occupational Psychology* 36 (October 1962): 215–231. J. Walker and R. Marriott, "A Study of Some Attitudes toward Factory Work," *Occupational Psychology* 25 (July 1951): 181–191. Richard Walton, "How to Counter Alienation in the Plant," *Harvard Business Review* 50 (November–December 1972): 70–81. Arthur Weinberg, "Six American Workers Assess Job Redesign at Saab Scandia," *Monthly Labor Review* 98 (September 1975): 52–53.

Job Definition, Role Clarity, and Their Impacts

John Ivancevich and James Donnelly, Jr., "A Study of Role Clarity and Need for Clarity for Three Occupational Groups," *Academy of Management Journal* 17 (March 1974): 28–36. John Rizzo et al., "Role Conflict and Ambiguity in Complex Organizations," *Administrative Science Quarterly* 15 (June 1970): 150–163. W. Clay Hamner and Henry Tosi, "Relationship of Role Conflict and Role Ambiguity to Job Involvement Measures," *Journal of Applied Psychology* 59 (September 1974): 497–499. Robert House and J. R. Rizzo, "Role Conflict and Ambiguity as Critical Variables in a Model of Organizational Behavior," *Organizational Behavior and Human Performance* 7 (June 1972): 467–505. T. F. Lyons, "Role Clarity, Need for Clarity, Satisfaction, Tension, and Withdrawal," *Organizational Behavior and Human Performance* 6 (January 1971): 99–110. Raymond H. Miles, "A Comparison of the Relative Impacts of Role Perceptions of Ambiguity and Conflict by Role," *Academy of Management Journal* 19 (March 1976): 25–35. R. H. Miles and M. M. Petty, "Relationships between Role Clarity, Need for Clarity, and Job Tension and Satisfaction for Supervisory and Nonsupervisory Roles," *Academy of Management Journal* 18 (December 1975): 877–883. J. R. Rizzo, R. J. House, and S. E. Lirtzman, "Role Conflict and Ambiguity in Complex Organizations," *Administrative Science Quarterly* 15 (June 1970): 150–163. Randall S. Schuler, "Role Perceptions, Satisfaction, and Performance: A Partial Reconciliation," *Journal of Applied Psychology* 60 (December 1975): 683–687; and "Role Perceptions, Satisfaction, and Performance Moderated by Organizational Level and Participation in Decision Making," *Academy of Management Journal* 20 (March 1977): 159–165. Andrew Szilogyi, "An Empirical Test of Causal Inference between Role Perceptions, Satisfaction with Work, Performance and Organizational Level," *Personnel Psychology* 30 (Autumn 1977): 375–388. Andrew Szilogyi et al., "Role Dynamics, Locus of Control, and Employee Attitudes and Behaviors," *Academy of Management Journal* 19 (June 1976): 259–276.

Chapter 11 Organizing and Coordinating Work Units

11

Learning Objectives

1. Know how to develop an organization chart for a firm.
2. Learn how to group jobs into departments in an effective manner.
3. Understand how to use the functional and product/service approaches to departmentation.
4. Learn how to effectively link and coordinate departments in a firm.
5. Learn how large an effective work group can be, including the optimal number of subordinates reporting directly to each manager (span of control) and number of levels in the hierarchy.

Chapter Outline

Introduction
Formalizing Organizations
Organization Charts
Organization Manuals
Standardization
How Do Firms Group Jobs?
Primitive Structure
Functional Departmentation
Product/Service Organization
Matrix Organization
How Big Can Work Groups Get?
Span of Control
Height of the Hierarchy
How Do Firms Get Units to Work Together?
Informal Unprogrammed Coordination
Programmed Nonhuman Coordination
Individual Coordination
Group Coordination
Summary
Questions
Case: Acme Office Furniture (AOF)

Introduction

In Chapter 10, you learned how tasks are organized into jobs that are meaningful for the employee and effective for the firm. This chapter addresses the next stage of the organizing process by considering three questions: (1) *How do we group jobs into work units?* (2) *How big can the work units get and still be effective?* (3) *How do we get the units to work together in achieving corporate objectives?* In examining these questions, you will also want to focus on why firms organize jobs into units.

In small and less complex firms, organization may be informal and change from day to day. Boutiques, small job shops, and offices may not spend much time organizing at all.

But for enterprises with larger and more complex objectives, and where time pressures are great, good organization leads to increased effectiveness. General Motors' current market position relative to Ford is strong evidence of the value of emphasizing organization. Their positions were reversed in the early years of the automotive industry, but General Motors passed Ford by and now has almost three times the business Ford has. Many attribute this feat to a great organizer, Alfred P. Sloan, Jr. (whose life is reviewed later in the chapter).

Besides its importance in achieving objectives, organization can also affect employee attitudes and performance. This will become clear as we discuss each aspect of organization.

In Chapter 10, we defined *organizing* as the management process by

Source: © King Features Syndicate, Inc., 1978. Reprinted by permission.

which work is divided up among units and employees (division of labor) and these units and jobs are linked together to form a unified system (coordination). Note some of the crucial elements in organization:

1. *Objectives:* We organize to achieve our objectives. We often hear people complaining about how disorganized they are. Stores will sell you little cards that say "Some day we have to get organized!" This is a typical problem of business enterprises. Organization helps clarify the objectives of the enterprise as they apply to work units.

2. *Formality of relationships:* A second characteristic of organization is the establishment of relationships that permit each person to know what must be done and how his or her job relates to other jobs. The first step in organizing is effective job design and job descriptions. But without formal relationships no one knows who is supposed to do what and how each person is supposed to work with others to get the job done.

3. *Stability/duration of relationships:* Effective organization requires some lasting stability in relationships at work. A firm cannot claim to be organized if each time an employee tries to get a part for a machine he or she has to go to a different person located in a different department. This is chaos. Effective organization requires reasonably long-lasting relationships among jobs, even if the employees in the jobs change.

Before proceeding to a consideration of the three questions noted above, we shall take a look at how firms formalize their organization.

Formalizing Organizations

In formal organizations, the manager describes the organizational relationships in written and graphic form as precisely as is practical. Changes thereafter can be made in formal or informal ways.

If you ask the manager or entrepreneur in a small firm how it is organized, he or she will tell you in general terms. As long as the organizational structure is well thought out and clearly communicated to the employees, this is quite adequate. What is most vital to effective organization is a thorough understanding on the part of all the members of the relationships involved. In Chapter 2 we saw that managers prefer verbal communication. In a small enterprise, verbal communication (with supportive nonverbal cues) serves well in developing this understanding.

Some medium-size and most large enterprises formalize their organizational structure with organization charts and manuals. The former present the organizational structure graphically; the latter describe it in writing. Organizations use these aids because it is difficult to communicate effectively to large numbers of people verbally. It is far more efficient to communicate information of this nature in written form.

These organization charts and manuals are the most frequently used and important means of formalization and standardization. Let us look briefly at each.

Organization Charts

The organization chart appears early in the formalization process. Several guidelines are used in its preparation:

1. The unit to be charted is usually represented by a rectangle (occasionally by a circle or some other geometric figure).
2. The most powerful unit is normally pictured at the top of the page. The distance below the top unit indicates the power of each lower unit.
3. Organizational relationships (who reports to whom) are indicated by lines between units.
4. When a power relationship is partial, it is represented by a dotted line. For example, if a personnel unit reports to a plant manager but the vice-president for personnel at the home office is responsible for the technical expertise of the unit, a dotted line runs from the vice-president to the unit. This limited power relationship is called functional authority. Management theory usually says that this functional authority is given by higher-level line executives to the staff executives.
5. If the firm distinguishes home office staff authority from line authority (see Chapter 14), staff units are shown to the side of the line organization structure.

The examples given here should help you understand organization charts. All are based on the same company. Figure 11.1 is an example of an organization chart showing the line executives (the president and the

Figure 11.1
A Line Organization Chart

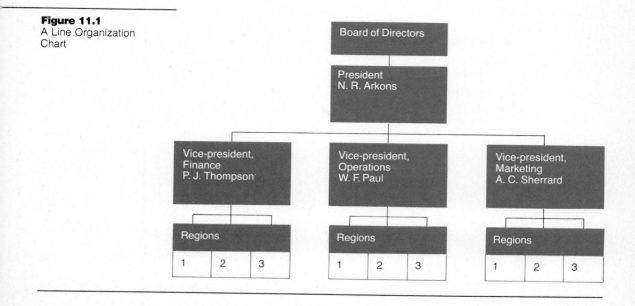

vice-presidents for finance, operations, and marketing). The vice-presidents report to the president, and regional managers report to each vice-president.

Figure 11.2 adds the staff vice-presidents (for simplicity, only three are shown). Note that staff units are shown to the right of the line hierarchy. In advising the line executives, the personnel department would begin at the vice presidential level and proceed down the hierarchy.

Figure 11.3 shows a more likely possibility. The personnel manager at Plant 3 reports to the plant manager, but personnel at headquarters tells him or her which tests and performance evaluation methods to use and provides the necessary technical training. This relationship is indicated by the dotted line. It is very important for organization charts to be accurate in showing power and responsibility relationships, especially when they are first drawn up.

Organization Manuals

Some organizations develop their formal organization structure further by means of organization manuals. These usually contain the following information:

Figure 11.2
A Line and Staff
Organization Chart

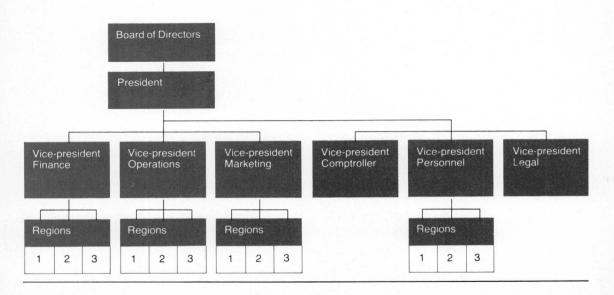

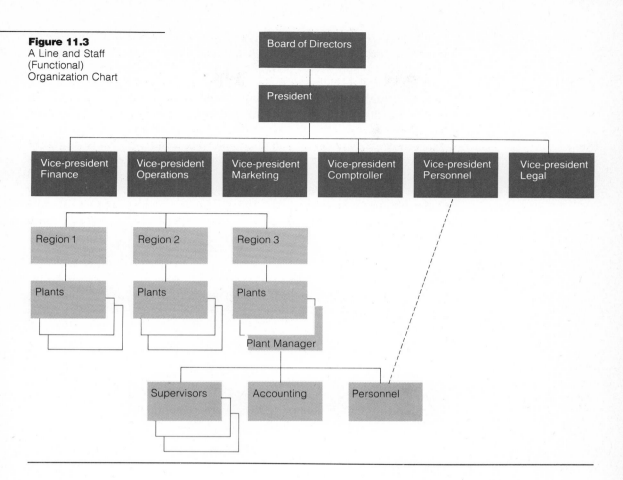

Figure 11.3
A Line and Staff
(Functional)
Organization Chart

- Organizational objectives
- Organizational policies and procedures
- Organization charts
- Job descriptions for key executives
- Guidelines for executive titles

Organization manuals are expensive to develop and maintain. Many managers do not like them. They prefer verbal communication and feel that manuals limit their freedom. Manuals are found primarily in very large organizations. Top managers usually delegate the preparation of these manuals to planning executives.

It is revealing, indeed, that when top executives are asked for their organization charts and/or manuals, they usually answer with some variation of the following: "You know, we don't have them here, although we probably should." Or: (very reluctantly) "Here they are, but they aren't up to date. I've been meaning to update them but haven't had a chance." Thus we must conclude that enterprises really operate on the basis of informal relationships developed interpersonally from day to day. They do not need formalities like charts and manuals, except when an employee is learning a new job. Informal relationships are not shown in these documents, and at times they are more important than the formal relationships. Nonetheless, charts and manuals do provide a *beginning point* for understanding how an enterprise is organized, especially a large enterprise. And they can help define relationships between jobs and people if properly developed, updated, and explained.

Standardization

The final approach to formalizing organization is *standardization*. Standardization of an organization's procedures and roles (jobs) means that the management examines the events occurring regularly and establishes within the enterprise approved ways of handling them. These standards are used in hiring, training, and evaluating employees and in running the organization.

Organizations vary in the degree to which they use standardization. Elements that are typically standardized in an organization with a more formal approach include:

- Written job definitions and specifications (Chapter 10).
- Written procedures and policies (Chapter 7).
- Carefully developed job titles and status differentials.

So if an organization believes that formal organizing is useful (and it is in larger organizations) it will develop and use organization charts and organization manuals and will also standardize job definitions and procedures.

How Do Firms Group Jobs?

After designing and defining jobs, the firm must determine how to relate the jobs to each other—how to group them into work units effectively. To understand how this is done, we will examine how jobs are grouped as a specific firm grows.

Primitive Structure

Our focal organization begins as a small toy manufacturing firm. Initially the entrepreneur assembled games that he had designed, with the help of his wife and children, in his basement. As sales grew, he rented an empty store building and hired high school students to work after school. Soon he had 5 full-time employees, then 10, then 15. At this point the enterprise had the primitive structure shown in Figure 11.4: a boss and several

Figure 11.4
A Primitive
(Informal)
Organization

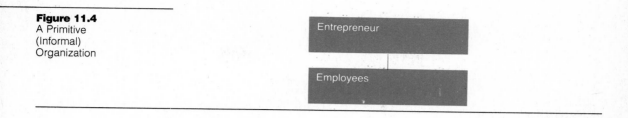

employees. In this structure the boss tells everyone what to do. Everyone expects the boss to organize the enterprise's activities and do all manageri-al jobs.

Functional Departmentation

As the enterprise developed further, the boss could not do all the managing. Informally, he began to ask one employee to help him with sales (probably calling on the smallest customers), another to help schedule employee time, another to hire people. They became his assistants. Eventually this structure became formalized; that is, the assistants became full-time specialists and the enterprise developed the *functional* structure shown in Figure 11.5.

Most firms use the functional approach to grouping jobs. Figure 11.6 represents a more fully implemented functional organization of the toy firm after ten years of successful growth.

As Figure 11.6 makes clear, grouping of duties into functional depart-ments results when jobs with similar technical content are grouped together into single functional units.

It is not by accident that the jobs are grouped in this way more than any other way today. There are significant advantages to functional grouping. These *advantages* are:

- It results in efficient usage of resources.
- It results in easier measurement of output and results.
- It prepares well-trained specialist managers efficiently.
- It gives status to major functional jobs.
- It maintains control at top management level.

Why are not all firms organized functionally? There are disadvantages to functional grouping of work units. The major *disadvantages* are:

Figure 11.5
Functional
Organization

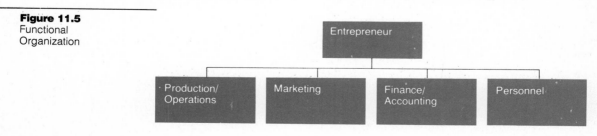

Figure 11.6
Functional
Organization Fully
Implemented

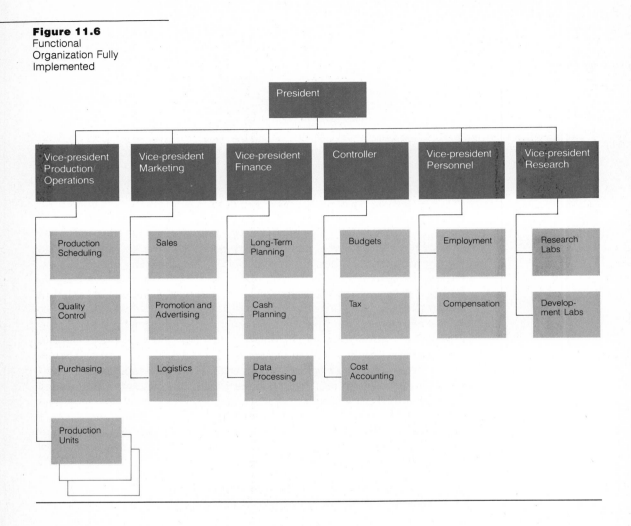

- The cost of coordination between functional departments is high.
- Close identification by a homogeneous group of specialists makes change difficult.
- It offers managers little preparation for general management.
- Conflict between departments is high.
- Client satisfaction can be lower compared to that obtained in other methods.

When dissatisfaction with functional organization rises—usually when the firm develops other product lines (diversification), especially fast-changing ones—top management often changes to product organization.

Source: Drawing by Lorenz; © 1977
The New Yorker Magazine, Inc.

Product/Service Organization

Business organizations can produce either products or services. A common approach to departmentation is to organize a division around the product or service. I will call this approach product/service departmentation. In product organizations specialists are grouped to perform all the duties necessary to produce an individual product or service. Most product firms, however, do not extend their grouping as far as the ice cream enterprise in the cartoon. Organization charts for typical product/service organizations are shown in Figures 11.7 (the recreational equipment manufacturer, now diversified) and 11.8 (an insurance firm).

As with functional organizations, there are advantages and disadvantages to product/service organizations. As Table 11.1 indicates, they are exact opposites of the advantages and disadvantages of functional organizations: What is an advantage under functional departmentation is a disadvantage under product/service departmentation and vice versa.

In addition, the product/service organization does place profit responsibility at the product/service division level—one step below president in our case.

A quick look at Table 11.1 shows that there are advantages and disadvantages to both styles. But they are not always of equal weight, and they are relative, not absolute. A manager must choose the set of advantages that are vital and the disadvantages he or she can live with.

There is very little research evidence that these supposed advantages and disadvantages always hold true. Arthur Walker and Jay Lorsch examined two plants that were alike in external and internal factors except that one used functional, the other product/service departmentation. They found that:

- The plant using functional departmentation was more efficient.

Figure 11.7
Product/Service
Organization for a
Recreational
Equipment Firm

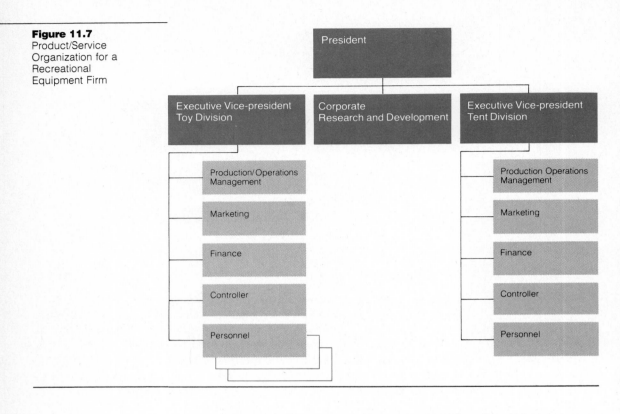

- Job satisfaction was higher in the plant using functional departmentation.
- The plant using product/service departmentation was better coordinated, and its communication was better.
- The plant using product/service departmentation solved problems more quickly and adapted to changing conditions more readily.
- The plant using product/service departmentation trained generalists better.[1]

Arthur Kover's study of an advertising agency resulted in the following findings:

- Product/service departmentation led to greater client satisfaction.
- Product/service departmentation improved coordination.
- Communication patterns changed when the organization shifted from functional to product/service departmentation. Communication with clients went up, but communication between specialists went down.[2]

In sum, managers should choose the form of departmentation that is critical to their success. Are efficiency and cost crucial? Then use

Figure 11.8
Product/Service
Organization for an
Insurance Firm

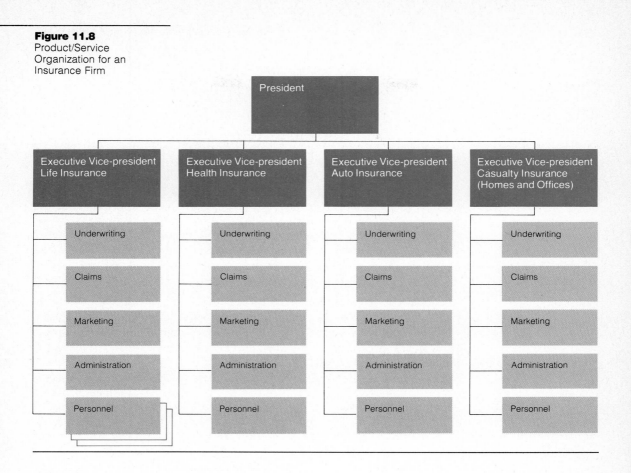

Table 11.1
Advantages and
Disadvantages of
Functional and
Product/Service
Approaches to
Departmentation

Factor	Functional Departmentation		Product/Service Departmentation	
	Advantage	Disadvantage	Advantage	Disadvantage
A. Efficiency of resource use	+			−
B. Coordination cost		−	+	
C. Willingness to adapt and change		−	+	
D. Ease of measurement of output and results	+			−
E. Preparation of broadly trained managers and employees		−	+	
F. Preparation of well-trained specialists	+			−
G. Interdepartmental conflict		−	+	
H. Client satisfaction		−	+	

Figure 11.9
An Enterprise
Divided into
Departments on the
Basis of Purpose
(Time)

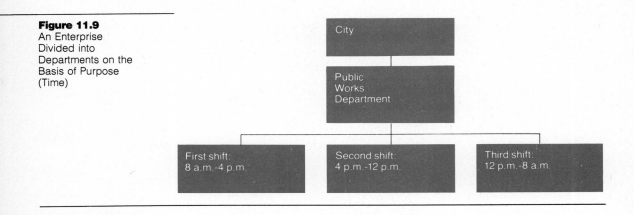

functional departmentation. Are coordination and getting the job done within narrow time limits crucial? Use product/service departmentation.

There are three variations of product/service departmentation. At lower levels in the organization, work units may be organized on the basis of time, as shown in Figure 11.9.

This system is often used when around-the-clock operation is essential.

Figure 11.10
An Enterprise
Divided into
Departments by
Purpose (Client)

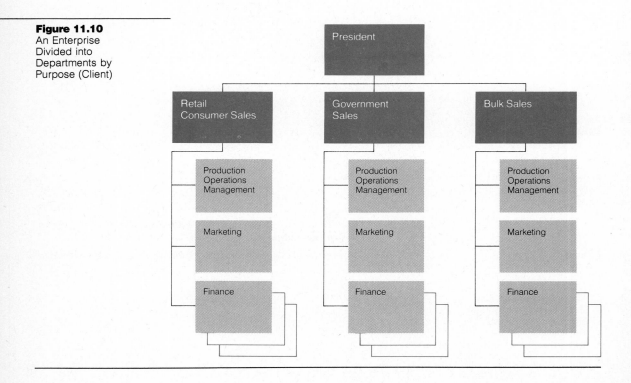

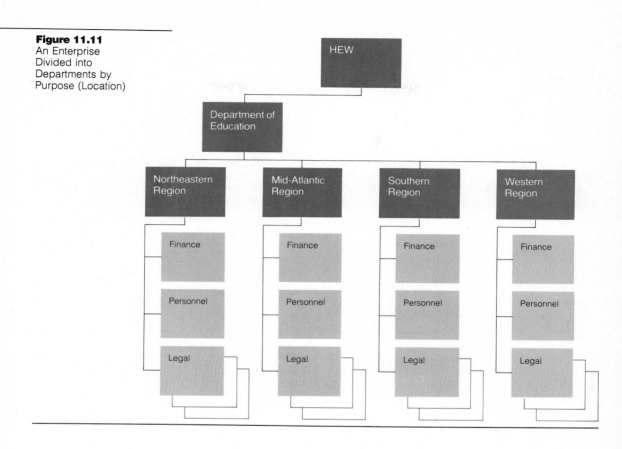

Figure 11.11
An Enterprise
Divided into
Departments by
Purpose (Location)

When there are three shifts, however, the second and third shifts usually do not contain all the functions necessary to run the operation. Some large organizations whose clients have very different needs may structure departments around individual clients rather than products, as shown in Figure 11.10.

And finally, in still another variation of product/service departmentation, geography is the principle of organization used, as shown in Figure 11.11. This approach is valid when geographical distances between units are significant and cause management problems.

All these variations of product/service grouping of jobs have roughly the same advantages and disadvantages as the more frequently used product/service departmentation itself.

Matrix Organization

In a way, matrix organization is an attempt to cross the product and functional approaches to organization in order to get the best (and avoid the worst) of both.

Fremont A. Shull, Jr.

Fremont A. Shull, Jr., professor of management and sociology, member of the gerontology faculty, and senior fellow of the Dean Rusk Center for International Law, University of Georgia, received his B.S. degree in business administration, his M.B.A. from Ohio State University, and his Ph.D. in economic theory from Michigan State University. He has been an assistant professor at Indiana University, a Ford Foundation Fellow at Carnegie Institute of Technology, professor and chairman of organization theory at Southern Illinois University, visiting professor of organization theory at the University of Kentucky, and research consultant at Glacier Institute of Management, Ruislip, England. He is listed in *Who's Who in America* and in *International Who's Who in Community Service.* He is also a Beta Gamma Sigma Distinguished Scholar.

   Shull made the first known academic presentation on the conceptualization of matrix organizational design at the Midwest Academy of Management in 1963. The design is composed of a set of organization strategies (rather than a standardized bureaucratic conceptualization); the importance of each of the strategies varies by organizational unit and type of organization. The primary applied proponent of the strategies is the National Aeronautic and Space Administration. Martin-Marietta also has long employed the model. For eighteen months in 1967–68, Shull was a research consultant and task-force leader under a NASA institutional grant at the University of Wisconsin, where he further refined the model.

   Shull has consulted on the application of matrix to the Alabama Welfare System, a nursing home, and the Delaware Correctional System. He has studied associated managerial perceptions and styles in a large electronics conglomerate. From these endeavors and others, he has been able to further elaborate on the design.

A matrix organization is an organization that uses a dual command system for many middle or supervisory managers.

They belong simultaneously to two groups—a functional specialist group and a product or project group—and they report to two superiors: a permanent boss in the functional part of the organization and one or more temporary bosses in the project (or product/service) part of the organization. Although matrix organization is relatively uncommon today, many large and complex organizations have used it to greater or lesser extent: Lockheed Aircraft, British Aircraft Corporation, Dow Corning, Procter & Gamble, Corning Glass, ITT, Texas Instruments, Citibank, British

National Health Service, and Harvard Business School.

The organization charts in Figures 11.12 and 11.13 will help clarify this organizational approach. Figure 11.12 portrays the organization of TRW Systems, one of the earliest users of matrix.

Note that the subproject manager, who reports to a lab manager within the operations/technical resources group as well as to an assistant project manager, is thus part of two work groups and must divide his or her energy and time between them. Figure 11.13 is the chart for the U.S. Environmental Protection Agency. Note here that if you are an Air Assistant Region I Manager, you report to EPA Director, Region I, and to a manager in the Air Bureau as well.

While matrix organization may seem unduly complex, sometimes it can

Figure 11.12
TRW Systems
Group: The
APM-SPM-WPM
Chain

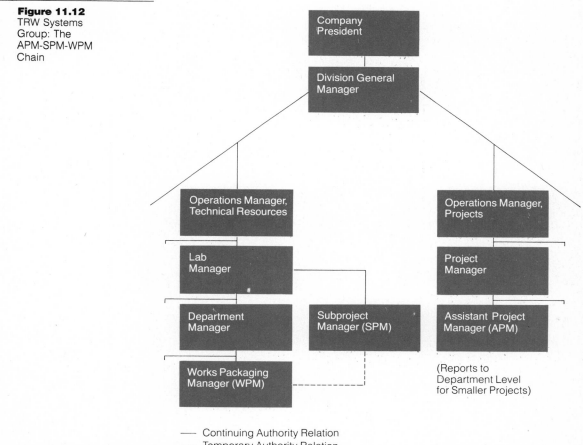

— Continuing Authority Relation
--- Temporary Authority Relation

Source: Stanley M. Davis/Paul R. Lawrence, *Matrix*, © 1977, Addison-Wesley, Reading, Massachusetts, Fig. 4.2, page 94. Reprinted with permission.

Figure 11.13
Organization of the
Environmental
Protection Agency

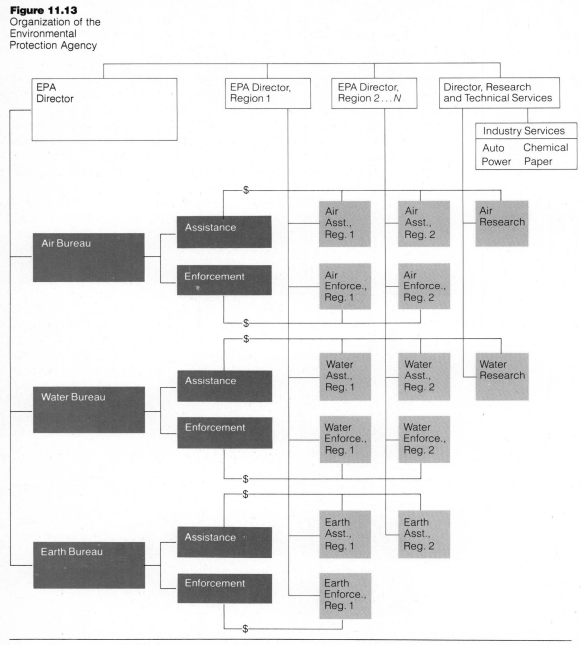

Source: Stanley M. Davis/Paul R. Lawrence, *Matrix,* © 1977, Addison-Wesley, Reading, Massachusetts, Fig. 7.3, page 176. Reprinted with permission.

be invaluable. It may, in fact, be essential. Why do firms use the matrix approach? If a government agency is a client—as in the case of TRW—it may require the firm to set up a project manager–matrix structure so that the agency will have a *single contact person* rather than a series of functional managers to negotiate and interact with. Matrix is also useful when exact meshing of times is important. For example, due to weather and other factors, NASA could only launch moon shots on certain days. Because all the subassemblies had to be done on exact dates, matrix was vital to the launching operations. Another virtue of matrix organization is that it can offer significant economies of scale. For example, some specialized engineering expertise may be necessary for a given project. If only part-time rather than full-time services of an engineer are required, two projects may share an engineer.

In sum, matrix is a compromise form of organization; it serves the needs of both customer and company. Often, it comes into existence through evolution rather than because top management chooses to develop a new approach to organization. A typical evolution might take place in the following steps: (1) Project managers are temporarily added to a functional organization for several short-term but important jobs. (2) The project manager system is made permanent for parts of the organization. (3) The system is extended throughout the organization; it becomes a mature matrix organization, where a majority of managers belong to two groups and are responsible to two superiors.

It makes many managers uncomfortable to have to report to two superiors. Traditional management theory suggests that it is most efficient (and less stressful) for managers (and employees) to have only one superior. This is called the principle of unity of command in traditional management theory. While matrix supporters admit that most persons prefer to have only one superior, they counter with the argument that in really complex enterprises this is not possible.

Problems which may arise in a matrix organization include:

- Power struggles between the two superiors (and their groups) can involve the manager.

- If both groups to which the manager relates are involved in all his or her decisions—not just those which require their expertise—decision making can be slowed down and costs increased.

- The corporate point of view can be lost in the struggle between groups.

In spite of problems, General Electric encouraged its managers to give matrix organization serious consideration:

We've highlighted matrix organization . . . not because it's a bandwagon that we want you all to jump on, but rather that it's a complex, difficult, and sometimes frustrating form of organization to live with. It's also, however, a bellwether of things to come. But, when implemented well, it does offer much of the best of both worlds. And all of us are going to have to learn how to utilize organization to prepare managers to increasingly deal with high levels of complexity and ambiguity in situations where they have to get results from people and components not under their direct control. . . . Successful experience in operating under a matrix constitutes better preparation for an individual to run a huge diversified institution like General Electric—where so many complex, conflicting interests must be balanced—than the product and functional modes which have been our hallmark over the past twenty years.[3]

In sum, managers face different kinds of organizational problems as the firm evolves. They must choose the approach to departmentation that will solve their particular problems.

How Big Can Work Groups Get?

The second organizational question that managers must answer is how big the work group can get and still be effective. The response will be found in part in Chapter 16, which discusses groups. The facet I wish to discuss here is how many employees a supervisor can manage effectively. This in turn affects how many levels there are within the firm.

In Chapter 2 you learned that there are three kinds of managers: top, middle, and supervisory. These three kinds of managers exist within the same enterprise and actually are on a scale ranging from the supervisor up to top management. Managers at highest levels tend to have the most power, and the amount of power tends to decrease in the middle levels and be much less at the supervisory levels. This phenomenon is called a *hierarchy,* or *chain of command.* Two related organizational aspects of a hierarchy are (1) the *number of levels* in it and (2) its managers' *span of control.* An enterprise can be classified as flat, medium, or tall, depending on the number of levels (jobs) in the longest "line" from worker to top executive (excluding assistants and secretaries). A manager's span of control (also called span of management) is the number of subordinates reporting directly to him or her.

Height of hierarchy and span of control are inversely related. Suppose an enterprise employs 1,000 people and chooses among three spans of control: 10, 20, or 100. It can easily be seen that the height of the hierarchy depends on this choice. In the case of a large span, each of 10 supervisors has 100 employees reporting to him or her. These 10 supervisors report to the president. This results in only two levels of managerial hierarchy, the supervisors and the president—a flat hierarchy.

With a small span of 10 employees, the firm needs 100 supervisors. They in turn must be supervised in groups of 10, so there are 10 middle managers reporting to the president. This makes three levels—a taller hierarchy.

Span of Control

As explained above, span of control—the number of people reporting to the manager—influences the height of the hierarchy: the smaller the span, the greater the height. This in turn increases the direct costs of management; the more managers needed, the greater the total amount of management salaries.

A series of studies were done to determine actual overall spans of control. Generally, these studies found that spans of control increase as enterprises get larger and that most top managers supervise five or six managers.

The figures reported are conservative, however. In reviewing the research, William Ouchi and John Dowling found that many such studies exclude assistants and helpers.[4] In the course of their investigations, they also discovered that many researchers oppose prescribing spans of control for all enterprises at all levels in view of individual differences among managers and jobs. Indeed, many factors influence the span of control, but the major ones are the people involved, the jobs involved, and the environment.

Personal Factors

Two personal variables affect the span of control. The first is *managerial preferences*. If the manager has a strong need for power, he or she may prefer a larger span of control. The manager who has strong social needs may prefer to interact with more rather than fewer subordinates. Since managers usually have some discretion over their span of control, this too could result in larger spans. Unfortunately, there are few studies on this subject.

The second personal factor is *competence*. A more competent supervisor may be *able* to supervise a larger group, so his or her span of control may be larger. Employee competence may also result in larger spans of control. Studies do not consistently support this relationship; at least two have found that the higher the competence, the lower the span of control.

Job Factors

The first of the job factors is the nature of the *manager's job*. Does the manager spend all his or her time in supervision or half of it? If the former, the span is likely to be larger. Few studies have been done on this aspect of management.

Other factors relate to the *employees being supervised*. The first is the relative importance of the job and the need of the subordinate to consult with the superior. In studying the reorganization of the state of Michigan in 1965, I noted a lot of talk about the governor's span of control—forty—being too large. Some of the department heads needed to see him daily, others once a year. (The chairman of the Apple Commission posed with the governor and the Apple Queen every year when the governor declared "Eat Michigan Apples Week.") Little research has been done on this factor, but it appears that the span should be computed on the basis of a weighted importance index, not sheer numbers.

Another factor is the *degree of similarity and standardization in the employees' work*. Researchers have found that the lower the variety in the job, the larger the span can be.

Another important variable is the *degree of interrelatedness in the department's work*. If there is a high degree of interrelatedness among the jobs in the department, more supervisory time and thus a smaller span of control is required. Little empirical research has been done on this subject, however.

Behavioral scientists have investigated a phenomenon similar to span of control: group size. The general conclusions are that *groups of five and seven* perform very well. Larger groups lead to clique formation and conflict, more problems of coordination, and lower participation and job satisfaction. Typical research showed a span of control median of eight and a mean of thirteen. But when adjusted for errors and when helpers and assistants were added, the median became almost twelve and the mean almost fifteen persons.

Environmental Factors

Technology also influences span of control. Studies have found that effective mass production companies have larger supervisory spans of control. The optimum for craft work is five and for automated work six. The optimum for mass production is forty to sixty.

Spans of control increase as *volatility* and *dependence* increase. They also increase as employees move farther apart *geographically*.

Conclusions

Much of the confusion resulting from research on span of control is due to the fact that researchers define span of control differently. Keeping this problem in mind, it is still possible to draw some reasonable conclusions concerning span of control. In sum, it is fair to say that spans of control should be *smaller* if:

- Managers prefer small departments. (Research shows, however, that managers of larger units are more satisfied than managers of smaller units.)
- The employees are not too competent.
- The manager must do part of the work, not just supervise employees.
- The jobs are unstandardized, dissimilar, and highly interdependent.
- The technology is craft or automated.

One approach to calculating the effective span of control is that of Lockheed. (See Table 11.2.) The size of the supervisor's work group is determined by a point system. Points are determined by a span-of-control index based on a series of span-of-control factors. Lockheed claims that it has experienced substantial savings in managerial costs as a result of establishing larger spans of control.

A sample of the spans of control for middle managers indicated by the Lockheed index is given in Table 11.3.[5]

Height of the Hierarchy

Two aspects of the relative flatness or tallness of an organization's hierarchy have been studied. One is the relationship between height and the size of the organization. The other is the effect the height of a hierarchy has on performance and job satisfaction of employees. A number of studies have found that as the organization grows in size, the height of its hierarchy increases.[6] In addition, research results indicate that the organization also gets taller—the height of its hierarchy grows—when its technology shifts from craft work occurring in job shops toward mass

Table 11.2
Weighted Index of Span of Control at Lockheed

Span Factor	Point Values for Each Factor				
Similarity of functions	Identical	Essentially alike	Similar	Inherently different	Fundamentally distinct
	1	2	3	4	5
Geographic contingency	All together	All in one building	Separate building, 1 plant location	Separate locations, 1 geographic area	Dispersed geographic areas
	1	2	3	4	5
Complexity of functions	Simple, repetitive	Routine	Some complexity	Complex, varied	Highly complex, varied
	2	4	6	8	10
Direction and control	Minimum supervision and training	Limited supervision	Moderate, periodic supervision	Frequent, continuing supervision	Constant, close supervision
	3	6	9	12	15
Coordination	Minimum relationships with others	Relationships limited to defined courses	Moderate relationships, easily controlled	Considerable close relationships	Extensive mutual nonrecruiting relationships
	2	4	6	8	10
Planning	Minimum scope and complexity	Limited scope and complexity	Moderate scope and complexity	Considerable effort required; guided only by broad policies	Extensive effort required; areas and policies not chartered
	2	4	6	8	10

Source: Harold Stieglitz, "Optimizing Span of Control," *Management Record* 24 (September 1962): 27. © 1962 The Conference Board. Reprinted by permission of The Conference Board.

Table 11.3	Supervisory Index[a]	Suggested Standard Span of Control
Middle Managerial Application of Weighted Index of Span of Control	40–42	4–5
	37–39	4–6
	34–36	4–7
	31–33	5–8
	28–30	6–9
	25–27	7–10
	22–24	8–11

[a]Total number of points on weighted index of span of control factors.
Source: Harold Stieglitz, "Optimizing Span of Control," *Management Record* 24 (September 1962): 29. © 1962 The Conference Board. Reprinted by permission of The Conference Board.

production or automation.[7] For example, Joan Woodward correlated this relationship in firms where a single system of production predominated.[8] She also noted a tendency to organize each system independently where two systems of production were combined, however. See Figure 11.14.

Studies of the effects of height of the hierarchy on the job satisfaction of employees and on their performance have provided some insights into employee motivation and behavior. Specifically, L. L. Cummings and Chris Berger noted the following two relationships: (1) The higher the level in the organization, the more satisfied the employee is (especially in taller organizations). (2) Higher-level executives in tall organizations and lower-level executives in flat organizations are more satisfied than higher-

Figure 11.14
Woodward's Levels of Management

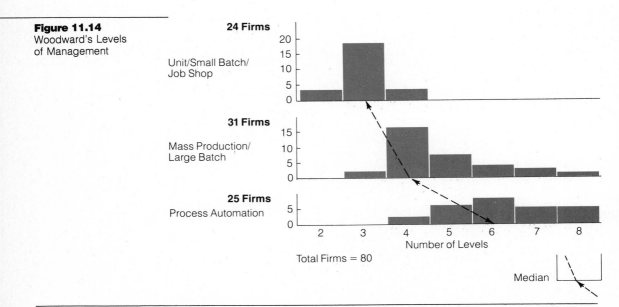

Total Firms = 80

Source: Adapted by permission from Joan Woodward, *Industrial Organization: Theory and Practice* (London: Oxford University Press, 1965), p. 52.

level executives in flat organizations and lower-level executives in tall organizations.[9]

How Do Firms Get Units to Work Together?

The third and final question you must be able to answer in order to organize effectively is how to relate the various work units to each other. This is done by coordination, or, as it is sometimes called, integration.

Coordination is the set of human and structural mechanisms designed to link the parts of the enterprise together to help achieve its objectives.

A great deal has been written about grouping jobs, but there is precious little on the subject of coordination. Still, there is greater emphasis on coordination today than in the past, as the systems approach evidences. One executive who was well known for his organizing and coordinating skills was Alfred P. Sloan, Jr., of General Motors.

Alfred P. Sloan, Jr.

Henry Ford's dominance of the auto industry was overthrown by the first and greatest of a new breed, Alfred Pritchard Sloan, Jr., who reconstituted General Motors in the 1920's so successfully that most large U.S. corporations, including Ford, have come to run on principles that Sloan developed. An M.I.T.-trained engineer, Sloan sometimes referred to his system as "scientific management," but a better term would be "rational structure of the decision-making process." He had built the Hyatt Roller Bearing Co. to the point where William C. Durant, the brilliant assembler of G.M., was glad to pay $13.5 million for Hyatt. Sloan liked and respected Durant, whose own operating style was intuitive. But too many decisions crowded in haphazard fashion on Durant's desk with its ten busy telephones. Sloan in 1920 produced a twenty-eight-page memo on how the management should be restructured, and he was about to resign when Durant was forced out by his largest stockholder group, the du Ponts. Sloan was soon at the top because he demonstrated an ability to marshal facts around the points of decision. His 1920 memo recognized that in so large an enterprise a high degree of operating authority must be left in the divisions. But he built a strong central staff and a system of forecasts against which performance was measured. Sloan, in short, dealt effectively with one of the fundamental problems of modern life: how to achieve cooperation among men who were—and needed to be—too individualistic to be commanded in the old sense, but who would accept an orderly framework of policymaking.

Source: *Fortune*, January 1975, p. 68. Reprinted by permission.

Clearly, if all the work is done by two people in one unit, there is little need for coordination. If the enterprise's work is divided into 1,000 units, each with thousands of employees, the need for coordination is naturally much greater. James Thompson pointed out that units can be linked in any of three ways: (1) pooled interdependence, (2) sequential interdependence, and (3) reciprocal interdependence.[10]

Pooled interdependence Subunits linked by pooled interdependence make contributions to the total enterprise but are not directly related. Purina Dog Chow plants in California and New York both contribute to Purina's profits, but they are not directly interrelated. The coordination between them is minimal.

Sequential interdependence When work units rely on other units earlier in the production chain, this is known as sequential interdependence. In a beer company, the production sequence is as shown below:

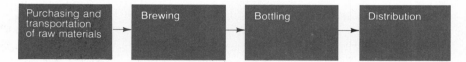

Greater coordination is necessary in sequential than in pooled interdependence, especially for later stages such as brewing, bottling, and distribution.

Reciprocal interdependence In this relationship the inputs of one unit become the outputs of the other and vice versa. The airlines provide an example of this kind of relationship:

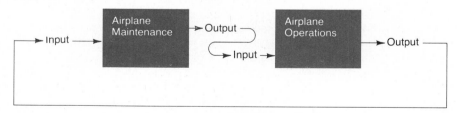

When maintenance finishes servicing a plane, the plane is an output of maintenance. The serviced plane then becomes an input to operations. When operations sees that a plane needs maintenance, the plane is an output of operations and becomes an input to maintenance. Obviously this close interrelationship leads to the strongest need for coordination between maintenance and operations.

There are four types of coordination which enterprises can use:

- Informal unprogrammed coordination
- Programmed nonhuman coordination

- Individual coordination
- Group coordination

As we discuss the ways to coordinate, I will describe which is best for each of these coordination conditions.

Informal Unprogrammed Coordination

A great deal of coordination comes about voluntarily, informally, without programming by the enterprise. It is impossible to anticipate, plan for, or coordinate all activities. So all enterprises rely on voluntary coordination to some degree.

Essentially, informal coordination is based on reciprocal understanding, shared attitudes, and powerful psychological mechanisms that motivate cooperation. Extensive departmentation leads to problems when voluntary informal coordination is used, but unprogrammed coordination exists in spite of this difficulty.

For voluntary coordination to work, the following conditions must be in effect:

- The employee must know his or her objectives and those of the unit.
- The employee must have a clear idea of what his or her job entails.
- Most of all, the employee must identify with the enterprise and its objectives. If the enterprise really means something to the employee, he or she will want to cooperate in attaining its objectives. This identification can be reinforced if the work groups identify with the enterprise.

Strong enterprise identification is often found in churches, hospitals, charities, and arts organizations and sometimes in business and government organizations, especially in times of crises such as wars, disasters, and economic malfunctions. A "let's pull together to get us through" attitude develops at such times.

Strong identification is often a result of careful employee selection and orientation (socialization). Identification is usually strongest in employees who have undergone a lengthy training process before entering the enterprise—for example, priests, ministers, nurses, and elite military groups such as commandos. Voluntary cooperation has been shown to work in some hospitals and some hospital procedures such as operations.

Thompson recommended this kind of coordination for all types of interdependence. But as enterprises get larger, or if the employees or the situation do not meet the necessary conditions, informal coordination needs to be supplemented by programmed coordination. Still, no enterprise can operate at all without *some* voluntary coordination.

Programmed Nonhuman Coordination

If not all the conditions for unprogrammed coordination are present, or if the organization is getting too complex or large for informal communication to be effective, the manager may develop programmed methods: standard operating procedures, rules, and what Thompson calls standardization. These can save the manager time if he or she spells out how to handle repetitive coordination problems in the form of a procedure, plan, or policy. Scheduling deadlines are an example of this approach. Of course policies have other purposes besides coordination (such as communication). These were discussed in Chapters 7 and 8.

Programmed nonhuman methods of coordination are used in all medium-size and large enterprises and in most small ones. Thompson recommends this kind of coordination for pooled interdependence linkages. Sequential interdependence linkages use it too, along with the methods described below.

Individual Coordination

Policies and other nonhuman coordination devices are not always understood by two parties in the same way. We tend to interpret them the way we want to. So what happens to coordination? There are two ways to handle this problem with individual coordinators.

The Hierarch The most typical approach is to have the coordination problem decided by the manager who supervises the two units with coordination problems. This assumes that the same superior supervises both units.

What happens here is that the "hierarch" hears out both sides. He or she sits in judgment and uses all the available sources of influence to get the two units to work out their problem. If this fails, the manager falls back on his or her authority and establishes a procedure for future interactions. To the extent that the decision is viewed as fair and workable, this solves the problem of coordination.

The Coordinator/Integrator In especially difficult areas the job of coordinating is large enough to be a separate position. The following positions in matrix organizations are typical:

- *Product manager:* an individual who serves as liaison for all functional areas and promotes improved sales and profits.
- *Project manager:* an individual who serves as liaison to all units for the duration of a project (e.g., Apollo).
- *Customer coordinator:* an individual who serves as a liaison to all functions for a major customer.
- *"Metropolitan Desk":* a unit to coordinate all information for clients or customers (e.g., HUD's Metropolitan Desk).

Creating the position of coordinator/integrator is expensive: It increases direct managerial costs. It is frustrating for the coordinators, since they have little formal authority yet are responsible for results. They have only certain influence mechanisms available to them. Though rarely used, this approach can be effective when timing is crucial and costs are not a major factor. Thompson recommended that individual coordinators be used in addition to nonhuman coordination in sequential interdependencies.

**Group
Coordination**

A number of devices can promote group coordination. For example, coordinating committees can be set up. Typically, representatives of the groups needing coordination will be on these committees, which may meet on a regular basis or as needed. Staff groups can also help in coordination. Effective use of groups and staffs will be discussed in more detail in Chapter 16. Thompson suggested the use of individual and group coordinators for sequential and reciprocal interdependencies among departments.

All the above-mentioned mechanisms of coordination can be effective. Of course to function well, they must be properly matched to the needs and interdependence relationships of the departments.

Summary

Once meaningful jobs have been designed, the next stage in the organizing process takes place—grouping jobs into work units, determining how big these units can get and still be effective, and getting these units to work together in achieving corporate objectives.

In small, less complex firms, much organization is informal and may change from day to day. But for larger and more complex objectives, and for outcomes with time pressures on them, good organization leads to greater effectiveness. Organization also can affect employee attitudes and performance. We organize to achieve our objectives, to formalize relationships, and to stabilize these relationships over time.

In formal organizations, the manager describes the organizational relationships in written and graphic form as precisely as practical. Changes thereafter can be made in both formal and informal ways. If an organization is formalized, an early document to appear is the organization chart. Guidelines for preparing this chart are given, and examples of several organization charts are diagrammed. Formal organization can be further developed by means of organization manuals. The final approach to formal organization is standardization: the enterprise examines the events occurring regularly and establishes approved ways of handling them.

The first question addressed by the chapter is how firms can effectively group jobs. The development of the organization strategy of one firm is followed through various stages. In the first stage, primitive organization, the boss tells everyone what to do. As the firm develops, it soon becomes impossible for the boss to manage everything. Then functional structure develops; assistants become full-time specialists handling one particular function such as personnel or office management. This grouping of duties into functional departments results when jobs with similar technical content are grouped together into single functional units. Advantages and disadvantages of the functional structure are explored.

When dissatisfaction with functional organization grows—usually when the firm enters other businesses—the firm may change to product/service organization. Product/service organization groups various specialists to perform all the duties necessary to produce an individual product or service offered. Three variations of product/service departmentation are illustrated: division by purpose (time), division by purpose (client), and division by purpose (location).

Matrix organization attempts to combine the advantages of both functional and product/service organization. A *matrix organization* is one which uses a dual command system for many or most managers; a typical middle or supervisory manager would belong simultaneously to two groups: a functional specialist group and a product or project group. Matrix organization tends to evolve rather than be imposed as a new approach.

The second organizational question that managers must answer is how big can the work group get and still be effective. Specifically, this chapter addressed how many employees a supervisor can manage effectively. *Span of control*, the number of subordinates reporting directly to the manager, and *number of levels in the hierarchy* were considered. These factors are inversely related: the smaller the span, the taller the hierarchy.

Major factors which influence the span of control are the people involved, the jobs involved, and the environment. The personal variables are managerial preferences and competence. The job factors include the nature of the manager's job, its relative importance, the need for the subordinate to consult with the superior, and the degree of similarity or standardization in the employee's work. Technology also influences spans of control. For example, effective mass production companies have very large spans of control at the supervisor's level of the hierarchy.

Research results are mixed concerning an ideal number for span of control, but some reasonable conclusions are that spans of control should be *smaller* if: (1) managers prefer smaller departments, (2) employees are not too competent, (3) the manager must do part of the work, not just supervise employees, and (4) the technology is craft or automated.

The relative flatness or tallness of an organization's hierarchy is a result of the number of managerial levels within the organization. Research findings regarding the relationship between height of the hierarchy and the size of the organization and the effects of height on employee satisfaction are briefly explored.

The final question addressed in Chapter 11 is how to relate the organizational work units to each other. This is done by coordination or integration. *Coordination* is the set of human and structural mechanisms designed to link the parts of the enterprise together to help achieve its objectives. Units can be linked in any of three ways: (1) pooled interdependence, (2) sequential interdependence, and (3) reciprocal interdependence. There are four ways to coordinate units: (1) informal unprogrammed coordination, (2) programmed nonhuman coordination, (3) individual coordination, and (4) group coordination. The chapter closes with a description of each of the coordination methods and its application to the ways units can be linked.

The final chapter on organization follows. It discusses the organization of the total enterprise.

Questions

1. What are the crucial elements of organization? Explain each of these elements briefly.
2. Your firm has just expanded from a small to medium-size organization. What means would you use to formalize and standardize its structure?
3. List the guidelines you would use to prepare an organization chart.
4. How important do you think organization charts and manuals really are to most managers? Why?
5. Explain primitive structure. When is it used?
6. When does an enterprise develop a functional structure? Differentiate functional structure from primitive structure.
7. Does product/service departmentation have advantages over the functional approach? What are they? When would you be most likely to adopt the product approach?
8. "Matrix is an attempt to cross the product and functional approaches to organization in an attempt to get the best of both." Explain why this is an accurate statement about the matrix structure.
9. How do personal characteristics of the manager, job factors, and environmental factors influence the span of control? When should spans of control be *smaller?*
10. Relate the height of the hierarchy to the size of the organization, to technology, to employee satisfaction.
11. Why is coordination necessary to relate the organization's units to each other? How can these units be linked, and what types of coordination work best with each method?

Notes

[1] Arthur Walker and Jay Lorsch, "Organizational Choice: Product versus Function," *Harvard Business Review* 46 (November–December 1968): 129–138.

[2] Arthur Kover, "Reorganizing in an Advertising Agency," *Human Organization* 22 (Winter 1963): 252–259.

[3] General Electric, *Organization Planning Bulletin*, n.p., n.d. Reprinted by permission.

[4] William Ouchi and John Dowling, "Defining the Span of Control," *Administrative Science Quarterly* 21 (September 1974): 357–365.

[5] Harold Stieglitz, "Optimizing Span of Control," *Management Record* 24 (September 1962): 25–29.

[6] For example, Ernest Dale, *Planning and Developing the Company Organization Structure* (New York: American Management Association, 1952); Richard H. Hall et al., "Patterns of Interorganizational Relationships," *Administrative Science Quarterly* 22 (September 1977): 457–474; and Martin McNulty, "A Question of Managerial Legitimacy," *Academy of Management Journal* 18 (September 1975): 579–588.

[7] Derek Pugh, "The Measurement of Organization Structures," *Organizational Dynamics* 2 (January 1975): 19–34.

[8] Joan Woodward, *Industrial Organization: Theory and Practice* (New York: Oxford University Press, 1965).

[9] L. L. Cummings and Chris J. Berger, "Organization Structure: How Does It Influence Attitudes and Performance?" *Organizational Dynamics* 5 (Autumn 1976): 34–49.

[10] James Thompson, *Organizations in Action* (New York: McGraw-Hill, 1967), chapter 5.

References

Introduction

Orlando Behling, "Some Problems in the Philosophy of Science of Organizations," *Academy of Management Review* 3 (April 1978): 193–201. J. Kenneth Benson, "Organizations: A Dialectical View," *Administrative Science Quarterly* 22 (March 1977): 1–20. John Child, *Organization* (London: Harper & Row, 1977). Michel Crozier and Erhard Friedberg, "Organizations as Means and Constraints of Collective Action," *International Institute of Management* (May 1976): Alan C. Filley and Ramon J. Aldag, "Characteristics and Measurement of an Organizational Typology," *Academy of Management Journal* 21 (December 1978): 578–591. John W. Meyer and Brian Rowan, "Institutionalized Organizations: Formal Structure as Myth and Ceremony," *American Journal of Sociology* 83 (September 1977): 340–363.

Formalizing Organizations

Charles McMillan et al., "The Structure of Work Organizations across Societies," *Academy of Management Journal* 16 (December 1975): 555–569. Derek Pugh, "The Measurement of Organization Structures," *Organizational Dynamics* 2 (January 1975): 19–34. Stanley L. Sokolik and I. Lawrence Richardson, "Preparing Organization Charts with a Computer," *Personnel Journal* 56 (November 1977): 575–577.

How Do Firms Group Jobs?

Arthur Kover, "Reorganizing in an Advertising Agency," *Human Organization* 22 (Winter 1963): 252–259. Paul Lawrence and Jay Lorsch, eds., *Studies in Organization Design* (Homewood, Ill: Richard D. Irwin, 1970). John J. Morse, "Organization Characteristics and Individual Motivations," in *Studies in Organization Design,* ed. Paul Lawrence and Jay Lorsch (Homewood, Ill.: Richard D. Irwin, 1970). Bernard Reimann, "Dimensions of Structure in Effective Organizations," *Academy of Management Journal* 17 (December 1974): 693–708. Fremont Shull et al., *Organizational Decision Making* (New York: McGraw-Hill, 1970). Arthur Walker and Jay Lorsch, "Organizational Choice: Product versus Function," *Harvard Business Review* 46 (November–December 1968): 129–138.

Matrix Organizations

Stanley Davis and Paul Lawrence, *Matrix* (Reading, Mass.: Addison-Wesley, 1977); and "Problems of Matrix Management," *Harvard Business Review* 56 (May–June 1978): 131–142. Jay Galbraith, "Matrix Organization Design," *Business Horizons* 14 (February 1971): 29–40. Andrew Grimes et al., "Matrix Model: A Selective Empirical Test," *Academy of Management Journal* 15 (March 1972): 9–31. Kenneth Knight, ed., *Matrix Management* (Westmead, England: Gowan Press, 1977). Kenneth Knight, "Matrix Organization: A Review," *Journal of Management Studies* 13 (May 1976): 111–130. Paul R. Lawrence, Harvey F. Kolodny, and Stanley M. Davis, "The Human Side of the Matrix," *Organizational Dynamics* 6 (Summer 1977): 43–61. Fremont Shull, *Matrix Structure and Project Authority* (Carbondale, Ill.: Southern Illinois University, Bureau of Business Research, 1965). Fremont Shull et al., *Organizational Decision Making* (New York: McGraw-Hill, 1970), pp. 187–226. H. R. Smith, "A Socio-Biological Look at Matrix," *Academy of Management Review* 3 (October 1978): 922–926.

Span of Control

Ernest Dale, *Planning and Developing the Company Organization Structure* (New York: American Management Association, 1952). Doris R. Entwisle and John Walton, "Observations on the Span of Control," *Administrative Science Quarterly* 5 (March 1961): 522–533. V. A. Graicunus, "Relationship in Organizations," in *Papers on the Science of Administration,* ed. Lyndall Urwick and Luther H. Gullick (New York: Institute of Public

Administration, 1937). James Healey, *Executive Coordination and Control* (Columbia, Ohio: Ohio State University, Columbia Bureau of Business Research, 1956). Robert House and John Miner, "Merging Management and Behavioral Theory: The Interaction between Span of Control and Group Size," *Administrative Science Quarterly* 14 (September 1969): 451–465. Allen Janger, "Analyzing the Span of Control," *Management Record* 22 (July–August 1960): 7–10. William Ouchi and John Dowling, "Defining the Span of Control," *Administrative Science Quarterly* 21 (September 1974): 357–365. Derek Pugh, "The Measurement of Organization Structures," *Organizational Dynamics* 2 (January 1975): 19–34. Roland Simonds, "Is Organization Structure Reflecting New Techniques and Theory?" *MSU Business Topics* 17 (Summer 1969): 65–71. Harold Stieglitz, "Optimizing Span of Control," *Management Record* 24 (September 1962): 25–29. Jon Udell, "An Empirical Test of Hypotheses Relating to Span of Control," *Administrative Science Quarterly* 10 (December 1967): 420–439. David D. Van Fleet and Arthur G. Bedeian, "A History of the Span of Management," *Academy of Management Review* 2 (July 1977): 356–372. Joan Woodward, *Industrial Organization: Theory and Practice* (New York: Oxford University Press, 1965).

Height of the Hierarchy

Rocco Carzo, Jr., and John Yanouzas, "Effects of Flat and Tall Organization Structure," *Administrative Science Quarterly* 14 (June 1969): 178–191. L. L. Cummings and Chris J. Berger, "Organization Structure: How Does It Influence Attitudes and Performance?" *Organizational Dynamics* 5 (Autumn 1976): 34–49. Ernest Dale, *Planning and Development in the Company Organization Structure* (New York: American Management Association, 1952). Edwin Ghiselli and Jacob Siegel, "Leadership and Managerial Success in Tall and Flat Organization Structures," *Personnel Psychology* 25 (Winter 1972): 617–624. David Hickson et al., "Operations Technology and Organization Structure," *Administrative Science Quarterly* 14 (September 1969): 378–397. Halsey Jones, "A Study of Organization Performance for Experimental Structures of Two, Three, and Four Levels," *Academy of Management Journal* 12 (September 1969): 351–365. Herbert Kaufman and David Seidman, "The Morphology of Organizations," *Administrative Science Quarterly* 15 (December 1970): 439–451. Stanley Nealey and Fred Fiedler, "Leadership Functions of Middle Managers," *Psychological Bulletin* 70 (October 1968): 313–329. Lyman Porter and Edward Lawler, "The Effects of Flat and Tall Organization Structures on Managerial Job Satisfaction," *Personnel Psychology* 17 (Summer 1964): 135–148. Lyman Porter and Jacob Siegel, "Relationships of Tall and Flat Organization Structures to the Satisfaction of Foreign Managers," *Personnel Psychology* 18 (Winter 1965): 379–392. Joan Woodward, *Industrial Organization: Theory and Practice* (New York: Oxford University Press, 1965).

How to Get Units to Work Together

Robert Aleshire, "The Metropolitan Desk: A New Technique in Program Teamwork," *Public Administration Review* 26 (June 1966): 87–95. Ivars Avorts, "Why Does Project Management Fail?" *California Management Review* 12 (Fall 1969): 77–82. Alan Filley et al., *Managerial Process and Organizational Behavior* (Chicago: Scott, Foresman, 1976), pp. 380–410. Basil Georgopoulos and Floyd Mann, *The Community General Hospital* (New York: Macmillan, 1962). Richard Hall, "Some Organizational Considerations in the Professional Relationship," *Administrative Science Quarterly* 12 (June 1967): 461–478. James Thompson, *Organizations in Action* (New York: McGraw-Hill, 1967), chapter 5. David Wilemon, "The Project Manager: Anomalies and Ambiguities," *Academy of Management Review* 13 (September 1970): 269–282.

Case for Chapter 11

Acme Office Furniture (AOF)

AOF is a medium-size manufacturer of office furniture. The firm, located in Iowa, has been growing fast in recent years, although profit margins have not kept pace with sales increases and increases in employment.

The president of AOF is Anne Fletcher. Fletcher was brought in from a larger firm when the previous president retired and the board felt that an outsider was needed to rejuvenate the firm, especially in terms of profitability. When Fletcher asked about some other success indicators, she found that absenteeism and turnover were up, quality was down, and the new-customer ratio was weakening.

The number of problems Fletcher faced was large, for most of the financial ratios had been weakening and production costs were increasing relative to past performance. Fletcher knew she could not run the firm the way her predecessor, Noel Lincoln, had. Lincoln had built up the business for the widow of the founder, Ed Upton, after Upton died. Essentially a salesman, he had let the organization take care of itself. "Just get enough orders—that's what keeps a firm going" was his belief.

Fletcher looked at the organization that Lincoln had left her (see Exhibit 1) and was not sure she could live with it. It had a large span of control. Fletcher felt that this was the time to centralize some of the decisions that had been left to drift. Yet she knew she could not make all the key decisions herself (nor did she desire to). She began to think about what she should do to make the organization easier to handle, yet not overly centralized.

Problems

You are a consultant hired by Fletcher.
1. Recommend a better organization to deal with the firm's problems.
2. Recommend the right span of control for this situation.
3. Justify your recommendations.

Exhibit 1
Organization Chart:
Acme Office Furniture

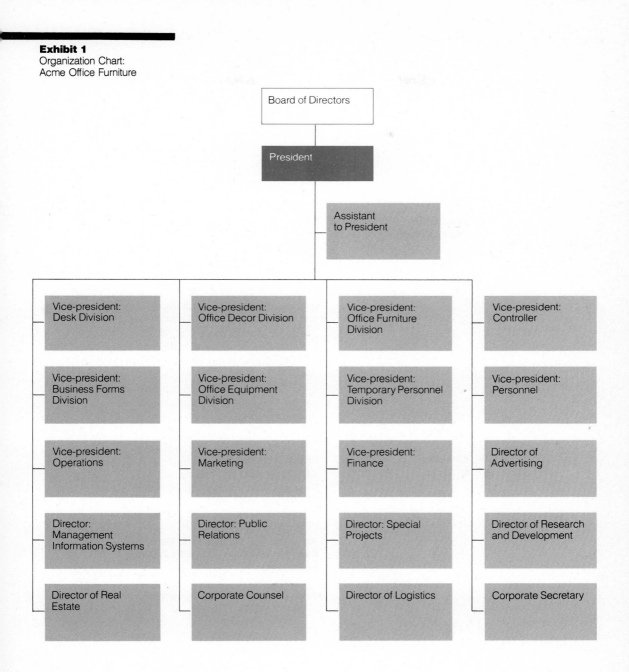

Chapter 12 Organizing the Total Enterprise

Learning Objectives

1. Develop an understanding of how strategy affects organization structure.
2. Recognize the importance of matching strategy with organization structure to achieve maximum effectiveness.
3. Know the most important external and internal factors which affect organization structure and their match with the three organizational styles.
4. Learn some principles that will help you identify when a change in organization structure and style is needed and what the appropriate change might be.
5. Know how to go about making an effective style decision when the significant determining factors do not agree.

Chapter Outline

Introduction

This chapter builds upon Chapters 10 and 11. Chapter 10 discussed how to organize jobs; Chapter 11 discussed how to organize jobs into units; and Chapter 12 examines how to group departments and units and coordinate them into total organizations. More specifically, this chapter discusses how strategy must match structure (departmentation) and how external and internal factors must match structure (organization style) for a firm to be effective (see Figure 12.1). As you will note, and as I will explain in more detail, organization style is a way of integrating all the aspects of organization I described in Chapter 11 except departmentation.

Figure 12.1
Factors Affecting
Organization Structure
of the Total Firm

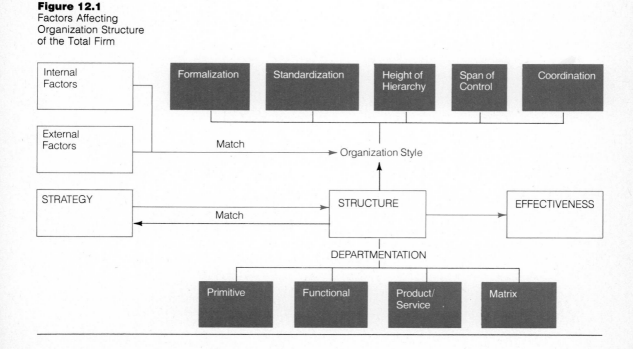

Strategy and Structure

Effective firms adjust their organization structure to fit their changing strategy. We discussed this briefly in Chapter 8 when I pointed out that once a strategy is chosen, it must be implemented by changes in people, changes in policy, and changes in organization structure. This relationship is well documented in the literature of management, and in its practice as well. As Alfred Chandler has shown—to cite one of many available examples—the most effective firms in the 1920s changed their structure arrangements from functional to product/service as they changed their strategy from growth in a single product/service line to growth in multiple product/service lines (diversification).[1]

Figure 12.2 further clarifies the relationship between strategy and structure (departmentation). Keep in mind that strategy determines a firm's growth and the complexity of the products/services it offers. Note that for the most part, as the firm grows, the structure shifts from primitive to functional to product/service to matrix. As the products/services offered become more complex, the structure shifts toward matrix. Of course if the size of the firm diminishes or the complexity of the products/services it offers is reduced, these shifts in structure take place in the reverse direction. For instance, a large firm may need to adjust its structure back to a functional design if it wishes to be efficient and effective.

Figure 12.2
The Relationship between Strategy and Structure in Effective Firms

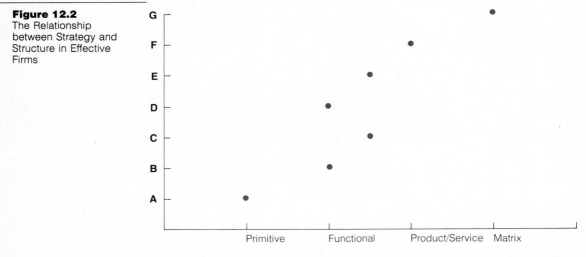

A. Small single product/service line firm; stable growth, growth, or retrenchment.

B. Medium single product/service line firm, stable growth or retrenchment.

C. Medium single product/service line firm: growth.

D. Large single product/service line firm; stable growth or retrenchment.

E. Large single product/service line firm: growth.

F. Large several product/service lines firm; stable growth, growth, or retrenchment.

G. Large multiple product/service lines firm; stable growth, growth, or retrenchment.

If you look again at Figure 12.1, you will note that a color arrow points from strategy to structure. This indicates that in most cases strategic change causes structural changes in effective firms. The small arrow from structure to strategy indicates that the present structure is a factor to be considered when strategic change is being contemplated. It can retard a decision to change the strategy. And if the strategic change is a small, incremental change, the structure need not be significantly changed.

Factors Affecting Organization Structure and Style

In Chapter 11, I described the following five characteristics of organization structure; formalization, standardization, height of hierarchy, span of control, and coordination. As you recall, each of these dimensions had various ways it could be implemented. (For example, spans of control can be small, medium, or large.) Much research was summarized to help you get an understanding of the relationships between structural elements. Table 12.1 ties together these organization characteristics into three types of organization styles: traditional, consultative, and participative. (These terms were used in Chapter 7 in reference to managers' approaches to determining objectives and are also used to describe leadership styles in Chapter 14.) Definitions of the three styles on the basis of the five structural characteristics appear in Table 12.1. They are used for illustrative purposes; firms frequently blend styles.

The crucial question in regard to these styles is when each is most effectively used. To make the firm as effective as possible, organization style should be chosen according to the internal and external factors that affect the firm's structure. There are perhaps an unlimited number of

Table 12.1
Organization Characteristics of Three Organization Styles

Organization Characteristic	Participative	Consultative	Traditional
Formalization (organization charts and manuals; detailed job descriptions, etc.)	Low	Moderate	High
Standardization (written procedures, policies, rules, etc.)	Low	Moderate	High
Height of hierarchy	Flat or matrix	Moderate or matrix	Tall
Span of control	Large	Moderate	Small
Coordination Mechanism	Informal/ nonprogrammed; a few nonhuman techniques[a]	Individual coordination and some nonhuman techniques[a]	Individual hierarch and nonhuman techniques[a]

[a] Nonhuman techniques include, for example, standard operating procedures and policies.

Table 12.2	Internal Factors	External Factors
Factors Affecting Organization Structure	Size of the firm	Technology
	Diversity of product/service line	Stability of the market
	Employee characteristics	Dependence on the environment

factors which could affect the structure of the firm. Those that appear to have the most significant impact are listed in Table 12.2.

Internal Factors

As Table 12.2 indicates, the most important internal factors that affect organization structure and thus influence organization style are (1) size of firm, (2) diversity of product/service line, and (3) employee characteristics. Table 12.3 shows how the three basic organization styles relate to these factors. Let's discuss each of these internal factors in more detail.

Size of the Firm

By size of the firm we mean the number of employees working for the organization.

Although these numbers are somewhat arbitrary, small enterprises employ one to 250 people; medium-size organizations, 251 to 1,000; and large organizations, over 1,000. Some might argue that size should be measured by amount of assets or sales (or the equivalent in nonbusinesses—revenue flow). But the correlation between these measures of size is over 0.95 in most studies. The exceptions are a few capital intensive organizations like oil refineries.

Size has some important effects on enterprises. For example, there is strong evidence that as units increase in size, job satisfaction decreases and absenteeism, turnover, and accidents increase. The size of support staff increases as a percentage of the total staff and then declines.

Table 12.3	Internal Factor	Participative	Consultative	Traditional
The Relationship between Internal Factors and Effective Organization Style	**Size of the firm**	Small	Medium	Large
	Diversity of products/services	High	Medium	Low
	Employee characteristics			
	Education	High	Moderate	Low
	Rearing style	Nonauthoritarian	Moderate	Authoritarian
	Location of rearing	Urban	Suburban	Rural
	Intelligence	High	Moderate	Low
	Experience	Wide	Moderate	Narrow

As size increases, the unit has a tendency to become more traditionally organized. Why? For two reasons. Larger numbers of people find it difficult or impossible to relate informally as the participative style requires. Ten to fifteen people can relate to each other rather informally; 500 cannot. As the number of people increases, the level of formality increases to cope with the complexity of employee interrelationships and communication problems.

The other reason larger enterprises tend to be traditional is that large size provides a greater opportunity to utilize the economics of specialization. The resultant structure encourages a traditional style.

Are all large enterprises necessarily traditionally organized, then? No. Consider two firms: Ralston Purina and McDonnell Douglas. Both are large firms. Ralston's employees tend to work at one of a large number of plants, all of which are small. McDonnell has essentially only two locations and concentrates large numbers of people at these locations. But the relevant factor is the size of the local unit. For example, Ralston subdivides a large number of people into smaller units and then has the smaller units organize themselves participatively. It might be that only the top executive at each location of an organization would need to relate to a traditional style (at the home office); he or she could introduce a participative style at the local plant, where the number of employees is relatively low.

Another way to deal with size is to make strategic changes. The company can merge (and increase size) or divest (and reduce size). Still, is it likely that McDonnell would break up its St. Louis complex of over 10,000 employees and assign them to fifteen medium-size plants all over the country? It is possible, but not too likely. Is Ralston likely to consolidate all its plants into a single large one? The technology and economies of scale tend to prevent major moves of this type. So generally we treat size as a given in the organizational situation and therefore as an influence on structure and style.

Research leads us to conclude that size does influence structure and that larger size usually leads to a traditional style. But there is no conclusive evidence that traditional style is *always* effective in larger organizations.

Of course, size alone does not dictate organization style. Only in combination with the other factors—internal and external—does it play a role in determining style.

Diversity of Products/Services

A firm has high diversity if it offers a large number of products and services which span more than one SIC (Standard Industrial Classification) code.[2]

An increase in internal diversity is accompanied by an increase in the external environment a firm must monitor. To illustrate, consider the impact of both high and low diversity on one department: marketing. The significance of level of diversity for the marketing department in two firms is summarized in Table 12.4.

The marketing department for Firm 1 has to perform its functions (personal selling, advertising, pricing, sales promotion) using only a few media. It has a short product list and only one distribution channel. The department in Firm 2 has a long product list—320 products—and uses many media to market its products. It also uses several distribution channels. Firm 2 is highly diverse, while Firm 1 is not. Clearly, the operations in Firm 2's marketing department are extremely complex compared to those in Firm 1's department. The decision making involved in coordinating marketing for 320 products by 1,000 salespeople in 50 different districts through 89 different advertising media requires sophisticated management.

In addition to its impact on internal operations, diversity enlarges the task of assessing and monitoring the environment. A large number of products/services requires a great variety of markets and marketing environments. Functional organization structures, for the most part, do not respond well to diversity. Indeed, diversity plays a leading role in determining organization structure and style. The more a firm diversifies, the greater its need to use a participative style. The less its diversity, the more easily it can use the traditional style.

Employee Characteristics

The final internal variable influencing organization structure and style is the "stock" of personnel employed at the enterprise. Many enterprises require employees with specific abilities. Oil refineries need chemical engineers; insurance companies need actuaries; the Securities and Exchange Commission needs lawyers. Organizations also vary in their percentage distribution of professional/technical, managerial, clerical, and

Table 12.4 Impact of Diversity on the Marketing Department in Two Firms	**Marketing Department, Firm 1**	**Marketing Department, Firm 2**
No. of products	3	320
No. of sizes per product	1	3
No. of channels used	1	4
No. of advertising media used	1	89
No. of salespoeple	10	1,000
No. of sales districts	1	50
No. of price lists	1	174
No. of sales promotion mechanisms (other than advertising)	0	5

operative employees. Obviously each of these groups contains some college graduates, but in almost all cases professional/technical and managerial employees have more education than operative employees. Thus certain departments or units are more likely to show particular educational patterns.

There is much evidence that work attitudes and preferences correlate with education. One possible modifier is child-rearing practices. But, in general, research suggests that education and intelligence are correlated with a preference for a participative organization style, as Table 12.5 indicates (see references listed for this section).

Research on organization behavior also suggests that people with more experience and education prefer more autonomy and responsibility and thus the participative style. There are individual differences, of course. An authoritarian or rural upbringing would reduce this preference. Several negative experiences with a participative style might reduce a preference for it, too. But in general, units whose employees are highly educated, intelligent, experienced people are likely to be more effective if they are organized participatively. More research is needed to confirm this theory, however.

We can see how these internal factors—the size of the firm, the diversity of its products and services, and the characteristics of its employees—all affect organizational structure. Now let's examine some of the external factors that affect structure.

External Factors

Three main factors in the environment of a firm play a role in determining the structure of an organization: (1) its technology, (2) the stability of the market, and (3) its dependence on the environment. The impact of these factors on organization style is summarized in Table 12.6. I will discuss each factor in turn.

Technology

The first external factor that influences organization structure and style is the technology of the enterprise. Of course once the technology is applied

Table 12.5 The Relationship between Workers' Education, Intelligence, and Experiences and Their Organization Style Preferences	**Factor**	**Participative**	**Consultative**	**Traditional**
	Education	High	Moderate	Low
	Intelligence	High	Moderate	Low
	Experience	Wide	Moderate	Narrow
	Child-rearing style of parents	Nonauthoritarian	Moderate	Authoritarian
	Location of upbringing	Urban	Suburban	Rural

Table 12.6
The Relationship
between External
Factors and
Organization Style

External Factor	Organization Styles		
	Participative	Consultative	Traditional
Technology	Small batch, automation, or nonroutine	In-between	Mass production or routine
Market stability (volatility)	Low	Moderate	High
Dependence	Low	Moderate	High

inside the enterprise, it becomes an internal variable as well. Here we will treat it primarily as an external variable.

The research on the relationship between technology and organization structure and style is more sophisticated than most organization research. But not all researchers define technology the same way. I will define it as follows:

Technology consists of the techniques (such as equipment, computers, forms, etc.) used on the inputs to the enterprise (such as money and materials) to accomplish the enterprise's objectives.

For example, the technology of an office could include a computer, standardized forms, typewriters, and the like.

Before noting the results of the research relating technology to structure and style, I want to summarize briefly the most influential work in this area—the research done by Joan Woodward between 1953 and 1971, which was introduced in Chapter 11.[3]

Woodward set out to see if there was one right way to organize. Her results were confusing until she hit upon the idea of classifying the firms according to their technology. The firms were classified into three groups: unit/small batch/job shop, mass production/large batch, and process automation. Using this new system of classification, Woodward found that:

1. Structure is related to the technology of the firm:
   a. The height of the hierarchy increases as the firm moves from small to mass production and then to automation (as shown in Chapter 11).
   b. Span of control is low for small batches and automation, high for mass production (as shown in Chapter 11).
   c. Ratios of managers to employees increase as the firm moves up the technology ladder from small batch to automation.
2. Successful organizations are those which match their organization structures to the kind of technology the firm faces. That is, if an organization's structure is related to its technology as specified in Item 1, it is more likely to be successful. For example, the most successful automated firms have the tallest hierarchies, while the most successful mass production firms have the widest spans of control.

In summary, Woodward found that the technology influences organization structure. In mass production, she noted, the technology leads to specialization because of the routineness of the output; in such cases the more the enterprise uses small span of control, strict chain of command, and a traditional style, the more successful it is. This pattern is found in most research.

Some additional conclusions of the research on technology and organization structure and style are as follows:

1. There seems to be a general correlation between the effectiveness of a firm and the suitability of the matches among its technology, structure, and style. (There is, however, not nearly enough research to support a firm conclusion along these lines.)
2. Technology is not *equally* influential in shaping the structure and style of all organizations and parts of organizations. It exerts the strongest influence in small, production-oriented units. It is least influential in upper levels of enterprises and in nonproduction units such as staff service. This is so because many factors influence structure and style, and sometimes they exert pressure in opposite directions.
3. With stable technology, as found in mass batch or mass production firms such as those in the automobile, food canning, and paper production industries, structure is most effective when it fits a traditional style.
4. In the case of changing technology, more flexible structural arrangements such as matrix organization and a corresponding participative style are most effective.

Market Stability

Market stability is a condition in which the market for the firm's products or services changes very little and very slowly.

Market volatility is the opposite of market stability.

When a market is stable, few decisions need to be made and little new information needs to be processed. When it is volatile, the reverse is true. One way to measure market stability is to determine the amount of market information a firm must process to survive.

Volatility can be measured by checking various industries' expenditures for research and development. (As firms spend more on research, new products and processes are invented and the rate of change—volatility—of the market increases.) Data of this sort indicate that the most volatile industries are communications equipment, aircraft, and missiles. The least volatile are textiles; lumber, wood products, and furniture; and food and kindred products. Volatility can also be measured as the percentage of change and/or the predictability of the changes in the market. For example, manufacturers of washboards have not experienced unpredictable changes in market since the introduction of the wringer washing machine. The market environment of fashion goods manufacturers changes all the time, but the managers know that these changes will affect either the spring line or the fall line. The kind of volatility most difficult to deal with results from wide market swings whose timing cannot be predicted.

In a study of environmental uncertainty, Ramon Aldag and Ronald Storey found some of the most stable markets in the industries listed below:[4]

- Vegetable oil
- Specialty machinery
- Auto parts and accessories
- Confectionery
- Meat packers
- Retail-department stores

They found the most volatile markets in their sample in the following industries:

- Drugs—ethical
- Drugs—medical and hospital supply
- Chemicals and chemical preparation
- Office and business equipment
- Electronics
- Photographic equipment

How does market stability affect organization structure? My own view is this: As volatility increases (as change accelerates) it is harder to effectively systematize (and organize traditionally) because things change too fast and because traditional organizations react too slowly. In general, the theory that stable conditions lead to traditional organization styles and volatile conditions lead to participative ones is reasonable. There is more evidence for this theory than there is for the theory that traditional styles are more effective in stable conditions and participative styles are more effective in volatile conditions. There is no evidence to support a conclusion that volatility *alone* leads to the participative style.

Dependence

The final external variable affecting organization structure and style is dependence.

Dependence is the relative loss of flexibility in choice of organization structure or enterprise strategy because of external pressures.

Independence is freedom to choose a strategy and organization structure without the need to consider the requirements of resource providers (suppliers, unions, stockholders, etc), regulators (government, community), and clients and customers.

Table 12.7 provides a few examples of companies that are relatively dependent on or independent of external forces. With its diversified ownership, AT&T is not as dependent on the wishes of the owners as Hallmark's management is on the wishes of the Hall family. Because New York Life Insurance Company is regulated by the State of New York, it is listed as relatively dependent on regulators. At the same time, however, New York City has less power to pressure a large firm like New York Life than a small firm, so New York Life is also listed as relatively independent of regulators. General Foods, with millions of customers, is less subject to pressure from one customer than McDonnell Douglas, which may have only twenty customers. With its huge market share, IBM can exert more pressure on competitors than can a small clothing manufacturer.

It is reasonable to assume that if an external force has concentrated power and wishes to dictate structural arrangements or strategy, the enterprise has a tendency to respond. If the enterprise is shielded from this problem, its strategists can base structure choices on other factors.

The other side of dependence is independence, when the management can choose the organization's structure as it sees fit. There is not a tremendous amount of research in this area, and what there is tends to be as much theory as it is research.

More studies have been conducted in nonbusiness than in business sectors. But all relevant studies show how the enterprise accommodates itself to dependence pressure through various mechanisms, including adjusting its organization structure and style to the force on which it is most dependent. Choice of structure and style is not always voluntary. If the firm is subject to government regulation and the government requires a

Table 12.7
Relatively Independent and Dependent Enterprises

Dependence Factor	Relatively Independent Enterprise	Relatively Dependent Enterprise
Resource Suppliers		
Stockholders (business)	AT&T	Hallmark
Unions	IBM	Chrysler
Suppliers: subparts	Ace Hardware Retailers	Jack's Paving
Regulators		
Government	Acme Hardware	New York Life Insurance Co.
Community	New York Life Insurance	Small clothing manufacturer
Clients/Customers	General Foods	McDonnell Douglas
Competitors	IBM	Small clothing manufacturer

strict control bureaucracy, its managers must modify its structure accordingly; it cannot use a participative style even if it wants to.

How Do We Organize If Different Factors Give Conflicting Signals?

When it comes to determining structure and style, the different internal and external factors often give management conflicting signals. It is my hypothesis that some of these factors are stronger indicators for a specific kind of organization structure and style than others; my estimate of their relative significance is given in Table 12.8.

Even if the various factors seem to be at odds with each other, it is usually still possible to choose the appropriate organization structure and style for a firm. I submit the following rules of thumb:

1. If five or six factors point to a single structure and style, adopt that structure and style.
2. If four or more factors point to one structure and style and the others to another structure and style, then examine the first four. If three of them are strong factors (as shown in Table 12.8), choose the structure and style they indicate.
3. If the strong factors point to two different structures and styles, compromise between the two—use a blend.

Summary

Chapter 12 discussed how managers group departments and units and coordinate them into total organizations. For firms to be effective, the organization's structure must be adjusted to fit its changing strategy. As the size of the firm changes as a consequence of the strategy, structure shifts from primitive to functional to product/service to matrix. Structure also shifts toward matrix as the product/service lines get larger and more complex.

Five characteristics of an organization—formalization, standardization, height of the hierarchy, span of control, and coordination—were described in Chapter 11. These organization characteristics form the basis for three organization styles: traditional, consultative, and participative. Table 12.1 defines the three styles in terms of these characteristics.

Three internal factors—size of the firm, diversity of product/service line, characteristics of the employees—and three external factors—technology,

Table 12.8
Estimates of Relative Impact of Internal and External Factors on Organization Structure and Style

Very Strong	Strong	Relatively Weak
Size	Technology	Dependence
Market stability		Characteristics of people
Diversity		

stability of the market, dependence on the environment—have a role in determining what the most effective structure and style are.

Size of the firm refers to the number of employees working for the organization. As size increases, the unit has a tendency to become more traditionally organized. Large numbers of people find it difficult or impossible to relate informally as the participative style requires.

Diversity plays a leading role in determining organization structure and style, too. A firm has high diversity if it offers a large number of products and services which span more than one Standard Industrial Classification (SIC) code. The more a firm diversifies, the greater its need to use a structure that permits participative organization style.

The stock of personnel employed at the enterprise is the final internal variable influencing organization structure and style. A unit whose employees are highly educated, intelligent, experienced people are likely to be more effective if its structure allows a participative style.

The external factors—technology, market stability, and dependence—also have an impact on organization structure and style. Successful organizations are those that match their organization structures and styles to the kind of technology the firm faces. Stable technology as found in mass production industries is effectively structured at the lowest levels using the traditional style. A firm where technology changes is most effective when structural arrangements are more flexible and the participative style can be used.

As regards market stability, stable conditions generally lead to structures that demand a traditional style, while volatile conditions lead to structures suitable to a participative style. Finally, there appears to be *no* general tendency that the greater a firm's dependence, the more appropriate a particular style or organization structure. Dependent firms appear to adjust structure and style to the force on which they are dependent.

In case different factors give conflicting signals as to what structure and what style are most desirable, they should be ranked according to their relative significance. The chapter closed with some basic principles to use in determining what organization structure and style to adopt in such cases.

Questions

1. Describe what type of structure fits the strategies listed in Table 12.1.
2. What type of structure would you probably find in a small enterprise? A medium-size enterprise? A large firm?
3. How do employee characteristics affect the firm's structure and style?
4. Summarize Woodward's research on technology and organization structure. Do you think technology has a strong impact on structure and style?
5. Explain how market stability and volatility are related to organization structure and style.
6. Compare the influence of dependence factors on the structure and style of a large manufacturing firm and of a similar small firm. How much

impact would dependence on suppliers have? On a union? On stockholders? On government? On customers? On competitors?

7. What factors have the strongest influence on structural choice and organization style?

8. You are planning a structural change at your firm, but the internal and external factors affecting the firm give conflicting signals regarding what would be the most effective structure and style. What guidelines would you follow in making the proper choice of structure and style?

Notes

[1] Alfred Chandler, Jr., *Strategy and Structure* (Cambridge, Mass.: MIT Press, 1962).

[2] SIC: Standard Industrial Classification. The federal government uses SIC codes to categorize different types of industries.

[3] Joan Woodward, *Industrial Organization: Behavior and Control* (New York: Oxford University Press, 1970); and *Industrial Organization: Theory and Practice* (New York: Oxford University Press, 1965).

[4] Ramon Aldag and Ronald Storey, "Environmental Uncertainty," *Proceedings of the Academy of Management* (August 1975).

References

Strategy and Departmentation

H.I. Ansoff and Richard Brandenburg, "A Language for Organizational Design," *Management Science* 17 (August 1971): 705–731. J. Thomas Cannon, *Business Strategy and Policy* (New York: Harcourt, Brace and World, 1968). Alfred Chandler, Jr., *Strategy and Structure* (Cambridge, Mass.: MIT Press, 1962). John Child, *Organization* (New York: Harper & Row, 1977). William F. Glueck, *Business Policy*, 3d ed. (New York: McGraw-Hill, 1980), chapter 7. John R. Montanari, "Managerial Discretion: An Expanded Model of Organization Choice," *Academy of Management Review* 3 (April 1978): 231–241. Jeffrey Pfeffer and Gerald R. Salancik, "Organization Design: The Case for a Coalitional Model of Organizations," *Organizational Dynamics* 6 (Autumn 1977): 15–29. Robert Pitts, "Strategies and Structures for Diversification," *Academy of Management Journal* 20 (1977): 197–208. H. Raymond Radosevich, "Strategic Implications for Organizational Design," in H. I. Ansoff, R. P. Declerck, and R. L. Hayes, *From Strategic Planning to Strategic Management* (New York: Wiley, 1976), pp. 161–180. Eric Rhenman, *Organization Theory for Long Range Planning* (New York: Wiley Interscience, 1973). Hans Thorelli, ed., *Strategy + Structure = Performance* (Bloomington: Indiana University Press, 1977). "Streamlining the Management at SCM," *Business Week,* February 21, 1977. Karl E. Weick, "Organization Design: Organizations as Self-Designing Systems," *Organizational Dynamics* 6 (Autumn 1977): 30–46.

Factors Affecting Organization Structure and Style

Henry Ogden Armour and David J. Teece, "Organizational Structure and Economic Performance: A Test of the Multidivisional Hypothesis," *Bell Journal of Economics* 9 (Winter 1978): 106–122. Richard Harvey Brown, "Bureaucracy as Praxis: Toward a Political Phenomenology of Formal Organizations," *Administrative Science Quarterly* 23 (September 1978): 365–382. Albert B. Cherns, "Can Behavioral Science Help Design Organizations?" *Organizational Dynamics* 5 (Spring 1977): 44–64. Robert Dewar and Jerald Hage, "Size, Technology, Complexity, and Structural Differentiation: Toward a Theoretical Synthesis," *Administrative Science Quarterly* 23 (March 1978): 111–136. William M. Evan, "Social Structure and Organizational Systems," *Organization and Administrative Sciences* 7 (Winter 1976–1977): 53–72. Jeffrey D. Ford and John W. Slocum, Jr., "Size, Technology, Environment and the Structure of Organizations," *Academy of Management Review* 2 (October 1977): 561–575. Robert H. Hayes and Roger W. Schmenner, "How Should You Organize Manufacturing?" *Harvard Business Review* 56

(January–February 1978): 105–118. Lawrence R. James and Allan P. Jones, "Organizational Structure: A Review of Structural Dimensions and Their Conceptual Relationships with Individual Attitudes and Behavior," *Organizational Behavior and Human Performance* 16 (June 1976): 74–113. Abraham K. Korman and Robert Tanofsky, "Statistical Problems of Contingency Models in Organizational Behavior," *Academy of Management Journal* 18 (June 1975): 393–397. Justin G. Longenecker and Charles D. Pringle, "The Illusion of Contingency Theory as a General Theory," *Academy of Management Review* 3 (July 1978): 679–683. Jay W. Lorsch, "Organization Design: A Situational Perspective," *Organizational Dynamics* 6 (Autumn 1977): 2–14. Fred Luthans and Todd I. Stewart, "The Reality or Illusion of a General Contingency Theory of Management: A Response to the Longenecker and Pringle Critique," *Academy of Management Review* 3 (July 1978): 683–687. Dennis J. Moberg and James L. Koch, "A Critical Appraisal of Integrated Treatments of Contingency Findings," *Academy of Management Journal* 18 (March 1975): 109–124. Donald V. Nightingale and Jean-Marie Toulouse, "Toward a Multilevel Congruence Theory of Organization," *Administrative Science Quarterly* 22 (June 1977): 264–280. Jon M. Shepard and James G. Hougland, Jr., "Contingency Theory: 'Complex Man' or 'Complex Organization'?" *Academy of Management Review* 3 (July 1978): 413–427. Leland M. Wooton, "The Mixed Blessings of Contingency Management," *Academy of Management Review* 2 (July 1977): 431–441.

Size of the Firm

Peter Blau, "A Formal Theory of Differentiation in Organizations," *American Sociological Review* 35 (April 1970): 201–218. Peter Blau and R. Schoenherr, *The Structure of Organizations* (New York: Basic Books, 1971). John Child, "Managerial and Organizational Factors Associated with Company Performance," *Journal of Management Studies* 11 (October 1974): 175–189; and 12 (February 1975): 12–28. John Child and Roger Mansfield, "Technology, Size, and Organization Structure," *Sociology* 6 (September 1972): 369–393. Ali Dogramaci, "Research on the Size of Administrative Overhead and Productivity: Some Methodological Considerations," *Administrative Science Quarterly* 22 (March 1977): 22–26. Frederick T. Evers, Joe M. Bohlen, and Richard D. Warren, "The Relationships of Selected Size and Structure Indicators in Economic Organizations," *Administrative Science Quarterly* 21 (June 1976): 326–342. Pradip Khandwalla, "Mass Output Orientation of Operations Technology and Organization Structure," *Administrative Science Quarterly* 19 (March 1974): 74–97. John R. Kimberly, "Organizational Size and the Structuralist Perspective: A Review, Critique and Proposal," *Administrative Science Quarterly* 21 (December 1976): 571–597. Marshall Meyer, "Size and the Structure of Organizations: A Causal Analysis," *American Sociological Review* 37 (August 1972): 434–441. Michael K. Moch, "Structure and Organizational Resource Allocation," *Administrative Science Quarterly* 21 (December 1976): 661–674. Jeffrey Pfeffer, "Size and Composition of Corporate Boards of Directors," *Administrative Science Quarterly* 17 (June 1972): 218–228. Louis R. Pondy, "Reply to Dogramaci: Suggestions for Improving Administrative Research," *Administrative Science Quarterly* 22 (March 1977): 27–29. Daniel Robey, M. M. Bakr, and Thomas S. Miller, "Organizational Size and Management Autonomy: Some Structural Discontinuities," *Academy of Management Journal* 20 (September 1977): 378–397.

Diversity of Products/Services

Robert Duncan, "Characteristics of Organizational Environments and Perceived Environmental Uncertainty," *Administrative Science Quarterly* 17 (September 1972): 313–327. David Murphy, "Decentralization: The Effects of Complexity," *Southern Journal of Business* 7 (November 1972): 79–86.

Employee Characteristics

Joseph Allutto and James Belasco, "A Typology for Participation in Organizational Decision Making," *Administrative Science Quarterly* 17 (March 1972): 117–125. Jay Lorsch and John Morse, *Organizations and Their Members* (New York: Harper & Row, 1974).

John Seiler, *System Analysis in Organizational Behavior* (Homewood, Ill.: Irwin–Dorsey Press, 1967), especially pp. 23–31 and 51–72.

Technology

Robert S. Billings, Richard J. Klimoski, and James A. Breaugh, "The Impact of a Change in Technology on Job Characteristics: A Quasi-Experiment," *Administrative Science Quarterly* 22 (June 1977): 318–339. Peter M. Blau et al., "Technology and Organization in Manufacturing," *Administrative Science Quarterly* 21 (March 1976): 20–40. Robert Blauner, *Alienation and Freedom* (Chicago: University of Chicago Press, 1964). Donald E. Comstock and W. Richard Scott, "Technology and the Structure of Subunits: Distinguishing Individual and Workgroup Effects," *Administrative Science Quarterly* 22 (June 1977): 177–202. Lex Donaldson, "Woodward, Technology, Organizational Structure and Performance: A Critique of the Universal Generalization," *Journal of Management Studies* 13 (October 1976): 255–273. David F. Gillespie and Dennis S. Mileti, "Technology and the Study of Organizations: An Overview and Appraisal," *Academy of Management Review* 2 (January 1977): 7–16. Charles A. Glisson, "Dependence of Technological Routinization on Structural Variables in Human Service Organizations," *Administrative Science Quarterly* 23 (September 1978): 383–395. Andrew Grimes and Stuart Klein, "The Technological Imperative," *Academy of Management Journal* 16 (December 1973): 583–597. Edward Harvey, "Technology and the Structure of Organizations," *American Sociological Review* 33 (April 1968): 247–258. David Hickson et al., "Operations Technology and Organization Structure," *Administrative Science Quarterly* 14 (September 1969): 378–397. Michael A. Hitt and R. Dennis Middlemist, "The Measurement of Technology within Organizations," *Journal of Management* 4 (Fall 1978): 47–67. Raymond Hunt, "Technology and Organization," *Academy of Management Journal* 13 (September 1970): 235–252. Mariann Jelinek, "Technology, Organizations, and Contingency," *Academy of Management Review* 2 (January 1977): 17–26. Robert T. Keller et al., "Uncertainty and Type of Management System in Continuous Process Organizations," *Academy of Management Journal* 17 (March 1974): 56–68. Thomas Mahoney and Peter Frost, "The Role of Technology in Models of Organizational Effectiveness," *Organizational Behavior and Human Performance* 11 (February 1974): 122–138. Lawrence Mohr, "Organization Technology and Organization Structure," *Administrative Science Quarterly* 16 (December 1971): 444–459. Jon L. Pierce and André L. Delbecq, "Organization Structure, Individual Attitudes and Innovation," *Academy of Management Review* 2 (January 1977): 27–37. S. Benjamin Prasad, "Thompson Technology Construct and Executive Compensation," *Management International Review* 17 (January 1977): 71–76. W. Richard Scott, "Organizational Structure," *Annual Review of Sociology* 1 (1975): 1–20. Gary G. Stanfield, "Technology and Organization Structure as Theoretical Categories," *Administrative Science Quarterly* 21 (September 1976): 489–493. James Thompson and Frederick Bates, "Technology, Organization, and Administration," *Administrative Science Quarterly* 2 (December 1957): 325–343. Joan Woodward, *Industrial Organization: Behavior and Control* (New York: Oxford University Press, 1970); and *Industrial Organization: Theory and Practice* (New York: Oxford University Press, 1965). William Zwerman, *New Perspectives on Organization Theory* (Westport, Conn.: Greenwood Press, 1970).

Market Stability and Organization Structure

Ramon Aldag and Ronald Storey, "Environmental Uncertainty," *Proceedings of the Academy of Management* (August 1975). Gerald Bell, "Formality vs. Flexibility in Complex Organizations," in *Organizations and Human Behavior,* ed. Gerald Bell (New York: Harper & Row, 1970), pp. 97–108. Tom Burns and G. Stalker, *The Management of Innovation* (London, Tavistock Institute, 1961). H. Kirk Downey et al., "Environmental Uncertainty: The Construct and Its Application," *Administrative Science Quarterly* 20 (December 1975): 613–629. Pradip Khandwalla, "Uncertainty and the Optional Design of Organizations" (Montreal: McGill University, 1975, mimeographed). Paul Lawrence and Jay Lorsch, *Organization and Environment* (Cambridge, Mass.: Harvard Business School,

1967). Richard Leifer and George P. Huber, "Relations among Perceived Environmental Uncertainty, Organization Structure, and Boundary-Spanning Behavior," *Administrative Science Quarterly* 22 (June 1977): 235–247. J. L. Metcalfe, "Systems Models, Economic Models and the Causal Texture of Organizational Environments: An Approach to Macro-Organization Theory," *Human Relations* 27 (July 1974): 639–663. Richard N. Osborn, "The Search for Environmental Complexity," *Human Relations* 29 (February 1976): 179–191. Johannes Pennings, "The Relevance of the Structural Contingency Model for Organizational Effectiveness," *Administrative Science Quarterly* 20 (September 1975): 393–410. Henry Tosi et al., "On the Measure of the Environment: An Assessment of the Lawrence and Lorsch Environmental Uncertainty Subscale," *Administrative Science Quarterly* 18 (March 1973): 27–36.

Dependence and Organization Structure

I. Adefolu Akinbode and Robert C. Clark, "A Framework for Analyzing Interorganizational Relationships," *Human Relations* 29 (February 1976); 101–114. J. Kenneth Benson, "The Interorganizational Network as a Political Economy," *Administrative Science Quarterly* 20 (June 1975): 229–249. Michel Crozier and Jean-Claude Thoenig, "The Regulation of Complex Organized Systems," *Administrative Science Quarterly* 21 (December 1976): 547–570. Michael A. DuBick, "The Organizational Structure of Newspapers in Relation to Their Metropolitan Environments," *Administrative Science Quarterly* 23 (September 1978): 418–433. Jerald Hage, "A Strategy for Creating Interdependent Delivery Systems to Meet Complex Needs," *Organization and Administrative Sciences* 5 (Spring 1974): 17–43. Richard H. Hall et al., "Patterns of Interorganizational Relationships," *Administrative Science Quarterly* 22 (September 1977): 457–474. David Jacobs, "Dependence and Vulnerability," *Administrative Science Quarterly* 19 (March 1974): 45–59. Ray Jurkovich, "A Core Typology of Organizational Environments," *Administrative Science Quarterly* 19 (September 1974): 380–394. Pradip Khandwalla, "Effect of Competition on the Structure of Top Management Control," *Academy of Management Journal* 16 (June 1973): 285–295. Thomas Kochen, "Determinants of the Power of Boundary Units in an Intraorganizational Bargaining Relation," *Administrative Science Quarterly* 20 (September 1975): 434–452. Curtis L. Manns and James G. March, "Financial Adversity, Internal Competition, and Curriculum Change in a University," *Administrative Science Quarterly* 23 (December 1978): 541–552. J. L. Metcalfe, "Organizational Strategies and Interorganizational Networks," *Human Relations* 29 (April 1976): 327–343. Dennis S. Mileti and David F. Gillespie, "An Integrated Formalization of Organization-Environment Interdependencies," *Human Relations* 29 (January 1976): 85–100. Sergio Mindlin and Howard Aldrich, "Interorganizational Dependence," *Administrative Science Quarterly* 20 (September 1975): 382–392. Johannes M. Pennings, "Strategically Interdependent Organizations," *Handbook of Organizational Design*, ed. Paul G. Nystrom and William H. Starbuck (Amsterdam: Elsevier Scientific, forthcoming). John R. Schermerhorn, Jr., "Information Sharing as an Interorganizational Activity," *Academy of Management Journal* 20 (March 1977): 148–153. Stuart M. Schmidt and Thomas A. Kochan, "Interorganizational Relationships: Patterns and Motivations," *Administrative Science Quarterly* 22 (June 1977): 220–234. Shirley Terryberry, "The Evolution of Organizational Environments," *Administrative Science Quarterly* 13 (March 1968): 590–613. James Thompson, *Organizations in Action* (New York: McGraw-Hill, 1968). Andrew H. Van de Ven, "On the Nature, Formation, and Maintenance of Relations among Organizations," *Academy of Management Review* 1 (October 1976): 24–36. Yoav Vardi and Tove Helland Hammer, "Intraorganizational Mobility and Career Perceptions among Rank and File Employees in Different Technologies," *Academy of Management Journal* 20 (March 1977): 622–634.

How Do We Organize If Different Factors Give Conflicting Signals?

John Child, "Organization Structure, Environment, and Performance: The Role of Strategic Choice," *Sociology* 6 (March 1972): 1–21. Richard Cyert and J. G. March, *Behavioral Theory of the Firm* (Englewood Cliffs, N.J.: Prentice-Hall, 1963). William F. Glueck, *Business Policy and Strategic Management* (New York: McGraw-Hill, 1980).

Case for Chapter 12

Aeronautical Systems Corporation

The Aeronautical Systems Corporation has experienced rapid growth in the past decade. Its current annual sales are approximately $250 million. The company employs 10,000 employees, a large proportion being highly talented engineers, technicians, and scientists. The company designs and manufactures complex custom-built electronics systems for the government, aviation firms, and other types of industrial organizations. Much of this work is done on a contract basis, where a number of companies are involved in the manufacture and construction of one major end product such as a missile, rocket, or booster, or a new type of aircraft. This company also has standardized product lines that are produced and distributed by six United States divisions, a Canadian division, and an international division.

A basic company objective is constant product and systems innovation of a highly technical and complex nature in fields where there are few competitors. Top management believes in a highly flexible organizational structure, which—in large part—entails organizing activities around highly talented personnel, rather than fitting people to an "ideal" organizational structure.

Following is an outline of the major manufacturing and distributing divisions and their major product lines:

1. Systems-Manufacturing Division, Los Angeles
   a. Space-Life-Support Systems
   b. Missile Systems
   c. Fluid Systems
   d. Flight-Electronics Systems
   e. Heat-Transfer Systems
   f. Environmental-Control Systems
2. Systems-Manufacturing Division, Phoenix
   a. Space-Power Systems
   b. Air-Pumping Systems
   c. Gas-Turbine Power Plants

   d. Pneumatic and Fluid-Control Systems
3. Research-Industrial Division, Los Angeles
    Manufactures and markets a line of industrial exhaust-driven
    turbo-chargers and specialized valves.
4. Research-Aviation Service Division, Los Angeles
    Conducts airplane modification work—including structural and system
    changes—and distributes several lines of turbine-powered executive
    aircraft in the Western states.
5. Electric Division, New York
    Manufactures a line of specialized industrial generating equipment.
6. Air Cruisers Division, New Jersey
    Manufactures fabricated products, aircraft-escape devices,
    missile-recovery systems, etc.
7. Systems Manufacturing, Ltd., of Canada
    Manufactures avionic systems such as temperature controls and static
    inverters.
8. Aeronautical Systems International, head offices in Geneva
    Controls a series of technical sales offices in Europe, and is also the
    holding company of subsidiaries in Japan, Great Britain, and West
    Germany.

On most major contracts, more than one of the company's divisions are
involved in the design, manufacture, and distribution of the systems or
company end product. Divisions 1 and 2, in particular, are highly
interdependent and interrelated in much of their work. Divisions 5 and
7 are the most autonomous in terms of their product lines and
operations. All of the divisions, however, have some standardized
products or systems, over which they have considerable operating
autonomy.

**Divisional
Organization**

To quote a current company manual:

Each manufacturing division is responsible for its own financial statement
and, therefore, enjoys a great deal of autonomy. The divisional manager,
assisted by an assistant manager, has a complete organization of managers
to control the operation of such departments as Engineering,
Manufacturing, Quality Control, Quotation Administration, Accounting,
Sales, and various service departments such as Personnel, Administrative
Service, and Plant Engineering and Maintenance. In addition to this basic
functional organization, Divisions 1 and 2 are further divided into
product-line organizations. Hence, the chief engineer, for instance, has a
chief-product engineer over each product line. Similarly, the sales manager
has complementary product-sales managers over each product line, and so
on.

The history of the Aeronautical Systems Corporation is one of deliberately planned internal growth through continuous investment in research and development of new products to supplement and complement existing products and systems capabilities. This policy has resulted in an unusually wide product mix, with uniquely complementary characteristics, that enables the development and production of complete, comprehensive accessory systems from components of various divisions and product lines. This practice has been exercised repeatedly and has established firm, practicable lines for inter-product group and inter-divisional collaboration in the creation of multiproduct systems.

Corporate Organization

To quote the company manual:

The corporation or head-office management consists of a board of directors, a chairman of the board, a president and an executive vice-president. All divisional and subsidiary managers report to the executive vice-president. He/she is assisted in his/her task by several corporation vice-presidents and directors who are responsible for policy direction to the divisions relating to matters such as law, finance, accounting, public relations, industrial relations, contract and quotation administration, engineering, material, product planning, manufacturing, quality control, and sales and service. The vice-president of Sales also has a complete Corporation-Marketing Organization, which is responsible for the sale of the corporation's products from offices throughout the free world.

Some additional comment on the corporate-level marketing organization is warranted here. Under the vice-president of Sales there are a number of sales forces organized on a customer basis; and within some of the customer groupings, there are also territorial breakdowns. For example, the following sales managers report to the vice-president of Sales:

1. Field Sales: Throughout the country, there are district sales offices, whose salespersons call on industrial customers.
2. Government Relations: This sales force deals with government contracts.
3. Airlines: This sales force deals only with airline companies; it consists of a number of regional offices.

Also reporting to the corporate vice-president of Sales are the manager of Engine Sales, whose sales force calls on both the airlines and government customers, and the manager of Special-Systems Sales (mechanical, electrical, etc.), whose sales force calls on all types of company customers. A director of Marketing Services also reports to this vice-president.

The head-office salespersons are the customer-contact persons for those systems and product lines that require joint developmental and manufacturing operations involving more than one division. These salespersons are the key disseminators of information between customers and those parts of the company concerned directly with the system or product being produced and sold to the customer. The divisional salespersons directly contact customers primarily where standardized products are involved and where the systems and products are under the autonomous control of a particular division.

Program Organization

To quote the company manual:

For the development of larger systems involving components of various types and requiring the coordinated efforts of several product-line organizations and more than one division, some form of program organization is used. The extent and exact composition of the program will vary with the size and complexity of the program involved.
A complete program organization consists of the following major positions:

Program Manager
System-Project Engineer
Contract Administrator
PERT Coordinator
Reliability Coordinator
Maintainability Coordinator
Value-Engineering Coordinator
Quality-Control Coordinator
Support-Service Coordinator
Manufacturing Coordinator
Material Coordinator

The subdivisions within the program organization follow the functional-line organizational structure in each Manufacturing Division. They draw on the strength, skill, and experience of existing line-organization people, combining them into a highly specialized group with a program of centralized responsibility and authority that comes directly from division and corporate management. This program structure has proven highly successful on many major programs such as the recent F-111 aircraft, Gemini, Apollo and SPUR space programs, and many others.

Program Manager

To quote the company manual:

The program manager has complete responsibility for the development of the systems in the program and complete authority to implement all activities necessary to insure contract compliance. He/she has overriding authority to alter decisions and to recommend alternate action, if such will enhance contract compliance, improve product reliability or quality, reduce development of fabrication costs, or reduce the time to develop the systems. The program manager reports any conflict between programs, regarding utilization of manpower or facilities, to the appropriate division managers. The division managers take appropriate actions to resolve such conflicts. The program manager must resolve all internal program conflicts involving compromise of costs, performance, product quality or reliability, or program scheduling. He/she has authority to request such action as is required to resolve any conflicts. The program manager represents the primary liaison and coordination point between the manufacturing division(s) involved and the customer. He/she authorizes all personnel conferences and correspondence at the technical and administrative levels between the division(s) and the customer. The program manager participates in all personnel-performance reviews for all key program members. He/she may recommend personnel changes when and if he/she deems such action necessary to the successful accomplishment of program tasks. He/she continually keeps abreast of all program developments, significant accomplishments, and important problems. He/she reports general program progress to division management on a biweekly basis and is responsible to the customer for all contractual reporting.

Problems

1. On one or more organization charts, depict the key organizational relationships discussed. You may make any assumptions you wish regarding specific titles of the personnel involved in cases where such titles have not been given.
2. What types of authority relationships does the program manager have with other company personnel (e.g., line, staff, functional, informal, formal)? Illustrate with examples.
3. Given this company's organizational structure and relationships, what significant organizational problems do you think are likely to arise? Illustrate with some examples involving personnel at different levels and in different departments or divisions.
4. In spite of any organizational problems that you might envision, do you feel that the overall organizational structure and authority relationships depicted are the most effective and practical for this particular company? Why or why not? If your answer is no, what are some of the more significant organizational changes that you would recommend?
5. How important do you feel technical as opposed to managerial skill is in effectively staffing the following positions in this company: (a) program manager, (b) divisional general manager, (c) corporate vice-president of Sales, (d) corporate manager of Special-Systems

Sales, (e) corporate manager for Government Relations, (f) divisional chief engineer, (g) divisional manufacturing manager, (h) executive vice-president, (i) president?

6. Discuss some of the advanced and more sophisticated planning and control techniques that may prove effective in the Aeronautical Systems Corporation.

7. Do you envision any serious directional, leadership, motivational, or communication problems in this company on the basis of the information provided? Illustrate with hypothetical examples in order to justify your answer if it is in the affirmative.

Chapter 13 Organization Change and Development

Learning Objectives

1. Examine the elements in the external and internal environment which influence organization change.
2. Learn basic principles for the effective implementation of organizational change.
3. Become familiar with the dimensions of organization change.
4. Compare and contrast organization changes based on changes in structure, changes in technology, and changes in people.
5. Understand what the organization development approach to change is.
6. Learn what some techniques for implementing organization development are.

Chapter Outline

Introduction
Causes
The Process of Organization Change
Reactions to Change
Negative Employee Responses to Change
Neutral Employee Responses to Change
Positive Employee Responses to Change
Dimensions of Organization Change
Elements to Be Changed
Changing the Structure of the Organization
Changing the Technology of an Organization
Changing the People of an Organization
Organization Development Approach to Change
OD Values and Assumptions
The OD Process
OD Activities
Is OD Effective?
Summary
Questions
Case: Hospital Departmental Consolidation

Introduction

In this chapter we will look at changing organizations and the people in them.

To change an enterprise is to make the enterprise different in some way in order to better achieve its objectives.

Change results from stimuli from both outside and inside the enterprise. Observers of modern organizations have found that *change takes place in all organizations and in all parts of an organization* but at varying rates of speed and degrees of significance. Change is more significant and more abrupt in some enterprises (for example, high-technology electronics firms) than in others (for example, lumber mills). And a firm's change takes place in all parts of an organization, but at varying rates of speed and degrees of significance. For example, the marketing department may face much more change, and more significant change, than its quality control department. So while change is important, it is necessary to keep the varying levels and rates of change in perspective. Indeed, in some organizations stability is so crucial to effectiveness that a strategy of no change at all is not only feasible but mandatory.

Causes

As I have noted above, change can come about because of two kinds of influences: external forces and internal forces. Any of the forces in the external environment discussed in Chapters 4, 7, 8, and 12 and listed below can be a major influence leading to change:

- The government
- The local community
- Customers and clients
- Suppliers (stockholders, unions, bankers, materials suppliers)
- Competitors

Competitors can cause change by increasing advertising, cutting prices, or increasing in number. Customers' attitudes toward the enterprise's products or services can become negative and so make change necessary. Radical changes in suppliers' technology can require change in the enterprise. And new government regulations are also often a strong force for change. In other words, the enterprise operates in an open system and thus is affected by what other institutions do.

Typical internal forces for change include:

- Changes in managerial objectives and policies.
- Changes in employees' attitudes and behaviors.
- Changes in technology (for example, the introduction of computers into personnel department operations).
- New conflicts between departments over roles to be played.

Many changes result from a combination of external and internal forces for change.

The Process of Organization Change

Organization change takes place over time. Larry Greiner has developed a model for the process, as shown in Figure 13.1.[1]

If you look carefully at the model you will note that it depicts six phases of change, which are similar to the stages of decision making discussed in Chapter 9. The top portion lists the stimuli for change and the bottom indicates the reactions of management. Let's discuss each briefly.

Phase 1

In this phase, management perceives a problem (pressure) from either external or internal forces. This perception arouses management to take some kind of action.

Figure 13.1
Greiner's Model of Organization Change

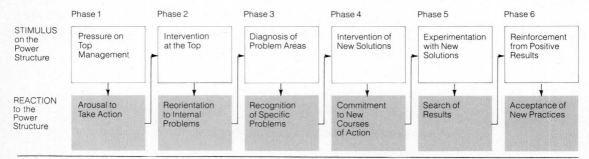

	Phase 1	Phase 2	Phase 3	Phase 4	Phase 5	Phase 6
STIMULUS on the Power Structure	Pressure on Top Management	Intervention at the Top	Diagnosis of Problem Areas	Intervention of New Solutions	Experimentation with New Solutions	Reinforcement from Positive Results
REACTION to the Power Structure	Arousal to Take Action	Reorientation to Internal Problems	Recognition of Specific Problems	Commitment to New Courses of Action	Search of Results	Acceptance of New Practices

Source: Larry Greiner, "Patterns of Organization Change," *Harvard Business Review* 45 (May-June 1967):126.
Copyright © 1967 by the President and Fellows of Harvard College; all rights reserved.

Larry Greiner

Larry E. Greiner received his B.S. degree from the University of Kansas and his M.B.A. and D.B.A. degrees from Harvard University. He began teaching at the University of Kansas School of Business Administration in 1960. He became a research fellow at the Harvard Business School in 1965, assistant professor in 1966, and associate professor in 1969. In 1973 he was appointed professor of organizational behavior at the University of Southern California. Professor Greiner's major field of study is organization change and development. His current research is concerned with stages of organization growth and structurally induced behavioral "diseases." Some of his publications are: "Breakthrough in Organization Development," *Harvard Business Review,* November–December 1964; "Patterns of Organizational Change," *Harvard Business Review,* May–June 1967; "Evolution and Revolution as Organizations Grow," *Harvard Business Review,* July–August 1972; "What Managers Think of Participative Management," *Harvard Business Review,* April–May 1973; "Can OD Be Fine-tuned for Bureaucracies?" *Organizational Dynamics,* Winter 1976; and "Reflecting an OD American Style," MacMillan Press, Spring 1977. His professional memberships include the Academy of Management, American Psychological Association, American Sociological Association, and Board of the Scandinavian Institutes for Administrative Research. He is currently chairperson of the OB Group at USC and chairperson for the OD Division of the Academy of Management. He also serves on the editorial board of the *Academy of Management Review.*

Phase 2	Management decides to intervene and focuses on internal problems flowing from the pressure.
Phase 3	Management decides to diagnose the direct cause-effect relationships. It does this by gathering data. If the problem is a sharp rise in absenteeism, data are collected on such factors as how long the problem has existed, in which units it is most severe, and what the possible causes are—supervisory style changes, lower pay, benefits relative to the economy, for example.
Phase 4	Alternative solutions are examined, and a preliminary choice is made. (For instance, in the absenteeism case, the new course of action may be a new supervisory training course focusing on effective supervisory leadership style.)
Phase 5	The firm experiments with the new solution. (A leadership training course is given in two of four divisions. Absenteeism is measured in all four divisions before and after the course is run.)

Phase 6

The results obtained in the experiment in Phase 5 were positive for the new solution (in our example, absenteeism dropped in the experimental divisions and did not in the other two). So the solution is given broader application and reinforced. (The leadership training course is used in the other two divisions, and periodic refresher courses for all supervisors reinforce the previous work. Supervisors are rewarded for their changed style and the consequent lower absenteeism of their employees.)

Reactions to Change

When change is initiated, both managers and employees may react adversely and even hinder it. Especially in Phase 1 of the change process, managers may react dysfunctionally to change in any of the following ways:

They may deny that change is taking place. When this happens, the firm may lose some of its effectiveness or even fail.

They may resist the change rather than determining how they can react in a functional way. When ball point pens were first introduced, for instance, fountain pen companies denied that people would buy them. Instead of reacting functionally—offering the public either ink or ball point pens—most ink pen firms went out of business or introduced ball points long after newer ball point companies such as BIC had taken most of their market away.

They may ignore the change. Managers who take this approach do not deny change is taking place; they simply put off decisions in the hope that it will go away. This was the reaction of many auto firms to the energy crisis and the demand for better gas mileage which flowed from the increased cost and decreased availability of gasoline.

Of course, managers can and often do react positively and functionally to change. This they can do in one of two ways. *They may accept change and adapt to it,* recognizing that it is a way of life. The many firms that have begun to conserve energy and so cut costs in response to the energy crisis have been successful in this approach. *Managers may also anticipate change and plan for it.* This is a more progressive approach. General Electric, to cite one example, is very active in studying the future. Years in advance of any actual changes, GM management identifies how it will adapt to possible future developments and sets up monitoring systems to determine whether anticipated changes are being realized.

Employees may exhibit one of three possible responses to proposed change: a positive response, a neutral response, or a negative one. Employees are likely to support change if it is directed at the *real* cause of the problem and is *an effective solution.* A neutral response—a "wait-and-see" attitude—is probably the most frequent reaction of employees.

A negative response occurs when employees resist change. They may do this either actively or passively. Most managers view resistance as bad. But is it? What if the employees see problems in the change that the manager has overlooked? Is management always right? When resistance is found, management might first reexamine the proposed change to see if it is *in fact* an improvement. If it is, then management must try to "work it through" with the employees.

Negative Employee Responses to Change

There are many reasons employees may react negatively to change. Some of the most common are listed below:

- *Ignorance of the need for change* The need for change must be crystal clear to affected employees because most people perceive most change as painful and threatening. Management needs to make the reasons *manifest* and be sure they are perceived as *real.* The ignorance may be due to poor management communication, actual ignorance on the part of the employees, or both.

- *A reaction to the agent of change* Employees may resist the change if the source of the proposal (a manager or consultant) is viewed as incompetent, unpleasant, or both. This type of reaction indicates a lack of interpersonal skills, leadership, communication skills, or all of these abilities on the part of the agent of change.

- *A loss for the employees* Some people who talk about change imply that it is possible for everyone to win through change and that it is "modern" to go along with the change. The fact is that in many changes, for economic or technical reasons, many of those affected by the change *lose.* You cannot expect people to support changes that will cause them to lose some or all of their need satisfactions or lower their level of need satisfactions. They can lose their jobs or get lower pay (and thus lose the means of assuring their physiological well-being); they can lose job security; they can be deprived of some degree of social interaction (and thus lower satisfaction of social needs). Change can lead to less status and power (recognition needs), require less ability (lower self-actualization), or require employees to do jobs in areas where their abilities are limited. Not surprisingly, people fight change if they are going to lose as a result of change.

- *A poorly planned change* Finally, people fight poorly planned change—change that comes too frequently because of poor planning (or none at all), poor communication of the change, or adverse consequences of the change.

Often people who resist change give *technical* reasons for their resistance: "It won't work—we tried it before," "the machine can't do that," and the like. The *real* reason might be that they feel they will lose as a result of the change. Just as people may quit because of a poor supervisor and say they wanted better pay, so they may say they are resisting change for technical reasons when their reasons are actually personal. After all, some people do not want to admit that they are trying to protect their job because they think that makes them appear too selfish. Besides, those who resist change are often perceived as "old fogeys" or reactionaries. The employees who take this tack are probably not resisting change but rather resisting being changed.

Neutral Employee Responses to Change

Employees are likely to respond neutrally to a proposed change if (1) they have some understanding of the need for change, (2) they do not react negatively to the agent of change, (3) their personal interests are not particularly threatened, and (4) the change seems to be adequately planned.

Positive Employee Responses to Change

Gene Dalton has modeled methods for instituting change that he believes lead to positive responses from employees and ultimately to success (see Table 13.1).[2]

Note that Dalton urges a four-pronged effort to produce positive responses.

Subprocess 1 Making explicit the goals and objectives of the change.

Subprocess 2 Building and replacing social ties disrupted by change.

Table 13.1
Dalton's Change Model

	Phase 1	Phase 2	Phase 3	Phase 4
Overall pattern of successful change effort	tension experienced within the system (unfreezing)	intervention of a prestigious influencing agent	individuals attempt to implement the proposed changes	new behavior and attitudes reinforced by achievement, social ties, and internalized values—accompanied by decreasing dependence on influencing agent (refreezing)
Subprocess 1	⟶	generalized objectives established ⟶	growing specificity of objectives—establishment of subgoals ⟶	achievement and resetting of specific objectives
Subprocess 2	tension within existing social ties ⟶	prior social ties interrupted or attenuated	formation of new alliances and relationships centering around new activities ⟶	new social ties reinforced—altered behavior and attitudes
Subprocess 3	lowered sense of self-esteem ⟶ ⟶	esteem building begun on basis of agent's attention and assurance	esteem building based on task accomplishment ⟶	heightened sense of self-esteem
Subprocess 4	⟶ ⟶	external motive for change (new schema provided) ⟶	improvisation and reality-testing ⟶	internalized motive for change

Source: Reprinted by permission from Gene Dalton, "Influence and Organization Change," in *Changing Organizational Behavior*, ed. A. Bartlett and T. Kayser (Englewood Cliffs, N.J.: Prentice-Hall, 1973), p. 159.

Subprocess 3
Building up the satisfaction level of affected employees' higher needs if the change has the potential to lower the level of satisfaction.

Subprocess 4
Improving the overall motivation set of affected employees.

Other research indicates that change is more likely to be successful if *employees participate in all phases of it, including*: (1) analysis of the data to see if change is needed, (2) consideration of alternative solutions, (3) choice of method and implementation. In other words, the bottom-up approach is essential to success *if the change is introduced over time, experimentally, and incrementally, rather than all at once.*

Dimensions of Organization Change

Now that we understand how change comes about and possible reactions to it, we need to know how it actually takes place. Obviously, the enterprise can be changed in a number of ways. Structure, technology, and people, however, are the major focuses of change. The scale on which change takes place can vary with respect to several dimensions.

Whatever its causes, organizational change has several dimensions, as shown in Table 13.2. The first dimension is its position on the planned-unplanned continuum—the *degree of planning* involved. The firm can just roll with the punches and let (unplanned) change happen or it can try to anticipate and manage it (planned change). This chapter focuses on planned change. I am convinced that planned change is more effective than unplanned change for reasons somewhat similar to those given in Chapter 7 to justify planning in general.

The second dimension of organizational change is its size and scope. Obviously, minor rearrangements of the functions in the corporate legal department at IBM will not have as much impact on the organization as the company's complete reorganization from a centralized to a decentralized structure which took place in past years. This chapter will focus on major programs of change.

Table 13.2
Dimensions of Organizational Change

Change Factor		
Degree of Planning	Unplanned change	Planned change
Size and Scope	Small changes Minor change	Large changes Major change
Initiation Point	Supervisors or employees (bottom)	Top managers
Time Dimension	Experiment and change over time	Change all at once
Elements to Be Changed	Structure Technology People	

Source: King Features Syndicate, Inc. 1976.

The third dimension of organizational change is the place within the enterprise where it is introduced: its *initiation point*. Does the change originate at the bottom of the structure, with employees or supervisors, or at the top, with the president? Organizational change comes about either by restructuring from the top down or from the bottom up. It seems reasonable to assume that the more the organization perceives itself as being in a crisis, the more likely it is to restructure from the top down; the less compelling the cause, the more likely it is to restructure from the bottom up. This chapter will discuss both top-down and bottom-up methods.

A fourth dimension of organizational change is the extent to which it is tested for effectiveness prior to implementation: the *time dimension*. On one end of the continuum is incremental change. In this approach the organization first tests the effectiveness of the change by means of one of several "pilot study" changes. If the results are positive, then the planned change is introduced step by step through the other parts of the organization. On the other end of this continuum is change that occurs throughout the organization simultaneously. It is reasonable to believe that the more a proposed change is perceived as crucial to survival, the more likely it is to be introduced in all parts of the organization at once. When the enterprise's survival is not at stake, it is sensible to change incrementally.

The final dimension consists of the *elements to be changed*—the enterprise's structure, the attitude and behavior patterns of its personnel, its technology, or some combination of these. A discussion of how change affects these elements will precede an examination of one program for instituting total and major organizational change.

Elements to Be Changed

In Figure 13.1 and the above discussion, we have noted that three elements of an organization (or some combination of them) can be changed: the structure of the organization, the technology, and the behavior of the people. Figure13.2 models how the change of each element is thought to lead to organization change.

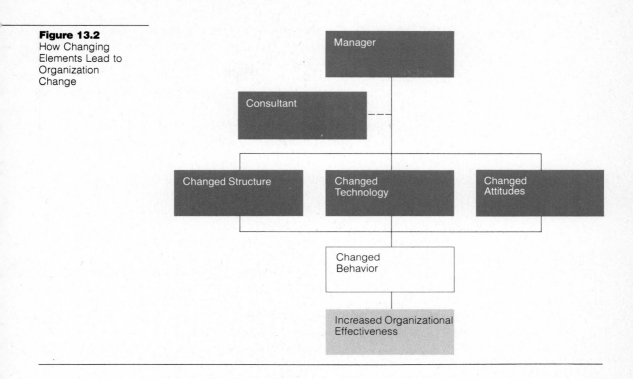

Figure 13.2
How Changing
Elements Lead to
Organization
Change

Manager

Consultant

Changed Structure

Changed Technology

Changed Attitudes

Changed Behavior

Increased Organizational Effectiveness

Figure 13.2 depicts the theory that whatever element is changed, employee behavior changes, leading to increased organizational effectiveness.

Changing the Structure of an Organization

In the preceding three chapters, we have considered a number of aspects of the formal organization structure, which are listed below. Each one (or all of these) can be changed by managers to improve organizational performance.

- Job design (changes can be made to permit more specialization or more enrichment).
- The clarity of job definitions.
- The basis of departmentation (for example, a change can be made from functional organization to product departmentation).
- The span of control (which can be increased or decreased) and therefore the height of the hierarchy.
- The organization manual and its description of policies and procedures.
- The clarity of the organization chart.
- Coordination mechanisms (such as policies and procedures).
- Power structure (for example, a change from centralized to decentral-

ized authority—an approach which is discussed in Chapter 14). Decentralization tends to (1) reduce the cost of coordination and increase the controllability of subunits and (2) increase the motivation of goal-oriented behavior through the use of smaller centers of decision, power, and information, giving greater flexibility and speed of response through local autonomy.

- Flow of tasks (social engineering involves modifying the flow of tasks to fit the flow of work, sometimes transferring significant numbers of people).

Structural changes to heighten effectiveness are quite common in business and government. D. Ronald Daniel reports that at least two out of every three large firms make major structural changes every other year.[3] The bigger the firm, the more likely it is to change. For example, nine out of the ten largest and sixteen of the twenty-five next-largest firms made a major change in the late 1960s.

Structural change, usually called *administrative reorganization*, has been the major method of change used in state, local, and federal governments, too. At the federal level, major structural changes took place under President Taft (1910–1912) and under President Harding (1920–1922). More changes occurred in 1932 under Hoover, in 1937–1939 under Roosevelt, in 1947–1949 (Hoover Commission 1) and in 1953–1955 (Hoover Commission 2) under Presidents Truman and Eisenhower. Usually the states reorganized shortly after each of these federal reorganizations following the federal lead in methods used. More recently, President Carter has proposed major changes in the federal government.

Changing the Technology of an Organization

The second mechanism of change is technology. Types of technology within the organization include:

- Equipment
- Techniques for doing work
- Production methods
- Engineering processes

A number of studies have indicated that when job technology changes, the organization changes. And not only the formal organization changes but also the informal organization—the way people interact at work (see Chapter 16). One study that demonstrated the relationships between technological change and organizational change is William Whyte's work on restaurant organization.[4] Whyte showed how as the restaurant grew in size and business, the problems of coordination between subgroups (waitresses, cooks, supervisor, bartenders, pantry runners) increased, as did problems of customer relations. Installation of a spindle in which lower-status waitresses could insert the food orders to higher-status cooks reduced status problems and improved coordination. Thus a small technological change functioned to reduce conflict and improve effectiveness.

Studies along similar lines have shown how the installation of new machinery changed organizational structure and behavior patterns in British coal mines.[5] When coal was mined by the old hand technology, small groups of workers made up the work group and a small span of control existed. When new automated equipment was introduced, spans of control increased—as did job dissatisfaction.

Managers have found they can use technology to change organizations and so reduce problems. For instance, installing equipment which prevents close interaction or even just moving employees physically apart can resolve or reduce conflict. To cite another example, patient monitoring by TV screen instead of personal visits by nurses has had an effect on job design, organizational relations, and patient relations in hospitals. And in many companies computerizing work has had a major impact on job design and organizational arrangements. Of the three elements of change, however, technology has been studied least, and we know the least about its significance to organization change.

Changing the People of an Organization

The final element of change in an organization is people. Whereas the changes in structure and technology are designed to create a new type of behavior in the enterprise by changing inanimate objects, the kinds of change we shall examine here are intended to influence the behavior of the people in the enterprise directly.

Advocates of the behavioral approach to organizational change contend that organizations are changed by modifying the skills, attitudes, and beliefs of the people in the organization. They believe the people will modify the structure and improve task performance after their attitudes and skills have improved.

Programs to change the people in an organization are run at three levels. On first level, training and development is provided for **individuals**. Such programs (either within the firm or outside it) are designed to improve the performance of individual managers and employees by improving their skills, knowledge, and attitudes. More effective selection methods may be included in programs of individual development; matching the right person with the right job can also lead to better performance. (These programs are discussed in more detail in Chapter 20).

The programs for managers are called *management development programs*. Some are skill and knowledge related. Programs of this sort could be aimed at increasing knowledge of computers (when computerization is introduced or the system is changed), teaching financial analysis and budgeting to those without these skills, and improving time management skills, to cite a few possibilities.

Other management development programs are designed to improve leadership and interpersonal skills (see Chapters 14 and 15). Generally, Kurt Lewin's model is the basis for these programs.[6] In Lewin's view, for a change in attitudes (and then perhaps behavior) to occur, an individual needs to go through the following stages:

- *Desire to change* Before any change can take place, the trainee must become aware of his or her shortcomings and become dissatisfied with the present state of affairs. The trainer and training group create this awareness and dissatisfaction.

- *Unfreezing* Support for present values or behavior patterns is removed. Once dissatisfaction with the present is created, the trainer questions the old values of behavior directly.

- *Conversion* The trainee is exposed to the new behavior pattern and attitude set and provided with strong evidence that they are better.

- *Refreezing* The new attitudes and behavior pattern are reinforced and integrated into the trainee's psychological constructs.

How these four stages take place varies with the individual program used, as will be seen in Chapter 20. Sensitivity training (T-groups), for example, is very unstructured. Other programs such as grid training are much more structured.

The second level of people change takes place in **small groups**. At this level, the purpose is to make the small group more effective in achieving objectives and to make the work more rewarding to group members. As with change at the individual level, training and development for small groups can be oriented toward improving job skills or interpersonal skills. Improved decision making at the group level, improved group communication skills, and improved job design are all goals of group programs designed to better job skills. Programs focusing on attitudes and interpersonal skills might be aimed at improving the satisfaction of social or interpersonal relationships. Small group training and development programs are also called *team building*.

The final level at which behavioral change can take place is the **whole organization**. When management tries to change the behavior of all the people in the organization at once, the program is called *organization development* (OD). Using OD, management can introduce programs such as job enrichment and MBO throughout the firm. The organization development movement is so important today that I will discuss it in the next section at more length.

Organization Development Approach to Change

Organization development is a planned change program which attempts to change the total organization using behavioral science knowledge to increase organizational effectiveness.

Normally, a consultant/change agent assists top management in the OD effort. OD is a relatively long-range program focusing on changing the behavior attitudes and performance of the total organization and groups of individuals within the organization. Rather than a one-time training and development program, it is an ongoing process. Action research is one of the mechanisms it uses to accomplish its objectives.

The OD movement probably started in the 1950s with Douglas McGregor's work at Union Carbide and Esso. The Survey Research Center at the University of Michigan strengthened it in the 1960s and 1970s. Today, firms such as Armstrong Cork, Corning Glass, Genesco, General Motors, Procter & Gamble, Texas Instruments, TRW, Abbott Labs, Celanese, Exxon, ITT, Lever Brothers, Polaroid, and Chrysler use it to some extent. In the service industries, firms such as American Airlines, Bankers Trust, 1st National Stores, Bank of New York, Federated Department Stores, Hotel Corporation of America, Jewel, and NBC have used it in varying degrees. Public organizations, too—MARTA(Atlanta); City of Kansas City, Missouri; and some hospitals, schools, and universities—have taken the OD approach to organization change.

But as a recent symposium of managers published by *Personnel* disclosed, OD is not universally used or admired.[7] Many of these managers had tried and discarded it.

OD Values and Assumptions

People serving as OD consultants and managers using OD in their enterprises hold certain values or assumptions about behavior. Kenneth Wexley and Gary Yukl contend that these values are those of Douglas M. McGregor.[8] Their first set of values arises out of the Theory Y perceptions described in Chapter 5:

- Employees have a need and desire for full growth and development at work when the work environment is supportive.

- Employees do not contribute as much as they could to the organization because their employer's management systems do not encourage them to contribute.

OD also rests on a set of values about group relationships. Some of these values and assumptions are:

Sheldon A. Davis
Vice President–Personnel

Sheldon A. Davis's career started with Specialty Papers Company in 1952 where he served as Personnel Director for four years. He then joined the Ramo-Wooldridge Corporation as a member of its Industrial Relations staff. In 1960 when they merged with Thompson Products to form TRW, Inc., Mr. Davis was Assistant Industrial Relations Director. During the next 15 years, he held a number of key personnel management positions, becoming a Vice President in 1968. In 1975 he was named Vice President and Director of Organization Development, with membership on TRW's Corporate Staff.

In 1977 Mr. Davis joined Digital where he took on worldwide responsibility for planning and implementation of the personnel programs conducted by Digital for their 40,000 employees in the areas of organizational and management development, employee relations, compensation, benefits, EEO, and recruiting. He is also a member of the Operations Committee, Digital's 13-member senior management group.

A recognized expert in organizational development, Mr. Davis has been a lecturer, consultant, teacher, and widely published author on personnel management and personal development topics. He has also produced several films on organizational development and has chaired seminars at MIT, Harvard, UCLA, Stanford, and other business schools.

His professional affiliations include charter membership in the International Association of Applied Social Sciences and he is also a member of the National Training Laboratories Institute. Mr. Davis holds a Bachelor's degree in Liberal Arts from Boston University where he graduated with honors in 1950. He received his MBA from Harvard University's Graduate School of Business in 1952.

- There is less interpersonal trust and support among group members than there should be at most firms.
- Leaders try to perform all the leadership responsibilities. This is impossible. Groups can help them with some of these responsibilities.
- Employees have a strong need to be accepted by other work group members. For this reason, cooperative effort by groups is an effective work approach.
- Open communications among group members should be encouraged to make groups more effective.
- Employees cannot fulfill their social needs unless they sense that their group has positive feelings about them.

The final set of assumptions and values on which OD advocates base their approach are those regarding how organizations should or do work, for example:

- Changes in one part or subsystem of a firm (such as personnel or technology) will be affected by and will influence the other subsystems.
- Managers are involved in their own groups as well as in overlapping work groups.
- Conflict resolution styles are critical to organizational effectiveness. Situations where one party to conflict wins and the other loses (zero sum games) are harmful to organizations.
- If OD is to succeed, the OD precepts must be reinforced by the enterprise's personnel–human resources systems.

Are these values and assumptions realistic and fair? Patrick Connor has reviewed the OD literature and raised a number of questions.[9]

First, he has pointed out, OD is mostly a set of norms and assumptions. There has been only about one scientific study of OD per year, and not all the findings are favorable to OD. In addition, OD consultants serve conflicting objectives: improving the "quality of work life" for the employees and improving organizational performance. Sometimes both objectives cannot be achieved simultaneously. Connor has also suggested that OD overemphasizes the interpersonal content of effectiveness—that other abilities plus motivation and role clarity have important impacts on effectiveness. And finally, he has noted that while OD focuses on work group influences on employees, employees are strongly influenced by significant people off the job as well. With these criticisms in mind, let's examine the process by which OD works.

The OD Process

OD is conducted in seven phases, as shown in Table 13.3. The OD process as practiced at General Motors is depicted in Figure 13.3. This is how General Motors explains the steps in its OD process:[10]

Table 13.3
Phases in the OD
Process

1. *Initial diagnosis*   The consultant seeks to determine the enterprise's problems.
2. *Data collection*   After the initial diagnosis, the consultant surveys the enterprise extensively to verify the diagnosis and to find possible solutions.
3. *Feedback and confrontation*   The consultant feeds these findings back to the group and sets priorities for change.
4. *Planning–problem solving*   The problem-solving groups begin to solve the problems chosen for solutions.
5. *Team building*   The consultant uses role play, sensitivity training, and games to strengthen the bonds of the problem-solving groups (teams).
6. *Intergroup development*   The consultant develops bonds between teams to build larger groups.
7. *Follow-up and evaluation*   The consultant analyzes the results against the objectives of OD.

- *Awareness* of a disturbance, of organizational problems of growth, identity, destiny, and revitalization; of human satisfaction and utilization of human resources; and of problems of organizational effectiveness.

- *Acceptance* of the nature of organizations, of the existence of alternative modes of organizational management, and of the range and depth of human and organizational potentialities.

- *Readiness and commitment to act* to undertake the change process and provide required resources and actions beyond mere verbal support.

Figure 13.3
Process of
Organizational
Development

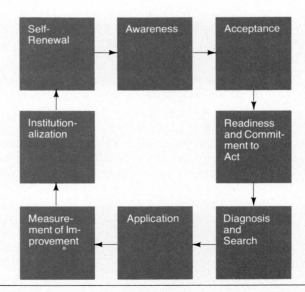

Source: Reprinted by permission of the publisher from "Organizational Research and Organizational Change: GM's Approach," by Howard C. Carlson, *Personnel,* July–August 1977, © 1977 by AMACOM, a division of American Management Associations, p. 21. All rights reserved.

- *Diagnosis* of problems and a *search* for solutions to gain an understanding of where the organization is, what produces disturbances, where the organization should be, and which improvement strategies are most appropriate to its needs and goals.

- *Application* of new behavior, to experimentally test new methods of operating, to modify organizational processes, and to seek congruency between organizational goals and individual needs.

- *Measurement* of the degree of improvement, of the means by which effective change occurs, and of the standards and methods by which organizations should be evaluated.

- *Institutionalization*, the incorporation into the management system of the principles of human resources management and the mechanism and strategies of organizational development.

- *Self-renewal*, a process for which a mechanism is required to assure that awareness of problems is regularly renewed, that organizational development is recycled, and that relevant values and practices are incorporated into the management system to ensure the continuity of the enterprise.

OD Activities

To implement organizational development, consultants and managers use a variety of activities. Some of the more frequently used techniques and certain of their characteristics as listed by Michael McGill are shown in Table 13.4.[11] Let's briefly discuss each one.

Survey Feedback Employee attitudes about such matters as leadership style, communications, and motivation are surveyed. The results of these surveys are reported in the aggregate to work groups. Then training and development are begun to change attitudes and thus, it is hoped, behavior in the direction desired.

Process Consultation A consultant observes managerial and work groups at work, analyzing such factors as communication patterns, leadership style, intergroup conflict and cooperation, and group decision making. On the basis of these observations, the consultant discusses what the situation is, offers alternatives to the current approach, and offers advice on how to implement the changes decided on by management.

Team Building The most popular approach today, team building combines the survey feedback and process consultation approaches. Its objective is to build cohesive and successful work groups either as the groups are beginning to be formed or after they have been functioning.

Table 13.4
Summary of
Organization
Development (OD)
Approaches

	Nature of the Plan	**Nature of Power**	**Nature of Personal Relationships**
Alternative approaches to OD	Sequentially structured Unstructured	Unilateral Shared Delegated	Impersonal Personal-Work Personal
Survey feedback	Structured	Unilateral	Impersonal
Process consultation	Unstructured	Shared	Personal-Work
Team building	Sequentially structured	Unilateral	Work
Laboratory training	Unstructured	Shared	Personal
Packaged approaches	Structured	Unilateral	Impersonal
Socio-technical systems	Structured	Shared	Impersonal to Personal-Work
Transactional analysis	Structured	Shared	Impersonal

Source: Reprinted by permission of the publisher from *Organization Development for Operating Managers*, by Michael E. McGill, © 1977 by American Management Associations, pp. 110–111. All rights reserved.

Laboratory Training This approach concentrates on creating attitude and behavior patterns that lead to open communication, group consensus solutions to conflict, free expression of emotions, and group decision making. The actual technique employed is T-group, or sensitivity training. Unstructured discussion groups, nonverbal exercises, and lecturettes on the new behaviors are used to accomplish the organization development objectives.

Packaged Approaches Two predesigned programs have been used widely in OD: Robert Blake and Jane Mouton's grid organization development and Gordon Lippitt's ITORP (Implementing The Organizational Renewal Process).[12] One of the chief mechanisms of grid organization development is the managerial grid—a matrix for examining leadership style. In six phases the program is explained, data about the organization are gathered, and implementation is begun. This prepackaged program is used to train managers at all levels, from the top down. The other well-known program, Lippitt's ITORP, is used less frequently than the grid.

Sociotechnical Systems This organization development approach focuses on matching the technical/production system of the firm with the people who work in it. Job enrichment (see Chapter 10) is one of its major strategies.

Table 13.4 continued

Nature of Pace	Nature of Price	Nature of Professional Relationships	Nature of Performance Criteria
Evolutionary	Inexpensive	Client (centered)	Product
Incremental	Moderate	Dual	Product-Process
Rapid	Expensive	Consultant (centered)	Process
Incremental	Moderate	1. Consultant 2. Client	Process
Evolutionary	Inexpensive	Consultant	Process
Incremental	Moderate	1. Consultant 2. Client	1. Process 2. Product
Evolutionary	Expensive	Client	Process
Incremental	Expensive	Consultant	Process
Incremental	Expensive	1. Consultant 2. Client	1. Product 2. Process
Incremental	Moderate to expensive	Client	1. Product 2. Process

Transactional Analysis Developed by Eric Berne, transactional analysis is a method of understanding an individual's interpersonal relationships with superiors, peers, and subordinates.[13] The analytical technique Berne uses is his description of the personality structure as composed of the Parent, the Adult, and the Child. Although Berne emphasizes the differences, I believe his analysis is an adaptation of Freud's superego, ego, and id. The analysis of interactions, communications, and behavior is much more direct in transactional analysis than in Freudian analysis, however.

For purposes of transactional analysis, each person's personality has a Parent, Adult, and Child ego state. The Parent tends to be righteous, dogmatic, evaluative, and protective. The Adult is the reasoning ego state. It seeks factual discussion in decisions and interactions. The Child is dependent, selfish, and rebellious. The Child desires immediate satisfaction, is emotional, and seeks approval.

When two people interact, one of the three ego states predominates. This leads to two possible transactions: *complementary* or *crossed*.

In the former, the ego states match. For example, both persons operate in the Adult ego state. Figure 13.4 exemplifies complementary transactions in a business setting. In the latter, the two persons operate in ego states that do not parallel each other. Figure 13.5 gives examples of these relationships between business associates.

Transactional analysis points out that all interactions involve "stroking." By this is meant any verbal or nonverbal signal of recognition and approval

Figure 13.4
Complementary
Transactions in
Parent, Adult, and
Child Ego States

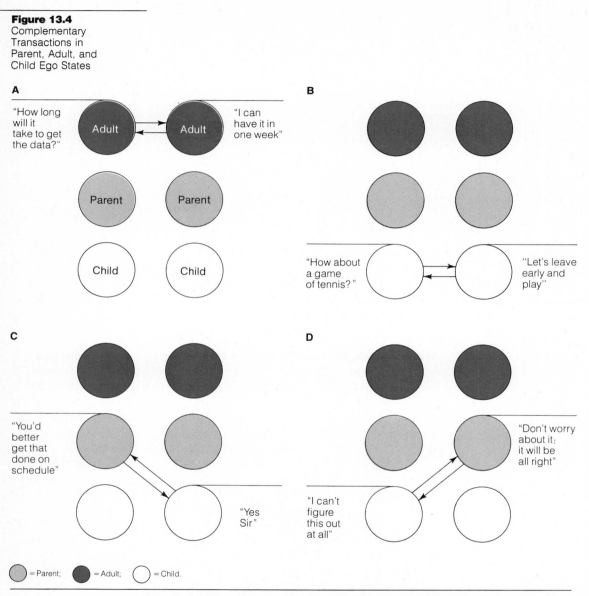

Source: Reprinted by permission from Muriel James, *The OK Boss* (Reading, Mass.: Addison-Wesley, 1975), p. 92.

or disapproval. Positive verbal stroking is shown in Figure 13.4 A, B, and D; negative verbal strokes are illustrated in Figure 13.5 A, B, and C. Managers can use an understanding of transactional analysis to become aware of the scripts (role patterns) people follow and to change these patterns if they so choose.

Figure 13.5
Crossed
Transactions in
Parent, Adult, and
Child Ego States

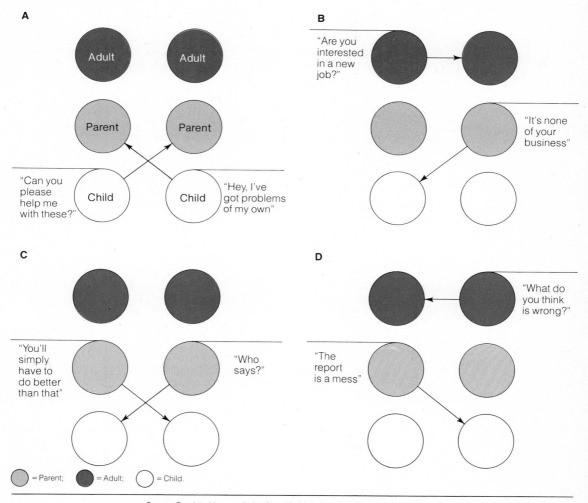

Source: Reprinted by permission from Muriel James, *The OK Boss* (Reading, Mass.: Addison-Wesley, 1975), pp. 94–95.

Is OD Effective?

How effective is organizational development? It is hard to say. Strauss notes that "as a rapidly evolving field, OD presents a moving target, making it difficult to define or criticize."[14] Strauss has identified eight common forms of OD, for example. Most of the relevant studies have been done by OD consultants, and most show positive results in terms of employee satisfaction. Strauss points out that since the consultants are in the business of selling OD, it is unlikely that they would report its failures. There have been studies indicating that OD increases productivity or organizational effectiveness, although in all the studies it was only one of several changes taking place at the time.

William Dunn and Fredric Swierczek have examined most or all the research on organizational change and arrived at the following general conclusions:[15]

- Change efforts in economic organizations will be more successful than change efforts carried out in other types of organizations.
- Two types of task environments—namely those which are long-term stable and short-term unstable—show the greatest proportion of effective outcomes of change.
- Change efforts in which the mode of intervention is collaborative will be more successful than change efforts undertaken with other modes of intervention.
- Change efforts in which the change agent has a participative orientation will be more successful than change efforts in which change agents share a nonparticipative orientation.
- Change efforts in which the solution is focused on a mix of organizational relationships will be more successful than efforts which focus on one relationship only.
- Change efforts directed at the total organization will be more successful than change efforts directed at lower levels.
- Change efforts employing standardized strategies which involve high levels of participation will be more successful than those which involve low levels of participation.

Table 13.5 summarizes their conclusions as well as some of my own. The results suggest that those strategies that are most explicitly oriented toward participative processes—namely, organization development and participative management—are associated with a greater share of effective change outcomes than others. OD is beginning to receive empirical support. Still, much more research is needed to clearly demonstrate all the conditions leading to its success in bringing about organizational change.

Summary

This chapter deals with overall organizational change. *To change an enterprise is to make the enterprise different in some way in order to better achieve its objectives.* Change can come about because of the influence of external forces, internal forces, or a combination of both. The forces in the external environment influencing change are the government, the local community, customers and clients, suppliers, and competitors. Internal forces include changes in managerial objectives and policies, employees'

Table 13.5

Characteristics of Effective and Ineffective Change Efforts Expressed in Frequencies Percentaged to the Independent Variable

Hypothesis	Percent Effective Cases	Percent Ineffective Cases	Total Number of Cases
Type of Organization			58
Commonwealth	100%	0%	8
Economic (business)	80	20	25
Service	64	36	25
Task Environment			53
Short-term/unstable	93%	17%	14
Long-term/stable	88	12	17
Short-term/stable	60	40	5
Long-term/unstable	47	53	17
Origin of Change Agent			62
Nonindigenous/external	90%	10%	10
Indigenous/external	69	31	16
Nonindigenous/internal	67	33	3
Indigenous/internal	63	27	33
Mode of Intervention			46
Delegative	100%	0%	2
Collaborative	91	9	22
Subordinate	54	46	13
Unilateral	44	56	9
Change Agent Orientation			50
Process	91%	9%	11
Participative	83	17	18
Engineering	71	29	14
Expert	43	57	7
Origin of Change Effort			63
Superordinate	87%	13%	15
External	72	28	7
Internal	61	39	41
Focus of Change Effort			53
First-line supervisors	100%	0%	3
Staff	91	9	11
Multiple focuses	84	16	19
Managers	83	17	12
Line	25	75	8
Focus of Solution			55
Mixed	91%	9%	11
Technological	83	17	6
Human	77	23	13
Task	73	27	11
Structural	57	43	14
Locus of Change			62
Division	83%	17%	17
Department	80	20	5
Total organization	70	30	33
Section	28	72	7
Standardized Strategy			56
Participative management	100%	0%	8
Organization development	89	11	18
Socioorganizational design	67	33	3
Institution building	67	33	9
Nonstandardized	61	39	18
Status of Methods			43
Multiple/untried	80%	20%	5
Single/untried	79	21	14
Multiple/proven	67	33	9
Single/proven	60	40	15

Source: Adapted by permission from William N. Dunn and Fredric W. Swierczek, "Planned Organizational Change: Toward Grounded Theory," *Journal of Applied Behavioral Science* 13 (April–May–June 1977): 135-157.

attitudes and behaviors, and technology and new conflicts over roles to be played.

There are six phases of change, which are similar to the stages of decision making. Management must perceive a problem, decide to intervene, diagnose the cause-effect relationships, examine alternative choices, and then choose and implement a preliminary choice. If the choice works out in an experimental trial in part of the organization, it is finally implemented throughout the enterprise.

Management and employees can have one of three reactions to the implementation of change: positive, negative, or neutral. Especially during the first phase of the change process, managers may react dysfunctionally by (1) denying the change is taking place, (2) resisting the change rather than determining how the firm can react in a functional way, or (3) ignoring the change. Managers respond functionally to change in one of two ways. Either they accept it when it comes, or they anticipate and plan for it.

Negative response to change can stem from ignorance of the need for change, reaction to the change agent, a feeling that the change will mean some kind of individual loss, or resistance to poorly planned change. A negative response is not always unwarranted. Employees may see problems that the manager has overlooked. Conditions which elicit a neutral response and methods for evoking a positive response are also outlined.

Organization change has several dimensions: (1) degree of planning, (2) size and scope, (3) point of initiation, (4) time dimension—the extent to which the proposed change is tested for effectiveness prior to implementation, and (5) elements to be changed. The last item deals with the major focuses of change in an organization: structure, technology, and/or people.

Structural change is used frequently in business and government. In fact, it is the major method of initiating change in state, local, and federal government. Structural elements that can be changed are job design, job definitions, departmentation, span of control, organization manual, organization chart, etc.

Changes in equipment, new techniques for doing work, new production methods, or new engineering processes are technological changes that lead to changes in the organization structure.

The final element subject to change is people. Advocates of trying to influence the behavior of employees directly rather than by changing inanimate entities such as technology and structure believe the people in the enterprise will modify the structure and improve task performance after their attitudes and skills have improved.

Programs whose purpose is to change people are run at three levels. The *individual* development approach includes such mechanisms as management development programs, grid training, and sensitivity training. The second level of people change is the *small group* level. As at the individual level, training at this level can be oriented toward improving job skills or interpersonal skills.

Finally, several of the methods for changing the behavior of people (or all of them) can be combined to try to change the whole organization. This type of program is called organization development (OD). *Organization development* is a planned change program which attempts to change the total organization using behavioral science knowledge to increase organizational effectiveness. Normally a consultant/change agent assists top management in the OD effort. The values upon which OD rests were outlined. OD is conducted in seven phases: (1) initial diagnosis, (2) data collection, (3) feedback and confrontation, (4) planning–problem solving, (5) team building, (6) intergroup development, and (7) follow-up and evaluation. Frequently used OD implementation techniques are listed in Table 13.4.

Most studies of the OD approach to organization have been done by OD consultants, and most show positive results. Since the consultants are in the business of selling OD, it is unlikely that they would report too many failures. Still, in an overall evaluation of the change methods, research results suggest that those strategies that are most explicitly oriented toward participative processes (OD and participative management) are associated with a greater share of effective change outcomes.

This chapter on organization change completes the material dealing with organizing the enterprise's resources. We turn next to Part 5, which examines leadership and effective relationships with superiors, colleagues, and groups.

Questions

1. Why is it necessary to keep the varying rates of change in perspective when planning an organization change?
2. If you were a manager, what forces in the external environment would you monitor to foresee the need for organization change? What internal forces?
3. Discuss the six phases of the change process and compare this process to the decision-making phases listed in Chapter 9.
4. Why do some employees exhibit negative reactions to change? Is a negative response always bad?
5. What is Dalton's four-pronged effort to insure positive response to change? Do you think his method is feasible?
6. How might a manager improve organizational performance by modifying organization structure?
7. How can changing technology change the organization? Use examples from the text and/or personal experience to illustrate this.
8. You are an advocate of the people approach to organization change. Explain this approach to your superior (its different levels, methods, and reasons why it is an effective approach).

9. What is organization development? What are its values and assumptions? Explain the process. Do you think this is the best approach to organization change?

Notes

[1] Larry Greiner, "Patterns of Organization Change," *Harvard Business Review* 45 (May–June 1967): 119–130.

[2] Gene Dalton, "Influence and Organization Change," in *Changing Organizational Behavior*, ed. Alton C. Bartlett and Thomas A. Kayser (Englewood Cliffs, N.J.: Prentice-Hall, 1973).

[3] D. Ronald Daniel, "Reorganizing for Results," *Harvard Business Review* 44 (November–December 1966): 96–104.

[4] William Whyte, "The Social Structure of the Restaurant," *American Journal of Sociology* 54 (January 1949): 302–310.

[5] Eric Trist and K. W. Bamforth, "Some Sociological and Psychological Consequences of the Longwall Method of Goal Getting," *Human Relations* 4 (February 1951): 3–38.

[6] Kurt Lewin, *Field Theory in Social Science* (New York: Harper & Row, 1964), chapters 9, 10, and appendix.

[7] "Is Organization Development Catching On? A Personnel Symposium," *Personnel* 54 (November–December 1977): 10–22.

[8] Kenneth N. Wexley and Gary A. Yukl, *Organizational Behavior and Personnel Psychology* (Homewood, Ill.: Richard D. Irwin, 1977), chapter 15. See also Douglas McGregor, *The Human Side of the Enterprise* (New York: McGraw-Hill, 1960).

[9] Patrick E. Connor, "A Critical Inquiry into Some Assumptions and Values Characterizing OD," *Academy of Management Review* 2 (October 1977): 635–644.

[10] Howard Carlson, "Organizational Research and Organizational Change: GM's Approach," *Personnel* 54 (July–August 1977): 11–22.

[11] Michael McGill, *Organization Development for Operating Managers* (New York: AMACOM, 1977).

[12] Robert Blake and Jane Mouton, *Building a Dynamic Organization through Grid Organization Development* (Reading, Mass.: Addison-Wesley, 1969); and Gordon Lippitt, *Organization Renewal* (New York: Appleton-Century-Crofts, 1969).

[13] Eric Berne, *Transactional Analysis in Psychotherapy* (New York: Ballantine Books, 1961).

[14] George Strauss, "Organization Development," in *Handbook of Work, Organization and Society*, ed. Robert Dubin (Chicago: Rand McNally, 1976).

[15] William N. Dunn and Fredric W. Swierczek, "Planned Organizational Change: Toward Grounded Theory," *Journal of Applied Behavioral Science* 13 (April–May–June 1977): 135–157.

References

The Process of Organization Change

Larry Greiner, "Patterns of Organization Change," *Harvard Business Review* 45 (May–June 1967): 119–130.

Reactions to Change

Lester Coch and John French, Jr., "Overcoming Resistance to Change," *Human Relations* 1 (August 1948): 512–532. Gene Dalton, "Influence and Organization Change," in *Changing Organizational Behavior*, ed. Alton C. Bartlett and Thomas A. Kayser (Englewood Cliffs, N.J.: Prentice-Hall, 1973). Alan Filley et al., *Managerial Process and Organizational Behavior* (Chicago: Scott, Foresman, 1976), chapters 21 and 22. Larry

Greiner, "Red Flags in Organization Development," *Business Horizons* 15 (June 1972): 17–24. Paul Hershey and Kenneth Blanchard, "The Management of Change," *Training and Development Journal* 26 (January 1972): 6–10; (February 1972): 20–24; and (March 1972): 28–33. Herbert Kaufman, *The Limits of Organizational Change* (University, Ala.: University of Alabama Press, 1971). Jay Lorsch, "Managing Change," in *Organizational Behavior and Administration*, ed. Paul Lawrence, Louis Barnes, and Jay Lorsch (Homewood, Ill.: Irwin, Dorsey Press, 1976).

Dimensions of Organization Change

Gerald Zaltman and Robert Duncan, *Strategies for Planned Change* (New York: Wiley, 1977).

Elements to Be Changed

Eliot Chapple and Leonard Sayles, *The Measure of Management* (New York: Macmillan, 1961). D. Ronald Daniel, "Reorganizing for Results," *Harvard Business Review* 44 (November–December 1966): 96–104. William F. Glueck, "Organizational Change in Business and Government," *Academy of Management Journal* 12 (December 1969): 439–441. Paul R. Lawrence, *The Changing of Organization Behavior Patterns* (Cambridge, Mass.: Harvard University Press, 1958). Harold Leavitt, "Applied Organization Change in Industry," in *Handbook on Organizations*, ed. James March (Chicago: Rand-McNally, 1965), pp. 1114–1167.

Changing the Technology of an Organization

Robert Blauner, *Alienation and Freedom* (Chicago: University of Chicago Press, 1964). James Taylor, "Some Effects of Technology on Organization Change," in *Tomorrow's Organizations*, ed. Jong S. Jun and William B. Storm (Glenview, Ill.: Scott, Foresman, 1973). Eric Trist and K. W. Bamforth, "Some Sociological and Psychological Consequences of the Longwall Method of Goal Getting," *Human Relations* 4 (February 1951): 3–38. Allan Warmington et al., *Organizational Behavior and Performance: An Open Systems Approach to Change* (Reston, Va.: Reston Publishing, 1977). William Whyte, "The Social Structure of the Restaurant," *American Journal of Sociology* 54 (January 1949): 302–310.

Changing the People of an Organization

Robert Kahn, "Organizational Development: Some Problems and Proposals," *Journal of Applied Behavioral Science* 10 (October–November–December 1974): 485–502. Kurt Lewin, *Field Theory in Social Science* (New York: Harper & Row, 1964), chapters 9, 10, and appendix. Newton Margulies and John Wallace, *Organization Change: Techniques and Applications* (Chicago: Scott, Foresman, 1973). James A. Waters; Paul F. Salipante, Jr.; and William W. Notz, "The Experimenting Organization: Using the Results of Behavioral Science Research," *Academy of Management Review* 3 (July 1978): 483–492.

The Organization Development Approach to Change

Clayton Alderfer, "Organization Development," *Annual Review of Psychology* 28 (1977): 197–223. Wendell French and Cecil Bell, *Organization Development* (Englewood Cliffs, N.J.: Prentice-Hall, 1973). Frank Friedlander, "OD Reaches Adolescence: An Exploration of Its Underlying Values," *Journal of Applied Behavioral Science* 12 (January–February–March 1976): 7–21. "Is Organization Development Catching On? A Personnel Symposium," *Personnel* 54 (November–December 1977): 10–22. Newton Margulies and Anthony Raia, *Conceptual Foundations of Organizational Development*

(New York: McGraw-Hill, 1978). Glenn Varney, *Organization Development for Managers* (Reading, Mass.: Addison-Wesley, 1977).

OD Values and Assumptions

Patrick E. Connor, "A Critical Inquiry into Some Assumptions and Values Characterizing OD," *Academy of Management Review* 2 (October 1977): 635–644. Kenneth N. Wexley and Gary A. Yukl, *Organizational Behavior and Personnel Psychology* (Homewood, Ill.: Richard D. Irwin, 1977), chapter 15.

The OD Process

Clayton Alderfer, "Organization Development," *Annual Review of Psychology* 28 (1977): 197–223. Robert Blake and Jane Mouton, *Building a Dynamic Organization through Grid Organization Development* (Reading, Mass.: Addison-Wesley, 1969). Howard Carlson, "Organizational Research and Organizational Change: GM's Approach," *Personnel* 54 (July–August 1977): 11–22. Gordon Lippitt, *Organization Renewal* (New York: Appleton-Century-Crofts, 1969). Michael McGill, *Organization Development for Operating Managers* (New York: AMACOM, 1977). Evert Van De Vliert, "Inconsistencies in the Argyris Intervention Theory," *Journal of Applied Behavioral Science* 13 (October–November–December 1977): 557–564. Glenn Varney, *Organization Development for Managers* (Reading, Mass.: Addison-Wesley, 1977). Kenneth N. Wexley and Gary A. Yukl, *Organizational Behavior and Personnel Psychology* (Homewood, Ill.: Richard D. Irwin, 1977), chapter 15.

OD Activities

David G. Bowers, "Organizational Development: Promises, Performances, Possibilities," *Organizational Dynamics* 4 (Spring 1976): 50–62. Gary Cooper, *Organization Development in the UK and USA* (New York: Petrocelli, 1977). Jerome L. Franklin, "Characteristics of Successful and Unsuccessful Organization Development," *Journal of Applied Behavioral Science* 12 (October–November–December 1976): 471–492. Robert Golembiewski, Keith Billingsley, and Samuel Yeager, "Measuring Change and Persistence in Human Affairs: Types of Change Generated by OD Designs," *Journal of Applied Behavioral Science* 12 (April–May–June 1976): 133–157. Bruce M. Meglino and William H. Mobley, "Minimizing Risk in Organization Development Interventions," *Personnel* 54 (November–December 1977): 23–31. Phillip Mirvis and David Berg, *Failures in Organization Development and Change* (New York: Wiley, 1977). Virginia E. Schein and Larry E. Greiner, "Can Organization Development Be Fine-tuned to Bureaucracies?" *Organizational Dynamics* 5 (Winter 1977): 48–61. George Strauss, "Organization Development," in *Handbook of Work, Organization and Society*, ed. Robert Dubin (Chicago: Rand McNally, 1976). Michael L. Tushman, "A Political Approach to Organizations: A Review and Rationale," *Academy of Management Review* 2 (April 1977): 206–216.

Is OD Effective?

William N. Dunn and Fredric W. Swierczek, "Planned Organizational Change: Toward Grounded Theory," *Journal of Applied Behavioral Science* 13 (April–May–June 1977): 135–157. Dan Gowler and Karen Legge, "Participation in Context: Towards a Synthesis of the Theory and Practice of Organizational Change, Part I," *Journal of Management Studies* 15 (May 1978): 149–175. Larry Short, "Planned Organization Change," *MSU Business Topics* 21 (Autumn 1973): 53–61. George Strauss, "Organization Development," in *Handbook of Work, Organization and Society*, ed. Robert Dubin (Chicago: Rand McNally, 1976). Noel Tichy, "Current Trends in Organizational Change," *Columbia Journal of World Business* 9 (Spring 1974): 98–111.

Case for Chapter 13

Hospital Departmental Consolidation

Janet Johns is the administrator of Suburban Memorial Hospital, a 275-bed hospital in an upper-class suburb located in a western state. Janet recently asked the new assistant administrator, Sam Donalds, to investigate whether a consolidation of the EKG, Pulmonary Function, and Cardio-Pulmonary Rehabilitation Departments would result in a significant savings to the hospital.

Background

The three departments do basically the same types of patient tests. As medicine has progressed, there has been a movement away from static (at rest) testing to dynamic (in motion) testing. Dynamic testing is used in the EKG Department for tests on the heart, in the Pulmonary Function Department for lung tests, and in the Cardio-Pulmonary Rehabilitation Department for both heart and lung tests.

At present there is a duplication of services and equipment among the three departments at Suburban Memorial. In addition, three separate technicians are employed as well as three different part-time physicians who work on a percentage basis, according to the volume of work.

The EKG and Pulmonary Function Departments make a significant contribution to Suburban's revenue. The contribution margin of Pulmonary Function has been 80 percent (for every $100 earned, the hospital spends only $20 to earn it), and that of EKG has been 60 percent.

Revenues for each department have been:

Department	Annual Revenue	Contribution Margin
EKG	$180,000	60%
Pulmonary function	260,000	80%
Cardio-pulmonary (new department, less than one year)	40,000	unknown

The total annual revenue of Suburban Memorial is $16.1 million, and the net income is $1.3 million. Mr. Donalds has calculated that a departmental consolidation could initially save the hospital $100,000 by selling duplicated equipment. In addition, the annual savings would amount to:

$ 44,000 personnel costs (fewer technicians needed, etc.)
  15,000 ordering and supplies reduction (no duplication, less ordering)
 125,000 reduced physician fees (only one physician would be needed)
  16,000 plant and facilities (can lease out space not needed after consolidation)
_____

$200,000 total

Therefore, the annual savings, in essence additional revenue, would be $200,000, in addition to the initial $100,000 received from the sale of equipment.

Physicians

Dr. Bartl, head of Pulmonary Function, is responsible for 80 percent of the pulmonary admissions to the hospital and about 4.7 percent of the total admissions. He is an extremely popular physician, attracting respiratory cases from well outside the normal service area of Suburban Memorial.

Dr. Neumann, head of EKG, controls 20 percent of the hospital's cardiac/internal medicine cases. She admits about 3 percent of the hospital's patients.

Finally, the head of the new Cardio-Pulmonary Rehabilitation Department, Dr. Hermann, controls 100 percent of those cases which at this point represent a negligible percentage of the hospital's total patient revenue.

All three physicians have more or less equal support from the medical staff.

Janet is wondering what to do about the physicians, *if* she decides to go through with the consolidation. One of the three physicians would have to be chosen (with a new reimbursement contract) to head this new department, or perhaps a new, salaried physician could be brought in. The combined workload would still be less than full-time.

However, Janet sees several problems with either of those two alternatives. First of all, the physicians who would be "excluded" from this new department might become resentful and start admitting their out-of-service-area patients to other hospitals. Janet and Sam have estimated a 25 percent probability that the three physicians would do so, which would mean a possible loss to the hospital of 15 percent of these physicians' admissions.

Janet has asked Sam to prepare a report of the situation, including his recommendations, which will be discussed at the next management council meeting.

Source: This case was written by Dorothy M. Hai and Richard C. Housley, Arizona State University, Tempe, Arizona.

Problems

1. If you were Sam Donalds, what would you recommend? Prepare the type of report Janet Johns has asked for, as if it were going to be presented to the management council.
2. Assuming the council votes for consolidation, prepare another report outlining your recommended strategy, which is designed to produce minimum alienation and maximum cooperation.

Case for Part Four

Peace of Mind Insurance Company

Beginning with the Chief Executive Officer and extending through the entire corporate ranks, the employees of the Peace of Mind Insurance Co. ("POM") have been generally proud of their reputation for stability, innovative approaches, professional competence, and financial strength. Their top-down organizational structure has worked effectively for several decades. Based in a large eastern city, POM markets (through the Independent Agency System) a full line of Property and Casualty[4] insurance products in all fifty states.[3] Internally, POM maintains product divisions,[1] whose managers are accountable for profit and efficiency of certain insurance lines.

In order to be able to provide a better service to its agents and insureds, and to get the benefit of local expertise, POM operates through a number of service offices located in key cities throughout the country. Each of the service office managers has responsibility for a specific geographic area (usually a single state or group of adjacent states).

Operating within a closely regulated industry, POM's policies, i.e., products, are largely controlled by governmental agencies in each state both as to rate (price) and as to form (coverages, conditions, etc.). Specific insurance policies which are routinely sold in one state may not be made available in a neighboring state as a result of differences in the two insurance department regulations.[2] The management of change which accompanies a newly available insurance product line[1] forms the basis of this case.

Synopsis of the Problem

POM's Commercial Insurance Division[1] had been generally well pleased with the results of its Commercial Combination Coverage ("CCC")[2] policy which it was marketing very successfully in most areas of the

1, 2, 3, 4 - See definitions on page 455 for greater clarity.

country. One exception to this was the area served by POM's Idaho Service Office, based in Boise, since the CCC had not previously been approved for use by that state's regulatory authorities.[3]

Since his staff had never worked with the CCC before, B. M. Miller, the POM manager of the Idaho office, was faced with a personnel problem when the CCC was approved for use in his area for the first time. He knew that the CCC was, essentially, a combination of several of POM's other non-life[4] insurance policies into a single contract. Although members of this Idaho staff had experience in handling one of the separate insurance lines elements, none of them had worked outside their own particular area and were thus unfamiliar with either the remaining elements of the "package" or its special rating and coverage features. Each staff member knew, however, that changing to the CCC format was both inevitable and impending.

This situation presented problems for employees at all levels of the operation. Most of POM's Boise office management felt that the primary difficulty would occur in the clerical support area, upon whom would fall the bulk of the procedural changes. Betty Barnet, supervisor of that clerical unit, surely would be called upon to manage the majority of the paperwork. This problem was compounded by the fact that most of the incumbent clerical personnel were older employees who had no interest in learning new or different duties. Virginia Taylor, one of the more likely candidates for the new duties, was becoming openly hostile to the idea. Virginia made it clear that she had no intention of getting involved in anything other than the job she had been performing (extremely well, by the way!) for many years.

Recognition and Definition of the Problem

In the sense of realizing that procedural changes were going to have to be made in their existing operations, "recognition of the problem" was pretty much forced onto Idaho's POM management by the October 1st announcement from the state insurance commissioner that the CCC had been approved. A few days later a lengthy wire arrived from POM's Commercial Insurance Division's top executive asking for details on how the CCC was to be handled locally. The final sentence requested, "What type of implementation assistance would be required?"

It was in the few days following receipt of this wire, in the discussions concerning the best way to answer it, that POM's Idaho management came to realize that in defining the new procedure their problem lay not so much in the "how" aspect (which could be handled by a few minor changes in the organization chart) as it did in the "who" considerations (when it became necessary to change the existing duties of the various members of the staff).

The problem, then, in B. M. Miller's eyes, had two distinct aspects, "structural" and "people," of which the latter was perceived to be by far the more complex. It was further recognized that within the broad "people" problem there was yet another distinction to be made—between "judgment-level" or "professional" employees versus the so-called clerical personnel. Upon closer examination, in view of the different age levels, general attitudes, adaptabilities, etc., it appeared highly probable that of these two groups, the clerical employees presented the more serious obstacle to a smooth transition.

Key Individuals Involved

The following Boise-based POM employees were to be most closely involved either in making or in implementing the final decision on the changes:

The Management Team

1. *Walter Osborn*, 38, Commercial Lines Underwriting Manager–Walt had been with POM for approximately 15 years and had been in the Idaho Office for the past 6. He had come up through the ranks of the underwriting department, was a good technician in the CCC area, and was an adequate, if not inspiring, administrator. He was somewhat budget-conscious and was therefore inclined to try and accomplish the changeover without going outside the present staff.

2. *Betty Barnet*, 32, Supervisor of the Commercial Lines Clerical Unit– Recently promoted from one of the positions she now supervised, Betty was also technically competent, had a good "feel" for the problems involved in the various jobs, and knew the members of the clerical unit well from having worked with many of them for the past several years.

3. *Joseph Schaeffer*, 30, Supervising Underwriter in Charge of Commercial Property–Joe had been with POM for approximately 4 years, prior to which he had been with a competing insurer in Illinois (which did allow programs similar to the CCC). Having had some limited experience in this area (including working with an occasional CCC for insureds with out of state plants), he was concerned with the problems presented by the narrow experience ranges of the clerical unit and felt that the use of outside talent should be considered.

4. *Robert Adams*, 37, Supervising Underwriter in Charge of Commercial Casualty–Bob had about 5 years with POM as a Casualty underwriter and prior to that had performed the same function for a competitor for approximately 8 years. Being thoroughly experienced in one of the two major areas of the CCC (plus having had a brief 6-month exposure to property underwriting) Bob was also considered a possibility to take over the CCC.

The Clerical Support

5. *Virginia Taylor*, 59, *Martha Murphy*, 52, *Grace Higgins*, 31—All three were Assistant Underwriters whose duties were primarily to provide clerical (rating, policy preparation, routine correspondence, etc.) support for the underwriters. Virginia and Grace worked with Joe and handled the property lines of business. Martha assisted Bob in the casualty lines. Virginia and Martha each had over 20 years with POM (mostly in the same areas in which they were presently working) and were extremely capable at their duties. Grace had been hired a little over a year earlier and, although she was intelligent and learning fairly quickly, she was still relatively inexperienced.

6. *Jerry Farmer*, 26, Junior Underwriter—Jerry had been with POM for about 2½ years and had no prior insurance experience before joining the company. During POM's rather extensive Training and Orientation program, Jerry had worked briefly in most of the various lines that the Idaho Service Office handled. He thus had a surface exposure to a broad range of jobs but had had little in the way of in-depth experience in any of them.

The On-Line Manager

7. *B. M. Miller*, 45, Idaho Service Office Manager—a career POM employee and head of the local operation for the past 2 years, Miller will have the final responsibility for the success or failure of the new venture. As was his usual pattern, Miller would make the decision after close consultation with his key managers, but the decision in the final analysis would be his alone. Being accountable for the over-all operation, Miller's concerns in this matter included quality of work which the new unit would produce (as this had a direct bearing on the profitability of his office), service to the agents, and, of course, budget considerations.

The Discussions

Throughout the several days following receipt of the instructions to develop a plan of operation for handling the upcoming changes, there were a number of formal and informal meetings between Miller, his key managers, and all of the members of the staff to be affected. By the time Idaho's management team met with Miller for the final time to make their recommendations, they were able to summarize the eight important considerations as follows:

1. Time and timing were crucial factors as the new procedures had to be completely installed before the new product "hit the market" in approximately 60 days. Miller had repeatedly emphasized his desire to be in a "go" position as soon as possible in order to provide the fastest and most professional service possible. He was acutely conscious of

POM's need to impress upon the agents POM's desire to be a primary factor in the CCC market, even though his current year budget did not allow any additional major expense;

2. None of the experienced supervising underwriters was particularly enthusiastic about the prospect of taking over the CCC, but all managers felt they would accept the decision even if another supervisor was selected;

3. Among the three possibilties on the present clerical staff, Virginia and Martha had both indicated that they were satisfied with their present duties and had no desire to change. Each was very competent in her own area and both were valued employees. Of the two, Virginia was the more outspoken on the subject. Grace, on the other hand, had not expressed her feelings on the matter at all;

4. Based on her knowledge of the individuals involved and their past experience, Betty expressed the opinion that while Virginia was probably the best prepared, even she would require considerable additional training and also that there was a real possibility that she would consider quitting rather than accept different duties. Grace, Betty believed, would be the one most likely to accept the new job willingly, but her lack of experience would create serious training problems, particularly in view of the limited time available. Martha was seen to be somewhere in the middle of these two positions in both attitude and qualifications;

5. There was a strong sentiment expressed by Joe Schaeffer in favor of either hiring from another insurance company or transferring experienced people from another POM office at the underwriting and/or the clerical level. This feeling was reinforced by the "people" and time difficulties mentioned above, plus the overload problems to the existing staff;

6. The Idaho Office held an advantage in that their interpersonal working relationships (at least among these key people) were very good, particularly between the underwriters and their individual assistants. Although the overall morale level of the office was probably just slightly on the positive side of indifferent or neutral, this particular group did seem to work well with and generally like and respect each other;

7. Technical help from CCC experienced personnel on a temporary, short-term basis could be arranged from the Home Office and other service offices;

8. It was agreed that, under the circumstances, the new unit should be established with only the minimum number of people necessary for the

immediate needs. Decisions on additional people to handle the expected increased flow of business would be deferred until later when more accurate volume predictions could be made. The initial unit would, however, continue as the nucleus of the larger one and was *not* to be merely a stopgap arrangement to be replaced later.

Following the approximately 90-minute discussion of the situation, the group presented its summary and recommendations: Namely, that Joe Schaeffer and Virginia Taylor be assigned the CCC responsibilities. Promotion to Joe's present slot should come from within the Boise office ranks. Miller promised to report back to them in the next day or so with his decision on the size and make-up of the CCC unit. Inwardly, however, he was concentrating on the other changes which seemed likely to occur.

Definitions

1. Commercial Insurance Division is a POM organizational unit which services larger business clients rather than personal customers. Example: The Widget Manufacturing Company may purchase fire, windstorm, difference-in-conditions, comprehensive general liability and 3-D Blanket crime coverage from POM's Commercial Insurance Division, via a POM service office facility.

2. Commercial Combination Coverage is a package of previously separate property or casualty insurance contracts. See 1 above.

3. Each insurance company in the United States is subject to the regulatory requirements of each state insurance commissioner in whose jurisdiction the insurer operates.

4. Property and casualty insurance broadly includes all insurance contracts *except* life or pension insurance arrangements.

Source: Professor Bruce D. Evans, The Graduate School of Management, University of Dallas, Dallas, Texas.

Problems

1. Identify the priority issues found in this case.
2. Discuss these issues showing understanding of the human aspects of management in the process, and
3. Propose what you perceive to be realistic solutions wherever feasible.

Part 5   Leading and Interpersonal Influences

5

The next four chapters focus on an analysis of the interpersonal skills the manager must develop in order to be effective. We will discuss leadership styles and sources of influence in dealing with employees; the interaction of the manager with peers and superiors; ways in which managers can relate to groups effectively; and the communication skills necessary to accomplish these leadership tasks.

Now

The Future

Chapter 14 Leadership of Employees

Learning Objectives

1. Learn principles of effective leadership.
2. Understand why leadership is a function of the leader, the work group, and the situation.
3. Be able to compare and contrast the various leadership theories discussed—trait theory, leadership behavior theory, Fiedler's contingency theory.
4. Determine which leadership style suits you best—traditional, consultative, participative.
5. Become familiar with the ways a leader can influence subordinates.
6. Learn to operate successfully within the political environment of the organization.

Introduction

The word *leadership* is an exciting one. All kinds of people have shown an interest in it—historians, philosophers, psychologists, politicians, executives. Whenever leadership is mentioned, people's names come to mind. In the business world some of those that come to mind are Thomas Watson, J. C. Penney, Ross Perot, J. Pierpont Morgan, Lorna Mills, and Mary Kay. In the military, George Patton and Douglas MacArthur, Robert E. Lee and Ulysses S. Grant, Joan of Arc, Napoleon, Alexius Comnenus, and Julius Caesar are names we associate with leadership qualities. Empress Catherine, Thomas Jefferson, Abraham Lincoln, Winston Churchill, and Margaret Thatcher are all well-known political leaders. Of course the names of other leaders, whose influence on history has been less positive, also come to mind: Bernie Cornfeld, Tamerlane, and Joseph Stalin.

Leadership, or influencing people effectively, is a fascinating topic. But if you are looking for a quick, precise explanation of the influence of a Napoleon over his subordinates, you are going to be disappointed. The topic is more complicated than it appears at first glance.

The theme of this chapter is twofold:

1. Leadership is a function of three factors: (a) the leader, (b) the work group, and (c) the situation.
2. Most managers can be or become successful leaders if they match their personality and leadership abilities with *the right work group* and *the right leadership situation*.

In this chapter I shall first define leadership and then examine each element of it. A discussion of the first major leadership theory, the trait or "great man" theory, will follow. (Two other theories of leadership—leader behavior theory and Fred Fiedler's contingency theory—will be discussed a little later in the chapter after necessary groundwork has been laid.) Next the work group and the leadership situation and how these two factors affect the manager's leadership will be considered.

An examination of leadership style—how the individual can apply the appropriate skills to the leadership situation and the work group—will also be included. Finally, I'll discuss how the individual acquires influence and the ability to exercise leadership as well as how a manager influences the work group and situation.

What Is Leadership?

There are many definitions of leadership. A basic one is:

Leadership is a set of interpersonal behaviors designed to influence employees to cooperate in the achievement of objectives.

If we are not careful, we may assign to leadership much the same definition that we assign to management. Leadership, however, is not planning or organizing behavior but rather motivating and controlling employees. It is the means used to accomplish organizational objectives.

Formal versus Informal Leaders

It is important to keep in mind that there are two kinds of leaders: formal and informal. In most employment situations the enterprise has a chosen "boss" or "leader." This is a formal leader, appointed by management or the organization's directors. In contrast, the informal leader is chosen by the group itself. This can happen in any social group—gang, bridge club, church organization, political party, or work group.

There are significant differences between how the two types of leaders emerge and how they influence the group. This will become clear when sources of influence are examined later in the chapter. Most managers are formally appointed leaders. But many consider the "ideal" manager a person who, in addition to being the formal leader, operates in such a way that he or she is the informal leader as well.

Why Is Leadership Important?

Leadership is important because top managers evaluate managers on their leadership potential. Thus it may be crucial to your career. Leadership is also important because it contributes to organizational effectiveness. For example, Robert Guest and associates have shown how significant leadership was in the success of a factory they called Assembly Plant Y.[1] Sally Coltrin and I found in a study we conducted in 1976 that effective leadership positively influenced the research productivity and satisfaction of very productive research professors.[2]

On the negative side, there are many studies which show that lack of leadership leads to lower employee satisfaction, higher grievances, and lower productivity. Richard Gabriel and Paul Savage have made a very strong case for their theory that the United States lost the war in Vietnam because the army then lacked strong, heroic leaders and that army leadership style and approach must be changed before the U.S. loses the next war as well.[3]

Still, leadership is not everything. It is only one aspect of management. Some contend that leadership accounts for about 15 percent of organizational effectiveness. In any case, 15 percent is an important figure, and it may be understated.

Why Does Anyone Want to Be a Leader?

You must be motivated to become a leader. According to Cecil Gibb, the motives for leadership include economic reward, primitive dominance, power over others, and status needs.[4] In terms of Maslow's hierarchy of needs, esteem recognition and self-actualization needs seem to be the main motivators of leadership behavior. In the McClelland-Atkinson scheme, the need for achievement and the need for power seem to be the strongest motivators of formal leaders.

Many who chose to be followers and not leaders may be more interested in affiliation or social needs and security needs. Leaders are willing to undergo the stresses and responsibilities of leadership to achieve their needs to exert power and influence. They are normally reinforced by higher salaries and other organizational rewards as well. Let us turn now to the first element of the leadership process: the leader.

Leadership and the Leader

When one thinks of a leader one thinks of a person like Douglas MacArthur. The son of a general and grandson of a federal judge, MacArthur was groomed to be a leader. He went to West Point and graduated as first captain of the corps of cadets and first in his class. He served with great distinction in wars in the Philippines in 1903, was appointed an aide to President Taft, made part of the general staff (1913), had a distinguished career in World War I, and was decorated nine times for heroism.

At age thirty-eight (1918), MacArthur was made a general. In 1919 he became superintendent of West Point. Later he became field marshall of the Philippines and led U.S. troops in World War II with great success and the lowest casualty rate of any U.S. general. As Supreme Commander for the Allied Powers, he revolutionized the Japanese government. He also led U.S. troops in Korea and was considered for presidential candidacy. Anyone who heard his "Old Soldiers Never Die" speech to Congress knows his abilities as an orator. MacArthur ended his career as a business executive—Chairman of the Board of the Remington Rand Corporation.

Here was a real leader. MacArthur had charisma of the sort that Elizabeth I, Mao Tse-tung, and Charles de Gaulle possessed. Freud's classic analysis of Moses showed that he was charismatic too. On the basis of these and other examples, some theorized that leaders are born to lead. These people were born with great abilities, educated at the right schools, and had families who encouraged them. The researchers tried to identify

H. Ross Perot

H. Ross Perot illustrates the free enterprise system at work. He saw the need for a service created by technological innovations, and he filled it.

Perot joined International Business Machines in 1957, where he was a highly successful salesman. During the five years he was at IBM, he realized that companies were selling computers faster than people could effectively learn to operate and use them.

On his thirty-second birthday, Perot left IBM to set up his own company, Electronic Data Systems, using $1,000 that he and his wife had saved. His goal was to build a company that would provide quality service. Under long-term contracts, EDS designs, installs, and operates data processing systems for its customers.

Perot serves as chairman of the board of the company, which has grown from one employee and $1,000 in 1962 to eight thousand employees in offices throughout the world and an income of $217,837,000 in 1978. The corporate headquarters for EDS is in Dallas, Texas.

the traits and characteristics leaders have. If that could be done, they believed, tests and interview schedules could be developed for use in the scientific selection of future leaders.

Traits and characteristics such as the following were identified as correlated with leadership.

- Physical size (relatively tall).
- Intelligence (more rather than less, but not too much more than the work group).
- Self-esteem/self confidence.
- Extroversion.
- Ambition—a high need for achievement and power.

This trait approach sounds great. But there is a problem; most of the leaders tested did not score significantly higher than the general management population on possession of the identified traits. Besides, there are many examples of leaders who did not have these characteristics. Hitler, Stalin, Napoleon, Charles Revson, and many other leaders could be described as short. Woodrow Wilson compensated for his low self-esteem by working harder and achieving much. The same is true of many business leaders. George Marshall, a great general, was an introvert.

The trait theory failed because leaders come in all varieties, shapes, colors, and sizes, even though as a group they show some tendency to be slightly more intelligent, ambitious, and extroverted than others and to have high self-esteem (or compensate for the lack of it). Nonetheless, certain *behaviors* do indicate leadership potential. We will look at these when we consider the behavioral theory of leadership.

Leadership and the Work Group

The second factor in the leadership process is the match between the leader and the work group, or "followers." The work group is a significant influence because it is there voluntarily. The group can reject the leader and quit, sabotage his or her leadership, or lower productivity. Even in very coercive leadership situations such as prison camps and the military, the leader can be rejected or even killed. (In Vietnam the euphemism for this was "fragging.")

Several aspects of the work group affect the leadership process. First, there are differences in abilities, skills, experience, and cognitive style. Some work groups are more experienced than the leader. Second, groups differ in their attitudes toward leadership and the needs/motives of the individuals within the group.

Third, groups differ in their expectations of the leader's personality, behavior, and leadership style. Such expectations are often based on experiences with past leaders. In *Backstairs at the White House* there is an account of the reactions of the staff to President and Mrs. Truman's homey, midwestern style.[5] Used to the aristocratic, eastern ways of the Roosevelts, the staff initially jeered and made fun of the Trumans.

Consider the following three employees:

- Joan: experienced, dedicated, responsible, hardworking; a good to excellent employee.
- Sam: sometimes like Joan—sometimes like Teresa.
- Teresa: partly experienced; in the job for the money; does only the minimum expected; a barely satisfactory employee.

It should be clear that leadership styles that are fruitful for Joan may not work with Sam and probably will not work with Teresa. Paul Hershey and Kenneth Blanchard theorize that effective leaders respond to these differences by using different leadership styles.[6] They suggest that the more mature, the more able and willing to accept responsibility, and the more experienced and educated the work group, the more the effective leader follows the leadership style I call participative. This leadership style will be discussed in a subsequent section of the chapter. George Graen and James Cashman suggest that the effective leader structures the task and decision making accordingly too.[7]

James MacGregor Burns has noted ways leaders can try to relate to the work group:[8] Leaders who choose to use *transactional leadership* relate to the work group with an eye to exchanging one thing for another. The attitude they adopt toward the work group is: "If you produce well, are loyal, are on time, and support me, I'll pay you well, get you better working conditions, praise you, get you promoted." In *transforming leadership,* the leader tries to assess what the work group's needs are, present and future, and engage each member of the group to his or her full potential. This leads to mutual stimulation and elevates employees into leadership roles. The leader who chooses to exercise *moral leadership* bases her or his relationship with the work group not only on power but also on mutual needs, aspirations, and values. The leader takes responsibility for his or her commitments and makes sure that promises are kept. Where moral leadership exists, followers are aware of possible alternative leaders but prefer the one they have.

Transactional leadership would seem to be effective with instrumentally oriented employees, while transforming and moral leadership would be more suitable for employees with strong work ethics (see Chapter 5 for discussion of these attitude sets).

Leadership and the Situation

The third factor in the leadership process is the leadership situation. Three aspects of the situation are relevant: (1) the organization's expectations, (2) the job and its characteristics, and (3) the opportunity to lead.

Leaders are affected by how their superiors and peers expect them to behave. Gerald Salancik and associates call these *expectations of the organization* the social structure.[9] Leaders must cooperate with superiors and peers to get the work done so they respond to how these people expect them to behave. The social structure provides leaders with a standard for what is acceptable; it is communicated to them in many ways—through policy statements and supervisors' evaluations, for instance.

The *job and the characteristics of the job* put limits on the leader's behavior. For example, jobs with high time pressures (such as surgeons during surgery and managers who must bid jobs under time pressure) limit the leader's behavior and style. The need for precision or careful attention to government regulations are job requirements that may bring out traditional leadership styles, as will be discussed later in the chapter. The repetitiveness of the task (or lack of creativity), the danger, and intrinsic interest or lack thereof also influence how a leader behaves.[10]

Some theorists contend that the situation—*the opportunity to lead*—brings forth the leader. Almost the opposite of the trait theory, this situational-environmental theory asserts that the leader emerges to meet the needs of the time and place and is determined by the situation. Thus Mao would not be known without a crisis; Hitler would never have been elected had it not been for the Great Depression.

But if the theory that a crisis gives rise to leadership is true, how does it explain the many occasions where crises arose and no leader appeared? In the business world we can identify numerous occasions of this type. For example, why did no leader come forward to handle the crisis that arose at Curtis Wright in 1945? Why did the firm (the largest builder of planes at the time) eventually leave the business and never again have the impact it had in 1945? Yet while a crisis situation may not necessarily produce the leader who can cope with it, the opportunity to lead can influence how significant an impact a leader can have.

Theories of Leadership

Many persons have developed theories of leadership and done research attempting to prove or disprove them. Rather than presenting an overwhelmingly long catalog of all these, I will discuss here only a few major theories that extend beyond the more common explanations of leadership as a function of the leader, the work group, and the situation.

Leader Behavior Theory

When most researchers gave up on the trait theory and attempting to isolate traits of leaders, leader behavior theory began to be recognized and used to help managers understand leadership. Instead of trying to identify who leaders were likely to be, based on individual traits, this theory tried to relate the behavior of effective leaders with desired outcomes such as higher employee productivity and satisfaction. The theme was: Let's see which behaviors lead to good results so we can train managers to behave in these ways. The major work was done on this theory at Ohio State University from about 1948 to the early 1960s by Ralph Stogdill and Carroll Shartle.[11]

After many detailed studies, Stogdill and Shartle found that two clusters of behaviors could be described. The stronger cluster was called *consideration*. Leaders whose behavior exhibits consideration convey warmth, respect, friendship, and mutual trust to their employees and establish a good rapport with them. Typically, they are accessible to employees, they explain their actions to employees, they treat them as equals, and they respond to their suggestions.

The second cluster of leadership behaviors was called *initiation of structure*. Behaviors in this cluster lead to good organization, good job definitions, clear relationships between the leader and employees, clear channels of communication, clear job instructions, and pressure for output/criticism of inadequate work. The manager also sets a good example of expected work behavior.

These two dimensions can be put into a matrix as is shown in Table 14.1. Initially leader behavior theory stated that the most effective leader was one who showed both high consideration and high initiation of structure (Cell 4). Some research supported this. Other research did not.

Table 14.1
Leader Behavior
Theory: Consideration
and Initiation of
Structure Matrix

		Low	High
Consideration	**High**	High consideration Low initiation of structure 3	High consideration High initiation of structure 4
	Low	Low initiation of structure Low consideration 1	High initiation of structure Low consideration 2
		Low	High Initiation of Structure

Path-Goal Theory

Robert House, who studied at Ohio State, extended the Ohio State approach and developed what he calls the *path-goal theory* of leadership.[12] One of his basic theses is that leader behavior will result in employee satisfaction and acceptance of the leader if the employees see that the behavior leads to the satisfaction of their present and future needs. Another is that leader behavior will result in good employee performance if the leader provides employees with good training, defines the job well, helps the employee to do the job well, and rewards the employee for effective behavior. This is similar to expectancy motivation theory discussed in Chapter 6.

Alan Filley, another Ohio State student, has drawn a number of conclusions based on leader behavior theory concerning how leader behavior relates to employee satisfaction and performance:[13]

- Employee satisfaction with the leader is dependent on the amount of consideration the leader shows the employee.

- Consideration behavior affects the employee's satisfaction more in stressful and unpleasant jobs.

- The leader who exhibits high consideration for the employee can increase the initiation of structure behavior without a decline in employee satisfaction.

- Consideration behavior given in response to good performance will increase future good performance.

- Initiation of structure which increases role clarity will increase employee satisfaction and performance.

- Initiation of structure in jobs where there is already adequate structure will lead to a decrease in employee satisfaction.

A leader who wishes to increase employee satisfaction, Filley advises, should adhere to the following principles:

1. Clarify the job if it is not clear.
2. Avoid giving too many instructions to experienced employees who already know their job well.
3. Avoid demanding greater levels of performance of those who are already performing well.
4. Help employees achieve more by providing them with the necessary resources—through more training and better tools and equipment—and protecting them from outside interference.
5. Show strong consideration behavior when the job is stressful or unpleasant.
6. Improve social skills.

A leader who wishes to increase productivity, Filley maintains, will give a great deal of consideration and significant rewards to employees already producing well and initiate more structure for employees *not* producing well.

Although the leader behavior approach to leadership received more support than trait theory, it has not received as much research support as desirable, probably because it does not take into account the third factor in the leadership process: the situation. Let's examine a theory which does.

Fiedler's Contingency Theory

Fred Fieldler's lengthy research led to his theory of leadership effectiveness.[14] It states that effectiveness comes from a good match between the leader's objectives and the degree to which the situation is favorable for the leader to control the situation.

How does Fiedler measure the leader's objectives? According to Fiedler's theory a leader is motivated by one of two objectives. Either the leader's highest priority goal is to accomplish a task or it is to establish worthwhile interpersonal relationships. These two objectives are related, respectively, to the need for achievement or power and the need for affiliation.

Fiedler developed an instrument called the least preferred coworker (LPC) scale. Table 14.2 is an example of the scale. He theorizes that the leader whose total LPC score is low—the person who is very *negative* about the coworker and who would score him/her as unpleasant, unfriendly, rejecting, etc.—has a high priority goal of accomplishing a task. The leader who has a high total LPC score, who would assign even the *least* preferred coworker moderately positive ratings, is motivated by interpersonal relationships. Thus the LPC score indicates how a leader is motivated.

But how does the leader determine how favorable his or her leadership position is? Fiedler suggests that three basic factors are involved: (1) the leader-employee relationship, (2) the task structure, and (3) the power of the leader's position.

Table 14.2
Least Preferred
Coworker Scale

Think of the person with whom you can work least well. He or she may be someone you work with now or someone you knew in the past. He or she does not have to be the person you like least well but should be the person with whom you had the most difficulty in getting a job done. Describe this person as he or she appears to you.

	8	7	6	5	4	3	2	1	
Pleasant									Unpleasant
Friendly	8	7	6	5	4	3	2	1	Unfriendly
Rejecting	1	2	3	4	5	6	7	8	Accepting
Helpful	8	7	6	5	4	3	2	1	Frustrating
Unenthusiastic	1	2	3	4	5	6	7	8	Enthusiastic
Tense	1	2	3	4	5	6	7	8	Relaxed
Distant	1	2	3	4	5	6	7	8	Close
Cold	1	2	3	4	5	6	7	8	Warm
Cooperative	8	7	6	5	4	3	2	1	Uncooperative
Supportive	8	7	6	5	4	3	2	1	Hostile
Boring	1	2	3	4	5	6	7	8	Interesting
Quarrelsome	1	2	3	4	5	6	7	8	Harmonious
Self-assured	8	7	6	5	4	3	2	1	Hesitant
Efficient	8	7	6	5	4	3	2	1	Inefficient
Gloomy	1	2	3	4	5	6	7	8	Cheerful
Open	8	7	6	5	4	3	2	1	Guarded

Source: Adapted from Fred E. Fiedler, *A Theory of Leadership Effectiveness* (New York: McGraw-Hill, 1967), p. 41. Used by permission.

Leader-Employee Relationship The leadership situation is more favorable for leaders who have strong employee support because they get along well with the employees and the work group respects them. This aspect of the leadership position involves both factors in the leadership process.

Task Structure Leaders enjoy a more favorable situation if they know exactly what to do and how to do it. A high degree of structure in the job—clear goals and tasks that can be easily evaluated, for example—makes this possible. It is hard to evaluate performance of unstructured tasks. This is part of the situation factor discussed earlier as part of the leadership process.

Leader's Position of Power Leaders in whom the firm vests the power to reward and punish subordinates have a more favorable situation than others. Pay, working conditions, and disciplinary measures can all be used as means of punishment and reward. Fiedler's theory can be modeled as shown in Figure 14.1.

The three types of situations—favorable, moderately favorable, and unfavorable—are indicated just below the figure. As you can see, managers with task motivation (a low LPC score) are most effective in moderately favorable conditions. Managers with relationship motivation are most effective in the most favorable and least favorable conditions.

Fiedler believes that it is easier to change the work situation than to change the leader's motivation and behavior. If the work situation is too difficult to change, he advises transferring the leader to a job situation that matches his or her motivation and behavior.

The research support for Fiedler's theory has been mixed but more positive than negative. Again, his model considers more of the factors in the leadership process than other theories. Still, it does not directly deal with leader traits other than one facet of motivation; it does not address work group characteristics other than how the group reacts to the leader; and it does not consider two of the three situational factors, the organization's expectations and the opportunity to lead.

Perhaps research support will not be substantial until we have a leadership theory which models all these factors. Figure 14.2 presents Jeffrey Barrow's summary of all the factors which could affect leadership effectiveness.[15] Note that on the left the factors affecting the leader

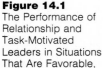

Figure 14.1
The Performance of Relationship and Task-Motivated Leaders in Situations That Are Favorable, Moderately Favorable, and Unfavorable.

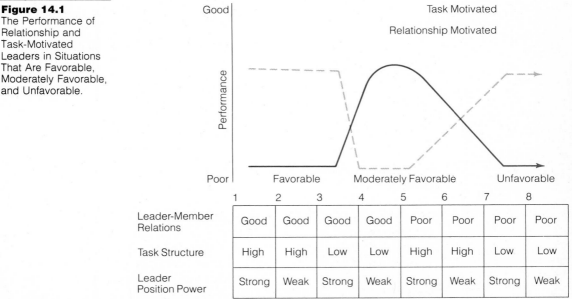

	1	2	3	4	5	6	7	8
Leader-Member Relations	Good	Good	Good	Good	Poor	Poor	Poor	Poor
Task Structure	High	High	Low	Low	High	High	Low	Low
Leader Position Power	Strong	Weak	Strong	Weak	Strong	Weak	Strong	Weak

Source: Adapted by permission of the publisher from "The Leadership Game: Matching the Man to the Situation," by Fred E. Fiedler, *Organizational Dynamics*, Winter 1976, © 1976 by AMACOM, a division of American Management Associations, page 11. All rights reserved.

Figure 14.2
Leadership
Effectiveness
Framework

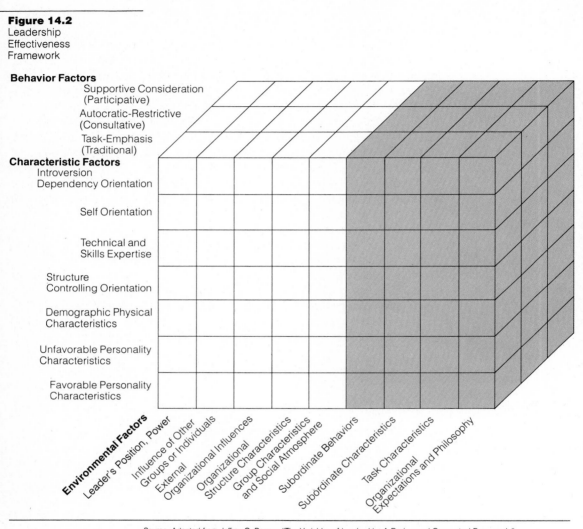

Behavior Factors

Supportive Consideration
(Participative)

Autocratic-Restrictive
(Consultative)

Task-Emphasis
(Traditional)

Characteristic Factors

Introversion
Dependency Orientation

Self Orientation

Technical and
Skills Expertise

Structure
Controlling Orientation

Demographic Physical
Characteristics

Unfavorable Personality
Characteristics

Favorable Personality
Characteristics

Environmental Factors

Leader's Position, Power

Influence of Other
Groups or Individuals

External
Organizational Influences

Organizational
Structure Characteristics

Group Characteristics
and Social Atmosphere

Subordinate Behaviors

Subordinate Characteristics

Task Characteristics

Organizational
Expectations and Philosophy

Source: Adapted from Jeffrey C. Barrow, "The Variables of Leadership: A Review and Conceptual Framework,"
Academy of Management Review 2 (April 1977): 242. Used by permission.

(personality, abilities, and background factors) are shown. The environmental factors—a combination of work group and situational factors—appear across the top. And on the bottom axis are presented what Barrow calls leader behavior factors and what most other theorists call leadership style.

How a manager exercises leadership is leadership style.

Leadership Styles

On the first page of this chapter, I pointed out that most managers can be successful leaders if they will match their *personality, preferences, and leadership abilities* with the *right work group* in the *right leadership situation.* All successful leaders are skilled managers of planning, organizing, and staffing. What I hope to do now is help you understand how and when to apply some of the theories of leadership so as to become a successful leader.

The first step in becoming a successful leader is to determine what your preferences are. One way of doing this is to obtain your LPC score. Table 14.3 is another instrument that may help. Table 14.4 provides an interpretation of the score you obtain in Table 14.3.

Table 14.3
Attitudes Influencing Leadership Style

In the section below you will see a series of statements. Please indicate your agreement or disagreement. Use the scale below each statement. For example:

It is easier to work in cool weather than in hot.

:	x	:	:	:
Strongly Agree	Agree	Undecided	Disagree	Strongly Disagree

If you think it is easier to work in cool weather, put an (X) above "agree"; if you think it is much easier to work in cool weather, put a mark above "strongly agree." If you think it doesn't matter, put a mark over "undecided" and so on. Put your mark in a space, not on the boundaries.

There are no right or wrong answers. We are interested in your opinion about the statements which follow.

1. The average human being prefers to be directed, wishes to avoid responsibility, and has relatively little ambition.

:	:	:	:	:
Strongly Agree	Agree	Undecided	Disagree	Strongly Disagree

2. Leadership skills can be acquired by most people regardless of their particular inborn traits and abilities.

:	:	:	:	:
Strongly Agree	Agree	Undecided	Disagree	Strongly Disagree

3. The use of rewards (pay, promotion, etc.) and punishment (failure to promote, etc.) is not the best way to get subordinates to do their work.

:	:	:	:	:
Strongly Agree	Agree	Undecided	Disagree	Strongly Disagree

4. In a work situation, if the subordinates cannot influence me then I lose some influence on them.

:	:	:	:	:
Strongly Agree	Agree	Undecided	Disagree	Strongly Disagree

5. A good leader should give detailed and complete instructions to subordinates rather than giving them merely general directions and depending upon their initiative to work out the details.

:	:	:	:	:
Strongly Agree	Agree	Undecided	Disagree	Strongly Disagree

6. Group goal setting offers advantages that cannot be obtained by individual goal setting.

:	:	:	:	:
Strongly Agree	Agree	Undecided	Disagree	Strongly Disagree

7. A superior should give his subordinates only that information which is necessary for them to do their immediate tasks.

:	:	:	:	:
Strongly Agree	Agree	Undecided	Disagree	Strongly Disagree

8. The superior's authority over his subordinates in an organization is primarily economic.

:	:	:	:	:
Strongly Agree	Agree	Undecided	Disagree	Strongly Disagree

Source: Adapted by permission from *Managerial Thinking*, by Mason Haire et al. Copyright © 1966, appendix 1. Reprinted by permission of John Wiley & Sons, Inc.

Table 14.4
Scoring of Attitudes
Influencing
Leadership Style
Scale

Question	Strongly Agree	Undecided	Strongly Disagree
1.	Traditional	Consultative	Participative
2.	Participative	Consultative	Traditional
3.	Participative	Consultative	Traditional
4.	Participative	Consultative	Traditional
5.	Traditional	Consultative	Participative
6.	Participative	Consultative	Traditional
7.	Traditional	Consultative	Partlcipative
8.	Traditional	Consultative	Participative

Five to eight items in any one of the three categories—participative, consultative, or traditional—is a strong indication of your managerial style. As you read the next few pages, perhaps you can relate the material covered to your own attitudes and obtain some picture of what your leadership style is likely to be. As should be obvious, the managerial attitudes that constitute a person's leadership style have a strong influence on how he or she will handle a managerial job.

The *crucial* managerial attitude or belief that influences leadership style concerns *the role of the manager in relation to that of the employees.* The manager who sees the employees as people who do the work under his or her direction is traditional. The leader who sees himself or herself as a colleague of the work group with certain extra responsibilities and different duties is participative.

Most managers do have a predominant, or core, style. It is the one they are most comfortable with. They will use this style much of the time. However, *all but a few managers have the ability to vary their style to fit varying circumstances or different people.* For example, a participative leader may become traditional and make all decisions, issue orders, and so forth in a crisis. Or a traditional leader may operate with a participative style in dealing with some especially trusted employees. Flexibility of this sort contributes to a manager's effectiveness.

I am about to discuss and distinguish between three leadership styles. The distinctions I will make are arbitrary. In fact, the styles are a continuum; that is, they blend into each other, as the schematic drawing by Robert Tannenbaum and Warren Schmidt in Figure 14.3 indicates.[16] Note that the manager's leadership style over nonmanagers is based on the freedom to act (a similar construct to Fiedler's favorableness).

Tannenbaum and Schmidt's continuum portrays how the leadership style that emerges is influenced by the relationship (they say interdependency) between the managerial and nonmanagerial employees. This relationship is also affected by the organizational environment and the larger society in which the organization operates, however. The attitudes and values of the organization and the society influence the relationships between managers and employees.

As Tannenbaum and Schmidt see it, the choice of a leadership style

Figure 14.3
Continuum of
Manager-Nonmanager
Behavior

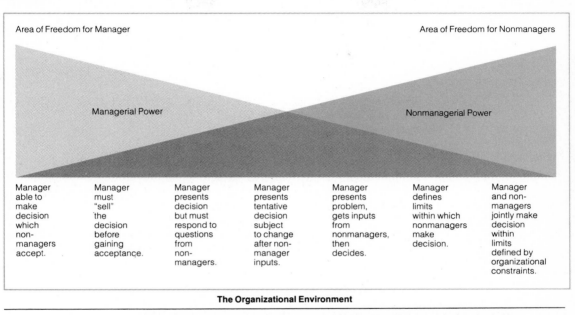

Area of Freedom for Manager

Area of Freedom for Nonmanagers

Managerial Power

Nonmanagerial Power

| Manager able to make decision which non-managers accept. | Manager must "sell" the decision before gaining acceptance. | Manager presents decision but must respond to questions from non-managers. | Manager presents tentative decision subject to change after non-manager inputs. | Manager presents problem, gets inputs from nonmanagers, then decides. | Manager defines limits within which nonmanagers make decision. | Manager and non-managers jointly make decision within limits defined by organizational constraints. |

The Organizational Environment

Sources: Adapted by permission from Robert Tannenbaum and Warren Schmidt, "How to Choose a Leadership Pattern," *Harvard Business Review* 36 (March–April 1958): 96; and "How to Choose a Leadership Pattern" 51 (May–June 1973): 164. Copyright © 1958, 1973 by the President and Fellows of Harvard College; all rights reserved.

depends on the situation, the managers, and the nonmanagers (work group), the three factors in the leadership process. Let me summarize what they have said, using my terms, *traditional, participative,* and *consultative.* This may help you decide what leadership style suits you best.

The Manager (Leader)

1. The greater the leader's preference for a particular style, the more he or she should use that style.
2. The greater the leader's belief in the nonmanagers' competence, the more likely he or she is to use the participative style.
3. The greater the leader's need to control the situation, the more likely he or she is to choose the traditional style.

The Nonmanagers (Work Group)

1. The more competent the nonmanagers, the more likely the use of the participative style.

2. The greater the nonmanagers' desire for independence and responsibility, the more likely the use of the participative style.
3. The more the nonmanagers identify with the objectives of the organization and believe its problems are important, the more likely the use of the participative style.

The Situation

1. The greater the size of the work group, the more likely the use of the traditional style.
2. The greater the geographic spread of the work group, the more likely the use of the traditional style.
3. The greater the time pressure to make decisions, the more likely the use of the traditional style.
4. The more effective and cohesive the work group, the greater the likelihood of the participative style.
5. The more complex the problem, the greater the likelihood of the participative style.

The consultative approach is chosen when the above factors contradict each other, show a mixed tendency toward the other two styles, and when the leader has a preference for that style. Now let's discuss these different styles.

Traditional Leadership Style

The most common leadership style in the United States and Canada is the *traditional style*. Our discussion of some of the theories of leadership has already touched on this style. For example, in leader behavior theory, a leader who ranks high in initiation of structure and low in consideration is a traditional leader. In Fiedler's contingency theory, a leader whose highest priority of goals is accomplishing the task is a traditional leader. And the managers described on the left side of Tannenbaum and Schmidt's manager-nonmanager continuum in Figure 14.3 are traditional. K mart management appears to operate in this traditional style. Most decisions are made at headquarters. Other units follow the lead of headquarters. A. Robert Abboud, chief executive officer of First Chicago Corporation, also seems to follow this style.

Robert McMurray has characterized the traditional leader as a "benevolent autocrat."[17] How does a traditional leader operate? Basically, the traditional leader believes that he or she is the boss, whose job it is to make decisions because many or most employees either cannot or do not want to take the responsibility. So traditional leaders make most decisions for themselves. They organize the job, communicate primarily through a chain of command, and pride themselves on designing the job and employment relationship so that the employees know what is expected of them and what will happen if they do not perform.

This does not mean that traditional leaders are unpleasant or mean, though participative leaders often stereotype them that way. (Note the stereotypical traditional leader in the cartoon here.) Douglas McGregor, a critic of the traditional style, believed that traditional leaders adhere to the following three propositions:[18]

1. Management is responsible for organizing the elements of productive enterprise—money, materials, equipment, people—in the interest of the organization's economic ends.
2. With respect to people, this is a process of directing their efforts, motivating them, controlling their actions, and modifying their behavior to fit the needs of the organization.
3. Without this active intervention by management, people would be passive—even resistant—to organizational needs.

The following three sections indicate how traditional leaders feel about their style of management as it relates to the factors of the leadership process.

The Nature of Leaders

The traditional style is very rewarding to leaders. That is why they like it. It takes care of their basic needs, of course, but by making them the center of

Drawing by Charles Saxon; © 1975 The New Yorker Magazine, Inc.

"If there are any calls, Miss Gilmore, I'll be on the fifteenth floor, breathing down some necks."

attraction and power it also fulfills their recognition, esteem, and self-actualization needs better than other styles.

In addition, the traditional style is the only one that makes sense to the managerial personality. As Robert McMurray has put it,

[Managers] are more likely to be hard-driving egocentric entrepreneurs who have come up in the business in careers where they had to keep power in their own hands: or they may be the victors in the give and take, no-quarter in-fighting for positions of power. . . . Such men cannot ordinarily bring themselves to use any concept of management other than a purely authoritarian one. . . . I suspect that no more than 10 percent of business executives . . . can use a [participative style].[19]

To be other than traditional, it would appear, one has to be manipulative.

It has been argued that managers using the traditional style make better decisions. Only the traditional style provides the uniformity that results from decision making by people who know the "big picture." Less than this, advocates of the traditional style maintain, leads to chaos or costly repercussions.

The Nature of Employees (and Work Groups)

Employees are raised in a society in which most leaders follow the traditional model: parents, teachers, priests, bus drivers, to cite just a few instances. So employees generally expect traditional leadership at work and work better when they get what they expect.

Moreover, employees can be lazy. It has been estimated that fewer than 25 percent of all employees can operate responsibly with the other styles of leadership. The rest want to know what to do and what is expected of them.

In addition, the traditional style takes care of employees' physiological and security needs. That is, if you do what the boss wants, you get paid well and keep your job. Everyone has basic needs to satisfy. Not everyone wants to exercise the higher needs at work, and the participative style is oriented toward satisfying the higher needs.

The Situation

Many jobs are unpleasant because of technological and cost considerations. Only a traditional leadership style can deal efficiently with employees working on unpleasant jobs.

Moreover, the traditional style is quicker. Decisions made by a good traditional leader will always be speedier than those made in a liberal style.

The traditional style is also simpler and easier to use than the others. The leader plans a structure, and the employees follow the plan.

In addition, the traditional style prevents the excessive duplication that always flows from involving more people in decision making, as the participative and consultative leaders do.

These, then, are the reasons traditional leaders give for using this style. McMurray goes so far as to say that the participative style is probably more humanitarian and more desirable, but it is not as practical or workable. Traditional leaders, aggressive, hard driving, self-reliant, get the work out and do their best to use human relations and build employee confidence in themselves. In sum, again quoting McMurry on behalf of the traditional model,

> [The traditional leader] structures his subordinates' activities for them; he makes the policy decisions which affect them; he keeps them in line and enforces discipline. He is like a good quarterback, who does not ask the line to decide what plays to attempt or what formations to use, but who tells them—and woe betide the hapless player who fails to follow his orders. He may encourage participation in the planning of a course of action, but much less frequently does he do so in its execution. He encourages participation by his subordinates prior to reaching his decision.
>
> I believe that a proper utilization of these insights and a proper application of the principles which grow out of them will result in the maintenance of nearly as high a level of morale, even under continued pressure for production, as is possible where the liked leadership is available.[20]

Consultative Leadership Style

In between the traditional and participative styles is the consultative style of leadership. The statements in the middle of Figure 14.3 describe this style. It is the second most frequently used leadership style.

Basically, the consultative manager functions in one of the three ways described below.

1. The manager prepares preliminary plans, makes preliminary decisions, and designs the organization. Then the manager asks for the employees' advice and counsel. Finally the manager makes the necessary decisions, executes the plans—sometimes accepting the work group's advice and sometimes not—based on the merits of the advice received from all sources, including the employees. Thus the manager consults with all concerned before taking action.
2. The manager divides up the managerial job and responsibilities assigning some parts of it to subordinates (with their consent, of course). These subordinates make their decisions and are responsible for their actions. This is a simplified explanation of a process called *delegation,* which will be discussed in depth shortly. An organization which has decisions made as close to the bottom of the organization as possible is called a *decentralized organization.*
3. The manager uses both of the above approaches.

Degree of Centralization

Degree of centralization is a measure of where decision-making authority is located: centrally (in the home office) or in local units. As indicated previously, an enterprise can place or parcel out decision-making power entirely or mostly at the top—in which case it is characterized by centralization—or it can parcel it out downward with appropriate controls by the delegation process described above.

Some contend that decentralization develops better managers, results in quicker decisions, and allows managers to satisfy their self-actualization and recognition needs. Traditionalists point to the very real costs of developing decentralization controls.

John Pfiffner and Frank Sherwood contend that accepting decentralization amounts to accepting a philosophy of life.[21] Many companies use it, including General Motors, Du Pont, and Sears. But since the evidence does not clearly favor one approach over the other, it makes good sense for an enterprise to use a productive combination of centralization and decentralization. That is, key policy decisions and staff services which yield economies of scale such as research and development, legal functions, and some purchasing are often best centralized. Centralization may also be beneficial if the enterprise is legally required to have uniform policies throughout all its departments and divisions.

Delegation of Authority

Commonly, the consultative leader delegates authority. This approach is traditional in that it assumes that all authority to make decisions resides in the leader. It is participative in that it recognizes the contributions dedicated and intelligent employees can make if given the chance.

Delegation is the achievement by a manager of specific, predetermined objectives for which the manager has final accountability by empowering and motivating subordinates to accomplish all or part of the specific results.

The specific results for which the subordinates are made accountable are clearly delineated in advance in terms of output required and time allowed, and the subordinates' progress is monitored continuously during the time period.[22] Delegation, therefore, requires that responsibility be clear, that those performing the duty be held accountable, and that managers monitor the results of delegation. Ideally, delegation takes place for the following reasons:

- Those who accept the delegated duties can do the job as well or better than the superior.
- The superior can be free to concentrate on more important duties or tasks for which he or she is better qualified.

Drawing by Whitney Darrow; © 1969 The New Yorker Magazine, Inc.

"To my mind, the secret of executive performance is the ability to delegate authority. For instance, nothing ever reaches this desk."

- Delegation helps develop the abilities of subordinates.
- Subordinates rewarded for performing delegated responsibilities well can achieve greater satisfaction.

Of course, some managers take delegation too far, as the cartoon indicates. According to Dale McConkey, delegation can fail for a number of reasons, which are listed below:[23]

- The duties or responsibilities delegated are not clearly understood by those involved.
- The time dimension of performance is not clear.
- The subordinate is delegated the responsibility to do something but not the authority or power base to get it done. (See final section of Chapter 15 for more on this.)
- Poor monitoring, feedback, and control systems give no indication that things are going wrong until it is too late.

The manager who adheres to the following principles, McConkey maintains, will be able to delegate responsibility effectively:[24]

1. Maintain control without stifling subordinates by establishing and using broad controls. (Often reluctance to delegate and to trust subordinates can be traced back to deficiencies in planning and control skills in the leader.)

2. Do not check constantly to see if subordinates are making mistakes. Continual checking is not a part of true delegation.
3. Determine what decisions can be best and properly made by subordinates and give them the authority to make these. This will allow you to concentrate your efforts on the crucial aspects of your position.
4. Discuss and try other people's ideas.

If properly designed and implemented, delegation can be effective and is a useful technique for the consultative leader.

Participative Leadership Style

The final leadership style, used by perhaps 10 percent of managers or in about 10 percent of decisions and managerial actions, is the participative style. The leader who chooses a participative style exhibits a high degree of consideration according to leader behavior theory. In Fiedler's model, the chief goal of the participative leader is interpersonal relationships. The descriptions on the right side of Figure 14.3 (Tannenbaum and Schmidt's continuum of manager-nonmanager behavior) fit participative leaders. The manager and nonmanager make decisions *jointly* within the limits defined by organization constraints. Jointly, they set objectives, draw up plans, organize, design control systems, and in general, manage.

As James MacGregor Burns described it, the role of the great leader is not diminished by a participative style—it "is only demythicized and demystified. That role is all the more legitimate and powerful if top leaders help make their followers into leaders. Only by standing on *their* shoulders can true greatness in leadership be achieved."[25] And M. Sami Kassem has cited Leo Tolstoy's insights into leadership expressed in *War and Peace*.[26] Tolstoy's message was that Napoleon, the traditional leader, failed and Kutuzov became the real leader because man must be free to live: "All man's efforts, all his impulses to life are only efforts to increase his freedom of action." Participative leaders allow their subordinates to increase their freedom.

Larry Greiner asked several hundred managers how participative leaders behave.[27] In their responses they described the participative leader as one who:

- gives subordinates a *share* in decision making.
- keeps subordinates informed of the true situation, good or bad, under all circumstances.
- stays aware of the state of the organization's morale and does everything possible to make it good.
- is easily approachable.
- counsels, trains, and develops subordinates.
- communicates effectively with subordinates.
- shows thoughtfulness and consideration of others.
- is willing to make changes in ways of doing things.

- is willing to support subordinates even when they make mistakes.
- expresses appreciation when a subordinate does a good job.

(The behaviors are listed in order according to the frequency with which they were mentioned; the first one was mentioned most often, the last one least often.)

Some firms—like Diamond Shamrock, Union Carbide, and others— have tried participative leadership. One of the most persuasive exponents of this style is Rensis Likert.[28] Likert's model of the different leadership styles has four components, which he calls systems. System 1 is a very negative, dictatorial style of leadership, an extreme version of the traditional style, based on mistrust and even fear of subordinates. System 2 roughly corresponds to the traditional style, System 3 to the consultative, and System 4 to the participative. Table 14.5 presents a comparison of the four systems with regard to a number of aspects of the management process.

Likert and his associates have done a great deal of research in the hope of demonstrating that System 4 (participative leadership) is more effective for the organization and more satisfying for the employee than the other leadership styles. But the results of his work have been mixed.

Industrial Democracy: The Ultimate Participative Style

The preceding discussion assumed that the individual manager is in a position to decide whether he or she will use a traditional or a participative leadership style. However, in many leadership situations the employees have a legal right to participate in decisions. This phenomenon is called *industrial democracy*. In its most participative form, the employees actually choose the manager (as in the Yugoslav self-management system). The degree of employee participation in such systems varies, as Figure 14.4 illustrates.

Obviously, if you are the manager of the employee-owned asbestos mine in Vermont or the employee-owned plywood plant in Oregon or the Yugoslav enterprise, you will be involved in a participative management style. If you are a manager in an industrial democracy system, you are legally required to involve employees in decision making, and this is likely to result in a participative leadership style.

Some of the participation schemes presented in Figure 14.3 have been around for many years. Whether we will see more of them in the future is anybody's guess.

Power, Influence, and Leadership

Throughout the chapter, I have referred to how much influence and power the leader has. This was explicit in Fiedler's theory in which leader position power is one of the conditions favorable for effective leadership. Although

Table 14.5
Organizational and
Performance
Characteristics of
Different Management
Systems

Organizational Variable	System 1	System 2	System 3	System 4
Leadership processes used				
Extent to which superiors have confidence and trust in *subordinates*	Have no confidence and trust in subordinates	Have condescending confidence and trust, such as master has to servant	Substantial but not complete confidence and trust; still wishes to keep control of decisions	Complete confidence and trust in all matters
Extent to which superiors behave so that subordinates feel free to discuss important things about their jobs with their immediate superior	Subordinates do not feel at all free to discuss things about the job with their superior	Subordinates do not feel very free to discuss things about the job with their superior	Subordinates feel rather free to discuss things about the job with their superior	Subordinates feel completely free to discuss things about the job with their superior
Extent to which immediate superior in solving job problems generally tries to get subordinates' ideas and opinions and make constructive use of them	Seldom gets ideas and opinions of subordinates in solving job problems	Sometimes gets ideas and opinions of subordinates in solving job problems	Usually gets ideas and opinions and usually tries to make constructive use of them	Always gets ideas and opinions and always tries to make constructive use of them
Character of motivational forces				
Manner in which motives are used	Fear, threats, punishment, and occasional rewards	Rewards and some actual or potential punishment	Rewards, occasional punishment, and some involvement	Economic rewards based on compensation system developed through participation; group participation and involvement in setting goals, improving methods, appraising progress toward goals, etc.
Amount of responsibility felt by each member of organization for achieving organization's goals	High levels of management feel responsibility; lower levels feel less; rank and file feel little and welcome opportunity to behave in ways to defeat organization's goals	Managerial personnel usually feel responsibility; rank and file usually feel relatively little responsibility for achieving organization's goals	Substantial proportion of personnel, especially at high levels, feel responsibility and generally behave in ways to achieve the organization's goals	Personnel at all levels feel real responsibility for organization's goals and behave in ways to implement them

Table 14.5
continued

Organizational Variable	System 1	System 2	System 3	System 4
Character of interaction-influence process				
Amount and character of interaction	Little interaction and always with fear and distrust	Little interaction and usually with some condescension by superiors; fear and caution by subordinates	Moderate interaction, often with fair amount of confidence and trust	Extensive, friendly interaction with high degree of confidence and trust
Amount of cooperative teamwork present	None	Relatively little	A moderate amount	Very substantial amount throughout the organization
Character of decision-making process				
At what level in organization are decisions formally made?	Bulk of decisions at top of organization	Policy at top, many decisions within prescribed framework made at lower levels	Broad policy and general decisions at top, more specific decisions at lower levels	Decision making widely done throughout organization, although well integrated through linking process provided by overlapping groups
To what extent are decision makers aware of problems, particularly those at lower levels in the organization?	Often are unaware or only partially aware	Aware of some, unaware of others	Moderately aware of problems	Generally quite well aware of problems
Extent to which technical and professional knowledge is used in decision making	Used only if possessed at higher levels	Much of what is available in higher and middle levels is used	Much of what is available in higher, middle, and lower levels is used	Most of what is available anywhere within the organization is used
To what extent are subordinates involved in decisions related to their work?	Not at all	Never involved in decisions; occasionally consulted	Usually are consulted but ordinarily not involved in the decision making	Are involved fully in all decisions related to their work
Are decisions made at the best level in the organization so far as the motivational consequences (i.e., does the decision-making process help to create the necessary motivations in those persons who have to carry out the decisions?)	Decision making contributes little or nothing to the motivation to implement the decision, usually yields adverse motivation	Decision making contributes relatively little motivation	Some contribution by decision making to motivation to implement	Substantial contribution by decision-making processes to motivation to implement

Table 14.5
continued

Organizational Variable	System 1	System 2	System 3	System 4
Character of goal setting or ordering				
Manner in which usually done	Orders issued	Orders issued, opportunity to comment may or may not exist	Goals are set or orders issued after discussion with subordinate(s) of problems and planned action	Except in emergencies, goals are usually established by means of group participation
Are there forces to accept, resist, or reject goals?	Goals are overtly accepted but are covertly resisted strongly	Goals are overtly accepted but often covertly resisted to at least a moderate degree	Goals are overtly accepted but at times with some covert resistance	Goals are fully accepted both overtly and covertly
Character of control processes				
Extent to which the review and control functions are concentrated	Highly concentrated in top management	Relatively highly concentrated, with some delegated control to middle and lower levels	Moderate downward delegation of review and control processes; lower as well as higher levels feel responsible	Quite widespread responsibility for review and control, with lower units at times imposing more rigorous reviews and tighter controls than top management
Extent to which there is an informal organization present and supporting or opposing goals of formal organization	Informal organization present and opposing goals of formal organization	Informal organization usually present and partially resisting goals	Informal organization may be present and may either support or partially resist goals of formal organization	Informal and formal organization are one and the same; hence all social forces support efforts to achieve organization's goals
Extent to which control data (e.g., accounting, productivity, cost, etc.) are used for self-guidance or group problem solving by managers and non-supervisory employees; or used by superiors in a punitive, policing manner	Used for policing and in punitive manner	Used for policing coupled with reward and punishment, sometimes punitively; used somewhat for guidance but in accord with orders	Largely used for policing with emphasis usually on reward but with some punishment; used for guidance in accord with orders; some use also for self-guidance	Used for self-guidance and for coordinated problem solving and guidance; not used punitively

Source: Rensis Likert, *The Human Organization: Its Management and Value* (New York: McGraw-Hill, 1967), pp. 4–10. Reprinted by permission.

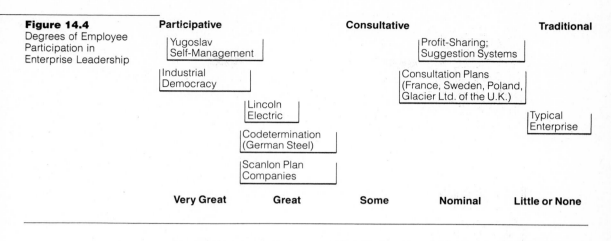

Figure 14.4
Degrees of Employee Participation in Enterprise Leadership

I have hinted at and touched on the subject, it makes sense at this point to clarify just how managers acquire power and influence and how they use it.

Sources of Leadership Influence and Power

Let's start with the position that to be a leader is to be able to influence subordinates at work. Political scientists, historians, sociologists, management specialists, and many others have discussed the sources of influence a manager or leader has at hand. Table 14.6 presents seven sources of influence discussed here and relates them to the terms important theorists have applied to them.

Legitimate Power

A person exercises *legitimate power* or authority if he or she is appointed to a leadership position by a "legitimate" authority. Cultural norms and values in most societies reinforce the idea that an officer has a right to lead troops, a manager to lead employees. This source of power or influence is available to all managers; managers receive legitimate power when they are appointed and retained.

Legitimate power has its greatest impact when employees accept the leader and when they are positively motivated to achieve the enterprise's objectives. When these conditions are present legitimate power is a strong influence base for the leader. Note, however, that if legitimate power is not reinforced by other sources of power, it can be less influential, and the organization's objectives may suffer as a result.

Monetary/Reward Power

A leader can influence some employees by using the pay system to reward or punish them. Employees who accept the objectives of the leader and

Table 14.6
Sources of Power and Influence Available to Leaders

Power Theorists and Their Terms

Source of Influence	Lasswell and Kaplan	French and Raven	Weber	Classical Management Theorists (Fayol, etc.)	Presthus	Bierstadt	Clark	Cartwright
Legitimate power		legitimate power	(legal) bureaucratic authority		legitimacy of formal position		constitutional officialdom	
Skill/expertise power	skill	expert power		experience, intelligence	authority of expertise	knowledge, skill, competence, ability	knowledge, expertise, power of information	expertise power
Monetary power		reward power					power over pay and jobs	positive sanctions
Affection power	affection for leader	referent power	patrimonial authority		power of rapport		popularity	
Respect (traditional) power			(traditional) patriarchal authority, charismatic authority	reputation of leader	legitimacy of deference	prestige of leader	social standing of leader	magnetism
Rectitude power				moral worth of leader				
Coercive power	physical power	coercive power				dominance		physical power

produce the quality and quantity of output desired receive higher financial rewards (and similar rewards such as better benefits and perquisites). This source of influence is available to most managers and entrepreneurs.

Monetary/reward power taps the physiological and security needs of the employees and the power needs of the leader. For it to be effective, money must be a strongly desired outcome for the employee *and* the reward system must directly tie pay with accomplishment of objectives. It is not always easy to get these conditions to coincide. The work group can offset monetary power by isolating and "punishing" those who respond to it. If the group is cohesive and influential, it can negate the influence of the leader's monetary or reward power.

Skill/Expertise Power

When a person's behavior indicates that he or she really knows how to get the job done (not just the everyday tasks but the tough and tricky ones as well), that person has influence. He or she can help others achieve their objectives. In such a situation group members will defer to the expert.

Ideally the manager has enough competence to have expertise power. To the extent, however, that the manager must depend on another person for expertise, that individual will have power over the manager and the work group.

Affection Power

Surely you have belonged to groups in which the leader was elected because "everyone likes her." When you like people, it is easier for them to influence you. Many people become leaders because they develop the ability to get employees to like them. This provides the basis for their influence. Ralph Stogdill has summarized the research in this area as follows:

[Research] suggests that being liked and accepted by group members gives
the leader more influence than if he [or she] is not liked or accepted.
Leaders high in power are better liked and accepted than those low in
power. Members desire acceptance by high power members of the
group.[29]

So if a leader can be not just accepted but liked by employees, peers, and superiors, he or she will have more influence over them.

Respect Power

Some leadership experts do not separate affection power from respect power. But surely you have been influenced by individuals whom you respected but did not like. In many cases you respected them for some of the reasons listed above (skill, for example).

Rectitude Power

In addition to respect power, a few theorists have speculated that some people are influential because they provide a moral example. These two bases of influence have not been studied in much detail, however.

Coercive Power

There are several varieties of coercive power. The first is physical. The slave laborers in Hitler's World War II factories or in the Soviet Union's Gulag Archipelago as described by Alexander Solzhenitsyn had direct experience with this. The closest equivalent in most work organizations is the power to fire an employee or to suspend him or her without pay. Taking away a person's job has many physical and psychological effects, as we have seen. Coercive power, then, appears to satisfy the leader's need for power and to affect the employees' lower (physiological and security) needs.

Coercive power does tend to induce compliance if the work group is unable to resist it. But even in Hitler's slave labor factories the "workers" sabotaged the output and worked very slowly by taking no iniative and requiring detailed instructions from the supervisors. In most work situations in the United States and Canada, coercive power is the leader's last resort. It should be used sparingly and fairly in order to avoid activating group cohesiveness in opposition to the leader. (Fortunately, situations such as the one shown in the following cartoon are relatively rare.)

The Political Environment of Leadership[30]

Besides being a formal framework for operations, organizations are political structures. Politics plays a significant role in a manager's life. Organizations distribute authority and set the stage for the exercise of power. They provide *opportunities* for managers to develop careers and platforms for the expression of individual interests and motives.

Do power and politics affect leaders? In the business context, politics involves reciprocity—"you help me and I'll help you." It also involves conflict over whose preferences will prevail in the determination of objectives, resource allocation, policy, and other areas.

Abraham Zaleznik says that politics in organizations comes from the following factors:

1. *Scarcity and competition* Managers cannot obtain all the power they want because authority is distributed. To get more power, they must cause someone else to give up some.

"At our last meeting eight members of the Board disagreed with
you and you said they'd be sorry."

2. *Constituents and clients* A manager cannot coordinate a position without
   the affirmation of subordinates and clients. And, in fact, a leader can
   become isolated and impotent if subordinates and clients withdraw
   affirmation and support.
3. *Power and action* The quantity of formal authority, expertise and
   reputation for competence, and the personal attractiveness of the
   manager determine how much power he or she has and what action he
   or she can initiate.

**Power is defined as the capacity to influence the conduct of others in a
desired manner and in such a way that the individual or group's own
conduct is not modified.**

I have just discussed theories of leadership as an important organizational
and managerial concern. But what is the basis upon which an effective
leader functions? A leader functions by using the various influence
mechanisms discussed in the previous section. These leadership influences
must take place within the political environment of the organization.
Recent literature views the leader as part of a political system where
politics connotes the use of authority and power to define goals, directions,
and other major parameters of the organization. Anthony Jay has
expressed this relationship between management and political action quite
strongly.

The root of the matter is that the great modern corporations are so similar
to independent or semi-independent states of the past that they can only
be fully understood in terms of political and constitutional history and
management can only be properly understood as a branch of
government.

Jay's statement is *extreme*. Nonetheless, in order to understand realistically
how to exist in an organization as an effective leader, a knowledge of
politics is a prerequisite. To function in the political sphere of organiza-

tions the leader needs to develop political expertise and tactics. A large part of these tactics are concerned with bargaining.

Bargaining is the process whereby two or more parties attempt to settle what each shall give and take, or perform and receive, in a transaction between them.

A set of bargaining tactics suggested by John Miner will be elaborated in the following chapter, which examines how managers can develop effective relationships with their superiors and colleagues.[33] Of course, as a manager you will sometimes have to function as a politician, so you may be interested in the set of guidelines for increasing your personal power developed by Walter Reichman and Marguerite Levy, which are presented in Table 14.7.[34]

The Limits of Power

The discussion so far has centered on how to acquire power or influence and how to use politics effectively. I cannot leave this subject without making several important points. First and foremost, be cautious in using the above guidelines in seeking and exercising personal power. As Lord Acton said, "Power corrupts; absolute power corrupts absolutely." How right he was! The American Constitution has checks and balances built into it to try to prevent the concentration of power in one branch of government or in the hands of any individual. Despite some close calls, this approach has proven fairly effective.

Most managers operate without such obvious checks and balances. Some abuse their power. But remember, employees can get back at such managers—they can quit, be absent, sabotage plans, paint the numerals on their tank, or report their activities to their boss or to Jack Anderson. This is called "blowing the whistle," and well-known examples include the

---

Table 14.7
Guidelines for
Increasing Personal
Power

1. Realistically assess the power you already hold.
2. Gain the support of other people.
3. Develop specializations and expertise where others need help.
4. Create a need for your specialized resource.
5. Form a wide range of working relationships and associations and make them known.
6. Conceal the extent to which another person's responses reward or punish you.
7. Minimize the pain of criticism.
8. Get complete information about the motives, knowledge, understanding, and attitudes of those with whom you are trying to increase your power.
9. Ingratiate yourself.
10. Become a part of the group before initiating innovations.

Source: Adapted by permission from Walter Reichman and Marguerite Levy, "Personal Power Enhancement: A Way to Executive Success," *Management Review* 66 (March 1977): 28–34.

aircraft brake scandal, the electrical conspiracy, and the Andersonville trial.

Power is an interesting phenomenon. It consumes some leaders. Once they have it, they will do almost anything to keep it. Others seem to be able to handle it. They are better people to work for, and they make more long-run contributions to organizational objectives. Really great leaders are able to separate the power associated with the office from themselves. Harry Truman is famous for constantly differentiating between the power of the presidency and his power as an individual. He viewed himself as a temporary occupant of the position (and of the White House) and realized that the deference given him as president was given just for a while. This came home very clearly the day after he left the White House. A reporter asked him, in effect, "What did you do today?" implying that he still had many world-shaking duties to perform. Truman's reply: "I took the suitcases up to the attic."

One of the strengths of our political system is the short tenure of its officeholders. One of the problems of the nonelective officials in many enterprises is that unless there is mandatory retirement they stay on and on and on, and soon the power of the office becomes the power of the person, a situation that can easily lead to abuses of power.

You must be aware of the limitations on managerial power if you are to perform effectively. It is true that some company politicians are interested in power alone. Most, however, are strong supporters of a "cause." This may be a more equitable EEO program, earning a larger market share, or getting better benefits for their employees. Usually, too, loyalty to a department or a profession serves to counterbalance more personal power seeking.

In sum, your career depends on securing power and operating realistically in the political environment of the organization. Power transforms individual interests into coordinated activities that accomplish variable ends. The effective leader incorporates power into her or his self-image, but the base of that power is in the political structure. It is derived from:

1. The quantity of formal authority inherent in each position relative to other positions.
2. The authority earned through professional abilities and a reputation for competence.
3. The respect and affection linked to an attractive personality.

Remember, organizations are political structures because people compete for power in an economy of scarcity. Underlying all the bases of social power is the consent of those over whom the power is exercised. If the leader is to be effective, those being led must grant their consent or respect or let the leader influence them. This is a significant point for leaders and would-be leaders to remember.

Summary

Chapter 14 begins the section dealing with the leadership process and the various relationships it involves. *Leadership* is a set of interpersonal behaviors designed to influence employees to cooperate in the achievement of objectives. It is the means used to accomplish organizational objectives. Leadership, or influencing people effectively, is a function of (1) the leader, (2) the work group, and (3) the situation.

What motivates a person to become a leader? According to Gibb, the motives of leadership include economic reward, primitive dominance, power over others, and status needs. Maslow's esteem-recognition and self-actualization needs seem to be significant motivators also.

The leader is the first factor in the leadership process. Study of such leaders as Douglas MacArthur led some theorists to conclude leaders are born (trait theory). Researchers began to try to isolate traits which could be used to identify leaders. This approach failed because others had about the same traits as successful leaders.

The second leadership factor is the match between the leader and the work group. The work group is a very significant influence on the leader. It can reject the leader, sabotage leadership, and lower productivity. Various ways of relating to the work group to enhance the leadership base were explored.

The third factor in the leadership process is the situation. The organization's expectations, the job and its characteristics, and the opportunity to lead—all aspects of the situation—limit or enhance the leader's position.

When the trait theory was found to be inadequate, alternative theories of leadership were developed. Leader behavior theory, which originated at Ohio State University, described two clusters of behavior: (1) consideration and (2) initiation of structure. The most effective leader was thought to be one who exhibited both high levels of consideration and initiation of structure behavior. Other researchers expanded on leader behavior theory, but studies have not overwhelmingly supported it and it does not take into account the situation, the third factor in the leadership process.

Fiedler's contingency theory of leadership states that effectiveness comes from a good match between the leader's objectives and the degree to which the situation permits the leader to control the situation. According to this theory, a leader is motivated by one of two possible top-priority objectives: (1) to accomplish a task or (2) to develop interpersonal relationships. Though research support for the theory is mixed, results are more positive than negative.

To become a successful leader you must become familiar with the available styles of leadership. The *crucial* managerial attitude that influences leadership style is *the role of the manager versus that of the employee.* The manager who sees the employees as working under his or her direction has a *traditional* style. If the leader operates as a colleague of the work group with certain extra responsibilities and duties, the style is *participative*. The *consultative* style is in between the traditional and participative.

The ultimate participative style is industrial democracy. Here the employees have a legal right to participate in decisions. In its most participative form, the employees actually choose the manager.

The final sections of the chapter clarified just how managers acquire power and influence as well as the political aspects of a leader's position in the organization. Leaders derive power and influence from seven sources: legitimate power, monetary/reward power, skill/expertise power, affection power, respect power, rectitude power, and coercive power. This power and authority is distributed throughout the organization in a political fashion.

Politics is the means by which power is distributed in an environment of scarcity and competition. It serves to resolve conflict over whose preferences will prevail in the determination of objectives, resource allocation, and policy, among other things. *Power* is the capacity to influence the conduct of others in a desired manner and in such a way that the individual's or group's own conduct is not modified.

The chapter concluded with a presentation of guidelines to increase personal power and the limits of power. Most managers can be or become successful leaders if they will match their personality and leadership abilities with the right work group in the right leadership situation.

Questions

1. Explain why leadership is a function of the leader, the work group, and the situation.
2. Define *leadership. Formal leader. Informal leader.* Do you think the formal leader and informal leader should be the same person?
3. "Some leaders are born to lead." Which leadership theory holds this? Have results of this approach to leadership been positive?
4. How does the work group affect the leadership process? Describe how you as a leader could try to relate to the work group using Burns's methods.
5. What are the three aspects of the situation that are relevant to the leadership process? Why is each relevant?
6. How does the leader behavior theory differ from the trait theory? How was it extended by Robert House and Alan Filley? Why do you think research support has not been as positive as desired?
7. Explain Fiedler's contingency theory. Do you think it is a valid approach to the leadership process?
8. Three styles of leadership were discussed: traditional, consultative, and participative. Describe each style. What style of leadership will you follow?
9. You are training a new group of middle managers. Explain the sources of influence available to them.

10. Do you believe an organization is a political entity and that you will be involved in political activity as a manager? If so, in what ways will you operate?

Notes

[1]Robert Guest et al., *Organization Change through Effective Leadership* (Englewood Cliffs, N.J.: Prentice-Hall, 1977).

[2]Sally Coltrin and William F. Glueck, "The Effect of Leadership Roles on the Satisfaction and Productivity of University Research Professors," *Academy of Management Journal* 20 (March 1977): 101–116.

[3]Richard Gabriel and Paul Savage, *Crisis in Command* (New York: Hill and Wang, 1978).

[4]Cecil Gibb, "Leadership," in *Handbook of Social Psychology,* ed. Gardner Lindzey and Elliot Aronson (Boston, Mass.: Addison-Wesley, 1969), pp. 877–920; "An Environmental Approach to the Study of Leadership," *Occupational Psychology* 25 (October 1951): 233–248.

[5]Gwen Bagni and Paul Dubov, *Backstairs at the White House* (New York: Bantam Books, 1979).

[6]Paul Hershey and Kenneth Blanchard, *Management of Organizational Behavior* (Englewood Cliffs, N.J.: Prentice-Hall, 1972).

[7]George Graen and James Cashman, "A Role Making Model of Leadership in Formal Organizations," *Organization and Administrative Sciences* 6 (Summer–Fall 1975): 143–165.

[8]James MacGregor Burns, *Leadership* (New York: Harper & Row, 1978).

[9]Gerald R. Salancik et al., "Leadership as an Outcome of Social Structure and Process: A Multidimensional Analysis," *Organization and Administrative Sciences* 6 (Summer–Fall 1975): 81–101.

[10]J. G. Hunt, "Different Non Leader Clarity Sources as Alternatives to Leadership," in *Proceedings of the Twelfth Annual Eastern Academy of Management,* ed. Blair Kolasa (1975); and Richard Osborn and James G. Hunt, "An Adaptive-Reactive Theory of Leadership: The Role of Macro Variables in Leadership Research," *Organization and Administrative Sciences* 6 (Summer–Fall 1975): 27–44.

[11]Ralph Stogdill and Carroll Shartle, *Methods in the Study of Administrative Leadership* (Columbus: Ohio State University, Bureau of Research, 1955).

[12]Robert House, "A Path Goal Theory of Leadership Effectiveness," *Administrative Science Quarterly* 16 (September 1971): 321–338.

[13]Alan Filley, *The Compleat Manager* (Champaign, Ill.: Research Press, 1978), chapter 6.

[14]Fred Fiedler, "The Leadership Game: Matching the Man to the Situation," *Organizational Dynamics* 4 (Winter 1976): 6–16; and *A Theory of Leadership Effectiveness* (New York: McGraw-Hill, 1967). Also Fred Fiedler and Martin Chemers, *Leadership and Effective Management* (Glenview, Ill.: Scott, Foresman, 1974); and Fred E. Fiedler and Albert F. Leister, "Leader Intelligence and Task Performance: A Test of a Multiple Screen Model," *Organizational Behavior and Human Performance* 19 (August 1977): 368–377.

[15]Jeffrey C. Barrow, "The Variables of Leadership: A Review and Conceptual Framework," *Academy of Management Review* 2 (April 1977): 231–251.

[16]Robert Tannenbaum and Warren Schmidt, "How to Choose a Leadership Pattern," *Harvard Business Review* 36 (March–April 1958): 95–101; and "How to Choose a Leadership Pattern," *Harvard Business Review* 51 (May–June 1973): 162–164, 168.

[17]Robert McMurray, *The Maverick Executive* (New York: AMACOM, 1974); and "The Case for Benevolent Autocracy," *Harvard Business Review* 36 (January–February 1958): 82–90.

[18]Douglas McGregor, "The Human Side of Management," *Adventure in Thought and Action: Proceedings of the Fifth Anniversary Convocation of the School of Industrial Management,* Massachusetts Institute of Technology, Cambridge, April 9, 1957, p. 1.

[19]McMurry, "The Case for Benevolent Autocracy," p. 83.

[20]Ibid.

[21]John Pfiffner and Frank Sherwood, *Administrative Organization* (Englewood Cliffs, N.J.: Prentice-Hall, 1960).

[22]This definition and description of the delegation process follows Dale McConkey, *No Nonsense Delegation* (New York: AMACOM, 1974).

[23]Ibid.

[24]Ibid.

[25]Burns, *Leadership.*

[26]M. Sami Kassem, "Tolstoy on Organization," *Business Horizons* 20 (April 1977): 9–15.

[27]Larry Greiner, "What Managers Think of Participative Management," *Harvard Business Review* 51 (March–April 1973): 111–117.

[28]Rensis Likert, *The Human Organization* (New York: McGraw-Hill, 1967).

[29]Ralph Stogdill, *Handbook of Leadership* (New York: Free Press, 1974).

[30]This section was researched and coauthored by Jean Marie Hanebury.

[31]Abraham Zaleznik, "Power and Politics in Organizational Life," *Harvard Business Review* 48 (May–June 1970): 47–60.

[32]Anthony Jay, *Management and Machiavelli* (New York: Holt, Rinehart and Winston, 1967).

[33]John Miner, *The Management Process,* 2d ed. (New York: Macmillan, 1978), chapter 10.

[34]Walter Reichman and Marguerite Levy, "Personal Power Enhancement: A Way to Executive Success," *Management Review* 66 (March 1977): 28–34.

References

Leadership of Employees

Cecil Gibb, "Leadership," in *Handbook of Social Psychology,* ed. Gardner Lindzey and Elliot Aronson (Boston, Mass.: Addison-Wesley, 1969), pp. 877–920; "An Environmental Approach to the Study of Leadership," *Occupational Psychology* 25 (October 1951): 233–248. Ralph Stogdill, *Handbook of Leadership* (New York: Free Press, 1974).

What Is Leadership?

Chester Barnard, "The Nature of Leadership," in *Organization and Management,* ed. Chester Barnard (Cambridge, Mass.: Harvard University Press, 1958), pp. 80–110. Alan Filley, Robert J. House, and Steven Kerr, *Managerial Process and Organizational Behavior* (Glenview, Ill.: Scott, Foresman, 1976).

Why Is Leadership Important?

Orlando Behling and Chester Schriesheim, *Organizational Behavior* (Boston: Allyn and Bacon, 1976). John Campbell et al., *Managerial Behavior* (New York: McGraw-Hill, 1970). Sally Coltrin and William F. Glueck, "The Effect of Leadership Roles on the Satisfaction and Productivity of University Research Professors," *Academy of Management Journal* 20 (March 1977): 101–116. Richard Gabriel and Paul Savage, *Crisis in Command* (New York: Hill and Wang, 1978). Robert Guest et al., *Organization Change through Effective Leadership* (Englewood Cliffs, N.J.: Prentice-Hall, 1977). Greg Oldham, "The Motivational Strategies Used by Supervisors," *Organizational Behavior and Human Performance* 15 (February 1976): 66–86.

Leadership and the Leader

Edwin Ghiselli, *Explorations in Managerial Talent* (Pacific Palisades, Calif.: Goodyear, 1971). Eugene Jennings, *An Anatomy of Leadership: Princes, Heroes and Supermen* (New York: Harper & Bros., 1960). William Manchester, *American Caesar* (Boston: Little, Brown, 1978). Chester Schriesheim et al., "Leadership Theory: Some Implications for Managers," *MSU Business Topics* 26 (Summer 1978): 34–40. Ralph Stogdill, "Historical Trends in Leadership Theory and Research," *Journal of Contemporary Business* 3 (Autumn 1974): 1–17. Victor Vroom, "Leadership," in *Handbook of Industrial and Organizational Psychology,* ed. Marvin Dunnette (Chicago: Rand McNally, 1976), pp. 1527–1551.

Leadership and the Work Group

James MacGregor Burns, *Leadership* (New York: Harper & Row, 1978). George Graen and James Cashman, "A Role Making Model of Leadership in Formal Organizations," *Organization and Administrative Sciences* 6 (Summer–Fall 1975): 143–165. Paul Hershey and Kenneth Blanchard, *Management of Organizational Behavior* (Englewood Cliffs, N.J.: Prentice-Hall, 1972). Ralph Katz, "The Influence of Group Conflict on Leadership Effectiveness," *Organizational Behavior and Human Performance* 20 (December 1977): 265–286. Bayard E. Wynne and Phillip L. Hunsaker, "A Human Information-Processing Approach to the Process of Leadership," *Organization and Administrative Sciences* 6 (Fall–Summer 1975): 7–25. Gary W. Yunker, "Theoretical Frontiers: A Critical Appraisal," *Organization and Administrative Sciences* 6 (Summer–Fall 1975): 45–57.

Leadership and the Situation

J. G. Hunt, "Different Non Leader Clarity Sources as Alternatives to Leadership," in *Proceedings of the Twelfth Annual Eastern Academy of Management,* ed. Blair Kolasa (1975). Richard N. Osborn and James G. Hunt, "An Adaptive-Reactive Theory of Leadership: The Role of Macro Variables in Leadership Research," *Organization and Administrative Sciences* 6 (Summer–Fall 1975): 27–44. Gerald R. Salancik et al., "Leadership as an Outcome of Social Structure and Process: A Multidimensional Analysis," *Organization and Administrative Sciences* 6 (Summer–Fall 1975): 81–101.

Leader Behavior Theory

Carl R. Anderson and Craig Eric Schneier, "Locus of Control, Leader Behavior and Leader Performance among Management Students," *Academy of Management Journal* 21 (December 1978): 690–698. David G. Bowers, "Hierarchy, Function, and the Generalizability of Leadership Practices," *Organization and Administrative Sciences* 6 (Summer–Fall 1975): 167–180. Charles N. Greene, "Empirical Frontiers: A Critical Appraisal," *Organization and Administrative Sciences* 6 (Summer–Fall 1975): 121–139. Gary Johns, "Task Moderators of the Relationship between Leadership Style and Subordinate Responses," *Academy of Management Journal* 21 (June 1978): 319–325. Steven Kerr and Chester Schriesheim, "Consideration, Initiating Structure and Organizational Criteria: An Update of Korman's 1966 Review," *Personnel Psychology* 27 (Winter 1974): 555–568. Harry Levinson, "The Abrasive Personality," *Harvard Business Review* 56 (May–June 1978): 86–94. Edwin Locke, "The Supervisor as 'Motivator': His Influence on Employee Performance and Satisfaction," in *Managing for Accomplishment,* ed. Bernard Bass et al. (Lexington, Mass.: Lexington Books, 1970), pp. 57–67. Chester A. Schriesheim, Robert J. House, and Steven Kerr, "Leader Initiating Structure: A Reconciliation of Discrepant Research Results and Some Empirical Tests," *Organizational Behavior and Human Performance* 15 (April 1976): 297–321. Ralph Stogdill, *Handbook of Leadership* (New York: Free Press, 1974).

Path-Goal Theory

Martin Evans, "The Effects of Supervisory Behavior on Path Goal Relationship," *Organizational Behavior and Human Performance* 5 (May 1970): 277–298. Alan Filley, *The Compleat Manager* (Champaign, Ill.: Research Press, 1978), chapter 6. Robert House, "A Path Goal Theory of Leadership Effectiveness," *Administrative Science Quarterly* 16 (September 1971): 321–338. Thomas C. Mawhinney and Jeffrey D. Ford, "The Path Goal Theory of Leader Effectiveness: An Operant Interpretation," *Academy of Management Review* 2 (July 1977): 398–411. Chester Schriesheim and Mary Ann von Glinow, "The Path-Goal Theory of Leadership: A Theoretical and Empirical Analysis," *Academy of Management Journal* 20 (September 1977): 398–405. John E. Sheridan, H. Kirk Downey, and John W. Slocum, Jr., "Testing Causal Relationships of House's Path-Goal Theory of Leadership Effectiveness," *Organization and Administrative Sciences* 6 (Summer–Fall 1975): 61–80.

Fiedler's Contingency Theory

Fred Fiedler, "The Leadership Game: Matching the Man to the Situation," *Organizational Dynamics* 4 (Winter 1976): 6–16; and *A Theory of Leadership Effectiveness* (New York: McGraw-Hill, 1967). Fred Fiedler and Martin Chemers, *Leadership and Effective Management* (Glenview, Ill.: Scott, Foresman, 1974). Fred E. Fiedler and Albert F. Leister, "Leader Intelligence and Task Performance: A Test of a Multiple Screen Model," *Organizational Behavior and Human Performance* 20 (October 1977): 1–14. Stephen G. Green and Delbert M. Nebeker, "The Effects of Situational Factors and Leadership Style on Leader Behavior," *Organizational Behavior and Human Performance* 19 (August 1977): 368–377. Albert Leister, Donald Borden, and Fred E. Fiedler, "Validation of Contingency Model Leadership Training: Leader Match," *Academy of Management Journal* 20 (September 1977): 464–470. Robert W. Rice, "Psychometric Properties of the Esteem for Least Preferred Coworker (LPC Scale)," *Academy of Management Review* 3 (January 1978): 106–118. Craig Eric Schneier, "The Contingency Model of Leadership: An Extension to Emergent Leadership and Leader's Sex," *Organizational Behavior and Human Performance* 21 (April 1978): 220–239. Chester A. Schriesheim, James M. Tolliver, and Orlando C. Behling, "Leadership Theory: Some Implications for Managers," *MSU Business Topics* 26 (Summer 1978): 34–40. Robert P. Vecchio, "An Empirical Examination of the Validity of Fiedler's Model of Leadership Effectiveness," *Organizational Behavior and Human Performance* 19 (June 1977): 180–206.

Leadership Styles

Robert Blake and Jane Mouton, *The New Managerial Grid* (Houston: Gulf Publishing, 1978). Arthur G. Jago and Victor H. Vroom, "Hierarchical Level and Leadership Style," *Organizational Behavior and Human Performance* 18 (February 1977): 131–145. Barbara Karmel, "Leadership: A Challenge to Traditional Research Methods and Assumptions," *Academy of Management Review* 3 (July 1978): 475–482. Pradip N. Khandwalla, "Some Top Management Styles, Their Context and Performance," *Organization and Administrative Sciences* 7 (Winter 1976–1977): 21–51. Paul C. Nystrom, "Managers and the Hi-Hi Leader Myth," *Academy of Management Journal* 21 (June 1978): 325–331. Greg R. Oldham, "The Motivational Strategies Used by Supervisors: Relationships to Effectiveness Indicators," *Organizational Behavior and Human Performance* 15 (February 1976): 66–86. Wickham Skinner and W. Earl Sasser, "Managers with Impact: Versatile and Inconsistent," *Harvard Business Review* 55 (November–December 1977): 140–148. Robert Tannenbaum and Warren Schmidt, "How to Choose a Leadership Pattern," *Harvard Business Reivew* 51 (May–June 1973): 162–164, 168. Victor Vroom and Philip Yetton, *Leadership and Decision Making* (Pittsburgh: University of Pittsburgh Press, 1973).

Traditional Leadership Style

"Abboud: Mr. Tough Guy of U.S. Banking," *Business Week,* June 28, 1976, pp. 90–93. David M. Elsner, "Links in a Chain: Those 1,215 K's Stand for Kresge, K Marts and the Key to Success," *Wall Street Journal,* March 8, 1977, pp. 1, 35. Robert McMurry, *The Maverick Executive* (New York: AMACOM, 1974); "The Case for Benevolent Autocracy," *Harvard Business Review* 36 (January–February 1958): 82–90.

Consultative Leadership Style

John Child, "Organization Structure and Strategies of Control," *Administrative Science Quarterly* 17 (June 1972): 163–177. Lee Donaldson, "The Aston Findings on Centralization," *Administrative Science Quarterly* 20 (September 1975): 453–460. David C. Limerick, "Authority Relations in Different Organizational Systems," *Academy of Management Review* 1 (October 1976): 56–68. Dale McConkey, *No Nonsense Delegation* (New York: AMACOM, 1974). Norman Maier and J. Thurber, "Problems in Delegation," *Personnel Psychology* 22 (Summer 1969): 131–139. John A. Patton, "Executive Accountability: Who Needs It?" *Management Review* 67 (December 1978): 17–21. Robert Yin and William Lucas, "Decentralization and Alienation," *Policy Sciences* 4 (September 1973): 327–336.

Participative Leadership Style

Chris Argyris, "Leadership, Learning, and Changing the Status Quo," *Organizational Dynamics* 4 (Winter 1976): 29–43. Warren Bennis, *American Bureaucracy* (Chicago: Aldine Press, 1970). James MacGregor Burns, *Leadership* (New York: Harper & Row, 1978). Thomas G. Cummings, "Self-Regulating Work Groups: A Socio-Technical Synthesis," *Academy of Management Review* 3 (July 1978): 625–634. H. Peter Dachler and Bernhard Wilpert, "Conceptual Dimensions and Boundaries of Participation in Organizations: A Critical Evaluation," *Administrative Science Quarterly* 23 (March 1978): 1–39. Margaret Molinari Duckles, Robert Duckles, and Michael Maccoby, "The Process of Change at Bolivar," *Journal of Applied Behavioral Science* 13 (July–August–September 1977): 387–399. William M. Fox, "Limits to the Use of Consultative-Participative Management," *California Management Review* 20 (Winter 1977): 17–22. Godfrey Gardner, "Workers' Participation: A Critical Evaluation of Coch and French," *Human Relations* 30 (December 1977): 1071–1078. Edmund R. Gray, "The Practice of Business—The Non Linear Systems Experience: A Requiem," *Business Horizons* 21 (February 1978): 31–36. Larry Greiner, "What Managers Think of Participative Management," *Harvard Business Review* 51 (March–April 1973): 111–117. Frank A. Heller et al., "A Longitudinal Study in Participative Decision-Making," *Human Relations* 30 (July 1977): 567–587. M. Sami Kassem, "Tolstoy on Organization," *Business Horizons* 20 (April 1977): 9–15. Rensis Likert, *The Human Organization* (New York: McGraw-Hill, 1967). Arthur M. Louis, "They're Striking Some Strange Bargains at Diamond Shamrock," *Fortune,* January 1976, pp. 142–156. "Participative Management at Work," *Harvard Business Review* 55 (January–February 1977): 117–127. Benson Rosen and Thomas H. Jerdee, "Effects of Decision Permanence on Managerial Willingness to Use Participation," *Academy of Management Journal* 21 (December 1978): 722–725. Richard E. Walton and Leonard Schlesinger, "The Supervisor in Participative Work Systems: Some Role Difficulties," *Proceedings of the Academy of Management* (January 1978). J. Kenneth White, "Generalizability of Individual Difference Moderators of the Participation in Decision Making–Employee Response Relationship," *Academy of Management Journal* 21 (March 1978): 36–43. D. Kent Zimmerman, "Participative Management: A Reexamination of the Classics," *Academy of Management Review* 3 (October 1978): 896–901.

Industrial Democracy: The Ultimate Participative Leadership Style

Klaus E. Agthe, "Mitbestimmung: Report on a Social Experiment," *Business Horizons* 20 (February 1977): 5–14. Paul Bernstein, "Workplace Democratization: Its Internal Dynamics," *Organization and Administrative Sciences* 7 (Fall 1976): 1–127. John Child, "Participation, Organization, and Social Cohesion," *Human Relations* 29 (May 1976): 429–451. Nancy Foy and Herman Gadon, "Worker Participation: Contrasts in Three Countries," *Harvard Business Review* 54 (May–June 1976): 71–83. G. David Garson, "The Codetermination Model of Workers' Participation: Where Is It Leading?" *Sloan Management Review* 18 (Spring 1977): 63–77. William Glueck and Dragoljub Kavran, "Worker Management in Yugoslavia," *Business Horizons* 15 (February 1972): 31–39. Eileen B. Hoffman, "The German Way of Industrial Relations: Could We, Should We, Import It?" *Across the Board* 14 (October 1977): 38–47. George Hespe and Toby Wall, "The Demand for Participation among Employees," *Human Relations* 29 (May 1976): 411–428. E. Linden Hilgendorf and Barrie L. Irving, "Workers' Experience of Participation: The Case of British Rail," *Human Relations* 29 (May 1976): 471–505. S. Benjamin Prasad, "The Growth of Co-Determination," *Business Horizons* 20 (April 1977): 23–29. Thoralf Ulrick Qvale, "A Norwegian Strategy for Democratization of Industry," *Human Relations* 29 (May 1976): 453–469.

Power, Influence, and Leadership

Robert Bierstadt, "An Analysis of Social Power," *American Sociological Review* 15 (December 1950): 730–736. Peter Blau, "Critical Remarks on Weber's Theory of Authority," *American Political Science Review* 57 (June 1963): 305–316. Dorwin Cartwright, "Influence, Leadership and Control," in *Handbook on Organizations*, ed. James March (Chicago: Rand McNally, 1965). Terry Clark, "The Concept of Power," *Southwestern Social Science Quarterly* 6 (December 1967): 271–296. William F. Dowling, "Consensus Management at Graphic Controls," *Organizational Dynamics* 5 (Winter 1977): 23–47. H. Gordon Fitch and Charles Saunders, "Blowing the Whistle: The Limits of Organizational Obedience," *Proceedings of the Academy of Management* (1975). J. R. P. French and B. Raven, "The Bases of Social Power," in *Studies in Social Power*, ed. Dorwin Cartwright (Ann Arbor: Institute of Social Research, 1959). John P. Kotter, "Power, Dependence, and Effective Management," *Harvard Business Review* 55 (July–August 1977): 125–136. James M. McFillen, "Supervisory Power as an Influence in Supervisor-Subordinate Relations," *Academy of Management Journal* 21 (September 1978): 419–433. Robert N. McMurry, "Power and the Ambitious Executive," *Harvard Business Review* 51 (November–December 1973): 140–145. Joseph Pichler, "Power, Influence and Authority," in *Contemporary Management*, ed. Joseph McGuire (Englewood Cliffs, N.J.: Prentice-Hall, 1974). Robert Presthus, "Authority in Organizations," *Public Administration Review* 20 (Spring 1960): 86–91. Gerald R. Salancik and Jeffrey Pfeffer, "Who Gets Power—And How They Hold on to It: A Strategic-Contingency Model of Power," *Organizational Dynamics* 5 (Winter 1977): 3–21. Ralph Stogdill, *Handbook of Leadership* (New York: Free Press, 1974). Max Weber, *The Theory of Social and Economic Organizations* (New York: Oxford University Press, 1947).

Political Environment of Leadership

This section was researched and coauthored by Jean Marie Hanebury.
Chris Argyris, "Double Loop Learning in Organizations," *Harvard Business Review* 55 (September–October 1977): 115–125. John Bryson and George Kelly, "A Political Perspective on Leadership Emergence, Stability, and Change in Organizational Networks," *Academy of Management Review* 3 (October 1978): 713–723. Bertrand de Jouvenel, *On Power* (Boston: Beacon Press, 1945). Edward J. Dunne, Jr., Michael J.

Stahl, and Leonard J. Melhart, Jr., "Influence Sources of Project and Functional Managers in Matrix Organizations," *Academy of Management Journal* 21 (March 1978): 135–140. A. J. Grimes, "Authority, Power, Influence and Social Control: A Theoretical Synthesis," *Academy of Management Review* 3 (October 1978): 724–735. Anthony Jay, *Management and Machiavelli* (New York: Holt, Rinehart and Winston, 1967). Bruce H. Kemelgor, "Power and the Power Process: Linkage Concepts," *Academy of Management Review* 1 (October 1976): 143–149. John P. Kotter, "Power, Success, and Organizational Effectiveness," *Organizational Dynamics* 6 (Winter 1978): 26–40. Harold D. Lasswell, *Power and Personality* (New York: Viking Press, 1948). Harold D. Lasswell and Abraham Kaplan, *Power and Society* (New Haven, Conn.: Yale University Press, 1950). Ian C. MacMillan, *Strategy Formulation: Political Concepts* (St. Paul, Minn.: West, 1978). Kenneth McNeil, "Understanding Organizational Power: Building on the Weberian Legacy," *Administrative Science Quarterly* 23 (March 1978): 65–90. Bronson T. Mayes and Robert W. Allen, "Toward a Definition of Organizational Politics," *Academy of Management Review* 2 (October 1977): 672–677. Ralph Nader, Mark Green, and Joel Seligman, "Who Rules the Giant Corporation?" *Business and Society Review* 18 (Summer 1976): 40–48. Robert Presthus, *Men at the Top* (New York: Oxford University Press, 1964). Walter Reichman and Marguerite Levy, "Personal Power Enhancement: A Way to Executive Success," *Management Review* 66 (March 1977): 28–34. Virginia E. Schein, "Individual Power and Political Behaviors in Organizations: An Inadequately Explored Reality," *Academy of Management Review* 2 (January 1977): 64–72. Ralph Stogdill, *Handbook of Leadership* (New York: Free Press, 1974). Eberhard Witte, "Power and Innovation: A Two-Center Theory," *International Studies of Management and Organization* 7 (Spring 1977): 47–70. Abraham Zaleznik, "Power and Politics in Organizational Life," *Harvard Business Review* (May–June 1970): 47–60. Abraham Zaleznik and Manfred F. R. Kets de Vries, *Power and the Corporate Mind* (Boston: Houghton Mifflin, 1975).

Cases for Chapter 14

A Supervisor's Day

Arthur Moment, aged twenty-four, is a supervisor at a large glass manufacturing plant in an eastern U.S. city. Arthur graduated from Cornell's business school, spent two years in the Peace Corps, and then entered the company's management training program. This supervisory job is really his first significant work experience.

Arthur has been a supervisor for three months. Recently his superior, David Thrasher, pointed out to him that the production of his units is dropping.

Thrasher: I think I know why, too, Moment. Recently I passed your Unit 1 when you weren't there and there was some goofing off going on. Later that day I passed your Unit 2, and it was the same there.

Moment: I'll look into it at once, Mr. Thrasher, and we'll get the production back up, you'll see.

What Arthur did not want to admit was that he knows there is goofing off but does not know what to do about it. Arthur's area of supervision includes two buildings. As the company grew, it added a small unit away from the main building, so Arthur's employees work in two places (see Exhibit 1). There are no windows in Unit 2's building and none near Unit 1's walls.

Unit 1 is composed of fifteen employees who are very similar in ethnic background, age, education, and experience. The employees are unionized and have worked for the company about seven to ten years each. Unit 2 consists of ten employees with twelve to fifteen years' experience with the company. They belong to the same union as the Unit 1 employees and are similar to each other in age, ethnic background, and education, although they are not the same age or from the same ethnic background as the Unit 1 employees. The workers at the two units do not get together at work.

When Arthur catches someone goofing off, the person usually passes it off as a brief interlude or makes remarks like "When the cat's away, ... Besides, we do our fair share." When Arthur tried to crack down, he found that the employees were using "lookouts" to warn the

Exhibit 1
Locations of Units 1
and 2, XYZ Glass
Works.

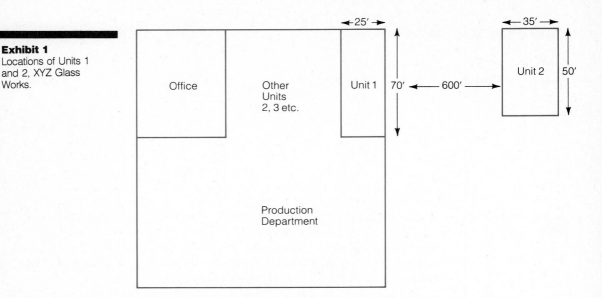

others when he was coming. Arthur is wondering what he should do
next.

Problem

You are Arthur's friend Sally Wurtzlebacher. Sally has years of
supervisory experience at Arthur's enterprise. Advise Arthur on how to
improve productivity and avoid future problems with Thrasher.

The Incident

William and Grace Cleary are both in their mid-forties, living in a
well-to-do section of a very posh resort town in Southern California.
They have five children and are well entrenched in the free-living society
life of Sunny Springs. Their small retail clothing chain affords them
ample time and money to do as they wish at this point in their lives.
May, their loyal employee for eighteen years, is comptroller of the firm.
She has worked for the firm almost from its inception. May has been
invaluable to the Clearys, both in their business and personally. She has
become a very close friend of the family. She is the narrator of the case.
Jill is a young woman who began working for the Clearys right after she
graduated from high school. She has no prior business experience.

"The other day was the last straw. It was the end of the month and all the office reports were due. Figures had just begun to arrive from the stores. Two of the girls in the office were out sick and we were really getting bogged down. I walked out into the warehouse and there did not seem to be a lot to do there. The other warehouse employees said Jill went across the street for a little while to the main store. Since the warehouse did not appear to have much to do, I borrowed one of the girls for a day to help me in the office. About an hour later when Jill returned she stormed into my office and started hollering and making a scene. Everyone was watching. She claimed the warehouse was very busy, twenty-five boxes had just arrived from Hawaii and had to be opened, checked, and distributed to the mainland stores. I tried to calm her down and explain that I was only using the girl for one day, but she would not listen. The office and the warehouse were in an uproar the rest of the day. It was chaos. She had no business talking to me that way. Besides, end-of-the-month figures have to be prepared right away in order to get the data to our computing firm on time. The merchandise in the warehouse was not going anywhere. The stores could wait a few extra days for the merchandise.

"I first came to work for Grace and William in 1953 when their business was still on somewhat shaky ground. I took the job because I was new in the area, having just separated from my husband, and this was the first job I found in my line of work. I was very worried that I would not find a job right away and I had two daughters to support. I knew I could not depend on my husband for support for the girls. Previously I had worked for fifteen years with the school board in their accounting department in the Los Angeles area. I had advanced to accounting supervisor at the time I left. There were no openings with the school in this resort town where I chose to reside for a combination of health and personal reasons.

"Although the Clearys could not pay me anywhere near my former salary, the job offered me more freedom and challenge. Their business was rapidly expanding, and I was to be in on some of the rewards of future expansion. None of this was fully laid out when I was hired, of course. We talked of the future at great length, but it was difficult and unrealistic to promise a piece of a dream.

"William Cleary had started his Hawaiian-wear business about five years earlier, but it did not amount to anything until he married Grace. She had a natural feel for the clothing business and really made their two stores into something special and unique. When I came they were opening their third store and about to have their second child. The Clearys, the children, the stores, and I were all like one big happy family. The business profited and by 1970 the stores numbered thirty. They were located from Hawaii to Florida and at points in between. By this time the Clearys had five children and my girls were grown and out on their own.

"Toward the latter part of the sixties business was exceptional. Financially the Clearys were doing very well. (Not long after I came to work for the firm, I advised the Clearys to incorporate as a private business for tax and legal reasons. Because of our relationship, I was made secretary-treasurer of the corporation and received a very small portion of the stock as compensation.) In 1968 a young girl was hired as warehouse help. The main office and warehouse for all the mainland stores was still located in Sunny Springs where the Clearys had started their business and continued to reside. Grace took a liking to this girl, Jill, and perhaps saw future potential in her. She took the girl under her wing and made Jill her assistant. Grace did everything concerning the business except the accounting, which was specifically my responsibility along with the six- to eight-member office staff I had. Still, because of my close relationship with the Clearys, there were times I did other things when they were out of town and sometimes even when they were in town, just to be helpful. More often than not, I traveled to the various stores to check out how they were doing and even did some of the buying. I worked many nights and weekends without complaining and without any extra pay. Lately, the Clearys have been spending less time at the office and more of their time playing tennis and getting involved with society affairs. Consequently, more responsibilities have fallen on my shoulders.

"Every summer the Clearys went on an extended vacation. It had always been implicitly understood that I was to handle all phases of the business during their absence. Many times, especially when we would be out at night together or when I would care for their children, they would tell me how important I was to the firm and to them. The Clearys always kept in touch when they were out of town and they would make any important decisions that were pressing at the moment. Still, I was responsible for keeping the business operating.

"The relationship between Jill and me had become increasingly strained, especially during the times when the Clearys were out of town. At first we had very little direct contact, but later she took responsibility for more areas and we were crossing each other's path more often. Last summer was particularly rough, and I was very worried about the situation for this summer. She was Grace's assistant and had been with the firm for approximately four years, but she was quite young and very inexperienced. She had never had a real job before working there. When Grace was out of town, Jill tried to take over all her duties. This was what she was supposed to do, but I felt I should have helped her whenever possible. There were many things about the "rag" business that she did not know and many things that she just could not do or did not understand. For example, when buying merchandise, we only accepted specific terms and we never gave out financial information to creditors. Our credit was good with United Factors, and we felt that should have been sufficient for any potential creditor. Jill was so gullible that she would tell any salesperson or anyone else, including our competitors, anything they asked. This could have proved very embarrassing. Also, she did not take into consideration other factors outside her immediate responsibility. For example, our payroll would have been heavy with overtime if I had not stepped in and told some of the warehouse staff that they would not be needed for the after-hours work that Jill had asked them to put in. These thoughts did not even enter her mind. She got into some projects to the exclusion of all other considerations.

"After the episode the other day in my office, whenever I came into the warehouse to see how things were going she gave me these disgusted looks and ignored me. I asked a question on a specific procedure, and she acted as if I were prying and only gave me a straight answer when I demanded it. I was getting the cold shoulder from a few of the girls in my office. I had always maintained a strong employee-supervisor relationship with the office employees, but the coldness was becoming too much to handle; the quality of their work was slipping. I was sure that Jill had been spreading vicious lies about me. We could not talk any more; she resented any help I tried to give. She should be grateful. After all, I was the one who had hired her in the first place; I gave her the first break she ever had.

"Grace was not yet aware of the difficulties Jill and I were having, but I doubted if I could have concealed them much longer. Our paths crossed every day and it was becoming apparent that she resented me. I realized she was young, but I had been in this business for nearly twenty years. I helped build this business into a successful venture. I sweated over every store opening. Jill should be thankful for any advice I gave her or for anything I did for Grace. She had only been with the firm for four years. What kind of comparison was that? Although she had made my life miserable, I was not about to leave. That was just what she wanted. She resented my relationship with Grace. I was well known in Sunny Springs and had a lot of friends there. I liked the small-town resort life. I was not about to go job hunting at that stage in my life! I needed to get Grace to see how vicious that girl really was and what a threat to the firm she could be. Jill had Grace so wrapped around her finger; she thought the girl was a wonderwoman or something."

Source: © Francis A. Yeandel, College of Business, University of Notre Dame. Used by permission.

Problems

1. What is the problem in this case?
2. What causes the problem? Is the problem caused mostly by individual differences in age, motivation, and training? Personnel problems? Organization problems?
3. What should the Clearys do to solve the problem(s) and prevent similar ones in the future?

Chapter 15 Effective Relationships with Superiors and Colleagues

Learning Objectives

1. Learn some techniques for relating effectively to superiors.
2. Be able to apply your knowledge of motivation, influence, and leadership theories to relate more positively to peers in workflow and service relationships.
3. Know how to differentiate between line and staff colleagues and some ways to influence each.
4. Learn some techniques for relating effectively to advisory and auditing personnel.
5. Understand how to apply general principles of politics and power sources to insure successful relationships with superiors, peers, and subordinates.

Chapter Outline

Introduction

In Chapter 14 we examined how a manager or entrepreneur could be most effective as a leader of employees. This chapter is designed to prepare you to deal effectively with two additional groups of people: superiors and colleagues.

Every manager has many roles to play. In private life one plays the roles of parent, spouse, child, and so forth. In work life there are other roles to play: superior, subordinate, and colleague. These roles are defined by people's expectations. This chapter will give you further insight into the differences and similarities between the role of a superior and that of a subordinate or a colleague.

Relating to Your Superiors

Obviously, superiors are people, so most of them are pleasant most of the time and unpleasant some of the time. A few are unpleasant most of the time.

A superior (boss) is the individual to whom an employee is responsible for his or her level of performance.

If you read some of the popular current management literature, you would think all there is to being successful is getting along with and outflanking your boss. In *Management and Machiavelli*,[1] for example, Anthony Jay implies that all you need to do is read Machiavelli's *The Prince* and apply its thesis. And the theme of the musical "How to Succeed in Business without Really Trying" is that the way to get to the top is by flattering your boss (and key power brokers like the boss's secretary); no talent is needed.

The Importance of Getting Along with the Boss

It should be apparent that some of your success as a manager depends on your relationship with your boss—not as much as "How to Succeed . . ." implies, but more than many feel is appropriate. Your superior determines the following:

1. How you are evaluated—which in turn affects your chances of promotion.

Source: © King Features Syndicate, Inc. 1975.

2. Your salary and benefits (within limits).
3. Possible transfers (if positions open up).
4. Your job: whether it is rewarding or not.
5. Your self-esteem (through feedback to you).
6. Your success in your job (through both instructions and feedback).
7. How you relate to others.

According to Michael Korda, to get power (from your boss) all you need is a winning, trustworthy smile.[2] His advice for dealing with bosses and peers includes the following pointers:

1. Always arrive late for business lunches so as to make your companion ill at ease.
2. Answer difficult questions with another question.
3. Project an air of mystery.
4. Get a corner office decorated in power colors (blue and touches of red) with low chairs and ashtrays just out of reach.
5. Speak softly with older executives. They will think they are going deaf.

Other writers imply that you can get ahead by trusting no one, maintaining positive mental attitudes, influencing the boss through his or her secretary or spouse, manipulating conferences, or joining the boss in social activities. Still, relating to a boss is not always easy, as the following incident, reported by Studs Terkel, illustrates:

My father got a phone call. His boss was chewing him out for something—in a tone and language that were humiliating. Here's my father who had worked for this company for thirty years. My father's a dignified man and he worked hard. God knows he's given that company all the years of his life. He doesn't have anything else. There are no hobbies. He wasn't close to any of his children. Nothing outside of work. That was it. He would get up in the morning and leave the house and come home 12–14 hours later, six days a week. That was it. Yet here he is at sixty and here's a guy chewing him out like he's a little kid. I felt embarrassed being there. I felt sorry that he knew I was watching that happen. I could see he was angry and embarrassed. I could see him concealing his feelings, sort of shuffling and scratching his head, in the face of higher authority. We went to lunch. We didn't talk about it at all.[3]

There is no doubt that your success depends on effective relationships with your superiors. But surely you do not believe they are so foolish that they cannot see through "intimidation," second-rate power plays, or third-rate fawning. To paraphrase Abraham Lincoln, you can fool some bosses all of the time and all bosses some of the time, but you cannot fool all bosses all of the time. So what does research tell us about relating to our superiors?

Influencing Superiors

There has been very little scientific research focusing on the relationship between superior and subordinate. But our discussions of motivation (Chapter 6) and influence and leadership (Chapter 14) theories can be applied to this area.

Insights from Motivation Theory

Superiors are people too. They have needs to be satisfied. As a subordinate, you can contribute to the satisfaction of the superior's lower (physiological and security) needs or his or her need for achievement by performing your duties well and thus helping your superior's unit achieve its goals. You contribute to the superior's social or affiliation needs by socializing with him or her, discussing problems, and providing sympathy as you would with any person.

You can also contribute to the satisfaction of the superior's recognition and esteem needs by recognizing what the superior does for the work group and saying so in word and deed. At one extreme, you can act like Lt. Fuzz. But superiors also have doubts and can benefit from constructive criticism. You can provide such feedback without becoming an insincere phony. When a superior wonders if he or she is getting anything out of the job, you can point out the positive side as well.

Insights from Influence Theory

You may recall the seven types of influence or power listed in Chapter 14:

1. Legitimate
2. Monetary
3. Skill/expertise
4. Affection
5. Respect
6. Rectitude
7. Coercive

Which of these do you think a subordinate exerts on a superior?

In general, subordinates do not have legitimate or monetary power over their superiors. In fact the superior usually has this power. Employee coalitions can exert an equivalent of *coercive power* over superiors, however. If employees all slow down or all work against the boss, output will drop. Or employees can "blow the whistle on the boss" in various ways. They can follow the rules to the letter—air traffic controllers are famous for this—or threaten to unionize. Robert McMurry suggests that "the most important strategy of power is for an executive to establish alliances and use passive resistance where necessary."[4]

Thus employees have available (usually as a last resort) the coercive influence of a coalition. Just as the ability to fire employees makes a superior's coercive power effective, the threat of employee slowdown or "sabotage" provides employees with a source of influence over superiors.

A second, more likely source of influence is *expertise* (which probably includes some respect). Most bosses do not have the expertise—or the time—to do the job as well as the employee. So to the extent that the boss needs the knowledge or skills the employee has, the employee can exert influence on the boss.

The final source of influence for a subordinate is *affection*. As I have mentioned before, if a superior likes a subordinate, he or she is more likely to be favorably inclined toward and influenced by that subordinate.

McMurry suggests that "the executive should take all the steps he [or she] can to ensure that he [or she] is personally compatible with superiors."[5] He suggests further that the executive become a persuasive person skilled at self-dramatization and radiating self-confidence.

Insights from Leadership Theory

If one accepts the premises of leadership style theory, traditional leaders will prefer subordinates who accept their direction and do what they are asked. As McMurry suggests, subordinates will get a clear, concise, unambiguous statement, in writing, of their duties and responsibilities, reporting relationships, and scope of authority and will be expected to respond appropriately.[6] The executive should establish clear communication channels upward.

One may assume that participative leaders will expect creativity and initiative from their subordinates. The subordinates would do well to act accordingly.

Motivation theory, influence theory, and leadership theory all provide insights into how to relate better to your boss. A good relationship should contribute to promotions, salary increases, better jobs, and a pleasanter work environment.

Relating to Peers

Relating to superiors is crucial to managerial effectiveness. But executives also need to interact with groups other than superiors and subordinates. Within the enterprise, these groups include colleagues and peers.

A colleague is another person at work of roughly equivalent status or rank who is neither a superior nor a direct subordinate and with whom the manager interacts to achieve enterprise objectives.

There are several kinds of colleagues: peers in the workflow process and managers of service, advisory, or auditing groups. Other relationships in the work environment are important, too— for example line-staff and committee relations, discussed in Chapter 16.

Colleagues control expertise and resources without which the manager normally has difficulty attaining his or her objectives. And relationships with colleagues are an important component of organizational success and employee satisfaction. Studies have shown that although lateral relationships (relationships with colleagues) are important in all organizations, they are likely to vary depending on the organizational environment. Thus in stable business environments crucial lateral relations are as follows:

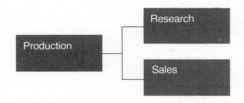

In rapidly changing environments the crucial relations are as follows:

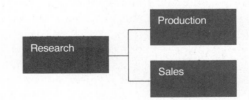

Colleague or lateral relations are especially difficult in many organizations for several reasons: (1) There is no clear-cut set of influence relationships; there is poor definition of who should initiate and when the other should respond. (2) Rewards for performance in two interacting units (and for two managers) are likely to be different. Research scientists do not have the same objectives and rewards that salespeople do. (3) Lateral relations are likely to be uncomfortable, tension producing, and much lengthier than vertical (superior-subordinate) relations. Because lateral relations are so

Leonard R. Sayles

Leonard R. Sayles, one of the best known management writers and scholars, received his Ph.D. from Massachusetts Institute of Technology. He is currently professor of business administration at Columbia University's School of Business. Previously, he taught at Cornell University, at the University of Michigan, at McGill University, and in Western Europe.

His well researched studies of contemporary organizations and his widely cited texts bridge the gap between organizational behavior and management. The results of these studies are used in hundreds of schools and management development programs in the United States and Canada and abroad.

Sayles has been a consultant to major corporations, to the National Aeronautics and Space Administration, to the National Academy of Sciences, and to the National Science Foundation. He has also served as a consultant for various programs designed to improve the management of health care and judicial services.

Sayles has received numerous awards for his research studies, including several Ford Foundation grants, two McKinsey Foundation awards, and various awards from professional societies in the fields of psychology and anthropology.

important and so difficult, I will examine them in more detail. The following discussion of how to develop effective relationships with different kinds of colleagues (workflow, advisory, service, and audit) is based on Leonard Sayles's approach.[7]

Influencing Peers in Workflow Relationships

The first lateral relationship is the workflow relationship. Each manager's section is part of the flow of work and thus has to deal with the units before and after it. Those units that come before a specific unit can usually cause it more problems than those that come after.

Consider Figure 15.1. If you are a manager in the brewing department of a beer company, you are dependent on a number of people and units to order the right amounts of malt, hops, and other ingredients and get them to you on time. The bottling line supervisors, in turn, are dependent on you to get the right amount of beer brewed on time.

Sayles studied problems in the relationship between purchasing departments and production departments. The typical problems that arose involved the following factors:

Figure 15.1
Workflow Relationships
at a Beer Company.

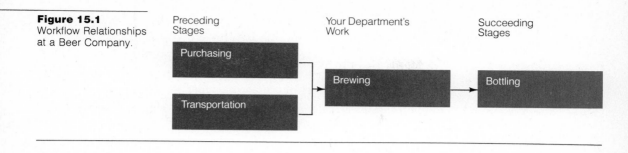

1. *Timing* Much dissatisfaction arises because of mutual pressures to rearrange schedules. In the example of the beer company, if the purchasing department does not order on time, your department is put behind, causing problems both for you and for the bottling department.

2. *Ways of working* A second potential problem is the way a preceding department does its work. For example, does the department before yours do its work in a way that facilitates the work in your department? In the manufacturing of parts, for instance, one group may provide the right number of parts on time, but the quality of the work may be poor, leading to inefficiences in the next department.

3. *Information* Often one department may not alert the next to problems ahead. This prevents planning how to deal with the difficulties and leads to bad feelings between the departments and managers involved.

Thus if you were the manager in the brewing department of the beer company of Figure 15.1, you would need to interact with the purchasing manager to deal with these kinds of problems. It is natural and necessary for peers and colleagues to relate to each other.

To understand this relationship better, consider the following study by Henry Landsberger.[8] He observed the personal interactions (face to face and on the phone) between production managers, schedulers, stock control managers, and sales liaison managers in two plants.

The first thing Landsberger found was how important peer relationships were. A large amount of time was spent interacting with peers. The sales liaison managers spent the most time in this way (about 60 percent), while the lowest average was for production managers (about 30 percent). The importance of lateral relations could also be measured in terms of suggestions for action: 45 to 55 percent of these came from peers, not from superiors or subordinates.

Finally, Landsberger found that certain issues came up again and again and had to be resolved. The conflicts usually came down to three issues: flexibility versus stability in production, short-run versus long-run costs, and departmental goal attainment versus plant goal attainment.

How can peer relations be organized and developed? Jay Galbraith suggests that there are several ways enterprises can help organize and develop peer relations at work:[9]

- *Direct contact* Encourage peers to interact and establish reciprocal relations. There is evidence that peer relations improve when managers' careers include wider experience across departments.
- *Liaison roles/integrating roles* Create positions whose purpose is to coordinate between departments.
- *Task forces* Create temporary groups of people from the departments involved whose job is to work out particular problems.

How Not to Relate to Peers

Some ways of relating work poorly. They include the following:

- Interacting directly only infrequently.
- Getting rules established at a higher level that favor your department over your peer's.
- Putting pressure on your peer's department by going to your boss and getting him or her to pressure your peer's boss.
- Interfering in your peer's department by giving orders to his or her subordinates.

How to Relate to Peers

Then what will work? Returning to motivation theory, you are likely to establish an effective working relationship with your colleague if you can help satisfy his or her needs: (1) Help get the work out, thereby helping the colleague meet his or her objectives and *physiological/safety* needs. (2) Interact with the colleague; get to know him or her and meet some of his or her *social* needs. (3) Treat the colleague with respect, thus satisfying some of his or her *esteem* needs.

Influence theory advises you of the following sources of power you can take advantage of in peer relationships: *skill/expertise* (when you can help the colleague solve problems), *affection* (when the colleague likes you), and *respect* (when the colleague respects you).

Leadership theory advocates increasing your influence by developing a transactional relationship ("I'll do this for you; you do this for me"). This is harder the further downstream in the workflow you are. The last department may depend on six prior departments; the first department depends on none.

In sum, you can effectively influence colleagues by using the following methods:

1. Interact with colleagues frequently. Get to know them and understand their problems.
2. Share information in a transactional relationship.

3. Try to be open about how quality problems affect the whole relationship.
4. If Steps 1–3 do not work, build a coalition of peers around the troublesome colleague and try to exert pressure that way.
5. If Step 4 does not work, try to get the workflow rerouted so that you are not so dependent on the troublesome colleague.
6. If all else fails, appeal through the hierarchy (to a mutual boss) and get rules established and hierarchical pressure put on the peer. Again, this is the method of last resort.

Influencing Peers in Service Relationships

Managers of service departments supervise activities needed by many departments. These activities are centralized for economic purposes. Some examples are specialized machine shops, typing pools, photocopying services, stores, mail rooms, computer services, design engineers, purchasing, maintenance, and hospital laboratories. If you are a manager of a service activity, your job relationships can be diagrammed as shown in Figure 15.2. Using the example provided in Figure 15.2, assume that you manage a typing pool. Four departments depend on you for typing service. This creates special problems for you as service manager, such as deciding priorities when several departments want service at the same time or deciding how much and what quality of service to provide on a limited budget.

Service relationships actually can be organized in three ways, as Table 15.1 shows. They may be provided on request, supplied on a programmed basis, or routinely supplied.

Leonard Sayles analyzed service departments and described the problems and pressures service department managers experience in the following way.[10] Service functions, he noted, become scarce resources. Service managers often are unable to satisfy all departments at the same time. When this happens, there is a tendency for the departments to compound the problem by increasing their requests for service and shortening the time in which service is needed in order to make sure they get their "fair share." Cost and quality then become serious problems and

Figure 15.2
Service
Relationships

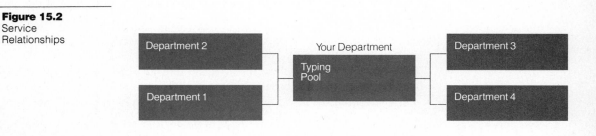

Table 15.1
Organization
of Service
Relationships

	Relationship of Service Unit to Head Operating Executive	Relationship of Head Operating Executive to Service Unit	Relationship of Service Unit to Employees of Operating Unit
Services supplied upon request.	Offers service when operating units request it.	Same as toward any outside contractor. The boss of the staff personnel is their own staff unit head.	Through operating unit's supervisors, issues such requests as required to make service effective.
Staff services supplied on a programmed basis.	Somewhat stronger than in the above relationship. Services are rendered on a programmed basis approved by higher authority and cannot be refused by operating unit head.	The direct chain of command of the staff personnel is to the staff unit head. Operating unit head must work.	Same as above.
Auxiliary services routinely supplied.	Services are a routine part of operations, not provided on request or specially programmed.	Same as above.	Service personnel can insist on regular procedures being followed. Routine communications flow directly between staff and operating personnel except in cases of sharp disagreement.

departments try to influence the service department manager with gifts, favors, good terms, or mutual protection. When this happens, Sayles observed, nonfavored departments are likely to use pressure tactics or appeal to the service manager's boss. The resultant problems are compounded by the difficulty of predicting service needs ahead of time and planning for them.

In his study of a purchasing department, George Strauss found that service managers' reactions to such pressure took the form of a series of mechanisms:[11]

1. *Rule-oriented tactics:* appealing to rules, such as written authorizations, to handle problems like priorities.
2. *Rule-evading tactics:* going through the motions of following the rules but acting according to personal preference.
3. *Personal-political tactics:* working through allies who support the department's position.

4. *Educational tactics:* explaining the service department's position and persuading the other departments to accept it.
5. *Organizational-interactional tactics:* getting procedures changed to fit desired patterns.

Sayles found that successful service managers did not accept conflict as inevitable but took the initiative and tried educational or organization-interaction methods in planning and scheduling the needed services. The successful service manager also protected employees from departmental pressure.

How does the service manager influence operating department colleagues to cooperate and help him or her do the job well and fairly? The manager will use skill/expertise power, affection power, or respect power most frequently and legitimate power or the equivalent of coercive power (threatening denial of the service request, for instance) only as a last resort. The adept manager interacts frequently, uses persuasion and education, and relates on a transactional basis with operating colleagues to promote such cooperation. In this way the manager not only improves the operating efficiency of the service department but also helps satisfy the achievement and affiliation needs of his or her colleagues.

How can an operating manager influence a service manager? Affection power, respect power, and skill/expertise power are important sources of influence. And developing a transactional relationship can serve the needs of both operating and service manager. Developing these relationships takes time. But it is vital to spend this time, for without it, objectives will not be reached.

A word of caution: honesty is important in transactional relationships. When an operating manager comes to a service manager with an emergency job, the service manager will generally try to help. But if all jobs are labeled emergency jobs, the service manager will rightly believe that the operating manager is a poor planner and pay less attention to his or her requests. The transactional relationship also implies that when one department has an emergency and the service manager asks the manager of another department to accept a delay on a job that is not an emergency, that manager does so without complaint.

Establishing reciprocity with the service manager makes sense as long as the relationship is not exploited. Again, the use of a proxy for coercive power (putting pressure on the service manager through the hierarchy) is risky and should be avoided until all other avenues have been exhausted.

Advisory, Audit, and Line-Staff Relations

The final relationship with colleagues to be discussed is that between line and staff managers or between advisory or audit managers and operating (or other staff) managers.

**The Advisory
Relationship**

A staff executive is a person whose role is to provide advice, counsel, and expertise to help line operating executives and their units achieve organizational objectives. A line executive is a person who is part of a direct chain of command.

The line-staff relationship is diagrammed in Figure 15.3. There are four possible line-staff relationships (see Table 15.2). Staff can be strictly advisory and located at headquarters (Type 1). It can consist of separate units located both at headquarters and at field units (Type 2). Or staff can be integrated with operating or line units (Types 3 and 4).[12] As you will note in the diagram in Figure 15.3, for example, if a regional sales manager seeks advice on a personnel issue (say, compensation guidelines from an employee relations manager, this is a Type 1 relationship. (Note colored arrows.)

The operating-advisory relationship can be a very troublesome one from the point of view of both operating and advisory personnel. As the line manager sees it, typical problems include the following:

1. *The adviser takes over.* The adviser starts giving too much advice and says or implies that it is not *advice* but rather what the manager *must do*. The operating manager views this as taking away the right to make his or her own decisions.
2. *The adviser interferes.* The line executive observes the adviser bypassing him or her and issuing directives or strongly "giving advice" to subordinates. Again, the operating executive views this as a reduction in his or her influence.
3. *Several advisers cause conflict.* In some cases, when several advisers or advisory groups are invited in, their advice is conflicting and/or contradictory. This is not viewed as helpful by the operating executive.
4. *The adviser will not help.* In a few cases operating executives want the adviser to make decisions in his or her area of expertise. Usually an adviser will avoid doing this. It is the operating executive's responsibility

Figure 15.3
The Line-Staff
Relationship

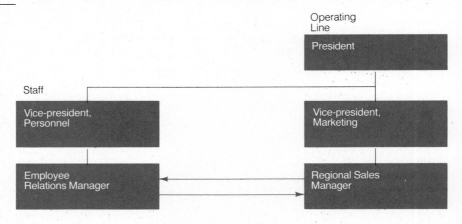

Table 15.2
Basic Line-Staff
Relationships

Type	Relationship of Staff Unit Employees to Head of Operating Unit	Relationship of Head of Operating Unit to Staff Unit Working in His or Her Department	Relationship of Staff Unit to Operating Unit Employees
Advisory	Many only volunteer suggestions, but may not necessarily have to wait to be invited.	May or may not have to avail himself or herself of suggestions.	Do not give or receive instructions.
Central staff and counterpart staff unit in operating department.		May or may not have to avail himself or herself of advice and suggestions of central staff unit; through chain of command, head of operating unit is boss of the staff unit in his or her department.	"Functional" relationship between central unit and employees of the staff unit in operating department; on matters of professional standards, mode of operation, etc., "suggestions" from the central unit have strong force and are to be disregarded only under special circumstances and with approval of head of operating unit.
Personnel assigned to operating unit by staff unit.	Assigned personnel are under administrative command of head of operating unit as to deployment on the job, discipline, hours of work, etc., but their "boss" is the head of the staff unit.	Head of staff unit may, with notice to head of operating unit, withdraw them from the job if he or she (head of staff) can supply replacements.	Relationships are those of any employees under direct supervision of head of operating unit; they carry on their own activities and work through normal channels within department.
A staff unit that is part of an operating organization unit.	Supply information and advise and recommend; decisions are made by operating head, and he or she issues instructions to operating personnel.	Direct relationship through chain of command.	Same as Type 3. Staff personnel do not issue direct instructions to operating personnel except under unusual circumstances (e.g., a safety or quality inspector shutting down an operation where emergency does not permit working through normal channels.

Source: *The Encyclopedia of Management*, 2d ed., edited by Carl Heyel, © 1973 Litton Educational Publishing, Inc. Reprinted by permission of Van Nostrand Reinhold Company, pp. 620–622.

to make the decision. Yet weaker operating executives want advisers to make decisions for them and grow unhappy with those who will not.

5. *The adviser takes credit for results.* Some operating executives believe advisers take credit for their decisions. This perception makes them unhappy since they feel the line executive should get credit and blame for all of the unit's results.

Staff advisers often feel that operating executives have too much power and do not pay attention to their advice and new ideas. This perspective on the line-staff relationship may result from any of the following line executive responses to their advice:

1. The line executive rejects the advice outright.
2. The line executive "files" the advice after sending a memo praising it (the bottom drawer approach).
3. The operating executive defends "his" or "her" interests against the adviser's by mobilizing support from colleagues or superiors (the political support approach).
4. The line executive finds as many errors (including typos) as possible and uses these to indicate that the project is ill-conceived and not worth carrying out (the pick-it-to-death approach).
5. The line manager agrees with the specialist's data analysis but argues that future statistics will be different and that the advice therefore is unsound (the future ploy).
6. The line executive simply avoids seeing the adviser by setting up conflicting appointments or using similar evasive tactics (the avoidance technique).

Operating line executives clearly hold most of the cards and, in addition, have legitimate power sources. The position of the staff is weaker. They can try to go along with line executives, compromise with them, or go over their heads (though the latter is dangerous).

The line-staff relationship often leads to frustration. Turnover is greater and satisfaction lower for staff than for line personnel. Since operating executives hold many advantages over staff advisers, most of the advice in the literature is aimed at helping staff advisers establish good relationships with line executives. Sayles proposed the following guidelines for developing such relationships:[13]

1. Types 1 and 2 staff advisers (Table 15.2) should report to their own staff executives.
2. Staff should be evaluated on their problem-solving abilities, not on the number of projects completed.
3. Staff should try to educate line employees in staff duties so they can take care of such duties themselves.
4. Staff should respond as soon as possible to requests for help from line executives. Line executives should take the initiative in obtaining help from staff.

5. Staff is successful if it builds support by doing small projects well before undertaking major ones.
6. Managers other than the staff executive should evaluate the staff work performed.
7. Staff should make sure the line manager gets the credit for the results of staff work.

William Whyte has suggested in addition that the effective staff adviser:[14]

1. Increases the frequency and regularity of interactions and contacts with line executives.
2. Learns the special circumstances of each line department before advising.
3. Builds an exchange relationship.
4. Sees that the line gets credit for the results.

As can be seen from these recommendations, advisory executives will be successful if they apply influence theory—if they build a power base on skill/expertise, affection, respect. Only in extreme cases should they try to use coercive power. From the standpoint of motivation theory, they must be careful of the line's recognition/esteem needs, utilize affiliation/social needs, and contribute to the physiological and safety needs of line executives.

As far as line executives are concerned, once they realize that the staff executive is there to help, they are usually glad to operate on a transactional basis. They should realize that the staff advisers have needs too and try to satisfy those social and esteem needs in dealing with them.

The Audit Relationship

Sayles believes that the audit relationship developed as organizations grew larger and more complex. No longer could top managers take the time to gather information on effectiveness and determine whether their policies were being carried out. So specialists with technical expertise were given the task of checking on operating managers. *Staff executives performing an audit appraise and evaluate the extent to which operating managers are meeting objectives, using resources properly, and following enterprise policies.* Their position, obviously, is a powerful one.

Among the staff specialists that may be involved in an audit relationship are accounting auditors (who check on budgets and use of finances) and personnel managers (who check on wage schedules, EEOC requirements, and the like). Figure 15.4 diagrams one such relationship.

From the operating manager's point of view, the problems in the auditing relationship include the following:

1. Auditors go directly to subordinates and so find out things managers do not know.
2. Several auditors may give contradictory "orders." Thus satisfying the demands of one requires violating the requirements of another. For

Figure 15.4
An Auditing
Relationship

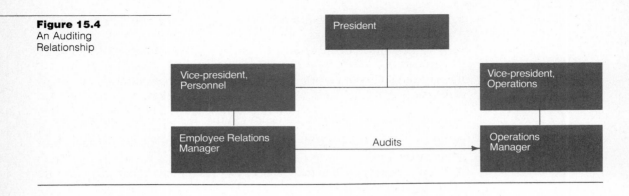

example, the personnel department's requirement that more handicapped employees be hired may exceed the budget requirements set by the accounting auditor.
3. Collusion can develop between an auditor and an operating manager. (This is a problem for the operating manager's superior.)
4. The auditor reports the findings to the operating executive's boss without first discussing it with the operating executive.

As in any other relationship, the operating executive can hinder the auditor's work by being unresponsive, not providing information, and so forth. Usually, however, auditors are too powerful for such tactics. Since they are so powerful, most of the "relating" is done by the operating executive. The behavioral theories we have examined suggest the following ways in which line executives can build good relationships with auditors.

Motivation Theory The operating manager can help the auditor fulfill his or her needs. Auditors do not have much chance to socialize. They are in different places each week, and they are generally feared. So being friendly and getting to know them can help satisfy their social/affiliation needs. Their esteem needs can be satisfied too if they are called on for advice on how to handle problems in their area of expertise—as long as the advice is *used*.

Influence Theory The operating executive's major sources of influence and power are affection and respect. In some cases the operating executives might have skill power as well.

Leadership Theory The operating executive should develop a transactional relationship and cooperate fully with the auditors in order to make their job quicker and smoother. In return, the auditors should inform the operating executive of their findings and suggest ways of implementing changes before reporting back to the home office.

Although it may appear that auditors hold all the cards, operating executives can have a positive impact on the audit relationship if they exercise interpersonal skills effectively.

Auditors have most of the sources of influence at their fingertips. They have coercive power and can stop workflow. They can cause people to be reprimanded or even fired. They have legitimate power, too, and they may also use skill, respect, and affection power. Ideally, auditors will develop a cooperative attitude—"I am here to help you meet your budget"—and then use affection, skill, and respect power to fulfill their function. They should rely on legitimate and coercive power only when other sources of influence do not work.

Impossible Relationships

Some enterprises try to combine advisory and auditing relationships in one department, sometimes even using the same person to do both. Lumping auditing and advisory duties into one job is poor practice. In such cases, operating executives never know when the auditor/adviser is auditing and when he or she is advising. Frequently, effective advising requires operating executives to reveal problems. Many executives would be reluctant to do so if they felt their revelations would be reported to higher-up executives. And sometimes that is exactly what an auditor must do.

Managerial Implications of Power and Politics

In this chapter the political and power sources and influences have been incorporated into the major discussions. But here are some overall guidelines which you can use in your relationships with superiors, colleagues, and subordinates. They are based on research by John Miner.[15]

1. Alliances should be established with superiors, peers, and subordinates so that when allies are needed they will be on your side.
2. Subordinates should be selected who are not only competent but reliable, dependable, and above all else loyal.
3. Be careful not to injure or alienate another manager who might be in a position to harm you. Do not alienate former colleagues.
4. Choose the time and place of your bargaining efforts so conditions are supportive of *your* goals.
5. If the outcome is uncertain, it is often better to support the aggressive efforts of someone else rather than being the leader yourself.
6. Attempt to divide and conquer your adversaries.
7. Work on and publicize adversaries' weaknesses.
8. Get your own expert in an area in which you lack expertise.
9. Sometimes it may be advisable to inflate your goals so that you can settle for less in the bargaining process.

Summary

One of the roles a manager must play is the crucial relationship role of subordinate to the boss. A *superior* (boss) is the individual to whom an employee is responsible for his or her level of performance.

Your superior determines: (1) how you are evaluated and your chances for promotion, (2) your salary and benefits, (3) your job and whether it is rewarding or not, (4) your success, and (5) how you relate to others.

The effective subordinate influences the superior by helping satisfy the superior's physiological, security, and achievement needs. It is also possible to influence superiors by utilizing skill/expertise, affection, and (if necessary, as a last resort) coalition/coercive power. Traditional bosses prefer subordinates who accept their direction and do what they are asked. Participative leaders expect creativity and initiative from their subordinates.

As a manager you will have to interact not only with superiors and subordinates but also with colleagues. A *colleague* is another person at work of roughly equivalent status or rank who is neither a superior nor a direct subordinate and with whom the manager interacts to achieve enterprise objectives.

Relationships between several kinds of colleagues (peers) were discussed: peers in the workflow process; managers of service departments; advisory, audit, and other line/staff personnel. Line and staff positions were differentiated from each other, and specific suggestions were given for the appropriate means of relating to each of these peer groups.

In all these positions, the power derived from affection and respect can be used to help the work relationship run smoothly. The development of a transactional relationship, that is, a give and take approach, is also helpful. Skill/expertise power is useful in forming effective relationships with workflow, service, and advisory peers. In some instances, skill is also a useful force in a relationship with an auditor. Some overall guidelines which you can use in your relationships with superiors, colleagues, and subordinates concluded the chapter.

In the next chapter we turn to effective relationships with groups.

Questions

1. Define *superior*. Why is it so important for you to get along with your superiors?
2. Use the insights you have gained from motivation, influence, and leadership theory to illustrate appropriate ways to influence your boss.
3. Using Sayles's and Landsberger's research, explain how important peer relationships are in workflow groups.
4. How would you establish an effective relationship with colleagues in the workflow group? Think of personal examples to illustrate this.
5. What did Sayles's research indicate about how service managers react to pressure? If you were a service manager how would you go about getting your operating department colleagues to cooperate with you?

6. Explain how the staff executive position differs from that of the line executive.
7. Why is the operating-advisory staff relationship such a troublesome one? Use Sayles's and Whyte's guidelines to explain how difficulties in this relationship can be avoided.
8. You are an operating manager who has always had trouble relating to auditors. What have you learned in this chapter which will help you develop a more positive relationship?

Notes

[1] Anthony Jay, *Management and Machiavelli* (New York: Holt, Rinehart and Winston, 1968).

[2] Michael Korda, *Power! How to Get It, How to Use It* (New York: Random House, 1975).

[3] Studs Terkel, *Working* (New York: Pantheon, 1974), pp. 564–565.

[4] Robert McMurry, "Power and the Ambitious Executive," *Harvard Business Review* 51 (November–December 1973): 140–145.

[5] Ibid., p. 141.

[6] Ibid.

[7] Leonard Sayles, *Managerial Behavior* (New York: McGraw-Hill, 1964).

[8] Henry Landsberger, "The Horizontal Dimension of Bureaucracy," *Administrative Science Quarterly* 6 (December 1961): 299–332.

[9] Jay Galbraith, *Designing Complex Organizations* (Reading, Mass.: Addison-Wesley, 1973), chapter 5.

[10] Sayles, *Managerial Behavior*.

[11] George Strauss, "Tactics of Lateral Relationships: The Purchasing Agent," *Administrative Science Quarterly* 7 (September 1962): 161–186.

[12] Carl Heyel, ed., *The Encyclopedia of Management* (New York: Reinhold Book Corporation, 1963), pp. 620–622.

[13] Sayles, *Managerial Behavior*.

[14] William Whyte, *Organizational Behavior* (Homewood, Ill.: Irwin, Dorsey Press, 1969), chapter 18.

[15] John Miner, *The Management Process*, 2d ed. (New York: Macmillan, 1978), chapter 10.

References

Relating to Your Superiors

Anthony Jay, *Management and Machiavelli* (New York: Holt, Rinehart and Winston, 1968). Michael Korda, *Power! How to Get It, How to Use It* (New York: Random House, 1975). Robert Ringer, *Winning through Intimidation* (New York: Funk and Wagnalls, 1975). Peter Smith et al., "Relationships between Managers and Their Work Associates," *Administrative Science Quarterly* 14 (September 1969): 338–345. Studs Terkel, *Working* (New York: Pantheon, 1974). Auren Uris and John Tarrant, *How to Win Your Boss's Love, Approval . . . and Job* (New York: Van Nostrand Reinhold, 1973).

Insights from Influence Theory

Gordon H. Fitch and Charles Saunders, "Blowing the Whistle: The Limits of Organizational Obedience," *Proceedings of the Academy of Management* (1975), p. 50. Robert McMurry, "Power and the Ambitious Executive," *Harvard Business Review* 51 (November–December 1973): 140–145. David Mechanic, "Sources of Power of Lower

Participants in Complex Organizations," *Administrative Science Quarterly* 7 (December 1962): 349–364. Allan Schwartzbaum, "Lateral Interaction and Effectiveness in Vertical Organizations," *Industrial Relations Research Association Proceedings* (1967), pp. 360–371. Robert Thornton, "Controlling the Technician," *MSU Business Topics* 22 (Summer 1974): 5–10.

Relating to Peers

James Hall and Joel Leidecker, "Lateral Relatives in Organization: Theory and Application," in *Dimensions in Modern Management,* ed. Patrick Conner (Boston: Houghton Mifflin, 1974). Richard Osborn and James Hunt, "An Empirical Investigation of Lateral and Vertical Leadership at Two Organizational Levels," *Journal of Business Research* 2 (April 1974): 209–221. Richard Osborn et al., "Lateral Leadership, Satisfaction, and Performance," *Proceedings of the Academy of Management* (1973), pp. 440–446.

Influencing Peers in Workflow Relationships

William Dowling, Jr., and Leonard Sayles, *How Managers Motivate* (New York: McGraw-Hill, 1971), chapter 9. Jay Galbraith, *Designing Complex Organizations* (Reading, Mass.: Addison-Wesley, 1973), chapter 5. Henry Landsberger, "The Horizontal Dimension of Bureaucracy," *Administrative Science Quarterly* 6 (December 1961): 299–332. Leonard Sayles, *Managerial Behavior* (New York: McGraw-Hill, 1964). Francis D. Tuggle, *Organizational Processes* (Arlington Heights, Ill.: AHM Publishing, 1978), chapters 3 and 8. Richard Walton et al., "A Study of Conflict in the Process, Structure and Attitudes of Lateral Relationships," in *Some Theories of Organization,* ed. Albert H. Rubenstein and Chadwick J. Haberstroh (Homewood, Ill.: Richard D. Irwin, 1966). William Whyte, *Organizational Behavior* (Homewood, Ill.: Irwin, Dorsey Press, 1969), chapter 18. Abraham Zalesznik, "Power and Politics in Organizational Life," *Harvard Business Review* 48 (May–June 1970): 47–60.

Influencing Colleagues in Service Relationships

Leonard Sayles, *Managerial Behavior* (New York: McGraw-Hill, 1964). George Strauss, "Tactics of Lateral Relationships: The Purchasing Agent," *Administrative Science Quarterly* 7 (September 1962): 161–186.

Advisory, Audit, and Line-Staff Relations

Philip Browne and Robert Golembiewski, "The Line Staff Concept Revisited," *Academy of Management Journal* 17 (September 1974): 404–417. Melville Dalton, *Men Who Manage* (New York: Wiley, 1959); and "Changing Staff-Line Relationships," *Personnel Administration* 29 (March 1966): 3–5, 40–48. Carl Heyel, ed., *The Encyclopedia of Management* (New York: Reinhold Book Corporation, 1963), pp. 620–622. Andrew Pettigrew, "The Influence Process between Specialists and Executive," *Personnel Review* 3 (Winter 1974); and "Towards a Political Theory of Organizational Intervention," *Human Relations* 28 (March 1975): 191–208. Leonard Sayles, *Managerial Behavior* (New York: McGraw-Hill, 1964). William Whyte, *Organizational Behavior* (Homewood, Ill.: Irwin, Dorsey Press, 1969), chapter 18.

Managerial Implications of Power and Politics

John Miner, *The Management Process,* 2d ed. (New York: Macmillan, 1978), chapter 10.

Cases for Chapter 15

Patience for a Patient

"You girls think you know everything! Who do you think you are, telling me what I can and cannot eat?" shouted Mrs. Marsini from her wheelchair. "I want that piece of chocolate cream pie, so you can just put it back on my tray." Laurie Brown tried to explain to the patient that it was impossible for her to do that unless she received a specific change in diet card from the dietician. At that point Mrs. Marsini completely exploded. "I talked to the dietician this morning and she agreed to allow me to have my desserts with supper. How many times do I have to go through this?" In an effort to avoid any further useless exchange of words with Mrs. Marsini, Laurie simply explained to her that she would check on the diet change as soon as possible. Mrs. Marsini left the cafeteria line still a bit perturbed, yet content with her pie.

Last night a similar confrontation had occurred with Mr. Baker on the dinner line, though Mrs. Marsini was a bit more difficult to handle. She had been a patient at Waverly Care Center since it had opened two years ago. In fact, without her financial contributions in the first initial months, the center probably would never have survived. She was one of various continuing-care patients at the institution, which meant that she would be there until the day she died. She was arrogant, demanding, and did not tolerate disagreement. Most importantly, however, she was a diabetic who had had several severe attacks in the past ten years brought on by her own refusal to follow doctor's orders.

Laurie held the title of diet technician for the Dietary Department of the care center. Actually she was a college student working during the summer at the same place she had held a job during her senior year of high school. She knew her job well, and besides that she really enjoyed it. She and two other girls of approximately the same age each worked two different shifts five or six days a week. Laurie generally had the 11:30–8:00 P.M. time slot and occasionally filled in on the 7:00–3:30 P.M. shift on her days off, if needed.

Upon arriving at 11:30 she would assist the other diet technician in preparing bed trays for any nonambulatory patients. They would then proceed to assist the other thirty or forty patients through the cafeteria line. Each patient had a specific diet card prepared by the dietician according to his or her individual medical problem or need. The diet technician's job was to help the patients select a salad, dessert, and entree according to the specifications of their diet cards and try to make sure they ate well. Laurie had become good friends with many of the patients (she was even one of Mrs. Marsini's favorites) and with all of the dietary staff, which included a dietician, the head of the dietary department, the cooks, dishwashers, a bartender, kitchen assistants, and dietary assistants who aided the diet technicians on the cafeteria line. At supper hour, 6:00–7:00 P.M., Laurie was the only diet technician on duty, which meant that she was responsible for the kitchen staff, the cleaning, and the closing of the kitchen after the meal was over. Things always went fairly smoothly, except when a message of a change in a diet failed to reach the person who needed to know about it. That person was Laurie.

Problems such as these were bound to keep appearing, especially since Waverly Care Center was still quite young and experimental. It was not a typical nursing home nor was it a hospital. Most of the patients fell into one of three categories: (1) continuing care (approximately ten to fifteen patients), (2) terminal (usually a maximum of four or five), and (3) the short-term goal patients, which made up the majority of all the patients at the center. This group usually consisted of patients recovering from an operation or waiting to be admitted to a nearby nursing home. Waverly also carried a day-patient program which involved therapy, recreational activities, and lunch at the facility. It was almost like a country club for some of the patients, such as Mrs. Marsini. This led them to forget sometimes that they were there for their health, not for a vacation. Still, they had their reasons for being cross or impatient. Many of them had spent full, vivacious lives; they were now essentially confined to one building day in and day out. It was the duty of the Waverly staff to understand the patients' situations and to work to help them through each day.

Laurie, although only a summer worker, was dedicated to achieving the main goal of the Waverly Care Center: to make the patients happy and comfortable and to give them the best care possible within the center's power. However, when confronted by Mrs. Marsini in front of the other waiting patients, Laurie felt humiliated and embarrassed by the apparent incompetence of the dietary staff. At the same time she resented the fact that Mrs. Marsini would make such a scene when every night she and her bridge club women would stay down at the cocktail hour until dinner was almost over. Then Laurie and the rest of the kitchen staff would run behind schedule. Mrs. Marsini would hold up the whole line with her usual complaints and remarks. This was all part of the routine night, yet Laurie knew what to do to avoid another unnecessary scene like the one she had just experienced.

After finishing with the rest of the hungry people, Laurie went immediately to complete the paperwork for the day. First, however, she pulled the cardex file for Mrs. Marsini. This file contained all the necessary dietary information on the patient, including her goals, intentions, and physical and emotional state. If there had been a diet change it would have first been recorded in the cardex and then written on the diet card the patient carried to meals. If possible, the person recording the diet change (either the dietician or diet technician) would also transmit the new information to the attending diet technician. Laurie reviewed Mrs. Marsini's file only to find that no diet change had been recorded. Either someone failed to record the information or Mrs. Marsini had just wanted to have a dessert. Laurie decided to go with the former explanation for several reasons.

First, during the course of the day in the Dietary Department of Waverly Care Center, there was often a rush of activity that forced everyone to concentrate only on immediate problems—such as the arrival of the peaches just an hour before lunch when peach pie was on the menu. Secondly, there had been several previous changes in Mrs. Marsini's diet card concerning desserts. When Laurie first started working in Dietary, Mrs. Marsini ate desserts at all times. Later, when she began to abuse this privilege, her doctor and the dietician decided to restrict her diet to a normal diabetic schedule without sugar. Since that time, Mrs. Marsini had complained bitterly every now and then about her diet. Laurie had thought there might be a diet change, but as of that night she had not been officially notified of any. Mrs. Marsini was the first person to inform Laurie that the dietician had given her approval for the change. For some reason, the dietician's written diet order had not been recorded in the cardex nor relayed orally.

Before leaving that night Laurie searched the diet technician's desk in search of the written order. She found it in the In Basket beneath various other papers. She recorded the diet change in the cardex file and on the patient's card and then wrote a note to the morning diet technician to remind her of the change. Laurie made sure she posted it in plain view where it would be seen as soon as the morning staff arrived. She finished her normal duties for the night and went home.

The following day Laurie arrived at work around 11:20. She went in to say hello to the head of Dietary, Barbara Schaeffer. Barb and she talked for a few minutes, and then Laurie told her about the prior night's incident. They discussed other similar occasions when a diet order had been misplaced or neglected. It was decided that a staff meeting for the diet technicians, diet assistants, and the dietician would be called for the following day. Laurie left Barb's office ready to begin her day's work. Later on that afternoon she sat down and began to prepare a few suggestions for the meeting. She did not want the other diet technicians to feel that they were solely responsible; she knew she had to present her ideas clearly and objectively. She also wanted to make a few proposals on how to alleviate some of the resentment on the part of a few of the elderly patients towards the younger dietary staff members. Laurie felt confident about the meeting. She hoped it would go well and that something constructive would be done about the problems at hand. After all, it was the health and well-being of all of the hundred patients in the nursing home that was at stake.

Source: Francis A. Yeandel, College of Business, St. Mary's College.

Problems

1. Who caused the problem at Waverly Care Center?
2. Did Laurie Brown handle this problem well?
3. How did Laurie Brown relate to her peers, subordinate, and superior—and patients?
4. What can Laurie Brown do to prevent these problems in the future?

Liberty Savings and Loan

Liberty Savings and Loan is a medium-size savings and loan firm headquartered in the Philadelphia area. Its president is John Barnesely, age fifty-five, who has spent twenty years with the firm. His experience is on the lending side of the business.

About five years ago Liberty decided to formalize and centralize some of its marketing activities such as advertising premiums. Among other things, Barnesely wanted to enlarge the marketing area (a staff function for a savings and loan firm) to include contact calls on builders, realtors, and potential large depositors.

Barnesely hired his first marketing director, Jim Johnson, from the marketing department of Pennsylvania's largest savings and loan company. Johnson did a good job setting up the department and getting it organized. Then, after three and one-half years on the job, Jim left to head the marketing department of another savings and loan.

John then hired Sonia Ramirez, a thirty-five year old M.B.A. graduate of Temple University. Ramirez had worked in the marketing department of a large savings and loan firm in Pittsburgh. She is married, has no children, and is the daughter of a successful entrepreneur in New York City.

She described her situation to the case writer as follows: "I've been on the job a year now and I'm very frustrated. I have developed four major marketing programs that I know would be successful. But only two branch managers have cooperated. Four others won't help."

The branch managers are:

- Arthur Steiner: 25 years old; B.S., SUNY–Buffalo; 4 years with Liberty. He cooperated.

- Ralph Paul: 33 years old; B.S., SUNY–Albany; 8 years with Liberty. He cooperated.

- Ernesto Oliva: 36 years old; B.S., SUNY–Binghamton; 7 years with Liberty. He refuses to cooperate.

- Willson Bolton: 47 years old; B.S., NYU; 10 years with Liberty. He makes many small criticisms of the programs and does not follow through.

- Juan Roderiquez: 42 years old; 2 years at New York Community College; 18 years with Liberty. He agrees to cooperate and then "forgets."

- Vincent Kybal: 28 years old; 2 years at California State University at Los Angeles; 4 years with Liberty. He loses the plans and does not follow through.

Problem

You work for Ramirez, and she has asked for your advice on how to increase her effectiveness with the branch managers. What are your suggestions?

Chapter 16 Effective Relationships with Work Groups

Learning Objectives

1. Learn techniques for managing a work group effectively.
2. Be able to differentiate between formal and informal work groups.
3. Realize the important role the informal work group plays in meeting each member's needs.
4. Learn what groups do for the firm.
5. Understand how groups develop and how an effective work group functions.
6. Develop an understanding of how you can handle conflict constructively in a manner which fits your leadership style.
7. Learn what makes a successful chairperson and/or committee member.

Chapter Outline

Why Are Work Groups Important?

What Is a Group?

The Informal Group

What Groups Do for Their Members

Social and Affiliation Needs

Identity, Recognition, and Ego/Esteem Needs

Security and Power Needs

Other Needs

Implications for Management

What Groups Do for Firms

Socialization of New Employees

Getting the Job Done

Decision Making

How Groups Form and Develop

Effective Groups

Factors in Groups Effectiveness

Groups Working against Organizational Objectives

Intergroup and Intragroup Conflict

Committees

Problems with Committees

Making Committees Effective

Summary

Questions

Case: The Day the Machine Department Had a New Supervisor

Case: Shepherd Manufacturing Company

Why Are Work Groups Important?

Thus far in this book, I have focused mostly on the processes and problems of managing individuals. Occasional references have been made to groups. For example, one definition of management was "getting things done through people." *People* is plural; it refers to a number of human beings. When I discussed decision making, I contrasted decision making by the individual with group decision making (Chapter 9). Clearly, the job of a manager involves handling group situations as well as individual problems.

The central concern of this chapter is managing groups of people. The subject is an important one because in fact, managers do manage groups of people—divisions, departments, or work units, for example. Groups are composed of individuals. But the group influences these individuals just as the leader does. Group pressures can affect the productivity and performance of the manager's department positively or negatively. Not infrequently, managers must help settle conflicts that develop within and between groups of employees. And as peers, managers spend much of their time—certainly at middle management and top management level—working in groups, which are usually called committees.

Thus successful managers must understand the dynamics of group behavior at work. This chapter focuses on human behavior in groups, drawing on the discussion of individual behavior presented in Chapters 5 and 6 and expanding it to material specific to group behavior.

What Is a Group?

Throughout your life you have been part of many groups. You and your brothers and sisters formed a group. You joined the Scouts or similar organizations, and these were groups. Your class at school was a group. At work, too, you will rarely operate alone. In most organizations, getting the work done takes a group effort.

There are various types of groups in an enterprise. To begin with, groups may be either formal or informal.

A formal group is a set of two or more people who see themselves as a group, are interdependent with one another for a purpose, and communicate and interact with one another on a more or less continuing basis.

In many cases (but not always) the members of a formal group work closely together physically. Formal groups are created (usually by managers) to fulfill specific tasks clearly related to the enterprise's purposes. They can be permanent, like departments in an enterprise, or temporary, like committees or task forces. Task forces are formed to achieve a purpose and then disband. But sometimes these "temporary" groups exist for years.

An informal group is a set of two or more people formed by mutual attraction of its members.

It is not formed by the firm. The informal group, which is also called a clique, usually supplements the formal group in achieving the firm's objectives. In addition, it plays a significant role in satisfying the needs of its individual members.

There are three types of informal groups (or cliques): the *horizontal clique* (a group of people who work in the same area and are of the same rank and status—for example, all supervisors); the *vertical clique* (a group of people of different rank and status within the same department); and the *mixed clique* (a group of people of different rank and status from different departments in different locations). The latter two types of groups may form because their members have known each other in the past or know each other off the job.

The Informal Group

In this section, I will try to give you a picture of a typical informal group. This example will serve as a reference point in the subsequent discussion of the purposes groups serve for their members and their firms.

In a job I held some years ago, I was part of an informal group. It consisted of about fifteen salespersons who called on grocery stores all day. To help you understand the purpose the informal group serves, let's discuss the typical salesperson's official job and day. The salespersons could not spend much time with their fellow salespeople. They had to "fight" all the time. The store owners or managers were clearly in positions of power, while the salespeople were "suppliants," always asking for something: an order for their product, a better shelf position, a display or feature. Occasionally they could offer managers or owners small rewards—a free lunch, tickets to sports events—but usually only once a year or so.

While sometimes the salespeople broke the routine for the owners and managers, telling stories and jokes or repeating community gossip, often the owners and managers were busy and did not want to talk to them. Or they were under competing pressure for the same space or order from "the office" or other salespeople. Then they would respond by being gruff, ignoring the salespersons, or even humiliating them. On some days, needless to say, the members of this informal group felt beaten down.

How does the informal group function here? These people worked alone, calling on stores by themselves. Nonetheless, the informal group influenced each individual member's work life. The group gathered for coffee and lunch and drinks after work. They also attended weekly sales meetings and twice-yearly or yearly national sales meetings together.

At these meetings—the official purpose of which was to introduce the sales force to new products, new advertising campaigns, price changes, and so forth—the salespeople were encouraged to tell their success stories. (Management saw this as an opportunity for older employees to train newer ones.) In addition, they recounted again and again their "classic" sales strategies. The common thread in these stories was, "How I fooled that SOB (buyer)." Usually the main character was an especially unpleasant buyer whom the salesperson oversold by playing on his or her weaknesses.

For example, one of Charlie's buyers, representing an independent group of stores, continually humiliated him. I asked him to sell this buyer 500 cases of a new product. In a classic sales strategy, Charlie exploited the buyer's weakness: hatred of chain stores.

Charlie: Well, Joe, this new product, Kool Pops, is really going to sell. In fact it's on allocation (limited sale). You're entitled to 500 cases, but I'm afraid your small stores couldn't handle that many. I'd hate to see you overloaded, so I suggest you take 250 and we'll give the other 250 to A&P or Kroger.

Joe: The hell you will! What do you mean my stores aren't big enough? I'm entitled to 500, and by God I get 500. You SOB, don't you dare give any of my cases to those . . . A&P and Kroger.

Each time this story was told there was uproarious laughter. Charlie now had the buyer right where he wanted him. He sold his quota and the buyer could not complain, since he had insisted that he needed all 500 cases. By telling this story Charlie got the recognition he needed, satisfied the group's social needs, and taught new salespeople some "tricks of the trade."

Whenever the group met, there was good-natured banter. Each individual was constantly reminded of his or her most outstanding "failings." John, a 300-pounder, was kidded about his eating and his fondness for gardening. He was the group's boss. Charlie, in spite of his ordinary looks and fifty years, was charged with being a stud and getting his orders by "performing" with the women in the buyers' offices. Bill, whose role was to appear befuddled (like a fox), always lost "small" orders only to send in bigger ones "by mistake." And of course Roy, who was bald, was "Curly" to the others. In the next section I will point out what was really going on in this group and how managers can facilitate or harm informal groups by their actions.

What Groups Do for Their Members

By becoming a member of a group, a person fulfills several types of needs:

1. Social and affiliation needs.
2. Identity, recognition, and ego/esteem needs.
3. Security and power needs.
4. Other needs—
   a. for stable work perceptions and norms.
   b. for information.
   c. for relief from boredom.
   d. for replacements for ill or absent employees.

Social and Affiliation Needs

In Chapter 6 Maslow's "social need" was described, as was McClelland's "need for affiliation." Through the friendship and support they offer, groups serve as the primary mechanism for satisfying these needs. The work group is the most likely place to find understanding, companionship, and comradeship at work. Job problems and often even personal problems can be discussed with group members. After all, many of us spend more waking hours per day with our coworkers than with anyone else.

Acceptance by others is a very rewarding experience, and we go to great lengths to obtain it and avoid rejection. The work group is usually the source of acceptance at work. If it becomes a source of rejection, an alternative source of acceptance is sought, often with great difficulty. So employees join work groups and work at being accepted in order to satisfy their need for affiliation (social need).

What was really going on with the salespeople in the informal group described above was fulfillment of their social needs. The banter, kidding, and talk among group members—called "schmoozing" by Robert Schrank—is a vital element in the group process that enables members to achieve their social needs.[1] Interpersonal interaction of this or some other sort is essential to survival. Recent research indicates that loneliness can even kill people.[2] Salespersons, auditors, and others who work alone need groups.

Remember that there are individual differences in the need for social interaction expressed through chatter, banter, horseplay, and the like. Some people prefer to work alone and produce more when doing so. It has been argued that southern European people prefer more social interaction of this type than northern Europeans, blacks more than WASPS, and so on. Rather than focusing on supposed ethnic differences, it probably makes more sense to realize that some individuals have a greater need for affiliation than others and that some jobs provide for this need better than others. In any case, output quantity and quality, costs, and employee satisfaction are more important than quiet, neat workplaces.

Identity, Recognition, and Ego/Esteem Needs

The second reason people become involved in work groups is that the groups can satisfy the recognition–ego/esteem needs described by Maslow. They can also make a significant contribution to a person's identity development. As discussed in Chapters 5 and 6, a major part of the identity of those for whom work is important comes from the workplace. Most middle-class and upper-class people (and many lower-class individuals as well) identify themselves as dentists, hospital administrators, personnel managers, or the like. The work group is the primary source of recognition and esteem for these individuals. Other people may not know what a biochemist is or how important he or she is to the lab, but the work group knows and provides the necessary feedback. Thus groups help us train ourselves in psychological adjustment, confirm our identity, and maintain self-esteem.

Groups also give us the feeling of "belonging." It is difficult to get such a feeling in most large organizations. The U.S. military establishment employs millions, the City University of New York thousands, and General Motors hundreds of thousands. To get a feeling of belonging within organizations like these one must be a member of a small work group.

So another need was being fulfilled when members of the sales force were encouraged to tell their success stories in the informal group. They were satisfying their recognition needs. Remember, they achieved when they were alone. No one saw it. Their discussion of their achievements served to satisfy their need for recognition as well as to train others. The third time Charlie told his classic story about fooling the buyer, everyone knew the facts. Everyone also recognized that it provided Charlie with self-esteem and energized him to go out and face hostile buyers again.

Security and Power Needs

Groups also help employees satisfy their security needs (Maslow) or their need for power (McClelland/Atkinson). If a group supports an employee against "arbitrary" demands by outsiders (other groups, managers, clients), it gives that employee more control over his or her destiny, a sense of power, and, therefore, dignity. The evidence is fairly strong that most employees join unions to protect themselves against what they perceive to be arbitrary or capricious acts by supervisors. Groups provide the employee with similar feelings of security. By joining groups employees hope to protect themselves against outside pressures.

Other Needs

Groups serve a number of purposes in addition to those just discussed. They help establish and stabilize perceptions of the workplace. They also serve as sources of information, of help when members are sick or absent, and of relief from boredom through mutual interaction.

Implications for Management

Some managers do not understand the value of groups. When they enter an office or workplace and hear chatter or banter, they scold the employees, telling them to "get to work and cut out this nonsense." This has the effect of *reducing* both employee satisfaction and productivity.

But, you say, group interaction can go too far, so that productivity suffers. This happens in a few cases. Before you react negatively to interaction, however, check the output. If it is high, you know the group is functioning well. If it is low, you may have to point out the need to increase it to the group.

What Groups Do for Firms

Groups perform at least three functions that are important to a firm's success:

1. Socialization of new employees.
2. Getting the job done.
3. Help in decision making.

Socialization of New Employees

Sociologists term the process of orienting new employees *socialization*. By this they mean teaching the new employee the work norms; that is, how to behave at work. In some cases groups "slow down" employees who are "working too hard" and showing up the other members. But they do the opposite, too. If an employee is not working hard enough, the group pressures him or her to "get in line." If an employee is lazy, comes in late, or fools around too much, the output of the whole group goes down. Or the slacker is noticed by bosses or other groups and the word gets around that that group is a "goof-off" group. Few groups want such a reputation. So the group pressures the slacker to meet the group's norms of output, work hours, and the like. This pressure takes the form of talking to the employee, shunning or ignoring him or her, or, in extreme cases, physical pressures. Thus the group orients and integrates the new employee into the enterprise's work rules and norms and keeps the employee under control.

After all, the supervisor cannot watch every employee all the time, but the group can.

Getting the Job Done

Although the enterprise is responsible for training the new employee and getting the work done, this is often accomplished by the work group. Usually the new employee gets some training on how to do the job. Rarely is this enough to get the job done well. The work group really teaches the employee how to cope with the job, how to handle the 1,001 variations on the techniques taught in the training program that are needed to get the job done.

Many parts of the job may have to be done by two or more people. Someone in the work group helps out at such times. For example, theoretically the departmental secretary types and the duplication operator runs the machine. In fact, when the duplication operator has a lot of work the secretary helps out by helping to collate the work. Then the duplication operator helps the secretary proofread the report just typed. They could work separately, but cooperation helps them both. Thus work groups facilitate both training and operations and therefore are beneficial to the enterprise.

Decision Making

Effective decision making is discussed in detail in Chapter 9. Here I want to point out that some decisions turn out better when several people with different backgrounds and training make them jointly than if one person makes them alone. Again, well-established groups that are operating effectively can make better decisions. This will be discussed more fully at the end of the chapter. Clearly, it makes sense for a manager to learn to work with and through groups instead of trying to prevent their formation. To do this, the manager should have an idea of how groups form and develop.

How Groups Form and Develop

Groups do not spring into being from nothingness. Their formation and development appears to take place in the following stages.

Stage 1: Initial Formation A number of people with the abilities necessary to achieve an organizational objective are assembled and assigned a task. At this stage of development it is important that individuals recognize the social need to belong to the group and that they be willing to give and receive friendship and other marks of affiliation. For it is in their self-interest to do so.

Stage 2: Development of Objectives At this stage the group seeks to establish common task objectives. To the extent that these objectives are clearly understood, are generally agreed on, and are relevant to the needs of individuals, they are more likely to be achieved.

Stage 3: Elaboration of Structure Coordination becomes paramount at this stage. Formal leaders are appointed by management, and communication is encouraged in an attempt to reinforce the structure.

Stage 4: Development of Leaders To supplement the formal leadership of the supervisor (boss or company executive), informal leaders develop. These are the people whom group members turn to when they encounter problems. Leadership studies have identified at least two leaders of work groups: the task leader (usually the formally appointed leader), who pays primary attention to formal achievement of objectives, and the social leader (informal leader), who provides "social maintenance." The informal leaders tend to be those who have the most status both on and off the job—in other words, the "right" education, skill, sex, age, seniority, ethnic background, and social mobility.

Ralph Stogdill gave us a shorthand for labeling these stages of group development.[3] Stage 1 he calls **Forming.** Stages 2 and 3, in which problems of development are confronted, are grouped under the label **Storming.** **Norming** is the term applied to Stage 4, when the group establishes its norms, and Stage 5—which Stogdill adds to the list—is dubbed **Performing.**

In addition to formal groups, smaller groups evolve within or across formal groups. It is important to be aware of these subgroups too.

Effective Groups

Not all groups operate equally effectively.

An effective work group is a work group whose members function as a team and participate fully in group discussions; whose objectives are clearly developed; and whose resources are adequate to accomplish its objectives.

Factors in Group Effectiveness

Let us briefly discuss factors that influence group effectiveness.

Size of group The effective group is relatively small. In fact some studies have come up with specific numbers; for example, seven is the ideal maximum for a decision-making group and fourteen is the maximum for a fact-finding group.

Theoretically, as a group gets larger it could become more effective. The potential for a greater variety of talents is higher. Members also have a better chance of finding people they like to work with. But the disadvantages of size more than offset the advantages. More effort must be used to get the group to function. Splinter groups may form. Larger groups take longer to function and may not be able to function at all. As the group gets larger, it becomes less efficient, since most members of necessity participate less. Thus, though the research in this area is tenuous, size is an important variable in group effectiveness.

Number of Members Groups with an even number of members make more accurate decisions because they are less likely than odd-numbered groups to resort to the simple process of voting. Odd-numbered groups work faster, however.

Eye Contact and Location of Members Groups whose members are located close together and can interact frequently and easily are likely to be more effective than those whose members are separated by greater distance. This may be due to the ability of the members to maintain eye contact if they are located close together. Eye movement, direction of gaze, and mutual eye contact are important nonverbal interactions that influence group effectiveness. The easier it is to communicate in person, the more likely the group is to be cohesive. Frequency of communication is also important. And, finally, the more isolated the group is from others by distance or other physical barriers, the more cohesive it becomes.

Cohesiveness Group cohesiveness is the degree to which group members are of one mind and thus can act as one body. Sometimes cohesiveness is thought of as group loyalty, group solidarity, or group pride.

Cohesiveness results from homogeneity of membership, stability of membership over time (the more stable, the more cohesive), and high status (the higher the status, the more cohesive the group). In general, cohesive groups are more effective. But it is a circular relationship. That is, as James Davis puts it, "there is nothing like success to increase group spirit and cohesiveness. A near universal finding is that cohesiveness generally increases with success." Cohesion and effectiveness also result when the group satisfies members' needs.

Group Norms Group norms are shared values about the kinds of behavior that are acceptable and unacceptable at work. They develop over time and are reinforced by group pressures on members to conform.

Norms can affect performance positively or negatively. The effects of norms on productivity or performance are affected by cohesiveness. In general, if the group if very cohesive and performance is a group norm, performance will be high. If the group is less cohesive, the norm will be less powerful.

Nature of Task Homogeneous groups (those whose members are alike in such areas as age, education, status, and experience) are better when the task or goal requires mutual cooperation and conflict-free behavior and when the task is simple. Heterogeneous groups are more effective when the task is complex, if speed is not important and if creativity is desirable. In sum, the ideal group is one which is effective from the *group's* point of view *and* one in which the group's norms coincide with the norms or objectives of the firm. A group of this sort arises out of group processes, effective leadership, and managerial processes.

Although the positive aspects of group behavior have been stressed in our discussion so far, groups can also be dysfunctional. Two kinds of problems can arise. One is when a cohesive and effective group works against management's objectives. The other is when conflicts arise between and within groups.

Groups Working against Organizational Objectives

Just as groups can organize to achieve organizational objectives, they can also resist or sabotage them, especially if the leaders fail to interpret these objectives effectively to the group. Groups that resist organizational objectives do not always develop randomly. Sometimes there are real conflicts in objectives between the group and the organization. For example, management's objectives of raising output standards can lead to the fear that jobs will be eliminated. A group may then try to protect less competent employees who cannot meet the new standards through a program of unified resistance. One of the challenges of management is to get groups working with rather than against the organization.

The literature and lore of management contain many cases of groups resisting management and hindering output. Let me present one example of what a cohesive work group can do to make a point and "fight management." A friend of mine was drafted and sent for basic Army training to the Armor Center, Fort Knox, Kentucky. He was part of a typical tank platoon. The platoon members got along well. Then they got a new commanding officer, an ROTC graduate with a swagger stick, an exaggerated opinion of himself, and a low opinion of the men. He worked them long hours, punished them frequently, and never praised them. The men let their performance drop in order to "send him a message." His response was to berate, punish, and overwork them even more.

The men then decided to "take action." They met for a few beers and planned their strategy. They had observed that the commanding officer (whom they called Little Napoleon) took special pride in the Company Day Room (a place designed for troop relaxation, consisting of pool tables, magazines, bulletin boards, and so on). Generally the Day Room was little used and little noticed, but "Little Napoleon" had privates in there waxing and polishing all the time.

The plan was to "send Napoleon a stronger message." One night after it was dark and Napoleon was gone, the group backed up a truck and emptied the day room of its chairs, card tables, pool tables, and so forth and dumped them in the Ohio River. Napoleon was financially responsible for this furniture. Believe it or not, this produced no change in the commanding officer. He redoubled his efforts to discipline the men.

At about this time the unit was to rotate to Europe. After Napoleon had turned in his equipment, the "crew" slipped into the motor pool and changed the numbers on a tank so that it was sent to the wrong unit in Germany. Napoleon was now out several million dollars. This incident finally convinced him that he was doing something wrong. He began to change, and eventually he got the group working with him toward achieving the objectives of the armor division.

Some research indicates that group problems do not develop as often in some groups as in others. Numerous studies have focused on this phenomenon. One of the most enlightening for the manager is that of Leonard Sayles.[4] Sayles describes how groups differ from each other but stresses that there is regularity in group behavior. Sayles observed 300 work groups in thirty companies, mostly in the auto and auto-related industries. He categorized the groups he observed as follows:

1. *Apathetic groups:* Members were relatively low-paid and low-skilled assembly line workers who were interdependent. It was hard to identify the leaders of these informal groups, if they had any.
2. *Erratic groups:* These groups were made up of semiskilled workers who worked together in smaller groups doing jobs that required interaction. Essentially, they all did the same job and were homogeneous. They tended to choose as their leaders big strong individuals who were autocratic. They also tended to be "loudmouths."
3. *Strategic groups:* Members of these groups were skilled employees (such as welders) whose jobs required judgment. Their jobs were not interdependent and were the better or key jobs in the plant. They chose as leaders several people who did their jobs well and represented the group quietly.
4. *Conservative groups:* These groups consisted of the most highly skilled workers in the plant (e.g., plant maintenance employees). They worked on their own. Their jobs were such that they could shut down the plant if they wanted to. They chose as their leader the most technically competent worker, who led quietly and stayed in the background.

Figure 16.1 is my summary of Sayles's characterizations of these four types of groups. Note that Sayles rated the groups on a series of dimensions important to managers ranging from how active they were in unions and

Figure 16.1
The Relationship
between Group Types
and Consequences

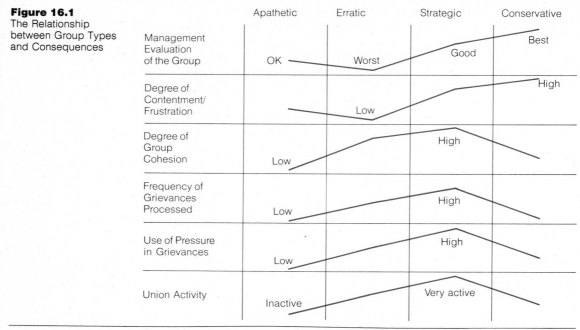

Source: Adapted from Leonard Sayles, *The Behavior of Industrial Work Groups* (New York: John Wiley & Sons, 1963), p. 39. Used here by permission of the author.

how many grievances they filed to how frustrated or contented they were at work. He found that the erratic groups tend to give management the most trouble. They are unpredictable; an action by management may lead to nothing one time but provoke a strike the next time. The apathetic workers tend to be continually and quietly frustrated. The strategic groups have a very rational approach. They make demands on management, but managers know where they stand with them. The conservatives are the "elder statesmen" and usually go about their business without any trouble. Generally speaking, management spends most of its time dealing with strategic groups and trying to keep erratic groups in line.

Groups can cause management problems (1) if they are cohesive and (2) if the work norm develops not into "a fair day's work for a fair day's pay" but into "let's do the minimum we can get by with." But why do negative norms develop?

Chapter 6 gives us one explanation of the development of negative norms: equity theory. If the group feels that it is underpaid, overworked, understatused, or in general receiving less than a fair output (reward) for its input (effort, abilities, etc.), trouble is likely to develop. There is only one way to deal with this situation: find out what the perceived inequity is and do something about it (raise pay, increase status, lower negative outputs, etc.).

In addition to rectifying the immediate problem, the manager may be able to ward off some future grievances by taking some of the following steps:

- Improve the group norms by leadership and interpersonal influence methods discussed in the previous two chapters; that is, improve the social rewards for the group.

- Improve the working conditions and financial rewards for the group, perhaps instituting a group incentive plan.

- Encourage competition between groups to increase the performance of a laggard group.

- A last resort, if all else fails, is to break up a problem group by transferring its members, laying them off, or even firing those who are the least productive.

Intergroup and Intragroup Conflict

The second kind of problem which can develop within or between groups is conflict.

Conflict is said to exist between two or more individuals or work groups when they disagree on a significant issue (or issues) and clash over the issue.

Figure 16.2 is a model that depicts how conflict takes place. Here the conflict situation is called an episode.

In his studies of conflict, Louis Pondy found that conflict is not a series of isolated incidents but a set of incidents; thus it is part of a process.[5] The present episode is partly influenced by preceding episodes. The present episode comes about because of conditions in the environment and other forces leading to latent (or less obvious) conflict. People perceive these conditions differently (see Chapter 5), and then the actual incident occurs (*manifest conflict*). It can be handled by various conflict resolution techniques. After the episode comes the *aftermath*, which includes hurt feelings on the part of the "loser" and good feelings on the part of the "winner."

Causes of Conflict

Conflict is a complex phenomenon. It rarely develops from a single cause. The major sources of conflict appear to be the following:

1. *Differences in group objectives* The parties involved in conflict may be pursuing quite different and opposing objectives. Management may be

Figure 16.2
The Dynamics of a
Conflict Episode

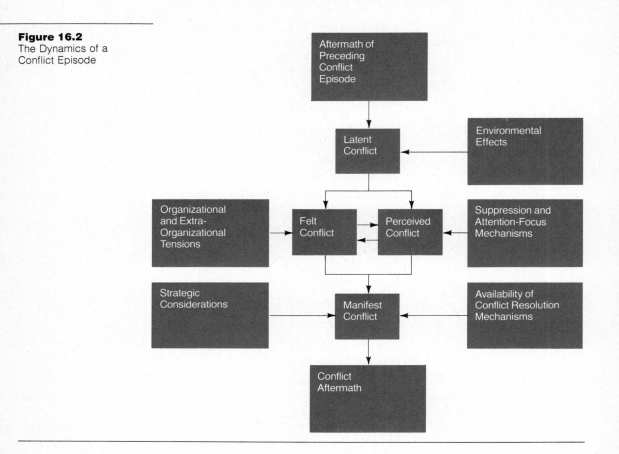

trying to keep costs down, while unions are seeking higher wages. One of the objectives over which conflict often develops is power. Often the leaders of one faction are fighting for increased power at the expense of another group. Perhaps (in McClelland's terms) they have a high need for power.

2. *Differences between individuals* Conflict may result from an inability to communicate because of differences in perceptions and attitudes toward a problem. It can be compounded by differences in personalities. Personal dislike acts as an information filter, causing conflicts that are really personality conflicts though on the surface they may seem to result from differences in perception.

3. *Differences resulting from job or structure* Some jobs call for more interaction with others. This provides more occasions for conflict. For example, a scientist working alone in his or her lab has fewer occasions for conflict than a manager of a typing pool. Poor structural design and

unclear relationships with overlapping authority patterns can also lead to conflict.

The greater the number of potential causes of conflict present in the situation, the greater the probability that conflict will develop.

Kinds of Conflict

There are various kinds of conflict: conflict within an individual, conflict between organizations, conflict within an organization. The latter is the focus of this section.

Organizational conflict takes two forms: interpersonal conflict and intergroup conflict. Interpersonal conflict is conflict between two or more people as individuals. A boss and a subordinate can come into conflict, or two supervisors can become involved in conflict. Intergroup conflict is conflict between two or more units (for instance, sales versus operations) or two or more groups (line versus staff, officers versus enlisted soldiers).

Conflict Management

Although generally viewed in a negative light, conflict can be of some value to the enterprise. It provides the opportunity for new leaders to arise and for the enterprise to examine and possibly change its objectives in order to respond to changing environments. Some believe that conflict relieves boredom. Franklin Roosevelt felt that conflict was necessary for effective policy making. By appointing advisers who would clash and then assuming the role of arbitrator in their disagreements, he believed he was able to weed the bias out of the opinions they offered.

When is conflict useful? William Evan, a contingency theorist, asserts that conflict is to be avoided in crisis organizations such as armies and in stable enterprises, but desirable in such volatile enterprises as R & D organizations.[6] Claggett Smith found that conflict is undesirable in most effective businesses but useful in effective unions and voluntary organizations.[7] Although there is not a lot of research on this subject, what there is tends to support the contingency position: Conflict is sometimes good, sometimes bad, and the manager should design a control and conflict resolution system to fit the amount of conflict that is desirable in his or her organization.

Conflict management includes all actions and mechanisms used by executives (or parties in conflict or independent third parties) to keep conflict from interfering with achievement of the enterprise's objectives.

What is done about conflict is in part a function of the attitudes of managers (and employees) toward conflict. Of course managerial attitudes toward conflict are closely related to leadership styles. Traditional leaders believe that conflict reflects a failure of managerial planning and control and so must be suppressed and dealt with severely. Participative leaders contend that conflict is normal, even desirable, and can be managed so that an equilibrium state is attained. Consultative leaders take the position that conflict sometimes arises, that it is more likely in some departments than in others, and that it should be both minimized and managed.

There are three functional approaches to managing conflict:

- Discuss the conflict fully with the parties involved and work it out.
- Solve conflict by majority rule, compromise, or hierarchical appeal.
- Suppress conflict by use of authority with subordinates; be competitive with peers; be persuasive with superiors.

Traditional leaders rely on dominance or power to settle a conflict; the person (or coalition) with the most power imposes the solution. Sometimes the solution is simply to suppress the conflict. The participative leaders try to work it out through bargaining, persuasion, problem solving, and confrontation. Consultative leaders try in-between mechanisms: discussion followed by a vote (majority rule); compromise (each gets part of the loaf); or political mechanisms, changing the structure, or if necessary, submitting the dispute to an impartial arbitrator or hierarch.

To summarize, the research evidence on conflict management indicates that conflict has many causes, that it does *not always* reduce productivity, and that there are many effective ways of reducing conflict. Thus it would seem that the "right" method for managing conflict depends on the nature of the enterprise and its managers.

Committees

Besides managing groups of employees, managers spend much of their time as members of committees and task forces and other such groups, which have a role in all aspects of the managerial process, from planning to control. In fact, some feel that managers rarely act alone anymore, as the Chas. Addams cartoon here indicates.

A committee is a group of two or more persons created to serve a particular purpose, make a decision, or make a recommendation.

Committees come in different varieties. A *board* or *commission* is a group of individuals appointed or elected to help manage an organization. Examples are the board of directors of a corporation, the board of trustees of a university, and the state parks commissions. The committees we usually find at lower levels are of two types. A *standing committee* is one appointed for a rather lengthy time to serve a specific purpose. A safety committee in a business and a promotions and tenure committee in a

Source: Drawing by Chas. Addams; ©1975 The New Yorker Magazine, Inc.

"There are no great men, my boy—only great committees."

university serve as examples. A committee appointed for a specific short-term purpose—to make a particular decision or recommendation, for example—is called an *ad hoc committee*. A committee created to review whether a merger offer for the corporation should be accepted, rejected, or counter-offered is one such ad hoc committee. A committee appointed for a specific purpose might also be called a task force (see Chapter 15).

Why are committees used? There are a number of good reasons, some of which are the same as reasons given for group decision making in Chapter 7.

- With more participants in discussion, recommendation, and decision making, there is likely to be greater acceptance by participants and their work units.

- With committees composed of representatives of affected units, potential coordination problems can be worked out before decisions are made.

- Committees diffuse power; sometimes decisions and problems are too important to give all the authority to settle them to a single person.

- If a committee is properly constituted, more experience and different backgrounds can be brought to bear on the issue or problem it is supposed to resolve.

- Committees can serve as fast and fully accurate communication- and information-processing devices.

- Committees can serve to provide newer managers with additional training and experience.
- Committees can be used to avoid lodging all the "blame" in one person when hard and unpleasant decisions must be made.

Committees are widely used in all kinds of organizations, including businesses. They tend to be disliked by most businesspersons in spite of this wide usage. *But committees are like people. They can be effective or ineffective.* It is a manager's job to make them effective both as a chairperson and a member.

Problems with Committees

There are a number of reasons managers generally dislike committees. They usually relate to problems some poorly-run or -constituted committees have encountered. For example:

- Committees are very expensive. This is not necessarily true unless a committee is asked to solve problems a single manager can solve.
- Committees are time-consuming. Poorly structured committees are indeed a waste of time.
- Committees can be poor decision makers. This is particularly true when they use the "group think" process described by Irving Janis in which they solve problems by accepting the decisions that involve the least amount of conflict—and that, consequently, are often mediocre.[8]
- Committees can be indecisive. Some authorities contend that committees are better at analysis than at recommendations and synthesis of data.
- Committees can lead to serious differences and conflict among members.
- Committees can be used as a guise to put off assumption of responsibility.

Making Committees Effective

Just as there are some good reasons for using committees, there are also some good procedures for increasing their productivity and effectiveness. Both chairpersons and members can contribute to the productivity of committees by attending to the guidelines set down in Table 16.1. Clearly, there is more to an effective committee than what takes place at the committee meetings. Committee members and chairpersons must prepare for the meetings and review—and sometimes even rework—the committee's actions after the meetings.

Care must also be taken by the person who establishes the committee if the committee is to be effective. The chairperson should be chosen carefully, with consideration given to how her or his ability and personality will suit the leadership role and relate to the committee's duties and

Table 16.1

Guidelines for
Increasing Committee
Effectiveness

Chairperson Prior to the Meeting	During the Meeting	After the Meeting
Limit committee size. (Some research indicates a committee of 5 is ideal; more than 15 is too big.)	Set the right tone; encourage participation by *all* members.	See that the secretary distributes the notes promptly.
Select members who are informed and who can act in a conscientious and reasonable manner.	Avoid dominating the meeting.	Make the same preparations for any follow-up meeting as for the first meeting.
Get a clear definition of the committee's responsibilities and authority.	Avoid competing with members for "equal time" in discussion.	Schedule meetings so that the committee work conforms to the specified timetable.
Communicate this definition along with agenda and supporting documents to members so they can prepare for the meeting.	Summarize discussion from time to time.	After the final committee meeting, thank members in person as well as in writing.
Call members, remind them of the time and place of the meeting, and clarify any points in agenda, etc., as necessary.	Keep discussion on the appropriate subject.	Communicate the results of the committee's work to the right authorities verbally and in writing, as required.
Choose a secretary to take notes and distribute them to members after each meeting.	Be interested and alert.	
Start the meeting on time.	End on time.	

Committee Members Prior to the Meeting	During the Meeting	After the Meeting
Read preparatory materials and develop preliminary ideas.	Be alert and attentive.	Rethink your initial position; reread the secretary's notes.
Consult with those you represent to gain their ideas and responses to your preliminary ideas.	Participate, being sure to state your position clearly.	Consult with those you represent for their responses and suggestions.
Arrive at the meeting on time.	Try to be as rational as possible, especially when responding to persons you do not like or to those who are severely critical of your suggestions.	
	Avoid dominating the discussion.	
	Encourage other members to participate.	

responsibilities. The date on which the committee's work is to be completed should be set clearly and early, and the chairperson should be reminded of it a short while before it arrives. Meeting times designed to restrict the committee's opportunities to indulge in overly long, unproductive sessions can also be suggested. The hours just before lunch or quitting time—11:00 A.M. or 4:00 P.M., for instance—are sometimes good choices. This ends our discussion of groups. With the general knowledge provided in this chapter of how groups function and what some of their benefits are, you should now be able to take steps to make the groups you are involved with function more smoothly and efficiently.

Summary

This chapter focused on managing groups of people. Groups are composed of individuals, all of whom influence each other. They also influence superiors.

Groups may be formal or informal. They may be permanent or temporary. Formal groups are created to accomplish specific tasks. Informal groups are formed by their members and can either help or hinder the achievement of the organization's needs. The interaction of a typical informal group—a group of salespersons—was described. Informal groups are important in fulfilling the recognition, social, and other needs of their members.

At least three functions of groups are important to a firm's success: (1) socialization of new employees, (2) getting the job done, and (3) help in decision making. Because of the significance of groups, it makes sense for a manager to learn to work with and through them.

A manager should also understand how groups form. The formation/development occurs in four stages: initial formation (Stage 1); development of objectives (Stage 2); elaboration of structure (Stage 3); and development of leaders (Stage 4).

An *effective work group* is one whose members function as a team and participate fully in group discussions; whose objectives are clearly developed; and whose resources are adequate to accomplish its objectives. Factors influencing group effectiveness include size of the group, number of members, eye contact and location of members, cohesiveness, group norms, and nature of the task. The ideal group is one in which the group's norms coincide with the norms or objectives of the firm.

Groups can be dysfunctional in two ways. They may resist or sabotage organizational objectives. Or conflict may develop within or between groups. *Conflict* is said to exist between two or more individuals or work groups when they disagree on a significant issue (or issues) and clash over it (them). Major causes of conflict appear to be (1) differences in group objectives, (2) differences between individuals, and (3) differences resulting from job or structure.

It is important to note that conflict does not always reduce productivity.

How conflict is handled is in part a function of what attitudes managers (and employees) have about it. Traditional leaders view conflict as a failure of managerial planning and control and suppress it. Participative leaders feel conflict is normal, even desirable, and can be managed so that an equilibrium state is attained. Consultative leaders realize conflict sometimes arises and feel that it should be minimized and managed. The preferred leadership style will influence the manager's approach to conflict. There are three basic approaches: (1) discuss the conflict fully with the parties and work it out; (2) solve conflict by majority rule, compromise, or hierarchical appeal; and (3) suppress conflict by use of authority with subordinates, competition with peers, and persuasion with superiors.

The final section of the chapter dealt with special groups such as committees and task forces. A *committee* is a group of two or more persons established to serve a particular purpose, make a decision, or make a recommendation. The reasons committees are used were given along with some guidelines for effective committee work.

Questions

1. Why is it important for you as a manager to be able to manage groups?
2. What is a formal work group? An informal group? What purposes do groups serve for their members? Use examples from the text and personal experience to illustrate this.
3. One of your office managers is always scolding the employees to stop chattering. Since productivity is high, how can you convince him or her the "chatter" is healthy and necessary?
4. Explain how groups form and develop. Why is it important for you as a manager to be familiar with this process?
5. What is an effective work group? Discuss the factors which can influence group effectiveness.
6. Why do groups sometimes resist or sabotage organizational objectives? According to Sayles, what kind of group is most likely to respond in this manner?
7. How would you as a manager try to handle the group in Question 6?
8. What is conflict? The text states conflict rarely develops from a single cause. Do you agree with this statement? List some possible causes of conflict.
9. You are a traditional manager. How do you feel about conflict, and how would you handle it? Answer the same question from the point of view of a consultative manager. A participative manager.
10. What can you do to be an effective chairperson of a committee? An effective committee member?

Notes

[1]Robert Schrank, *Ten Thousand Working Days* (Cambridge: MIT Press, 1978).

[2]James Lynch, *The Broken Heart: Medical Consequences of Loneliness* (New York: Basic Books, 1977).

[3]Ralph Stogdill, *Individual Behavior and Group Achievement* (New York: Oxford University Press, 1959).

[4]Leonard Sayles, *The Behavior of Industrial Work Groups* (New York: McGraw-Hill, 1963).

[5]Louis Pondy, "A Systems Theory of Organizational Conflict," *Academy of Management Journal* 9 (September 1966): 246–256.

[6]William Evan, "Conflict and Performance in R and D Organizations," *Industrial Management Review* 7 (Fall 1965): 37–46.

[7]Claggett Smith, "A Comparative Analysis of Some Conditions and Consequences of Intraorganizational Conflict," *Administrative Science Quarterly* 10 (March 1966): 504–529.

[8]Irving Janis, *Victims of Group Think* (Boston: Houghton Mifflin, 1972).

References

Why Are Work Groups Important?

Chris Argyris, "The Incompleteness of Social-Psychological Theory," *American Psychologist* 25 (October 1969): 893–908. James Davis, *Group Performance* (Reading, Mass.; Addison-Wesley, 1969). Sara Kiesler, *Interpersonal Processes in Groups and Organizations* (Arlington Heights, Ill.: AHM Publishing, 1978), chapters 2, 4, and 7. Edgar Schein, *Organizational Psychology* (Englewood Cliffs, N.J.: Prentice-Hall, 1970). Alvin Zander, *Motives and Goals in Groups* (New York: Academic Press, 1971).

The Informal Group

André Delbecq, "How Informal Organization Evolves," *Business Perspective* 4 (Spring 1968): 17–21. Gerald Graham, "Interpersonal Attraction as a Basis of Informal Organization," *Academy of Management Journal* 14 (December 1971): 483–495. Fred Katz, "Explaining Informal Work Groups in Complex Organizations," *Administrative Science Quarterly* 10 (September 1965): 204–223. William Reif et al., "Perceptions of the Formal and the Informal Organization," *Academy of Management Journal* 16 (September 1973): 389–463. Donald Roy, "Efficiency and 'the Fix': Informal Intergroup Relations in Piecework Machine Shop," *American Journal of Sociology* 60 (November 1954): 255–266. Robert Schrank, *Ten Thousand Working Days* (Cambridge, Mass.: MIT Press, 1978).

What Groups Do for Their Members

Solomon Asch, "Effect of Group Pressure upon the Modification and Distortion of Judgments," in *Group Dynamics: Research and Theory,* ed. Dorwin Cartwright and Alvin Zander (Evanston, Ill.: Row Peterson, 1953), pp. 151–162. Theodore Caplow, *Two against One: Coalitions in Triads* (Englewood Cliffs, N.J.: Prentice-Hall, 1968). J. M. Chertkoff, "A Revision of Caplow's Coalition Theory," *Journal of Experimental Social Psychology* 3 (April 1967): 172–177. Barry Collins and Bertram Raven, "Group Structure: Attraction, Coalitions, Communication and Power," in *Handbook of Social Psychology,* ed. Gardner Lindzey and Elliot Aronson (Reading, Mass.: Addison-Wesley, 1968). Kenneth J. Gergen, *The Psychology of Behavior Exchange* (Reading, Mass.: Addison-Wesley, 1969). James Lynch, *The Broken Heart: Medical Consequences of Loneliness* (New York: Basic Books, 1977). Robert Schrank, *Ten Thousand Working Days* (Cambridge, Mass.: MIT Press, 1978). Marvin Shaw, "Why People Join Groups," in *Group Dynamics,* ed. Marvin Shaw (New York: McGraw-Hill, 1971).

How Groups Form and Develop

William A. Gamson, "A Theory of Coalition Formation," *American Sociological Review* 26 (June 1961): 373–382. S. S. Komorita and Jerome M. Chertkoff, "A Bargaining Theory of Coalition Formation," *Psychological Review* 80 (May 1973): 149–162. Ralph Stogdill, *Individual Behavior and Group Achievement* (New York: Oxford University Press, 1959). Noel Tichy, "An Analysis of Clique Formation and Structure in Organizations," *Administrative Science Quarterly* 18 (June 1973): 194–208.

Effective Groups

Larry Cummings et al. "The Effects of Size and Spatial Arrangements on Group Decisionmaking," *Academy of Management Journal* 17 (September 1974): 460–475. David M. Herold, "Improving the Performance Effectiveness of Groups through a Task-Contingent Selection of Intervention Strategies," *Academy of Management Review* 3 (April 1978): 315–325. J. Jackson, *Norms and Roles: Studies in Systematic Social Psychology* (New York: Holt, Rinehart and Winston, 1976). Leonard Sayles, *The Behavior of Industrial Work Groups* (New York: McGraw-Hill, 1963). Ralph Stogdill, "Group Productivity, Drive and Cohesiveness," *Organizational Behavior and Human Performance* 8 (August 1972): 26–43. Edwin Thomas and Clifton Fink, "Effects of Group Size," *Psychological Bulletin* 60 (July 1963): 371–384. Andrew van de Ven and André Delbecq, "Nominal versus Interacting Group Processes for Committee Decision Making Effectiveness," *Academy of Management Journal* 14 (June 1971): 203–212.

Intergroup and Intragroup Conflict

Ronald Corwin, "Patterns of Organizational Conflict," *Administrative Science Quarterly* 14 (December 1969): 507–520. Gordon Darkenwald, "Organizational Conflict in Colleges and Universities," *Administrative Science Quarterly* 16 (December 1971): 407–412. John Dutton and Richard Walton, "Interdepartmental Conflict and Cooperation: Two Contrasting Studies," *Human Organization* 25 (Fall 1966): 207–220. William Evan, "Conflict and Performance in R and D Organizations," *Industrial Management Review* 7 (Fall 1965): 37–46. Alan Filley, *Interpersonal Conflict Resolution* (Chicago: Scott, Foresman, 1975). Ralph H. Kilmann and Kenneth W. Thomas, "Four Perspectives on Conflict Management: An Attributional Framework for Organizing Descriptive and Normative Theory," *Academy of Management Review* 3 (January 1978): 59–68. Susan Lourenco and John Glidewell, "A Dialectical Analysis of Organizational Conflict," *Administrative Science Quarterly* 20 (December 1975): 489–508. Robert Nye, *Conflict among Humans* (New York: Springer Publishing, 1973). Louis Pondy, "A Systems Theory of Organizational Conflict," *Academy of Management Journal* 9 (September 1966): 246–256; and "Organizational Conflict: Concepts and Models," *Administrative Science Quarterly* 12 (September 1972): 296–320. Richard B. Robinson, "Conflict Management: Individual Preference and Effectiveness," *Proceedings of the Academy of Management* (1978). Claggett Smith, "A Comparative Analysis of Some Conditions and Consequences of Intraorganizational Conflict," *Administrative Science Quarterly* 10 (March 1966): 504–529. James Sorensen and Thomas Sorensen, "The Conflict of Professionals in Bureaucratic Organizations," *Administrative Science Quarterly* 19 (March 1974): 98–105. Ross Stagner, "Conflict in the Executive Suite," in *American Bureaucracy,* ed. Warren Bennis (Chicago: Aldine Press, 1970), pp. 85–95; and "Corporate Decision Making," *Journal of Applied Psychology* 53 (February 1969): 1–13. Kenneth W. Thomas, "Pedagogy—Toward Multi-Dimensional Values in Teaching: The Example of Conflict Behaviors," *Academy of Management Review* 2 (July 1977): 484–489. James Thompson, "Organizational Management of Conflict," *Administrative Science Quarterly* 4 (March 1960): 389–409. Daniel F. Twomey, "The Effects of Power Properties on Conflict Resolution," *Academy of Management Review* 3 (January 1978): 144–150. Richard Walton, "Interpersonal Confrontation and Basic Third Party Functions: A Case Study," *Journal of Applied Behavioral Science* 4 (July–August–September 1968): 327–344. Richard Walton and John Dutton, "The Management of Interdepartmental Conflict: A Model and Review," *Administrative Science Quarterly* 14 (March 1969): 73–84. Richard Walton et al., "Organizational Context and Interdepartmental Conflict," *Administrative Science Quarterly* 14 (December 1969): 522–542. Mayer N. Zald and Michael A. Berger, "Social Movements in Organizations: Coup d'Etat, Insurgency, and Mass Movements," *American Journal of Sociology* 83 (January 1978): 823–861.

Committees

Alan Filley, "Committee Management: Guidelines from Social Science Research," *California Management Review* 13 (Fall 1970): 13–21. Alan Filley et al., *Managerial Process and Organizational Behavior* (Glenview, Ill.: Scott, Foresman, 1976). Ray Golde, "Are Your Meetings Like This One?" *Harvard Business Review* 50 (January–February 1972): 68–77. Jay Hall, "Decisions, Decisions, Decisions," *Psychology Today* 5 (November 1971): 86–88. Irving Janis, *Victims of Group Think* (Boston: Houghton Mifflin, 1972). George Manners, "Another Look at Group Size, Group Problem Solving, and Member Consensus," *Academy of Management Journal* 18 (December 1975): 715–724. George Prince, "How to Be a Better Meeting Chairman," *Harvard Business Review* 47 (January–February 1969): 98–108. Victor Vroom and A. G. Yago, "Decision Making as a Social Process," *Decision Sciences* 5 (October 1974): 743–769.

Cases for Chapter 16

The Day the Machine Department Had a New Supervisor

Particular Electronics Corporation is a relatively small electronics firm located in a major midwestern city. The company manufactures a variety of small electrical appliances such as outlet plugs and specially wound cords. A privately owned corporation, Particular Electronics has shown profit each year of its existence since it was purchased by Ed Montgomery and Bill Watkins in 1970. However, profit margins on many items were slim as Particular had as its major competition, small household operators in the Far East, especially Hong Kong. In order to compete with such low-wage competition, Particular had to be cautious about its wages as well. To accomplish this, the company adopted a policy of using only part-time help in its factory operations; employees included students, retirees, foreign nationals, etc. This strategy, coupled with sophisticated time- and labor-saving devices (innovations of Montgomery and Watkins), and the fact that Particular was nonunion, enabled them to ease some of the competitive pressure which they faced. It must additionally be noted that Particular's competitive edge also stemmed from its extremely creative approach in meeting customer needs, solid engineering, and a willingness to take customer orders that larger competitors ignored.

Organization

Most of the products made by Particular pass through each of the three major manufacturing departments: cutting and winding, machining, and assembly. Because of this production flow, a great deal of cooperation and close coordination is needed between the departments. The organization of Particular is described in Exhibit 1.

The Incident

On a Friday in January of this year, an unusual combination of events occurred at Particular. To begin with, Dick Ruthman, plant manager of Particular, was absent—as he was every Friday to attend classes at a local university where he was pursuing an M.B.A. degree. Then, about 10:00 that morning, Sandra Bandor, machine department supervisor, received a phone call informing her that a fire had occurred in her

Exhibit 1
Particular's
Organization
Structure

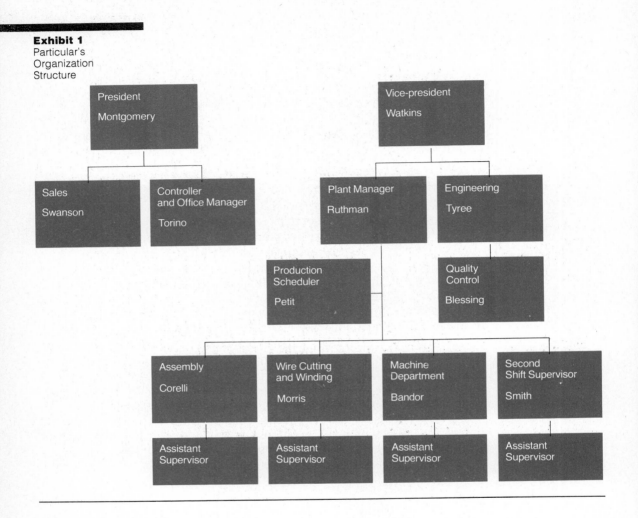

apartment and her sister had been slightly burned in the blaze. Bandor
went back to her department visibly upset but did not say anything to her
work crew. She was in tears when she left for home a few moments later.
To further complicate matters, Sandra's assistant supervisor was not at
work that day because of a death in her family.

Roberta Torino, Particular's controller and office manager, was aware
of the dilemma Sandra's departure would cause, especially with the
concurrent absences of the plant manager and the assistant machine
department supervisor. Frequently involved in factory matters, and also
mindful of the organization's small size and informality, Roberta decided
to act to fill the supervisory void in the machine department. She told Joan
Petit (production scheduler): "You will have to watch the jobs they are

working on, and make sure they are working on the right ones according to the daily schedule." Joan was selected by Roberta for this task, even though she had had only two months of experience, because she was familiar with the jobs the machine department was working on that day.

Upon reaching the machine department, Joan told the women she was taking over for the day because Sandra had gone home. The women seemed to be upset by this news. Some even stopped work and started talking to one another. Joan decided to seek out Liz Candelli, supervisor of the assembly department and senior supervisor on the floor. The two women discussed the situation in Liz's office, which, because of the large glass window, was clearly visible to the women in the machine department. Joan wondered out loud whether she should separate the two informal leaders of the department who seemed to be talking the most and generally causing disruption among the other department personnel.

When Joan returned to the machine department after her discussion, she found some of the workers were still standing around in small groups and talking. Two of them, the informal leaders, were again the most vocal and demonstrative. It was then that Joan decided to separate the two ringleaders by assigning them to operations which were physically distant from each other. One of the ringleaders told Joan, "Nothing personal, honey, but we don't like to be told what to do by that bitch in the assembly department." Joan assured her that the assignments were strictly her idea.

Another woman (the other ringleader) told Joan that she was going home at noon. Joan later found out that she had been the assistant supervisor in the machine department at one time but had been demoted to the ranks about a year before this incident. Joan said nothing but could not help noticing that none of the women looked very happy and that they were working at a very low level of output.

Confused and concerned with what appeared to be a work stoppage, Joan decided to seek executive advice this time. After a brief recitation of her story to Ed Montgomery, Bill Watkins, Roberta Torino, and Rod Tyree (the engineering director), the two owners of the company decided that they would not get involved in the situation. They explained to Joan that the chain of command dictated that Dick Ruthman should handle the problem when he came in on Monday. Moreover, they did not want to "go over Ruthman's head." Rod Tyree, however, asked for and received permission to talk to the machine department women. Rod said he thought he might be able to "calm them down."

The women told Rod that they were not really angry toward Joan Petit but that they resented very much the job reassignments which they believed Liz Candelli had suggested to Joan. Moreover they felt Candelli was trying to punish them through Joan's intervention. A few women did, however, ask Tyree by whose authority Joan Petit came to be the machine department supervisor that day. Tyree's efforts to calm the women proved somewhat fruitful insofar as none of the women left early, and all stayed on the job.

**Postincident
Events**

When Dick Ruthman heard the story of Friday's events, he decided to call a meeting of the entire machine department, including Sandra Bandor and Joan Petit. Joan felt the two ringleaders should be punished. Dick, however, only told the women that Joan had his support whenever she was given a supervisory assignment and that everyone should "just forget the whole thing."

Source: This case was prepared by Donald J. Petersen, College of Business, Loyola University, Chicago, Ill. Reprinted by permission.

Problems

1. What problems at Particular are illustrated by this incident?
2. How might this situation have been handled more effectively?
3. Describe the situation with reference to the organization and its employees, the behavior of those involved, and the attempts to resolve the problems.
4. What might be done to salvage this situation?

**Shepherd
Manufacturing
Company**

Charles Johnson, the new foreman of the drill press department at Shepherd Manufacturing Company, was wondering how to deal with what appeared to be a solidly formed clique comprised of ten of the twenty-one drill press operators in his department. These particular operators all worked on adjacent drill presses, bantered back and forth during working hours, ate lunch together, and frequently were involved together in after-hours social functions.

Ike Ramey, the union shop steward for the drill press department, seemed to organize most of the clique's after-hours functions, and his leadership within the group was also quite apparent on the job. It appeared obvious to Charles, after only a week in this department, that every time he made a request of these ten men the operator would look to Ike for his approval before he would cooperate. Already, on two occasions, Ike had come to Charles as spokesman for "his men" regarding matters having nothing to do with the union or his position as steward.

The situation appeared particularly intolerable in that the youngest man in the department had come to see Charles at lunchtime today while the others were out. He complained that he was being forced to hold down his output. This young man, Johnny Rivers, said that Ike had mentioned to him on several occasions that he should hold his completed plates down to fifteen per hour. Johnny had told his foreman that it was easy for him to turn out twenty-five per hour, even though he had only been on the job for three weeks. He found the work much more boring and even made more mistakes when working at such a slow pace. Yesterday he had resumed his former pace of twenty-five plates per hour and had already today been called a "fink" by one of his coworkers and a "rate-buster" by another. Then shortly before lunchtime, he found that his lunch box had mysteriously disappeared. Although he knew exactly where it had been left, his questions of his fellow workers had brought only knowing smiles but not his lunch.

As Charles leaned back in his chair thinking over the situation existing in his department, he could hear the men laughing and talking as they returned from lunch.

Source: This case was prepared by Roland B. Cousins, College of Business, University of Southwestern Louisiana, Lafayette, La. Reprinted by permission.

Problems

1. What can Charles Johnson do to increase productivity at Shepherd?
2. Did Charles handle Johnny Rivers properly?
3. What can Charles do to better manage Ike Ramey?

Chapter 17 Effective Communication

Learning Objectives

1. Understand the communication model as it applies to effective interpersonal and organizational communication.
2. Learn some guidelines for effective communication.
3. Be aware of the ways individual differences influence word meanings.
4. Learn some guidelines for effective listening.
5. Understand how nonverbal signals enhance messages and indicate they have been received.
6. Learn to choose the appropriate media, time, and channels of communication to ensure that your messages are received.

Chapter Outline

Introduction to the Communication Process

As I noted in Chapters 2 and 3, most managers spend the bulk of their time communicating. They are involved in two kinds of communication: interpersonal and organizational.

Interpersonal communication is the process of exchanging information and transmitting meaning between two people or in a small group of people.

Organizational communication is the process by which managers systematically give information and transmit meaning to large numbers of people within the organization and to relevant individuals and institutions outside it.

Many communication theories rely on the observations of Aristotle, who lived centuries before Christ.[1] He thought interpersonal communication consisted of three key elements: the speaker, the speech, and the listener. Modern theorists, too, have contributed to our understanding of communication, adding several elements to Aristotle's classic model. The communication model shown in Figure 17.1 reflects this expanded communication theory.

How does this model work? First the sender has the idea for the

Figure 17.1
A Communication Model

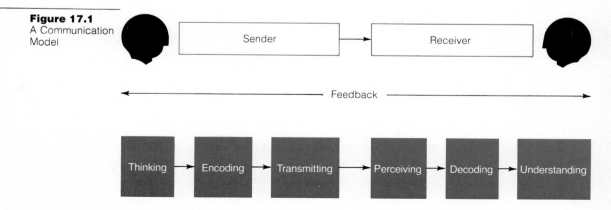

message (1, thinking). Then the sender encodes the message into the form in which it will be transmitted: words, bodily movements such as gestures, or other symbols such as writing (2, encoding). Next the message is sent verbally, either in speech or in writing (3, transmitting). Then a formal or informal channel—the route through which messages pass—is chosen. After these three steps, the sender has completed the initial phase of communication.

At this point, the receiver must decode the message. Decoding, or interpretation, is affected by how the receiver perceives the symbols and nonverbal behavior of the sender (4 and 5, perceiving and decoding). The communication process is complete when the reader comprehends the message (6, understanding).

Another important element to consider is feedback. At the time that person-to-person communication is taking place, cues are sent between the sender and receiver which affect the process of communication.

The Importance of Communication

Before examining the various ways that managers communicate, it is necessary to understand what communication means to the effective manager. Communicating is important for a number of reasons.

Managers Spend Most of Their Time Communicating You will recall from our earlier analysis of the various types of managers and their duties that many experts contend that 75 to 95 percent of a manager's time is spent communicating. For example, in the study of two chief executives discussed in Chapter 8, Neil Snyder and I observed that the average percent of time our subjects spent in direct communication (telephone calls, scheduled meetings, unscheduled meetings) was 64 percent.[2] Additionally, these chief executives spent approximately half of the remaining 36 percent of their time in some activity related to the process of communication. Clearly, good communication skills are crucial to managerial success.

Communication Is Needed for Managerial Effectiveness To achieve effectiveness in other managerial functions, one has to be an effective communicator. Almost every aspect of management involves communication. According to Mel Grosz, "planning and control, two principal responsibilities of management, are essentially information-processing activities."[3] It takes communication to make these processes work. And research by Donald Kirkpatrick indicated that mistakes in judgment may be due to errors in communication more than 75 percent of the time.[4] In the situations he observed, these mistakes frequently resulted because the receiver did not understand the message.

Communication Leads to Power Power is often attained through effective communication. Communication skills are also essential for exercising power or leadership. Consider, for example, the impact of Franklin Roosevelt's communications on the downhearted, depressed Americans of the 1930s: "The only thing we have to fear is fear itself." And remember how Churchill persuaded the almost-beaten British in 1940 to contribute more "blood, sweat and tears" to the war effort. Consider how Hitler mobilized a cultured, advanced nation like Germany. You do not have to know German to understand the powerful words and gestures he used to convey the message "Germany over all." Executives in business and other enterprises do not usually have the impact that these political leaders did. But communication skills of the first order were required for J. C. Penney to revitalize his company after the Great Depression and for AMC's Roy Chapin to turn his company back from the brink of ruin in the seventies.

Good Communication Leads to Organizational Effectiveness There is reasonable evidence that if an organization is effective in its communications it will be effective overall. In fact, Chester Barnard, probably one of the best businessmen and management theorists the United States has ever produced, indicated that communication is the key to management:

The coordination of efforts essential to a system of cooperation requires an organized system of communication. Such a system of communication implies centers or points of interconnection and can only operate as these centers are occupied by persons who are called executives. It might be said that the function of executives is to serve as channels of communications.[5]

Fred Allen, chairman and chief operating officer of Pitney Bowes, attributes a substantial portion of the company's enviable performance record to its effective communication program: "While our results cannot be attributed solely to our communication program, it clearly deserves much of the credit."[6]

For all these reasons, it is important for managers to understand how to communicate and what tools and media to use. The rest of the chapter will focus on these subjects.

Building Blocks of Communication

Language and nonverbal behavior are the building blocks of communication. You must have a basic knowledge of words, their meanings, and the nonverbal signals that modify what words convey to be an effective communicator.

**Language as
a Tool of
Communication**

Language—words and the way we combine them—is the basis for almost all the forms of communication in which we engage. To encode a message we use words.

**Effective
Encoding**

Encoding means, simply enough, "using the 'right' words to reach the receiver." There is an old anecdote about the boys at a British school sitting in the chapel pews listening to an Anglican missionary talk about his missionary work in Africa. After a few sentences in English the missionary shifted into Swahili for the rest of the talk. This missionary could have been effectively communicating to his parishioners in Africa but had ceased to communicate in England.

Words have many meanings. One expert has pointed out that the 500 most often used words in the English language have *an average* of twenty-eight different meanings. In this respect English is no different from the 3,000 other languages used on the earth.

What words convey is determined by the meanings ascribed to them, the way they are used in a sentence, the overall context in which they are used, and the setting in which they are used.

We learn the meanings of words the way we learn other things. In Chapter 5 we reviewed how influences such as parents, friends, school, and jobs give meaning to attitudes. This is how we learn words as well. The meanings of words change, too. The slang from my college days is meaningless today; "living in your own space" and other current expressions will someday be equally meaningless.

The same language differs according to geographic location, too. An American who travels in England finds that hundreds of our words have no meaning there. To communicate, the traveler has to learn the equivalent British words. Here are some examples:

North American Word	**British Word**
hood (of car)	bonnet
trunk (of car)	boot
windshield	windscreen
vacation	holiday
clothes pin	peg
blue book (for exam)	script
truck	lorry
elevator	lift

Just as the American in England must ask to get on the *lift* and watch out for the *lorry,* so the manager must communicate with words understandable to the board of directors, the vice-president, the janitor, or the photocopy machine operator. Each may speak a different language.

In sum, to communicate effectively it is important to keep several facts in mind. First, words mean different things to different people. Second, they vary in degree of abstraction. Third, language, by its very nature, is incomplete. It should be supplemented with nonverbal cues, and ideas should be expressed in several ways. Fourth, language reflects not only the personality of the individual but also the culture of his or her society. And finally, language creates a social reality. Thus some guidelines for effective encoding would include the following:

- Communicate with the right degree of intensity for the message.
- Avoid rambling; have the message thoroughly encoded before delivering it.
- Do not deliver the message too quickly.
- Use some repetition to make sure the receiver gets and understands important concepts.
- Watch for feedback cues showing lack of understanding, and repeat the message when such cues are received.
- Use simple and direct wording.
- Phrase the message in such a way as to tap the receiver's needs (see Chapter 6).

Nonverbal Communication

When we communicate, we use nonverbal signals to get our message across. Randall Harrison, an expert on nonverbal communication, estimates that no more than 35 percent of the social meaning of a message is conveyed by words used in face-to-face communication.[7] The rest is conveyed nonverbally or is lost. I will first briefly mention the forms of nonverbal communication that are used infrequently at work and then describe those used more frequently.

Nonverbal Signals

The sign of the cross sends a message. So does an auto horn or a siren. In baseball, signals are used to send specific messages. Status symbols are the most frequent application of nonverbal communication at work. They include offices with windows, large desks, and badges of authority. In some· workplaces, wearing a suit separates a manager from the white-shirt-and-tie clerk and the blue-overalls worker.

Touch and Body Movements

Which is the more powerful way of communicating a love relationship: saying "I love you" or kissing? Just as touching and body movements are important ways to communicate in one's personal life, so they play a part in communicating at work.

One typical way of communicating is the greeting or farewell handshake. Among southern Europeans and Latin Americans, an abrazzo (hug) is substituted. The strength of the handshake/abrazzo can communicate very effectively.

The whole body and its movements can communicate. When slumped, the body may indicate dejection; when lax, indifference; or when tense, apprehension. Tapping of the foot or fingers may indicate boredom. How one applauds may measure degree of enthusiasm; how one nods may indicate extent of agreement. These and other body movements can be important elements in the communication process.

Space/Distance Factors

The physical distance a communicator puts between himself or herself and the receiver may influence the communication process. As John Keltner puts it,

The space factor is particularly noticeable in small-group meetings. I recently worked with a seminar, the first few meetings of which were in a regular conference room, which was so arranged that members of the group sat at long tables arranged in a hollow square. There was open space in the middle, and a number of unused chairs allowed the group to break down into subgroups separated by empty chairs. While the group was meeting under these conditions, there was a very low level of close personal interaction in the sessions. At the suggestion of one of the members, we moved across the street to a dingy little cellar, less than one third the size of the conference room, in which old end-up cable drums had been arranged closely together in a tight circle. There were just enough and all members could gather around the drums only if they sat very close together. Almost immediately after moving to this setting, the tone of the meetings changed from impersonal to a highly personal interactive atmosphere.[8]

Time and Communication

According to Edward Hall, "time talks."[9] How fast we speak and the gestures we use may indicate the intensity of our message. Whether we are on time to a meeting may indicate how important we consider the subject to be discussed. Also, pausing during verbal communication allows nonverbal behavior to reinforce the words spoken.

Facial Expressions

Have you ever seen how Marcel Marceau communicates with his face? We communicate many messages in this way. A frown, for example, signals discontent. Raised eyebrows indicate shock or disbelief, and tightened jaw muscles or squinting often means antagonism. Eyes tell a story too. Many managers learn more by "reading" their boss's eyes than by listening to what he or she says.

Nonverbal Voice Communication

How the voice is used sometimes says as much or more than the words used. Several aspects of voice inflection contribute to communication (see Figure 17.2):

- *Pitch* (relative highness or lowness of tone): Variety of pitch leads to interest on the part of the receiver. A high pitch can mean antagonism; a low pitch, complacency.
- *Quality:* The calmer the quality, the greater the clarity of the message.
- *Volume:* The louder the volume, the greater the emphasis.
- *Rate and rhythm:* A very fast rate bores the audience. Faster rates, shorter comments, and more frequent pauses often indicate anger or fear. Too many pauses can mean indecision, tension, or resistance.

Nonverbal Communication and Managers

By now it should be clear that nonverbal behavior is a very important part of communication. It should be used to *reinforce* the words spoken. Most nonwritten communication is a mixture of verbal and nonverbal "signals." Some varieties of mixed communication are illustrated in Figure 17.3.

In effect, nonverbal communication reinforces the verbal message. Thus managers need to communicate through both verbal and nonverbal media. For example, suppose a supervisor asks a new employee if he understands the job. The employee nods and says yes. But an examination of his facial expression and body tension may indicate that the answer really should be no. Shouting into the telephone instead of talking in your normal tone of

Figure 17.2
Voice Inflection and
Communication

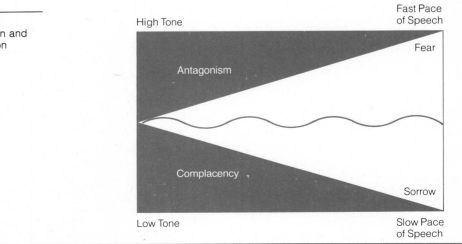

Source: George Porter, "Non Verbal Communications," p. 4, reproduced by special permission from the June 1969 *Training and Development Journal*. Copyright 1969 by the American Society for Training and Development, Inc.

Figure 17.3
Examples of Mixed
Verbal/Nonverbal
Communication

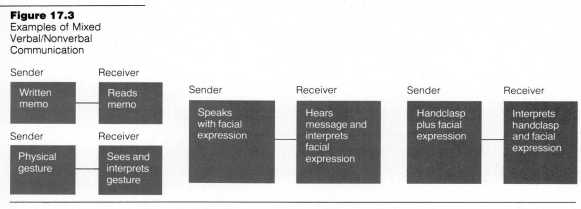

Source: George Porter, "Non Verbal Communications," pp. 3–4, reproduced by special permission from the June 1969 *Training and Development Journal*. Copyright 1969 by the American Society for Training and Development, Inc.

voice is a form of verbal communication (words) and nonverbal communication (inflection/loudness).

Of course in addition to using nonverbal methods to send more effective messages, managers should be observant of messages sent nonverbally as well as verbally by superiors, peers and subordinates. Sensitivity to nonverbal messages enhances the accuracy with which the receiver interprets the message and thus the entire communication process.

Verbal Communication Media

There are two basic ways we communicate verbally. Verbal communication takes place (1) when we speak and (2) when we write. Let's examine what is involved in effectively using the two basic communication media: speech and writing.

Oral Communication

The most frequently used medium of communication is speech. Most managers spend most of their time talking. Speech or oral communication may occur when people are face to face or when they cannot see each other. When people are facing each other, nonverbal communication can be used to enhance oral communication. When they cannot see each other—for example, when they are on the telephone—only the choice of words and tone of voice serve to convey the message. This is why many people find the telephone a problematic method of communication.

Although communication between individuals might seem to be a simple process, Raymond Ross's model of it in Figure 17.4 indicates just how complicated it can be.

As Ross has pointed out, interpersonal verbal communication is a process of *mutual* influence, "a transactional process involving cognitive

Figure 17.4
Transactional
Communications
Model

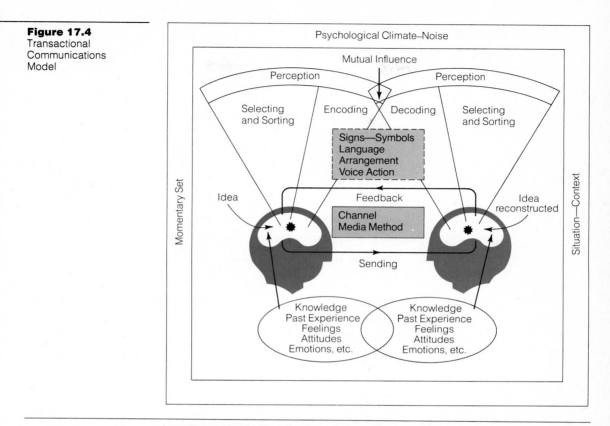

Source: Raymond S. Ross, *Persuasion: Communication and Interpersonal Relations*, © 1974, p. 58. Reprinted by permission of Prentice-Hall, Inc., Englewood Cliffs, New Jersey.

sortings, selecting, and sharing of symbols in such a way as to help another elicit from his own experience a meaning or response similar to that intended by the source."[10]

As Figure 17.5 indicates, differences in communicators' backgrounds (experience, education, upbringing) can create barriers to accurate

Figure 17.5
Conditions for Effective
Verbal Communication

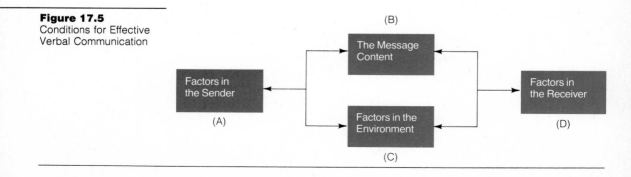

communication. In Chapters 5, 6, and 14, respectively, we have seen how individuals differ in their attitudes, perceptions, and emotions; in motivation and participation; and in leadership styles. I do not intend to review all of this information. Instead, I will concentrate on barriers which prevent effective verbal communication, focusing particularly on the face-to-face encounter.

Barriers to Effective Oral Communication

What factors can prevent us from using our knowledge of language and nonverbal signals to communicate effectively? There are two kinds of barriers to effective oral communication: environmental barriers and receiver barriers.

Environmental Barriers to Communication

Environmental barriers to effective communication are often lumped under the label "noise." Interruptions by other people or stimuli such as a telephone or alarm can prevent effective communication. Sometimes it is possible to avoid interruptions of this sort—for example, by stopping phone calls during an interview. While noise is definitely an environmental barrier, it is not the only one. Problems with the communication channel can arise. The path a message follows may be wrong. Sometimes there is not enough time to communicate as thoroughly as is desirable; time pressure becomes a barrier to communication.

Status and power differences in the communicating parties can also interfere. Indeed, a receiver can be so aware of status differences that he or she focuses on them instead of on the message being communicated. For example, if the president of a firm is trying to communicate to a janitor, it probably is useful for the president to get up from behind the desk and talk to the janitor side by side. The cartoon below illustrates the wrong approach to status differences.

Receiver Barriers and How to Overcome Them

The receiver of a message controls four factors that can hinder or help communication. The sender must be aware of these and try to offset them when they become barriers.

1. *Decoding-translating.* The receiver may misunderstand or mistranslate the message. If the sender is alert and encourages feedback, he or she can send the message again (redundancy), using different verbal and nonverbal media to correct this problem.
2. *Evaluative attitudes.* Some receivers evaluate certain concepts negatively or may react adversely toward certain topics. The topic of unions may be taboo with some people, while the subject of religion may be off limits for others. Again, the sender tries to offset this problem by

"Come in, Frank. I've been eager to communicate downward to you."

recognizing it, being sensitive to it, and utilizing his or her knowledge of motivation in trying to influence the communication process. In such cases, what is needed is what William Keefe called "open minds: the forgotten side of communication."[11]

3. *Degree of interest.* The receiver may not get involved or may listen only partially (selective perception) to the sender's message. This is a difficult problem to cope with. Sometimes you can pick it up in the feedback. When you are communicating to groups of people, some of the receivers will be getting the message, others not. The best you can do to create interest is to try to make your communication interesting by building in messages that contribute to the satisfaction of the receiver's needs. Try to show why the receiver should be listening—how he or she can benefit from the message.

4. *Degree of trust in the sender.* One of the most difficult barriers to overcome is distrust. Before you can communicate effectively, you must be perceived as honest and knowledgeable and viewed with goodwill.[12] Trust develops out of rapport. To lay the groundwork for a relationship of trust, the sender must first establish some common basis for beginning the discussion. Then the sender's qualifications should be introduced. Slowly, a relationship of reciprocal trust can be built up.

So far we have discussed how a sender can communicate more effectively by using language well and understanding the processes of communication. Emphasis has been placed on the sender's side of communication, because the manager is often a sender. Still, the manager must also be a receiver at times. He or she may need help or counsel, receive instructions from superiors, or get complaints from clients. Accordingly, effective listening is an important management tool.

Effective Listening

Listening is probably the weakest link in the oral communication process. When it is inadequate it is a more serious receiver barrier than all those noted above. Poor listening includes not hearing what was said at all, hearing only part of what was said, hearing information incorrectly, or forgetting the message. Unfortunately, it is a common occurrence. One study found that the typical person retained only 50 percent of a message ten minutes after receiving it and only 25 percent of it forty-eight hours later. Poor listening of this sort can lead to lack of performance as well as conflict between the communicators.

There are a number of factors that have a negative impact on listening. Probably the most significant is the fact that a receiver can hear four times as fast as a sender can speak. Thus the receiver can think about the message (or lots of other things) in between the transmission of the words of the message. Other barriers to good listening are listed below:

- *Lack of interest:* It is a poor listening technique to pretend to be attentive when you are not interested in or paying attention to the subject being communicated.

- *Emotional words or topics:* Emotions can interfere with your ability to listen. For example, it is difficult to concentrate on the subject of a communication when you are upset over a personal crisis.

- *Inefficient note taking:* If you get bogged down in the details of the subject, you may miss the main point of a message.

- *Interruptions:* Do not allow interruptions to continue once they occur.

- *Selective listening:* It is poor practice to listen only for facts, letting your mind wander when the subject matter does not involve facts.

- *Personal dislike:* You may be tempted not to listen closely if you do not like the sender.

- *Anticipating the message:* The feeling you "know what the speaker is going to say" may be misleading and interfere with your getting the message.

- *Response preparation:* Avoid using the time during which you are receiving the message to develop your response to what you think the message will be.

Experts on listening describe three kinds of listening styles. *Mechanical listening* is characterized by most of the shortcomings just described. The receiver who is listening mechanically is only going through the motions of listening. *Evaluative listening* is superior to mechanical listening. But although the receiver pays more attention, evaluative listening is characterized by jumping ahead and judging the intent of the speaker. *Empathetic listening* is the ideal listening style. The receiver gives his or her full attention to the speaker. Evaluation is avoided, and the sender trusts and likes the speaker. According to Carl Rogers, empathy is created when the receiver restates what the sender says before responding to it.[13] This gives the sender a chance to clarify the message if it has been misinterpreted.

Listening training can help people improve their listening skills. Aurelius Abbatiello and Robert Bedstrup conducted an experiment in which they trained their subjects.[14] Their trainees listened to a series of tapes. The first tapes were short and simple; later ones became progressively longer and harder to understand. In the more difficult ones, for example, the messages were poorly organized, delivered with negative emotions (such as anger), and garbled with background noise. The subjects in this training program increased their retention rate from 25 to 90 percent. And not only was their retention rate 90 percent at the end of the course, but it was still the same a year later.

Even if you do not have access to listening training, however, you can improve your listening by practicing the following techniques:

- Stop talking and listen.
- Establish rapport with the sender; put the speaker at ease.
- Indicate willingness to listen; look interested, do not engage in other activities, and show empathy.
- Reduce distractions; hold telephone calls and choose a quiet place to communicate.
- Allow time for discussion.
- Listen patiently to the *full* message.
- Keep your emotions in check; do not get angry or lose your temper. Recognize your emotional involvement in some topics and try not to argue or criticize.
- When you are not sure of part of the message, restate what you think you heard in the form of a question.
- When you feel that something is missing (after noting what you did not hear), ask simple, brief, direct questions to get the information needed.

Telephone Communication

Telephone conversation is of course a form of oral communication. Although most executives prefer it to written communication, it is a more difficult medium than face-to-face communication because the phone makes all supplementary nonverbal messages except speed of delivery and tone of voice impossible. Since few nonverbal clues are available, effective

Source: *Wall Street Journal.* Reprinted by permission.

"What a day! Eleven busy signals, nine answering services and ten recorded announcements!"

telephone communication requires that the sender and receiver observe all the techniques for effective listening and sending behavior given above.

Many executives spend a great deal of their communication time on the telephone. Neil Snyder and I found that the two executives we observed in our study spent an average of 6 percent of their working days talking on the telephone.[15] Unfortunately, managers often make very inefficient use of the telephone. Indeed, much of the hectic pace of the typical manager's day is due to lack of telephone management. Here are some suggestions for more efficient telephone use:

- Answer it promptly.
- Call other executives after 10:30 A.M.
- Identify yourself at the beginning of every conversation.
- Speak distinctly, keeping the receiver close to your mouth.
- Have a secretary place your calls to save time. Group your phone calls and make them all together; have the secretary place the next call while you are completing the first one.
- When you are very busy, control interruptions by having a secretary take messages. If you have no secretary, use a recording device to answer the phone and take messages.

These are commonsense ways to save time and avoid interruptions in telephone use. Again, the key point about telephone communication is that your use of words, communication speed, and tone must compensate for the lack of nonverbal means of communication. The phone is quick but it is a tricky medium. In sum, it is reasonable to conclude that for oral communication to be effective a number of conditions must be met (see Figure 17.5). First, the sender must encode the message in words (and nonverbal cues) that will effectively convey it to the sender. Second, the message content must be well organized. Third, there should not be too many "noise" factors in the environment which obscure the message. And finally, the receiver must be willing to listen to and accept the message and able to decode it.

Written Communication

The alternative to oral communication is written communication. Managers prefer to communicate orally, in part because oral communication is quicker. But the main reason they prefer oral communication is that it allows them to supplement their words with nonverbal cues more easily than does written communication. Written communication does have significant advantages, however. Because it provides a record of the message, it improves the receiver's rate of retention. And it is effective in transmitting complicated messages to large numbers of people.

Many forms of written communication are used in business—reports, memoranda, letters, and enterprise newsletters and news magazines. Excellence in written communication is important in management. Good written messages are composed according to the following rules:

1. Prepare a rough draft of important messages to make corrections possible.
2. Draft the message with the receiver and his or her needs clearly in mind.
3. Think through the facts of the message *ahead of time.*
4. Keep the message as brief as possible; eliminate all unnecessary words and ideas.
5. If the message is long, place a summary of the report on the first page. (This summary should make the main points clear, with page references for details on each item.)
6. Organize the message, stating the most important points first. (This way

Source: © The Wall Street Journal. Reprinted by permission.

"Finally, the great American memo."

if the receiver reads only the first few points, the main message will get across.)

7. Give the message a title that clearly conveys its subject.
8. Use simple words and short, clear sentences.

Figure 17.6 is an example of a memo. Which of these eight suggestions do you feel it follows? Which does it violate?

Figure 17.6
A Memorandum for
Evaluation

January 14, 1980

TO: All Biweekly Hourly Employees

FROM: Smedley Jones
        Assistant Director
        Personnel Department

SUBJECT: Time cards

This is to advise you of a cut-off date for turning in time cards. Effective immediately, to be paid on the two-week schedule, you must sign your time card and turn it in to your departmental secretary by 11:00 A.M. *Thursday, the day after the pay period ends.*
   If your time card is not turned in by the deadline, you will *not be paid* until the *next payroll* is submitted.
   Please sign the enclosed form and return to Sally Arthur, indicating you have received this notice and understand the procedure.

SJ/SA

Enclosure

How do you feel the employee who has been handing in time cards on time felt about being required to sign a statement that he or she had read the memo? The message was received clearly. But there was strong negative reaction to the methods used in this memo.

Reading ability and readability are both important to effective written communication. To be of use, messages must be readable. The more closely they adhere to the eight rules listed above, the more readable they will be. Good reading ability on the part of the receiver is essential, too. The receiver must be able to read and understand the message. The appendix to this chapter presents some techniques for getting the most out of reading.

Selecting the Appropriate Medium for Communication

Thus far I have focused on techniques of oral and written communication. As I have noted, managers generally prefer to communicate orally. Still, the way a message is delivered should vary according to what it is. After surveying seventy-two supervisors, Dale Level developed the following guidelines on when and when not to use oral communication, written communication, or a combination of both:[16]

- Oral communication by itself is *most* effective:

to reprimand an employee for work deficiency.
to settle a dispute among employees about a work problem.

- Oral communication by itself is *least* effective:
to communicate information requiring future employee action.
to communicate information of a general nature.
to communicate a company directive or order.
to communicate information about an important company policy change.
to promote a safety campaign.

- Written communication by itself is *most* effective:
to communicate information requiring future employee action.
to communicate information of a general nature.

- Written communication by itself is *least* effective:
to communicate information requiring immediate employee action.
to commend an employee for noteworthy work.
to reprimand an employee for work deficiency.
to settle a dispute among employees about a work problem.

- Oral communication, then written communication, is *most* effective:
to communicate information requiring immediate employee action.
to communicate a company directive or order.
to communicate information on an important company policy change.
to communicate with your immediate supervisor about work problems.
to promote a safety campaign.
to commend an employee for noteworthy work.
(The supervisors did not feel that any message would be ineffective if this method were used.)

- Written communication, then oral communication:
The supervisors did not view this as a frequently used method of communicating.

Communication Channels

A communication channel is the route along which a message passes, that is, the chain of personnel who pass the message on.

There are two kinds of communication channels: formal and informal (See Figure 17.7). Organizations establish *formal* communication channels when they set up structural relationships. In other words, the boss-employee and departmental relationships described in an organization chart define the formal channels. In large organizations these channels are carefully delineated. Lists of people who should receive information and the order in which they are to receive it—sometimes called *routing lists*—are established. A great deal of information passes through these formal channels of communication.

Figure 17.7
Formal and Informal
Channels of
Communication

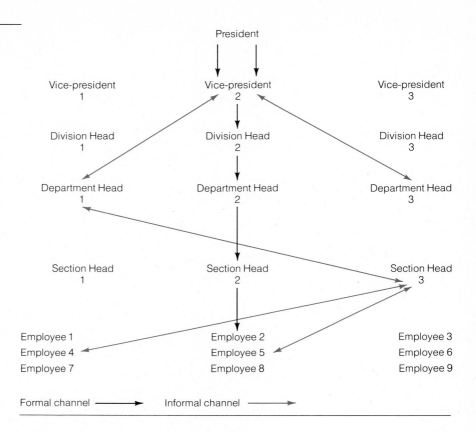

Informal channels, usually called the *grapevine,* exist along with formal channels. These are any channels that do not follow the formal chain of command. Note that in Figure 17.7 the formal channels move directly down (and up) the chain of command while the informal channels move in several directions.

Informal Communication: The Grapevine

Every organization has grapevines. They have several advantages over formal channels of communication, and they fulfill a number of needs.

Grapevines Are Fast Grapevines exist because they get information to people much faster than formal channels. Most people prefer to know important information sooner rather than later.

Grapevines Are Accurate Studies indicate that the grapevine is 80–95 percent accurate. The "inaccuracy" normally takes the form of incompleteness rather than wrong information.

Grapevines Are Efficient Grapevines selectively handle a lot of information. Formal channels have a way of sending information to people who do not need it. The unwanted information may sit on one desk for a long time

Figure 17.8
Grapevine Patterns

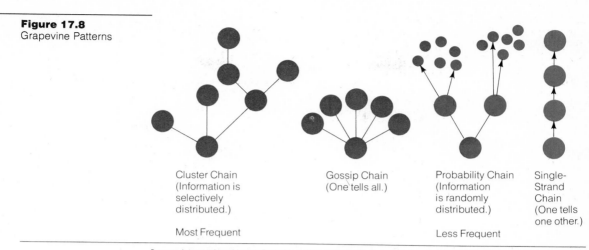

Cluster Chain
(Information is
selectively
distributed.)

Gossip Chain
(One tells all.)

Probability Chain
(Information
is randomly
distributed.)

Single-
Strand
Chain
(One tells
one other.)

Most Frequent

Less Frequent

Source: Adapted from *Human Behavior at Work* by Keith Davis, p. 377. Copyright © 1977 by McGraw-Hill Book Company. Used with permission of McGraw-Hill Book Company.

before it is passed on. Almost never is the formal system faster or more efficient than the grapevine.

Grapevines Fulfill People's Needs Grapevines are based not on hierarchy but on need or desire to communicate: they are made up of people who like each other and want to communicate. Thus they serve social needs, and through speed and accuracy they help fulfill security needs as well. In a way they satisfy recognition needs too. The "communication center" gets recognition when people call him or her to find out "what's going on."

How Grapevines Work

Keith Davis has studied how the channels of the grapevine work.[17] Figure 17.8 illustrates four grapevine patterns Davis found: the single-strand chain, the probability chain, the gossip chain, and the cluster chain. In the cluster chain, by far the most common pattern, A tells several others (B, R, F) the message. Only some of these employees pass the information on (F, C), and only some of those to whom they pass it on tell others. As more people learn the information, the grapevine quiets down. Davis calls this pattern a cluster because each link leads to another cluster of people rather than to just one person. Only a few people, however, assume the role of liaison and start the clusters. Most people learn the information but do not spread it. In Davis's study, 68 percent of an executive group heard the information but only 20 percent spread it; in another study, 81 percent of the executives observed obtained information over the grapevine, but only 11 percent communicated it to others.[18]

Generally the grapevine involves oral communication. Davis, however, has shown that written communications may be passed along the grapevine when a grievance covers more than one location (see Table 17.1).

Employees become active on the grapevine when they have news that is fresh and is likely to be "hot." Jay Knippen studied the grapevine in a large grocery store employing 170 people.[19] (Because of turnover he actually studied 216 employees over time.)

Although the managers in his study accounted for only a few of the 170 employees, they initiated almost 50 percent of the grapevine information. On average, they passed information on to almost eight other people. The typical employee gave only four other people information obtained from the grapevine. Many management books report cases of managers who try to suppress the grapevine. But Knippen found managers active in its use.

Managers, Knippen found, knew about 79 percent of what was passed along the grapevine. Employees knew only 42 percent. Managers got a bit more than half their information from outside the store, but they spread information primarily in their own department. Employees got 78 percent from inside, 22 percent from outside the store, and they too spread the information primarily within their department.

Managers and the Grapevine

The manager who uses a traditional leadership style typically discourages the grapevine, preferring to limit communication to formal channels insofar as possible. The manager who favors a participative style, on the other hand, will use the grapevine frequently and formal channels rarely.

Since grapevines are ubiquitous, speedy, and accurate, managers should think of them as a good communication channel rather than try to eliminate them. They should learn who the liaison people in the informal network are and give those people information to be communicated. It is particularly important to be able to use the grapevine this way to correct incomplete or inaccurate information that is being passed along it.

I once heard of an executive who was in the habit of handing out $20 bills for information about activities and attitudes of employees in the firm. He explained the practice thus: "Look, I have to know what's going on out in the plant. So I have my communication network for finding out." Few executives need a network of paid spies to find out what is going on in their workplace. They should be able to find out through the grapevine.

Formal Communication: The Chain of Command

Most large organizations establish chains of command through which communications of an official nature are expected to flow. As Figure 17.7 indicates, the formal channels parallel the management hierarchy. Almost all written communications—policy statements, letters, memorandums, and official company publications such as newsletters, newspapers, and magazines—are passed along these formal channels.

Table 17.1
Actual Transcript of a
Teletypewriter
Grapevine over a
Company Private Wire
between Two
Warehouse Clerks in
Separate Cities

IS JOE* THERE GA[1]

YES

PUT HIM ON TELEX PLS[2] GA

THIS JOE

THIS SUE AND I AM A LITTLE CURIOUS ABOUT UR[3] TELEX YESTERDAY   COAST CLEAR NOW   SO WHAT DO THEY ASK YOU GA

THE FIRST STUPID QUESTION WAS THEY WANTED TO KNOW WHAT HAPPENED TO CERTAIN ITEMS THAT WERE ON THE INVENTORY ONE MONTH AND NOT ON THE NEXT MONTH   I TOLD THEM IT WAS ONLY LOGICAL TO ASSUME THEY WERE SOLD   SO THEY ASKED TO WHOM   TOLD THEM TO LOOK IT UP ON THEIR COPIES OF THE DR'S[4] GA

UR ANSWER WAS PRETTY GOOD   UR RIGHT   THINGS LIKE THAT COME UP ALL THE TIME BUT UNFORTUNATELY I HAVE TO FIGURE OUT MOSTLY FROM HERE   WHAT ELSE JOE GA

THEY SAID MY INVENTORY WAS SHORT 25 TONS AND WANTED TO KNOW WHY   I ASKED THEM FOR THE FIGURES THEY USED AND I CHECKED IT OUT ONLY TO FIND THEY CANT EVEN COPY THE RIGHT FIGURES DOWN GA

WELL SOMETIMES I GUESS THEY MAKE BOBOS[5] LIKE THAT BUT UR LUCKY ONLY BEING OFF 25 TONS   WE WERE OFF 400 TONS AND IT TOOK ME AWHILE TO FIND IT   WHAT ELSE

THIS IS PROBABLY THE FUNNIEST   I PAY THE LOCAL PAPER HERE EVERY MONTH FOR ADVERTISING AND WHEN OUR STATEMENTS COME HERE FROM CHICAGO THEY NEVER HAVE ANYTHING CHARGED TO ADVERTISING WHICH AMOUNTS TO A FEW THOUSAND A YEAR   I ASKED ABOUT IT AND THEY WERE SURPRISED   I GUESS THEY DONT LOOK AT THE COPIES OF THE CHECKS THAT I MAKE OUT GA

WELL THEY SURE LOOK AT OURS BECAUSE THEY CONSTANTLY ASK US WHY AND TO WHOM AND WHAT FOR WE PAID THIS AND THAT   THE ONLY ONE WHO KNOWS ABOUT CHECK COPIES IS MAX SMITH AND I THINK HE KEEPS GOOD TRACK OF IT BUT U[6] ARE RIGHT THAT IS FUNNY   OH GOOD GA

ANYWAY I REMEMBER GEORGE TELLING ME ABOUT UR PROBLEM AND I JUST WANTED TO LET U KNOW U WERE NOT THE ONLY ONES THAT KEEP IN DAILY COMMUNICATION WITH CHICAGO GA

I THINK IT WAS VERY NICE OF U AND AS FAR AS I CAN SEE I HAVE IT WORSE THAN U SO MY COMPLIMENTS TO YOU AND THANKS AGAIN FOR UR CONCERN GA

THATS ABOUT ALL FROM HERE GA

OK JOE BIBI[7]

Key: *All names are disguised.

[1]Go ahead.

[2]Please.

[3]"Your" or "you are," depending on the sentence.

[4]Delivery receipts.

[5]Errors; "boo-boos."

[6]You.

[7]Bye bye.

Source: *Human Behavior at Work* by Keith Davis, p. 48. Copyright © 1972 by McGraw-Hill Book Company. Used with permission of McGraw-Hill Book Company.

Formal channels are subject to problems that slow down the communications that pass through them. They often need help from the grapevine. Overload and clogging, especially in times of crisis, can afflict formal channels. Another problem is that as the organization gets larger, formal channels have to be used to communicate lengthy rules, regulations, and policies. In many ways, then, the formal channels *supplement* the grapevine or serve the purpose of communicating *official* communication. Finally, formal channels are often very bureaucratic. People who do not want to allow certain information to enter the informal network often tell the sender to "go through channels," assuming that this will slow it down or kill it.

Outward Communication

In this chapter I have focused on communicating *inside* the enterprise. Obviously there must also be communication between the enterprise and entities outside it: the general public, competitors, the government, and so forth. Communications of this sort are normally part of the organization's marketing or public relations activity. They were touched on very briefly in Chapter 4.

Improving Communication in Organizations

Oral and written communication can be improved in many ways. I have already mentioned some of these ways. At this point, I would like to present some general principles for developing a good overall program of communication in an organization.

Good communication is often a consequence of *training programs*. Clayton P. Alderfer, for example, has developed a program for improving intergroup communication.[20] Such programs can help in enterprises where communication between departments or units is poor.

Really important communications call for *repetition*. More than one medium and more than one channel should be used. For instance, an oral communication via the grapevine could be followed by a written communication on the same subject sent through the formal channel.

For especially important communications, the manager should set up a *follow-up and feedback system* to determine whether a message is received and whether it has the desired results. One simple way of accomplishing this is to contact those to whom the communication was directed, ask if they have received it, and in addition, ask how they are responding to it.

Effective managers develop a *climate of trust*. This aids them not only in sending messages but also in receiving information. Managers who wish to establish a climate of trust must not punish senders who are subordinates for delivering unpleasant news. If they do, they will receive unpleasant news only after it is too late to do anything about it. One way to encourage communication is to have an "open-door" policy—to tell senders that the doors are always open and information, whether pleasant or not, is desired. Again, it is important for managers who wish to promote such a policy to be receptive to the sender even when they receive unpleasant news.

Other means of encouraging communication include using suggestion boxes and sounding boards. Douglas Curley has described how General Electric personnel executives regularly gather information on predesignated subjects from a cross-section of employees.[21] Other firms encourage or even require managers to eat in the employee cafeteria from time to time and urge employees to discuss items of concern with managers. Some organizations sponsor social events to develop rapport between managers and employees and thus encourage communication.

Effective firms *regulate the flow of information* to employees so that communication channels are not overloaded. Managers avoid sending too much information through the formal or informal channels at the same time. Especially when important messages are sent, other communications are delayed so as not to distract the receivers' attention.

Timing is important, too. Information must be sent far enough ahead so that the receivers can respond to it on schedule but not so far in advance that they may forget it by the time action is required.

According to Donald Kirkpatrick, there are some times when communication should be avoided:[22]

- When the receiver is preoccupied with other matters such as mental or emotional problems.
- When the receiver is too busy to listen adequately.
- When the receiver is likely to be interrupted frequently.
- When the receiver is angry, frustrated, or in a bad mood.

It is also important to communicate in the right *place.* Table 17.2 presents Kirkpatrick's examples of proper places for certain types of communications.

Summary

Most managers spend the bulk of their time communicating. A communication model was given in Figure 17.1. Steps in the communication process include thinking, encoding, transmitting, perceiving, decoding, and understanding. Thus both the sender and receiver participate in the communication process.

Communication is important to a manager for a number of reasons: (1) Managers spend most of their time communicating. (2) Communication is vital to managerial effectiveness. (3) Communication skills are essential for exercising power or leadership, and (4) Good communication leads to organizational effectiveness.

Language—words and how they are combined—is the basis for every

Table 17.2
The Proper Place for
Communication

Nature of Communication	Proper Place
Constructive criticism	In private. Remove as much anxiety as possible. Avoid interruptions.
Praise	Where convenient. In front of other people if appropriate.
Formal interview (employment, performance appraisal, etc.)	In private. Create an "at ease" atmosphere. Avoid interruptions.
Work assignment	Where convenient and natural. At work place of subordinate or in office of the boss.
Discussion of a problem	In private. Avoid interruptions.
Request for ideas	Wherever convenient.
Information	In private, if confidential. Where convenient, if not confidential.

Source: Donald L. Kirkpatrick, *No Nonsense Communication* (Brookfield, Wis.: K&M Publishers, 1978), p. 60.

form of communication. Words mean different things to different people; it is important to choose words that have the right connotation for the receiver.

Nonverbal signals enhance or inhibit our verbal communications. Such signals include touch and body movements; space and distance between sender and receiver; time or speed of communication; facial expression; and pitch, quality, volume, rhythm, and rate of the voice.

Both oral and written communication were discussed. Guidelines were provided for making both as effective as possible. The principles below serve to summarize the more detailed analyses that were offered in the chapter on what techniques result in effective communication. They apply to all forms of communication.

1. Logically analyze what the message is before preparing the message.
2. Encode the message in words that are meaningful to the receiver.
3. Encode the complete message. (One of the most frequent sources of miscommunication is when the sender condenses or overly shortens the message. The sender must be sure to encode all crucial elements of the message if she or he wishes to communicate effectively.)
4. Transmit the message with sincerity, using reinforcing verbal and nonverbal symbols and minimizing status differentials between sender and receiver. Trust is essential to effective communication.
5. The receiver should be trained to listen effectively and be encouraged to provide feedback and ask questions to clarify items in the message which are not understood.
6. Communication is more effective if it is provided at the right time with the right media and sent through the right channels.
7. The sender should develop a feedback and control system to assure that the messages are received, understood, and given a response.

A **communication channel** is the route along which a message passes—that is, the chain of personnel who pass the message on. When boss-employee relationships and departments are created, formal communications channels are set up. Informal channels called grapevines also exist. Grapevines occur in four patterns: the single-strand chain, the probability chain, the gossip chain, and the cluster chain. Managers can use both formal and informal channels to make their communications effective. Grapevines are fast, accurate, and efficient means of conveying a message. They also fulfill employees' needs. Formal channels follow the superior-subordinate hierarchy; most written communications are routed through them.

Questions

1. Distinguish between interpersonal and organizational communication. In what ways are they similar? Different?
2. Outline the communication model and explain how each step takes place in a typical communication.
3. Why is communicating effectively important to a manager?
4. What do managers need to know about language before they can become effective communicators?
5. Do you think nonverbal signals have a significant impact on communication? What are these nonverbal cues? How does each affect communication?
6. What are the communication media managers use most frequently?
7. How would you overcome receiver barriers which impair verbal communication?
8. You are a personnel manager who has the job of training your firm's middle management in effective listening techniques. What guidelines would you give these managers?
9. How do telephone communications differ from other oral communications? Do the same guidelines apply to both?
10. When are written communications most likely to be used? How can you make sure your written communications are effective?
11. What is a communication channel? A formal channel? An informal channel? Give the strengths and weaknesses of these two types of channels.
12. List some general principles of effective communication.

Notes

[1]Aristotle, *Rhetorica*, in *The Works of Aristotle*, ed. W. D. Ross, 12 vols. (Oxford: Clarendon Press 1908–1952), vol. 11.

[2]Neil Snyder and William Glueck, "Mintzberg and the Planning Literature," *Proceedings of the Academy of Management* (1979), p. 403.

[3]Mel Grosz, "General Theory of Management Communication," mimeographed (Providence, R.I.: Institute of Management Sciences, Research Committee on Management Measurements, 1969).

[4]Donald Kirkpatrick, *No Nonsense Communication* (Brookfield, Wis.: K&M Publishers, 1978).

[5]Chester Barnard, *Functions of the Executive* (Cambridge, Mass.: Harvard University Press, 1938).

[6]Fred Allen, "Ways to Improve Employee Communications," *Nation's Business* 63 (September 1975): 54–56.

[7]Randall Harrison, "Non Verbal Communication," in *Dimensions in Communication,* ed. J. H. Campbell and H. W. Harper (Belmont, Calif.: Wadsworth, 1970).

[8]John Keltner, *Interpersonal Speech Communication* (Belmont, Calif.: Wadsworth, 1970), pp. 116–117.

[9]Edward Hall, *The Silent Language* (New York: Doubleday, 1959).

[10]Raymond Ross, *Persuasion* (Englewood Cliffs, N.J.: Prentice-Hall, 1974).

[11]William Keefe, *Open Minds: The Forgotten Side of Communication* (Belmont, Calif.: Wadsworth, 1970), chapter 9.

[12]Aristotle, *Rhetorica.*

[13]Carl Rogers, "In Retrospect: 46 Years," *American Psychologist* 29 (February 1974): 115–123.

[14]Aurelius Abbatiello and Robert Bedstrup, "Listening and Understanding," *Personnel Journal* 48 (August 1969): 593–596, 638.

[15]Snyder and Glueck, "Mintzberg and the Planning Literature."

[16]Dale Level, Jr., "Communication Effectiveness: Method and Situation," *Journal of Business Communication* 10 (Fall 1972): 19–25.

[17]Keith Davis, *Human Behavior at Work,* 4th ed. (New York: McGraw-Hill, 1972), pp. 261–273.

[18]Ibid.

[19]Jay Knippen, "Grapevine Communication: Management Employees," *Journal of Business Research* 2 (January 1974): 47–58.

[20]Clayton P. Alderfer, "Improving Organizational Communication through Long-Term Intergroup Intervention," *Journal of Applied Behavioral Science* 13 (April–May 1977): 193–210.

[21]Douglas G. Curley, "Employee Sounding Boards: Answering the Participative Need," *Personnel Administrator* 53 (May 1978): 69–73.

[22]Kirkpatrick, *No Nonsense Communication.*

[23]Snyder and Glueck, "Mintzberg and the Planning Literature."

[24]Mortimer Adler and Charles Van Doren, *How to Read a Book* (New York: Simon & Schuster, 1972).

[25]Snyder and Glueck, "Mintzberg and the Planning Literature."

[26]Adler and Van Doren, *How to Read a Book.*

References

Introduction to the Communication Process

Aristotle, *Rhetorica,* in *The Works of Aristotle,* ed. W. D. Ross, 12 vols. (New York: Oxford University Press, 1908–1952, vol. 11. Mel Grosz, "General Theory of Management Communication," mimeographed (Providence, R.I.: Institute of Management Sciences, Research Committee on Management Measurements, 1969).

The Importance of Communication

Fred Allen, "Ways to Improve Employee Communications," *Nation's Business* 63 (September 1975): 54–56. Chester Barnard, *Functions of the Executive* (Cambridge, Mass.: Harvard University Press, 1938). Mel Grosz, "General Theory of Management Communication," mimeographed (Providence, R.I.: Institute of Management Sciences, Research Committee on Management Measurements, 1969). Richard C. Huseman, John

D. Hatfield, and Robert D. Gatewood, "A Conceptual Framework for Analyzing the Communication-Productivity Relationship," mimeographed (Athens, Ga.: Department of Management, College of Business Administration, University of Georgia, 1976). Donald Kirkpatrick, *No Nonsense Communication* (Brookfield, Wis.: K & M Publishers, 1978). Paul M. Muchinsky, "Organizational Communication: Relationships to Organizational Climate and Job Satisfaction," *Academy of Management Journal* 20 (December 1977): 592–607. Neil Snyder and William Glueck, "Mintzberg and the Planning Literature," *Proceedings of the Academy of Management* (1979).

Building Blocks of Communication

Cathrina Bauby, *O.K., Let's Talk about It: Dynamics of Dialogue* (New York: Van Nostrand Reinhold, 1972). David Berlo, *The Process of Communication* (New York: Holt, Rinehart and Winston, 1960), chapters 7 and 8. Kim Giffin and Bobby Patton, *Fundamentals of Interpersonal Communication* (New York: Harper & Row, 1971), chapters 5–7. William Keefe, *Open Minds: The Forgotten Side of Communication* (New York: AMACOM, 1975). John Keltner, *Interpersonal Speech Communication* (Belmont, Calif.: Wadsworth, 1970), chapter 9. Charles K. Ogden and I. A. Richards, *The Meaning of Meaning* (New York: Harcourt, Brace and World, 1956).

Nonverbal Communication

Kim Giffin and Bobby Patton, *Fundamentals of Interpersonal Communication* (New York: Harper & Row, 1971). Bernard Gunther, *Sense Relaxation: Below Your Mind* (New York: Collier, 1968). Edward Hall, *The Silent Language* (New York: Doubleday, 1959). Randall Harrison, "Non Verbal Communication," in *Dimensions in Communication,* ed. J. H. Campbell and H. W. Harper (Belmont, Calif.: Wadsworth, 1970). John Keltner, *Interpersonal Speech Communication* (Belmont, Calif.: Wadsworth, 1970), chapter 6. George Porter, "Non-Verbal Communications," *Training and Development Journal* 23 (June 1969): 3–8.

Oral Communication

William Keefe, *Open Minds: The Forgotten Side of Communication* (Belmont, Calif.: Wadsworth, 1970), chapter 9. Fritz Roethlisberger, "The Executive's Environment Is Verbal," in *Management and Morale* (Cambridge, Mass.: Harvard University Press, 1941). Raymond Ross, *Persuasion* (Englewood Cliffs, N.J.: Prentice-Hall, 1974).

Effective Listening

Aurelius Abbatiello and Robert Bedstrup, "Listening and Understanding," *Personnel Journal* 48 (August 1969): 593–596, 638. Donald Kirkpatrick, *No Nonsense Communication* (Brookfield, Wis.: K&M, 1978). Martin Maloney, "Semantics: The Foundation of All Business Communications," *Advanced Management* 19 (July 1954): 26–29. Ralph Nichols, "Listening Is Good Business," *Management of Personnel Quarterly* 1 (Winter 1962): 2–10. Carl Rogers, "In Retrospect: 46 Years," *American Psychologist* 29 (February 1974): 115–123. Carl Rogers and Fritz Roethlisberger, "Barriers and Gateways to Communication," *Harvard Business Review* 30 (July–August 1952): 46–52.

Telephone Communication

Joseph Cooper, *How to Get More Done in Less Time* (New York: Doubleday, 1962), chapter 10. Neil Snyder and William Glueck, "Mintzberg and the Planning Literature," *Proceedings of the Academy of Management* (1979).

Written Communication

A. S. Burack, *The Writer's Handbook* (Boston: The Writer, 1972). H. Dudley Dewhirst, "Influence of Perceived Information Sharing Norms on Communication Channel Utilization," *Academy of Management Journal* 14 (September 1971): 305–315. Rudolph Flesch, *The Art of Reasonable Writing* (New York: Harper & Row, 1949). Donald Kirkpatrick, *No Nonsense Communication* (Brookfield, Wis.: K&M, 1978). J. S. Lindauer, *Communicating in Business* (New York: Macmillan, 1974).

Selecting the Appropriate Medium for Communication

Dale Level, Jr., "Communication Effectiveness: Method and Situation," *Journal of Business Communication* 10 (Fall 1972): 19–25. Arlyn Melcher and Ronald Beller, "Toward a Theory of Organization Communication: Consideration in Channel Selection," *Academy of Management Journal* 10 (March 1967): 39–52.

Communication Channels

Samuel B. Bacharach and Michael Aiken, "Communication in Administrative Bureaucracies," *Academy of Management Journal* 20 (September 1977): 365–377. Keith Davis, *Human Behavior at Work*, 4th ed. (New York: McGraw-Hill, 1972), pp. 261–273. Marshall Scott Poole, "An Information-Task Approach to Organizational Communication," *Academy of Management Review* 3 (July 1978): 493–504.

Informal Communication: The Grapevine

Keith Davis, *Human Behavior at Work*, 4th ed. (New York: McGraw-Hill, 1972), pp. 261–273. Robert Hershey, "The Grapevine: Here to Stay but Not beyond Control," *Personnel* 43 (January–February 1966): 62–66. Jay Knippen, "Grapevine Communication: Management Employees," *Journal of Business Research* 2 (January 1974): 47–58. Barbara Marting, *A Study of Grapevine Communication Patterns in a Manufacturing Organization* (D.B.A. thesis, Arizona State University, 1970). Jim Montgomery, "'Did You Know . . . ?' Rumor-Plagued Firms Use Various Strategies to Keep Damage Low," *Wall Street Journal,* February 6, 1979. Harold Suttona and Lyman Porter, "A Study of the Grapevine in Governmental Organizations," *Personnel Psychology* 21 (Summer 1968): 223–230. Eugene Walton, "How Efficient Is the Grapevine?" *Personnel* 38 (March–April 1961): 45–49.

Formal Communication: The Chain of Command

Stephen Grover, "Most Firms' House Organs Emphasize Employee News and Avoid Controversy," *Wall Street Journal,* January 7, 1978. Robert Katz and Robert Kahn, *The Social Psychology of Organizations* (New York: Wiley, 1978), chapter 9. Thomas Kindre, "Corporate Policy Programs and Communications Media," in *Handbook in Modern Personnel Administration,* ed. Joseph Famularo (New York: McGraw-Hill, 1972), chapter 72. Norman Maier et al., *Superior-Subordinate Communication in Management* (New York: American Management Association, 1961).

Outward Communication

James Hynes, "Managing the Unmanageable: Harnessing Creativity in Corporate Communications," *Business Quarterly* 43 (Autumn 1978): 68–73. Otto Lerbinger, *Designs for Persuasive Communication* (Englewood Cliffs, N.J.: Prentice-Hall, 1972). Raymond Ross, *Persuasion* (Englewood Cliffs, N.J.: Prentice-Hall, 1974), chapters 4–10.

Improving Communication in Organizations

Clayton P. Alderfer, "Improving Organizational Communication through Long-Term Intergroup Intervention," *Journal of Applied Behavioral Science* 13 (April–May 1977): 193–210. John Athanassiades, "The Distortion of Upward Communication in Hierarchical Organizations," *Academy of Management Journal* 16 (June 1973): 207–226. Bradford Boyd and J. Michael Jensen, "Perception of First Line Supervisor's Authority: A Study of Supervisor-Subordinate Communication," *Academy of Management Journal* 15 (September 1972): 331–342. Douglas G. Curley, "Employee Sounding Boards: Answering the Participative Need," *Personnel Administrator* 53 (May 1978): 69–73. Donald Kirkpatrick, *No Nonsense Communication* (Brookfield, Wis.: K&M, 1978). Karlene Roberts and Charles O'Reilly, III, "Failures in Upward Communication in Organizations: Three Possible Culprits," *Academy of Management Journal* 17 (June 1974): 205–215.

Appendix 17.1: Effective Reading

Mortimer Adler and Charles Van Doren, *How to Read a Book* (New York: Simon & Schuster, 1972). Neil Snyder and William Glueck, "Mintzberg and the Planning Literature," *Proceedings of the Academy of Management* (1979).

Appendix 17.1

Effective Reading

Effective listening is required on the part of the receiver if oral communication is to be effective. Similarly, successful written communication requires effective reading. Two quite different kinds of reading can be of value to the manager: inspectional reading and analytical reading.

Inspectional Reading

Inspectional reading (also called skimming or prereading), focuses on reading through material in a limited amount of time. Its goal is to examine a report, book, etc., in a superficial way in order to find out what it is about. Neil Snyder and I found in the study we conducted that the chief executives read 94 percent of the books, reports, and other written material they received in this manner.[23]

All written material received by a manager should be given an inspectional reading. In this way the manager can determine whether it should be given an analytical reading as well. Mortimer Adler and Charles Van Doren give the following suggestions for effective inspectional reading:[24]

- Look at the title page and preface of the report or book. Read each quickly. Note subtitles. This gives the scope and angle of the work.
- Study the table of contents to get an idea of the structure of the work. This is like looking at a road map before taking a trip.
- Check the index and estimate the range of topics covered and the authors (or reports) referred to.
- Look at the sections or chapters whose titles sound most useful. Read their summary statements (usually on the opening and closing pages) carefully.
- Turn the pages of these chapters or sections, dipping in here and there. Read a paragraph or two, but never more than several pages in sequence. This will give the flavor of the relevant material.

This quick skimming should give you an idea of whether the report or book is worth reading in more detail. If a more thorough reading seems warranted, read the report or book through quickly without stopping to look up words, ponder the material, or understand it. Adler and Van Doren call this superficial reading.

To make most effective use of the report or book, use the following techniques:

- Answer the following basic questions:
  What is it about?
  What was said (in detail) and how?
  Is it true (in whole or in part)?
  What is its significance?

- Read with a pencil or pen.
  Make sure you understand major points (circle key words and phrases).
  Mark the margin beside very important points or sections that are too long to underline.

- For the ten or so most important items in the report (book), place a star in the margin.

- Keep track of a sequence of items by numbering them in the margin.

- Write comments on key points in the margins.

**Analytical
Reading**

Finally, in more important instances you will want to read the book analytically. The purpose of analytical reading is to obtain an in-depth understanding of the content of the communication. The chief executives in the study Neil Snyder and I did read 6 percent of their reading materials in this way.[25] To improve your analytical reading ability, proceed in the following steps:

- Find out what the report (book) is about:
- Classify the report (book) according to kind and subject matter.
- State what the whole report (book) is about with the utmost brevity.
- Enumerate its major parts in order; outline these parts as you have outlined the whole.
- Define the problem or problems the author has tried to solve.
- Interpret the report's (book's) contents:
  Come to terms with the author by interpreting key words.
  Grasp the author's leading propositions by dealing with the most important sentences.

Know the author's arguments by finding them in, or constructing them out of, sequences of sentences.
Determine the problems the author has solved and those he or she has not; of the latter, decide which ones the author knew he or she had failed to solve.

- Criticize the report (book) as a communication of knowledge.
- General maxims of intellectual etiquette:
Do not begin criticism until you have completed your outline and interpretation of the report (book). (Do not say you agree, disagree, or suspend judgment until you can say "I understand.")
Do not disagree in a cranky way.
Demonstrate that you recognize the difference between knowledge and personal opinion by presenting good reasons for any critical judgment you make.
Show where the author is uninformed.
Show where the author is misinformed.
Show where the author is illogical.
Show where the author's analysis or account is incomplete.

Note: Of these last four, the first three are criteria for disagreement. Failing in all of these, you must agree, at least in part, although you may suspend judgment in the light of the last point.

Most reading improvement programs focus primarily on reading speed. In fact, the effective reader reads at several speeds: quickly for less important items, more slowly for more difficult or significant material.

Most ineffective readers *subvocalize;* that is, they move their lips with the words. Poor readers also *fixate*—that is, go over and over certain words or passages—sometimes as often as five or six times. Thus the way to improve their reading speed is to get the eye to move as fast as the brain can. Adler and Van Doren suggest the following method for increasing your reading speed: "Place your thumb and first two fingers together. Sweep this 'pointer' across a line of type, a little faster than it is comfortable for your eyes to move. Force yourself to keep up with your hand. You will very soon be able to read the words as you follow your hand."[26] This can triple your reading speed.

Communication Exercises

Nonverbal Communication

1. Go to a work area where the noise is so loud that people cannot easily talk to one another (for example an auto factory, or lumber mill, or where punch presses are in operation). List ways in which employees communicate nonverbally or get around this problem of communication. Rate the effectiveness of these methods.

2. Keep track of all the nonverbal messages you respond to tomorrow. Identify those that have the greatest and the least effect on your behavior. What conclusions can you draw on the basis of your record of responses?
3. What nonverbal messages do your instructors send? During one week observe carefully and write down the nonverbal messages sent to you by each of several instructors.

Communication Barriers and Effective Listening

4. List things that distract you most from listening. Then discuss the list with others to see if there is a pattern of distractions.
5. Ask someone to read a case in this book and tell you what it is about. Then repeat what you think you have heard. Evaluate how well you listened.

Telephone Exercises

6. Observe someone in an office for two hours. Record how he or she uses the telephone. Prepare a set of suggestions to improve the observed person's telephone behavior.

Written Communication

7. Analyze a paper you have written according to the principles given for effective writing, and determine how you could improve it.
8. Prepare a set of rules to use when writing your next report or paper. Keep it by your typewriter and read it *before* you write your papers.

Effective Reading

9. Analyze how you read the last required reading in a course prior to reading Chapter 17 and determine how you could have read it to make better use of your time and improve your comprehension.
10. Reread Appendix 17.1. Prepare a set of guidelines for *when* you would use inspectional reading and analytical reading at work and/or in school.

Grapevine

11. The next time an organization you are in has a message to get out to its members, note the time of the official notice and start the message simultaneously through the grapevine. Beginning the next day, ask the

members of the organization if they heard the message, how they heard it, when they heard it, and determine how completely they understood it. Summarize your findings and compare them with the results of research on the grapevine noted in this chapter.

12. Reread the section on the grapevine. Determine what pattern the grapevine followed in Question 11—cluster chain, gossip chain, probability chain, or single-strand chain. Why do you think your grapevine followed this pattern?

Case for Part Five

**Valpo
Industries**

Doug Slater, plant supervisor in charge of the evening and midnight turns at Valpo Industries in New Haven, Tennessee, closed the door of his small office and eased into the soft leather chair behind his cluttered desk. The ten-thirty whistle had just signaled the midnight turn employees to their work stations, and Doug anticipated that the time remaining before twelve would be uneventful. He recalled that there had been problems in the past. When production orders started to back up on the big welders five months ago, the main office decided to put in an extra eight-hour shift at the plant. This necessitated an overlap of an hour and a half between the second and third shifts, and it created a few scheduling difficulties at first. However, the overlap period had been operating rather smoothly during the last month as the men became accustomed to doubling up on their machines.

When the phone rang, Doug hissed a silent curse to himself.

"Doug here."
"Doug, this is Gus. You better get down here to 15. We've had some big trouble."
"What is it, Gus?"
"I'll have to fill you in once you're here. All I can say is hurry!"

Department 15 was situated at the north end of the building and was the largest department in the plant. It was in Department 15 that six giant welding machines fabricated steel parts of various shapes and sizes that were cut and assembled in the other sections of the plant. When Doug arrived he noticed a crowd gathered at one of the large doorways that led to the oil supply area outside. Gus Hoffman, second shift foreman for 15, approached Doug.

"Dammit all, Doug, another problem with one of those third-shift boys! I just don't see how poor Tom can put up with all this. . . ."
"Hold on, Gus. Settle down. Now tell me what happened so we can get something done about it."

"Jack Metcalf, that big maintenance man, reported to Tom that someone was snooping around outside with a flashlight. Tom went out to the yard to check it out while Jack went up to the front gate to back Tom up. I had just picked up the phone to call you when I heard Tom yell. I ran outside and saw Tom rubbing his head. Jack had grabbed that huge chain we use to lock up the gate to the yard and cornered the guy before he could run out."

"Jack didn't have to use the chain on the guy, did he? And who is this guy anyway?"

"Jack would have taken the man's head off if he hit him with that twenty-pound chain. The guy just froze in his tracks when he saw Jack. The man's name is Richard Johnson; he's one of the welders from the third shift. He didn't report in at 10:30. Johnson said that he was just trying to get in through the side door by the employees' locker room. He said he forgot his safety glasses and didn't want to walk through the plant. Jack and Tom are holding him now waiting for the police to arrive. Johnson looks pretty drunk to me."

"Why did you call the police in on this; was Tom hurt?"

"No, he was just stunned. It seems Tom caught Johnson by surprise. Johnson panicked and threw his flashlight at Tom. The flashlight glanced against Tom's head and knocked him down. He said he was feeling all right and told me he wanted to get the police here so he could press assault charges against Johnson."

"Okay, Gus, get these men back to work. I'll try to talk Tom into going to the hospital and getting his head checked. I suppose he'll be tied up most of the night if he's going to file a complaint. How about staying on a few extra hours, Gus, and I'll get a first-shift foreman to come in and relieve you around 3 A.M."

"Well, I don't like the idea of working third shift, but I guess there's no way out of it. You just make sure you get someone in here. I don't want to be in here all night."

"Don't worry, Gus, and thanks a lot. Send Tom and Jack up to my office as soon as they're finished with the police. I've got to get a report started on this."

Doug sullenly walked back to his office. He was concerned about Tom. It seemed a shame that this should happen to such a nice guy. Ever since Tom took over third shift he'd had problems with absenteeism and drinking on the job. It just seemed that those inner-city men that personnel hired never worked out for Tom. But Tom wanted to work midnights. He felt it would give him more time to work on his farm.

As Doug entered his office and got a stack of forms out of his desk, he started to wonder whether Tom would think of leaving the company because of tonight's incident. It didn't seem likely, but it might happen. Doug hoped not. Tom had been with Valpo for nearly twenty years. Before he had been made a foreman, Tom had been one of the hardest workers in the plant. In fact, he had a couple of records for parts produced on the welders. He was a good foreman too, and when he was on the second shift last year his department had the highest production level in the company. A couple of local competitors had tried to lure Tom away recently, and Doug began to worry that Tom might decide to accept one of those offers after what happened.

The next day, Doug received the latest production reports for the previous month. He noticed that the third shift was still rated far behind the other shifts in parts per hour (see Exhibit 1). He began to wonder whether a piece-rate wage would bring production up, but then he remembered that both management and the union opposed the idea.

Exhibit 1
Department 15:
Production Report,
May 15–June 15

Welder 1

Shift	Total Hours	Total Parts	Down Hours	Parts per Hour
1	160	1690	10.5	11.3
2	160	1543	11.6	10.4
3	130	1037	12.2	8.8

Welder 2

Shift	Total Hours	Total Parts	Down Hours	Parts per Hour
1	160	1326	5.8	8.6
2	160	1385	2.6	8.8
3	130	678	9.0	5.6

Welder 3

Shift	Total Hours	Total Parts	Down Hours	Parts per Hour
1	160	2173	7.0	14.2
2	160	1871	6.6	12.2
3	130	1046	7.0	8.5

Welder 4

Shift	Total Hours	Total Parts	Down Hours	Parts per Hour
1	160	2056	5.4	13.3
2	160	2412	5.4	15.6
3	no operator	. . .	. . .	. . .

Welder 5

Shift	Total Hours	Total Parts	Down Hours	Parts per Hour
1	160	1852	8.2	12.2
2	160	1874	6.4	12.2
3	130	866	14.6	7.5

Welder 6

Shift	Total Hours	Total Parts	Down Hours	Parts per Hour
1	160	2100	10.0	14.0
2	160	2163	9.8	14.4
3	130	954	12.2	8.1

Machine Capacity

Welder 1 . . . 13 parts per hour

Welder 2 . . . 11 parts per hour

Welder 3 . . . 15 parts per hour

Welder 4 . . . 17 parts per hour

Welder 5 . . . 15 parts per hour

Welder 6 . . . 15 parts per hour

Doug was just beginning to put the finishing touches to his report of the previous night's incident when the phone rang. It was Jim Mitchell, the plant manager, calling from the main office.

"Doug, Watkins in personnel just briefed me about the trouble you had with Johnson last night. Have you got a report on it yet?"

"I've just about finished it up, Jim. It should be on your desk before you leave the office this afternoon."

"How about Tom, is he all right?"

"The X-rays were negative, but the doctor advised him to take things easy for a few days."

"I imagine we'll be hearing from the union on this. I understand that Johnson joined the union a couple of months ago."

"We shouldn't have to worry about the union. Johnson was late for work, he didn't report in that he would be late, he was drunk, and he assaulted a foreman on company property. The company rules are pretty clear in calling for discharge. I told the shop steward of Johnson's dismissal last night. I waited until this morning to tell Johnson. He wasn't in any shape last night to really understand what was going on. When I talked to him this morning he didn't show any surprise at being discharged."

"I just hope that's the end of it, Doug. You realize I've got to go into bargaining with the union over a new contract in three months. I'd like to be sure our relations are pretty good by then. I've also been looking at the latest production report. I'm beginning to think opening up a third shift for Department 15 was a pretty bad idea. We just barely cover our operating expenses, not to mention the beating we've been taking in personnel losses. We just can't seem to get good men to work midnights. I'm seriously thinking of shutting down the third shift and telling our salespeople we can't handle any more new orders for a while. Look, Doug, I've got to go out of town for the rest of the week, so check into that for me. I'll expect your opinion when I get back."

Doug heard a knock on the door as he was hanging up the phone. It was Bill Benedict, the shop steward for third shift.

"Yeah Bill, come on in. What brings you in so early?"

"Well, Doug, it's about last night."

"The union's not going to try to get Johnson reinstated, are they!"

"We don't think so, Doug. It seems that it would be a losing battle. We talked about it at a meeting we just had, and the consensus was that there is something more important at issue here."

"What are you trying to say, Bill?"

"Let me ask you something first, Doug. Do you believe that a rule is fair only if it is applied equally without exception?"

"Of course! A rule is reasonable only if it can be used fairly. That's what I try to do all the time. So, what's your point? Are you going to tell me that it was unfair to dismiss Johnson because the rules are unreasonable?"

"Doug, that's exactly where the union disagrees with you. Company rules state that any employee who assaults or physically threatens to do bodily injury to another employee on company property is subject to immediate discharge. The union feels that Jack Metcalf violated that rule when he threatened Johnson with that chain. We decided to file a grievance against Metcalf. We want him discharged or we'll push for Johnson's reinstatement with back pay."

"You've got to be kidding, Bill! You were there last night and you saw Johnson's condition and what he did to Tom! What should Jack have done, stand there and let Johnson run off? Besides, Jack had no way of knowing it was Johnson out there. It was pretty dark last night. What did Jack have to say about all this at your meeting?"

"He wasn't there, Doug. Metcalf's not a union member. Look, Doug, now is not the time to argue about it. We'll have plenty of time to hash things out at the grievance meeting next week. I've got to get home and get some sleep before work tonight, so I'll see you later."

Bill half slammed the door on his way out. Doug got up to get some aspirin. He felt a tremendous headache building up in the back of his neck. He wondered whether he should call Jim Mitchell up and give him the bad news now or wait until Jim came back from his trip. Either way, he thought, his neck would still be in a noose.

Source: Francis A. Yeandel, St. Mary's College, Notre Dame, Indiana.

Problems

1. What are the problems at Valpo?
2. What are the causes of the problems?
3. Does the leadership have anything to do with the problems? Communication? Interpersonal relationships? Group behavior?
4. If you were Doug, what would you do about the problems?
5. If you were Gus, what would you do about the problems?

Part 6   Controlling Organizational Resources

We have discussed how managers are responsible for planning and organizing the firm's resources and how interpersonal skills such as leadership and effective communication structure the manager's job. But these processes are not enough to achieve organizational objectives. Controls are necessary too.

This section defines control, discusses various types of control, and examines who is involved in control and what can and should be controlled. The budget is a complex and important topic so a separate chapter, Chapter 19, is devoted to this control tool.

Chapter 18 Controlling for Effective Results

Learning Objectives

1. Understand what control is and why it is a necessary managerial tool.
2. Learn some mechanisms for controlling a work unit.
3. Be able to recognize when cybernetic controls are possible and when a noncybernetic approach should be used.
4. Know how to adjust your approach to control to fit your leadership style.
5. Learn how to control your use of time effectively.

Chapter Outline

What Is Control?
The Process of Control
Cybernetic and Noncybernetic Controls
Types of Control
Who Is Involved in Control?
What Can and Should Be Controlled
Methods of Control
Self-Control
Group Control
Policies and Procedures
Budgets
Management Information Systems
External Audits
Special Reports
Project Controls
Step 1

Step 2
Step 3
Personal Observation
Control, Cybernetic Controls, and Managerial Style
Examples of Controls in Business Functions
Controls for Finances
Controls for Marketing
Production/Operations Management Controls
Personnel and Labor Relations Controls
Overall Control
Summary
Questions
Appendix: Controlling the Use of Your Time
Case: Honest Employees
Case: Ajax Foundry

What Is Control?

Thus far, I have discussed how managers, entrepreneurs, and family business executives must set objectives for the enterprise and develop plans to meet these objectives. I have also discussed how executives design organizations to facilitate the achievement of their plans and objectives. In addition, I have shown how interpersonal skills such as leadership and effective communication aid executives in achieving objectives and plans. In this chapter and the following one, I will describe internal controls used by firms and examine the role they play in increasing the firm's effectiveness.

Controls are necessary to achieve objectives. Table 18.1 summarizes the relationship between control and increased effectiveness found in nine studies. As you will note, most of the research has shown that good control leads to greater organizational effectiveness.

If we lived in a perfect world where all managerial plans were fulfilled, control would not be necessary. But the world is far from perfect. Factors in the environment change. These changes affect organizational plans. Employees make mistakes. And not all employees are motivated to achieve the results needed to keep the enterprise on its planned course. They may not do their jobs at all. So control is necessary to resolve problems and adjust plans and objectives or take corrective action as the need arises.

The term *control* has a somewhat negative connotation. This should not be. As William Newman has pointed out, controls are normal, pervasive in all societies and organizations, and positive.[1] Just as a thermostat is a positive device to keep heating and air conditioning systems functioning well, so controls in firms are positive aids in achieving desired ends.

Control is the managerial skill that helps ensure effective acquisition and use of the enterprise's resources and achievement of its objectives.

Controls are implemented to avoid situations like the one in the cartoon here. Effective controls have a number of characteristics. First, they are *cost effective.* This means that they involve as little cost as possible in terms

Table 18.1

Research on the Relationship between Control and Effectiveness

Researcher(s)	Setting	Findings
Farris and Butterfield	16 banks in Brazil	The greater the control, the greater the effectiveness. Effectiveness is greater if the manager at a lower level perceives the manager at the next level as having greater control over him or her than is actually the case.
Lawrence and Lorsch	6 American companies	The greater the control, the more effective the firm. But the firms in stable industries use conservative control mechanisms; those in volatile industries use liberal mechanisms.
Woodward	100 British companies	Effective control leads to organizational effectiveness. The control mechanisms vary, however. Effective small-batch firms use behavioral control based on single measures of effectiveness. Effective automated firms use mechanical controls (output controls). In mass production both behavioral and output controls are used, but on an infrequent (not continuous) basis.
Bell	204 employees in 30 departments of a Connecticut hospital	Control leads to effectiveness. The more routine the job, the greater the use of behavioral control (personal supervision). The more volatile, the greater the use of output control. This confirms the Ouichi and Maguire study.
Khandwalla	80 large American firms	The more volatile the environment (as measured by type of competition), the greater the control in effective business.
Tannenbaum	104 League of Women Voters units	The greater the amount of control, the greater the effectiveness.
Bowers	40 life insurance agencies	The greater the amount of control, the greater the effectiveness as measured by job satisfaction and organization development (not by growth, sales, or turnover). Greater control costs more, too.
Turcotte	2 state government agencies	Higher performance is found where output measures are clear; the control-level executives are high; and the control system emphasizes and helps achieve high output. Not all measures of output are equally high.
McMahon and Perritt	2,537 line managers in 12 plants of a large and successful mass production technology firm	The greater the control, the greater the effectiveness.

of time and money while still maintaining their value. Second, they are *acceptable to employees*. Controls, like laws, are not effective if the persons subject to them feel they are unnecessary, poorly designed and implemented, or harmful to their psychological well-being. Controls must be designed to fit the personalities of the employees. It is important for controls to be

"Dame Fortune smiles and Dame Fortune frowns,
but we have to face the stockholders."

well designed in several respects. In addition to suiting employees, they must also fit the plans the firm has. Sometimes design is overdone. Controls need only be as detailed as the plans they help implement. A fourth characteristic of effective controls is that they are *strategic*. It is impossible and undesirable to try to control all aspects of a firm. Controls should focus only on the most important objectives and the most valuable resources. Finally, controls must *measure and be objective*. Ideally controls measure specific behaviors and outputs. Vague control standards are more difficult to administer.

The Process of Control

Control is an ongoing process which may be defined in terms of its subparts, which are shown in Figure 18.1 and described below.

Setting Objectives Objectives must be set in measurable terms for individuals as well as work groups. This occurs during planning if planning is done well. By clarifying what is desired of the enterprise and of the individuals and groups within it, MBO serves as the link between planning and control.

Figure 18.1
The Control Process

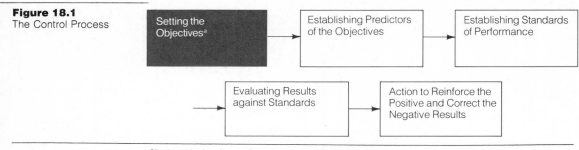

aSetting objectives is part of the planning process. It is also the beginning of the control process.

Establishing Predictors of the Objectives Effective managers do not wait for a specific time to find out whether objectives are being achieved. They look for regular, reliable, and prompt indicators. For example, weekly or monthly sales results highlighting problems by product/service and territory provide managers with the opportunity to help define and correct those problems. An effective flow of information and a feedback system are vital components of a system for determining whether objectives are being achieved or not.

Establishing Standards of Performance Insofar as possible, each objective should specify quantitatively the minimum acceptable standards of performance. These standards may be based on past performance projected into the future; established by managerial judgment; or for some units, developed through detailed studies such as time studies for individual jobs.

Evaluating Results against Standards When the manager sees results early enough to act on them, he or she determines which are critical, which bear watching, and which can be temporarily ignored based on the amount of their divergence from standards and the significance of the items involved. Thus, for instance, a 5 percent shortfall in sales in the firm's smallest territory on a minor product is not the same as a 30 percent loss on its largest product in its biggest territory.

Action to Reinforce the Positive and Correct the Negative Results Many people have the idea that control is only negative. This is not so; leadership style determines whether the impact of control is negative or positive. The effective manager regularly reinforces outstanding employee performance and positive responses of work units to the organization's objectives and plan. When there are problems, the manager attends to the most serious first, determining what they are and then deciding how to help improve the problem employee or unit's performance. Corrective action is taken only if the employee or unit does not perform up to capacity after receiving help.

Thus the control process serves to *prevent* disasters by determining how the enterprise is faring relative to its objectives and plans and taking action to ensure good results.

Cybernetic and Noncybernetic Controls

The process described above is a cybernetic control process.

Cybernetic control is a system of control through which a critical resource is held at a desired level by a self-regulating mechanism.

Many experts believe it to be the most desirable system of control. As Geert Hofstede has pointed out, however, it is not universally applicable.[2] For cybernetic control to work, standards must be set, actual results must be reliably measured, standards and results must be compared, and the resulting comparison must be fed back to management for action.

Most nonbusiness organizations (universities, cities, and museums, for instance) do not meet these conditions. Nor do most segments of business firms that are not involved in either production, operations, or sales—research and development, advertising, personnel/labor relations, engineering, legal, and accounting departments. In such units and organizations, objectives and standards are frequently missing, unclear, or shifting; results of activities are difficult to measure accurately and reliably; and feedback information is often unavailable, not timely, or undependable.

Noncybernetic controls are control systems which do not meet all of the criteria for cybernetic controls (as in the case of nonbusiness enterprises). The most typical example of noncybernetic control is a budget. But budgets can be designed such that they can be either cybernetic or noncybernetic (See Chapter 19). Later in the chapter it will become clear how control varies between organizations which are and are not likely to be able to use the cybernetic control process fully.

Types of Control

Three types of control are distinguished according to *when* control is exerted. The first of these is *feedforward* or *steering* control. In this type of control emphasis is on a future time frame. With accurate forecasting of what will happen, we can take action before a total operation is complete to ensure its success. Thus, for example, adjustments were made during the mission to the moon to help land the astronauts on the moon. Sometimes these controls, which modern developments such as real time computers have made possible, are called *in process* controls.

The second kind of control has been called the *yes–no* control. With this kind of control, work is stopped at various predetermined times or when certain events take place and cannot continue without a screening decision to go ahead. Examples of such controls include spending limits on projects and quality controls at various points in the operations process.

George Eastman

The quiet man with the camera stayed on his knees as the rhinoceros charged. It was only five feet away from him when the white hunter at his side shot it dead. The guide remonstrated with the camera buff for not having fled. "Well," said George Eastman, "you've got to trust your organization." Eastman Kodak was built by a man who met every threat by an effort to strengthen his organization. He hadn't been in business a year when he began to get complaints from customers that his photographic dry plates didn't work. After 472 experiments, Eastman concluded that nothing was wrong with his formula; the trouble lay in a component, a gelatin he bought from a British chemical company. Thereafter, he tried to control by integration every essential ingredient in his product. (Eastman's chemicals division now has sales approaching $1 billion.) He did for photography what Ford did for automobiles: cut costs to a level where the average man—or child—could enter the market. In 1900 his Brownie camera sold for $1 and a roll of six-exposure film for 15 cents. Eastman's most enduring contribution was in corporate research. No company has ever been better served by R and D. In the early sixties, Bell & Howell teamed up with Du Pont in an attempt to break into the color-film market. Senator Charles Percy, who was then chairman of Bell & Howell, recalls, "Du Pont film was very good but Kodak's film kept improving and sending us back to the drawing boards." When he was seventy-eight, Eastman, a bachelor, arranged that his fortune go to philanthropic projects. Next he had a doctor diagram exactly where his heart was. Then Eastman, methodical to the last, went home and put a bullet into it. His note said, "My work is done, why wait?" But his work went on in the organization he designed to keep moving ahead.

Source: *Fortune*, January 1975, p. 71. Reprinted by permission.

The final type of control is *post action* control. With this type of control, when the operation is completed the results are reviewed. Although nothing can be done about the cycle that was completed, the review serves as a guide to ways for preventing future mishaps.

Clearly, steering control is the only one that can be considered a cybernetic control.

Who Is Involved in Control?

Just as every manager plans, leads, and communicates, every manager controls. Top managers approve the control system and philosophy and review its results. One example of a top manager who made a significant impact on control in his firm is George Eastman.

Others besides top managers are important to effective control systems. Staff executives in accounting, personnel, and other areas help design the control systems. Line executives in all functions are responsible for administering controls for their units.

What Can and Should Be Controlled?

Some management books proclaim that all facets of the business for which there are set objectives should be controlled. For example, control should be exercised with regard to the market share objective, the profitability objective, and other objectives discussed in Chapter 7. But as was indicated when describing cybernetic versus noncybernetic controls, firms are limited in the degree to which they can control their operations.

According to William Ouchi, we can try to control two effects: output and behavior (see Figure 18.3).[3] To effectively control output, it is necessary to have reliable and valid measures of the output. This is relatively easy for the tin can plant and the insurance agency used as examples in Figure 18.2. But what is the output of the U.S. Foreign Service? Assuming it is better international relations, how can it be reliably and validly measured? Instead this service goes through the motions of control (thus the term ritual). Its main control is highly selective hiring standards. And if a baseball team wishes to study double plays, it is difficult to measure the output of a specific player—since it by definition involves more than one.

To effectively control the behavior of employees, it is necessary to

Figure 18.2
The Effects of Output Measures and Knowledge of Transfer on Control Methods

		Knowledge of Transfer (Means/Ends)	
Output Measures	Good	Example: Tin Can Plant Control Methods: Behavioral and Output	Example: Insurance Agency Control Method: Output
	Poor	Example: Baseball Team (Double Plays) Control Method: Behavioral	Example: Foreign Service Control Method: Ritual
		Perfect	Imperfect

Source: Adapted by permission from William G. Ouchi, "The Relationship between Organizational Structure and Organizational Control," *Administrative Science Quarterly* 22 (March 1977), p. 98.

thoroughly understand the production function: how inputs go through a transfer process and become outputs. If this is known, we can observe and control employee behavior. This process is basically well known for the production of tin cans. It is not well known in the foreign service.

So before we design control systems to follow the cybernetic output or behavior approach, both the output measures and means-end transfer must be known and perfect. As we discuss the control methods next this must be kept in mind.

Methods of Control

Effective managers use nine methods of control. Some of these have been discussed earlier in the book and will be mentioned only briefly here. Others will be discussed in more detail. Figure 18.3 ranks these methods according to the frequency with which they function.

Control mechanisms that are almost always present and persistent are self-control, group and ideological controls, and policy control. These will be discussed first, for they are the most important control devices. Management information systems (MIS) and audits provide information needed for control on a regular basis. Finally, three devices are used occasionally, as needed; special project controls (when they exist), special

Figure 18.3
Control Devices and the Frequency with Which They Function

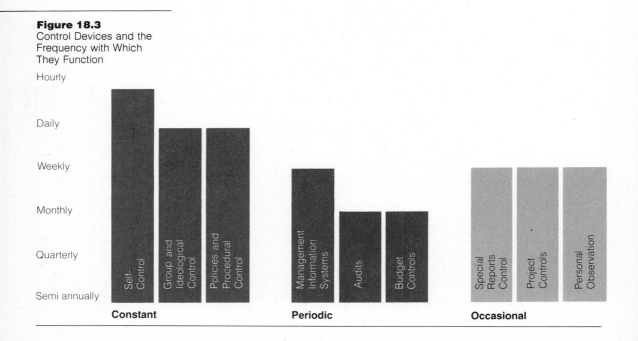

reports (to supplement regular reports in special circumstances), and personal observation. The lighter colored bars indicate that potential lengths of time vary.

Self-Control

An enterprise cannot exist unless its employees exert enough self-control to do what is expected of them most of the time on most work-related matters. This means giving their employer a fair day's work for a fair day's pay, coming to work on time, respecting the enterprise's property, obeying work rules, and so on. The employees' egos, guided by their superegos, are the main source of this self-control, though orientation and training contribute to it. Employees' work attitudes also serve to reinforce their self-control.

Some enterprises reinforce self-control by asking employees to report their activities. Most salespersons' duties are recorded on "call sheets" reporting their activities. University professors report their service activities in this way. Many staff employees keep records of their activities. Librarians tally the number of inquiries they have received. Personnel specialists report the number of employees counseled or interviewed for a job. Research and development employees record their activities. Some of these can be checked by other control methods.

Group Control

As discussed in Chapter 11, groups also control individuals—in regard to both output and behavior. Group norms for work exert pressure on the individual to perform and to follow work rules and policies. Some organizations place great emphasis on group control and develop a strong ideology in their members or employees that stresses doing a good job and behaving properly to achieve the ends of the organization. Many of the organizations that do this are noneconomic ones such as churches, museums, and charities. Many business organizations take this approach, too, however. The strong identification with their companies that employees at IBM, Texas Instruments, Procter & Gamble, and Lincoln Electric feel causes them to be more readily influenced by attitudes of their work group and so encourages them to exert self-control. Without this type of group ideological control, it is difficult for managers to control behavior and output of employees.

Policies and Procedures

The formulation of policies and procedures was discussed in connection with planning in Chapter 8. Policies and procedures are one kind of steering or feed forward control device. They reflect the past experiences of many executives at many levels of the firm. They are guides for managers to use in controlling the behavior and output of employees. They may be concerned with any number of things—ways to deal with the firm's resources and equipment, times employees must be present, and other matters of a similar nature.

Employees know the probable consequences of breaking these policies and procedures. Properly implemented, policies and procedures which are up to date, clearly and fully communicated, and have involved employee input can function as a powerful reinforcement to group control and self-control. If policies are violated and if a feedback system has been established, managers can take action to see that objectives are still achieved in time.

Budgets

A very significant control device used in most enterprises is the budget—one of the three regularly scheduled control devices shown in Figure 18.3. Budgetary control is so important (and complicated) that it is treated in the next chapter as a separate unit.

Management Information Systems

Another control device which is used on a regular schedule is the management information system (MIS). The MIS serves many aspects of the management process. It is used for planning and communication as well as control.

A management information system is the system developed by a firm to collect, process, and distribute information about the operations of the firm to its executives and others.

In most organizations the MIS involves at least three systems, which are likely to be the following:

1. Personnel systems which trace the flow of employees in the firm: those entering and leaving the firm, their pay, benefits, seniority, location, etc.
2. Financial systems which trace the flow of money into, through, and out of the firm.
3. Goods and services which trace the flow of materials, subassemblies, etc. into, through, and out of the firm.

In many organizations, the MIS is manual. Units submit reports to upper-level managers on a regular basis. In larger organizations, much of the MIS is computerized. Earlier in the seventies, it was envisioned that one perfectly integrated system would serve the total MIS needs of the organization. This has rarely come to be. Still, only the advances in computer technology have enabled many organizations to develop and use an effective MIS. Before computerization, the data these organizations obtained were not timely enough to be used for control or planning systems.

Many early MISs were developed by staff specialists who knew how to use the hardware. The reports that were printed out were in forms that few managers were able or wanted to use. Today, effective firms have a better system. MIS operators determine information needs and timeliness deadlines from all levels of managers. They then design the system to develop the required data and send reports when the user can use them and in the form in which the user needs them. Managers request and get reports measuring the current status relative to each objective to be achieved. For example, reports on profitability, sales, market share, efficiency (as indicated by low inventory levels) can be delivered in time to take action. In this way, the MIS is used to help control the enterprise's outputs.

For example, Table 18.2 is a report from a company MIS on sales. It reveals that some salespersons are behind and some ahead of their quotas. With this kind of information, managers can take action to determine why in each case and to bring each salesperson closer to desired quotas and objectives.

As noted earlier, managers can absorb only so much information and have only a certain amount of time for control. A manager who is not selective will be inundated with reports. Key strategic control items may be buried when this happens. Effective managers delegate the control of less significant items and objectives to subordinates. They receive MIS reports and use a strategic approach to control, concentrating only on those items necessary to meet the most important objectives.

External Audits

General management practice requires that the financial systems of a firm be examined on a regular basis by an outside accounting firm. The professionals in these firms (called certified public accountants in the

Table 18.2
A Sales by
Salesperson Report

No.	Salesperson Name	Current Month			Year to Date		
		Quota	Actual	Variance	Quota	Actual	Variance
0120	John Nelson	1200	1083	−117	3600	3505	−95
10469	Lynn Sherry	1000	1162	+162	3000	3320	+320
19261	Darvin Upshaw	800	1090	+290	2400	2510	+110
20234	Janie Evans	1500	1305	−195	4500	4110	−390
61604	Travis Burke	2000	2333	+333	6000	6712	+712
62083	Cathy Hager	1000	990	−10	3000	2319	−681
63049	Steve Jenner	1100	1250	+150	3300	2416	−884
64040	Sam Moseley	1050	985	−65	3150	3020	−130
	Totals	9650	10198	548	28950	27912	−1038

Source: Raymond McLeod, Jr., *Management Information Systems* (Chicago: Science Research Associates, 1979), p. 247. Reprinted by permission.

United States and chartered public accountants in Canada) are trained to make sure that the financial statements of an enterprise are honest and accurate. Thus they function to protect the rights of present and future stockholders.

Rather than examining every detail of every financial statement, accountants use a sample to conduct an audit. They check to be sure that certain assets (those in their sample) claimed on the financial statements actually do exist. For example, they will verify the existence of a number of items listed under inventory, equipment, furniture, and current assets such as cash in the bank. To the extent that accountants are thorough and more clever than any thieves who may be on the payroll, the external audits help management control the use of assets and other resources in the enterprise.

Special Reports

When managers determine from regular reports or other control mechanisms that certain areas of their firm need to be analyzed in greater depth, they have special reports developed. The analysts who compile these reports may be either employees of the firm or outside consultants. Managers themselves may gather information to help determine the cause of a control problem. If they have the time and expertise, they may even conduct the entire study that serves as the basis for a special report.

Special reports vary in content and nature; some may be statistical, others may not. A longitudinal analysis of past production costs with a projection into the future as shown in Figure 18.4 is an example of a statistical report. Note that the authors of the report first plotted actual monthly expenditures. Then they plotted the moving average to obtain the trend. The moving average is simply the previous twelve months' cost

Figure 18.4
A Longitudinal Analysis of Sales Costs, 1975–1980

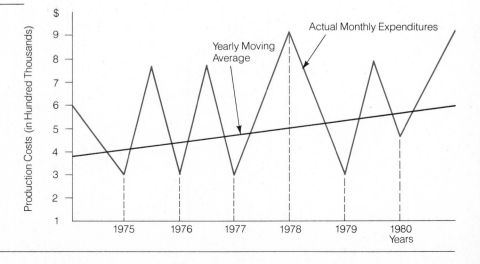

divided by twelve. If asked for, they could have plotted the trend to 1982. A manager might also have asked the analysts who compiled this report to check how previous cost reduction programs in mid-1975, mid-1976, and mid-1978 worked. From Figure 18.4, we can see that the 1975 and 1976 programs may have had some effect but that 1978's program did not. On the basis of this information, the manager might decide to use a variation of the 1975 and 1976 programs should cost reductions be necessary.

Special reports are not limited to analyses of internal data. They may focus on comparisons of internal data with external data such as costs of competitors, government figures, or industry figures available through trade associations. Some examples of special reports are operational (internal) and management audits. Unlike external audits, *operational audits* are performed by staff employed by the firm. They are also not performed on the expected schedules of the external auditors. Large firms hire their own special staffs to perform operational audits. Medium-size and small firms use managers from outside the unit to perform the audits.

Operational audits are generally designed to protect assets (as are external audits), but they can also be used to determine the extent to which all aspects of the firm are in line with company policies and plans. For example, audits of the purchasing department may check into conflicts of interest and cost efficiency (whether the purchasing agent buys from the suppliers with lowest costs, best quality, and best service, for instance). In sum, operational audits are a systematic way of determining whether the units are following the planned steps needed to meet company objectives.

A *management audit* is an analysis of the total operations of a firm by external experts. Its purpose is to determine the firm's overall effectiveness. Various management audits have been developed. William Greenwood has developed a set of approximately 400 questions designed to evaluate about 200 aspects of a firm's management.[4] Jackson Martindale's American Institute of Management has a similar package of about 300 questions.[5] The answers to the questions are scored, and the firm is rated on the basis of its total score. Ten thousand points is a perfect score. Three thousand five hundred points relate to managerial processes, 2,400 to the quality of management, 1,400 to sales vigor, etc. An excellent rating on the Jackson evaluation is 7,500 points. A perfect score is 10,000.

Project Controls

Various techniques have been developed over the years for controlling specific projects. Several will be discussed here. The Gantt Chart, developed early in this century, is a frequently used control mechanism in firms which have many unrelated projects. Figure 18.5 presents a Gantt Chart in its simplest form. For each project listed with its supervisor in the chart, the upper bar records the production schedule; the lower bar records what part of that schedule has been accomplished. On most Gantt Charts, the bars are movable strips of plastic, with different colors to indicate schedule and actual progress. At a glance, the manager can see whether a project is on time, ahead of time, or behind time. If it is behind time, of course, action must be taken to put it back on schedule. An examination of Figure 18.5 reveals the following information:

- Project 330 was completed ahead of schedule.
- Projects 127 and 415 are on schedule.
- Projects 226 and 563 are behind schedule.
- Project 651 had not been started as of March 20.

Control measures are necessary on Projects 226 and 563. Gantt Charts have been widely used. They are, however, useful only if the information on them is accurate and if the managers take action on the conditions they show to be in need of correction.

Other techniques are available for controlling projects which are interrelated; Gantt Charts are not useful in such cases. If, for instance, Project 127 had to be completed before Project 330 could be started, a Gantt Chart would be of no value in controlling the two. Network analysis as is found in PERT (Program Evaluation and Review Technique), CPM (Critical Path Method), and Milestone Budgeting is used for controlling interrelated projects. PERT will be described here as representative of this type of control mechanism.

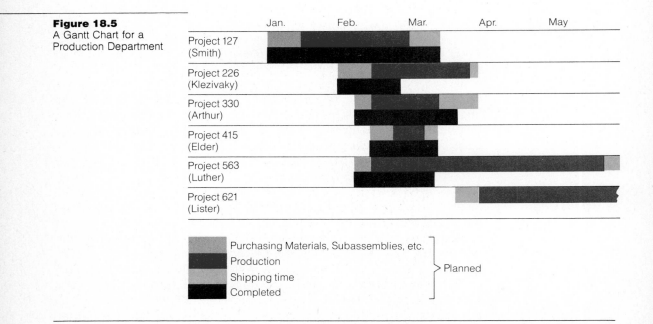

Figure 18.5
A Gantt Chart for a Production Department

For PERT to work, the basic procedure described below must be followed:

Step 1

Prepare a list of all activities and accomplishments necessary to complete the project. Begin this by listing the necessary accomplishments (sometimes called milestones)—for example, negotiating and signing contracts for materials and subassemblies, getting permits, hiring and assigning employees, producing Major Subassembly 1, producing Major Subassembly 2, and packing and shipping the product. Activities are the tasks necessary to attain these accomplishments.

Step 2

Estimate the time between accomplishments or events. First, three people most familiar with the activity must make three estimates:
1. Optimistic time (the shortest time it could take if everything ran perfectly).
2. Pessimistic time (the longest time it could take if everything went wrong).
3. The most probable time.

Then a weighted average of these times is computed and inserted into the PERT network. Assuming the optimistic time is 2 weeks; the pessimistic time, 6 weeks; and the most probable time, 4 weeks, the calculation would be:

$$\frac{2 + 6 + 4}{4.5} \text{ (the three times)} \atop \text{(most probable or expected)}$$

Step 3

Combine the activities, accomplishments and times into a PERT network. As many activities as possible should be performed simultaneously.

Figure 18.6 is an example of a PERT network. Each letter in the figure stands for an accomplishment. For example, A-B is contract and design time. These network codes are supplied in supporting documents. The circled numbers indicate the number of weeks between accomplishments. It is important to note that the length of the lines in the network do not indicate time. The total time for the project is sixteen weeks (the sum of the numbers along the flow.)

Network analysis such as PERT has had an up and down career. The military and many government contracts used to require them. That is not always the case today. Some experts contend that the use of network analysis necessitates good planning and makes more effective control systems possible. Critics point out that this is true only when the managers are able to estimate times for accomplishments accurately. This can be

Figure 18.6
A PERT Network

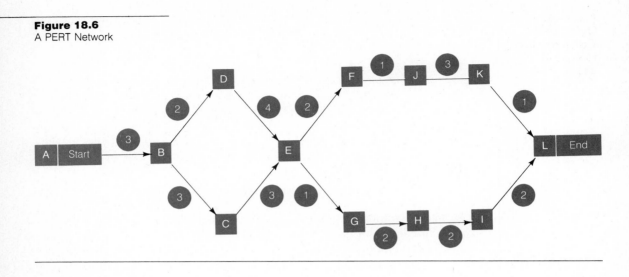

difficult, especially if some accomplishments are dependent on outside vendors. Network analysis can be costly, too. But for projects such as the space program's moonshots, where time is of the essence, it can be of great value.

**Personal
Observation**

Each manager is expected to influence and control employees' behavior and outputs. Chapter 14 described the many ways a manager can reinforce self-control and group control. More often than not, managers find they must spend most of their control time working on a few problem employees. Most managers report that approximately 5 percent of the employees under their direction cause them approximately 95 percent of their control problems.

To make personal control work, managers must have set objectives and standards which the employees know and find acceptable. They must visit crucial workplaces where reports, audits, and MIS results indicate the greatest problems exist. There they observe behavior and output and interview employees to gain additional insight into the nature of the problems. In addition to the information they gain in this way, their personal intervention often serves to facilitate the correction of the problems.

Some managers visit all work units occasionally to check the reliability of reports they receive. If time is available, this can be a good practice but it can also be a costly use of managerial time. Where time is severely limited, it makes more sense for managers to "manage by exception"—to observe and investigate only those units where reports indicate the greatest control problems exist and where the problems are of strategic import for the successful achievement of the firm's objectives.

Control, Cybernetic Controls, and Managerial Style

We have now discussed nine kinds of controls. Are each of them equally useful in conditions which allow cybernetic controls or prevent them? Some can be used in all sett.

- Self-control
- Group control and ideology
- Policies and procedures
- Budgets
- Periodic reports
- Personal observation

But even when these mechanisms are used, *how* they are used varies. In situations where objectives or standards are not clear—the foreign service, personnel departments, a museum, for instance—what do managers look for when they observe? What do reports examine? What do policies say? Hofstede contends that control in these situations consists primarily of self-control and group control supplemented by judgmental evaluations by superiors that budgets are properly spent.[6] Attitude surveys of consumers of the firm's product or service can also contribute somewhat to control. But control devices like MIS and most audits are not useful; supervisors must make trusting and judgmental evaluations of feedback results.

In organizations or subunits where cybernetic controls are appropriate, all nine control devices can be of value. Which ones are actually used depends on cost considerations and the leadership style of management. Table 18.3 indicates which control devices are most commonly associated with each of the three leadership styles described in Chapter 14.

As far as output controls are concerned, traditional managers believe it is necessary to control most important factors in detail. Participative leaders trust their subordinates to exercise control over these factors on their own. (Consultative leaders, as usual, are in-between, exhibiting some of the characteristics of traditional and some of participative leaders in their approach to control.) Participative leaders expect employees to impose self-control while traditional leaders exert control to see that objectives are reached. Traditional leaders also tend to control the means by which people perform their jobs.

Participative leaders are concerned only with attainment of objectives. As far as behavior control is concerned, note the differences in who sets the controls. Traditional managers set control standards, check frequently, and use rules, SOPs and personal observation. Participative managers depend on the work group to set its own controls and monitor results.

The control tools used (such as the budget) probably do not vary by organizational style. But how they are used and how many are used is where the differences come into play. Differences will result from the leadership style of the managers, the competence of the work group, and how critical or strategic items being controlled are to the enterprise's achievement of its objectives.

Table 18.3
Characteristics of the
Control Exercised by
Participative,
Consultative, and
Traditional Managers

	Leadership Style		
Control	**Participative**	**Consultative**	**Traditional**
Degree of Control			
Number of elements controlled	Few (Most crucial)	Few (The most crucial and next most crucial)	Many
Specificity of control	General	Some general Some specific	Specific controls
Control devices used	Self-control	Self-control	Detailed policies and procedures
	Group controls General policies and procedures	Group controls Somewhat specific policies and procedures	Budgets Special reports
	Budgets General audits MIS Project controls as needed	Budgets Specific audits MIS Project controls as needed	Specific audits MIS Project controls
	Large span of personal control (Occasional observation)	Moderate span of personal control (Regular observation)	Small span of personal control (Frequent observation)
Determination of control standards	Determined jointly by work group and manager	Set by manager after consultation with work group	Determined by manager

Examples of Controls in Business Functions[7]

Specific devices have been developed for controlling each aspect of a business. You will encounter more detailed presentations of many of these devices when you study finance, production/operations management, marketing, personnel and labor relations, accounting, and research and development in more depth. For illustrative purposes, however, I will include brief descriptions of some of them here.

Controls for Finances

Auditing, of course, provides some control over the financial aspects of an enterprise. Breakeven analysis and budgets are two other financial control devices. Breakeven analysis was discussed in Chapter 9. Budgets will be discussed in the next chapter. In addition, financial ratios are used to analyze financial statements—chiefly income statements and balance sheets—and control financial resources. There are four basic areas of ratio analysis: liquidity, activity, profitability, and leverage analysis. These will be explained using as an example the fictitious ABC company.

Liquidity Ratios

Liquidity is a measure of a firm's ability to meet its short-term obligations. Short-term obligations are any current liabilities, including currently maturing long-term debt. A firm uses current assets to pay off current liabilities. Therefore, one indication of a firm's liquidity is the current ratio: current assets divided by current liabilities.

$$\text{ABC Co. current ratio} = \frac{\text{Current assets}}{\text{Current liabilities}} = \frac{\$464,259}{\$121,570} = 3.82.$$

Most analysts believe a current ratio of 2 is desirable. A large current ratio is not necessarily a good sign; it may mean the organization is not making the most efficient use of these assets. The optimum current ratio will vary from industry to industry, with the more volatile industries having higher current ratios.

Since slow-moving or obsolescent inventories could cause the current ratio to overstate a firm's ability to meet short-term demands, the quick ratio is sometimes preferred for assessing liquidity. The quick ratio is current assets minus inventories, divided by current liabilities.

$$\text{ABC Co. quick ratio} = \frac{\text{Current assets} - \text{Inventories}}{\text{Current liabilities}}$$

$$= \frac{\$104,736}{\$121,570} = 0.86.$$

A quick ratio of 1 would be typical for American industries. Although there is less variability in the quick ratio than in the current ratio, stable industries would be able to operate safely with a lower ratio.

Activity Ratios

Activity ratios demonstrate how effectively a firm is using its resources. By comparing revenues and expenses with the resources used to generate them, efficiency of operation can be established. The asset turnover ratio indicates how efficiently management is employing its assets. It is obtained by dividing sales by total assets.

$$\text{ABC Co. asset turnover} = \frac{\text{Sales}}{\text{Total assets}} = \frac{\$908,785}{\$718,795} = 1.26.$$

Industry figures for asset turnover will vary, with capital intensive industries having a much smaller ratio.

Another activity ratio is inventory turnover, which is obtained by dividing sales by average inventory for the year. The norm for American industries is 9, but whether the ratio for a particular firm is higher or lower normally depends upon the product sold. Small, inexpensive items usually turn over at a much higher rate than larger, expensive ones.

$$\text{ABC Co. inventory turnover} = \frac{\text{Sales}}{\text{Inventory}} = \frac{\$908,785}{\$359,523} = 2.53.$$

The accounts receivable turnover measures the average collection period on credit sales. If the average number of days on credit sales varies widely from the industry norm, this may be an indication of poor management. A figure that is too low could indicate the firm is losing sales because of a restrictive credit policy. If the ratio is too high, too much capital may be tied up in accounts receivable, and management may be increasing its chance of bad debts. Because of varying industry credit policies, a comparison for the firm over time or within an industry is the only useful analysis.

$$\text{ABC Co. accounts receivable turnover} = \frac{\text{Sales}}{\text{Accounts receivable}}$$

$$= \frac{\$908,785}{\$\ 97,182} = 9.35.$$

On the basis of a 360-day year, the average collection period for ABC Company is thirty-nine days.

$$\text{ABC Co. average collection period} = \frac{360}{9.35} = 39 \text{ days.}$$

Profitability Ratios

Profitability is the result of an organization's management, operating, marketing, and sales. The profit margin is an important ratio. It is calculated by dividing net earnings by sales. There is wide industry variation, but the average for American firms is 5 percent.

$$\text{ABC Co. profit margin} = \frac{\text{Net earnings}}{\text{Sales}}$$

$$= \frac{\$\ 41,725}{\$908,785} = 0.0459 = 4.6\%.$$

A second useful ratio for evaluating profitability is the return on investment (ROI), found by dividing net earnings by total assets.

$$\text{ABC Co. return on investment} = \frac{\text{Net Earnings}}{\text{Total assets}}$$

$$= \frac{\$\ 41,725}{\$718,795} = 0.06 = 6\%.$$

It is often difficult to determine causes for lack of profitability. If the return on investment ratio is low, it can be broken down into two other key ratios, the profit margin and asset turnover ratios, to provide management with clues to the firm's lack of success.

$$\text{Return on investment} = \text{Profit margin} \times \text{Asset turnover}$$

$$= \frac{\text{Net earnings}}{\text{Sales}} \times \frac{\text{Sales}}{\text{Total assets}}$$

This may show that the lack of profitability is due to a low profit margin (expenses that are too high or prices that are too low) or to low sales generation on assets.

Leverage Ratios

Leverage ratios identify who has supplied the firm's capital requirement—owners or outside creditors. The term *leverage* refers to the magnification effect of debts' fixed costs on profits or losses. The most common ratios computed are debt/equity and debt/total assets.

There are several variations of these ratios, but the ones presented here define debt as long-term liabilities and equity as the total of stockholders' equity.

$$\text{ABC Co. debt/equity ratio} = \frac{\text{Debt}}{\text{Equity}} = \frac{\$175,863}{\$421,362} = 0.42.$$

$$\text{ABC Co. debt/total assets ratio} = \frac{\text{Debt}}{\text{Total assets}} = \frac{\$175,863}{\$718,795} = 0.24.$$

Because of the possible magnification of losses in poor years, debt/equity ratios over the 0.5 norm are usually considered safe only for the most stable industries.

Controls for Marketing

In addition to the budget, one of the most basic controls for the marketing unit of a firm is the sales forecast. In Chapter 9, various forecasting methods were discussed.

The marketing department prepares sales forecasts based on past sales patterns, the presence or absence of new products and services, the increase or decrease in competition, and additional expenditures for advertising, sales promotion, and personal selling. It can and does forecast unit sales. It also forecasts revenue flowing from these sales by multiplying unit sales times price. Current pricing policies (price increases and temporary or permanent discounts) affect the revenue flow. These data are used, together with reports and MIS per day, week, month, quarter, half-year, or year as a standard for determining what actions should be taken to assure the achievement of sales objectives.

Marketing units also use formal product development planning and control devices. As new products or services are market tested, costs and sales are compared and controlled according to the standards (planned units and costs) set in the formal planning stage.

Production/ Operations Management Controls

Aside from the finance unit, production/operations management has the most fully developed functional controls in most organizations. Several such controls were described earlier. The appendix to Chapter 9 illustrated methods of inventory control. PERT and Gantt Charts were discussed as planning and control devices. Production/operations management units also have elaborate quality control systems such as Zero Defects Programs and product sampling (autos, for instance, are tested as they come off the line).

**Personnel and
Labor Relations
Controls**

The personnel department exercises two kinds of controls: (1) control of individual employee performance and (2) control of overall personnel performance. Performance appraisal evaluations serve to evaluate, reward, and control the performance of individuals. Various schedules, forms, and interviews are used to examine how employees have been performing relative to expected behaviors. These systems are described in more detail in Chapter 20.

Overall personnel performance can be controlled by auditing the degree of compliance with personnel policies. Checklists are also used. Probably the most scientific mechanism for this type of control are personnel ratios. These ratios are developed by gathering statistics and comparing them to statistics on the firm's past performance and the performance of similar effective organizations. Some of the more frequently used ratios are given in Table 18.4.

Table 18.4
Personnel Evaluation
Ratios

Effectiveness ratios
Ratio of number of employees to total output—in general.
Sales in dollars per employee for the whole company or by organizational unit (business).
Output in units per employee hour worked for the entire enterprise or organizational unit.
Scrap loss per unit of the enterprise.
Payroll costs by unit per employee grade.

Accident ratios
Frequency of accident rate for the enterprise as a whole or by organizational unit.
Number of lost-time accidents.
Compensation paid per 1,000 hours worked for accidents.
Accidents by type.
Accidents classified by type of injury to each part of the body.
Average cost of accident by part of the body involved.

Organizational health ratios
Number of grievances filed.
Number of arbitration awards lost.

Turnover and absenteeism ratios
Attendance, tardiness, and overtime comparisons by organizational unit as a measure of how well an operation is handling manpower loading.
Employee turnover by unit and for the organization.

Employment ratios
Vacations granted as a percentage of employees eligible.
Sick-leave days granted as a percentage of man-days worked.
Military leaves granted per 100 employees.
Jury duty leaves granted per 100 employees.
Maternity leaves granted per 100 employees.
Educational leaves granted per 100 employees.
Personal leaves granted per 100 employees.
Employment distribution by chronological age.
Employment distribution by length of service with organization.
Employment distribution by sex, race, national origin, religion.
Managerial distribution by chronological age, sex, race, national origin, religion.
Average age of work force.
Average age of managerial work force.

Source: William F. Glueck, *Foundations of Personnel* (Dallas: Business Publications, Inc., 1979), p. 491. © 1979 by Business Publications, Inc. Reprinted by permission.

Two of the most common evaluations are those of turnover and absenteeism. Turnover is the net result of the exit of some employees and entrance of others. Three formulas used in analyzing turnover are given below:

$$\text{Separation rate} = \frac{\text{Number of separations during the month}}{\text{Total number of employees at midmonth}} \times 100. \quad \textbf{(1)}$$

$$\text{Quit rate} = \frac{\text{Total quits}}{\text{Average work force}} \times 100. \quad \textbf{(2)}$$

$$\text{Avoidable turnover} = \frac{\text{Total separations} - \text{Unavoidables}}{\text{Average work force}} \times 100. \quad \textbf{(3)}$$

Formula 1 is the most general and is the one recommended by the Department of Labor. Formula 2 tries to isolate a specific type of turnover (quits). Formula 3 is the most refined; it discounts quits by those groups that can be expected to leave: part-timers and women leaving for maternity reasons. These data can be refined further by computing turnover per 100 employees by length of employment, by job classification, by job category, and by each organizational unit.

Other measures used to evaluate and control overall personnel performance are absenteeism rates.

Absenteeism is the failure of employees to report for work when they are scheduled to work.

Tardiness is partial absenteeism, in that employees report late to work.

Absenteeism is undesirable because of its costs and the operating problems it causes. Absenteeism's costs to the enterprise include the costs of benefits, which continue even when workers are absent, so benefit costs are higher per unit of output. Overtime pay also may be necessary for the worker who is doing the job for the missing worker. Facilities may be underutilized and productivity may drop because of reduced output due to understaffing. There also may be increased break-in costs for replacements, substandard production, the need for more help from supervisors and peers, and increased inspection costs.

How is absenteeism computed? The standard formula recommended by government bodies and used by over 70 percent of those who compute absenteeism is:

$$\frac{\text{Number of employee days lost through job absence in the period}}{\text{Average number of employees} \times \text{Number of work days}} \times 100.$$

Most others use a variation of this formula, such as

$$\frac{\text{Total hours of absence}}{\text{Total hours worked (or scheduled)}} \times 100.$$

These measures can be used to determine and thus help control personnel costs and resources.

Overall Control

Some firms use control devices to analyze how well plans are meeting objectives. Management by objectives (discussed in Chapter 7) is one of the devices most frequently used to gain overall control. In firms where financial objectives predominate, the return on investment (ROI) measures mentioned earlier are also used for this purpose. Under the guidance of Harold Geneen, ITT gained a reputation for its focus on return on investment planning and control methods.

Return on investment has been calculated in various ways. One well-known conceptualization of ROI originated at Du Pont. J. Fred Weston and Eugene F. Brigham have developed a modification of the Du Pont system, which is presented in Figure 18.7.[8] As they point out:

It brings together the activity ratios and profit margin on sales and shows how these ratios interact to determine the profitability of assets. . . .

The right side of the figure develops the turnover ratio. That section shows how current assets (cash, marketable securities, accounts receivable, and inventories), when added to fixed assets, give total investment. Total investment divided into sales gives the turnover of investment.

The left side of the figure develops the profit margin on sales. The individual expense items plus income taxes are subtracted from sales to produce net profits after taxes. Net profits divided by sales gives the profit margin on sales. When the asset turnover ratio on the right side of [the figure] is multiplied by the profit margin on sales developed on the left side of the figure, the product is the return on total investment (ROI) in the firm. This can be seen from the following formula:

$$\frac{\text{Sales}}{\text{Investment}} \times \frac{\text{Profit}}{\text{Sales}} = \text{ROI.[9]}$$

Properly defined and communicated, ROI can become a powerful control tool to aid in achieving the financial objectives of the firm.

Normally at this point, I would discuss making controls effective. Since this is only the first chapter of a two chapter unit on control, I will postpone this discussion to the end of Chapter 19.

Summary

Control is the managerial skill that helps ensure effective acquisition and use of the enterprise's resources and achievement of its objectives. It enables management (1) to anticipate problems, (2) to act to adjust the plan, or (3) to take corrective action when the plan is not being met. Controls are positive aids to achieving desired ends. Effective controls are cost effective, acceptable to employees, and well designed. They are also strategic, measurable, and objective.

Figure 18.7
Modified DuPont
System of Financial
Control Applied to
Walker-Wilson

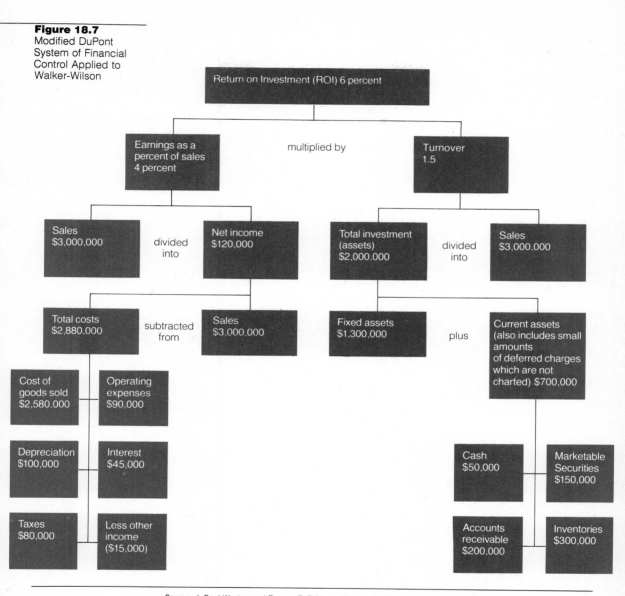

Source: J. Fred Weston and Eugene F. Brigham, *Managerial Finance*, 5th ed., (Hinsdale, Ill.: Dryden Press, 1975), p. 36. Copyright © 1975 by Dryden Press, a division of Holt, Rinehart and Winston. Reprinted by permission of Holt, Rinehart and Winston.

The most effective process of control involves: (1) setting objectives, (2) establishing predictors of the objectives, (3) establishing standards of performance, (4) evaluating results against standards, (5) acting to reinforce the positive and correct the negative results. This process is called cybernetic control. It can work only if there is a standard, if actual results are measured reliably, and if the information obtained from a comparison of the standard and results is fed back to management for action.

Most nonbusiness organizations and units in business firms that do not involve production, operations, or sales do not meet the above conditions. Therefore, they cannot use the cybernetic approach.

Control can be categorized according to *when* the control is exerted. *Feedforward* or *steering (in process)* control uses the future as a time frame of control. In *yes–no* control, work stops at predetermined times or when certain events take place and cannot continue without a screening decision to do so. In *postaction* control situations, results are reviewed when the operation is completed.

Firms are limited in the degree in which they can control their operations. To control output effectively, it is necessary to have reliable and valid measures of output. To effectively control the behavior of employees, it is necessary to understand thoroughly the production function: how inputs go through a transfer process and become outputs.

Self-control, group and ideological control, policies and procedural control, management information systems, audits, budget controls, special reports, project controls, and personal observation are all methods of control.

Unless each employee exercises *self-control*—and does what is expected at work most of the time on most work related matters—no enterprise can exist. Self-control stems from the employee's ego, orientation, training, and work attitudes.

Group control affects individuals, both in output and behavior. Group norms of doing a good job exert pressures on the individual to perform and to follow work rules.

Policies and procedures are guides to action for managers to use in controlling behavior and output of employees. They can, for example, protect the firm's resources and equipment and require employees' presence for appropriate work times.

Budgets are regularly scheduled control devices discussed in Chapter 19.

A *management information system (MIS)* is the system developed by a firm to collect, process, and distribute information about the operations of the firm to its executives and their users of information. Advances in computer technology have made possible the development of sophisticated MIS systems.

The financial systems of a firm must be examined by a professional accounting firm on a regular basis. These *external audits* make sure that the firm's statements are honest and accurate and thus protect the rights of present and future stockholders.

When certain areas of the firm need analysis in more depth, managers require *special reports*. These reports can be statistical or nonstatistical and may require comparisons of internal data with external sources such as costs of competitors, government figures, or industry data. Some examples are operational (internal) audits and management audits.

There are various kinds of *project controls*. Two of these are Gantt Charts and PERT.

Personal control and observation is another method of control. The manager sets objectives and standards which the employees know and that are acceptable and visits and observes crucial workplaces where data indicate serious problems exist. Through personal influence, the manager resolves problems, making it possible for objectives to be met.

In organizations or subunits where cybernetic controls are appropriate, all control devices can be used. Which ones are used depends on cost considerations and the leadership style of the manager.

For each area of a business specific control devices have been developed. Finance uses budgets, breakeven analysis, and various financial statements and ratios to analyze and control financial resources. Marketing sets up sales forecasts and other formal product development planning and control devices. Production/operations management units use PERT and Gantt Charts as scheduling and control devices.

Personnel uses two kinds of control devices: those directed at the performance of individuals (performance appraisal evaluations) and those directed at the overall performance of personnel. The latter include auditing for compliance with personnel policies, checklists, and personnel ratios.

In addition, firms have mechanisms for establishing overall control. These include MBO and return on investment (ROI). The Du Pont conceptualization of ROI as modified by Weston and Brigham brings together activity ratios and profit margin on sales and shows how these ratios interact to determine the profitability of assets.

The chapter is followed by an appendix which will help you learn how to control your time more effectively. The next chapter is devoted to one particular method of control, the budget, and ways of ensuring that all control mechanisms used are effective.

Questions

1. Your immediate subordinates feel control is a negative process. Explain what control is and why it is a positive process.
2. Describe some of the characteristics of effective controls. How could you make sure that your firm's controls were designed effectively?
3. Diagram the control process. Describe each phase in the process, linking it with the subsequent phase.
4. You are a manager of a research and development department. Are you likely to use cybernetic controls? Why or why not?
5. There are nine methods of control which effective managers use. What are the most important of these methods? How will you make use of self-control in your career as a manager? Do you think you will be controlled by your peer group?
6. What is a management information system? How would you use MIS to control your enterprise's outputs?

7. Describe project control mechanisms like the Gantt Chart and PERT network. Do you think these mechanisms are useful to managers? Why or why not?

8. You have chosen to follow the traditional leadership style as a manager. How are you likely to feel about the use of control? Compare your approach to that of a participative leader.

9. Describe some control devices used by one of the following departments of a firm: finance, marketing, or P/OM.

10. You are a personnel manager. What two kinds of control do you use? What control mechanisms do you use with each kind?

Notes

[1] William Newman, *Constructive Control* (Englewood Cliffs, N.J.: Prentice-Hall, 1975).

[2] Geert Hofstede, "The Poverty of Management Control Philosophy," *Academy of Management Review* 3 (July 1978): 450–461.

[3] William G. Ouchi, "The Relationship between Organizational Structure and Organizational Control," *Administrative Science Quarterly* 22 (March 1977): 95–113.

[4] William Greenwood, *A Management Audit System* (Carbondale, Ill.: School of Business, Southern Illinois University, 1967); and *Business Policy: A Management Audit Approach* (New York: Macmillan, 1967).

[5] Jackson Martindale, *The Appraisal of Management* (New York: Harper & Row, 1962).

[6] Hofstede, "Poverty of Management Control Philosophy."

[7] This section was coauthored with Elizabeth Gatewood, University of Georgia.

[8] See J. Fred Weston and Eugene F. Brigham, *Managerial Finance,* 5th ed. (Hinsdale, Ill.: Dryden Press, 1975).

[9] Ibid., p. 35.

References

What Is Control?

Robert Anthony and John Dearden, *Management Control Systems* (Homewood, Ill.: Richard D. Irwin, 1976). Gerald Bell, "The Influence of Technological Components of Work upon Management Control," *Academy of Management Journal* 8 (June 1965): 127–132. David Bowers, "Organizational Control in an Insurance Company," *Sociometry* 27 (June 1964): 230–244. Samuel Eilon, *Management Control* (London: Macmillan, 1971). George F. Farris and D. Anthony Butterfield, "Control Theory in Brazilian Organizations," *Administrative Science Quarterly* 17 (December 1972): 574–585. Giovanni Giglioni and Arthur Bedeian, "A Consensus of Management Control Theory: 1900–1972," *Academy of Management Journal* 17 (June 1974): 292–305. Xavier Gilbert, "Does Your Control System Fit Your Business?" *European Business* 4 (Spring 1973): 69–76. Geert Hofstede, "The Poverty of Management Control Philosophy," *Academy of Management Review* 3 (July 1978): 450–461. Pradip Khandwalla, "Effect of Competition on the Structure of Management Control," *Academy of Management Journal* 16 (June 1973): 285–295. Paul Lawrence and Jay Lorsch, *Organization Environment* (Cambridge, Mass.: Harvard Business School, 1967). J. Timothy McMahon and G. W. Perritt, "Toward a Contingency Theory of Organizational Control," *Academy of Management Journal* 16 (December 1973): 624–635. William Newman, *Constructive Control* (Englewood Cliffs, N.J.: Prentice-Hall, 1975). William Ouchi, "The Transmission of Control through Organizational Hierarchy," *Academy of Management Journal* 21 (June 1978): 173–192. William G. Ouchi, "The Relationship between Organizational Structure and Organizational Control," *Administrative Science Quarterly* 22 (March 1977): 95–113. William Ouchi and Mary Ann Maguire, "Organizational Control: Two Functions," *Administrative Science Quarterly* 20 (December 1975): 559–569. Jeffrey Pfeffer and Gerald Salancik, *The External Control of Organizations* (New York: Harper & Row, 1978).

Bernard Reimann and Anant Negandhi, "Strategies of Administrative Control and Organizational Effectiveness," *Human Relations* 28 (May 1975): 475–486. Arnold Tannenbaum, *Control in Organizations* (New York: McGraw-Hill, 1968). William Turcotte, "Control Systems, Performance, and Satisfaction in Two State Agencies," *Administrative Science Quarterly* 19 (March 1974): 60–73. Joan Woodward, *Industrial Organization: Behavior and Control* (New York: Oxford University Press, 1970).

What Can and Should Be Controlled?

Edwin G. Nelson and John L. J. Machin, "Management Control Systems Thinking Applied to the Development of a Framework for Empirical Studies," *Journal of Management Studies* 13 (October 1976): 274–287. William G. Ouchi, "The Relationship between Organizational Structure and Organizational Control," *Administrative Science Quarterly* 22 (March 1977): 95–113; and "The Transmission of Control through Organizational Hierarchy," *Academy of Management Journal* 21 (June 1978): 173–192. Charles Perrow, "Hospitals, Technology, Structure and Goals," in *Handbook of Organizations,* ed. James March (Chicago: Rand McNally, 1965). T. Kenaston Reeves and Joan Woodward, "The Study of Managerial Control," in *Industrial Organizations: Behavior and Control,* ed. Joan Woodward (London: Oxford University Press, 1970). James Thompson, *Organizations in Action* (New York: McGraw-Hill, 1967). John Todd, "Management Control Systems: A Key Link between Strategy, Structure and Employee Performance," *Organizational Dynamics* 5 (Spring 1977): 65–78.

Methods of Control

James A. Anderson, "Planning Control Systems to Include Human Factor," *Managerial Planning* 25 (July–August 1976): 30–35. John B. Miner, "The Uncertain Future of the Leadership Concept: An Overview," *Organization and Administrative Sciences* 6 (Summer–Fall 1975): 197–208. William G. Ouchi and Jerry B. Johnson, "Types of Organizational Control and Their Relationship to Emotional Well Being," *Administrative Science Quarterly* 23 (June 1978): 293–317. David Smith, "Control and Orientations to Work in a Business Organization," *Journal of Management Studies* 15 (May 1978): 212–221. Peter F. Sorensen, Jr., "Control and Effectiveness in Twenty-Seven Scandinavian Voluntary Organizations," *Journal of Management Studies* 13 (May 1976): 183–190. Francis Tuggle, *Organizational Processes* (Arlington Heights, Ill.: AHM Publishing, 1978), chapter 7.

Management Information Systems

Anders Edström, "User Influence and the Success of MIS Projects: A Contingency Approach," *Human Relations* 30 (July 1977): 589–607. Phillip Ein-Dor and Eli Segev, "Information-System Responsibility," *MSU Business Topics* 25 (Autumn 1977): 33–40; and "Organizational Context and the Success of Management Information Systems," *Management Science* 24 (June 1978): 1064–1077. John C. Henderson and Paul C. Nutt, "On the Design of Planning Information Systems," *Academy of Management Review* 3 (October 1978): 774–785. Edward Lawler and John Rhode, *Information and Control in Organizations* (Santa Monica, Calif.: Goodyear, 1977). David Nadler, Philip Mirvis, and Cortlandt Cammann, "The Ongoing Feedback System," *Organizational Dynamics* 4 (Spring 1976): 63–80. Kamal E. Said, "A MIS for Problem Detection, Diagnosis, and Evaluation," *Managerial Planning* 26 (March–April 1978): 4–8.

Special Reports

William Greenwood, *A Management Audit System* (Carbondale, Ill.: School of Business, Southern Illinois University, 1967); and *Business Policy: A Management Audit Approach* (New York: Macmillan, 1967). Jackson Martindale, *The Appraisal of Management* (New York: Harper & Row, 1962).

Project Controls

Further information on these project tools are available from any standard production/operations management text. Some examples include Elwood Buffa, *Basic Production Management* (New York: Wiley, 1975); Richard B. Chase and Nicholas J. Aquilano, *Production and Operations Management: A Life Cycle Approach* (Homewood, Ill.: Irwin, 1977); and Norman Gaither, *Production and Operations Management* (Hinsdale, Ill.: Dryden Press, 1980).

Control, Cybernetic Controls, and Managerial Style

Cortlandt Cammann and David A. Nadler, "Fit Control Systems to Your Managerial Style," *Harvard Business Review* 54 (January–February 1976): 65–72. Geert Hofstede, "The Poverty of Management Control Philosophy," *Academy of Management Review* 3 (July 1978): 450–461. Anthony Hopewood, *An Accounting System and Managerial Behavior* (London: Haymarket, 1974).

Appendix 18.1

Controlling the Use of Your Time

The most valuable resource most managers have is their own time. In this appendix I will give you some ideas on how to get control of your time. Though the guidelines presented below are intended primarily to help you improve your on-the-job time management, they can also be applied to your off-the-job life.

To make more effective use of your time you must (1) determine how you spend your time; (2) analyze how you use your time; (3) set priorities and develop a time use strategy; and (4) implement an effective time plan.

Step 1: Determining How You Use Your Time

Studies of how managers use their time are not very helpful if they ask managers to estimate their own time usage. Such studies are notoriously unreliable. Managers consistently overestimate the time devoted to production and underestimate the time spent on other matters such as employee problems.

The first step toward better control of your time is to learn how you use your time now. Only through recording and observational methods can you do this effectively. The recording can be done by you, a secretary, or a friend. Usually you can be more thorough. One way of keeping such a record is by using a device leased by Extensor Corporation for $200 per week. The device beeps randomly during the day. At each beep you punch a button on a keyboard to indicate what you are doing at that moment. Extensor recommends a five-week study period for an accurate picture of how you use your time.

Another approach is to use the work-sampling method; that is, time uses are recorded for a shorter but *typical* period such as one week or several random hours in a week. Record how each block of time is used.

A third approach to time use study is to keep a log. This log will vary according to the type of managerial job you have. The more standardized the job, the more abbreviated the symbols in the log can be. Exhibit 18.1 is an example of a log for a supervisor. For this system to work well the following hints should be kept in mind:

Exhibit 18.1
Time Log for a
Marketing Supervisor

Date _____
Time _____

Start	End	Total	Activity	With Whom	Initiation	Action/Notes
8:00	9:00	60	M	Region 1 Salespeople	S	Discussed entry of Smith Brothers Region 1 Market. Action: discuss with boss our reaction.
9:00	9:05	5	TP	Arthur's Wholesale	S	Set up appointment.
9:05	9:50	45	TR	John Artis (Salesperson)	S	While on way, Artis briefed me on Smith Brothers problem at Arthur's.
9:50	10:00	10	WT	Artis	—	Waiting for appointment.
10:00	10:30	30	C	Artis; John Arthur (Buyer)	S	Discussed Smith Brothers campaign with buyer and how we should respond.

Initiation	Activity	Functional Code
O = Other	I = Individual discussion	P = Personal activities
S = Self	C = Conference	F = Financial and accounting problems
	TP = Telephone	M = Marketing/customer relations/logistics
	W = Writing correspondence, reports	E = External/public relations
	R = Reading	O = Operating problems
	T = Thinking	PP = Personnel problems

- Carry your log with you at all times.
- Note your comments immediately or you will forget the details.
- Make your entries short, but be specific.
- Record the *smallest* uses of time, *especially interruptions.*
- Subdivide long periods. (For example, a meeting may cover three areas: finance, accounting, and marketing.)

Now that you have a record of your activities during a typical period you are ready for Step 2.

**Step 2:
Analyzing How
You
Use Your Time**

Time analysis can be done in several ways. The first way is to total the categories and see how much time you spend in various activities such as personal time, telephone calls, conferences, and individual discussions. Then you can examine how you allocate time to functional areas and analyze the flow of activities. This includes a study of the time taken up by interruptions.

Next your time can be divided into four categories: creative, preparatory, productive, and overhead:

- *Creative time* is time devoted to planning future activities, new product ideas, and the like.
- *Preparatory time* is time spent in setup activities such as gathering facts in preparation for a conference.
- *Productive time* is time spent actually doing the job.
- *Overhead time* is time spent on correspondence and reports, paperwork, public relations, and so forth.

In analyzing your use of time you should ask yourself the following questions:

1. *Should anyone be doing this activity at all? Does it serve any purpose?* For example, suppose you always start the day by meeting with three assistants. Is this conference really needed? What purpose does it serve? Maybe it should be eliminated.
2. *If the activity needs to be done, should I be doing it?* If a subordinate can do it equally well (with a little experience), then you should not be doing it. But if you decide to delegate the activity, do not oversupervise.
3. *If I should do it myself, can it be done in less time? How?*
4. *Do I keep punctually to my time schedules or do I waste subordinates' time?*
5. *Do I keep a pile of overhead duties (correspondence to be signed, etc.) at my elbow to be done while waiting for telephone callers to get on the line or visitors to show up?*

Step 3: Setting Priorities and Developing a Time Use Strategy

The preceding step serves the purpose of getting you to realize how you spend your time. The next step is much harder: deciding what to do with your time.

Your time is divided into several categories: work, pleasure, sleep, personal hygiene, self-development, travel. You set personal priorities among these categories. Some people become "workaholics" and eliminate the pleasure category, maybe self-development, and sometimes sleep. Only you can set priorities like these, and your allocation of time is a reflection of your life-style, beliefs, and attitudes.

But how do you set priorities within the work category? The story is told of a top executive who asked a consultant to make his time use more efficient. He paid the consultant $25,000 for the following advice: At the end of each day make a list of the important things you did not get done today. The next day use it as your job list. Do the jobs in order of their importance, starting with the most important or difficult ones.

To take advantage of this advice you must be able to set your priorities—to come up with that list, then rank the items in order of importance. The list should be shorter as a result of Step 2. Still, if there are six items on the list, which three should you do first? It is frequently pointed out that 80 percent of your results come from the vital 20 percent of your activities. Thus the importance of setting priorities should be evident.

Step 4: Implementing an Effective Time Plan

A basic element of effective time management is developing a time budget for the week. This may be easier for you if you follow the suggestions below:

- Assign substantially long periods of continuous time (without interruptions) to major tasks (production time). Control interruptions during crucial periods by accepting no visitors or phone calls.
- Block out time for creative planning, preparation, and overhead activities. Creative planning and preparation time should be used in a quiet place away from your desk, if possible.
- Group together related kinds of work to save starting and stopping time. Put all phone calls together and get your secretary to dial the next one when you signal that you are almost through with the current one.
- Schedule top-priority projects early in the week.
- Budget decision times to reduce procrastination.
- Reserve an average amount of time for unanticipated crises and time over which you have no control (for example, conferences initiated by others).
- Schedule your least interesting jobs at your peak energy periods so they will get done.
- Postpone shorter projects until you have started long ones. This will motivate you to complete the long ones once they are started.
- Make better use of meetings. Prepare an agenda with time allocated to each topic. Schedule meetings so that they will be naturally cut off by lunchtime or the end of the work day.

The above suggestions constitute a strategy for controlling your time usage that can work on the job, in school, or during leisure time. People who control and plan their time get more done and are more effective on most jobs.

Cases for Chapter 18

Honest Employees	Recently a fast-food chain that was concerned about robberies installed television cameras in some of its stores on an experimental basis. They were focused on the cash register. The chain explained the purpose of the experiment to its employees and said it did not know if it could justify the expense for the full chain.

A few months after the installation one of the accountants pointed out an interesting phenomenon. The accountant had compared the cash register receipts before and after the installation of the cameras and found that the number of small sales rung up after the installation was substantially higher than before. "It seems to me that some of the employees were taking some sales as 'tips' before we installed the cameras. Now they think we're watching. This should help profitability."

At the same time, the personnel manager began to get complaints about "Big Brother" in the exit interviews of some of the employees who quit. He followed this up and found that a number of employees were really upset because they felt that they were being watched by the bosses.

The security specialist pointed out that not one of the outlets with the cameras had been robbed. The stores had prominent signs warning thieves about the cameras.

The cameras are very expensive. The additional cash in the cash registers covered 10 per cent of the cost of the cameras. At the stores without the cameras (used as "control" stores) there was one robbery. The total "savings" from additional cash and "lack of robberies" equaled 25 per cent of the cost of the cameras. |

Problem

You are the manager in charge of this firm. Since the three-month trial period is over, should you remove the cameras (they are leased)? continue the experiment another three months? expand the experiment? Explain your answer.

Ajax Foundry

Ajax Foundry has a large plant in Arizona. Each employee's job has been analyzed using time and motion studies. Each employee therefore is responsible for a certain amount of output. The company also uses a common recording and control device: the time clock.

On one particular job some of the employees, who had been selected on the basis of their skill, were getting the job done an hour and a half before quitting time. All but one of these employees would leave early. That employee would stay around and punch the whole section out on the time clock at the end of the shift. This "job" was rotated among the members of the section.

One day the plant manager caught one employee punching out all the employees in the section. The next day he met with them. He reminded them that according to company rules this action justified firing them all. He explained that in this case he would just warn them that if it happened again he would have to fire them. At this point John Sikes, the informal group leader, spoke up: "Look, Mr. Paul, we do good work. We do all our work. Why not put this job on a 'get the work out, then go home' basis?"

The plant manager said, "I wish I could do that, but as you know, you guys are unionized. If I put the job on that basis the senior men could apply for your jobs and bump you from them. The contract says they have that right, and you know this would happen because they would want to leave early. Frankly, many of the senior men are not as skilled as you guys, and production quality would drop."

The employees continued to work fast. But since they had to stay around, they tended to wander around the plant, distracting other workers, reducing their productivity, and lowering their morale ("those guys must have cushy jobs"). And as they started messing around, the accident rate increased by 5 percent.

Problem

You are the assistant plant manager. What recommendations would you give Mr. Paul on this control and morale problem?

Chapter 19 Budgeting Control

19

What Is a Budget?

Chapter 18 described the control systems used by managers in detail—all except for the most pervasive nonhuman system, the budget. Budgeting is a complex and important topic. That is why it has been given its own chapter. Probably no other nonhuman system of control can be found in more enterprises than budgets. And once budgets are installed, managers get attached to them, as the cartoon here indicates.

Budgets and the Budgeting Process

A budget is a statement of future expenditures and revenues that quantifies management's plans to control the use of financial and other resources.

A budget is a tool for both planning and control. A forecast, however, is the predominant planning tool (see Chapter 8). The budget is more important in control. A budget exercises control in two basic ways: (1) it

"Oh, it's great here, all right, but I sort of feel uncomfortable in a place with no budget at *all*."

limits the amount of resources that can be used by a unit; and (2) it sets a standard for production—the budgeted amount of output must be produced or management must know why it is not. When a manager's report indicates that his or her unit is not meeting budget standards, the superior takes action. Thus actually a budget is a plan accompanied by a description of how actual events should correspond to the plan. Figure 19.1 demonstrates how budgets are related to planning.

In Chapters 7 and 8 I showed how top managers set objectives, choose a strategy, and then begin to implement it by establishing functional policies. Budgets are part of this implementation phase. Comparison of actual expenditures to the budget provides the feedback necessary to the planning process and helps the firm realize its objectives.

Robert Anthony and John Dearden have noted the following characteristics of budgets:[1]

- A budget is stated primarily in monetary terms. Occasionally parts of it involve other quantitative terms such as units to be sold or produced.

- Typically, a budget covers a one year period. In a few volatile businesses there may be two budgets. The fashion industry has one for fall and one for spring lines.

- Total commitment by management is necessary to achieve the budgeted objectives.

- Preliminary budgets are prepared by lower-level managers and approved by higher-level managers.

- Sometimes budgets can be changed—but only under previously specified conditions.

- During the year to which the budget applies, actual performances are compared to budgeted performance. If variances (differences) exist, they are analyzed and explained by subordinates to superiors.

Steps in Budgeting

Essentially, an enterprise begins its budgeting procedure with the projected receipts of the firm. In a business, this figure is based on the sales forecast. For other organizations it is a forecast of receipts from various

Figure 19.1
Relationship of Planning Process to Budget

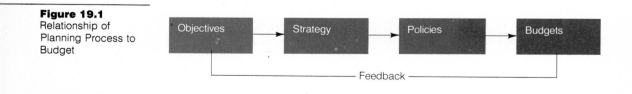

sources of funds. For a state university, for example, the sources include the state legislature, student tuition, research grants, gifts, and profits from ancillary enterprises such as food service, bookstores, and sports. Receipts from each of these sources are forecast and then totaled to estimate gross receipts.

At this point, subsidiary budgets are developed—for example, the operating budget, financial budgets, the capital budget, expense budgets. The operating budget specifies materials, labor, overhead, and other costs. Financial budgets project cash receipts and disbursements; the capital budget projects major additions or new construction. The expense budgets project expenses not covered in other budgets, such as marketing costs.

The summary budget (profit and loss or income statement) subtracts the total obtained by combining the subsidiary budgets from the projected receipts. The remainder is a profit or loss (in the nonprofit sector these might be called surpluses or deficits, excess revenues, or other terms). Various other kinds of graphs, statements, and presentations can be developed to exemplify the summary budget.

Viewed in more detail, the process by which a budget is drawn up and administered can be analyzed as a series of steps. These steps are described below.

Step 1 *Top management initiates the budgeting process.* It does this by communicating the objectives of the firm for the period. It also announces the assumptions it uses—the predicted economic and competitive conditions, for instance—to set these objectives. Another budget-related duty of top management is to send out the timetable for preparing and reviewing budgets at various levels. Often this timetable is prepared by the budget department (or administration).

Step 2 *The budget department (in large firms) or administrator communicates information and offers advice and counsel to the units preparing the budgets.* This unit prepares the forms and procedures for developing a budget. It helps those preparing budgets with technical problems and in preparation. It makes sure that budgets are received on time. If there are budget specialists at divisions, it trains these persons and coordinates their work. Normally, the budget department is part of the Vice President–Controller's office.

Step 3 *Each unit prepares a preliminary budget for the next period.* Normally the unit begins with the previous period's budget and performance against this budget. Next the unit states how the next period will differ from the current period. So the unit proposes the next year's budget based on the past budget plus or minus expected changes. This shows how the unit's management expects to achieve its objectives.

On the cost side, how much inflation will there be eighteen months from now? What will the interest rate be? What about the cost of coal to heat the

Source: Drawing by Hamilton;
© 1976 The New Yorker Magazine, Inc.

"Sometimes ballpark figures aren't in the ballpark."

buildings? Accountants have developed methods to *try* to cope with these uncertainties, but this aspect of budgeting is not an easy process.

Conceptually, the budgeting process sounds easy. In practice, however, there are serious problems involved in budgeting. Estimating both revenues and costs is very difficult. In the case of an automaker, for example, how many new cars will the company sell? This depends on factors such as the economy, competitors' products, and how consumers evaluate its product compared to competing products. The company's pricing and market image affect this estimate, as do product quality, engineering, the aggressiveness and reliability of dealers, and other factors. Managers often handle this by making their best guesses. They use the expression "in the ballpark" for these estimates. Sometimes they miss, as the cartoon indicates.

To illustrate the uncertainties involved in making such estimates, consider the case of a college. On the revenue side, how does the administration know how many students will enroll (and pay their tuition), what the legislature will appropriate, how many grants the college will get (or lose), how many gifts it will receive?

Step 4 *The preliminary budgets developed in Step 3 are reviewed and approved.* The budget department analyzes and reviews each unit's past performance and determines whether its projections are realistic given likely future conditions. After comparing the budgets of the various units, the budget department submits them to top management along with recommendations for approval or adjustment. Top management examines and approves the budgets if they are consistent with past performance, anticipated revenues, and the firm's strategy.

The allocation of funds among the firm's units is the basic feature of this step in the budget process. It is a very difficult task involving hard questions: Who gets the money to hire more people, buy new furniture or machinery, build a new building? In most enterprises resources are scarce and every unit cannot be given what it wants (and says it needs). The allocation of funds can be crucial to the success of a unit (and to the career of its manager). Loss of marketing funds for TV spots at a strategic time, for example, can wreck a unit's results. Because the decisions involved are so difficult, they are often made by a budget committee or a number of managers.

Step 5 *The budget performances of units are evaluated during the year.* The budget department and line managers review how well each unit has done in sticking to its budget. If a unit's performance in this regard is poor, then action can be taken to remedy the situation. After review and evaluation, if it is believed the unit had a reasonable budget, the unit is encouraged to meet the budget.

Step 6 *In the unusual event that a unit's budget turns out to be unreasonable in practice—usually because of unforeseen difficulties—then the budget department can recommend a revised budget.* Top management approves or rejects this revision just as it did the entire current budget. Effective control requires that budget revisions that favor the unit are not too easy to obtain. If they are, units may be less motivated to meet the firm's standards of performance (as quantified in the budget), and overall performance could very well drop.

The Purpose of a Budget

A budget has three general purposes: (1) to preserve the enterprise's capital resources, (2) to promote the efficient use of capital, and (3) to help achieve the financially oriented objectives of the enterprise. Glen Welsch lists a number of reasons firms take the trouble to establish a budgeting control system, including the following:[2]

- It aids in planning in that it forces management to consider basic policies and set and communicate objectives.
- It leads to periodic company self-analysis.
- It leads to efficiency in the use of resources.
- It helps clarify specific responsibilities within the organization.
- It helps achieve objectives by useful implementation of the strategy.

Thus in addition to their control function, budgets are also important in a number of management tasks. For example, in defining specific standards and objectives for managers, the budget is a valuable aid in the MBO process as well as in the performance evaluation and development of managers (see Chapter 20).

The Structure of Budgets

For the budget to be used as an effective control device, firms must divide up their organization into units which are meaningful for budget purposes—units that contain the necessary people and other resources to achieve specific budgeted objectives. Such units are often called "responsibility centers." A responsibility center is a unit whose manager is held responsible for achieving certain budgeted results. There are four kinds of responsibility centers, which correspond to the four basic concerns of a budget: investment, profit, expense, and revenue.

Investment Centers Budget units whose criterion of control is *return on investment* (ROI) are investment centers. As indicated in the previous chapter, return on investment is measured by dividing income by investments:

$$ROI = \frac{Income}{Investments.}$$

The investment figure is obtained by subtracting current liabilities from assets. Any unit whose budget objective is measured not just in terms of revenue generated, costs, or profit but rather in terms of how well the profit earned approximates the ROI objective set by the firm can be considered an investment center.

Profit Centers The budget objective of profit centers is of course profit:

$$Profit = Revenue - Expenses.$$

Profit centers can exist at departmental, divisional, and many other levels. Accountants get involved in many discussions over ways of measuring profits, especially the cost side. The contribution margin approach focuses on variable costs (which are discussed later in the chapter). Direct profit measures attempt to measure costs with all costs which can be directly attributable to the unit.

Expense (Cost) Centers In investment or profit centers the manager is expected to relate inputs and outputs in budgeting. But some units in a firm—legal, administrative services, and other staff departments—have little or no output or revenue. Thus their budgets are based on a fair and reasonable assessment of the costs of the services they provide. Such assessments may be purely discretionary (based on judgment) or based to some extent on standard costs.

Revenue Centers Whereas cost centers have no output or revenue, revenue centers have no costs or expenses for inputs. Typically, revenue centers are sales units. They are responsible for meeting sales budgets but only slightly concerned with the costs of manufacturing. In essence, revenue centers prepare sales budgets for each unit and salesperson in the organization.

The firm establishes its control structure as it sets the responsibilities at each level. Financial theorists advocate emphasizing investment over profit centers on the grounds that ROI is a more appropriate budgetary control criterion than profit. Many accountants and control experts urge firms to minimize the number of their expense and revenue centers because the efficiency of the control device for those budget units is not as great as for investment or profit centers. Of primary importance, however, is that the control structure meet the needs of management in providing effective control.

In its most fully developed form, the enterprise develops budgets for all major uses of funds. These normally include the following:

- A sales or receipts budget.
- An operations or production budget.
- A cash budget.
- A capital expenditures budget.
- Expense budgets.

Variable Budgets

The kind of budgets I have just listed are based on the assumption that revenues and costs will not change during the budget period and that those who develop the budget can predict what these revenues and costs will be. Yet these two conditions do not exist at all times.

In Chapter 8 we examined the contingency approach to planning. In that approach, a number of possible future states are determined and planned for. When one of the states becomes reality, the corresponding plan is put into effect. Thus if State 1 comes to be, Plan 1 is implemented. In budgeting, a similar approach is used. It is called variable or flexible budgeting.

Managers and budget specialists divide costs into three categories, which are explained below: fixed, variable, and semivariable. The different methods used to classify costs into each of these categories are discussed in accounting books.[3]

Fixed costs are those which do not change no matter how many or how few products or services are sold or produced. Examples include property taxes, rent, some research costs, minimum salaries, and marketing expenditures. Total fixed costs are not a factor in a variable budget since they remain the same.

Variable costs are those costs which increase directly in proportion to increases in volume of output and decrease proportionately when volume decreases. Examples include direct materials costs, some labor costs, and some utilities costs. These costs are directly related to variable budgets. If sales and production increase above budgeted figures, then adjustments need to be made.

Semivariable, semifixed costs increase as volume increases but not in direct proportion. An example is advertising. Adding one unit of advertising does not increase sales by one unit. We have some instances where when advertising decreased, sales increased. The tobacco industry found that even when it was prohibited from using TV advertising and not all of the millions of dollars was spent on other kinds of advertising, sales *increased*.

Just as costs can vary, so can revenues. How do budget experts devise a budget with these variances? They develop a variable budget, of course.

Table 19.1 presents a variable budget which portrays several possible outputs (volume/machine hours) and how the budget would vary for each, assuming that costs are stable. Note that foremen's salaries are regarded as fixed, other expenses as semifixed, and direct labor as variable.

It is difficult, if not impossible, to represent variable expenses and variable revenues per volume on a table. Computer simulation, however, makes it possible to budget for a number of possible variations in cost and revenue factors. Variable budgets are more expensive to draw up, but they are also more realistic than single assumption budgets.

The Human Influence on Budgets

The budgetary process I have described above is the ideal way of drawing up budgets. Research and common experience indicate that this is not always the way budgeting is done.

As indicated earlier, the question of who gets the most money from the budget has a major effect on the work environment as well as on the career of managers. If, as a manager, you "lose the budget battle," your employees will have to do more work with fewer helpers and less desirable equipment. They will feel that you have failed them and treat you accordingly.

The "budget battle" has been examined by Jeffrey Pfeffer and G. Salancik, who studied the budgeting process at the University of Illinois.[4]

Table 19.1
A Variable Budget

Volume/machine hours[a]	250,000	300,000	350,000
Percentage of plant utilization	50	60	70
Foremen's salaries	$12,000	$12,000	$12,000
Indirect labor	10,000	12,000	14,000
Other expenses	17,500	21,000	24,000
Totals	$39,500	$45,000	$50,000

[a]Assume for simplicity that 1 unit is produced per machine hour.
Source: Adapted and revised from Glen Welsch, *Budgeting: Profit Planning and Control* (Englewood Cliffs, N.J.: Prentice-Hall, 1976), p. 330. Used by permission.

They found that the powerful departments (those with national reputations and major committee appointments) got more than their "fair share" of the budget. These departments had established good peer and superior relations, which gave them considerable influence on the budget.

One of the manager's most important jobs is to make sure the unit gets its fair share of the budget. Since so much rides on the budget, the budgeting process becomes very political. The interpersonal influence and political skills described in Chapters 14 and 15 are very important at budget times. Competition between units (and thus between peers and managers) can be fierce. If the budget process becomes too competitive, however, it is very harmful for the enterprise. Cooperation and coordination may decline to zero.

Henry Tosi has looked into the budgetary process and found that in addition to highly political behavior it can also lead to:[5]

- *Negative reactions toward the budget specialists:* If a unit does not get the budget it wants, its members may treat budget specialists badly.

- *Gamesmanship and overstatement of needs*: A unit may overstate its needs in the expectation that the budget will be cut. The rationale for the overstatement is that it will put the adjusted budget at just the level desired. John F. Hulpke and Donald Watne have demonstrated that this is what school districts do.[6] They also understate their expected revenue—an item Tosi does not discuss—but which is the obvious other side of the coin to overstatement of needs.

- *Covert Information Systems*: If the budgetary process is kept secret, much time is expended by managers to determine how they and their unit did relative to other units. They tend to overestimate the differences in favor of competing departments.

What can managers do to offset these human problems? Solutions offered include more participation, less secrecy, and more trust by all concerned in budgeting. But to suggest such solutions may be naive. If there are not enough resources to go around in some years (not always the case, of course), some departments will lose and some will win. Participation and openness may not be able to eliminate the desire of each unit to come out on top in the budget process—or the sting of losing in the budgetary competition. Control is necessary. Budgets are an essential part of controlling, but some side effects may not always be positive.

Designing and Implementing Controls with Humans in Mind

In chapter 18, I said I would discuss the conditions under which all controls—budgetary and otherwise—would be accepted by employees. Let's do so now. Control may be met by one of three employee responses: positive cooperation, neutral acceptance, or negative resentment and evasion. A manager's job is to design and implement controls with humans in mind so as to make them effective. Let's review the conditions in which controls evoke these different types of responses.

Positive and Neutral Reactions to Budgets

Controls lead to voluntary compliance (neutral) or support (positive) when they exhibit *technical competence* and when they involve *managerial-subordinate participation and communication*. The control process must be competently designed and operated. This means that the following characteristics should be present:

- The information and data used in the control system are accurate and up to date. This gives the system credibility.
- The control system is not overly developed. That is, the number of standards to be met is reasonable and it is clear which are of primary and which of secondary importance.
- The feedback system is accurate and timely so that the manager becomes aware of problems in time to act if necessary.

A number of studies have found that controls meet with acceptance and cooperation if the subordinates participate in the design phase, understand why the standards are needed, believe them to be both fair and attainable, and are included in the communication network. This permits employees to see that the controls give the firm the necessary structure for effectiveness; they recognize this as needed; and they view controls as supporting the vast majority of employees who are doing a good job.

Negative Reactions to Budgets

Poorly designed (technically incompetent) controls or controls that are perceived as arbitrary (imposed from above) can lead to a series of negative results, some of which are enumerated below:

1. *Fudging the records or beating the system* One of the more typical responses to poorly designed or arbitrary controls is to try to beat the system. There have been many studies of this response, but one of the most fascinating is Melville Dalton's *Men Who Manage*.[7] It is full of accounts of the ways managers get around what they perceive to be unfair controls. Here are a couple of examples:

- "The office" pressured quality control to lower its reject rates. The inspectors reported only a fraction of the rejects, secretly sending most of them back to the production department.
- Middle managers and supervisors wanted their offices redecorated. The budget would not allow it. So the maintenance department redecorated the offices and charged the expenses as a maintenance cost. In exchange, the managers did not report maintenance errors and backlogs.

2. *Horse trading* If top management sets unrealistic budgets and control systems, supervisors and middle managers will begin to horse trade. If they have found in the past that their realistic budget requests were cut 20 percent, they will inflate their requests by 20 to 25 percent. When top management realizes what is going on, the budget is cut further, which leads to an escalation of the horse trading. This can be compounded by competition among units, which keep bidding each other up until no one knows the real needs of any unit.

3. *Cost inefficiencies* Often, in order to meet unit budgets on time, excessive overtime is put in, quality controls are lowered, and break-downs result. Soviet managers frequently take this route. If the controls are poorly designed and require only a certain number of units, it is cheaper for the Soviet manager to run too many shoes in size 9A than are needed. This fills the quota; if more 8B's are needed, that is too bad. Other observers of Soviet budgets have noted that quotas are often set in pounds. So the manager of a Soviet nail factory produces mostly bigger, heavier nails. It is easier to meet the quota on time this way than by producing twice the number of smaller nails.

4. *Overemphasis on the short run* Imposed controls can lead to an overemphasis on meeting the immediate budget in spite of what is happening to long-run results. Salespeople often oversell a customer to meet their current budget, knowing that in the long run they will lose business. Some units sell assets in order to make short-run figures look better. Others lay off employees, knowing they will have to rehire and retrain them later. Deferring maintenance costs also makes the books look better, but it costs more when a new machine must be bought.

5. *Reduced coordination* Various studies have shown that very strict controls lead to tunnel vision—an overconcern with meeting standards regardless of the effects on other departments. Coordination suffers under these conditions.

6. *Feelings of tension or pressure* Studies have also indicated that strict controls can lead to the feeling that controls are simply pressure tactics. This often results in tension among lower-level employees, who then react negatively to management.

**Making
Controls Work**

Do these negative results mean that the enterprise should forget about controls? No. Even though some units may fudge their reports, controls still lead to improved performance. For example, in one situation described by Dalton, parts inspectors were used to cut down on theft of parts and excessive parts inventories. Even through the inspectors abetted the thieves by distributing their inspection schedules, the inspections still caused the theft rate as well as the costs of parts inventories to decline. Even bad control systems control.

Simply put, you need controls to police the worst managers and employees, those who are so inefficient or unethical that without controls they would abuse the enterprise and their peers. We may fondly desire to do away with police and armies. But this clearly cannot be done. Until all managers and employees are honest and hardworking the enterprise cannot do without controls.

There are different kinds of controls. Well-designed and carefully operated controls work better than those that are poorly designed and badly run. Controls will work better when employees are made aware of the need for them and allowed to participate in their design.

Summary

This chapter dealt with budgeting, a complex and important aspect of control. A **budget** is a statement of future expenditures and revenues that quantifies management's plans to control the use of financial and other resources. No other nonhuman system of control can be found in more enterprises than budgets.

The budgeting procedure begins with a projection of receipts of the firm for the budget period. Subsidiary budgets are then developed. The summary budget (a profit and loss or income statement) subtracts the totals of the subbudgets from the receipts budget. The remainder is a profit or loss. The budgeting process can be broken down into six basic steps.

In *Step 1* top management initiates the process by communicating the objectives of the firm for the period and sends out the timetable for preparing and reviewing budgets at various levels. In *Step 2* the budget department or administrator communicates information and offers advice and counsel to the units preparing the budgets. Next in *Step 3* each unit prepares a preliminary budget for the next period. In *Step 4* the preliminary budgets are reviewed and approved. Finally in *Step 5* the budget performances of units are evaluated during the year. In the unusual event that the budget turns out to be unreasonable—usually because of unforeseen difficulties—there is a *Step 6*, in which the budget department recommends a revised budget.

The organization is divided into budget units called "responsibility centers." The responsibility center is a unit whose manager is held responsible for achieving budgeted results. The four types of responsibility centers correspond to the four kinds of budgeting objectives. An *investment center* is a budget unit whose criterion of control is return on investment. The budget objective of a *profit center* is profit. A unit whose budget objective is to establish fair and reasonable costs for services is an *expense or cost center*. Typically a *revenue center* is a unit responsible for meeting a sales budget but not too concerned with the costs of manufacturing.

In its most fully developed form, the enterprise develops the following budgets to control all major uses of funds: (1) a sales or receipts budget, (2) an operations or production budget, (3) a cash budget, (4) a capital expenditures budget, and (5) expense budgets. These budgets assume that revenues and costs will not change during the budget period and that they can be accurately predicted. Since this is not always the case, managers and budget specialists often use variable budgets. The approach of variable budgets is similar to that of contingency planning.

To set up a variable budget, costs are divided into three categories: fixed, variable, and semivariable/semifixed. Revenues will vary also. Variable budgets are more expensive to draw up, but they are also more realistic than single assumption budgets.

The question of who gets the most money in the "budget battle" brings the human element into the budgeting process and makes the process very political. Complications such as negative reactions towards budget specialists, gamesmanship and overstatement of needs, and covert information systems often result. To offset these problems, more participation, less secrecy, and more trust among all concerned in budgeting should be encouraged.

The final sections tied the subject matter of Chapter 18 and this chapter together with guidelines for designing and implementing controls with humans in mind. Control can have one of three effects on employees: (1) positive cooperation, (2) neutral acceptance, or (3) negative resentment and evasion. Positive or neutral responses are likely to result when the control process is competently designed and operated. If subordinates participate in the design phase, understand why the standards are needed, believe them to be both fair and attainable, and are included in the communication network, acceptance is also likely.

Negative reactions such as fudging the records or the system, horse trading, cost inefficiencies, overemphasis on the short run, reduced coordination, and feelings of tension or pressure can result when controls are poorly designed (technically incompetent) or perceived as arbitrary (imposed from above).

This chapter completes the section on control. The final section in the text begins with a discussion of human resource management.

Questions

1. What is a budget? How is it both a planning tool and a control device?
2. According to Anthony and Dearden, budgets have certain characteristics. What are these?
3. Review and briefly summarize the steps in the budgeting process.
4. What do you see as the most serious problem involved in the budgeting process?
5. Your new assistant does not understand the purposes of a budget. Explain them to him or her. Use some of Welsch's reasons to show why it is worth the trouble to set up a budget.

6. What are the four kinds of budget responsibility centers? What criterion is each based on?

7. Compare the variable budget to contingency planning. Is this budget approach better than the single assumption approach? Why?

8. How should you as a manager be involved in the budgeting process to see your unit gets the funds it needs?

9. Reactions to your firm's control system have become increasingly negative. What can you do to make responses more positive or neutral?

Notes

[1] Robert Anthony and John Dearden, *Management Control Systems* (Homewood, Ill.: Richard D. Irwin, 1980).

[2] Glen Welsch, *Budgeting: Profit Planning and Control* (Englewood Cliffs, N.J.: Prentice-Hall, 1976).

[3] Ibid., for example.

[4] Jeffrey Pfeffer and Gerald R. Salancik, "Organizational Decision Making and Political Process: The Case of the University Budget," *Administrative Science Quarterly* 19 (June 1974): 135–151.

[5] Henry Tosi, "The Human Effects of Budgeting Systems on Management," *MSU Business Topics* 22 (Autumn 1974): 53–63.

[6] John F. Hulpke and Donald A. Watne, "Budgeting Behavior: If, When, and How Selected School Districts Hide Money," *Public Administration Review* 36 (November–December 1976): 667–674.

[7] Melville Dalton, *Men Who Manage* (New York: Wiley, 1959).

References

Budgets and the Budgeting Process

This chapter derives much of its material from the following sources: Robert Anthony and John Dearden, *Management Control Systems* (Homewood, Ill.: Richard D. Irwin, 1980). Glen Welsch, *Budgeting: Profit Planning and Control* (Englewood Cliffs, N.J.: Prentice-Hall, 1976). J. Fred Weston and Eugene Brigham, *Managerial Finance*, 6th ed. (Hinsdale, Ill.: Dryden Press, 1978).

The Structure of Budgets

Robert Anthony and John Dearden, *Management Control Systems* (Homewood, Ill.: Richard D. Irwin, 1980). Jay Lorsch et al., *Understanding Management* (New York: Harper & Row, 1978), chapter 6.

The Human Influence on Budgets

Frederick S. Hills and Thomas A. Mahoney, "University Budgets and Organizational Decision Making," *Administrative Science Quarterly* 23 (September 1978): 454–465. Geert H. Hofstede, *The Game of Budget Control* (London: Tavistock, 1968). John F. Hulpke and Donald A. Watne, "Budgeting Behavior: If, When, and How Selected School Districts Hide Money," *Public Administration Review* 36 (November–December 1976): 667–674. William H. Mobley and Bruce M. Megline, "A Behavioral Choice Model Analysis of the Budget Allocation Behavior of Academic Deans," *Academy of Management Journal* 20 (December 1977): 564–572. William Newman, *Constructive*

Control (Englewood Cliffs, N.J.: Prentice-Hall, 1975). Jeffrey Pfeffer and Gerald R. Salancik, "Organizational Decision Making and Political Process: The Case of the University Budget," *Administrative Science Quarterly* 19 (June 1974): 135–151. Val Ridgeway, "Dysfunctional Consequences of Performance Measurements," in *Readings in Organizational Theory,* ed. Walter Hill and Douglas Egan (Boston: Allyn & Bacon, 1966). D. Gerald Searfoss and Robert Moncska, "Perceived Participation in the Budget Process and Motivation to Achieve the Budget," *Academy of Management Journal* 16 (December 1973): 541–554. Henry Tosi, "The Human Effects of Budgeting Systems on Management," *MSU Business Topics* 22 (Autumn 1974): 53–63. Aaron Wildavsky, "The Political Economy of Efficiency: Cost-Benefit Analysis, Systems Analysis, and Program Budgeting," *Public Administration Review* 26 (December 1966): 292–310.

Designing and Implementing Controls with Humans in Mind

Chris Argyris, "Human Problems with Budgets," *Harvard Business Review* 31 (January–February 1953): 97–110. Selwyn Becker and David Green, "Budgeting and Employee Behavior," *Journal of Business* 35 (October 1962): 392–403. Joseph Berliner, *Factory and Manager in the U.S.S.R.* (Cambridge, Mass.: Harvard University Press, 1957). Melville Dalton, *Men Who Manage* (New York: Wiley, 1959). Frank Jasinski, "Use and Misuse of Efficiency Controls," *Harvard Business Review* 34 (July–August 1956): 105–112. Raymond Miles and R. C. Vergin, "Behavioral Properties of Variance Controls," *California Management Review* 8 (Spring 1966): 57–65.

Case for Chapter 19

The Man in the Middle

"Sometimes I think my position is quite impossible. There is no way I can reconcile the pressures from corporate headquarters with the reality of the situation in my company." Jack Walker was reflecting on his first three years' experience as general manager of the Small Engineered Products European division of the Blake White Corporation, a large diversified U.S. owned multinational. Jack, an Australian, was located in Germany. Corporate headquarters was in Baltimore, U.S.A. Blake White had five separate divisions, all with European operations, each of which reported directly back to the U.S. office. Forty percent of Blake White's sales and 30 percent of its profits were generated in Europe.

"The trouble really is the budgeting and planning system. The Corporate Planning Department at HQ requires an elaborate five-year plan with detailed projections of sales, P & L statements, cash flows, balance sheets, etc. Frankly I think what they ask for is ridiculous, but all operating units have to provide the data. The planning process takes an immense amount of time and culminates in an annual review with the chief executive officer. This is the only time each year I sit down with him for an extended discussion, so naturally I put a lot of time into preparing for this meeting. Then we have the annual budgets. They are almost a standing joke now in the company. Usually by period 9 we have had at least three revisions from the original, all of which take considerable time. Sometimes I think the most rapidly growing part of my organization is the controller's department. Plenty of increased output there, but it doesn't always help the bottom line. The difficulty with the budget is we do our forecasts in periods 3 and 4 of the previous year, and in present-day circumstances these forecasts are often very inaccurate quite early on in the new budgeting year. The corporation is so big now, though, that it takes at least eight months to compile the following year's budgets and it is very difficult to make substantial changes to the figures once the process is rolling.

"However, these are really small problems compared with the impact of the monthly variance returns on my top management group. Sometimes they don't know whether to laugh or cry. In spite of the budget revisions, the variances are often enormous and for reasons which are quite beyond our control. As general manager, I have to take the role of Corporate HQ and appear to take the figures seriously. But it is a difficult role to take with any conviction, and I am not sure by doing so I am improving my relationship with my senior management group.

"Then there is compensation. We are supposed to have a management bonus scheme based on performance against budget. Even when budgets seemed to have longer lives than they do now there were some well-known cases in the company of people who put everything into a two-year high-return period, got promoted, and left an impossible situation for those who followed. Some of those fast promotion guys are now highly placed in the company. But now the whole idea of a bonus based on performance against budget is ridiculous. We are all working twice as hard to offset rising material and labor costs and falling order books, but there is no way we can beat budgets which are strongly influenced by historical performances when they are set. I know we all agree with them at the outset, but really it is hard to resist when you have pressures from HQ, too little time, and serious operating problems to contend with. You know it really is time you academics came up with a better planning and budgeting system. If something doesn't happen soon at Blake White, there are going to be an awful lot of demotivated managers who will not take the system seriously. Then I fear we may lose some good men. Hey, didn't I read an advertisement for a new Professor of Business Policy at your Management School? Maybe I should apply for that and then I might have time to sort out these problems for the Blake White Corporations of the world."

Source: This case was prepared by C. J. Constable, IMEDE, L'Institut pour l'Etudes Methodes de Direction de l'Entreprise, Lausanne, Switzerland.

Problems

1. What is the problem at Blake White?
2. Is the problem the planning and control system or Jack?
3. If you were Jack's superior, how would you reply to Jack's complaints?
4. What, if anything, would you do about Jack's complaints about planning and control systems? About compensation systems?

Case for Part Six

This case takes place within a College of Business of an eastern United States university which prided itself on its efficiency and effectiveness. In the last few years, it has had budget problems.

As business has become a more popular major, the number of students has increased in the college. But because of financial difficulties within the university the amount of money budgeted for the college did not increase in real dollars, and inflation more than offset the dollar increases.

The college could not hire more faculty, but it did not increase entrance requirements and thus reduce the number of students. Instead, it scheduled the faculty to teach more classes and increased the number of students in each class. As the number of students increased so did the cost of supplies. For example, the amount of copying paper used for tests, course outlines, and similar uses increased more than the budget allowed.

Faculty job satisfaction has been decreasing for at least five years for a number of reasons, four of which are noted here. First, the work load has increased. With increases in the number of students, for some faculty the work load has increased 60 percent over a two year period. Because of budget shortages, the amount of support provided faculty has also decreased during this time. For example, faculty members have received fewer hours of help for grading. The number of research assistants who help the faculty by doing library searches, computer runs, etc. has also decreased substantially.

Second, salaries have decreased in terms of real dollars. Over a five year period, the average faculty member has actually suffered a pay cut. That is, the typical pay "raise" was often *one-half* the inflation rate of the previous year.

Third, faculty raises were granted in three categories: merit (above average), average, none. Each department had to have 25 percent zero raises to generate the money to provide merit raises. Merit raises were paid *not* to those who taught the most or wrote the most articles or did the most research but to the department chairpersons and their friends.

And finally, the dean was selected against the will of the majority of the faculty. Even after her hand-picked department chairpersons went to the president to ask for her removal, the president refused.

Each year faculty morale has declined more. This decline can easily be measured in the increased rate of faculty turnover and absenteeism. Many faculty members have begun coming to the university for classes only. Many have refused to serve on committees. The rest of their time they spend either on personal matters or in increased consulting work with which they supplement their pay.

Exhibit 1
The College of
Business

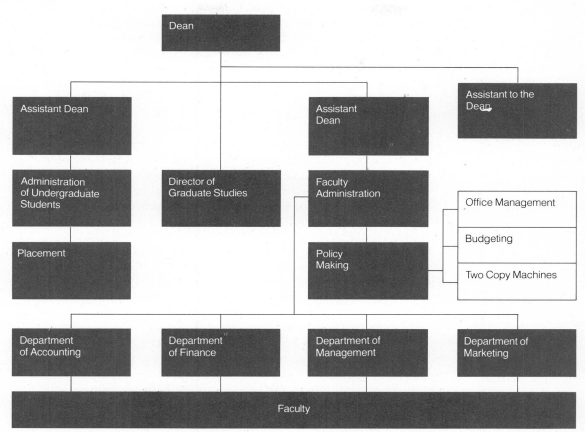

Organization Prior to the Change

Exhibit 1 is an organization chart of the college with a description of the copying system prior to the change. Since the dean had been rejected by the faculty but not the president, the dean had little influence in the college. She took little interest in internal administration. She did, however, have discretionary funds with which to give project money to faculty members who had supported her.

The key actors in this case are the assistant to the dean, the assistant dean, the department heads, and the faculty. In the old system the assistant to the dean, a woman of about forty with ten years of experience, ran the office, handled budgeting, and supervised the copier.

A faculty member could have copying work done in one of two ways: (1) The faculty member gave the work to the departmental secretary or his or her graduate assistant. This person then handed the copier operator a chit (signed by the department head) counting the number of copies and charging the copying to the appropriate department. (2) If the faculty member was in a hurry or the secretary or assistant was ill or busy, the faculty member could supervise the copying. Then the faculty member signed a chit and handed it in. Since there were only about forty faculty members, the copier operators knew them.

Then, the assistant to the dean left the college for a better job. The assistant dean was replaced by an associate professor aged thirty-five. The new assistant to the dean was a man with seven years' experience (elsewhere, not in the college) and about age thirty.

As the faculty had become demoralized, it had become more difficult to be a secretary at the college. Although turnover tended to be high because the primary source of secretarial staff had been student wives, it increased to about 150 percent per year.

Instead of addressing himself to the secretarial turnover and other issues, the new assistant to the dean involved himself in visible projects. He reorganized the dean's bulletin board: new lettering was provided. He cleaned up a storage room. He decided that faculty storage of their publications was inappropriate in this room. So he sent letters to the faculty telling them they had three days to pick up their books and monographs or they would be discarded. When one faculty member pointed out that although his grant had paid for the publication of his book there, he had allowed the college to sell them and keep the $50.00 per month this generated, the assistant to the dean told him verbally that those books could stay.

The assistant dean was busy too. He was concerned that about $75.00 per month was "lost" on the copy machine. It was lost because there were no chits to account for some of the copying and no department could be charged for the cost.

The assistant dean discussed this problem with the company the machines came from and with the dean of the Arts and Sciences College. He did not discuss this with the faculty, the departmental secretaries, or the department heads.

Instead, he and the assistant to the dean issued the memo shown here as Exhibit 2 to department heads, the memo shown here as Exhibit 3 to departmental secretaries, and the memo shown here as Exhibit 4 to faculty. A new control device called the auditron was put on the copying machines after the memos were received. Now the only way a faculty

Exhibit 2
Memo to Departments
and Unit Heads
Regarding Auditron

TO: **Administrative Units: Using IBM Copier II in Room 90**
SUBJECT: Auditron Meter

In order to more efficiently monitor the copies made on the IBM Copier II in Room 90 we have decided to install an Auditron Meter System on April 25.

Departments that wish to use the copy machine will need to purchase an Auditron meter. There is a $25.00 one-time charge for the meters which can be purchased from IBM. IBM representatives indicated that Auditrons will be delivered two weeks after receipt of a purchase order. An Auditron meter for personal copies will be available in the Dean's Office.

The cut-off date for copy billing for this fiscal year will be April 25. From that date on billings will be based on the Auditron meter readings. The $13.00 monthly rental charge for the Auditron meter receptacle will be prorated.

Attached is a list of guidelines for use of the IBM Copier II in Room 90 under the new system. Copy chits will continue to be used for copying on the machine in Room 84.

If you have any questions, please contact me.

Sincerely,

Marc Blackwell
Assistant to the Dean

Exhibit 3
Guidelines for Use of
Copy Machine in
Room 90

1. Each School, Department, or other administrative unit that plans to use the copy machine in Room 90 will need an Auditron meter.
2. In order to make copies, faculty and staff will have to pick up the Auditron meter from their department office. Copies cannot be made without an Auditron.
3. An Auditron meter for personal copies will be available in the Dean's Office.
4. The copies made on each Auditron will be charged to the departmental E&E account.
5. Grant and other special accounts can have a separate Auditron or if departments prefer, they can keep records of copies made on the department Auditron that should be charged to a grant account.
6. Auditrons must be brought to the Dean's Office, Room 90, the first thing the morning of the first of the month so that a meter reading for billing purposes can be taken. No copies should be made on the Auditron before the reading is taken on the first day of the month. The department secretary or assistant should indicate the number of copies metered on their Auditron that should be charged to a grant account.
7. The copy machine in Room 90 can be used for 10 or less copies. The total of number copies in one run cannot exceed *200*.
8. The copy machine in Room 84 can be used for 10 or more copies. Chits will continue to be used for copying on this machine.

Exhibit 4

Use of IBM Copy
Machines

IBM in Room 90—Necessitates Auditron

1. All requests for copy work must be brought to the departmental secretary at least *four* hours in advance of the time needed.
2. The Auditron will be kept under lock in the departmental office when not in use and will be used only by the departmental secretary.
3. The departmental secretary will make copies twice a day at *11:00* and *4:00*.
4. The departmental secretary will maintain a record of all copy work requested and post the exact number of copies to the appropriate account.
5. A maximum number of 10 copies per page is permitted, and the total number of copies in one run cannot exceed 200.
6. The departmental secretary will render an accounting of use of the department's Auditron to the Assistant to the Dean on the first working day of each month.
7. Private use of the IBM in Room 90 may be made with the Auditron kept by the receptionist in Room 90.

IBM in Room 84—Necessitates Chits

1. Faculty members must bring requests for copy work to the departmental secretary.
2. Chits will not be issued to faculty or other staff members.
3. Ordinarily the departmental secretary will take work to Room 84 twice a day at *11:00* and *4:00*.
4. Ordinarily the departmental secretary will pick up work from Room 84 twice a day at *10:00* and *3:00* the following morning.
5. Tests, syllabi, and other work entailing more than 10 copies per page or more than 200 copies in total should be submitted *at least 48 hours in advance*.
6. Private use of the IBM in Room 84 will not be made.

member could get copying done was to have the departmental secretary do it or charge it to his or her personal account.

The secretaries now became part-time copier operators. Copier operators were paid much less than the secretaries. Copy operating jobs were viewed as lower-status jobs by the secretaries. The secretaries spent about three hours per day running the machines, since faculty and graduate students could not do it so easily. They also spent time checking out the auditron accounts to balance them weekly.

This also meant that for three hours per day the secretaries were not in the department offices to answer the phone or talk with the students or faculty. It gave less motivated secretaries a place to be other than at her desk—"I was at the copier." Two of the departmental secretaries quit. They felt they were not using their skills properly.

Departmental secretaries were given assigned times when they were allowed to use the copiers. The faculty was very upset. They could not have class handouts copied quickly if the assigned times for the machines were given to other departments. So they gave fewer handouts—or delayed them. Because secretaries were running copy machines, students could not get advice and outsiders could not reach the departments or find out when faculty would be in. But the new system kept close track of the copier costs.

Problems

1. Do you think the faculty is justified in staying away from the office except at class time?
2. What are some of the major problems the new assistant dean should be handling?
3. Will the new copying system have a significant impact in controlling faculty dissension?
4. What systems of control should be instituted to make faculty/administration relations less caustic?

Part 7 Managing Human Resources

7

The final two chapters in the text focus on staffing and management of human resources and how to build a managerial career. Involved in human resource management are human resource planning, recruitment, selection, orientation, performance appraisal, training and development, compensation, and discipline. The importance of these processes and the manager's role in them are explained in Chapter 20.

These same processes are essential to the development of a management team, the subject of Chapter 21. Suggestions on how to plan your career, land the job of your choice, and start your new job are also included in Chapter 21, along with a look at some of the personal challenges managers commonly face.

Now

The Future

Chapter 20 Staffing and the Management of Human Resources

Introduction

This chapter is concerned with how managers, with the help of personnel, assure that there are people present in the firm to do the jobs needing to be done. An additional subject of the chapter is the manager's responsibility for seeing that employees experience enough satisfaction and development on the job that they will wish to remain and contribute to the firm.

Management of human resources is that function of all enterprises which provides for effective utilization of people to achieve both the objectives of the enterprise and the satisfaction and development of the employees.

Management of human resources includes many activities which will be described in more detail in the chapter. Some of these activities are (1) human resource planning; (2) recruitment, selection and orientation; (3) performance appraisal; (4) training and development; (5) compensation and rewards; and (6) discipline. For most organizations, human resource management is one of the most important, if not the most important, function. After all, in almost every organization the most valuable resource is the human resource.

Effective *management of human resources* or *staffing*—the two terms are synonymous—will lead to a number of desirable consequences. It will, more specifically, do the following for the firm:

- Help achieve the firm's objectives.
- Make efficient use of the work force.
- Provide the firm with well-trained and motivated employees.
- Increase employee job satisfaction and self-actualization to the fullest.
- Develop and maintain a quality of work life which makes employment in the department personally and socially desirable.[1]

Some firms are well-known for emphasizing the management of human resources as a vital management function. These include IBM, Exxon, American Telephone & Telegraph, Lincoln Electric, Hormel, Armco Steel, and General Electric. J.C. Penney is widely recognized for its

James Cash Penney

James Cash Penney's long and illustrious career paralleled the growth of American retailing from the days of the small general dry goods store on "Main Street" to the emergence of the large national department store chain, a transition he played a dominant role in bringing about. The foundation for his business success was deeply rooted in a strict moral and ethical code instilled in him by his Baptist minister father and equally devout mother.

Penney gained his first retail experience in a job procured for him by his father in the J. M. Hale & Bro. Dry Goods Store in their native Hamilton, Missouri. He earned $2.27 a month. After moving to Colorado for health reasons, he went to work in 1898 with Tom Callahan, a well-established merchant who operated a small chain of Golden Rule dry good stores in the Rocky Mountain states, and Guy Johnson, manager of the chain's Evanston, Wyoming, store. In just a few years, Penney became a partner with a one-third interest in the business. The founding of the J. C. Penney Company dates from April 14, 1902, when he became the manager of the chain's new store in Kemmerer, Wyoming.

By 1907 Penney was in business for himself and had dreams of building a chain of stores. By 1911 he had established the first central office for the firm in Salt Lake City. In January 1913 the name Golden Rule was dropped, and the chain was incorporated as the J. C. Penney Company. The following year the base of operation was shifted to New York City.

positive approach to managing human resources, which no doubt results from its founder's attitude toward people.

Human Resource Planning

Human resource planning is the process which helps provide adequate human resources to achieve organizational objectives.

It includes forecasting future needs for employees of various types; comparing these needs with the present work force; and determining the numbers and types of employees to be recruited or phased out of the employment group.

Forecasting human resources demand is a joint activity of the unit manager and the personnel manager. Usually the unit manager begins his or her forecast by preparing a list of jobs by name and number of jobholders for each job. The number and skills of the current personnel are evaluated. Then the effects of expected losses due to retirement, promotion, and other causes are considered. The unit manager must answer two

J. C. Penney has been credited with the introduction of profit sharing in national retailing. His partnership plan enabled each manager who saved enough from the store's earnings to buy a one-third interest in a new store, provided an individual capable of opening and managing the new link in the chain had been trained. Even though the original profit-sharing plan has undergone revision with the rapid expansion of the company, the underlying operating concept has remained intact to this day.

True to the spirit of his partnership concept, Penney turned over the presidency in 1917 to one of his most able associates and relinquished active day-to-day administration of the company. At age forty-one he became the company's first chairman of the board. He remained a member of the board of directors until his death at age ninety-five. During this period, Penney embarked upon several major philanthropic endeavors, principally the Penney Retirement Community in Florida, the Christian Herald Association, and several public-spirited agricultural and livestock breeding pursuits. He also provided scholarships to deserving and needy college students, among other charitable endeavors.

In answer to countless young people who sought his advice on their career goals, Penney said, "Any young person of ordinary intelligence who is not afraid to work, plays the game fairly, is willing to make all necessary sacrifices to achieve his goal, and keeps everlastingly at it should succeed in spite of obstacles and handicaps. Success has no secrets."

Source: Information courtesy of J.C. Penney Co.

questions: whether those losses will require replacement and what the unit's projected growth needs in personnel will be. To project personnel needs, the unit manager analyzes the unit's product or service demand by projecting current trends. The total organization's personnel manager adds these up to prepare a statement of the total organization's human resource needs.

After determining the employment needs of the enterprise, the personnel manager must then assess the present supply of employees in the organization. This is done by means of a skills inventory.

A skills inventory in its simplest form is a list of names, certain characteristics, and skills of the people working for the organization. It provides a way to acquire these data and makes them available where needed.

Skills inventories range from being simple pieces of paper, forms, and 3″ × 5″ cards to being sophisticated computer information systems. Their degree of sophistication is related to the size, complexity, and volatility of the organization. In smaller, manually compiled and used skills inventories, the data are entered on cards. In more advanced systems of this kind the cards have notches or loops which can be "pulled" by the use of long metal bars. Enterprises such as IBM, RCA, and the U.S. Civil Service Commission use computerized inventories that have a wide variety of applications. With these systems managers can even plan employees' careers, not to mention define the business.

.ion cisions in ıman esource ʹlanning

Once the demand for people has been forecast and compared to supply, there are several managerial decisions to be made. Figure 20.1 provides a picture of what these action decisions are and how they come about. As indicated in the figure, in conditions with no variances—when the existing employment supply meets the employment demand—managers have few decisions to make. Such an exact match is rare. When there is a surplus of employees, the work force is first reduced by attrition; as people retire or leave, they are not replaced. Then work sharing may be initiated. In this approach, all employees work fewer hours. Finally, layoffs and terminations are used. These are very difficult decisions.

Figure 20.1
Employment Planning
Action Decisions

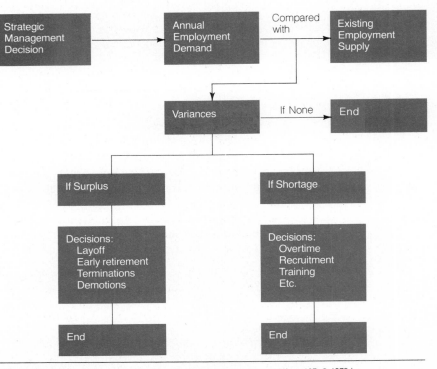

Source: William F. Glueck, *Foundations of Personnel* (Dallas: Business Publications, 1979), p. 107. © 1979 by Business Publications, Inc. Reprinted by permission.

How does a manager decide whom to lay off or terminate? Two criteria have been used: merit and seniority. The most common practice has been to lay off or terminate last the employees with the longest record of continuous employment (the greatest seniority) in the firm. A new approach is to lay off or terminate those with lower merit ratings. Thus employees who do the job best are kept; those who perform poorly are not.

Recruiting Employees

If human resource planning action decisions indicate a shortage of employees, the firm engages in recruiting.

Recruiting is that set of activities an enterprise uses to attract job candidates who have the abilities and attitudes needed to help the enterprise achieve its objectives.

How much effort a firm must put into recruiting is influenced by the labor market at the time. If there is a surplus of labor, even informal recruiting efforts will attract more than enough applicants. When full employment is present in an area, skillful recruiting may be necessary to attract good applicants.

Where does a firm get its recruits? Table 20.1 shows that this varies according to the kinds of employees desired. As the table indicates, firms

Table 20.1
Recruitment Sources by Type of Employee

Sources	Blue Collar	White Collar	Managerial, Technical, Professional
Internal			
Job posting and bidding	●	●	
Friends of present employees	●	●	
Skills inventories	●	●	●
External			
Walk-ins, including previous employees	●	●	
Agenices			
Temporary help		●	
Private employment agencies		●	
Public employment agencies[a]	●	●	
Executive search firms			●
Educational institutions			
High school	●	●	
Vocational/technical	●	●	●
College and universities			●
Other			
Unions	●		
Professional associations			●
Military services	●		●
Former employees	●	●	●

[a]Normally called U.S. Employment Service.
Source: William F. Glueck, *Foundations of Personnel* (Dallas: Business Publications, 1979), p. 130. © 1979 by Business Publications, Inc. Reprinted by permission.

use skills inventories and seek recruits by asking present employees to help recruit their friends and relatives. They may also use job posting and bidding. In this underutilized approach, the firm puts a list of the job openings on bulletin boards and in the company newspaper. Those interested apply or "bid" for the job.

External sources for recruiting include employment agencies, schools and associations, and former employees. People who walk in and fill out applications for jobs on their own or in response to want ads are a major source of entry-level employees. As Table 20.2 shows, the want ad—whether it appears in newspapers, professional journals and media, or both—is the most frequently used method of external recruiting. For positions that are difficult to fill, managers or personnel specialists ("Recruiters" in Table 20.2) recruit at schools and conventions. Once recruitment is completed, it is time to select and hire from among the applicants.

Selection of Employees

When there are more than enough applicants for a position, the manager is faced with deciding which is the best one. In the past, the manager made this decision without concern for government requirements. But in recent years, the governments of various states have passed laws and regulations to guarantee equal employment opportunity to certain groups. The federal government also regulates selection practices.

Generally, the government determines whether a selection practice has an adverse impact on hiring and discriminates on the basis of age, race, sex, religion, or national origin. If selection procedures have *unequal impact* on prospective employees, they must conform to U.S. regulations such as the *Guidelines for Employee Selection Procedures* issued by the

Table 20.2
Methods of Recruiting for Various Types of Employees

Method	Blue Collar	Gray Collar	White Collar	Managerial, Professional, Technical
Media advertisements				
Newspaper want ads	●	●	●	●
Professional journals and other media	●	●	●	●
Recruiters				●
Computer matching services				●
Special-event recruiting				●
Summer internships				●
Coop programs	Select Highly Skilled	Select Highly Skilled	Select Highly Skilled	●

Source: William F. Glueck, *Foundations of Personnel* (Dallas: Business Publications, 1979), p. 133. © 1979 by Business Publications, Inc. Reprinted by permission.

U.S. Equal Employment Opportunity Commission (EEOC) and the *Federal Executive Agency Guidelines* for firms with federal contracts and funds. These guidelines apply to almost all employers with fifteen or more employees.

Much has been said about how tough, complex, and unreasonable the federal selection guidelines are. There is some truth in these complaints. Nonetheless, the selection guidelines require adequate development and validation of selection procedures, an activity industrial psychologists have recognized and called for as essential to good placement practices for decades.

The selection decision is usually made by the unit manager. Some selection decisions may be delegated to personnel managers, however.

Selection Criteria

To make an effective selection decision, a manager must establish what criteria to use. Specifically, the manager must determine what characteristics and skills a person must have to meet the firm's needs. Effective selection criteria are based *not* on what the manager would *like* to have but rather on what, in the firm's experience, the characteristics of successful employees have been.

- Educational level and achievement (for example, college graduate in upper half of his or her graduating class).

"What we're really looking for is a not-too-bright young man with no ambition and who is content to stay on the bottom and not louse things up."

Source: The Wall Street Journal.

- Experience (five years of selling experience, for example).
- Physical characteristics (for instance, ability to lift thirty pounds without strain).
- Skills: *Interpersonal skills* (a salesperson, for example, must be able to interact easily with people and communicate well). *Mechanical skills* (for example, the person must be able to cut metal to within a 1/4″ tolerance).

The Selection Process

A firm will use a variety of steps in the selection process. Figure 20.2 models the *complete* process. Few employers use all six steps in hiring all employees. Because of space limitations, not all of the steps can be discussed in detail here.

Step 1: Preliminary Interview

Different firms handle Step 1 in various ways. For entry-level jobs, applicants often just walk into the employment office. A personnel specialist or operating manager will spend a few moments with applicants in order to do a preliminary screening. The firm has developed rough

Figure 20.2
Process Model for a Typical Selection
Decision When All Possible Steps Are Used
(Private and Third Sector[a])

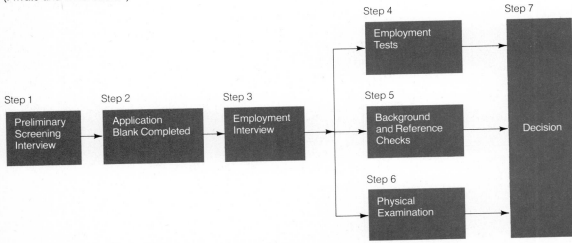

[a]Other institutions in society that are neither government nor profit oriented, i.e., museums, colleges, etc.
Source: William F. Glueck, *Foundations of Personnel* (Dallas: Business Publications, 1979), p. 155. © 1979 by
Business Publications, Inc. Reprinted by permission.

guidelines to be applied in order to reduce the time and expense of actual selection. These guidelines might, for example, specify minimum education. Only those who meet the criteria established in these guidelines are interviewed. In smaller organizations, if the applicant appears to be a likely candidate for the position the preliminary screening can proceed as an employment interview (Step 3).

Step 2: Application Blank

Applicants who come to an employment office are asked to complete an application blank after a screening interview. Recruiters at conventions, schools, colleges, and universities often have interested persons fill out application blanks also. Proper use of application blanks can be effective in selection. If an employee looks satisfactory during the preliminary interview and his or her application blank indicates that selection criteria are met, then the manager interviews the applicant.

Step 3: Employment Interview

Employment interviews are part of almost all selection procedures. Most studies indicate that the interview is the *most important aspect* of the selection decision. There are three general types of employment interviews: structured, semistructured, and unstructured. The main difference between these types of interviews is in the interviewer's approach. The type of interview used depends both on the kind of information desired and the purposes to be served.

In the *structured interview,* the interviewer prepares a list of questions in advance and does not deviate from it. In many firms a standard interview form is used. The interviewer notes the applicant's responses to the predetermined questions on this form. Many of the questions asked in a structured interview are "forced choice" in nature. In forced choice, the evaluator must choose from a set of descriptive statements about the employee. The interviewer indicates the applicant's response with a check mark on the form.

In the *semistructured interview,* the major questions are prepared in advance. The interviewer may also prepare some probing questions in certain areas. This approach allows for more flexibility than the structured approach. The interviewer is free to probe into those areas that seem to merit further investigation. With less structure, however, reliability of results can become a problem. Still, the semistructured interview combines enough structure to facilitate the exchange of factual information with adequate freedom to develop insights.

The *unstructured interview* involves little preparation. The interviewer may or may not make a list of possible topics to be covered. The advantage here is the freedom it allows the interviewer to adapt to the situation and to the changing stream of applicants. Yet while spontaneity is an advantage of this approach, under the control of an untrained interviewer, digressions, discontinuity, and eventual frustration for both parties may result.

Generally speaking, structured or semistructured interviews provide the most reliable and useful data. Managers who are involved in employment interviews for their departments usually take one of these two approaches.

Step 4: Employment Tests

Some firms use tests to provide some of the data on which the decision makers base selection of applicants. Personnel specialists do the testing and then provide the appropriate manager with the test scores and keys. Tests vary from paper and pencil tests to job simulations or job samples.

Step 5: Reference Checks and Recommendations

Often applicants are required to submit references—names of people for whom the applicant has worked—or letters of recommendation. These indicate how well the applicant did at her or his last or previous job. Studies show that this has been a common practice for white-collar jobs.

For a letter of recommendation to be useful, it must meet certain conditions:

- The person who writes it must know the applicant's performance level and be competent to assess it.
- The person who writes it must communicate the evaluation effectively to the potential employer.
- It must be truthful.

If the applicant chooses the references, the first two conditions may not be met. With regard to the third condition, many people are reluctant to write what they really think of the applicant, for he or she may see it. Thus often a letter of recommendation either glosses over the applicant's shortcomings or overemphasizes his or her good points. For these reasons, written references have not been found to be too reliable a selection tool.

When there is need to verify information obtained from an applicant, a phone call to the applicant's previous supervisors can be valuable. The firm may want to contact a number of persons in order to cross-check opinions or to probe further on doubtful points. Most firms combine telephone checks, written letters of recommendation, and data obtained from the employment interview in making selections.

Step 6: Physical Examination

Some firms require a physical exam or medical questionnaire as a means of assuring that healthy people are hired and providing baseline data for worker's compensation claims. This aspect of the selection process is handled by the personnel department, which reports its findings to the manager doing the hiring.

Table 20.3 gives some indication of how frequently each of the above steps is part of the selection process. It presents the proportion of different types of employees that become involved in each of the steps in applying for a job.

How Do Managers Make Selection Decisions?

There are three types of approaches managers can take to selection decisions. In the *random choice or chance approach,* the selection decision is based not on any reasoned evaluation of applicants but rather on some purely mechanical and arbitrary device. For example, a decision might be made prior to conducting interviews to choose the third applicant interviewed. Or the manager might put the names of all the applicants in a hat and draw one out. In the *emotional-clinical approach,* the manager unconsciously picks the applicant who was most likable in the interviews. The six-step process just described, the *systematic-quasirational approach,* is the most systematic approach based on rational selection techniques. It is called quasirational in recognition of the fact that unconscious emotional choices are likely to enter into the selection decision.

Of course the different steps in the selection process may produce conflicting results. One approach to reconciling contradictory results is that of Lawrence Jauch, who recommends preparing a matrix of the results (as

Table 20.3
Frequency of Use of Various Methods of Selection

	Proportion of Employees on Whom Method of Selection Is Used			
Method	**Blue Collar**	**Gray Collar**	**White Collar**	**Managerial**
Preliminary screening interview	Over 90%	Over 90%	Over 90%	50%
Application blank	Over 90%	Over 90%	Over 90%	a
Employment interview	Over 90%	Over 90%	Over 90%	Over 90%
Employment tests	Very few	Very few	Most	Very few
Background/ reference checks	Very few	Very few	Over 90%	Over 90%
Physical examination	Most who will do heavy or dangerous work	Very few	Very few	Very few

aSubmit resumes which serve the same purpose.

illustrated in Table 20.4), comparing them systematically, and selecting the best person accordingly.[2]

Persons who are hired must be introduced to the job in a way which is useful to them and to the firm. This process of introduction, known as orientation, is discussed next.

Orienting New Employees

Orientation is the set of actions which introduces new employees to the firm, the job, superiors, and work groups.

Effective orientation reduces the startup costs that invariably occur when an employee is new and saves supervisory and coworker time in the startup as well. It brings the employee's production level closer to standard sooner than would otherwise be the case. A good orientation program also reduces the amount of anxiety and hazing a new employee experiences and helps the employee develop realistic job expectations, positive attitudes toward the employer, and job satisfaction. As a result of all these benefits, employee turnover is reduced.

Although the personnel department does part of orientation, the most crucial aspect of the program is how the manager and the work group handle it. Orientation programs vary from quite informal, primarily verbal efforts to formal schedules which supplement verbal presentations with written handouts. Formal orientation programs, which are usually developed when a large number of employees must be oriented, often include a tour of the facilities or slides, charts, and pictures of them. Generally, formal programs cover the items listed below:

Table 20.4
Selection Decision Matrix for Paired-Comparison Technique[a]

Criteria	A–Mr. Black	B–Mr. White	C–Ms. Neutral	D–Ms. Other
		Candidates		
Education	College grad	High school grad	High school grad	2 years college
Test scores	130	110	115	120
Experience	None	5 years	8 years	2 years
Job knowledge	Above average	Excellent	Excellent	Average
Past performance	Excellent	Average	Above average	Above average
Desire	Above average	Average	High	Above average
Stability	Low	Average	High	Below average
Interviewer 1	1	3.5	2	3.5
Interviewer 2	2	3	1	4
Interviewer 3	2	4	3	1

[a]In this technique the names of the persons to be selected are placed on separate sheets in a predetermined order so that each person is compared to all others on all criteria.
Source: "Systemizing the Selection Decision," by Lawrence Jauch. Reprinted with permission *Personnel Journal*, copyright © November 1976.

- History and general policies of the enterprise.
- Descriptions of the enterprise's services or products.
- Organization of the enterprise.
- Safety measures and regulations.
- Personnel policies and practices.
- Compensation, benefits, and employee services.
- Daily routine and regulations.

The following are some guidelines for conducting an effective employee orientation:

1. Orientation should begin with the most relevant and immediate kinds of information and then proceed to more general policies of the enterprise.
2. The most significant part of orientation is the human side, giving new employees knowledge of what supervisors and coworkers are like, telling them how long it should take for them to reach standards of effective work, and encouraging them to seek help and advice when needed.
3. New employees should be "sponsored" or directed by an experienced worker or supervisor in the immediate environment who can respond to questions and keep in close touch during the early induction period.
4. New employees should be gradually introduced to people with whom they will work rather than given a superficial introduction to all of them on the first day. The object should be to help them get to *know* their coworkers and supervisors—not just to give coworkers' and supervisors' names.
5. New employees should be allowed sufficient time to adapt to the work situation before demands on them are increased.

Many efficient firms create feedback mechanisms to determine to what extent an orientation program is carried out for new employees. This is often done by asking the newly hired employees and their superiors to complete forms containing questions about the orientation process.

Performance Appraisal

After a new employee is on the job for a while, it is necessary to determine how well she or he is doing. This is called performance appraisal.

Performance appraisal is the system used by firms to regularly and systematically evaluate the employee's performance to determine how well he or she is meeting minimum standards or objectives.

A good performance appraisal serves a number of purposes. First, it encourages *employee development*. Performance appraisal also serves to determine which employees need more training and to evaluate the results of training programs. In addition, it enhances the employee-supervisor counseling relationship and encourages supervisors to observe employee behavior in order to be better able to help employees.

Performance appraisal is also important in the distribution of *employee rewards*. It helps the enterprise decide who will receive pay raises and promotions and who will be laid off. Thus it reinforces employees' motivation to perform and so improves the enterprise's performance. Finally, performance appraisal is vital to *human resource planning*. It serves as a significant input to skills inventories and personnel planning.

Performance appraisal is usually completed by a superior for each employee. Less frequently a committee of supervisors does the appraisal, and a peer evaluation supplements it. Occasionally an employee's subordinates are asked to appraise her or him. This type of appraisal also supplements that of the employee's superiors.

In most firms employees are appraised yearly, either on the anniversary of their hiring date or on a day set according to an appraisal schedule set up on the basis of job type. Often new employees—considered on probation—receive more frequent appraisals. Appraisals are probably most effective when performed more than once a year—semiannually or quarterly. Only about 10 percent of employees, however, are appraised more often than twice a year.

One of the most crucial aspects of performance appraisal is the criteria managers use to appraise employees. It is vital that these criteria be:

- *Relevant*—reliable and valid measures of the characteristics being evaluated and as closely related to job output as possible.
- *Unbiased*—based on characteristics, not the person.
- *Significant*—directly related to enterprise goals.
- *Practical*—measurable and efficient for the enterprise in question.

The criteria used by managers depend on the nature of the job and the purpose of the performance appraisal. Whether the appraisal should consider actual or potential performance also affects the criteria used and depends on the primary purpose of the evaluation. There are three principal purposes of performance evaluation: (1) improvement of performance, (2) promotion considerations, and (3) pay adjustments. If the manager's main purposes are improved performance or pay adjustments, the emphasis should be on *actual* performance. If the main purpose is possible promotion, the emphasis must be different—more like that of the selection decision for the position into which the employee may be promoted. Then past performance on one job must be projected to possible performance on a different one. This type of evaluation is made easier if the employee has had experience that is relevant to the new job. But again, its emphasis is different from that of an evaluation of actual performance, and it is much more difficult.

There are many different performance appraisal systems that can be used. Most firms require the manager to appraise employees, record the appraisal on a form, and have a discussion interview with each employee. An example of the most typical form, the graphic rating scale, is given in Table 20.5. Using a graphic rating scale, the manager rates an employee by checking a series of boxes. Typically, these ratings are then assigned points. For example, in Table 20.5, *outstanding* may be assigned a score of

Table 20.5
Typical Graphic Rating Scale for Performance Appraisal

	Out-standing	Good	Satis-factory	Fair	Unsatis-factory
Quantity of work Volume of acceptable work under normal conditions Comments:	☐	☐	☐	☐	☐
Quality of work Thoroughness, neat-ness, and accuracy of work Comments:	☐	☐	☐	☐	☐
Knowledge of job Clear understanding of the facts or factors pertinent to the job Comments:	☐	☐	☐	☐	☐
Personal qualities Personality, appear-ance, sociability, leadership, integrity Comments:	☐	☐	☐	☐	☐
Cooperation Ability and willing-ness to work with associates, super-visors, and sub-ordinates toward common goals Comments:	☐	☐	☐	☐	☐
Dependability Conscientious, thorough, accurate, reliable with respect to attendance, lunch periods, reliefs, etc. Comments:	☐	☐	☐	☐	☐
Initiative Earnestness in seeking increased responsibilities. Self-starting, unafraid to proceed alone? Comments:	☐	☐	☐	☐	☐

Source: William F. Glueck, *Foundations of Personnel* (Dallas: Business Publications, 1979), p. 214. © 1979 by Business Publications, Inc. Reprinted by permission.

4 and *unsatisfactory* a score of 0. (In some plans, the scores for more important traits may be weighted.) Total scores are then computed. Managers are often asked to explain each rating with a sentence or two.

After the manager has completed the appraisal, it should be discussed with the employee in a performance appraisal interview. Some enterprises use split evaluations to accomplish the different purposes of the appraisal process. Thus in evaluation for developmental purposes, the ratings are communicated to the employee and appropriate counseling takes place, while the ratings of the evaluation to determine pay, promotion, and other rewards are not given to the employee. In any case, employees are generally asked to acknowledge whatever aspects of the evaluation are communicated to them, usually by signing a receipt form.

The following are some suggestions for conducting an effective appraisal interview:

1. Superiors and subordinates should prepare for the meeting and be ready to discuss the employee's past performance against the objectives for the period.
2. The manager should put the employee at ease and stress that the interview is not a disciplinary session but a time to review past work in order to improve the employee's future performance, satisfaction, and personal development.
3. The manager should budget the time so that the employee has approximately half the time to discuss the evaluation and his or her future behavior.
4. The manager should structure the interview to combine positive comments (reinforcements) with constructive criticism. Some techniques for doing this are described in Table 20.6.
5. The superior should budget the time for the interview using the employee's rating as a basis. For example, if the employee is an 85 on a scale of 100, 85 percent of the time should be spent on positive comments to *reinforce* the employee's good performance.
6. The final aspect of the interview should focus on *future* objectives and

Table 20.6
Suggestions for Structuring an Effective Performance Appraisal Interview

The interview should be private, between the employee and the evaluator.

Open with *specific positive remarks*. For example, if the employee's quantity of work is good, the superior might say: "John, your work output is excellent. You processed 10 percent more claims than were budgeted."

Sandwich performance shortcomings between two positive result discussions. Be specific, and orient the discussion to *performance* comments, *not personal* criticisms. Stress that the purpose of bringing the specific issues up is to alleviate the problems in the *future,* not to criticize the past.

Probably no more than one or two important negative points should be brought up at one evaluation. It is difficult for many people to work toward improving more than two points.

Conclude with *positive* comments and overall evaluation results.

how the superior can help the employee achieve enterprise and personal goals.

Properly done, the interview contributes importantly to the purposes of performance evaluation.

Through the performance appraisal process, it may become clear that the employee could improve performance or satisfaction by receiving additional training. Most firms do provide training for their employees.

Training and Development

The environment changes, and employees frequently must learn new skills. When new production or service techniques arise, training can often improve employee performance.

Training is the systematic process of altering the behavior of employees to increase organizational goals.

The formal purposes of training are:

- To improve the quantity of output.
- To improve the quality of output.
- To lower the costs of waste and equipment maintenance.
- To lower the number and costs of accidents.
- To lower turnover and absenteeism and increase employees' job satisfaction (since training can improve the employees' self-esteem.)
- To prevent employee obsolescence.

Managers are involved with training in a number of ways. As managers note shortcomings in performance, they prepare a list of training needs. As they read and talk to others, they learn about new techniques that may improve production or service. They then communicate the needs they see for training programs to the department responsible for developing such programs.

As training programs are developed, the managers identify the employees who can benefit most from these specific training experiences. Thus managers have a crucial role in trainee selection.

Managers also have some impact on the content of training programs. In discussing the training needs and potential programs with trainees, managers can gain valuable insights into employee preferences on length of program, training content, and training methods. Then they can feed this information back to the training program developers. In addition, managers who have expertise in the subject area of a proposed training program may be asked to serve as trainers for employees throughout the enterprise.

Probably the most widely used method of training (formal and informal) is on-the-job training. The employee is placed in the real work situation and taught how to function properly by an experienced employee or the supervisor. Although on-the-job training is apparently simple and relatively inexpensive, if it is not handled properly costs in damaged machinery, unsatisfied customers, misfiled forms, and poorly taught workers can be high. To prevent such problems, managers who train must be carefully selected on the basis of their motivation and rewarded for doing a good job.

One approach to systematic on-the-job training is the *job instruction training (JIT)* system developed during World War II. In this system, the trainers first train the supervisors, who in turn train the employees. Table 20.7 presents the JIT instructions given to supervisors on how to train new or present employees in the War Manpower Commission's bulletin, "Training within Industry Series in 1945."

Another frequently used on-the-job training technique is *job rotation*. In this approach, the trainee is taught the skills necessary for several jobs in succession over a period of time. Thus when the training program is complete, the trainee can be used in several positions.

Training that does not take place on the job—whether it is done in organization classrooms, vocational schools, or elsewhere—is off-the-job

---

Table 20.7
Job Instruction
Training (JIT) Methods

First, here's what you *must do* to *get ready* to teach a job:
1. Decide what the learner must be taught in order to do the job efficiently, safely, economically, and intelligently.
2. Have the right tools, equipment, supplies, and material ready.
3. Have the workplace properly arranged, just as the worker will be expected to keep it.

Then, you should *instruct* the learner by the following *four basic steps:*

Step I—*Preparation* (of the learner)
1. Put the learner at *ease.*
2. Find out what he already knows about the job.
3. Get him interested and desirous of learning the job.

Step II—*Presentation* (of the operations and knowledge)
1. *Tell, show, illustrate* and *question* in order to put over the new knowledge and operations.
2. Instruct slowly, clearly, completely, and patiently, one point at a time.
3. Check, question and repeat.
4. Make sure the learner really knows.

Step III—*Performance try-out*
1. Test learner by having him perform the job.
2. Ask questions beginning with *why, how, when,* or *where.*
3. Observe performance, correct errors, and repeat instructions if necessary.
4. Continue until you *know he knows.*

Step IV—*Follow-up*
1. Put him "on his own."
2. Check frequently to be sure he follows instructions.
3. Taper off extra supervision and close follow-up until he is qualified to work with normal supervision.

Remember—If the learner hasn't learned, the teacher hasn't taught.

Source: William F. Glueck, *Foundations of Personnel* (Dallas: Business Publications, 1979), p. 246. © 1979 by Business Publications, Inc. Reprinted by permission.

training. Off-the-job training is used when the manager feels that she or he is less skilled than people outside the work unit at imparting training necessary to improve performance or employee satisfaction. Organizations with the biggest training programs often use off-the-job training. Indeed, most of the 50,00 trainers and the $100 billion spent on training in the U.S. are in off-the-job training. The most frequently used methods for off-the-job training are the conference/discussion, programmed instruction, computer-assisted, and simulation approaches.

Compensation

To retain well-trained and well-motivated employees, managers must not only reward them with praise, but also see to it that they receive the best pay and benefits the firm can afford. Managers have an important role in influencing four aspects of the compensation process: (1) the pay level decision, (2) the pay structure decision, (3) incentive compensation programs, and (4) benefits and services decisions.

Pay Level Decisions

Managers differ as much as employees do. One major difference among managers manifests itself in the pay level strategies they adopt. The choice of a pay level strategy is a significant strategic decision. There are three basic pay level strategies managers can choose from: high, low, or comparable.

The High Pay Level Strategy The managers who choose this strategy pay employees better than average wages and salaries. The assumption behind this strategy is that "you get what you pay for." These managers believe that paying higher wages and salaries will enable them to attract and hold the best employees. Thus in their opinion this is the most effective long-range policy.

An example of a company with a high pay level strategy is Procter & Gamble. One of the firm's family executives, William Cooper Procter, was responsible for introducing what was at the time a highly innovative approach to employee compensation.

The Low Pay Level Strategy At the opposite extreme is the low pay level strategy. In this case, the managers may choose to pay at the minimum level needed to hire enough employees. This strategy may be used because this is all the enterprise can pay—the ability to pay is restricted by other internal or external factors. Or the managers may be trying to maximize short-run profits or to live within a tight budget.

The Comparable Pay Level Strategy The most frequently used strategy is to set the pay level at the going wage level. The wage criteria are

William Cooper Procter

The essence of business is how people relate to people: producers to consumers, management to labor. Whoever improves these relations exercises business leadership. In 1883 when Cooper Procter, fresh out of Princeton, went to work for Procter & Gamble, the firm was already forty-six years old and had been so successful under the direction of his grandfather and father that no obvious challenge faced the scion. Cooper Procter, however, transmuted his silver spoon into a golden reputation as a pioneer in more equitable treatment of the work force.

With Procters running the office and Gambles in charge of production, the firm had taken an early lead over numerous other Cincinnati soapmakers partly because of a strict policy of giving honest weight and consistent quality to customers. Cooper Procter soon found a new dimension in which to deploy this ethical tradition. Starting at the bottom, he picked up a keen sympathy with the workers' sense of economic insecurity and with feelings that today would be called "alienation." He was a junior executive when he persuaded his elders in 1885 to shorten the workweek to five and a half days and in 1887 to establish what seems to have been the first profit-sharing plan in a sizable U.S. company.

Profit sharing, Cooper argued, made sense on business as well as on humanitarian grounds. P.&G. then had a 50 percent labor turnover and had been plagued by small but costly strikes. "The root of existing trouble," said young Procter, "lies in the fact that the employee takes no interest in his work and has no consideration for his employer's property or welfare." Profit sharing didn't change that attitude overnight, but strikes and turnover diminished. In 1894, P.&G. had only six severances from a staff of more than 600. Later, when profit sharing had been tied to a stock-ownership plan, the company could point to small fortunes amassed by longtime employees.

In 1923, Procter put through his boldest stroke of labor relations: the company guaranteed most employees forty-eight weeks of work in every year. To do that Procter had to restructure its merchandising by selling directly to retailers. Sales increased as, once again, concern for the workers turned out to be also good for profits. When in 1930 Procter stepped down after twenty-three years as head of the company, sales had risen from the 1907 level of about $20 million to over $200 million.

Source: *Fortune,* January 1976, p. 20. Reprinted by permission.

comparable wages, perhaps modified by cost of living or purchasing power adjustments. Thus the policy of a manager of this type is to pay the current market rate in the community or industry, ±5 percent or so.

These three strategies are usually set for the firm as a whole, although the strategy might have to be modified for a few hard-to-fill jobs from time to time. Managers who wish to reward their employees will try to increase the pay level to high pay strategy. Or more likely they will try to influence the pay structure decision or individual pay decisions.

Pay Structure and Individual Pay Decisions

So far I have discussed only overall pay levels. Within a firm, there are structures of pay ranging from entry-level wages to the president's salary. Personnel managers use a tool called job evaluation to establish the pay differences between jobs.

Job evaluation is the formal process by which the relative worth of various jobs in the organization is determined for pay purposes.

Essentially, it attempts to relate the amount of the employee's pay to the extent that her or his job contributes to organizational effectiveness. What often happens is that job evaluation downgrades or does not elevate the pay grade of employees in a manager's section. A manager then attempts to get personnel to consider the manager's input and interpretation of the job.

Job evaluation simply establishes pay for a job. The final step is to determine the individual pay for each person within a pay grade. This comparison leads to setting the pay of each individual, within the pay ranges that have been established. This is called *individual pay determination.* It is done first when the employee is hired. It then takes place each year (or in some cases more frequently) when the employee's pay is reconsidered, often tied to performance appraisal. Essentially, the issue is: Given that a job can pay varying amounts within a range, which pay rate should this individual receive? A *crucial* aspect of setting pay is individual pay determination. The manager is the key decision maker here. Usually, the manager examines the performance appraisal score and seniority and decides the pay of each employee. This pay is a crucial determinant of the employee's job satisfaction, and it often affects the employee's performance.

Most employees receive pay on the basis of the hours worked. Some firms also pay incentive amounts based either on the amount of output or on making a quota. Perhaps the oldest form of compensation is the *individual incentive plan.* In this plan the employee is paid for units produced. One example is *straight piecework.* In this form an employee is guaranteed an hourly rate (probably the minimum wage) for performing an expected minimum output (the standard). For production over the standard, the employer pays so much per item produced. The standard is set through work measurement studies, as modified by collective bargaining. The base rate and piece rates may develop from pay surveys. There are variations on the standard piecework system.

Commissions are paid to sales employees. Straight commission is the equivalent of straight piecework and is typically a percentage of the price of the item. A variation of this incentive plan is to pay the salesperson a small salary and a commission or bonus when he or she exceeds standard (the budgeted sales goal).

Are individual incentives effective? Research results are mixed. Most studies indicate that incentives increase output. But although production increases, other things can decline. For example, in sales a straight commission can lead to poorer servicing of accounts, and individual differences affect this.

Incentive systems may be designed to affect results besides performance. For example, employers may use them to try to lower absenteeism and turnover. At least for some employees, incentive pay may lower satisfaction, however. Employees may be dissatisfied if they have to work harder or if they feel manipulated by the system.

Benefits and Services

Benefits and services are also part of the compensation decision. For most firms, compensation is divided in such a way that the employee receives two-thirds of it in the form of pay and one-third in benefits and services. Typical benefits include vacations, holidays, health and life insurance, and counseling. These kinds of tax-free rewards can be important to employees, but it is essential that managers determine whether employees prefer more benefits or more pay before deciding what benefits and services to provide.

Of course sometimes discipline, rather than rewards, is in order. When employees are not rated well on performance appraisal forms or get into trouble, managers must take disciplinary action.

Discipline of Employees

The final aspect of human resource management to be discussed is discipline. Most managers dislike having to use discipline, even though they are aware it is necessary for maintaining effectiveness. Discipline styles are related to the leadership styles discussed in Chapter 14. Managers bring these styles to bear as they deal with disciplinary problems.

The Disciplinary Process

In order to provide for effective discipline, a firm must establish a disciplinary process. Figure 20.3 is a model of this process. As you will note, the first activity in the process is the establishment of work goals and

Figure 20.3
Elements in a
Disciplinary System

Elements in a Disciplinary System

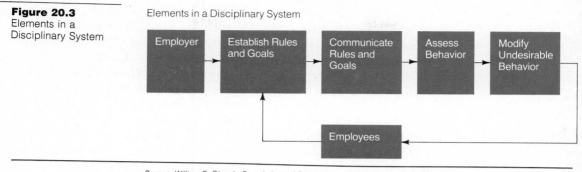

Source: William F. Glueck, *Foundations of Personnel* (Dallas: Business Publications, 1979), p. 477. © 1979 by Business Publications, Inc. Reprinted by permission.

behavior rules. Through whatever method is used (time and motion studies, examination of past performance or performances by others, management by objectives), a set of minimally acceptable *work goals* is developed. *Behavior rules* cover many facets of on-the-job behavior. They can be categorized as concerning behavior that is directly or indirectly related to work productivity. Both categories are often negatively described as prohibited behavior. Table 20.8 lists some examples of employee behavior rules.

The second important element in the disciplinary process is the communication of the goals and rules to all employees. Unless employees are aware of the rules, they can hardly be expected to follow them. Naturally, if employees or their representatives participate in the formation of the rules, their cooperation in observing them will be more likely.

Table 20.8
Examples of Employee
Behavior Rules

I. Rules Directly Related to Productivity
   A. Time rules
      1. Starting and late times
      2. Quitting times
      3. Maximum break and lunch time
      4. Maximum absenteeism
   B. Prohibited-behavior rules
      1. No sleeping on the job
      2. No leaving workplace without permission
      3. No drinking on the job
      4. No drug taking on the job
      5. Limited nonemployer activities during work hours
   C. Insubordination rules
      1. Penalties for refusal to obey supervisors
      2. Rules against slowdowns and sit downs

   D. Rules emphasizing laws
      1. Theft rules
      2. Falsification rules
   E. Safety rules
      1. No-smoking rules
      2. Safety regulations
      3. Sanitation requirements
      4. Rules prohibiting fighting
      5. Rules prohibiting dangerious weapons
II. Rules Indirectly Related to Productivity
   A. Prevention of moonlighting
   B. Prohibition of gambling
   C. Prohibition of selling or soliciting at work
   D. Clothing and uniform regulations
   E. Rules about fraternization with other employees at work or off the job

Source: William F. Glueck, *Foundations of Personnel* (Dallas: Business Publications, 1979), p. 478. © 1979 by Business Publications, Inc. Reprinted by permission.

Employees must be convinced that work goals and behavior rules are fair and related to job effectiveness for discipline to be effective.

Rules, like laws, need regular updating to achieve the respect and acceptance necessary for discipline at work. It is useful for managers to seek employee advice when changing rules. One objective in formulating or reformulating rules should always be to minimize their number.

The third element of the disciplinary process is the mechanism of assessment. In most firms, performance appraisal is that mechanism. Last, the process includes a system of administering punishment or attempting to motivate change. This usually involves administration of discipline by the managers, the courts, or through grievance procedures.

The firm's disciplinary systems usually are hierarchical. Discipline is administered to most nonunion employees by their supervisor, who also appraises them. When an employee is found to be ineffective, the supervisor decides what needs to be done. In a hierarchical system, supervisors who may be arbitrary, wrong, or ineffective themselves sometimes act as police officer, judge, and jury over the employee.

If hierarchical systems are to be effective and fair, managers must administer discipline equitably. There have been a few studies of the extent to which they do. The best study on the subject found that even in companies with a well-developed discipline system, discipline was unevenly administered.[3] Others have found that prejudice against minorities or union members has led to inequitable discipline. The data these studies provide on management of discipline offer good reason for having systems of appeal besides the open-door policy available to employees.

Disciplinary Actions

If discipline is called for, the manager can apply a series of sanctions to improve future performance or behavior. These vary from counseling to jailing the violator, as the military does on occasion. In counseling, the most frequently used method of disciplinary action, the manager explains to the employee why the violation significantly affects productivity and states that it should not happen again. Sometimes the manager may push counseling to the "chewing out" stage. Counseling works in most cases when behavior rules are violated and performance is poor.

If a second or more serious violation takes place, the manager again counsels the employee. But this time the manager enters the incident in the employee's personnel file and lets the employee know this has been done. If the violation was sufficiently serious, the employee may also be given an oral or written warning.

When counseling and a warning do not result in changed behavior and a transfer is not appropriate, the next step is disciplinary layoff. If damage resulted from the employee's behavior, deductions may be made from his or her pay over a period of time to pay for the damage. The layoff is usually of short duration, perhaps a few days up to a week.

The ultimate punishment is discharge. To many inexperienced managers, discharge seems to be the solution to *any* problem with a difficult employee. But often discharge is not possible because of seniority rules, union rules, too few replacements in the labor market, or for other reasons. Discharge has many costs—the costs of recruiting, selection, appraisal, and training a replacement as well as the loss that results during the period in which the newly hired employee is not as productive as the former employee was. In addition, many firms pay severance pay. There are indirect costs, too, in the effect firing a coworker has on other employees. If the action is taken in a blatant case of severe inability or deviant behavior, this is not too much of a problem. Too often, however, the facts are not clear and coworkers feel the employer has acted unfairly. Some employees may be distressed enough to seek employment elsewhere. Others may reduce productivity in protest or join a union.

This concludes our consideration of the management of human resources. The final chapter in the text deals with your managerial career and the unique problems you will encounter as a manager.

Summary

Chapter 20 explored how managers, with the help of personnel, assure that adequate human resources are available for the firm. *Management of human resources* is that function of all enterprises which provides for effective utilization of people to achieve both the objectives of the enterprise and the satisfaction and development of the employee. The activities included in human resource management are (1) human resource planning; (2) recruitment, selection, and orientation; (3) performance appraisal; (4) training and development; (5) compensation and rewards; and (6) discipline.

Human resource planning is the process which helps provide adequate human resources to achieve organizational objectives. First, the human resource demand must be forecast. To do this, a list presenting jobs by name, number of jobholders, number and skills of present personnel, and the effects of expected losses due to retirement or promotion is compiled.

When the firm's needs have been determined, the availability of those presently employed must be checked. A skills inventory is used. *A skills inventory* is a list of names, certain characteristics, and skills of people working for the organization.

Next the demand forecast is compared to the supply. When there is a surplus, the work force can be reduced by attrition, work sharing, and layoffs or terminations. When there is a shortage of employees, the firm must recruit. *Recruiting* is that set of activities an enterprise uses to attract job candidates who have the abilities and attitudes needed to help the enterprise achieve its objectives.

The manager must then select the best applicant from the recruits. The selection process *can* include up to six steps: (1) a preliminary screening interview, (2) completion of an application blank, (3) an employment interview, (4) employment tests, (5) background and reference checks, and (6) a physical examination.

The employment interview is the most important aspect of the selection decision process. There are three general types: structured, semi-structured, and unstructured. In the *structured* interview the manager prepares a list of questions in advance and does not deviate from it. In the *semistructured* interview the major questions are prepared in advance but the interviewer may include some probing questions which allow more flexibility. In the *unstructured* interview, the interviewer may not even prepare a list of possible topics to cover. The first two approaches provide the most reliable, useful data.

Following the selection steps above, managers can use three types of approaches to the selection decision: *random choice or chance,* an arbitrary nonrational choice; *emotional-clinical,* the choice of the most likable candidate; or the *systematic-quasirational* approach, the six-step process just described.

Once the applicant is chosen, he or she must be introduced to the job. *Orientation* is the set of actions which introduces new employees to the firm, the job, superiors, and work groups. How the manager and the work group handle orientation is crucial.

After the employee is on the job for a while, performance appraisal is used to determine how well he or she is doing. *Performance appraisal* is the system used by firms to regularly and systematically appraise the employee's performance to determine how well he or she is meeting minimum standards or objectives.

The criteria used to appraise employees depend on the purpose of the appraisal. Whether the evaluation should be based on actual or potential performance also depends on the primary purpose of the evaluation. Most firms require the manager to appraise employees, record the appraisal on a form such as the graphic rating scale, and have a discussion interview with the employee.

Sometimes the appraisal process indicates an employee should receive additional training to improve performance or satisfaction. *Training* is the systematic process of altering the behavior of employees in a direction to increase organizational goals.

In on-the-job training the employee is placed in the real work situation and shown how to do the job by an experienced employee or the supervisor. Two frequently used on-the-job methods are job instruction training (JIT) and job rotation. Off-the-job approaches such as organization classrooms, vocational schools, etc. are necessary when the manager or other employees in the work unit cannot impart the necessary training well.

Compensation in the form of pay, benefits, and services is necessary to retain the well-trained and well-motivated employee. The manager is active in the compensation process, influencing the pay level decision, the pay structure decision, incentive compensation programs, and benefits and services decisions.

There are three pay level strategies available to the manager: high, low, or comparable. Pay structures range from entry pay to the president's salary. *Job evaluation* is the formal process by which the relative worth of various jobs in the organization is determined for pay purposes. This process attempts to relate the amount of an employee's pay to the extent that her or his job contributes to organizational effectiveness. The manager must determine the individual pay for each person within a pay grade.

In most firms, two-thirds of total compensation goes to pay, one-third to benefits and services. It is important to determine whether employees prefer more benefits or more pay.

A good discipline system is necessary for maintaining the firm's effectiveness. The disciplinary process includes: (1) establishing rules and goals, (2) communicating rules and goals, (3) assessing employee behavior, and (4) modifying undesirable behavior. If employees or their representatives participate in the formation of rules, their cooperation is more likely.

When rule infractions occur, the firm's system of administering punishment or attempting to motivate change is put in operation. Most systems are hierarchical—administered to most nonunion employees by their supervisor. If these systems are to be effective and fair, managers must administer discipline equitably.

Counseling, the most frequently used method of improving poor performance or behavior, is usually effective. A written or oral warning may be the response to second violations. If counseling and a warning do not result in changed behavior, the next step is disciplinary layoff. The ultimate punishment is discharge, but discharge has many costs, including its effect on other employees.

Questions

1. For most organizations, human resource management is one of the most important, if not the most important function. What is human resource management? Why is it important to the manager?
2. How do you go about forecasting a work unit's human resource needs? How do you use the firm's skills inventory?
3. Your forecast indicates your unit faces a shortage of several key employees. How will you go about recruiting applicants for these vacancies?
4. You have to decide what selection criteria to use in filling the above vacancies. What general guidelines will you follow in establishing these criteria?
5. There can be six steps in the complete selection process. Briefly describe each of these steps.

6. You have successfully recruited and selected the necessary employees. Describe the orientation process you will use to introduce them to the firm and their job. What does effective orientation accomplish?

7. What purposes does a good performance appraisal serve?

8. The performance appraisal criteria used by managers depend on the purpose of the evaluation. Explain this statement. When should the evaluation be based on actual performance? Potential performance?

9. Following the performance appraisal process, you discover a few of your employees need additional training. How would you as a manager be involved in this process? Compare on-the-job to off-the-job training methods.

10. Explain the three pay level strategies. Under what conditions would each strategy be likely to be used?

11. Define the job evaluation process. What does it attempt to do?

12. Discuss the various forms of compensation including the individual incentive system, commissions, and typical benefits and services firms provide.

13. How would you go about establishing a disciplinary system for your firm? Outline each step in the process.

14. What are the direct and indirect costs involved in the ultimate disciplinary action, discharge?

Notes

[1]The benefits derived from human resource planning stated here are discussed in greater detail in the following: Clyde Benedict, "A Personnel Perspective—Today," *Personnel Administrator* 20 (November 1975): 27–30. Bureau of National Affairs, David Babcock and John Boyd, "PAIR Department Policy and Organization," in *PAIR Policy and Program Management,* ed. Dale Yoder and Herbert Heneman, Jr. (Washington, D.C.: Government Printing Office, 1978). Fred Foulkes, "The Expanding Role of the Personnel Function," *Harvard Business Review* 53 (March–April 1975): 71–84. James Henderson, "What the Chief Executive Expects of the Personnel Function," *Personnel Administrator* 22 (May 1977): 40–45. Walton Burdick, "A Look at Corporate and Personnel Philosophy," *Personnel Administrator* 21 (July 1976): 21–26.

[2]Lawrence Jauch, "Systemizing the Selection Decision," *Personnel Journal* 55 (November 1976): 564–566.

[3]Phillip Shaak and Milton Schwartz, "Uniformity of Policy Interpretation among Managers in American Industry," *Academy of Management Journal* 16 (March 1973): 77–83.

References

This chapter draws heavily on my books: *Personnel: A Diagnostic Approach* (Dallas: Business Publications, 1978); and *Foundations of Personnel* (Dallas: Business Publications, 1979).

Human Resource Planning

Bruce Coleman, "An Integrated System for Manpower Planning," *Business Horizons* 13 (October 1970): 89–95. George Milkovich and Thomas Mahoney, "Human Resources Planning and PAIR Policy," in *PAIR Handbook,* vol. 4, ed. Dale Yoder and Herbert Heneman, Jr. (Berea, Ohio: American Society of Personnel Administrators, 1976). James

Walker, "Evaluating the Practical Effectiveness of Human Resource Planning Applications," *Human Resource Management* 13 (Spring 1974): 19–27.

Recruiting Employees

Bureau of National Affairs, Paul Wernimont, "Recruitment Policies and Practices," in *Staffing Policies and Strategies: ASPA Handbook,* ed. Dale Yoder and Herbert Heneman, Jr. (Washington, D. C.: Government Printing Office, 1974). Dave Dahl and Patric Pinto, "Job Posting: An Industry Survey," *Personnel Journal* 56 (January 1977): 40–42. William Glueck, "Decision Making: Organization Choice," *Personnel Psychology* 27 (Spring 1974): 77–93. Michael Ornstein, *Entry into the American Labor Force* (New York: Academic Press, 1976). Robert Sibson, "The High Cost of Hiring," *Nation's Business* 63 (February 1975): 85–88.

Selection of Employees

Bureau of National Affairs, *Selection Procedures and Personnel Records,* Personnel Policies Forum, Survey 114 (Washington, D. C.: Government Printing Office, 1976). Richard Chase, "Working Physiology," *Personnel Administration* 32 (November 1969): 47–53. Lawrence Jauch, "Systemizing the Selection Decision," *Personnel Journal* 55 (November 1976): 564–566. Clemm C. Kessler III and Georgia Gibbs, "Getting the Most from Application Blanks and References," *Personnel* 52 (January–February 1975): 53–62. William Owens, "Background Data," in *Handbook of Industrial and Organizational Psychology,* ed. Marvin Dunnette (Chicago: Rand McNally, 1976). Frank Schmidt et al., "Job Sample vs. Paper and Pencil Trades and Technical Tests: Adverse Impact and Examinee Attitudes," *Personnel Psychology* 30 (Summer 1977): 123–131. W. Wilson, "Toward Better Use of Psychological Testing," *Personnel* 39 (May–June 1962): 55–62.

Orienting New Employees

Warren Boe and Thomas Stone, "A Comparison of Three Placement Methods," *Proceedings of the Academy of Management* (1973), pp. 372–377. Earl R. Gomersall and M. Scott Myers, "Breakthrough in On-the-Job Training," *Harvard Business Review* 44 (July–August 1966): 67–71. Joan Holland and Theodore Curtis, "Orientation of New Employees," in *Handbook of Modern Personnel Administration,* ed. Joseph Famularo (New York: McGraw-Hill, 1972), chapter 23. Daniel Ilgen and William Seeley, "Realistic Expectations as an Aid in Reducing Voluntary Resignations," *Journal of Applied Psychology* 59 (August 1974): 452. John Van Maanen, "Breaking In: Socialization to Work," in *Handbook of Work, Organization, and Society,* ed. Robert Dubin (Chicago: Rand McNally, 1976). John Wanous, "Organizational Entry: From Naive Expectations to Realistic Belief," *Journal of Applied Psychology* 61 (February 1976): 22–29.

Performance Appraisal

Bureau of National Affairs, *Employee Performance: Evaluation and Control,* Personnel Policies Forum, Survey 108 (Washington, D. C.: Government Printing Office, 1975); and *Labor Policy and Practice—Personnel Management* (Washington, D. C.: Government Printing Office, 1974). Larry Cummings and Donald Schwab, *Performance in Organizations* (Glenview, Ill.: Scott, Foresman, 1973). Cal Downs and David Spohn, "Case Study of an Appraisal System in an Airline," *Proceedings of the Academy of Management* (1976). Kirt Duffey and Robert Webber, "On 'Relative' Rating Systems," *Personnel Psychology* 27 (Summer 1974): 307–311. Ronald Grey and David Kipnis, "Untangling the Performance Appraisal Dilemma: The Influence of Perceived Organizational Context on Evaluative Processes," *Journal of Applied Psychology* 61 (June

1976): 329–335. Michael Kelley, "Subjective Performance Evaluation and Person-Role Conflict under Conditions of Uncertainty," *Academy of Management Journal* 20 (June 1977): 301–314. W. K. Kirchner and Marvin Dunnette, "Identifying the Critical Factors in Successful Salesmanship," *Personnel* 34 (September–October 1957): 54–59. Alan Locher and Kenneth Teel, "Performance Appraisal: A Survey of Current Practices," *Personnel Journal* 56 (May 1977): 345–354. Douglas McGregor, "An Uneasy Look at Performance Appraisal," *Harvard Business Review* 53 (May–June 1975): 89–94. J. Sidney Shrauger, "Responses to Evaluation as a Function of Initial Self-Perceptions," *Psychological Bulletin* 82 (1975): 581–596. Patricia Smith, "Behaviors, Results, and Organizational Effectiveness," in *Handbook of Industrial and Organizational Psychology,* ed. Marvin Dunnette (Chicago: Rand McNally, 1976). Paul H. Thompson and Gene W. Dalton, "Performance Appraisal: Managers Beware," *Harvard Business Review* 48 (January–February 1970): 149–157. Robert Zawacki and Robert Taylor, "A View of Performance Appraisal from Organizations Using It," *Personnel Journal* 55 (June 1976): 290–292, 299 ff.

Training and Development

Eric Berne, *Transactional Analysis in Psychotherapy* (New York: Ballantine Books, 1961). Bureau of National Affairs, Dale Yoder and Herbert Heneman, Jr., *Training and Development: PAIR Handbook* (Washington, D. C.: Government Printing Office, 1977); and *Training Employees,* Personnel Policies Forum, Survey 88 (Washington D.C.: Government Printing Office, 1969). Robert Burnaska, "The Effects of Behavior Modeling Training upon Manager's Behaviors and Employee's Perceptions," *Personnel Psychology* 29 (Fall 1976): 329–335. Theodore Currey II, "Why Not Use Your Line Managers as Management Trainers?" *Training and Development Journal* 31 (November 1977): 43–47. William Franklin, "A Comparison of Formally and Informally Trained Journeymen in Construction," *Industrial and Labor Relations Review* 26 (July 1973): 1086–1094. A. P. Goldstein and Melvin Sorcher, *Changing Supervisor Behavior* (New York: Pergamon Press, 1974). Irwin Goldstein, *Training: Program Development and Evaluation* (Monterey, Calif.: Brooks/Cole, 1974). M. Gould, "Counseling for Self-Development," *Personnel Journal* 49 (March 1970): 226–234. D. L. Kirkpatrick, "Techniques for Evaluating Training Programs," *Journal of the American Society of Training Directors* 13 (November 1959): pp. 3–9; and "Determining Training Needs," *Training and Development Journal* 31 (February 1977): 22–25. Newton Margulies and Anthony Raia, *Conceptual Foundations of Organization Development* (New York: McGraw-Hill, 1978). Joseph Moses and Richard Ritchie, "Supervisory Relationships Training: A Behavioral Evaluation of a Behavior Modeling Program," *Personnel Psychology* 29 (Fall 1976): 337–343. Jack Retting and Matt Amano, "A Survey of ASPA Experience with Management by Objectives, Sensitivity Training and Transactional Analysis," *Personnel Journal* 55 (January 1976): 26–29. Roger Roderick and Joseph Yaney, "Developing Younger Workers: A Look at Who Gets Trained," *Journal of Management* (Spring 1976): 19–26. Edward Rundquist, "Designing and Improving Job Training Courses," *Personnel Psychology* 25 (Spring 1972): 41–52. Stanley H. Steelman, "Is There a Payoff to OD?" *Training and Development Journal* 30 (April 1976): 18–23. George Strauss, "Organization Development," in *Handbook of Work, Organization and Society,* ed. Robert Dubin (Chicago: Rand McNally, 1976). S. B. Utgaard and R. V. Davis, "The Most Frequently Used Training Techniques," *Training and Development Journal* 24 (February 1970): 40–43.

Compensation

Robert Ashall and John Child, "Employee Services: People, Profits, or Parkinson?" *Personnel Management* 4 (Fall 1972): 18–22. Bureau of National Affairs, *Employee Health and Welfare Benefits,* Personnel Policies Forum, Survey 107 (Washington, D.C.: Government Printing Office, 1974); *Paid Leave and Leave of Absence Policies,* Personnel Policies Forum, Survey 111 (Washington, D.C.: Government Printing Office, 1975); Mitchell Meyer and Harland Fox, "Profile of Employee Benefits," *Basic Patterns in Union*

Contracts (Washington, D.C.: Government Printing Office, 1975); and *Wage and Salary Administration,* Personnel Policies Forum, Survey 97 (Washington, D.C., Government Printing Office, 1972). Donald Carlson, "Responding to the Pension Reform Law," *Harvard Business Review* 52 (November–December 1974): 133–144. Edward Deci, *Intrinsic Motivation* (New York: Plenum, 1975). John Deardon, "How to Make Incentive Plans Work," *Harvard Business Review* 50 (July–August 1972): 117–124. A. J. Geare, "Productivity from Scanlon-Type Plans," *Academy of Management Review* 1 (July 1976): 99–108. Mary Hopkins and Marcia Wood, "Who Wants to Retire?" *Personnel Administrator* 21 (October 1976): 38–41. Robert Kelly, "Job Evaluation and Pay Plans: Office Personnel," In *Handbook of Modern Personnel Administration,* ed. Joseph Famularo (New York: McGraw-Hill, 1972). Linda Krefting and Thomas Mahoney, "Determining the Size of a Meaningful Pay Increase," *Industrial Relations* 16 (February 1977): 83–93. E. E. Lawler, Jr., *Pay and Organizational Effectiveness* (New York: McGraw-Hill, 1971). E. R. Livernash, "Wages and Benefits," in *Review of Industrial Relations Research,* ed. Woodrow Ginsbert et al. (Madison, Wis.: Industrial Relations Research Association, 1970). Herbert Meyer, "The Pay for Performance Dilemma," *Organizational Dynamics* 3 (Winter 1975): 39–50. Mitchell Meyer and Harland Fox, *Early Retirement Programs* (New York: National Industrial Conference Board, 1971). Alan Miller, "How Companies Can Trim Employee Health Benefit Claims," *Harvard Business Review* 56 (January–February 1978): 608. Alan Nash and Stephen Carroll, *Management of Compensation* (Monterey, Calif.: Brooks/Cole, 1975). Stanley Nealey, "Compensation Fungibility," *Proceedings of the Industrial Relations Research Association* (1977), pp. 154–159. Thomas Patten, *Pay* (Glencoe, Ill.: Free Press, 1977). Robert Paul, *Employee Benefits Factbook* (New York: Martin Segal, 1976). Robert Sbarra, "The New Language of Executive Compensation," *Personnel* 52 (November–December 1975): 10–18. Bruce R. Uly, "Compensation Management: Its Past and Its Future," *Personnel* 54 (May–June 1977): 30–40. Marc Wallace, "Type of Control, Industrial Concentration and Executive Pay," *Proceedings of the Academy of Management* (1976). William Werther, "A New Direction in Rethinking Fringe Benefits," *MSU Business Topics* 22 (Winter 1974): 35–40.

Discipline of Employees

Claire Anderson, *"The Marginal Worker: A Search for Correlates"* (Ph.D. diss., University of Massachusetts, 1976). Bureau of National Affairs, *Employee Conduct and Discipline,* Personnel Policies Forum, Survey 102 (Washington, D.C.: Government Printing Office, 1973); and Richard Healey and Timothy Walsh, "Security Policies, Programs, and Problems," in *PAIR Policy and Program Management,* ed. Dale Yoder and Herbert Heneman, Jr. (Washington, D.C.: Government Printing Office, 1978). Susan Halpern, *Drug Abuse and Your Company* (New York: American Management Association, 1972). Ken Jennings, "The Problem of Employee Drug Use and Remedial Alternatives," *Personnel Journal* 56 (November 1977): 554–560; and "Verbal and Physical Abuse toward Supervision," *Arbitration Journal* 29 (December 1974): 258–271. Edward Levin and Tia Denenberg, "How Arbitrators View Drug Abuse," *Arbitration Journal* 31 (June 1976): 97–108. Mark Lipman, "What You Can Do about Employee Theft," *Nation's Business* 64 (May 1976): 63–65. Roger Mager and Peter Pipe, *Analyzing Performance Problems* (Palo Alto, Calif.: Fearon, 1970). John Miner, *The Challenge of Managing* (Philadelphia: Saunders, 1975). William G. Scott, *The Management of Conflict: Appeal Systems in Organizations* (Homewood, Ill.: Richard D. Irwin, 1965). Philip Shaak and Milton Schwartz, "Uniformity of Policy Interpretation among Managers in American Industry," *Academy of Management Journal* 16 (March 1973): 77–83. Lawrence Steinmetz, *Managing the Marginal and Unsatisfactory Performer* (Reading, Mass.: Addison-Wesley, 1969). Jerry L. Wall, *Industrial Espionage in American Firms* (Ph.D. diss., University of Missouri, Columbia, 1974).

Cases for Chapter 20

**Moder
Aircraft, Inc.**

Moder is a medium-sized company that supplies subassemblies for major aircraft firms. It ships its parts to all the major airframe manufacturers as well as firms that make executive aircraft and similar products. Its president is Jason Fleming.

Recently Fleming has seen many articles about equal employment opportunity for women and minority groups. He wondered how his company would be evaluated on this issue. So he asked the personnel vice-president to prepare a report on Moder's employees. Exhibit 1 is that report.

After looking the report over, Fleming called the personnel vice-president, Elling Takover, into his office. The following is an excerpt from their discussion.

Fleming: "El, tell me the truth. If a government guy came in here, what'd happen?"

Exhibit 1
Moder Aircraft,
Inc., Employee
Analysis

Level of Employees	Employees by Sex			Employees by Ethnic Group					
	Male	Female	Total	White	Black	Hispanic American	American Indian	Asian Pacific Islanders	Total
Top management	100%	0%	100%	100%	0 %	0 %	0%	0%	100%
Middle management	99	1	100	99	0.5	0.5	0	0	100
Technical	93	7	100	97	1.5	1.5	0	0	100
Supervisory	89	11	100	94	2	4	0	0	100
Clerical	1	99	100	79	11	10	0	0	100
Operative	92	8	100	61	28	11	0	0	100

Takover: "We'd be in trouble, boss."

Fleming: "It's not like we discriminated. We hired minorities long before others did. But most of our managers are engineers or ex-engineers. How many female engineers are there? Black engineers?"

Takover: "I'm not sure that'd cut much ice. We really have an EEO problem, I think. Maybe we haven't been as socially responsibile as we thought."

Problem

Takover is asked by Fleming to recommend some preventive action. You are Takover. What do you recommend?

Alberta Mobile Homes, Ltd.

Alberta Mobile Homes, Ltd. (AMH) is a small manufacturer of mobile homes and modular homes located in Calgary, Alberta, Canada. The firm has about 250 employees.

Alice Butkus, president of AMH, recently attended a seminar on personnel administration in Calgary conducted by Professor Warren Simpson of the University of Calgary's business school. After the session was over, Butkus approached Simpson and asked him if he'd be willing to come to her firm and provide consulting help for several personnel problems.

"Sure, I'd be delighted," replied Simpson. A few days later, he went to AMH to begin the project.

Butkus introduced the problem this way: "Look, Warren, we seem to be having problems with our promotion and evaluation system here. Let me describe two incidents that have come up just in the last two months. We're in a growth industry. We've doubled our work force in the last year and a half. This means we need to move some people up, but we are having the darnedest time with it.

"Recently, George Drester, the head of our plant, came to see me. He said he'd been wrestling with this problem for months. He'd promoted Jay Gilbreth to supervisor about six months ago. Jay was good at his job before, but he's not a good supervisor. His employees don't like or respect him. Jay himself seems aware of the situation. George is wondering what he can do about Jay.

"Then there's the case of Ed Bankhead, the head of marketing. He needs to recommend someone for promotion to sales manager. I've been asking him to do so for weeks, and no recommendations yet. See what you can do about it, will you?"

With this send-off, Simpson went to meet Bankhead. After some preliminaries, he came to the point. "Look, Ed, I'm here to see about establishing some policies about promotion. Frankly, Alice gave you as a case in point. She's wanting to know what you've done about the sales manager's job."

Bankhead shifted around in his chair. He then described in some detail the persons he was thinking about:

1. James Prior: ten years' experience in construction sales, lots of personality, no supervisory experience, high school graduate.
2. Helen Cortney: four years' sales experience for AMH, the best salesperson of the bunch, college degree in business, no supervisory experience, very quiet, almost introverted.
3. Matt Dotler: older, 12 years' experience selling, 5 of it for AMH, outgoing personality. He supervised two men with his previous company.

"Frankly, Warren," Bankhead said, "I'm leaning towards Helen. I figure the best salesperson is bound to make the best sales manager. But I really don't have a lot of facts and figures to back up my choice. How should I go about this, anyway?"

Simpson said he would make a recommendation on this shortly. Next he visited Drester. "What am I going to do about Jay?" asked Drester. "He's not cutting it."

Simpson pressed Drester and asked him how he "knew" that Gilbreth's employees didn't like or respect him. "How isn't he cutting it?" he asked. He quickly determined that these were just Drester's general impressions, not based on a lot of evidence. He also learned that Drester had not tried to discuss the issue with Gilbreth or tried to counsel or help him.

Source: Reprinted with permission from Glueck, William F., *Personnel: A Diagnostic Approach* (Dallas, Texas: Business Publications, Inc., 1974).

Problem

You are Professor Simpson. Write the report to Butkus, copies of which will go to Drester and Bankhead. The report should include recommendations on:

1. How to decide on a sales manager and if possible whom Bankhead should recommend.
2. What to do about Drester and Gilbreth.
3. Recommendations for improving promotion, evaluation, and counseling at AMH.

Chapter 21 Managing Managerial Careers

Learning Objectives

1. Learn how to take the initiative in job search and sell yourself.
2. Be aware of the problems facing the new manager and how an effective orientation program helps overcome them.
3. Be able to follow the guidelines for developing a career plan for a successful managerial career.
4. Learn how managerial performance appraisal, management development, and compensation differ from those of other employees.
5. Know some ways to handle the unique challenges which face the dual career couple.
6. Examine your personality for Type A characteristics and your ability to handle stress.
7. Learn what problems to expect during the mid-life crisis and how to cope with these.

Chapter Outline

Introduction
Recruiting and Selecting Managers
Practical Application: Recruiting and Selection
Orientation Programs for New Managers
Practical Application: The Young Manager's Career Problems
Career Planning and Development
Practical Application: Your Career Plan
Establishing Your Career Objectives
Career Planning for Family Business Executives and Entrepreneurs
Performance Appraisal for Managers

Management Development
On-the-Job Management Development
Off-the-Job Management Development
Compensating Managers
Staffing for the Entrepreneurial or Family Business
Maintaining Managerial Health
Managing Stress
Dual Career Couples
Managing the Mid-Life Crisis
Overcoming the Mid-Life Crisis
Summary
Questions

Introduction

In Chapter 20, I discussed how firms manage human resources and staff the enterprise with effective employees. In this chapter I will discuss how a firm develops a management team to lead the firm. I will also address the subjects of how you should plan your managerial career and some of the challenges it will offer you.

A managerial career is a sequential set of work roles or jobs in an enterprise or a series of enterprises.

Understanding how firms manage their managerial resources is vital to your future—both in developing a successful career and in fulfilling your role in the management process. This applies whether your career objectives are primarily success oriented (as in the cartoon) or development oriented. Let's begin with a discussion of how firms recruit and select managers.

Recruiting and Selecting Managers

In Chapter 20, you learned that managers are recruited from inside the firm by use of the skills inventory. Recommendations from the network of executives within the firm are a much more important source of recruitment information. Managers are recruited from outside sources too. External recruitment may take place at colleges and universities, at professional meetings, and through executive search firms (private employment agencies specializing in executives). A few managers are recruited from coop programs and summer internships. And many are recruited in college placement service interviews and through walk-in interviews and write-ins (résumé mailings).

Firms use want ads for executives, too. Some places they advertise are the *Wall Street Journal*, professional journals (such as the *Personnel Administrator*, a journal for personnel managers), and in major metropolitan newspapers such as the *Los Angeles Times*, the *Kansas City Star*, the *Chicago Tribune*, the *New York Times*, and the *Atlanta Journal*.

In many ways managerial selection is similar to employee selection. For

Source: Drawing by Stan Hunt; © 1976 The New Yorker Magazine, Inc.

"That's enough, Foster. It's time to go now."

example, the criteria for selection are established based on the characteristics and skills of successful managers already in the firm. It is not easy, however, to pinpoint the characteristics and abilities that make managers successful. Nor is it easy to establish reliable ways to select managers using these criteria. Norms for lower-level jobs such as clerks or typists are more readily obtained than for managerial positions because those jobs generally require more specific, measurable skills.

The tools used for managerial selection include the employment interview, application blanks, and reference checks. In a few larger firms, a technique for selection (and performance appraisal) called the assessment center is used. An assessment center combines several methods of evaluating applicants. The applicants spend several days performing exercises, management games, and mock selection interviews. The decision makers, who are specially trained, observe their performance and rate them. Although relatively new and expensive, the assessment center appears to be a useful approach for selection and performance appraisal of managers.

With all this in mind, let's consider how you can assure yourself of the best chance of getting the job you want.

Practical Application: Recruiting and Selection

To be recruited for the job you want, you must take the initiative. You should take as many interviews as possible at the college placement service. You should attend professional meetings that have placement services. You should apply in person and by mail to the firms you are most interested in. Your initial contact should be well planned and carefully prepared. It should include an explanation of why you applied to the firm and how your skills fit the firm's needs exactly.

Finally, to be a successful applicant, you must make use of all possible informal networks. Members of your sorority, fraternity, and/or social clubs who have graduated and are already employed and friends of your parents are good contacts. Faculty members at your college or university may also be able to provide you with some leads and contacts. In general, successful applicants market themselves. Remember, the product that has the best advertising and product quality and can be found in the most stores sells the best. So you, the applicant (product), must check into all sources of jobs and use good advertising (résumés, letters of recommendation, good grooming, etc.). Do not be shy. You have lots to offer.

The selection phase is the next hurdle in getting a job. Prepare for the interviews. Learn all you can about the company. Anticipate questions and prepare answers. Do the best you can on the tests. All these aspects of the selection process are very important.

Especially if your grades were good, the subjects you took were relevant, the school you attended has a good reputation, and you have some work and extracurricular experience, you will have a good chance of getting the job of your choice. Do not sell yourself short!

Orientation Programs for New Managers

Once you are hired, the next step is orientation. What orientation is and why it is done was discussed in Chapter 20. The difference between employee and managerial orientation is that most management orientation is more formal and is usually called a management training program.

After recruits have been selected to become managers, there are two different approaches to their orientation. The first is to orient them briefly and let them go to work. This is the approach most organizations use with other types of employees. The second is to orient them in a management training program. When this is done, the recruits are not assigned positions until after they have completed the program.

The most effective management training programs:

- Are short (of four to five months' duration, if possible).
- Use on-the-job training.
- Minimize classroom teaching.
- Encourage high expectations in trainees.
- Provide trainees with frequent feedback on their progress or lack of it.

Perhaps most crucial to an effective management training program is an effective supervisor for the trainee. Too often the trainers see themselves as failures because they have not been promoted beyond a certain point. They may haze recruits and give them tough experiences. Instead, new managers should have a supervisor who understands their problems and wants to get them off to a good start. If good orientation does not take place, the new manager will face more of what I call the young manager's career problems.

Practical Application: The Young Manager's Career Problems

As you start your careers you face a number of problems. An understanding of these problems may put them in perspective and help reduce some of the turnover that characterizes the early years of many managerial careers.

Anxiety Typically, the young manager is anxious over whether he or she will be successful and can hold the job. This is a problem that many younger managers hide from each other. You may be afraid that admitting it will indicate immaturity. In fact, however, it is quite normal. Proper orientation programs can help you reduce such anxiety to manageable dimensions. An understanding superior and peers can help. If you find very competitive peers and a supervisor who expects high confidence and lack of anxiety, this can accentuate the problem. Too much attention to these anxious feelings will reduce your chances of success: Psychic energy that could be channeled into job behavior is used to control the anxiety.

A variation of this problem is concern over whether you are in the right job. If you had few job offers, the job may appear to be your only choice. You may not be happy about it and may long for other choices. If you had several offers, you may wonder whether you made the right choice. Chances are that if you gave serious thought to the matter you made the right choice. An understanding of cognitive dissonance may help reduce anxiety.

The Expectations Problem Some young managers come out of college with the expectation that they will shortly earn per year what their parents took twenty years to get and that although they will spend a short time "learning the business" (say, a year or two), they will soon be making significant managerial decisions. This problem is compounded if the recruiters promised these young managers more than they can deliver.

Such expectations are found especially in people who have not worked before, and often in graduates of the most prestigious schools. In addition, new managers may expect that their supervisor's main job is to give them frequent feedback (normally, glowing), just as they could expect grades at frequent intervals while they were in school.

If you are put in a standardized job, with little or no exposure to major decisions and an indifferent supervisor who may "review your progress" only annually (if that often) and on unknown criteria, you may develop an acute case of the expectations problem. This may be compounded if your supervisor is much older—a situation that can create variations of the parent-child problem (which you may have been through only recently).

The expectations problem varies in intensity. In most cases young managers are anxious. But consider the two managers in Table 21.1. It should be easy to see that Mary might have a slight expectations problem, but Constantine is likely to have a serious one. To the extent that your conditions are like Mary's, you will be better able to cope with the expectations problem.

In fact young managers must think carefully to determine whether they have an expectations problem or whether they have been put in a "dead-end" job—one with no future promotion possibilities. In the latter case the manager should follow the guidelines for successful career planning and development presented later in the chapter. A good management training program and supportive superiors and peers can reduce anxiety and expectations problems to manageable size for most young managers.

Career Planning and Development

Once a manager is on the job, she or he must develop a career plan for success. Exactly how to do this will be explained shortly. Some firms help their managers develop careers for themselves. An example of career development by an organization is the approach taken by a major telephone company. The typical career path it uses to develop a general

Table 21.1
An Example of How Differences In Background Affect Expectations

Factor	Manager 1 Mary	Manager 2 Constantine
1. Income of family	Low	High
2. College financing	Worked way through with little or no parental help	Parents paid
3. College attended	Community college	Harvard
4. Parent's position	Supervisor, small firm	Vice-president, large firm
5. First supervisor		
a. Age	32	50
b. Leadership style	Middle of the road	Very conservative
c. Future	Up the ladder	Present job
d. Performance evaluation method	MBO, critical incident method,[a] frequent feedback	Annual cursory graphic rating scale
6. Nature of first job	Varied	Standardized in hierarchy
Expectations Problem	Slight	Serious

[a]In this evaluation method, personnel specialists and operating managers prepare lists of statements of very effective and ineffective employee behavior. Then examples of outstandingly good or bad behaviors are logged for individual employees during the evaluation period.

Figure 21.1
Typical Career Path for
General Manager in a
Major Telephone
Company

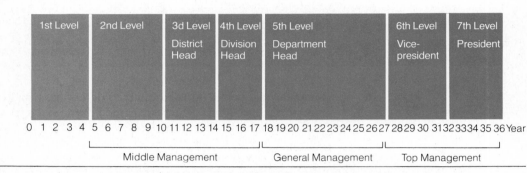

Source: William F. Glueck, *Foundations of Management* (Dallas: Business Publications, 1979), p. 269. © 1979 by
Business Publications, Inc. Reprinted by permission.

manager is given in Figure 21.1. Table 21.2 lists the steps in an actual
career for a general manager with this firm. It also offers a college tuition
reimbursement plan if the managers choose to further their formal
education. But since most firms do not have career development programs,
it will be your responsibility to plan your own career.

Table 21.2
Career Path of a
General Manager in a
Major Telephone
Company

Level	Job Title	Location	Department	Years in Position
1st	Staff assistant	Home office	Commercial	2½ years
1st	Manager	District office, small city	Commercial	1½ years
2nd	Unit manager	Home office	Commerical	1 year
2nd	Data sales manager	Home office	Commercial	2½ years
2nd	Rate engineer	District office	Commercial	1½ years
3rd	District manager	District office	Commercial	1½ years
3rd	College employment representative	Home office	Personnel	1 year
3rd	Corporate headquarters	New York	Human resource development	2 years
4th	College relations director	Home office	Personnel	1 year
4th	Division manager	Division office	Commercial	3½ years
5th	Assistant vice-president, personnel	Home office	Personnel	5 years

Source: William F. Glueck, *Foundations of Personnel* (Dallas: Business Publications, 1979), p. 269. © 1979 by
Business Publications, Inc. Reprinted by permission.

Practical Application: Your Career Plan

This section concentrates on the planning of your future career in management or as an entrepreneur. Career planning is not a science. But the consensus of research (and common sense) is that planning for the future is more likely to lead to the achievement of your goals than not planning. Of course luck is a factor, as I pointed out in Chapter 2. But if you have a plan, you are more likely to be able to exploit the opportunities that luck presents. Keep in mind the following axioms of career planning:

- Each individual must assume primary responsibility for his or her career planning.
- With a well thought out career plan you have a better chance of having a rewarding career.
- Career planning does not guarantee success, but it allows you to take advantage of circumstances.
- Once you have made a career plan, it takes courage to carry it out.

Joe, Fred, and Carol

Joe is about to graduate from State U with a degree in business, He has heard that the job market is tough, but he does not start worrying about it until November. He interviews at the placement office and in his home town. He takes the first job offer he gets: a job in a bank. Years later he vaguely hates the job and wishes he had never gotten into banking.

When Fred was going to graduate in six months, he visited one of his professors and got some career advice. Together they planned a career with a nearby sports organization. Fred loves his job.

Carol was thinking about taking a job with a large financial institution. She consulted with her professors, and they convinced her that big business was not for her. Instead, they helped her get a job with a promising entrepreneurial firm. Carol loves her job.

Most students drift into a career instead of planning it, with predictable results. Career planning can help you avoid becoming a Joe.

How to Plan a Managerial Career

Career planning consists of the six steps presented in Figure 21.2. The first step is to prepare a list of what you are looking for in a career. Crucial questions you must ask yourself to answer include the following:

1. How hard do I like to work?
2. Do I like to be my own boss, or would I rather have someone else take the responsibility?
3. Do I like to work alone, with a few others, or with large groups?
4. Do I work evenly or in bursts of energy?

Figure 21.2
Career Decision
Strategy

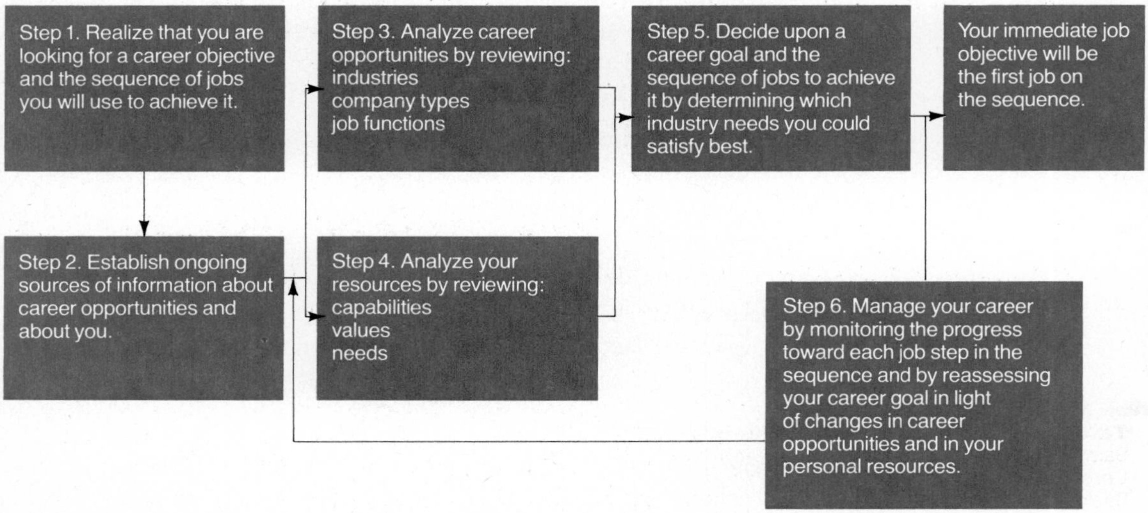

Step 1. Realize that you are looking for a career objective and the sequence of jobs you will use to achieve it.

Step 2. Establish ongoing sources of information about career opportunities and about you.

Step 3. Analyze career opportunities by reviewing:
industries
company types
job functions

Step 4. Analyze your resources by reviewing:
capabilities
values
needs

Step 5. Decide upon a career goal and the sequence of jobs to achieve it by determining which industry needs you could satisfy best.

Step 6. Manage your career by monitoring the progress toward each job step in the sequence and by reassessing your career goal in light of changes in career opportunities and in your personal resources.

Your immediate job objective will be the first job on the sequence.

Source: Adapted by permission from Benedetto Greco, *How to Get the Job That's Right for You* (Homewood, Ill.: Dow Jones–Irwin, 1975).

5. Do I want to work near home? in warmer climates? ski country? Does location matter? Am I willing to be mobile?
6. How much money do I want? Am I willing to work for less if the job is interesting?
7. Do I like to work in one place or many, indoors or outdoors?
8. How much variety do I want in my work?
9. What kind of job or work is appealing to me?

The list of questions is potentially limitless. What you must do first is rank the more important ones so that you know the trade-offs, since you will not find one job that satisfies all your wants.

Questions relating to your potential employer might include the following:

1. Do I have a size preference: small, medium, large, none?
2. Do I have a sector preference (private, nonprofit, public sector)?
3. What kinds of industries interest me? (This is usually based on interests in their products or services. Do you like mechanical objects? counseling people? This is a crucial question.)
4. Does the sector or product or service have a good future that will lead to greater opportunity?

Suppose at this point that you have determined that what you really want is the following: a position near home in a small firm in the toy industry that you can buy out someday. By making this determination you have narrowed your choices. Your next step is to prepare a list of your comparative advantages to help you sell yourself to the employers you have chosen. You also prepare a résumé (a sample is shown in Table 21.3). Your list of advantages should include the following items:

1. **Education**
   grades
   courses
   skills developed
2. **Experience**
   variety
   relevance to company

Table 21.3
Sample Résumé for College Graduate Seeking Management Job.

Personal Information	John Roerger 2745 Artis Rd. Chicago, IL 60600 (314) 476-8765	Born: December 12, 1955 5'8", 170 lbs. Health: Excellent

Educational Experience

Sampson High School, 1969–1972

Chicago Junior College, 1972–1974

Northern Illinois University, 1974–1976
B.S. (Business Administration)
Gradepoint Average: 3.1 (4.0 system)

Extracurricular Activities and Honors

Member, S.A.M.; President, 1975–1976
Beta Gamma Sigma Business Honorary
Dean's List, 1974–1975, 1975–1976
Delta Sigma Pi Fraternity
Northern Illinois Debate Team, 1974–1976

Work Experience

Part-Time Jobs: (1) Sales: J. C. Penney and Company, 1972–1974
(2) Computer Programmer, Northern Illinois University, 1974–1976
Summer Jobs: 1972, 1973, 1974, 1975: J. C. Penney and Company
I earned 75% of my college expenses.

Position Desired

Management Trainee, Sales, Finance, or Operating Supervisor leading to challenging career. Location, company size open.

References

Mr. Samuel Logan, J. C. Penney and Company, Chicago, IL 60600—supervisor of my work at Penney's, 1972–1974 and summers.

Dr. Henry Higgins, Computer Center, Northern Illinois University, DeKalb, IL—supervisor of my work, 1974–1976.

Dr. Eileen Jones, Department of Marketing, Northern Illinois University, DeKalb, IL—my adviser at Northern Illinois University.

amount
skills developed
3. **Personality and personal characteristics**
interpersonal skills
conscientious/ambitious
leadership skills
4. **Contacts with company**
businesspeople
bankers
professors

**Establishing
Your Career
Objectives**

For career planning to be successful you must have specific goals or objectives. These are usually stated in the terms listed below:

1. The number of people you want to supervise by a certain age (e.g., 500 by age thirty-five).
2. A target salary per year by a certain age (e.g., $35,000 per year by age thirty-five).
3. A specific title by a certain age (for example, vice-president by age forty).
4. A colleague goal (for instance, to be working with at least four compatible colleagues by age twenty-five).
5. Your desire to run your own business or not.
6. Your life-style objectives.

As should be clear by now, because of individual differences these objectives will vary. What is important is setting your goals precisely. A word of caution: Do not become inflexible. If your goal is to become a millionaire by age thirty-five and you are nearly thirty-five, be willing to wait until you are thirty-six.

Guidelines for Successful Career Planning and Development

Recently *Business Week* summarized the success stories of several fast-rising young managers in large companies.[1] The stories tended to have a number of characteristics in common, which I will briefly summarize here. The young managers gained experience in several fields, including finance. Thus they became generalists early. After a few years of experience (and before age thirty), they obtained an M.B.A. This helped advance their career. (A recent study by the Association of M.B.A. Executives found that upon graduation, the average starting salary for an M.B.A. is $3,305 per year higher than that of his or her counterpart with a bachelor's degree.)[2]

Business Week's fast-rising managers did not leave the company when their promotion progress slowed down just a bit. But if there was a significant slowdown, they changed jobs, especially when they were in their twenties and thirties. They realized that career goals such as "make your age in salary" are guideposts, not inflexible requirements. Still, they did not want to spend too much time in any single job. Their general rule of thumb was two years in early jobs, five years as a vice-president. When they stopped learning, they pushed for transfer or promotion.

To maintain their flexibility and general competence, these managers switched from line to staff and back to line jobs. Line positions, however, predominated. They enhanced their chances for success by working in such a way that their bosses looked good and by developing their style so that they were noticeable. They gained their reputation as innovators by taking jobs that gave them exposure.

Eugene Jennings has studied successful managers for years. His eight career success rules (many similar to the principles *Business Week's* managers followed) are listed below:[3]

1. Maintain the largest number of job options possible.
2. Do not waste time working for an immobile manager.
3. Become a crucial subordinate to a mobile superior.
4. Always favor increased exposure and visibility.
5. Be prepared to nominate yourself for jobs that come open. Define your corporation as a market of jobs.
6. Leave a company when your career has slowed too much.
7. Rehearse quitting. It is a cruicial act.
8. Do not let success in your present job preempt your career plan. You will stop moving up.

Many of these rules imply that a career plan is only useful to the upwardly mobile. This is not the case. Even though luck is important in career success, any career will be more effective if it is well planned.

Career Planning for Family Business Executives and Entrepreneurs

What about the person who plans to become an entrepreneurial or family business executive? It is a good idea, if possible, for the future family business executive to acquire experience in at least one other firm before entering the family business. Preferably, this should be a successful firm in a similar business in another location. This allows the executive to become successful independently of the family (which is very important psychologically) and provides perspective for the family experience. A good career plan for a future family business executive is to work two to five years in a nonfamily business before entering the family business.

An entrepreneur or future entrepreneur can follow one of two patterns: direct entry or postponed entry. In the most frequent pattern, *postponed entry,* the entrepreneur-to-be works for others for a period of ten years or so before opening her or his own firm. In this pattern the potential entrepreneur learns the business and develops his or her capital (and entrepreneurial plan) while working for another firm in the same business. The entrepreneur builds capital by saving her or his salary and making a believable case with a bank (or friends) in order to be able to borrow the rest later. Many entrepreneurs fail several times before making it. If the capital is used up, the entrepreneur must go back to work for someone else and try again.

In the *direct entry* pattern the entrepreneur borrows from relatives, friends, or businesspeople to start the business directly after finishing school. This is a much less frequent pattern, but with luck the entrepreneur can succeed more quickly using this approach.

Performance Appraisal for Managers

All that was said in Chapter 20 about performance appraisal of employees applies to managers too. Except that the higher the level of the employee, the more difficult it is to measure performance directly and thus the greater the reliance on personality criteria. If a division fails to achieve its budget, is it due to the manager's failure, to the economy's dip, or to increased competition? This question is harder to evaluate—a lot harder to evaluate than whether John Smith made twenty-five baskets or less yesterday (if twenty-five is the standard).

Some of the appraisal techniques used to evaluate managers are the same as those used to evaluate other employees. MBO is one technique for appraising managers that is growing in use. The assessment center discussed previously is another.

Performance appraisal is an important tool in the development and promotion of managers. To earn an exceptional performance appraisal, your management skills must be up-to-date. Management development programs help achieve that goal.

Management Development

Although few firms have career development programs, most medium-size and large firms have management development programs designed to serve the same purposes as the training programs for other employees that were discussed in Chapter 20. In other words, they are designed to prevent obsolescence and to improve productivity and employee satisfaction. In smaller firms, where management development programs are not formally structured, managers are encouraged to keep up-to-date by taking courses at universities or short courses offered by professional associations. As in employee training programs, both on-the-job and off-the-job approaches are used in management development.

On-the-Job Management Development

Firms that have a program of on-the-job development plan a series of ways to develop managers while they are working. Three techniques that are used are (1) coaching and counseling programs, (2) transitional experiences, and (3) rotation and transfer programs.

Coaching and Counseling This technique for on-the-job development is simple enough in theory and can be effective if well run. The manager receives regular coaching and counseling on how to do the superior's job. This makes sense because the manager must do the superior's job when the superior is on vacation, on site visits, or out of the office for some other reason. The superior takes the manager into his or her confidence, shows how the job is done, encourages the manager to make recommendations, and allows the manager to make some of the decisions and handle some of the problems.

For this system to work, the superior must have confidence in the manager's ability and be consultative or participative in leadership style. Also, the enterprise must reward the superior for taking this approach. Many organizations will not promote the superior unless he or she has a well-trained replacement ready to take over. This is one kind of reward system. Another kind is a system of formal rewards (raises, promotions) tied to the development of subordinates. If this latter system is used, the performance appraisal criteria must clearly include development of subordinates as a factor to be evaluated. If managers are not rewarded for developing subordinates, the coaching/counseling system will work primarily when the manager's motivational or social and recognition/esteem needs are satisfied by helping others.

Transitional Experience The second technique listed above for developing managers while they are working is transitional experience. In this method, instead of transferring a superior and appointing a replacement the same day, the enterprise announces the change in advance. For a specified period the manager does the superior's job with the help and advice of the superior. The first time through a difficult experience the superior does the job with the manager watching; then the roles are reversed.

This concentrated, realistic program of coaching and counseling in transition works well when the superior is willing to share his or her methods with the manager, when the superior is knowledgeable, and when an enterprise is willing to expend extra time and money to pay two managers to do the job (for weeks, sometimes months, depending on the level of the job). It also avoids many of the potential problems of coaching and counseling discussed earlier.

Rotation and Transfer The third method is to develop a rotation and transfer program so that all managers who are perceived to have potential for promotion receive a variety of experiences in terms of both function and location.

Off-the-Job Management Development

Many larger and some medium-size organizations try to develop their managers' abilities and attitudes through *company-sponsored* off-the-job courses and conferences. For example, they may establish a program at a university so that executives can receive training or have an opportunity to examine certain attitudes. If it is large enough, the organization's own staff may run these programs, sometimes supplemented by university faculty or consultants.

It is in the firm's interest to have a well-trained and motivated managerial team. Management development is one way of achieving this. Another is a rewarding compensation system.

Compensating Managers

Much of what was said in Chapter 20 about pay and benefits for employees applies to managers too. In this section I will discuss forms of compensation specific to managers. Business managers are rewarded with salaries, bonuses, perquisites, stock options, performance shares, and book value devices.

Salaries Top managers are paid top salaries. Consider, for example, the 1977 salaries (and in some cases bonuses) of the presidents or chief executive officers (CEOs) of the firms listed below:

Rapid American	$916,000
ITT	776,000
Exxon	518,000

And the figures for the total cash remuneration received by the president or chief executive of the following firms are equally impressive:

Halburton	$1,593,000
J. Roy McDermott	1,223,000
White Consolidated	706,000

Most studies have found that the salaries below the CEO level are based on a percentage of the CEO's salary. For example, the second highest executive is usually paid about 71 percent of the CEO's salary in most industries, while the third highest is paid 55 to 60 percent.

Bonuses A bonus is a payment in addition to salary. It can be paid now or in the future. In the latter case, it is called a deferred bonus. The size of bonuses and deferred bonuses varies with the size of the company. The larger the company, the greater is the proportion of bonuses making up total annual compensation.

A majority of large firms pay bonuses on the theory that increased profitability and other advantages will result. Bonuses involve large expenditures of funds. They vary in size from 80 percent of top executives' salaries to 20 percent of the salaries of lowest-level participants.

Perquisites In addition to salaries and bonuses, managers can receive special perquisites and extras ("perks"). Typical perks are: a better office, a good office location, a company car, reserved parking, a car for personal use, and first-class air tickets. Other perks managers may receive are subsidized insurance, free club memberships, a company airplane, subsidized loans, and free or subsidized financial counseling.

Why do managers want perks? In terms of Abraham Maslow's hierarchy of needs, perks fulfill the physiological and especially the recognition needs of the manager. And a company car, club membership, financial counseling, and so on provide the manager with nontaxable income, a factor which is particularly important to those in high tax brackets.

Stock Options and Other Stock-Related Rewards Over the years, firms have also rewarded managers with stock options. A stock option is a right to buy the company's stock below the market price for a set period of time. Because the tax advantages of stock options were recently reduced, new ways of compensating managers who hold or wish to purchase company stock have been developed. Some of these are listed below:

- *Market value purchases* The company lends the manager money at low interest rates to buy company stock at current market value. The manager repays the loan by direct payment or receives credits on the loan payments for staying with the company and/or achieving a performance goal.

- *Book value purchases* The executive is offered a chance to buy the company stock at book value (or some similar nonmarket value measure) but can resell it to the company later, using the same formula price.

- *Exercise bonuses* Payment to the manager when he or she exercises a stock option that is equal to or proportionate to the option gain is called an exercise bonus. This helps the executive keep the stock rather than sell it to pay the taxes on the gain.
- *Performance shares and performance units* Performance shares grant stock units to the manager in the future (such as five years later) if performance targets are met. These units appreciate or depreciate as the stock does. Performance units are performance shares paid in cash instead of stock. The units are compensation unless they are to be used to buy stock.

Staffing for the Entrepreneurial or Family Business

Family businesses and entrepreneurial firms have some unique characteristics with regard to the aspects of staffing I have discussed above. I will consider these briefly here before proceeding to another subject.

When planning for its executive team, the entrepreneurial/family firm will use the tools of similar-sized managerial firms. An additional consideration for these firms, however, is the extent to which the family will supply executives for the firm. This aspect must be planned, especially if the family wishes continuity or wants always to have family members in certain key positions. Sometimes few or no family members are interested in the firm. This often happens when the grandchildren or great-grandchildren of the founder are due to take charge. In such cases the family may pressure some of its members to enter management.

A more frequent and more difficult problem arises when there are more family members who wish to manage the firm than there are positions available. Usually the firm tries to maintain a balance between family and nonfamily executives. If there are four family members interested in two positions, some difficult personal and political decisions must be made. Often these decisions are made in family councils.

Sometimes the decisions are based on abilities alone. In other cases trade-offs develop. For example, if one branch of the family has furnished an executive fairly recently, the other branch is given a "turn." Such decisions can play havoc with family relationships. Sometimes they can be institutionalized to prevent difficulty. At *Sunset*, one brother runs the magazine, the other the book company. But what happens when their children decide to enter the business?

Often such problems are handled by education. One heir is urged to become a lawyer and head one end of the business; another is urged to get an M.B.A. in marketing. Or one child is designated to run the business, another given stock but encouraged to become an independent professional.

The career paths of family executives are different too. Although a family member may start in the mail room and rotate through jobs like other trainees, it is clear to most employees that better things await him or her. Just as Prince Charles is given a series of minor ceremonial duties to prepare him to be King of England, so the family executive is oriented and developed in such a way that he or she will be ready to take over at the appropriate time.

It is obvious that a family executive is evaluated differently. Evaluation by his or her superior is less important than how the family executives view his or her progress. This is complicated by personal relations within the family: "You know, I never liked cousin George when we went to St. Paul's together." It is not always pleasant to be evaluated in this way.

Finally, the compensation of family executives differs significantly from that of nonfamily executives. Perhaps the family executive is paid more than similar managers. More likely, the compensation includes in addition to pay and benefits, partial payment in voting stock of the concern, in amounts and combinations that are usually carefully planned by tax lawyers and accountants. This, again, may be complicated by family politics. Should the family members be treated "equally" even if one makes a greater contribution to the enterprise's success? Who gets control of the firm? Alliances can be formed to dislodge a relative who is generally disliked. In short, sometimes it is almost impossible to separate family and business life.

In the above sections I have discussed most of the ways firms manage managerial resources. I wish to turn now to a consideration of three key human problems or challenges a manager may have to meet: maintaining good health, adjusting to life with a spouse who also has a career, and coping with the mid-life crisis.

Maintaining Managerial Health

What you do at work affects your health, how long you live, and how you live. Meyer Friedman and Ray Rosenman suggest that heart attacks are caused *not* by lack of exercise, *not* by cholesterol, *not* by cigarette smoking, but by behavior patterns (including behavior at work).[4] And as you know, more Americans die of heart attacks than of any other cause. Lengthy studies by these researchers led to the characterization of two types of managerial personalities, Type A and Type B, given in Table 21.4. According to Friedman and Rosenman, if you are or become a Type A, you will have a heart attack in your 30s or 40s, not in your 70s. Type A behavior is partly a matter of personality and partly a result of the way some enterprises work. If you want to live longer and if the enterprise wants your services longer, examine the Type A checklist and determine what you must do to modify your behavior. Enterprise personnel policies can be adjusted to help managers become Type B's—successful, healthy individuals—as shown in the Type B checklist.

Table 21.4
Characteristics of
Type A and Type B
Managers

Type A Characteristics	Type B Characteristics
•You *always* move, walk, and eat rapidly.	•You are completely free of Type A characteristics.
•You feel impatient with the pace of things. You almost cannot restrain yourself from hurrying others.	•You never suffer from a sense of impatience or urgency.
•You do several things at once. For example, you listen to someone else while thinking about another matter.	•When you play, you do so for fun, not to exhibit your superiority.
•You feel vaguely guilty when you relax or do nothing for several hours or days.	•You relax without guilt and work without agitation.
•You attempt to schedule more and more in less and less time. You have a chronic sense of urgency.	•You feel no need to display your superiority or discuss your accomplishments.
•When meeting another "A," you want to challenge him or her.	
•You believe you are successful because you do things faster than others.	
•You evaluate everything in terms of numbers.	
•You use "Type A" nervous gestures (clench fist, bang hand on table, etc.).	
•You always bring the conversation around to topics that interest you.	
•You express the last few words of a sentence much more rapidly than the first few words, and you overlap and accentuate key words more than necessary.	
•You do not have time to enjoy life.	

Source: Meyer Friedman and Ray Rosenman, *Type A Behavior and Your Heart* (New York: Knopf, 1974). Reprinted by permission.

Managing Stress[5]

We have explored the manager's world presenting the human aspects which individuate each manager and the skills such as communication skills the manager uses; the processes involved in planning, organizing, and controlling the firm; and the leadership styles and influences which make up the managerial role. All the factors, processes, techniques, and influences which operate within the organization define the manager's environment, and they all have one crucial impact on the manager—stress.

Hans Selye, the most prominent researcher in this area, defines *stress* as the nonspecific response of the body to any demand.[6] The body is constantly adapting to stress-producing factors by changes in its structure and chemical composition. In that sense, stress-producing factors are not necessarily negative. In fact, much current research sees them as a positive challenge to many successful managers. The need to achieve and the rewards gained from meeting deadlines are for these individuals an impetus to do their best. Some companies are starting to recognize that reducing stress may not be in the best interests of these individuals.

But some managers cannot handle stress-producing factors well. For these individuals, they represent a failure of routine methods for handling threats and can result in maladaptive behavior.

The causes of stress lie inside the individual and in the organization. Look back over the things you have learned about the individual. If the needs, attitudes, emotional makeup, and personality do not match the particular demands of the position, the individual will experience stress. Life events also can change a person's ability to cope with a previously satisfactory situation. Experiences such as the death of a spouse, divorce, marital separation, personal illness or injury mean an individual must exert more effort to adapt effectively to everyday job-related, stress-producing factors.

The organization also pressures individual managers and employees. This can have a negative impact on both the achievement of the firm's objectives and meeting the individual's needs. Because stress in these instances involves an inability to cope, it must be dealt with in a defensive manner. Stress-producing factors related to the organization include lack of role clarity; work overload; conflicting, incomplete and/or confusing communications; and underutilization of abilities, interpersonal or group conflict, mental strain, poor planning and controlling techniques. Unstable, fast-changing goals and technologies also cause stress.

What are the results of an inability to tolerate stress-producing factors? It can result in apathy, job dissatisfaction, depression, physical illness or accident, or even in violent acts directed against the organization. The stress resulting from an inner conflict between the manager's or employee's needs for efficiency, profit, productivity, and self-actualization can result in emotional strain and feelings of futility. Symptoms of stress to look for in yourself and others include departure from characteristic patterns of action and interactions that are erratic with regard to volume, direction, and content. For example, feeling overly tired when you are normally an energetic person may mean you are encountering more stress than you can cope with.

How can the negative effects of stress be minimized? The organization can take several steps, including those listed below:

- Introduce new criteria for selection and placement to screen out individuals who are prone to stress.
- Use the screening to match the individual with a position having the optimal level of stress-producing factors.
- Set up training programs to teach individuals how to cope with job-related stress.
- Work to minimize and control role ambiguity, poor planning techniques, and other stress-producing factors in the organization.

The individual can use several methods for coping with stress:

- Noncompetitive physical exercise programs
- Transcendental meditation

- Transactional analysis
- Encounter groups
- Biofeedback
- Behavior modification
- Psychotherapy

As a manager, you can help subordinates cope with stress by nonevaluative listening, frequent feedback about job performance, eliminating role conflict and role ambiguity, and making job demands compatible with subordinates' needs and capabilities.

In sum, stress-producing factors can add spice to your job as a manager. Or they can be a threat to your career and your well-being. You must learn to evaluate your own and your employees' capacity to handle stress and must realize that there will be times when this capacity is modified by both individual and organizational stressors.

Dual Career Couples

As is often pointed out, work life overlaps with personal life. Indeed, just as problems and aspects of the manager's work life can cause stress and affect his or her health and performance on the job, so can factors in the manager's personal life. One challenge that arises more and more often in managers' personal lives is that of finding a life-style and way of managing a career that make it possible to maintain a satisfactory long-term relationship with a life partner, usually a spouse, who also has a career.

Each year the percentage of the labor force made up of women increases. In the past there were a few managers whose wives had separate careers. But it was assumed that the wife's career was secondary to the husband's and that if he was transferred, she went along.

Today we see more couples like the Lawrences. Harding Lawrence is president of Braniff Airways. Mary Lawrence is president of Wells, Rich and Company. We also find dual career couples like these:

- *Mary and John* Mary is a manager for a large retail firm. John is a college professor.
- *Howard and Sally* Howard is a manager for an insurance company. Sally is the head nurse at a local hospital.
- *Jerri and Sandy* Jerri is a lawyer working for a large corporation. Sandy is a manager for another corporation.
- *Bob and Marlyn* Bob and Marlyn are both executives with one firm. (*Business Week* recently reported many examples like Bob and Marlyn.)

This pattern is relatively new. When it first appeared, there was a gloomy prognosis. As Homai Madani and Cary L. Cooper point out, the predictors forecast high stress, messed up marriages, and confused children of such marriages. Although for some couples this has come true, Madani and Cooper's summary of the research indicates that most marriages are strengthened when both partners have careers and that the children are changed but not necessarily for the worse.[7]

Francine S. Hall and Douglas T. Hall are a dual career couple. They have studied the phenomenon extensively.[8] Their findings indicate that partners must make accommodations if the relationship is to be lasting and that some do not. Generally, partners in a successful dual career relationship display the following characteristics:

- They have a mutual commitment to both careers and see themselves as a working team.
- They have a willingness to consider alternative careers if one partner is transferred.
- They develop family goals and set priorities between family and career goals.
- They are flexible in their career timetables.
- They are expert in time management and have high energy levels to keep the relationship, household, and both careers going.

Too often, organizations' human resource management policies work to the disadvantage of the partners in dual career couples. Effective firms are now beginning to adjust their personnel policies to make better use of the resources these individuals offer. Some of the changes that are necessary are:

- The reduction and/or elimination of nepotism rules. The only rule necessary is that one partner must not report to or work for the other.
- A willingness to expand counseling services to include dual career counseling.
- The development of clear conflict of interest rules for partners in dual career couples who work for competitors.
- A change in benefit programs to avoid unnecessary duplication between partners. The ideal is a cafeteria approach to benefits.
- Sensitive recruiting and a willingness to help find a position for the applicant's partner. This may involve joint job offer bargaining.
- A willingness to schedule career changes and promotions flexibly in consideration of both partners' needs.
- Adaptibility in the amount of travel required for jobs.
- Flexibility in transfers and relocation.

The last item in this list is the most difficult issue in adjusting organizational policy to accommodate dual career couples. Few enterprises have faced up to it yet. Still, dual career couples have successfully used a number of approaches in coping with this problem. In some cases, both partners have declared that they absolutely will not move. Using another approach, managers have asked for and sometimes been given career paths other than the old transfer system. In other cases, managers have made a condition of their acceptance of a transfer that their partners find a suitable position in the new location. Sometimes the transferring company has helped relocate the partner. Though the process is slow, old rules like "you move when we tell you, where we tell you, or your future is zero with us" are being modified.

Managing the Mid-Life Crisis

For many persons, the period between ages thirty-five and forty-three is an unstable, troubled time. Since we spend most of our waking hours at work, this condition sometimes manifests itself in the workplace more than at home. It is important for managers to understand this mid-life crisis because it helps them understand their superiors' problems, their parents' problems, and a period that they will experience themselves.

The great Italian poet Dante wrote, "Midway on the path of life I found myself in a dark woods." He expressed the mid-life crisis well. Studies indicate that everyone or almost everyone in the work force experiences the mid-life crisis. Researches at the Menninger Clinic and the California Institute of Technology have found that they have all experienced it. Lee Stockford of the California Institute of Technology has found that five out of six managers and professionals experience it and that one out of six never recover. Experts point out that although it is frequently denied, it is necessary to experience this crisis. Otherwise the person feels weighed down and does not go through the later phases of life effectively.

What is the mid-life crisis like? In a word, *depression*. This does not mean merely "feeling down." This depression leads to insomnia and vulnerability to illnesses. In the more serious cases it leads to abandonment of one's career, alcoholism, mental illness, marital difficulties, divorce, and suicide. The mid-life crisis is likely to be most serious when the person is under job stress and is vulnerable because of problems at home, and when the job or economic environment is antagonistic. The individual experiencing the least severe form of a mid-life crisis has trouble concentrating on and doing the job well and can find no meaning in the job or in life itself.

How does the mid-life crisis hit managers? Four sets of factors seem to come together at this period. Each can set off the crisis and each reinforces the others to make it worse.

Problems in Personal Life At age forty a person is at least halfway through life (the American male tends to live sixty-seven to seventy-two years, the female a few years longer). At this point the manager realizes that he or she is on the down-side, especially since his or her parents may die during this period. The manager's children begin to leave home, and marital problems may develop. Aging has set in: vision becomes less sharp; hair grays and/or thins; weight is hard to lose; sexual activity declines. The fact of human mortality becomes abundantly clear.

Broken Dreams Most of us, but especially managers, have dreams or expectations of reaching certain job, status, and money goals. Rarely are these dreams or expectations met. Often these goals are set to be reached by age forty. But they are rarely met, because the more ambitious a person is, the higher the goals and the harder it is to reach them. So the manager suddenly realizes that he or she "didn't make it." Feelings of failure arise, and the manager asks, "What's the use?" These feelings are compounded when the manager compares himself or herself to the *few* people who have achieved much more, a very unfavorable comparison indeed.

Broken Relationships Many managers receive help during their early years from a mentor—an executive higher up in the hierarchy. This relationship tends to be broken at this stage because the mentor is older and less influential or perhaps retired. It may also be broken when the manager decides that "it's time I grow up and achieve on my own." This break has been compared by psychiatrists with the break from one's parents. Thus the mid-life crisis may be considered a second painful adolescence.

The Competition Seems Worse Job competition seems especially tough at this stage. Everyone seems to be after your job. There is a terrible feeling of rivalry, the feeling that you have no friends and must constantly defend yourself and your job. In many companies this feeling may be compounded by the naming of a younger president. If the new president is forty-one and you are forty-two, what future do you have?

Overcoming the Mid-Life Crisis

The first step toward overcoming the crisis is awareness. This should be coupled with the realization that for the majority who survive the crisis, although life (and work) is different, it is not over. After Dante went through the dark woods he wrote his masterpiece, *The Divine Comedy*. In a few fields (notably the sciences) major contributions are made before age forty. But in most jobs, including management, a person's highest output comes during his or her forties.

In addition to facing the crisis, managers should be aware that life will be different. Erik Erikson points out that after the crisis the dominant mode becomes caring.[9] The manager's leadership style begins to change. He or she becomes a mentor. (The enterprise can help managers overcome the mid-life crisis by offering management development programs that emphasize updating and mentor skills such as counseling. Also, the enterprise should build in opportunities for discussing the manager's feelings during performance appraisal and should provide other counseling opportunities.)

The manager's personal life should be enriched by "renegotiating" and renewing the marriage and making new and closer personal friendships. Almost all research indicates that we survive life's traumas better with friends. People without friends literally die of loneliness—sometimes immediately, but in most cases a little at a time.

The mid-life crisis is serious. But with the right steps it can be conquered, and the manager can go on to a very rewarding life.

In summary, a career in the management of a corporation, a family business, or an entrepreneurship can be more rewarding if the manager plans the career and develops it according to plan. Yet as I have indicated in this final chapter, it is also vital to career success that the manager be aware of significant challenges and problems that may arise and know some ways to deal with them.

Summary

A *managerial career* is a sequential set of work roles or jobs in an enterprise or a series of enterprises. This chapter has discussed how a firm develops a managerial team, how you as a manager should plan your career, and some of the challenges you will face.

The managerial recruiting and selection process is somewhat similar to that of other employees. Inside recruitment involves the use of skills inventories and recommendations of other managers within the firm. Major external sources of recruits are college placement offices, professional meetings, executive search firms, and want ads in major newspapers and professional journals.

Criteria for selection are based on successful managers in the firm, although evaluating what makes successful managers is more difficult than evaluating success criteria for lower-level employees. The employment interview, application blank, and reference checks, supplemented by the assessment center at larger firms, are the tools of selection. Successful applicants sell themselves through résumés, letters of recommendation, personal appearance, and other forms of advertising.

The most effective management orientation programs are short, use on-the-job training, minimize classroom teaching, encourage high expectations in trainees, and provide trainees with frequent feedback on their progress. Problems facing new managers such as anxiety and expectations that are too high can be overcome with a good orientation program.

Most firms do not offer these career planning programs, so it is the individual's responsibility to develop his or her own career plan. Career planning consists of the six steps presented in Figure 21.2. Remember that career planning does not guarantee success, but it allows you to take advantage of circumstances.

Performance appraisal is an important tool in the evaluation, development, and promotion of managers. Some of the appraisal techniques used for managers are the same as those used for other types of employees. MBO and the assessment center are additional appraisal tools.

Most medium-size and large firms have management development programs which are training programs for managers. Both on-the-job and off-the-job approaches are used. On-the-job techniques include coaching and counseling programs, transitional experiences, and rotation and transfer programs. Off-the-job techniques include courses and conferences to develop managerial abilities and attitudes.

The salaries of top managers are high. Good managers are rewarded with salaries, bonuses, perquisites, stock options, performance shares, and book value devices.

The staffing process for the management team of the entrepreneurial or family business firm relies on the same tools used by managerial firms of similar size. However, the extent to which the family will supply executives for the firm is an additional and sometimes problematic consideration.

As a manager you will face personal problems linked to career challenges. Maintaining health, coping with stress, being a partner in a dual career couple, and meeting the mid-life crisis are some of the career-related challenges a manager faces.

Friedman and Roseman found two managerial personality types: Type A and Type B. Type A individuals are prone to heart attack in their thirties or forties.

The problems associated with individual and organizational stress are closely related to the problem of maintaining good health. Some managers see stress as a positive challenge and companies are starting to recognize that reducing stress for these individuals may not be in their best interests. In others, the inability to tolerate stress can result in apathy, job dissatisfaction, depression, physical illness or accidents, even violent acts against the organization.

Another problem many managers face is coordinating their careers with their personal relationships. Dual career couples are an increasing phenomenon as each year the percentage of women in the work force increases.

The period between ages thirty-five and forty-three can be an unstable, troubled time. It is at this time that the mid-life crisis, a form of depression, occurs. This crisis is likely to be most serious when the person is under job stress and is vulnerable because of problems at home, and when the job or economic environment is antagonistic. Specifically this crisis centers on problems in personal life, broken dreams, broken relationships, and the perception of increased competition.

This completes our consideration of management and the managerial career. An appendix has been added to the text to give you an idea of what a managerial career would be like in the public and not-for-profit sectors.

Questions

1. What is a managerial career? Describe how managers are recruited.
2. What methods are used in the managerial selection decision? What approach will you use to get the job of your choice?
3. How important is a manager's orientation experience to his or her early success on the job? What part does the supervisor play in this orientation?
4. Why should you bother to plan your career?
5. Describe some methods of evaluating and improving managerial performance. Why is it more difficult to appraise managerial performance?
6. Describe typical on-the-job and off-the-job management development techniques.
7. How are managers compensated? How does compensation affect managerial motivation?
8. In what ways do entrepreneurship and family business personnel practices differ from others?
9. In what ways does work influence a manager's health? How can a manager reduce the possibility of a heart attack?
10. If both spouses have careers, how do they come to grips with conflicts in their career progress? How can organizations help such couples?
11. What problems will you face at the mid-life crisis? How can you deal with these?

Notes

[1] "Plotting a Route to the Top," *Business Week*, October 12, 1974, pp. 127–130, 132 ff.

[2] Association of MBA Executives, *The Master of Business Administration* (1975).

[3] Eugene Jennings, "Success Chess," *Management of Personnel Quarterly* 9 (Fall 1970): 2–8.

[4] Meyer Friedman and Ray Rosenman, *Type A Behavior and Your Heart* (New York: Knopf, 1974).

[5] This section was researched and coauthored by Jean Hanebury.

[6] Hans Selye, *The Stress of Life* (New York: McGraw-Hill, 1978).

[7] Homai Madani and Cary L. Cooper, "The Impact of Dual Career Family Development on Organisational Life," *Management Decision* 15 (November–December 1977): 487–493.

[8] Francine S. Hall and Douglas T. Hall, "Dual Careers: How Do Couples and Companies Cope with the Problems?" *Organizational Dynamics* 6 (Spring 1978): 57–77.

[9] Erik Erikson, *Adulthood: Essays* (New York: Norton, 1978).

References

Some of the sections of this chapter are based on my *Foundations of Personnel* (Dallas: Business Publications, 1979).

Recruiting and Selecting Managers

Orlando Behling and Henry Rodkin, "How College Students Find Jobs," *Personnel Administration* 32 (September–October 1969): 39–42. John P. Campbell et al., *Managerial Behavior, Performance, and Effectiveness* (New York: McGraw-Hill, 1970). Edwin Ghiselli, *Explorations in Managerial Talent* (Pacific Palisades, Calif.: Goodyear, 1971). William Glueck, "Decision Making: Organization Choice," *Personnel Psychology* 27 (Spring 1974): 77–93. Robert Simison, "Sifting Seniors," *Wall Street Journal*, March 30, 1977.

Orientation Programs for New Managers

Joan Holland and Theodore Curtis, "Orientation of New Employees," in *Handbook of Modern Personnel Administration*, ed. Joseph Famularo (New York: McGraw-Hill, 1972), chapter 23. Daniel Ilgen and William Seeley, "Realistic Expectations as an Aid in Reducing Voluntary Resignations," *Journal of Applied Psychology* 59 (August 1974): 452. Ronald Pilengo, "Placement by Objectives," *Personnel Journal* 52 (September 1973): 804–810. Edgar H. Schein, "How to Break in the College Graduate," *Harvard Business Review* 42 (November–December 1964): 68–76. John Van Maanen, "Breaking In: Socialization to Work," in *Handbook of Work, Organization, and Society*, ed. Robert Dubin (Chicago: Rand McNally, 1976). John Wanous, "Organizational Entry: From Naive Expectations to Realistic Belief," *Journal of Applied Psychology* 61 (February 1976): 22–29.

Practical Application: The Young Manager's Career Problems

Melville Dalton, *Men Who Manage* (New York: Wiley, 1961). M. L. Moore et al., "Predictors of Managerial Career Expectations," *Journal of Applied Psychology* 59 (February 1974): 90–92. Victor Phillips, Jr., *The Organizational Role of the Assistant To* (New York: American Management Association, 1971). L. B. Ward and Anthony Athos, *Student Expectations of Corporate Life* (Cambridge, Mass.: Harvard Business School, 1972). Abraham Zaleznik, "Power and Politics in Organizational Life," *Harvard Business Review* 48 (May–June 1970): 47–60.

Career Planning and Development

Theodore Alfred, "Checkers or Choice in Manpower Management," *Harvard Business Review* 45 (January–February 1967): 157–169. Association of MBA Executives, *The Master of Business Administration* (1975). Howard Becker and Anselm Strauss, "Careers, Personality, and Adult Socialization," *American Journal of Sociology* 62 (November 1956): 253–263. Richard Bolles, *What Color Is Your Parachute?* (Berkeley: Ten Speed Press, 1972). Donald Crane, "An Experimental Program in Career Planning," *Proceedings of the Academy of Management* (1975). Gene W. Dalton, Paul H. Thompson, and Raymond L. Price, "The Four Stages of Professional Careers: A New Look at Performance by Professionals," *Organizational Dynamics* 6 (Summer 1977): 19–42. Lawrence Ferguson, "Better Management of Managers' Careers," *Harvard Business Review* 44 (March–April 1966): 139–152. John Fernandez, *Black Managers in White Corporations* (New York: Wiley, 1975). William F. Glueck, "Career Management of Managerial, Professional, and Technical Personnel," in *Manpower Planning and Programming,* ed. Elmer Burack and James Walker (Boston: Allyn & Bacon, 1972), pp. 239–255. Benedetto Greco, *How to*

Get the Job That's Right for You (Homewood, Ill.: Dow Jones–Irwin, 1975). Thomas Gutteridge, "The Hardest Job of All: Career Planning," *MBA* 7 (October 1973): 19–23. Bernard Haldane, *Career Satisfaction and Success: A Guide to Job Freedom* (New York: American Management Association, 1974). Margaret Higginson and Thomas Quick, *The Ambitious Woman's Guide to a Successful Career* (New York: AMACOM, 1975). Theodore A. Jackson, "Turned Off by Your Job? Knowing Yourself Is Essential," *Industry Week*, February 12, 1973, pp. 54–57. Eugene Jennings, "Success Chess," *Management of Personnel Quarterly* 9 (Fall 1970): 2–8. Michael L. Johnson, "Plan Your Career—Or Wing It?" *Industry Week*, September 30, 1974, pp. 32–37. Marion Kellogg, *Career Management* (New York: American Management Association, 1972). Rosalind Loring and Theodora Wells, *Breakthrough: Women into Management* (New York: Van Nostrand Rheinhold, 1972). Edith Lynch, *The Executive Suite: Feminine Style* (New York: AMACOM, 1973). David Moment and Dalmar Fisher, *Autonomy in Organizational Life* (Cambridge, Mass.: Schenkman, 1975). Robert F. Pearse, *Manager to Manager II: What Managers Think of Their Managerial Careers* (New York: AMACOM, 1977). "Plotting a Route to the Top," *Business Week*, October 12, 1974, pp. 127–130, 132 ff. Alan Schoonmaker, *Executive Career Strategy* (New York: American Management Association, 1971). Charles Vance, *Manager Today, Executive Tomorrow* (New York: McGraw-Hill, 1974).

Performance Appraisal for Managers

James Goodale and Ronald Burke, "BARS Need Not Be Job Specific," *Journal of Applied Psychology* 60 (June 1975): 389–391. Ronald Grey and David Kipnis, "Untangling the Performance Appraisal Dilemma: The Influence of Perceived Organizational Context on Evaluative Processes," *Journal of Applied Psychology* 61 (June 1976): 329–335. Alan Locher and Kenneth Teel, "Performance Appraisal: A Survey of Current Practices," *Personnel Journal* 56 (May 1977): 345–354. Joseph Moses et al., "Standards and Ethical Considerations for Assessment Center Operations" (Paper delivered at the Third International Congress on the Assessment Center Method, Quebec, May 1975). Patricia Smith, "Behaviors, Results, and Organizational Effectiveness," in *Handbook of Industrial and Organizational Psychology*, ed. Marvin Dunnette (Chicago: Rand McNally, 1976). Paul H. Thompson and Gene W. Dalton, "Performance Appraisal: Managers Beware," *Harvard Business Review* 48 (January–February 1970): 149–157. Robert Zawacki and Robert Taylor, "A View of Performance Appraisal from Organizations Using It," *Personnel Journal* 55 (June 1976): 290–292, 299 ff.

Management Development

Robert Blake and Jane Mouton, *Critique* (Austin, Tex.: Scientific Methods, 1976). David Casey and David Pearce, eds., *More than Management Development* (New York: AMACOM, 1977). Donald Ely and John Morse, "TA and Reinforcement Theory," *Personnel* 51 (March–April 1974): 38–41. Charles H. Kepner and Benjamin B. Tregoe, *The Rational Manager* (New York: McGraw-Hill, 1965). Newton Margulies and Anthony Raia, *Conceptual Foundations of Organization Development* (New York: McGraw-Hill, 1978). Jack Rettig and Matt Amano, "A Survey of ASPA Experience with Management by Objectives, Sensitivity Training and Transactional Analysis," *Personnel Journal* 55 (January 1976): 26–29. H. Stanley Steelman, "Is There a Payoff to OD?" *Training and Development Journal* 30 (April 1976): 18–23. George Strauss, "Organization Development," in *Handbook of Work, Organization and Society*, ed. Robert Dubin (Chicago: Rand McNally, 1976).

Compensating Managers

John Deardon, "How to Make Incentive Plans Work," *Harvard Business Review* 50 (July–August 1972): 117–124. Stanley Nealey, "Compensation Fungibility," *Proceedings of* the *Industrial Relations Research Association* (1977): 154–159. Paul Robert, *Employee Benefits Factbook* (New York: Martin Segal, 1976). Robert Pitts, "Incentive Compensation and Organization Design," *Personnel Journal* 53 (May 1974): 338–344, 348 ff. Robert Sbarra, "The New Language of Executive Compensation," *Personnel* 52 (November–December 1975): 10–18. "Special Privileges," *Wall Street Journal*, September 18, 1975. U.S. Chamber of Commerce, annual surveys on fringe benefits published in *Nation's Business*, U.S. Department of Labor Statistics. Marc Wallace, "Type of Control, Industrial Concentration and Executive Pay," *Proceedings of the Academy of Management* (1976).

Maintaining Managerial Health

Herbert Benson, "Your Innate Asset for Combating Stress," *Harvard Business Review* 52 (July–August 1974): 49–60. Meyer Friedman and Ray Rosenman, *Type A Behavior and Your Heart* (New York: Knopf, 1974). Harry Levinson et al., *Men, Management, and Mental Health* (Cambridge, Mass.: Harvard University Press, 1966). Herbert Meyer, "The Boss Ought to Take More Time Off," *Fortune*, June 1974, pp. 140–142, 229–230 ff.

Managing Stress

Robert Albanese, *Managing: Toward Accountability for Performance* (Homewood, Ill.: Richard D. Irwin, 1978), chapter 13. Clifton D. Bryant, *The Social Dimensions of Work* (Englewood Cliffs, N.J.: Prentice–Hall, 1972). Andrew J. Du Brin, *Human Relations: A Job Related Approach* (Reston, Va.: Reston, 1978), chapter 4. "Executive Stress May Not Be All Bad," *Business Week,* April 30, 1979, pp. 96–103. David R. Frew, *Management of Stress* (Chicago: Nelson-Hall, 1977). James Gavin and Jeffrey Greenhaus, "Organizational Tenure, Work Environment Perceptions, and Employee Mental Health," *Journal of Vocational Behavior* 8 (April 1976): 247–258. Edward Gross, "Work, Organization, and Stress," in *Social Stress*, ed. Sol Levine and Norman Scotch (Chicago: Aldine, 1970), chapter 3. David R. Hampton, Charles E. Summer, and Ross A. Webber, *Organizational Behavior and the Practice of Management* (Glenview, Ill.: Scott, Foresman, 1973). Ari Kiev, *A Strategy for Handling Executive Stress* (Chicago: Nelson-Hall, 1974). Richard A. Morano, "How to Manage Change to Reduce Stress," *Management Review* 66 (November 1977): 21–25. Hans Selye, *The Stress of Life* (New York: McGraw-Hill, 1978). Kurt R. Student, "Changing Values and Management Stress," *Personnel* 54 (January–February 1977): 48–55. Ogden Tanner, *Stress* (Alexandria, Va.: Time-Life, 1976).

Dual Career Couples

Lotte Bailyn, "Career and Family Orientations of Husbands and Wives in Relation to Marital Happiness," *Human Relations* 23 (April 1970): 97–113. Mary Bralove, "Working Partners," *Wall Street Journal*, May 13, 1975. R. Paul Duncan and Carolyn Cummings Perrucci, "Dual Occupation Families and Migration," *American Sociological Review* 41 (April 1976): 252–261. Michael Fogarty et al., *Sex, Career, and Family* (London: Allen and Unwin, 1971). Max Gunther, "Your Wife Is None of Your Company's Business," *True*, January 1970. David Hacker, "Where Couples Learn to Mix Job and Family," *Wall Street Journal*, April 20, 1974. Francine S. Hall and Douglas T. Hall, "Dual Careers: How Do Couples and Companies Cope with the Problems?" *Organizational Dynamics* 6 (Spring 1978): 57–77. Lois Hoffman and Ivan Nye, *Working Mothers* (San Francisco: Jossey Bass, 1975). Linda Holstrom, *The Two Career Family* (Cambridge, Mass.: Schenkman, 1973). Homai Madani and Cary L. Cooper, "The Impact of Dual Career Family Development on Organisational Life," *Management Decision* 15 (November–December 1977): 487–493. John Schermerhorn, Jr., et al., "Women in Management," *Proceedings of the Academy of Management* (1975). Robert Seidenberg, *Corporate Wives: Corporate Casualties* (New York: AMACOM, 1973). Alfred Stoess, "Conformity Behavior of Managers and Their Wives," *Academy of Management Journal* 16 (September 1973): 433–441. Harry Wellbank et al., "Planning Job Progression for Effective Career Development and Human Resources Management," *Personnel* 55 (March–April 1978): 54–64.

Managing the Mid-Life Crisis

Erik Erikson, *Adulthood: Essays* (New York: Norton, 1978). "Executives and the Mid-Life Crisis," *Dun's Review* 105 (June 1975): 48–51. Barbara Fried, *The Middle Age Crisis* (New York: Harper & Row, 1976). Emmanuel Kay, *The Crisis in Middle Management* (New York: AMACOM, 1974). Harry Levinson, "On Being a Middle Aged Manager," *Harvard Business Review* 47 (July–August 1969): 51–60. Robert Pearse and Purdy Pelzer, *Self-Directed Change for the Mid-Career Manager* (New York: AMACOM, 1975).

Exercise

Your Career Plan

Complete this career planning guide for yourself.

List your career objectives:

1. *Title (by year)*
2. *Salary (by year)*
3. *Number of people supervised (by year)*
4. *Colleagues (type desired)*

List your comparative advantages:

1. *Education*
Courses (be specific)
Grades (be specific)
Skills developed

2. *Experience*

	Jobs Held	Time in Job	Skills Developed
A.			
B.			
C.			
D.			

Summary (variety, relevance of jobs to job sought)

3. *Personality*
Interpersonal skills (be specific)
Ambitions
Leadership (style and ability)
4. *Contacts/references by level*
A.
B.
C.
D.

List the characteristics of the job you want:
1. *Size of enterprise (small, medium, large)*
2. *Location*
3. *Sector (profit, nonprofit, public)*
4. *Industries (in order of preference)*
Future of Industry Good, Average, Poor
A.
B.
C.
D.
E.
5. *Manager, entrepreneur, or family business executive*
6. *Amount of responsibility (great, average, low)*
7. *Amount of variety (great, average, low)*
8. *Amount of money (great, average, low)*
9. *Other*

List the firms that fit the above characteristics (in order of preference):
1.
2.
3.
4.

List the kinds of jobs at these firms that you can realistically fill now (in order of preference):
1.
2.
3.
4.

Prepare a job-seeking strategy to get Job 1 at Firm 1.

Case for Part Seven

Progress Industries, Inc.

Progress Industries, Inc., is a medium-size manufacturing plant in a small town in central Illinois. Progress was established in 1922 and has since been producing products primarily made of sheet metal. These products are of two general types and result in two divisions in the company.

These divisions are the tank division and the funeral products division. The tank division is the larger of the two, having approximately two hundred hourly or nonsalaried employees, while the funeral division employs approximately 100 people. The tank division produces truck tanks and trailers, which are made of mild steel, stainless steel, or aluminum, depending on their intended use, and also produces fertilizer tanks. The funeral division manufactures caskets made of copper, bronze, and steel and also does some burial vault work.

The factory is departmentalized on a basis of the different processes which are necessary in the production of the tanks or caskets and also by type of tank. Each department has a separate function to perform. Each of these departments is managed directly by a foreman, the duties of whom will be explained later.

Progress is located in a small farming community where it is the main industry and employs a large percentage of the labor force. Workers are drawn also from neighboring small towns within a twenty mile radius. Major competition for industrial workers comes from the large surrounding cities of Mattoon, Decatur, and Champaign, which are twenty-five, thirty-five, and forty miles away, respectively.

The plant is a union shop represented by the International Union of Operating Engineers, AFL-CIO. There is presently a three year contract in effect which expires June 10, 1980.

Wallace Dicks, vice-president of operations, recognizes that Progress has had more than its share of problems. It has been constantly plagued by low productivity but always seems to make a profit. This profit has not necessarily been a result of good management, but rather of the low labor expenses incurred. "There is a trade-off between these wages and productivity; however the total expense per unit produced probably works out the same. That is, poor wages play a part in the poor productivity of workers; therefore they will take longer to accomplish a task."

One of the other factors that must be considered is turnover. There is cost when new people must constantly be trained to replace people who quit. Progress management realizes that it must strive to make the quality worker stay with the company. The company must meet workers' needs, if it hopes to get many years of service from them.

At Progress, for the fiscal year from October 1976 to September 1977, the rate of employee turnover was 57 percent. This is the figure for factory workers alone, many of whom were high labor grade (long-term and experienced) employees. In addition to this, Progress has lost the following key individuals during the last twenty months:

- 2 vice-presidents
- 3 division managers
- 3 plant superintendents
- 3 assistant plant superintendents
- 7 foremen

Also lost during this period were a sales manager, an engineer, a data processing supervisor, a personnel manager, an invoice clerk, and two experienced truck drivers. Five of these positions had to be filled with inexperienced people from outside the firm. Some of the people who left felt their jobs with Progress were not fulfilling their needs any longer. This concerned Dicks, who stated, "The company wants its product to be of high quality, produced with few mistakes and as little labor time as possible. Therefore, the management must strive to show workers how, if they produce in this manner, they will be provided with some type of goal or need satisfaction."

One of the production workers in the shop noted that the hourly employees felt that "the company really doesn't care about our welfare." This feeling was only evident in a department where the foreman was younger and did genuinely care about the workers. The workers there recognized the foreman's concern for them and seemed to appreciate it but still had a negative feeling about the "company," or upper-level management. For them, the job became a tiresome task and in many cases was just a source of income until a better job could be found. According to one employee, "It takes more than just a handshake from the president and a Christmas bonus to make someone feel appreciated, and this is the extent of the management's efforts at Progress."

Progress appears to use money as a primary motivational device. The company is not known for its high wage scale, and raises in pay of the average factory worker have seldom exceeded twenty cents per hour at a given time. Exhibit 1 shows the labor grade system in the union agreement and the accompanying rates of pay.

Labor grades are offered upon request of the foreman. The offers are then posted on the bulletin board and workers are allowed to bid on the new labor grade. Final say on the matter of who receives the promotion rests with the plant superintendent. Several employees felt this was a mistake. Comments included:

I don't object to his having a voice in the matter, but I do feel that the major portion of this decision should be the foreman's. He knows what we can do.

I also feel that the changes in labor grades are too few and far between after an employee's first four or five years. These are the men who are most needed, since they are experienced, and should receive more recognition, not less.

One employee of the tank division stated, "I think the merit raise system employed by Progress is very vague and ineffective. No one really understands it." The merit policy is explained in Exhibit 2. Furthermore, employees felt there is not enough money involved in these increases.

There have also been other incentives tried at Progress. One was aimed generally at rewarding departmental performance and was given as a monthly bonus. This did not seem to be very effective. According to a foreman, "I noticed that one of the most industrious and highly valued employees in my department flaunted his 'whopping' bonus of $1.74." Another incentive program which brought smirks to the faces of employees was the institution of a system, again on a departmental basis, that rewarded the departments having the fewest days lost per month with S&H green stamps.

An additional problem area at Progress, which is related to low productivity, is poor supervision. This is more serious on the foreman level than on any other as far as each individual worker is concerned. The

Exhibit 1
Progress
Industries, Inc.:
Labor Grade
System in the
Tank Division

Labor Grade	Wage Effective June 9, 1978
15	$4.40–$4.73
12	4.23– 4.53
8	4.04– 4.36
7	3.87– 4.19
6	3.70– 4.02
5	3.53– 3.85
4	3.36– 3.68
3	3.19– 3.51
1	2.91– 3.14

Exhibit 2
Progress
Industries, Inc.:
Merit Pay Raise
Policy, Article XIX,
Section 2 of the
Union Contract

Merit increases are figured as follows: Each foreman rates all of his or her people. The average rating in each department is then figured. We then take a department with a median average and add or deduct from each individual in other departments the difference in the average of this department and the others. This gives each individual the rating points we use in determining pay. Then we give the following merit increases if they can be given within the employee's labor grade. Employees at the top of their labor grade do not get a merit increase.

	Low ⅓ of Labor Grade	Mid ⅓ of Labor Grade	High ⅓ of Labor Grade
10 pts. or more below average	0.06	0.05	0.05
1 to 9 pts. below average	0.08	0.06	0.05
Average to 9 pts. above	0.11	0.09	0.07
10 pts. or more above	0.14	0.12	0.10

foreman is the manager that the individual worker has the most direct contact with. The foremen feel a need for more formal training, especially in the area of human relations.

Still another problem at Progress, which also deals with cooperation, is communication between departments. "I personally have seen one department be forced to expend much more time and effort to do a job which could be done more quickly and easily by another department with more facilities. The problem is not one of awareness. People who have the authority to deal with this just haven't seemed to do anything about it," stated a foreman in the tank division.

There also seems to be a major problem that has just recently been brought to the surface. Some of the older, more experienced shop workers possess a great deal of knowledge about certain facets of tank production that is not written down anywhere. If they were to become unable to work, there would be no way of replacing all that necessary knowledge.

When managers were asked how to motivate their employees several replies were received. One opinion was that the recent changes in supervisory personnel would help remedy the situation. Monetary policies of motivation were mentioned in different ways. Two respondents felt that the present system of monetary reward (the labor grade and merit system) was sufficient, while another leaned toward a year-end bonus of $500 for meeting a set production schedule. Most agreed a back-up system for replacing key employees and filling key positions in the plant was necessary. On the whole, Dicks seems to be aware of some existing problems, but no effective action has been taken. It seems as if plans are being made to try to remedy some of the situations that exist, but as yet nothing positive seems to have resulted.

Source: This case was prepared by K. Mark Weaver, University of Alabama, University, Alabama, and John T. Wholihan, Bradley University, Peoria, Illinois.

Problems

1. Will an increase in compensation increase the productivity of Progress employees? Why or why not?
2. What action can the company take to increase productivity? to decrease turnover?
3. What can be done to make sure the company retains the necessary production knowledge of key employees after they leave the company?

Comprehensive Cases

Harrison, Inc.

Harrison, Inc., is a small firm in Milwaukee, Wisconsin. Its business at present involves the installation of flooring, walls, and ceilings in commercial buildings.

The company historically has been well run and profitable. Founded by the late John Harrison, Sr., in 1960, the company then concentrated on installation and sales of floor tile. Harrison would approach potential buyers, acquire installation contracts, and then hire workers to install the tile.

Noting the increased interest in acoustical tile, Harrison diversified his business by adding to his product-service mix in 1962. This decision was wise, for by 1970 new-product sales exceeded sales of floor tiles.

Always on the alert for new products that would fit into the company's line, Harrison added wall partition products to its list of installation services in 1969.

A Family Firm

Harrison had been a tile salesman for another firm, but he longed for the pleasures and pains of his own business. Psychologists have not often studied the motives of people who form their own firms. This decision often means that they will work longer hours for less money and with a high risk that they will lose all their investments and have no job at all. The failure rate of new small businesses is high. William Henry, analyzing the thematic apperception tests of successful entrepreneurs, concluded that the firms were mother substitutes for men with oedipal complexes. But some people do have a desire for the independence and success that entrepreneurship can bring, and Harrison seems to be one of them. He knew the construction business, and by watching cash contracts and careful bidding for jobs, he avoided the bankruptcy that most similar businesses experience.

In 1975 Harrison became ill, and he died in June 1976 after a lengthy illness. He was succeeded in the presidency by his twenty-six year old son John. The younger Harrison had received a bachelor of education degree from Wisconsin State University at Whitewater and had spent three years in the Air Force before entering the business during his father's illness. His experience in the business was limited to part-time work while in high school and college.

The casewriter interviewed young Harrison and asked him what the outlook was for his business. He replied:

This has always been a profitable business, but in the last few years we've suffered setbacks in sales and profits. But some of this is due to slowdown in the construction industry in the last five years. I think we're just about over the slump period. We should see a reversal in the sales situation over the next few years.

I'm more concerned about other aspects of our operations. It seems like a lot of inefficiencies and poor practices have crept into our work in recent years. Dad was in poor health much of that time, and I guess he just didn't realize what was happening.

One main problem is that our jobs are poorly coordinated. We usually have three crews working on large projects: a floor crew, a wall crew, and a ceiling crew. Changes in work procedures and work schedules for one crew can completely wreck the plans of the other crews. Yet, in most instances, none of the crews knows what each of the other crews is doing. Sometimes it's like we're three different companies working on the same job.

Another problem is a lack of good supervision. Oftentimes I find workers just loafing around, waiting for some types of material or just waiting for further instructions. Invariably, the supervisor in charge is up to his elbows in another job—doing things that the foremen should be doing. This sort of thing may have been permitted in the past, but we're simply too big now. We need supervisors who will be supervisors.

Yes, I'm anxious to get a few things straightened out—to really shake things up around here. The trouble is, any time I mention changes, I meet with resistance. For example, I met with the supervisors last week to try to iron out the problem I was just telling you about. They agreed to do a better job of supervision, but the last on-site visit I made revealed that the problem is worse, if anything.

At first I thought that such resistance was due to the fact that I am fairly young and inexperienced. People seem to resent being told what to do by a newcomer. But now I'm beginning to think that some people around here are just plain stubborn. I can tell you one thing: a few heads are going to roll unless things improve pretty soon!

The casewriter then asked Harrison to describe briefly the business as he saw it in view of its history and possible future. He described it as follows:

In the past, Harrison served both residential and commercial customers. Presently, the company limits its business to commercial customers. You see, it is difficult to compete in the residential market, since the small contractors selling in that market are not unionized and are therefore able to do the job cheaper. And we didn't want to spread ourselves too thin. Typically, we lay the floor, put up wall and ceiling work for medium-to-large stores and office buildings. We try to work out a "package" deal with our customers. That is, we prefer to do all the basic interior work—floors, walls, and ceilings—ourselves. These three jobs require a certain amount of coordination, and it is usually better to have one outfit doing them rather than many. We do, on occasion, contract to do just a portion of the interior work. Profitwise, these jobs have not been as satisfactory.

Harrison continued:

We offer a total interior service, you see. The floor line consists of vinyl tile, carpeting, and other resilient coverings. The ceiling line includes acoustical board material, illumination panels, and suspension hardware. We do some plastering work, but most of the wall work involves installation of drywalls. The company has developed its own line of drywalls, which features metal studs and channels rather than the more common wood studs and bases. These light and nonpermanent wall partitions have been especially popular in remodeling.

How the Firm Evolved

When the company began operations, Harrison, Sr., performed a wide range of tasks himself. He did all the selling, ordered materials, scheduled and supervised operations, and handled all bookkeeping and accounting routines. He employed a secretary and four or five workers. More workers were added as the business grew. Then, as the company began taking on simultaneous projects, it became necessary to hire foremen for each project, and supervisors to supervise the foremen. Salespeople were hired to help Harrison find new business.

Presently, the organization consists of about 110 employees, sixty-five of whom are skilled or semiskilled laborers. At the management level there are two vice presidents, an accountant, and three production supervisors. Exhibit 1 shows what the organization presently looks like.

Thomas Oslin is the vice-president in charge of production and also serves as general manager. Forty-eight years old, Oslin began working for Harrison in 1966. Before that, he worked for a firm which manufactures acoustical ceiling material. Besides having responsibility for all production activity, Oslin is in charge of the main office and

Exhibit 1
Harrison, Inc.:
Organization Chart

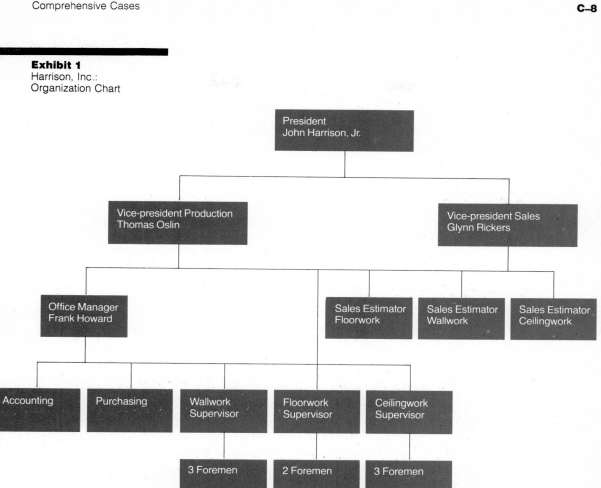

accounting department. Frank Howard, the office manager, reports directly to him.

Reporting to Oslin are three production supervisors. One is in charge of drywall construction, another supervises ceiling operations, and the third is responsible for floor installation. These persons schedule and control all production activity. Each supervisor assigns work crews to their jobs, ensures that needed supplies are on hand at the work sites, and coordinates work activities with the other two supervisors. The foremen working on specific projects report to these men. All three supervisors have worked for Harrison for many years and have "risen through the ranks."

The vice-president of sales is Glynn Rickers. Rickers worked in the construction business for eighteen years before coming to Harrison. He started as a sales estimator and was promoted to vice-president in 1973.

Rickers is knowledgeable in all aspects of the company's business and works closely with Oslin in planning and scheduling jobs.

Three sales estimators work directly under Rickers. They are responsible for locating new business and for preparing price estimates for bids. They also assist customers in selecting materials and color schemes. All three have had considerable experience in the interior finishing business. One man previously owned an acoustical tile company.

The Firm's Operations

Jobs at Harrison are obtained either by bids or by negotiated sales. Most Harrison business is a result of bid jobs. Typically, a job is announced in a trade magazine or in a construction service bulletin to which the company subscribes. When a potential job is announced, Rickers sends sales estimators to review the plans with the building owners and architects. Guided by the blueprint plans, the sales estimators compute the costs for materials and labor. Estimates of cost are made as close as possible to actual direct costs, with overhead, error allowance, and profit margin added on.

Rickers emphasized the importance of accurate cost estimation: "Most firms lose their shirts because they underestimate costs," he said. "A good estimator can determine almost exactly what the labor and materials needs will be from a good set of plans. A poor set of plans can throw estimates off seriously. We give ourselves a large error margin if plans are not specific. Overall, we've done a pretty good job of bidding most projects. Sometimes we're caught off guard by unforeseen hikes in wages or materials prices, but this is unusual."

Rickers said that the firm tries to make a 13 percent operating margin on most projects. He added that it was not always possible to obtain such a margin, particularly if a number of other firms are anxious to obtain a given project. Profits for most companies have been generally lower during the construction decline of recent years.

A small proportion of jobs are obtained through direct negotiation with general contractors. In most such instances, contractors have worked with Harrison in the past or desire a specific skill or material available only from Harrison. Some interior materials businesses have salespeople who solicit sales by calling on architects and contractors. Rickers does not feel that this marketing approach is worthwhile, particularly since most of Harrison's work involves rather large projects for which bids are necessary.

There are dozens of firms in the Milwaukee area that install floor, wall, or ceiling material. However, only four firms engage in all three types of activities on a large commercial scale. Harrison, Jr., said that his company has about 25 percent of the commercial market and that this market percentage has remained fairly constant for the past five years. Harrison presently limits its market to the immediate Milwaukee area.

The other three firms are Bischoff Construction Company, Arrighi Services, Inc., and Pulaski Interiors. Bischoff is the leading firm, having about 35 percent of the commercial market. But in addition, it has as much residential business as commercial. An old, well-established and respected firm (founded in 1925), it originated as a family concern but is no longer dominated by the family. Its bids are always competitive, yet it stresses quality workmanship as well. It does not do as much wall business as Harrison.

The third firm, Pulaski Interiors, was founded in the depression and has about 20 percent of the commercial business. Its share of the market has been declining. Pulaski, whose son was killed in the Korean War, seems to have lost interest in the business as he nears retirement in about 1981. Pulaski's business is about the same size as Harrison's.

The newest entry is Arrighi Services. At present it gets only 5 percent of the commercial business, but it has a fairly large residential business. It also offers wider services, including painting and decorating. The business is about two-thirds the size of Harrison but growing fast. Harrison feels that Arrighi cuts a few corners and has been getting more bids than it should of late.

Like other firms tied to the construction business, these firms find that their business fluctuates considerably. Construction activity is both seasonal and cyclical. Seasonality does not affect firms doing interior work as much as it does firms doing outside work, since workers inside are afforded protection from the elements. Nevertheless, most companies like Harrison do a greater amount of work during the warm months. All construction activity is dependent upon a number of political and economic variables, including interest rates, rate of business growth, employment rates, etc. Recessions in construction activity are often rather prolonged, and marginal companies are sometimes forced to go out of business during such periods. The level of manpower in this labor-intensive industry fluctuates in proportion to the level of construction activity

Once the job is obtained, a sales ticket and work ticket are filled out. The sales ticket is sent to the accounting office, and the work ticket is sent to the production department. As soon as the production supervisors receive the work ticket, they begin planning operations. Materials for the job are ordered, and manpower assignments are tentatively made. The production supervisor must keep in close contact with the general contractor to determine the exact date when the job will begin. When the job is ready for Harrison to begin operations, the material is sent to the job site from the warehouse and labor is scheduled.

The accounting office records job expenses as they accrue. Actual material costs and labor costs are compared to bid cost estimates on a weekly basis. Wide variances between bid and actual costs are reported immediately to Oslin, who investigates the discrepancy and takes corrective action, if necessary.

To explain more about his operations, Harrison took the casewriter on a visit of several work sites. He explained what he considers the production problems to be. He said:

For one thing, our work crews can never seem to follow schedules. You see, work crews for the three basic operations—wall work, ceiling work, and floor work—are scheduled so that the needed workers are available for each successive phase of a project. But if one crew gets behind, this delays the starting time for the next crew. For example, if the wall crew is delayed in finishing a job, the ceiling crew cannot begin on time.

Since there is often no more work for the ceiling crew to do, they are temporarily idle. This is not because of a lack of planning, but subsequent changes in work assignments throw projects off schedule. What happens is that the wall superintendent sees that he's getting a little behind on one project, so he shifts men over from another. This delays work on the other project and throws everything off schedule. Tom Oslin and I have talked over the problem a great deal but haven't come up with any workable solutions. He claims that you just have to expect so much slack in the work schedule.

On a later day, the casewriter visited with the production vice-president, Oslin. Earlier a worker had told the casewriter that he should talk to Oslin, since "he runs the whole place, anyway."

The casewriter asked Oslin about the production problem mentioned by Harrison. He replied rather sharply:

No, I don't think we have poor supervision or poor work conditions. John seems to think that something is wrong when every single man is not working every single minute of the day. But this just isn't always possible. Things happen which upset even the most carefully planned schedules. I try to keep in touch with the production supervisors about scheduling and work assignment changes. We work things out the best way we can.

But I'll tell you one thing, we do have a supervisor problem. Our three supervisors are spread too thinly. Right now, for instance, we have four major projects under way. It's impossible for each supervisor to be everywhere at once, although sometimes it's almost necessary for him to do so. We need more supervisors. That's the only solution.

The casewriter asked several other questions and at one point commented that a worker had said he really ran the Harrison company. Oslin replied:

Oh, sure, I guess you might say that I did run the place for quite a while.

Mr. Harrison, Sr., became so sick that he even stopped coming to work. He left everything in my hands. The business would have gone to pieces if someone hadn't taken over. But now that John, Jr., is here, things are different. There's only room for one man at the top, and right now that's him. I'm careful not to infringe on his authority. Sometimes that's difficult, because many people still look to me for instructions and guidance. I discourage this. I'm trying to help John, Jr., all I can.

Asked to comment on Harrison's abilities as president, he said:

Well, you can't learn everything there is to know about this business overnight, but John is working hard and learning fast. He's interested in the business. Sometimes, though, I think that there could be better communication between John and the rest of us. He makes a lot of decisions without talking them over with anyone. Some guys resent this. But I'm not going to say anything. As I said before, he's running this show, not me.

Financial Management

Frank Howard, the company's accountant, told the casewriter about the financial problems that are unique to the business.

For one thing, we must pay for materials and labor long before we receive payment from the customer. Furthermore, the customers retain a certain amount to assure the completion of a job. Usually, 10 to 15 percent of our accounts receivable consists of such funds. Because of these factors, we must manage our money more carefully. This involves sound financial planning. Also, it's imperative that we maintain a good relationship with the bank. Since there are relatively few fixed assets to serve as collateral in this business, most banks want prompt payment. Yes, many firms in this business fail because they lack financial management capabilities.

Harrison recently investigated the possibility of computerizing such operations as accounting, inventory control, cost estimation, and profit planning. He decided that there is not enough work to justify the purchase of a computer but feels that it may be worthwhile to contract with an outside computer service in the future. Presently, the office force handles the bookkeeping, payroll, and job-cost records. Howard personally keeps track of delinquent accounts receivable. Entries to all accounts are made by hand and checked by machine.

Howard's department also handles purchasing functions. Purchases are made for inventory and in response to specific job requests. All materials are stored in a new warehouse building having rail access. Howard explained that since there is ample storage space, he usually goes ahead and orders materials as soon as he finds out that they will be needed.

Sometimes we have all the materials for a job as much as 3 months in advance of the time they are needed. This way we avoid the possibility of work stoppage due to the late arrival of materials.

I think we've done a good job managing our assets. You're welcome to look at our financial records if you wish.

Harrison has had nearly a 40 percent sales decline from 1974 to 1975. Much of this is no doubt due to bad economic conditions. But not all.

Profitability has declined. The ratio of net profit to sales has been falling, and deficits appeared in 1975 and 1976. Some of the losses are due to a rise in variable costs and increases in selling and administrative costs. The costs of materials and labor have also risen at the same time that competition for bid business has intensified. All of this has put serious pressures on the firm's financial health.

Some Final Comments

As the casewriter was getting ready to leave, he was pondering the challenges and problems at Harrison. Running through his mind were some of Harrison's earlier comments about his dream for the firm. He had said:

I want to get things shaped up around here first—make the most of what we have now. But my real hopes are far beyond that period. I dream of a firm that is growing and expanding. We've entrenched ourselves—cut out our share of the pie. But we've been standing still—we still think of ourselves as a small outfit. It's about time our managerial thinking caught up to our size and we did some long-range thinking instead of operating only on a day-to-day basis.

The casewriter wondered if Harrison was capable of fulfilling those dreams.

Problems

You are a consultant called in by Harrison. Analyze this case and make suggestions to Harrison for improving the managerial effectiveness at Harrison, Inc.

Mixing Blood and Business: A Family Company in Crisis

The Waterloo and Sons Insurance Company

The Waterloo and Sons Insurance Company was formed to provide insurance coverage for commercial automobiles. Its clients consisted of a wide variety of businesses who insured their company cars and the private cars of employees who used their cars for company purposes. The company was built on the reputation and selling ability of Dudley F. Waterloo, Sr. Mr. Waterloo pioneered the development of comprehensive protection plans for the trucking industry and was responsible for many of the innovations which have now become accepted standards in this very large and specialized area of insurance underwriting. In due time Dudley F. Waterloo, Jr., Jason R. Waterloo, and Willy T. Waterloo joined the payroll of Waterloo and Sons Insurance Company.

Dudley F. Waterloo, Sr., moved into semiretirement as chairman of the board, and Dudley F. Waterloo, Jr., became president and chief executive officer of Waterloo and Sons. Buddy Richardson is serving as manager of the area of personal and noncommercial insurance. Wendal Dickson is serving as manager of the commercial automobiles department. The newly developed area of life insurance is currently without a manager, and all three of the employees report to the president. The three employees are Jason R. Waterloo, Willy T. Waterloo, and William Thompson.

Waterloo and Sons Today

On February 7, 1977, an agreement to conduct an organizational audit between the managers of Waterloo and Sons and Wellington and Associates was discussed and reached. The purpose of the audit was to systematically, critically, and impartially review and appraise the current organizational structure and the management of this organization. The analysis of the organization and management of it was accomplished in two major phases:

1. An organization audit questionnaire which was completed by thirty-two of the employees.
2. Personal interviews conducted with thirty-two employees.

Findings

The findings resulting from the data gathered by the above-stated methods are shown in Exhibits 1 through 5.

Discussion of Major Findings

The following represents a discussion of the major weaknesses or concerns that emerged from the audit. The strengths of the organization have been presented in tabular form but will not be formally discussed.

Exhibit 1
Employee
Attitudes toward
Working
Conditions

Factor	Satisfied	Neither One nor the Other	Dissatisfied
My job	24	5	3
My pay	17	3	12
My fringe benefits	32	0	0
My opportunities for advancement	16	5	11
My fellow employees	24	7	1
My supervisors	25	5	2

Exhibit 2
What Employees
Like Most about
Working at
Waterloo and Sons

Items most often mentioned by employees were:
1. The people—good working relationships.
2. The fringe benefits.
3. Job freedom and responsibility.
4. The family atmosphere.
5. Openness and frankness of communications between and among managers and employees.

Exhibit 3
What Employees
Like Least about
Working at
Waterloo and Sons

Items most often mentioned by employees were:
1. Lack of organizational direction in the form of:
    a. Long-range plan(s).
    b. Ability of top management to organize.
2. Opportunities for advancement.
3. Pay.

Exhibit 4
What Employees
Consider the Major
Strengths of
Waterloo and Sons

Items most often mentioned by employees were:
1. The name and its history of service to its customers.
2. The transportation department.
3. Its market position.
4. Continually attempting to improve the organization.
5. The president.

Exhibit 5
What Employees
Consider the Major
Weaknesses of
Waterloo and Sons

Items most often mentioned by employees were:
1. Lack of long-range plans and goals.
2. Top management is spreading itself too thin—selling, supervising, and servicing—and as a result there is a lack of selling in all areas.
3. Lack of profit in the life insurance department and the conflict between life insurance and other departments.
4. The Waterloo family situation.

Top Management

The Chief Executive Officer The data collection generated a large amount of information on the president. Typical comments were: "I don't feel that Dudley, Jr., is a good administrator. He will ask your ideas on Monday and on Tuesday nothing will happen." "Dudley, Jr., likes to sell; I'm not sure he likes to manage." "Dudley, Jr., spends so much time on things like the mayor of Waterview and chairman of this and that. He needs to spend more time managing." "Dudley, Jr., needs to initiate what he wants done and how he wants it done. We have talked about a three to five year plan, yet nothing has been done."

"Dudley, Jr.'s influence is strong in the wrong way. He will demand that we get things done *now*. If Dudley, Jr., has a friend who needs a quote, you have to drop everything and take on that piece of work, even if it is a bad risk." "Dudley, Jr., asks us to get quotes for his friends even if they are bad risks. If we object, Dudley, Jr., pounds the desk and says 'Give me a quote, I don't care.' We waste a lot of time getting quotes on business that will be rejected." "Dudley, Jr., manages from crisis to crisis. He needs to confine himself to management and delegate more." "Due to lack of long-range planning and crisis management, we waste human resources." "It is impossible for the president to sell, service, and yet manage." "Our president does not need to be involved in day-to-day insurance; he needs to manage the company." "Dudley, Jr., puts out fires when he should be providing us with overall direction." "I would like to see him move into a public relations and selling position and find an administrative assistant to manage the company." (See Exhibits 1 through 5.)

Corporate Objectives and Direction

The Planning Function A major problem within the organization (Exhibits 3 and 5) is the lack of a formal planning system within the firm. A planning system is the hallmark of a well-managed and successful firm. This planning includes such areas as:

- Corporate planning
- Marketing planning
- Organizational planning
- Manpower planning
- Facilities planning
- Financial planning

The perceived lack of formal planning voiced by the employees and management is a major criticism of the organization and its top and middle management. Without formal planning the organization lacks direction and a valid basis for judging its progress. If an organization cannot define where it is attempting to go in the next year, the next five years, and so forth, it is impossible to define programs for achieving those goals (since they are undefined) and secondly, there is no means of judging performance since no guidelines exist.

Job Descriptions and Duties

The Selling Function A general statement that emanated from the data was that people were not sure of exactly what they were supposed to do. This general criticism is applicable to the clerical and support positions as well as the professional staff.

It is a damaging criticism regarding the professional staff as it relates specifically to the selling function. Most of these people are being asked to sell, supervise, and service within their specific areas. While we have spoken earlier to the supervisory function, the roles of selling (the solicitation of new business and the upgrading of existing business) and servicing (day-to-day maintenance and handling of matters pertaining to existing business) must be addressed.

The selling function seems to be taking a secondary position to the servicing function. While it cannot be denied that the servicing of existing business is of critical importance, the generation of new business (selling) is the lifeblood of the firm.

Financial data and customer lists were not available for this study. Based upon our discussions, it is highly probable that *real gains* (deflated dollars) in premium dollars and/or net profit have not been realized by the firm over the past several years. Furthermore, it is probably a valid inference that the composition of clients by most departments has not substantially changed in the same period.

Both of these conditions, if true, would point to the lack of emphasis on the selling function. This condition is detrimental to the firm.

A Full Service Firm

The Life Department Major criticisms of the life insurance department of the firm were found. Examples of typical comments are: "The Life Department has been a thorn in our side. They write so little business, yet we are carrying them and their losses. Life has to prove itself." "The Life Department is just a place for Jason and Willy to work. Life operates at a loss, and yet they have a great deal of influence." "They are unprofitable in Life, yet they are directing the company." "There is conflict between Life and the rest of the company" (see Exhibit 5).

As can be seen, much of the criticism of this department stems from perceptions relating to the profitability of this department. There is also some concern regarding the personnel in this area; however, that situation will be discussed in another section.

The continued failure of the department to generate profit is the primary concern.

A Family Business

While this area was presented as a strength and a factor that makes the firm a nice place to work, it also was presented as a problem.

Waterloo Family Situation (the Life Department) The comments regarding the Office of the President have referred to Dudley F. Waterloo, Jr. Much criticism of the Life Department centered on Jason and Willy in that department. Typical comments included: "The Life Department has caused discontent; Jason and Willy are not doing their jobs, yet they are directing the company." "Jason is not well liked. He is intelligent, yet no one is close to him. He gives the image that 'I'm a family member and therefore I am better.'" "The Life Department is just a place for Jason and Willy to work. Life operates at a loss; yet they have a great deal of influence." "Willy and Jason don't contribute to the company. We are carrying them."

Source: © 1977 by Jack L. Simonetti, D.B.A., and Nick Nykodym, Ph.D., of the University of Toledo.

Problems

1. What are the major problems at Waterloo?
2. What organizational changes would you recommend and why?
3. Which personnel changes would you recommend and why?
4. Which procedural changes would you recommend and why?

Production Department

KCDE-TV is one of two television stations in Tuttle, a city of 100,000 population with a metropolitan area of 175,000.

KCDE-TV (and radio) for some time had serious morale problems, especially in the television production department. KCDE employed eighty-five people in six departments: general office, data processing, news, engineering, radio, and television production. The television production group formed the single largest department, about twenty people. The functional areas of the production department are: announcing, directing, switching, camera operating, and videotape operating. (See Exhibit 1 for a description of these functions.)

As is the case with many small- to medium-size stations, KCDE was looked upon as a training ground by members of both management and staff. This was a reason offered by management on occasion for not granting a raise to an employee. It was suggested to the employees that if they wished to remain at KCDE they had better accept their present wage as the maximum for the forseeable future. They then would find it necessary to move on to a bigger city if they expected to be paid more for the same job. The turnover, especially in the radio and production departments, was high.

Each employee negotiated his or her own salary with management since there was no union representation. There was no published salary range, but staff members knew that the approximate ranges in 1970 were as follows:

Announcers	$850-950/mo.
Directors	850-925
Switchers	775-825
Videotape Operators	750-825
Camera Crew	700-750

Exhibit 1
Functional
Areas of the
KCDE-TV
Production
Department

Announcers are responsible for performing live commercials and programs and for providing audio recordings for locally produced slide, film, and videotape commercials. Since the workload is variable, they typically have other duties, e.g., writing commercial copy or reading news for the radio station.

The *director* is ostensibly the most creative member of the crew. He or she is responsible for the "on-air" presentation. He or she either recommends a set for a commercial or program or approves an idea presented by some other member of the crew. During the actual broadcast or recording session, the director is in charge of all activities.

The *switcher*, sometimes referred to as the technical director, performs the physical operations at the control board required to put various video sources on the air and to mix the sources at the director's command. This person is also responsible for loading slides and film on the various projectors.

The *videotape operator* loads and "cues" videotapes on the videotape machines for the playback of commercials and programs on the air. He or she also sets up the machines for the recording of commercials and programs. The videotape machines are extremely complicated and quite difficult to operate, requiring a practiced touch for trouble-free operation.

The *camera operators* use the large studio cameras, moving them on the director's cue and selecting the shots the director asks for. They do the actual construction of the sets and most of the lighting, sometimes under the direct supervision of the director.

An additional member of the operating crew is an *engineer*, who is not a member of the production department. She or he is expected to provide technical advice to the director. The engineer's primary responsibility, however, is the maintenance of the expensive, complicated electronic gear.

The salaries were based on a forty-eight hour, six day week. Much conversation among the crew members centered around what they all agreed was a low pay scale. As one of the crew members put it regularly in conversation: "Nowhere else can you work a six day week, a night shift, and virtually every holiday for such lousy money."

Benefits were another sore point. The company made group insurance available, but there was no retirement program. Though it provided paid vacations, the company paid the vacationing employee for two forty hour weeks. The two week paycheck then was less by sixteen hours of overtime what the employee was accustomed to receiving.

Working conditions with regard to physical comfort and safety were adequate and about average for the industry.

It was a common feeling among the crew members that they were being "used" to one degree or another by management. They knew that many general office workers for the city's major private employers and the state government were making more money than they, working better hours and shorter weeks. Adding salt to the wound was the feeling that the television job required infinitely more creative ability than the general office worker needed or had. At the same time, most felt their jobs were intrinsically interesting, and far more challenging than office or administrative work.

Great animosity was directed toward the assistant general manager of the station. His previous post was chief engineer of the station, where he was tagged with the nickname "Overkill" by some members of the engineering department. This name was inspired by his tendency to overreact to situations. On one occasion he had fired an employee for smoking in the television control room. Though parts of the studio and control areas were posted against smoking, members of the staff looked upon this regulation as trivial. Care was taken not to smoke only when the assistant general manager was in the immediate area.

More than once "Overkill" threatened to have a vital piece of equipment removed, "unless you guys take better care of it." The threats were obviously hollow, since the station could not operate without the equipment. He had been heard to refer to the operating crew and the engineering department, or various members, as "coolies."

The leader of the production department itself was not spared the crew's wrath. Every member of the crew looked upon Gary Brown, the production supervisor, as one of the switchers put it, as "a miserable, two-timing s.o.b." More than one of the crew had had the experience of making a request for a raise, only to find some weeks later that the production supervisor had "forgotten to take it up," or to be counseled that "this just isn't the right time to ask." It had been observed by everyone in the production staff that Gary often delivered different versions of a story to upper management than he gave to his subordinates. It was generally felt that he always sided with management, especially "Overkill," rather than backing his subordinates.

The general manager of the station, Gordon Frederick, was a retired military officer and an ex-mayor of the city. He was active in political causes and was out of town frequently, leaving the day-to-day operation of the station to the assistant general manager. Most of the staff members looked upon Frederick as being a slightly befuddled autocrat since he conducted regular "inspections" when in the building and indulged a fetish for small detail, such as seeing that the flags were removed from the flagpole in front of the building promptly at sunset. He was responsible for, and for the most part the author of, a booklet of company rules and regulations called the Blue Book. In the Blue Book were voluminous descriptions of each job title within the organization, and page upon page of rules pertaining to coffee breaks, use of company telephones, and virtually every other activity within the building.

The Blue Book was treated with varying degrees of contempt by most staff members and with utter contempt by the production department. Those who had been in the military service insisted parts of the Blue Book text were lifted wholesale from military manuals. It was felt that the book's only value was to management, in that some obscure regulation could be used to chastise an employee, while other rules were totally ignored. For example, the Blue Book stated that the company had a policy against members of the same family being employed. However, "Overkill's" son, Steve, worked as a full-time camera operator; one of the director's wives worked in the office; and the husband of the TV program director served as a technician.

The Blue Book also contained rules for communication between departments, management feeling being that the rank and file of one department should not communicate directly with their counterparts in other departments in matters of operations. For example, if a news announcer became upset at a camera operator, director, or any other member of the production staff in connection with a newscast, she or he was to inform the news director, who would then take the matter up with the production supervisor. This rule was totally ignored.

Though the Blue Book delineated a very rigid chain of command, it was fairly common for orders to the production crew to come from "Overkill," the program director, or Brown, the production supervisor. On occasion, in the case of an equipment failure or similar emergency, these orders would conflict, resulting in confusion until the three decided upon a common plan.

Job security was felt to be nonexistent. Many of the workers felt directly threatened by "Overkill" and verbally expressed their fear of his capricious behavior.

Seemingly arbitrary changes of shift upset some of the crew. In early spring of 1970, one of the directors was moved to the position of videotape operator. Though his salary was left at its old level, this move involved a real loss of prestige. No explanation was given to members of the crew. A camera operator was promoted directly to the position of director, bypassing several switchers. Again, there was no explanation.

Sabotage, in the name of "games," became quite common among the operating crew. It was not too unusual for a film projector to be misthreaded, causing the film to be torn to ribbons when the projector was started, resulting in program down-time. Program sets would occasionally topple over during a videotaping session, or microphones would refuse to work. One favorite trick was the tripping of master light breakers for the control room areas. Another was pounding on the wall of an area where an announcer was on the air. One of the more ingenious acts involved the wiring of a prop telephone on the TV news set. The phone was then rung during a newscast, causing the news announcer to "break up." Though members of management never appeared to suspect sabotage, its occurrence was by no means rare.

Also in the spring of 1970, Ron E., an announcer, came to work for KCDE radio. The television and radio control areas were adjacent to one another, and some of the announcers worked both radio and television. There was a great deal of social contact between employees of both sides.

At the end of his first pay period, Ron became tremendously upset. His check totaled about $50 less for the two week period than he thought it would be. According to Ron, the radio station manager had hired him at $900 a month, but his first check was paid at the rate of $800 a month. Ron promptly complained to his supervisor, and the matter was taken to the general manager. He informed Ron that the radio station manager did not have the authority to hire an announcer at such a salary as Ron had been promised. There was no offer to compromise on the salary. Frederick offered to pay Ron's moving expenses back to the city he had left just weeks before. Ron's answer was, "And what the hell am I supposed to do for a job if I do return?" Feeling he had no choice, Ron accepted the lower salary.

In May, about a month after the salary episode, Ron began questioning other employees about the possibility of unionizing the station. His idea was met with great enthusiasm by the members of the production department. More than one of them indicated that though they did not like unions, they liked the management of KCDE even less. The few holdouts expressed fear for their jobs, but no one expressed any pro-management thoughts.

Several meetings were held with union representatives and the union formally notified Frederick of its intention to organize the production department. This action was met with disbelief on the part of Frederick, followed soon by a meeting to stress to employees that "the door is always open, and you know we're interested in your problems." Union 'horror' stories soon followed, accompanied by a frigid atmosphere and veiled threats by both sides. Rumor generation reached very high levels.

In early August, Ron E. was fired for "inattention to duties." He filed an unfair labor practices suit against the station management with the National Labor Relations Board. The filing of the suit served to freeze the unionization proceedings until the suit was resolved.

In the meantime, Frederick, Brown, and "Overkill" turned to a well-known management consulting firm for help in analysis of the organizational and personnel problems.

Source: © Patrick Fleenor, Seattle University, Seattle, Washington.

Problems

1. What are the major problems at KCDE?
2. What are the major causes of the problem: motivation, use of change agents, leadership style, pay and personnel policies, organization structure?
3. What steps would you take to remedy KCDE's problems?

Appendix

A Career in Public and Not-for-Profit Sectors of the Economy

Managing Public and Nonprofit Enterprises

Some of you, by chance or choice, may wind up as managers in a nonbusiness setting. Do the principles of management set forth in this book apply to the managers of the employment security office of the government? or the postal service? or the administration of Greenlawn Hospital? Do they apply to the vice-president for finance of New York University? the business manager of the Seattle Opera Company? the business vice-president of the Episcopal Diocese of Southern Ohio?

I believe the answer is yes—for the most part. Most of what was said in Chapters 5, 13, 14, 15, 16, 17 and 20 applies. In fact most health care facilities, universities, churches, and similar organizations are run like small or medium-size businesses. The federal government is similar to a large business; state and local government services are like small and medium-size businesses.

People are similar in all organizations. Small groups exist in all organizations. Leadership styles vary in all organizations. Planning, organization, and control need to be performed in all enterprises. Job enlargement is the same in a university machine shop as in a private sector machine shop. A laundry worker's job in a hospital probably is not much different from an equivalent job in a business-run laundry.

Note, however, that I left out Chapters 4, 6, 7, 8, and 9. Chapter 6 discussed the motivation of people. It is *possible* (though there is little evidence here) that some employees working for some nonbusiness enterprises are more dedicated to the objectives of the enterprise than the employees of some businesses. For example, church secretaries may receive more satisfaction from helping others than they would from working for a foundry. So they may work for less pay. In other words, the motives people have for working for an enterprise like a church, an opera company, a hospital, or a university might be different from the motives of business employees. The jobs must be designed to satisfy these needs. This difference could also affect leadership style, control style, and so forth.

A second difference may lie in the objectives of the enterprise. This was pointed out in Chapter 7. Thus the Orthodox Church in America does not have the same objectives as Mattel Toy Company. Moreover, the nonbusiness enterprise may not be as profit oriented as a business. This will depend on the ranking of objectives by the enterprise. It is true that there are hospitals that are operated for profit, but many nonprofit hospitals will improve the quality of patient care even if it means no net surplus is added in a given year. Such differences in objectives can have an effect on reward systems, on job development, and on how the manager spends his or her time.

A third difference may be found in the environmental forces faced by nonbusiness enterprises. (Internal forces may differ, too.) In this final part of the chapter we cannot discuss all these differences. But I do want to say a few words on how these differences affect the life of the manager in the public and nonprofit sectors.

The Public Manager

The public manager is an individual who manages an enterprise whose primary source of revenue is local, state (provincial), or federal taxes and similar flows of funds. In what ways does the managerial job differ in the public sector from the equivalent job in the private sector? First of all, the public sector enterprise can seek different objectives and, usually, more objectives than the private sector enterprise. And most of these objectives are very hard to measure. It is more difficult to design planning and control systems if objectives are broadly defined.

Secondly, the public manager faces more uncertainty more frequently than the private manager. This is a consequence of the environment in which he or she operates. Thus the public manager must seek resources and support from the hierarchy. But the hierarchy can include a split between the executive branch (president, premier, governor, city manager) and the legislative branch (Congress, the legislature, the city council). These groups may choose to have a political fight over any given program. Then there is the press or the media, whose business it is to expose the "useless, inefficient bureaucrat." And out-of-office politicians are continually feeding the media information to expose the misdeeds—past or present—of public managers.

Politicians can interfere with the public manager's operations, and the remnants of the spoils system found in the "merit system" often lead public managers to prostitute their procedures in order to keep the politicians happy and/or off their backs.

Thus environmental forces have a much stronger impact on the job of the public manager than on that of most private managers. The public enterprise's "suppliers" (executive and legislative branches) and customers and pressure groups are highly interrelated, with the public manager in the middle, often subject to close scrutiny because the press want good stories or the politician wants to get elected. Business managers, by contrast, face neither of these threats. This greater dependence on a complicated and conflicting environment provides the major difference between the public manager and the business manager.

In addition, just as there is diversity in the jobs of business managers, so there is variety in those of public managers. Some technical jobs are little affected by the political process. A technician in the Weather Bureau or a researcher in a government lab are examples. I would hypothesize that successful public managers who must deal with the political environment need more leadership ability, greater ability to deal with peers, and more tolerance for ambiguity and change than most business managers. The difficulties of the public manager's job may help explain Bruce Buchanan's findings that businesspeople are much more involved in their work and identify more strongly with their company than public managers.[1]

Some private managers are involved in joint public-private projects where they become exposed to the political process itself. Comsat is an example of such a project. I once studied a steel company that was owned half by private sources, half by the government. The board was half private and half public. It operated fairly well, but its members had different expectations. For example, the government directors pressed for more profit than the private sector directors felt was appropriate for the safety of the workers. Public managers need to be more skilled in dealing with complex environments and with a situation that involves greater dependence on the outside environment.

The Hospital Administrator

There are over 7,000 hospitals in the United States, employing well over 2 million people. (Hospitals are in the public sector in Canada.) About 15 percent of these hospitals are proprietary (for profit) hospitals. About half are nonprofit community hospitals, and the rest are run by governments at several levels: federal (Veterans Administration and military), state (mental hospitals), and local (city-run hospitals). In my opinion, hospitals are *the* most difficult enterprise to manage.

First of all, none of the hospitals' "customers" really want to be there. By definition most are not well, and therefore they can be difficult to handle. The hospital's employees are quite different in background, varying from the poorest-trained and paid employees in America (food service, janitorial, housekeeping) to some of the best-trained people employed anywhere. Large numbers of hospital employees are professionals (nurses, medical technicians, occupational therapists, dietitians) who identify with professional objectives that sometimes conflict with the objectives of other groups in the enterprise.

The objectives of the hospital are many and hard to measure. Frequently cited are quality patient care, creative health research, effective training of physicians and other health professionals, financial solvency, growth in size, and variety of health care. The trustees' objectives may include prestige in the community.

In no other institution that I can think of can outsiders come in, use the facilities for their own business, and not be financially responsible to the hospital. Yet physicians are not employees of hospitals. They have the highest status of all the people involved in hospitals, use the facilities to cure their patients, yet may be on the staffs of several hospitals.

The hospital's "suppliers," in addition to suppliers of materials, can include donors, the state, and "third-party" groups—Blue Cross, insurance companies, Medicare/Medicaid (government bodies)—which can question and withhold payments if hospitals "violate their contracts." The hospital is also subject to suits for improper care as well as to competition from the plush new hospital down the street.

At the center sits the hospital manager (or administrator). He or she is responsible for the survival and prosperity of the hospital and patient care. The successful hospital administrator must understand the work motivations (and status needs) of professional employees, deal with sick customers, fend off third-party payees, raise money from trustees and friends of the hospital, manage volunteers who want to help (and often get in the way), and keep physicians from leaving the staff. And if the hospital fails a customer, it does not mean a return order but pain, suffering, and sometimes death.

Hospital administrators, too, must be able to deal with more ambiguities than most business managers. They must be able to get conflicting groups to work toward common objectives and stay financially viable. The leadership qualities needed are *extraordinary*.

Health care is a "growth industry" in our society. We need to produce more health care administrators capable of staffing these challenging (and rewarding) jobs.

The University Manager

There are about 3,000 colleges, junior colleges, and universities in the United States, with about 6 million students and somewhat less than 1 million faculty members. They range from small colleges with fewer than 500 students and a faculty of about 30 to vast multicampus systems like the State University of New York, the University of California, and California State Universities and Colleges, with budgets of hundreds of millions, students in the hundreds of thousands, and faculties in several college organizations.

The official objectives of colleges and universities include teaching and dissemination of knowledge, research (creation of new knowledge), and service to society. But the more complex institutions of higher education also

- Counsel students on personal problems.
- Provide for the health needs of students and the community.
- Provide job placement services.
- Run cultural programs.
- Provide intercollegiate athletic programs that gross hundreds of thousands of dollars on football weekends.
- Run "hotels" (dormitories) for students.
- Provide food service for students and the college or university community.
- Operate buildings and grounds services.
- Run museums, radio stations, and newspapers.
- Provide for the religious needs of students and the community.

The major elements in higher education span a variety of offices and functions. (1) The *board of trustees* represents the people of the state (in the case of a state-supported institution) or the alumni, donors, church, or similar supporting groups (in the case of a private university). (2) The *faculty members* see themselves as independent professionals attached to the college; they are responsible for curriculum, granting degrees, and academic counseling. (3) The *students* spend two to four (or more) years at the college until the degree or program is completed. The student is there to learn and develop himself or herself socially for the transition period between childhood and adulthood. (4) The *academic administration* consists of a set of officers who are responsible for the use of the college or university's resources. (5) The *professional support staff* are the people who help the faculty educate students and do research. This group includes librarians, audiovisual aids specialists, lab technicians, extension specialists, and counselors. (6) The *business staff* is made up of people who run the "business side" of the university—dormitories, food service, development, sports, ancillary services, admissions, personnel, buildings and grounds, maintenance, etc.

The ultimate power in a university lies with the board of trustees. The president's job is to see that the university survives. He or she needs to get enough money from tuition, gifts, grants, foundations, the legislatures, and alumni to keep the university open. The president must see that the business side of the university is efficient and the academic side effective. This includes recruiting and holding good students and competent faculty.

You may choose someday to enter university management—as a controller or personnel officer, for example. The higher administrative offices in a college or university are usually held by former faculty members. Someday colleges may change this policy and hire professional managers as presidents (the way hospitals are headed by administrators, not physicians). The problem with academic administrators is that most of them have *no* professional training as managers. Yet they are asked to manage very complex, fragile organizations. The provost, vice-president, or president may have been a good (or satisfactory) Milton scholar, research biologist, theologian, or anthropologist. But he or she may know nothing about administration, or only what he or she has learned through "on-the-job training" as a department chairperson or dean. In the long run, I expect many of the positions now held by academics to be held by professional managers. Only academic matters (curriculum, degree approval, faculty recruiting and development) will be the concern of academics.

Colleges and universities are exciting institutions to manage. They have had a lot of problems recently. For example, in the 1960s they had to deal with riots. In the 1970s, seas of red ink appeared in the account books. The differences between business and university management include different objectives, and hard-to-measure objectives at that. (What is quality research? How much "service" should be done—and which kind? What is good teaching?)

The environmental forces are different, too: "suppliers" include politicized legislatures or governors. The legislature may fight budget battles with the governor, with the university in the middle. Donors may want their names perpetuated. Alumni may be dissatisfied with the way the college is being run. An old joke has a new college president asking his predecessor, who was retiring after a very successful career, "How do you get to be successful in this job?" The retiring president answers, "Really, you just have to try to satisfy the important groups and remember what they want: Give the alumni a winning football team; allow the student rules to be flexible enough so they can have sex and beer; and give the faculty enough parking places."

Thus university managers must deal with a volatile budget situation, changing student demands, and a generally dissatisfied faculty. Most faculty are trained to be critical of students, their peers, and society as a whole. This critical attitude leads to dissatisfaction with the present and to creative new approaches. So faculty usually are critical of university administrators.

Still another group has started to put pressure on universities: the federal government. Universities get large amounts of federal money to fund research, student loans, and scholarships; to build buildings; and for other purposes. Therefore universities are subject to federal pressure to hire and promote members of minority groups, among other things.

In sum, universities are complex enterprises to run, but this makes their management more challenging.

Arts Management

Another set of smaller enterprises that can benefit from effective management are arts organizations: ballet troupes, symphony orchestras, opera companies, theater groups, museums, and similar enterprises. Museums are usually among the smallest of these enterprises. Musical and theater groups can employ several hundred people, but still are relatively small enterprises. General Motors, by contrast, employs 600,000 people. A large hospital (1,500 beds) may employ 4,500.

Arts organizations derive their funds from donations, foundations, government grants, and ticket sales or admission charges. Almost all have continuous money problems as they try to balance their budgets while inflation eats away at their endowments.

The employees of musical and theater groups generally are professional artists, 98 percent of whom are dedicated, underpaid people who are in the job because they love it. Museum employees are headed by professionally trained curators who purchase and arrange their collections. Artists are not normally employed by museums.

Many arts organizations survive because of the dedication of volunteers who work for the institution for nothing, helping to raise money, sell tickets, and the like. In some communities these volunteer groups have high social status.

Managers have a lot to offer an arts organization. First of all, management tools can improve the efficiency of the operation if the manager is sensitive enough to know where he or she can cut costs without impairing the quality of the performance. Marketing skills are desperately needed by most arts organizations. Additional sources of revenue can be generated. For example, the Smithsonian Museum started a magazine; it "franchises" its collection for royalties; textile firms make sheets using its patterns; toy firms make replicas of old toys; and so forth. Most museums now have "stores." Many run TV auctions. Especially for the individual who loves great art, ballet, music, or theater, the job of business manager of an arts organization might be the right career choice.

A good example of a very successful arts manager is Glynn Ross, the great manager and developer of the Seattle Opera Company.[2] He has built it into one of the most artistically and creatively outstanding companies in the world. Yet it is fiscally sound.

Managing Voluntary Organizations and the "Third Sector"

There are many other nonprofit enterprises in our society that need managers: churches, community groups, consumer groups, public and private elementary and secondary schools, libraries, political parties, unions, charity organizations, social groups, country clubs, and so forth. Some authors refer to these enterprises as the "third sector."

In each case the manager must determine how the enterprise differs from a "main line" business in employee motivation, enterprise objectives, and environmental forces. The manager can then adapt his or her leadership practices, communications, planning and control, organizational style, and other management tools to the setting.

I encourage some of you to consider contributing your talents and life to helping manage in the public and not-for-profit sectors. There are many opportunities there for very rewarding careers.

Notes   [1]Bruce Buchanan, "Government Managers, Business Executives, and Organizational Commitment," *Public Administration Review* 34 (July–August 1974): 339–347.

[2]See Winthrop Sargent, "The Ring's the Thing," *New Yorker,* June 26, 1978, pp. 35–50.

References   ### The Public Manager

Joseph L. Bower, "Effective Public Management," *Harvard Business Review* 55 (March–April 1977): 131–140. Bruce Buchanan, "Government Managers, Business Executives, and Organizational Commitment," *Public Administration Review* 34 (July–August 1974): 339–347. Robert Golembiewski and Michael Cohen, *People in the Public Service* (Itasca, Ill.: F. E. Peacock, 1968), chapter 1. Nicholas Henry, "Paradigms of Public Administration," *Public Administration Review* 35 (July–August 1975): 378–386. Andrew P. Kakabadse, "Corporate Management in Local Government: A Case Study," *Journal of Management Studies* 14 (October 1977): 341–351. Barry D. Karl, "Public Administration and American History: A Century of Professionalism," *Public Administration Review* 36 (September–October 1976): 489–504. Robert Levine, *Public Planning: Failure and Reduction* (New York: Basic Books, 1971). Laurence E. Lynn, Jr., and John M. Seidl, "Bottom-line Management for Public Agencies," *Harvard Business Review* 55 (January–February 1977): 144–153. Michael Murray, "Comparing Public and Private Management: An Exploratory Essay," *Public Administration Review* 35 (July–August 1975): 364–371. Alan Otten, "Politics and People: On Managing," *Wall Street Journal*, February 12, 1976. Richard L. Schott, "Public Administration as a Profession: Problems and Prospects," *Public Administration Review* 36 (May–June 1976): 253–259. Jay Shafritz, "Political Culture: The Determinant of Merit System Viability," *Public Personnel Management* 3 (January–February 1974): 39–43. Carl W. Stenberg, "Contemporary Public Administration: Challenge and Change," *Public Administration Review* 36 (September–October 1976): 505–507. Gary Wamsley and Mayer Zald, "The Political Economy of Public Organizations," *Public Administration Review* 33 (January–February 1973): 62–73. Earl Warren, "Value and Quality of the Career Public Service," *Public Administration Review* 34 (July–August 1974): 390–394.

The Hospital Administrator

Vaughn Blakenship and Ray Elling, "Organizational Support and Community Power Structure: The Hospital," *Journal of Health and Human Behavior* 3 (Winter 1962): 257–269. Max Densmore and Donald Klein, "Health Care's Response to the Consumer: Patient Representatives," *Proceedings of the Academy of Management* (1975). Amitai Etzioni, "Alternative Conception of Accountability: The Example of Health Administration," *Public Administration Review* 35 (May–June 1975): 279–286. Christopher Forrest et al., "The Changing Role of the Hospital Administrator," *Proceedings of the Academy of Management* (1976). Basil Georgopoulous and Floyd Mann, *The Community General Hospital* (New York: Macmillan, 1962). Paul Gordon, "The Top Management Triangle in Voluntary Hospitals," *Academy of Management Journal* 4 (December 1961): 205–214. Robert Makowski, "Hospital Planning: Synthesis and Restatement," *Hospital Progress* 54 (April 1973): 24–28. Harold Wilensky, "The Dynamics of Professionalism: The Case of Hospital Administration," *Hospital Administration* 7 (Spring 1962): 6–24.

The University Manager

J. Victor Baldridge et al., *Policy Making and Effective Leadership* (San Francisco, Calif.: Jossey-Bass, 1979). John D. Millet, *New Structures of Campus Power* (San Francisco, Calif.: Jossey-Bass, 1979). Kenneth P. Mortimer and T. R. McConnell, *Sharing Authority Effectively* (San Francisco, Calif.: Jossey-Bass, 1979).

Arts Management

Winthrop Sargent, "The Ring's the Thing," *New Yorker,* June 26, 1978, pp. 35–50.

Managing Voluntary Organizations and the Third Sector

Diane Borst and Patrick Montana, eds., *Managing Non-Profit Organizations* (New York: AMACOM, 1977). Richard Cyert, *The Management of Non-Profit Organizations* (Lexington, Mass.: Lexington Books, 1975). Michael McGill and Leland Wooten, "Management in the Third Sector," *Public Administration Review* 35 (September–October 1975): 444–455. Brian O'Connell, *Executive Leadership in Voluntary Organizations* (New York: Associated Press, 1976). Charles Reimnitz, "Testing a Planning and Control Model in Non-Profit Organizations," *Academy of Management Journal* 15 (March 1972): 77–87.

Name Index

Subject Index